PHILOSOPHICAL PERSPECTIVES FOR EDUCATION

PHILOSOPHICAL PERSPECTIVES FOR EDUCATION

Carlton H. Bowyer

The University of Alabama

Scott, Foresman and Company

Two things, chiefly, are required in a philosopher—1. Cultivation of talents and of skill, so as to use them for various ends. 2. Readiness in the use of all means to any ends that may be chosen. Both must be united; for without knowledge one can never become a philosopher; yet never will knowledge alone constitute a philosopher, unless there is added a fitting combination of all his knowledge and skill into unity, and an insight into the harmony of the same with the highest ends of human reason.

No one can call himself a philosopher who cannot philosophize. Now, it is only by practice and independent use of one's reason that one can learn to philosophize.

—Immanuel Kant, *Introduction to Logic*

Library of Congress Catalog Card Number 70–91951.
Copyright © 1970 by Scott, Foresman and Company, Glenview, Illinois 60025.
Philippines copyright 1970 by Scott, Foresman and Company.
All Rights Reserved. Printed in the United States of America.

Regional offices of Scott, Foresman and Company are located in Atlanta, Dallas, Glenview, Palo Alto, Oakland, N.J., and London, England.

*To my wife, Jane Mehl Bowyer,
my father, Carlton W. Bowyer, and in fond
memory of my mother, Elsie Hodges Bowyer.*

Preface

Writing is not easy for me, and it has been a long stretch between the first outlines of this text and its completion. Many times I have asked myself the question which is sure to be asked by those who notice my efforts: Why, in view of the plethora of educational works, many of them excellent texts, have I labored so long and hard to add one more to the number? I have attempted to delineate the rationale for my effort as clearly as I am able in the Introduction, but perhaps it would not be superfluous to relate here how I happened to write this textbook and to state the purpose I hope the work will serve.

It would be difficult to pinpoint the actual inception of my idea for the book as it developed over a period of years until gradually the text, in a manner of speaking, came into its own being. Perhaps the initial impetus occurred some fifteen years ago when I first taught the undergraduate course which was required by the state of Missouri for teacher certification. Or perhaps the idea began to take shape even earlier when, as a graduate student at the University of Missouri, I had the good fortune to know a number of excellent teachers who stressed ideas, and who insisted upon the sort of analysis and critical thinking that I came to believe is the most valuable aspect of an education. Among these outstanding teachers were the late Professors M. G. Mehl, W. W. Carpenter, and A. C. Benjamin, and certainly Professor W. E. Drake, to whom my debt is twofold. It was largely due to him some years later when we were colleagues at the University of Texas that I began the actual writing of the manuscript which developed into the present text.

By that time I had taught the required undergraduate course in principles of education (I use the term here to include educational history, philosophy, theory, and sociology) in six institutions located in four different states. The course title and catalogue description differed considerably from one state to another which seemed to reflect a lack of consensus about the exact nature of the required course. I felt that such a generalized requirement for teacher certification could only be justified on the grounds that it would contribute in some way to the professional competency of the teacher, and regardless of the importance one must accord to history and philosophy of education and to educational sociology, I did not believe that a subject-matter orientation of these disciplines would have any practical merit for those planning to teach in the public schools.

Teaching, at best, is a difficult, highly complex activity, and there are simply not enough hours in a teacher preparation program for us to be sure that the neophyte is properly equipped for the task which faces him after graduation. For example, few students preparing to teach in the elementary and secondary grades have time in their heavy schedules of required course work and practice teaching for courses which deal specifically with the tools of critical thinking and analysis. This alone, in my view, is sufficient reason for those of us teaching the one required course in the area of principles of education, regardless of the course title or description, to present the material in such a way that it will be practical and relevant to the needs of those in the teacher education program. Our particular function must be to help the student recognize the significant relationships between teaching, learning, and society, to assist him to synthesize the discrete elements of teacher education into some kind of conceptual structure, and to encourage his ability to develop the philosophical and educational perspectives necessary for his professional task.

I soon discovered that the greatest difficulty in this regard was to find a satisfactory textbook. I discovered any number of excellent educational histories, educational philosophies, or combinations of the two, but, although purely chronological or system-oriented books can be splendid references, they were not what I needed for a text. The available concept-oriented texts were also in many cases good reference books, but most were either too superficial for the task or the concepts were not related to historical development or to educational thought. Therefore, I was forced to depend largely upon lectures and classroom discussions supplemented by a variety of readings and some combination of the many paperbacks that are available. But I continued my search for a textbook structured upon basic concepts such as value, knowledge, intelligence, thinking, educational theory, and teaching; a text which is not strictly a history and philosophy of education but which gives close attention to the historical and educational developments of basic concepts; a text which suggests the kinds of problems contemporary educators must deal with for the purpose of showing how the elements of critical thinking further understanding and help find solutions to educational problems.

Generally speaking, the foregoing text description outlines the approach and the emphasis I have used in the required undergraduate course for a number of years, and I feel that it has been successful enough to merit the time and labor that have gone into the writing of this textbook. I believe it is a work many will find useful, even though they may disagree with my views about the required course, as the open-ended discussions are designed to be adaptable to a variety of approaches to the foundations of education. The material is sufficiently ample for a subject oriented approach, and I believe it is flexible enough to allow for class elaboration according to a teacher's special interests and scholarship. The readings provide excellent material for analysis and can serve as extensions of the chapter materials, or simply as exercises in critical thinking.

There have been radical changes in every area of life during the past decade, and the predominant surge seems to be a search for the truth or for what those under thirty call "telling it like it is." All over the country students are protesting against the status quo of the establishment. They protest against the sort of teaching which follows the traditional and safe prescriptions of educational techniques, and demand education that is "meaningful." I interpret this as a cry for help, and it must not go unheeded. We have a responsibility to the youth of America, and we fail miserably unless we point the way to make our vast store of knowledge relevant to everyday living by teaching students how to relate, to structure, and to analyze information. I make no claim that the neophyte will find in the pages of this book any pat solutions to the classroom difficulties which will confront him in his teaching. But it is my hope that by the close of this study he will, by example and by practice, have learned to approach these problems, whatever they may be, with understanding and critical judgment and to deal with them intelligently and effectively.

It would be impossible to acknowledge individually all of those who have contributed in some way to the completion of this text, for the number is a panorama of teachers, students, colleagues, other friends, and members of my family, whose influence, encouragement, and assistance have been invaluable. Among others, I am indebted to James G. Hunt of Scott, Foresman and Company for first envisioning some promise in my initial efforts and to those of the staff who have been unusually patient and helpful. I am especially grateful for the encouragement and constructive criticisms of Professor Israel Scheffler of Harvard University and to the authors and publishers who so graciously consented to allow portions of their works to be reprinted here.

Table of Contents

Introduction

Philosophical Perspectives for Education is a study of educationally related activities which stresses the use of philosophical concepts and methodologies as one base of interpretation. The philosophical materials are
organized both topically and historically, and the approach differs somewhat from the more traditional view associated with philosophical foundations of education and philosophy of education in that greater emphasis is
given to the variety of ways in which the cognitive skills have been developed by philosophers and educators such as Plato, Aristotle, Kant, Dewey,
and others.

It would be presumptuous to claim that logical and linguistic analyses
—studies in their own right—are taught here. But the emphasis is such that
the student will begin to acquire and develop cognitive skills such as
inquiry, analysis, explanation, prediction, and verification during the course
of the study. The approach taken here is intended to serve the purpose of
alerting the neophyte to the importance of these cognitive skills as he begins
to engage in the process of building his own conceptual structures in order
to obtain and utilize knowledge. The historical consideration of their use
is demonstrative of the significance of logical and linguistic analyses and
of acceptable means of verification of conclusions in the achievement of
the philosophical perspectives which are essential for successful teaching.

The emphasis which is now being given to teaching and learning
technologies has raised serious questions about existing teacher education
patterns. The idea that education is merely amassing of "fact" is as out-
moded as the pony express. Those who cling to the meaningless debate of
subject matter versus method are out of step with current movements in
education which recognize that "knowing how" and "knowing that" are
integral parts of the learning process. Twentieth century knowledge explosion is so great that a college graduate who has had no occasion to keep
up with the new math needs a refresher course in order to help his children

1

with their homework. Subject matter in many areas is in a state of flux, and new information accumulates so rapidly that by the time it has sifted to the public school level it is already obsolete. It seems likely that the increase of knowledge between this century and the next one will be greater than it was during the centuries between the early Greeks and the Enlightenment.

Teacher education programs today bear little resemblance to normal schools at the turn of the century when little more was offered than a review of subject matter and experience in practice teaching. We realize that more than propositional and procedural knowledge are required to meet the demands made on teachers today, and outstanding scholars emphasize the need for a teacher training curriculum that stresses the development of cognitive skills. Jerome Bruner has stated:

> It would seem, from our consideration of man's evolution, that principal emphasis in education should be placed upon skills—skills in handling, in seeing and imaging, and in symbolic operations, particularly as these relate to the technologies that have made them so powerful in their human expression.[1]

Teacher training programs are beginning to emphasize the needs Bruner cites. The new programs that are concerned with the development of critical abilities for the basis of intellectual growth draw upon newly developing analytical philosophies that stress linguistic analysis, and many of the new programs include study in structures of knowledge, structures of the curriculum, curriculum theory, computer-assisted instruction, theories of learning, and the discipline of education. The ability to understand more intelligently comes from close attention to critical thinking and methods of inquiry. Several scholars have used the phrase "disciplined intellectual activity" to describe the newer movements in philosophy and education. Israel Scheffler characterizes these methods of inquiry and philosophical activity as "rational reflection, critical analysis of arguments and assumptions, systematic clarification of fundamental ideas."[2] Rational reflection is to be logical; critical analysis is to reduce vagueness and ambiguity without dogmatism; and the systematic clarification of ideas is to engage in discourse that follows the principles of logic. Philosophical perspectives are based on these elements.

Marc Belth[3] has noted the mathematical, scientific, philosophical, and educative modes of reasoning. Although there are differences among these modes, Belth recognizes common elements that are related to the traditional logical categories of the deductive and the inductive. According to

---

[1] Jerome Bruner, "Education as Social Invention," *Toward a Theory of Instruction* (Cambridge, Massachusetts: The Belknap Press of Harvard University Press, 1966), p. 34.
[2] Israel Scheffler, *Philosophy and Education* (Boston: Allyn & Bacon, Inc., 1958), p. 3.
[3] Marc Belth, *Education as a Discipline* (Boston: Allyn & Bacon, Inc., 1965), pp. 8–9.

Belth's analysis, there is a closer correlation between the philosophical and the educative than there is between the educative and the mathematical or between the educative and the scientific. The relationship between the philosophical and the educative can be described by the term conceptualization. Belth, in making this relationship, speaks of teaching as an activity which entails both the content and the methodological dimensions of education and which is directly related to the task of describing and analyzing the type of thinking that is required for excellent teaching.

The typical program today for the preparation of teachers invariably includes a course that is variously designated by certification agencies as the principles, theory, or philosophy of education. The nature of the required course varies from one state to another and even in the same institution from one instructor to another. It is possible, however, to note one or two general tendencies in the course which is required to fulfill the certification requirements. Either the course will be one in the area of the foundations of education, usually the philosophical foundations, or it may be one in the area of educational philosophy, usually an introduction to philosophy of education. Unfortunately, the two views are not only disparate and thus insulated from each other, but in many instances this required course will have no relationship to the other aspects of the teacher preparation program and will have little practical value for the neophyte teacher.

One of the earliest suggestions for the point of view explicit in the foundations of education came in 1896 from a United States Commissioner of Education, W. T. Harris (1835–1909). Harris, an American philosopher and educator, holding the position of Commissioner from 1889 to 1906, expressed the view that, since education is based on sociology or the science of civilization, American teacher education needed a particular instrument for the development of social-consciousness. The suggestion undoubtedly grew out of the general trend at the turn of the twentieth century to think in terms of a community of individuals. Already the increasing emphasis on science, technology, and national economy was beginning to change our way of looking at things, and Commissioner Harris was convinced that education must keep abreast with the times.

Fortunately for American education, the educators who dominated the scene in the early 1900's—men such as John Dewey (1859–1952), Harold Rugg (1886–1960), and George S. Counts (1889–   )—were social minded, and they pioneered the social foundations movement. These men were the avant garde, the kinds of educators who have no fear of asking nor of being asked probing questions about the relationship among educational ideals, practices, and outcomes. Like Commissioner Harris, they felt there should be a closer relationship between the school and society, and the basic theme of social foundations at the beginning of the movement was the idea of social reconstruction through education. John Dewey believed this was certainly a step in the right direction, although it was not precisely what he envisioned for the foundations. He wrote in *The Sources of a Science of Education:*

> The important thing is to discover those traits in virtue of which various fields are called scientific. When we raise the question in this way, we are led to put emphasis upon *methods* of dealing with subject-matter rather than to look for uniform objective traits in subject-matter. From this point of view, science signifies, I take it, the existence of systematic methods of inquiry, which, when they are brought to bear on a range of facts, enable us to understand them better and to control them more intelligently, less haphazardly and with less routine.[4]

John Dewey's concern about the narrowness of educational research discipline and subject-matter orientation led to his original design for the foundations as an observation-centered reasoning about scientific data from the established sciences. But increasing public demands and societal needs alerted educators to an awareness of social obligation, an awareness which dominated the implementation of the social foundations concept to such a degree that only in the past few years has it begun to function according to Dewey's insights into the need for a separate and unique area within education. What Dewey wanted was a broadened concept of method whereby educational problems, viewed in terms of social and historical influences, are considered rationally and critically. What actually occurred was a shift to a subjective sort of moral doctrine or social philosophy, with the purpose of directing social change.

The foundations movement in education then had its beginning as the social foundations and gradually came to include the historical and the philosophical aspects. It was a broadly conceived subject with the primary purpose of making education useful to society by first making it useful to the individual. Difficulties in the movement developed rapidly, for some educators began to interpret the social foundations in a very narrow sense. These educators began to write about the "sociology of education" and tried to force the foundations concept into the mold of a laboratory science where it could be subjected to batteries of tests and measurements. The effort to gain the respectability of a science for education had the result of turning the foundations concept into a battleground for the conflict between the science-oriented and the art-oriented. The development of the scientific interpretation of the foundations of education was frightening to those who were the art-oriented and who feared the dehumanizing tendencies of the scientific. The battle lines were drawn between content and method, between the traditional and the progressive, between art and science. Everywhere educators uncapped their pens or sharpened their pencils and leapt into

---

[4] John Dewey, *The Sources of a Science of Education* (New York: Horace Liveright, 1929), pp. 8–9.

the fray. The battle-scarred foundations became an essay in keeping the peace. As Charles Brauner characterizes it:

> In sum, the foundation movement strove to establish *education as a literary discipline* operating between the exacting scholarly and logical demands of philosophy and the careful, detailed attention to literal description prerequisite to empirical science.[5]

The foundations movement gained momentum during the twenties and thirties at Teachers College, Columbia University, and at the University of Illinois during the fifties. Distinct areas for study began to emerge, and soon the divisions between the areas became too rigid to support a single course entitled the foundations of education. Those who were concerned with the psychological foundations of education parted company entirely from the others and in some cases attempted to align themselves with the experimental psychology taught in colleges of arts and sciences. The historical foundations of education concentrated upon the impact of social, economic, political, and religious forces in past societies; the social foundations of education attempted to bring about an understanding of the school by exploring contemporary social forces such as class structure, pressure groups, urban living, and the like; and the philosophical foundations of education looked to the philosophical structures of value theory, epistemology, and metaphysics as the most relevant concepts for understanding the school in American society.

A required course for teacher certification offered in the area of the philosophical foundations most often stresses the mastery of the various theories promulgated by philosophers about these fundamental concepts in philosophy. The stress is most apt to be placed upon comparing and contrasting the theories, and it is left to the student to discover what relevancy these concepts have for his educational thinking or practice. On the other hand, if the required course is offered in the area of philosophy of education, it is likely to be system-oriented. That is, the content is centered on exemplars of systems such as realism, pragmatism, and idealism. Again, stress is placed upon the mastery of the details of the system and the student urged to develop his own philosophy of education by using the models as guide lines.

There can be no quarrel with the view that those who have chosen to enter the teaching profession should be required to have some knowledge of philosophical systems and of educational theories. In this regard, there is nothing inherently wrong with either of the aforementioned approaches, and this study borrows heavily from both areas. However, if one decides to build a house or to erect a building, one needs a good deal more than a warehouse of building materials. One needs to know the nature of the vari-

---

[5] Charles J. Brauner, *American Educational Theory* (Englewood Cliffs, New Jersey: Prentice-Hall, Inc., 1964), p. 223.

ous materials in order to determine which can be used to the greatest advantage; one needs to know the basic principles of structure and design in order to formulate detailed plans for the building; and one needs to be able to use the various tools that are necessary.

Following this line of reasoning, it becomes eminently clear that even a perfect storehouse of philosophical and educational information will be relatively meaningless to the neophyte who has not learned how to use the tools of thinking in order to structure his data. Not only is mere acquaintance with philosophers, philosophical systems, and educational theories insufficient for the task of building practical ideas about education, it is pointless to wait until students are ready for advanced study in philosophy of education in order to begin the development of critical abilities which arise out of some sort of theoretical framework. I believe that an essential aspect of teacher training ought to be the stimulation of educational inquiry, and toward that end it is a purpose of this text to encourage students to develop the ability to discriminate among meanings, to clarify meanings, to formulate hypotheses, to recognize logically sound alternatives, and to distinguish between truth and probability.

The distinguishing feature of *Philosophical Perspectives,* therefore, is primarily a matter of emphasis. The study is based on the idea that cognitive skills can be the focal point for viewing education and philosophy. Drawing upon concepts in philosophy and upon the writings of philosophers about education, we will concentrate upon developing the ability to systematize and structure the cognitive skills in such a way that they become tools for philosophizing about education. In sum, we are concerned here with the kind of activity which leads to the development of critical and analytical thinking and which encourages the organization of ideas to form a conceptual structure.

The term *structure* is used in many different contexts. We speak of the structure of a molecule, a painting, a bridge, or a building. We speak of the structure of the English language, a curriculum, a society, or a metaphysical concept. But in all cases, the fundamental principle of structure is one of relationships. A precise definition of a term with such a broad range of uses poses a number of problems, but for our purposes we shall define structure as: *The arrangement and interrelation of parts that combine, or are combined, in such a way as to make an individual contribution to the general character of the whole, which in turn dominates the ordering of the parts.* Specifically, the structure of a molecule is the arrangement and relationships between the various atomic constituents of the molecule; the structure of a curriculum is the arrangement and the relationships between the various subjects and educational activities. Structure may indicate the levels of qualities, such as the structure of a society, or it may describe the combination of components, such as the structure of a building. We see that in some instances structure is *discovered,* while in other cases, structure is *planned* and is the result of individual or group activity. For example, we discover the structure of a molecule, but we plan the structure of a bridge.

When we speak of man's conceptual structure, where the referent is the relationship between all of the individual concepts and ideas, we become involved both with *discovery* of structure and with *planned* or *conscious structuring*. The conceptual structure of an individual begins to evolve out of individual experiences that contribute to attitudes, knowledge, and beliefs. The initial awareness of any order or structure to the developing concepts is *discovered* by the individual. At the point of such discovery or awareness the individual may begin consciously to alter and amplify his ideas which contribute to the total conceptual structure. The relationship between the parts and the whole becomes circular in a causal sequence. The complexity and the various levels of a conceptual structure will become evident as we study the history of philosophical ideas about education.

Chapter One provides an introduction to the tools of inquiry as they relate to education. Chapters Two through Five develop the philosophical concepts of value, intelligence, empiricism, and knowledge as they are related to changing views about the nature of reality. Chapter Six deals with social philosophies and their relevance for education. Chapter Seven is concerned with the beginnings of modern educational theorizing. Chapter eight provides examples of: 1) different levels of criticism about educational thought and practice and 2) contemporary educational issues. Chapter Nine concludes the study with a look at the philosophic and educational enterprises as they affect the new teacher who must make choices that in turn affect the future of the individual students. The readings at the end of each chapter have been selected to amplify the main topics of discourse and have been drawn from both the classics and modern sources in order to illustrate the historical continuity of philosophical concern and to illustrate the applicability of models of the past to contemporary problems. The entire text is designed to illustrate the importance of awareness of underlying philosophical principles in order to make critical and analytical judgments and in order to form a conceptual structure that will be significant for educational choices.

An Introduction to Philosophy, Education, and Elements of Critical Thinking

The title of our text, *Philosophical Perspectives for Education,* implies a view that brings into focus educational ideals and educational practices. Certainly the two are interrelated, and both depend upon ideas and practices that have preceded them. No concept is independent of history, and students cannot come to a meaningful understanding of modern educational concepts without some knowledge of the background of educational thought and practice.

Historically we associate ideas about education with philosophy. At one time the term *philosophy* was used to describe all wisdom, all knowledge, all of man's intellectual endeavors. Even today, in the face of a high degree of specialization, no intellectual activity is isolated from philosophy, because analysis, criticism, systematization, and organization are all philosophical endeavors. A philosophical system, by definition, is an organized whole, and thus we expect philosophers such as Plato, Aristotle, Kant, and others to have ideas about education in keeping with the particular system each attempted to build. It is indeed the case that their ideas about education grew out of their philosophical views which is one reason for examining the traditional philosophies in this text. A second reason is to help the reader recognize that one's individual philosophical attitudes largely determine his educational aims and choices.

Since one aspect of the philosophical foundations of education is the relationship between traditional philosophical views and educational processes, some knowledge of philosophy, elements of critical thinking, and the history of philosophical attitudes is a necessary condition for this study. The primary purpose of this chapter is to satisfy that condition. The first section of the chapter supplies the reader with an introduction to the essential philosophical vocabulary and background material for the study. The reader who might have had courses in philosophy will find the section helpful for purposes of review and for its concentration upon those philosophical ideas and terms which are especially pertinent to educational concepts. The second section of the chapter is an overview of education and provides an educational frame of reference comparable to the philosophical frame of reference provided in the first section. The final section and reading widen the base for later discussions about educational theories, directives, and practices, by presenting basic elements of critical thinking. "Formal Logic" by Harold Larrabee has been selected for the reading at the end of the chapter to underscore the importance of logic, a sometimes neglected aspect of teacher education programs.

Philosophy—"The Love of Wisdom"

> Man was a poet before he learned to be a philosopher; and a philosopher before he learned to be a scientist. Man's intellectual life began in the rank and luxurious vegetation of stories, images, and pictures of every kind, their variations sprouting in all directions.[1]

Whether or not we agree with the above quotation, it is interesting to speculate about the origins of philosophy. We realize that we can no more pinpoint the precise beginning than we can know for sure exactly how, and at what point in time, man first learned to use weapons for self-defense and to obtain food. Even the artifacts that have survived the ages leave room for speculation, and we can only imagine the sort of wonderings and gropings for answers that primitive man must have experienced in his attempt to explain and to understand the apparently random happenings of birth and death and other events of nature. We can be reasonably sure, however, that the beginnings of philosophical speculation occurred at whatever point man began to abstract meaning from his experiences. An attempt to be systematic in his efforts to find answers to the larger questions, such as the nature of life and death and the reason for our being, surely started man on a course of philosophizing that extended into all areas of his intellectual activity. Man's capacity for reasoning sets him apart from the rest of the animal kingdom, but it is the use of his intellectual abilities to give thought to the "why's" and the "wherefore's" of the world that results in a higher level of living than other species can realize.

One's philosophy is definitive in respect to his life, as it represents the meaning and significance attributed to the individual human experience. One's philosophy is probably more descriptive of the individual than any other single factor, as genuine philosophizing wells up from one's unique existence and helps one person to relate to another. Accordingly, it appears that authentic existence is not exclusively an existentialist theme but one with significance for all men. At the same time, extreme views about existence that place one on an esoteric level apart from the rest of the world are gainless, for man obviously cannot live alone. John Dewey has

---

[1] William L. Reese, *The Ascent from Below* (Boston: Houghton Mifflin Company, 1959), p. 362.

drawn an analogy between individuals and letters of the alphabet to demonstrate that the connections between individuals are as important to society as the connections between letters are to language. Living as he does with others of his kind in a world of flux, man feels the need for guiding principles which he comes by in a variety of ways. The sources can range from superstition, subjective attitudes that do not relate to the realities of the world and various forms of authority, to a philosophical view of the universe, or what we call a *world view*. It is self-evident to most thinking people that it is desirable to achieve a world view, a view in which the particulars, the individual concepts or ideas, are flexible and subject to necessary changes without destroying the whole view. But the process of acquiring such a view is arduous and exacting. It requires a philosophic attitude, knowledge about philosophic methods, and a sensitivity to philosophic problems.

The Philosophic Attitude

The philosophic attitude is characterized by open-mindedness, is marked by a willingness to debate, and by the disposition to investigate all areas of belief. Those who exhibit the philosophic attitude respect other people and their opinions. They avoid the straitjacket of authoritarianism for there is nothing in the philosophic attitude to support egoism. Judgment about the nature and the quality of actions, about the motives that prompt the actions, and about the consequences of the actions themselves, is unceasing. Beliefs and commitments are open to continued investigation, and freedom of inquiry prevails.

The oft-heard statement that one should "be philosophic" about some tragedy carries the implication of blind acceptance in the face of adversity. This is contrary to the philosophic quest for truth which does not allow passive or blind acceptance of any event or experience. The philosophic attitude is characterized by the sort of questioning disposition that even questions the nature of the questions. It would be a mistake, however, to confuse questioning with philosophizing. There are no "why's" more persistent or penetrating than those of a child determined to have all of the answers, yet his random questions are a far cry from those of the philosopher who orders and directs his inquiries and who relates and structures the results to serve as a base for further investigations. This brings us to a consideration of philosophic methods.

Philosophic Methods

A method is the procedure used to attain an end; it is the planned way a thing is done. Philosophers have used a variety of methods for the pursuit of truth, but all are attempts to relate the logic of inquiry through the formulation of hypotheses to the logic of proof. The methods can be variously described by terms such as exploration (discovery), explanation, inference, and prediction.

One of the early philosophic methods is the *dialectic*, debate by question and answer. Originally the dialectic was associated with the *Socratic method* which leads to a conclusion, step by step, by the means of pointed questions designed to elicit responses. Plato conceived the dialectic to be the science of first principles, differing from other sciences by doing away with hypotheses. The Platonic dialectical reasoning begins with generally accepted opinions and attempts to reach the premises on which the opinions rest. Aristotle distinguishes between that sort of reasoning and what he calls *demonstrative reasoning* which moves syllogistically from true premises to true conclusions.

The dialectic, however, has taken on rather special meaning in modern philosophy. One of these occurs in Immanuel Kant's "Transcendental Dialectic." Kant, in his discussion of the limits of human reason, uses dialectic to refer to the difficulties that arise when man's reason attempts to reach beyond the realm of objects that are observable through the senses, or as Kant calls it, the phenomenal world. (See Chapter Five.) A second special meaning of the term dialectic occurs in the writings of Georg Wilhelm Friedrich Hegel. He uses the term dialectic to refer to universal speculative processes which are exhibited in nature, and he describes the process as a movement from thesis (an occurrence) to its antithesis (the opposite occurrence) to a synthesis (the unity of the opposites). (See Chapter Six.) This process was adopted by Karl Marx and became the basis of his dialectical materialism.

Other methods that philosophy has inspired—in addition to the *Socratic method,* the *synthetic method* developed by Plato, Aristotle, and the medieval thinkers, the *transcendental method* developed by Kant, and the *dialectical method* which is promoted by Hegel and dialectical materialists—include: the *ascetic method* proposed by Plotinus, Augustine, and the mystics; the *psychological method* of inquiry into the origin of ideas which was used by Descartes and by the British empiricists; the *intuitive method* involving the immediate perception of reality; the *reflexive method* of metaphysical introspection; the *eclectic method;* and the *positivistic method* of Comte, Spencer, and the logical empiricists which attempts to apply scientific procedures to philosophy.

Philosophic methods, for the most part, employ *deductive reasoning* which moves from the general to the less general, from the universal to the particular. Conclusions are drawn from given postulates. Some examples of *deductive reasoning* are: *apodictic reasoning* moving from propositions where something is asserted as *necessary; problematic reasoning* moving from propositions where something is asserted as possible; *assertoric reasoning* moving from propositions where something is asserted as *true;* and *eristic reasoning* which is a polemic employing specious premises for the purpose of winning an argument. It should be noted, however, that while deductive reasoning is most typical of philosophic methods, it is not used exclusively. *Inductive reasoning,* where the movement is from particulars to the general, from the individual to the universal, and conclusions sum up the observed facts, is especially characteristic of scientific methods, but most philosophic methods make some use of it. The *positivistic method,* which attempts to apply scientific methods to philosophical problems, makes extensive use of *inductive reasoning.*

One approach to a better understanding of philosophic methods is to contrast philosophy with science. But it should be understood that the distinctions we make here are a matter of degree and emphasis, for there are different interpretations of the nature and task of philosophy and of science. We noted earlier that a method is the way of doing something according to a plan. Clearly, the tools we use, the techniques we employ, the overall plan we follow in order to accomplish a particular end, will vary according to our subject matter. Herein lies a clue as to one way we might contrast philosophic methods with scientific methods.

Generally speaking, the areas of philosophical investigation include religion, value, the ends and purposes of life, and beauty in the arts. Philosophy is concerned with all aspects of human experience. It is interested in the real aspects and in the ideal possibilities of concepts and in their worth and their meanings. Philosophy has an intellectual criterion of truth, it is rational, and knowledge, according to some philosophers, can be gained *a priori* as well as *a posteriori.* The subject matter of philosophical investigation tends mainly to be mental and nonsensory, and the method involves criticism, evaluation, and synthesis.

Science, for the most part, is interested in the nature of things as they are observed and strives to eliminate the subjective factor. Science has a sensory criterion of truth, is empirical, and knowledge is thought to be gained after experience. The subject matter of scientific investigations is predominantly sensory, and the method involves observation, the construction of means, and the control of processes.

Both philosophy and science are interested in the exploration of particulars, their meanings, and in the relationship between the particulars and the larger scheme of things. But because the philosopher raises questions of purpose, the philosophic emphasis is on the "why" of phenomena. The scientific emphasis, on the other hand, is on the description of the laws of phenomena. Philosophy attempts to combine particulars into interpretive syntheses, to seek the total significance, and the philosophic method is more synthetic and synoptic. Science attempts to analyze the whole into its constituents, and the scientific approach is more analytic and descriptive.

Philosophic Problems
René Descartes (1596–1650) wrote that ". . . . Philosophy is like a tree, of which Metaphysics is the root, Physics the trunk, and all the other sciences the branches that grow out of this trunk, which are reduced to three principal, namely, Medicine, Mechanics, and Ethics."[2] Since Des-

---

2 René Descartes, *Meditations and Selections from the Principles of Philosophy,* trans. John Veitch (La Salle, Illinois: The Open Court Publishing Company, 1955), p. 119.

cartes' time, as the various areas of knowledge broadened to become more and more complex, there was a gradual separation between philosophy and the sciences which became independent disciplines. The broad philosophical categories came to be metaphysics, epistemology, axiology, and logic which traditionally referred to the nature of reality, to structure of knowledge, to questions of value, and to correct reasoning. During the past few decades the pressures of twentieth century living have contributed to a gradual shift in the emphasis placed upon philosophical problems, and there has been a corresponding change or evolution in terminology.

"Metaphysical" has come to mean the supranatural. A metaphysical problem may be a scheme of explanation which attempts to transcend the inadequacies of ordinary thought, or it may be a disagreement about the nature of reality. Traditionally, metaphysics included ontology, or the science of being, and cosmology, or the science of fundamental causes and processes. Cosmology is the branch of metaphysics that theorizes about reality, that considers the possible origins and causes of the cosmos. A major part of cosmologic speculation deals with the nature of man in relation to metaphysical concerns such as freedom, purpose, God, and existence. However, the theoretical nature of metaphysical answers has been the cause of a good deal of dispute in the history of philosophy, and a number of modern philosophers have turned away from many of the traditional problems, limiting their attention to the meaning of existence (ontology). Thus, in many instances we find the term ontology replacing the term metaphysics.

Epistemology refers to the theory or science which investigates the origin, structure, methods, and validity of knowledge. There are various views regarding the relative priority of epistemology and metaphysics (or ontology). The dominant view, which was held by Descartes, Locke, Kant, and Dewey, is that investigations of the limits of knowledge must come before any metaphysical speculations. The opposite view was held by metaphysicians, such as Spinoza and Hegel, who adopted a view of knowledge consonant with their metaphysics. An intermediate view is that epistemology and metaphysics are interdependent. There is an intimate relationship between epistemology and psychology, for psychological studies of perception, memory, and imagination provide essential data for epistemological interpretations. Nevertheless, they are two distinct areas of study, for their treatments of the cognitive processes of the mind are radically different.

Theory and study of value had its rise in Plato's Idea of the Good, and Christian philosophy later built upon Aristotle's identification of the highest value with final cause in God as "a living being, eternal, most good." Values were also metaphysically grounded in scholasticism and in Spinoza's system. The study of value theory became an independent investigation with Kant's *Critiques,* although it remained related to investigations of metaphysical and epistemological problems. Axiology is the modern term for the search into: 1) the nature of value; 2) the types of value; 3) the criterion of value; and 4) the metaphysical status of value.

Logic deals with the laws and criteria of validity in thought and demonstration. It is the science of formal principles of correct reasoning directed toward the insurance of sound conclusions. Many of the principles and procedures of logic were first developed by Aristotle. His syllogistic reasoning, or what is referred to as Aristotelian logic, is an important aspect of all introductory logic courses. Logic is concerned with the elements of correct reasoning, a special kind of thinking that deals with inferences or conclusions that may be drawn from certain premises. The logician is interested in the correctness of the completed process rather than with the psychological aspects of thinking.

Although one need not necessarily study logic in order to reason correctly, some knowledge of the general principles of logical methods will assist even the keenest thinker. Such knowledge gives one the benefit of easily applied methods for testing the correctness of his reasoning, as well as that of others. Since it is a major purpose of this study to encourage the development of critical thinking, the last section and reading for this chapter will concentrate upon the primary aspects of language analysis and logic.

Systematic Philosophy

In order to qualify as a system of philosophy, an intellectual position should provide a coherent scheme of answers to the metaphysical, the epistemological, and the axiological, or to current variations of these problems. This does not preclude the possibility of other ways of ordering one's thinking, but as H. R. Smart states: ". . . a mere classification is logically a weak device, useful only to the extent that it affords some help in dealing, on an empirical level, with recalcitrant material that temporarily at least resists a more systematic, more theoretically profound treatment."[3] Additional ways of ordering philosophical problems have been suggested by John Dewey[4] and others,[5] but Smart's criticisms are no less applicable to their suggestions.

The contemporary philosophical scene has many "isms" which are often designated as systems or schools of philosophy, and some of the changes in philosophy have been the result of splinter groups that have developed their own variations of some main theme. These derivatives and fragmentations may well be the sign of genuine philosophical enterprises, but we shall concentrate here upon five of the main systems of philosophical investigation. These are naturalism, idealism, realism, pragmatism, and logical empiricism.

Naturalism is a philosophy that accepts nature as the whole of reality. All of the many interpretations of nature revolve around the common rejection of the supernatural and the otherworldly. Whatever exists can be

[3] H. R. Smart, *Philosophy and Its History* (La Salle, Illinois: The Open Court Publishing Company, 1962), p. 57.
[4] John Dewey, *Quest for Certainty* (London: George Allen & Unwin Ltd., 1929), pp. 286–287.
[5] W. E. Hocking, Brand Blanshard, Charles W. Hendel, and John Herman Randall, Jr., *Preface to Philosophy*: *Textbook* (New York: The Macmillan Company, 1946), p. 431.

said to exist in nature and forms a part of the naturalist's view of the world. "If you ask, what causes nature itself, the answer is—nature *is* the total system of causes; each phase of the universe leads to and explains the next phase; hence nature, as it now is, is completely explained by nature as it has been. To ask for a cause of nature outside of nature, a 'First Cause,' a 'God,' is meaningless."[6]

Another aspect of the common beliefs held by naturalists is adherence to concepts of evolution and continuity. Little attention is given to interpreting change and process as progress, as such an interpretation would imply a "higher" purpose and goal. According to the naturalist, when change does occur it is the result of the interplay of forces and energy in nature and human intelligence, for there is nothing that exists outside of nature.

There are different types of naturalism, each stressing some variation of the main theme. These include romantic naturalism as exemplified by Jean Jacques Rousseau, critical naturalism as found in the writings of Auguste Comte and Herbert Spencer, and materialistic (mechanistic) naturalism as represented in some of the early Greek philosophies. Romantic naturalism sees nature as good and virtuous. This idea of harmony and beauty in the natural world is almost a "mother nature" view. Critical naturalism is sometimes called humanistic naturalism. The stress is upon continuity and process in nature. Materialistic naturalism emphasizes the atomistic, or "bodies moving in space" interpretation of nature. The whole of nature may be viewed in mechanical terms, in which case even mental processes are thought to be purely physical connections. Naturalism, which is scientific and empirical, has appeal for a great many thinkers. Others, who believe there is more to nature than can be revealed by the senses, reject naturalism in favor of idealism.

The term idealism made its appearance late in the seventeenth century. It was first used to describe the Platonic Ideas which had been incorporated into Christian and Scholastic theism. It was later used to describe the epistemological doctrines of Descartes and Locke. Early in the eighteenth century the term was applied to theories such as acomism and immaterialism which deny the existence of a physical world. D. D. Runes' *Dictionary of Philosophy* lists dozens of idealisms that are defined by further classification, such as Platonic idealism, personal idealism, objective idealism, and moral idealism. All of these relate in a general way to the mental or spiritual, and all attempt to go "beyond" the observable for some more ultimate substance.

Idealism—regardless of the particular type—is a system of thought which regards reality as essentially spiritual or as the embodiment of mind or reason. Thus reality is identified with perceptibility, the basic interpretive principle is ideal, and the mental is the only knowable life. Idealism is the alternative to materialism. Unlike materialism, idealism emphasized the supra or nonspatial, the incorporeal, and the nonsensuous. Most ideal-

---

[6] W. E. Hocking, *Types of Philosophy*, Third Edition (New York: Charles Scribner's Sons, 1959), p. 25.

ists believe that the natural world is only the appearance of reality which is authored by thought. The view emphasizes the person or the self, and idealists believe that the existence of the world and individual selves depends upon a Self who is Creator and Sustainer. There are many philosophers who reject the idealist position because it tends to ignore the world as it is sensed and because it leads one to the security of an absolute. Among the critics of idealism are those who call themselves realists. These are followers of a belief that is in some respect a lineal descendant of naturalism.

We have noted that there are different forms of naturalism and of idealism. The same is true of realism, which makes it difficult to pinpoint the distinguishing features of realism and to define the realist point of view. One element that the various forms of realism do have in common is a rejection of the idealist theory of knowledge that the various qualities of experience depend upon a knower for their existence. Realists believe that the universe is composed of real entities that exist in themselves. These entities can be known, and their existence is not dependent upon a knower or perceiver. Although realists can agree on this point, they do not all agree when they attempt to build a metaphysical system. Here their views range from pluralism to dualism to monism.

The realist's epistemological views include epistemological monism where it is held that objects are *presented* in consciousness, and epistemological dualism where objects are thought to be *represented*. The monists define mind as a relation between the organism and an object, while the dualists identify the mind more closely with the organism. Realists do have a common tendency to view the world as the mechanism described by the physical sciences, and they generally believe in determinism, in orderliness in the universe, and in the objectivity of science. The unifying thesis of realism is that knowledge is thought to have a universal character and comes to man through his sensory capacity. The realists have a confidence in their assertions about reality and value which is most disconcerting to pragmatists.

Pragmatism is primarily a method of knowing, a method that emphasizes the experimental and the problematic, and for this reason some interpreters argue that it should not properly be called a system. Certainly the pragmatists make no deliberate attempt to construct a metaphysical system, as they believe that man's knowledge is limited by his sensory capacity. Rather, in the attempt to understand man and his society, pragmatism "orders" the experienced world. But there are those interpreters who maintain that the pragmatic principles of knowing and values can be viewed as metaphysical principles, and these maintain that pragmatists do inadvertently describe a metaphysical system. They claim that one metaphysical concept of pragmatism is that the constantly changing world of sense and intellect constitutes all of reality, and that it is a metaphysical concept that nothing in the world is guaranteed, and that man is a crucial factor in whatever progress is made toward the betterment of society. But pragmatism does reject all absolutes and stresses the precarious nature of man, morality, and society.

Charles Sanders Peirce (1839–1914) and William James (1842–1910) were the originators of pragmatism which is often thought to be the spirit of the modern era in America. According to Peirce and James, certain elements of pragmatism can be found in the thinking of Socrates, Aristotle, Bishop Berkeley, and David Hume. Many contemporary thinkers react strongly against pragmatism, but a large segment of American society has accepted the principles of relativism, cooperation, problem solving, and pluralism and exhibits a concern for all actions and their consequences.

Education is a primary concern of the pragmatist, and the concepts of utility, progress, democracy, and technology are crucial to the pragmatic view of education. The pragmatist asserts that the process of education is learning to reconstruct one's experience intelligently. The child, rather than subject matter, is considered central to education, and the child's interests, aspirations, likes, and dislikes are apt to be the keys to the educational program. The pragmatic goal of education is to develop individuals who can function adequately in our *present democratic* context and who are capable of creative responses for *future actions.*

Logical empiricism is another comparatively recent development in the Western philosophical tradition. The movement had its inception in views developed by members of the *Vienna Circle* which was founded by Moritz Schlick in 1924 at the University of Vienna. Contemporary logical empiricists trace their heritage to the empiricism and positivism of John Locke, David Hume, and John Stuart Mill. Other influences have been the positivism of Auguste Comte, the scientific methodology that developed in the middle of the nineteenth century, and the symbolic logic and logical analysis of language developed by Alfred North Whitehead, Bertrand A. W. Russell, and Ludwig Wittgenstein. The views that were developed in the Vienna Circle were first called logical positivism, but those who could not accept the narrowness of the positivist verification principle, limited as it was to actual observation through the senses, began to refer to themselves as logical empiricists. The forerunners of modern-day logical empiricism have been described by Jørgen Jørgensen as follows:

> The forerunners of logical empiricism are, in the opinion of the members of the movement themselves, all those philosophers and scientists who show a clear antimetaphysical or antispeculative, realistic or materialistic, critical or skeptical, tendency—as well as everyone who has contributed essentially to the development of their most important methodological instrument: symbolic logic.[7]

It is a basic thesis of logical empiricism that only those things which can be verified constitute genuine knowledge. The logical empiricists claim

---

[7] Jørgen Jørgensen, *The Development of Logical Empiricism* (Chicago: University of Chicago Press, 1951), p. 6.

that there are two types of statements which are capable of verification: 1) analytic or formal statements such as those found in logic and mathematics whose truth depends upon definition; and 2) empirical or factual statements whose truth depends upon actual observation or testing by recognized scientific procedures. Logical empiricists have also accepted the view that language analysis is a fundamental role of the philosopher, for they claim that disagreement among philosophers is due to the ambiguities of conventional language. The logical empiricists disagree as to whether their efforts should be directed toward the analysis of everyday language usage, or whether they should be directed toward the construction of an artificial language system. The former claim that if they concentrate on everyday usage they will be able to use statements from ethics, aesthetics, and law, as well as from the natural sciences. The latter group restrict their range to the natural sciences, logic, and mathematics, but they claim a greater precision than the ordinary language analyst.

Education

When a group of children appearing on a television program were asked what education is, one boy replied, "It's what you get when you go to school." Another child said, "It's what you learn when you're little so you can make a lot of money when you get big." Still another replied, "It's what makes you smart." We hardly expect definite answers from children of seven or eight years, but it is doubtful that many adults would be more explicit if the same question were put to them.

Education is taken pretty much for granted in America today. Most people agree that chances for success are in proportion to the amount of education a person acquires, and children are sent to school five days a week as a matter of course. They get through one grade so that they may be passed to the next grade. When students finally reach high school, they try to make grades that will qualify them for admission to some college or university where they can obtain a degree that will help them find a good job. Much of our lives we spend time doing the things that we "ought." This is not to suggest that the things we do as a matter of course are necessarily wrong, or that they are things that should not be done. It *is* to suggest that it is an act of dehumanization to engage in any sort of activity or routine without some attempt to understand the nature and the implications of the activity. The following advertisement for Eaton's Hi-Line report covers is an indication of this sort of dehumanization:

> The student might be considered the product of an educational factory. A product of thousands of painstaking learning operations contributing to educational growth, to the making of the product, the student.
>
> The analogy goes far enough when it is understood that, like all products, the student must eventually be sold. He must sell himself to businessmen for the job wanted, to educators for graduate work and fellowship opportunities. . . .

Is this really what education is all about? Do you like to think of yourself as a product? Do you view the children you will be teaching as so much raw material to be processed in assembly-line style? Do you believe that education is merely the means to an end, that it is an end in itself, that it is an activity that continues throughout life, or that it really doesn't matter what it is?

Pick up almost any current magazine and glance through the table of contents. In almost every case you will find at least one article dealing with some aspect of education, for education is a subject of general interest—one that concerns all of us in one way or another. There will be articles by educators, laymen, teachers, and parents, each with some claim to authority, for there is a bit of the educator in each of us. You will find education viewed as a scapegoat and as a panacea; as the only hope for a better future and as the reason for our present moral decline; as a reflection of societal ills and as a shaper of society! You will find education described as all things to all people, and you may well begin to wonder if the different writers can possibly be talking about the same thing.

It is self-evident that if we are to engage in meaningful discussions about educational goals, educational directives, and educational problems, we shall need more than a dictionary definition of what we mean by education. Whether we agree that education is the act of educating, the discipline of mind or character through study or instruction, or a science dealing with the principles and practices of teaching and learning, we need to be more definite in order to be sure that we communicate ideas.

As you begin to examine your own views about education, as you read a variety of educational articles and engage in discussions about them, you will probably discover that each person has a view of education in keeping with his personal goals and the objectives of his society. This being the case, an attempt to define education without reference to a cultural context is meaningless. While this is not intended to be a study of the history of education, it is to our advantage to consider briefly the range of educational emphases and directives in relation to the nature of the society producing them.

Indoctrination

Indoctrination is the oldest and least complex form of education. Although in modern parlance the term carries the connotation of imposing a partisan or sectarian point of view on others and is often used in a derogatory sense, to indoctrinate literally means to teach, to instruct in the rudiments or principles of learning. We can only speculate, as we did concerning the beginnings of philosophy, about the first sort of education known to man; but it is reasonable to suppose that in the broadest sense of the word, indoctrination must go back to the very beginnings of mankind. When the caveman taught his young how to chip arrows and blades from pieces of flint, how to use the hides of animals for coverings; when he taught them how to sew the hides together with strips cut from leather, or with sinews, using needles made of small bones, how to protect themselves from the elements, and how to make fire; when the caveman taught his young all of these things, and more, he was educating by indoctrination. Had it not been for this kind of transmission of knowledge and techniques from one generation to another, we should probably be living much as our cavemen forefathers lived. If each generation had to start fresh, without benefit of lessons from the preceding generation, there could be little in the way of progress.

As the social structure began to evolve from the family group to the clan, and from the clan to the tribe, the mechanics of living became more and more complex. Such complexities gave rise to the specialization of skills and occupations, and this in turn led to the need for a system of apprenticeship. Again indoctrination was probably the most efficient method, and the most successful apprentice was one who learned to do exactly as his master had done before him. In early societies, innovation was most likely the result of accident or happenstance and must have been the exception rather than the rule. We cannot be sure at what point in his evolution man became aware of the future or whether he had such an awareness from his earliest beginning. But skeletal remains, tools, and other artifacts bear witness to burial customs and to primitive religious rites that indicate a real concern for a life after death. We can only imagine the primitive gropings for explanations of life and death, but we can be reasonably certain that "answers" were passed from father to son so that succeeding generations might know how to live in this world; so that they might know how to placate whatever gods, forces, or fates were believed to have power over the lives of men, in order to continue some sort of existence after death.

Salvation

The transmission of any belief or faith in the supernatural might properly be called education for salvation. While education with an emphasis on man's salvation is not necessarily limited to any particular religion or to any particular time in history, the term salvation is usually associated with Christianity. Christianity began as an antiworldly movement of protest, and in early Christianity the emphasis on otherworldliness gave rise to the extreme of asceticism. The early Christians did not trust the educated people of their time who were interested in the things of this world, for Christianity promised and emphasized salvation in another world. Within only a few generations, however, this religion of consolation for the humble and the unhappy became an established church with its own government, property, and power in the secular as well as in ecclesiastical affairs.

Education in such a church-dominated society was obviously authoritarian in nature, and was oriented toward man's salvation. Indoctrination thus took on the meaning of inculcating principles or doctrines with a partisan or sectarian point of view. The view of education for salvation cannot be dismissed as merely an historical curiosity, however, for a glance at history reveals the close relationship between all religiously oriented cultures and religious authoritarianism in education. Nevertheless, this sort of indoctrination is considered by most sophisticated societies of the contemporary world to be antithetical to a democratic education.

Self-Development

Education for self-development can only flourish in a society where a concern for temporal matters dominates a concern for eternal matters and where there is a democratic system of education. Such an emphasis obviates indoctrination and authoritarianism and can only exist in an open society where nothing is immune to inquiry or criticism. It was not until the growth of national self-consciousness in the late nineteenth century that Americans began to work out their own theories of education, giving primary emphasis to self-development.

Actually, the germinal idea of education for self-development may have occurred in the Socratic attack upon the Sophists who professed their ability to teach the youth of Athens any subject by apprenticeship. Certainly the Platonic belief that triggered the attack was instrumental in bringing about a changed view of education in Western civilization. The Platonic idea of recalling knowledge from the soul of man—an unfolding of existing knowledge (a view that will be discussed in the following chapter)— brought a new stress on the individual. It was thought that each individual had a particular function to fulfill in life and that education should be designed to draw out the knowledge each person required in order to realize a predetermined function. This emphasis on self-development was metaphysical in nature, and in that regard differed from current views, even though we accept it as the forerunner of education for self-development.

After the advent of Christianity which emphasized salvation of the soul, the idea of education for self-development did not reappear until the seventeenth century in the works of the English philosopher John Locke (1632–1704) who believed that a child is born with unformed capacities which are developed by individual experiences (Chapter Four). Following Locke, the humanitarian movement, especially the romanticism of Rousseau (Chapter Five), increased the interest in education for self-development. The idea found further expression in the writings of John Dewey (1859–1952) who emphasized the progressive activities of education. Dewey's idea that gradual self-development should be directed along the lines of self-discipline was compatible with the American ideal which emphasizes the uniqueness, worth, and responsibility of the individual in society (Chapter Seven).

The idea of education for self-development has led educators to different conclusions about the curriculum, for there are several possible interpretations of the self which is being educated. Those who see creativity as the distinguishing feature of man are inclined to stress a subjective self-development. Whether the distinction is thought to be that man is simply a symbol-creating animal or that man is a creature with an inherent creative impulse, the curriculum is apt to lean heavily on the fine arts and the humanities. Those who view man as a rational animal—either rational by nature, or with the potential of rationality that can be developed—are apt to stress the sciences and technology as essential for self-development. The extremity of the views is responsible for many of the controversies about the nature of education and about teaching methods, and the divergent viewpoints appear to form an unresolvable dichotomy. However, as we consider recent educational developments we will see that the modern trend is toward a synthesis of the two.

Education in Modern Society

There is no end to the educational issues that are debated by educators and laymen. Should education and the institutions designed for education be used by society for the purpose of a societal betterment? Or should they be instruments to help the individual toward self-development? If the latter, what are the determinants of self-development? What constitutes an educated person? Is teaching an art, or a science? Is method or content more important to education? We have said that the view one takes of man is significant in making educational choices. The view of man that emphasizes the subjective or the creative impulse in man stresses fine arts in the curriculum; the view that emphasizes the objective or the rational in man stresses science and technology in the curriculum. Let us consider briefly the extremes of both views.

There are many who believe that activities in the arts have not had a significant influence on society since the Renaissance, but such a view does not appear to take into consideration the fact that from the nineteenth century on more and more works of art have come to be publicly displayed or performed. Today works of art are no longer the exclusive property of the wealthy or the patrons of the arts but belong to the people. The result is the increasing power of the artist to affect the attitudes of the people. Much art of the recent decades has been experimental and rebellious and has gradually claimed an appreciative audience among those who experience a sort of vicarious liberation from the pressures of the modern world through the expression of the artist. This feeling of liberation through the arts has had a profound effect on the thinking of many who suffer a loss of individuation in the space age. These people feel that twentieth century art reflects the futility of man's venture into space without a corresponding interior expansion and point out that our best art is inwardly focused. Those who look to the arts as salvation from the dehumanizing effects of technology believe that the artist senses a new relation to reality. They insist that only through art can we feel at home in our own time and that only the artist can show us how to move into the future with the necessary creative initiative.

Those who believe the sciences and technology to be disruptive forces turn to creativity as the talisman against this twentieth century onslaught. They believe that creativity, like works of art, belongs to the people. No longer is it thought that creativity is due to divine inspiration, madness, or genius; rather, the creative impulse is thought to be inherent in every human being. Never in history has there been such a profusion of amateur actors, Sunday painters, coffee house poets, kitchen ceramicists, and hobbyists of all descriptions. As the individual turns from the turmoil and anxiety he believes to be engendered by contemporary preoccupation with the sciences, he emphasizes the creativity in business, advertising, cooking, and embroidery.

On the other hand, as members of a society become more and more preoccupied with the sciences and technology, there will be a shift in values. The science-oriented are suspicious of the subjectivity of the artist, and favor the scientific pattern of investigation which is based on disciplined empirical observation, and calls for rigorous, exacting proof—the sort of proof that extends beyond all aspects of personal belief. Science, subject to experimentation and testing, involves the ordering of empirical knowledge about the universe, society, and the individual and, according to the science-oriented, provides the most reliable and practical knowledge. The science-oriented counter the charge of dehumanization by pointing to the scientific miracles in all areas of human endeavor, advances that free man from the shackles of superstition, sentimentality, and tradition.

The claim is often made that man's only real progress has been in the sciences and technology. The claim is supported by contentions that medicine and general technology provide the knowledge which contributes to the alleviation of human suffering and adds to the life span of the individual; that science as a specialized body of knowledge contributes to industry and productivity so that America is the most affluent nation in the world; that advances in military science make America the most powerful nation; that through scientific and technological advances man's universe has expanded beyond his wildest imaginings. Surely by any measure, scientific and technological achievements have been so spectacular that it was not surprising that educational researchers in the nineteenth century began to look to scientific techniques for the solution of problems in education.

The development of a "science of education" can be traced to the writings of Johann Friedrich Herbart (1776–1841) who is generally credited with the beginning of the science of psychology; the works of G. Stanley Hall (1844–1924) who contributed to the scientific study of child development; the works of Edward L. Thorndike (1874–1949) on animal intelligence; the investigation of Joseph M. Rice (1857–1934) which gave impetus to the testing movement in educational research; and the works of Charles Judd (1873–1946) in scientific curriculum development. The introduction of teaching machines in the 1920's by psychologist Sidney Pressey was the beginning of a technological revolution in education, and the electronic computer has led to a computer-based instruction concept in educational circles that is alternately praised and condemned by educators.

Those who react against such innovations do so on a humanistic basis and claim that education by machines has dehumanizing tendencies. Many feel that an emphasis on the "practical" is highly impractical and contributes to the idea that the acquisition of a diploma is an educational finale. Students concentrating on science and technology, it is claimed, have no time for the rudiments of a "liberal" education and no interest in developing their aesthetic and creative aspects. Certainly on the surface, the disparity between art-oriented and science-oriented attitudes points the way to an intellectual schism, to a divergency of values, aims, and goals. The contrariety, if it were a reality, would infinitely complicate the task of the educator, for it would be impossible to satisfy both views. Although the extremes are seldom actualities, the differences between the opposing views of the art-oriented and the science-oriented are sufficient to create a certain amount of confusion about educational choices and goals unless it is recognized that modern education is a sturdy fabric made up of the differences we have broadly outlined.

Elaborating on the analogy, the sciences and technology form the warp of the fabric, and the fine arts and the humanities form the woof of the fabric of modern education. It is the tightness of the weave that determines the strength of the product. The interwoven fabric is a far more accurate representation of modern education than either the warp or the woof alone. The combination is representative of a truly liberal education—one which provides a grounding in the traditional basic subjects as well as an acquaintance with the new ones which have grown out of modern science and technology. The fabric represents a structured relationship of self-development in the fullest sense of the word.

The idea should begin to emerge that perhaps many of our educational problems stem from an insistence on an either/or position which is not feasible or desirable within our democratic framework. This is not to suggest a conceptual potpourri drawn from an emotional and intellectual grab bag, nor to advise an indiscriminate acceptance of all views. Our analogy of an educational fabric makes it eminently clear that unstructured data, ideas, and experiences are merely a jumble of raw material, meaningless until woven into some sort of design. It would make as little sense to utilize all new materials simply because they are new as it would to reject them out of hand because they seem to be at odds with accepted ideas.

Without belaboring the point, the idea emerges that many of the so-called educational controversies are comparable to optical illusions. For instance, a pattern may seem to change according to one's point of view, but the design remains the same. Regardless of the particular view one has of education, there are qualities that remain constant. Modern education is a deliberate activity. Ideally, it is an activity for all people. The common, basic elements of education are thought to be reading, writing, the communication of ideas, and the ability to compute. Education is systematic. There is a correlation between ability levels and the complexity of subject matter. Education has the overall purpose of preparing the individual for the good life which implies that educational choices are related to individual values and goals. Education is a discipline concerned with the formation of concepts, and we are becoming increasingly aware in this connection of the importance of methods of inquiry and systematic approaches to problem solving. Language analysis is an essential element of educational inquiry, and the purpose of the concluding section of the chapter is to introduce the student to the rudiments of this procedure.

Language and Critical Thinking

As we shall see later in our study, the role of the teacher has been considerably altered by twentieth century technological developments. No longer is it thought to be sufficient for a teacher merely to present or to dispense information to the students. Contemporary emphasis in teaching is on activities such as analyzing, evaluating, synthesizing, and structuring information. All of these activities provide the tools for clear and critical thinking. It should be noted, however, that the term *thinking* is used in a variety of ways. For example, consider the following statements:

1. I *think* you should study for this examination.
2. I *think* that I shall go to the bookstore.
3. I want a book, but I can't *think* of the name of it.
4. I *think* that I shall become a teacher.
5. I was just sitting here *thinking* about what a wonderful vacation I had last summer and *thinking* about what it will be like next year.
6. I shall have to *think* about your offer before I can decide what action to take.

Each of the foregoing statements uses the term *think* or *thinking*, yet in each case the term has a different meaning. The first two statements express an attitude or a feeling and are statements of belief. It would be more accurate to substitute the word *believe* or *feel*, for *think*. The third statement expresses a lapse of memory, and *remember* would be a more accurate term than *think*. The fourth statement is primarily one of belief but may also express *desire*. The fifth statement would be more precise if the terms *remembering* and *wondering* were substituted for the two uses of the term *thinking*. No one of the first five statements has the essential qualities of critical thought, for there is no choice between alternatives and no analysis of fact and implication. Consider, however, the way the term *think* is used in the sixth statement. Here the term is not used to express feeling, belief, desire, recollection, or speculation but is used to indicate the sort of thinking which does involve analysis and choice.

Critical thinking (sometimes called rational reflection, reflective thinking, or rational thought) means to be analytical about beliefs, ideas, experiences, and facts. It requires close attention to clarity of language and meaning, to methods of inquiry, and knowledge about procedures that insure correct reasoning. The importance of critical thinking has long been recognized, and throughout the centuries there has been considerable controversy over whether it is a process that can be taught or if one develops the ability through example and practice. The Herbartian formal steps were designed to develop processes of thinking, but the method was not successful as the application of the steps required too much rigidity. In recent years mathematics and the natural sciences stress discovery and inquiry with a view toward promoting critical thinking, and more and more curricula, both in high schools and in colleges, require courses in logic. As we have previously noted, this study is designed to encourage the development of critical thinking by way of example, by study of the basic elements of language and logic, and by practice.

According to the Harvard Report on *General Education in a Free Society:*

> The final ground of the policy for the study of literature here outlined is perhaps this: long-continued close contact with excellent work, the best of its kind, has a formative and ordering power especially upon minds still plastic, growing, and active in imitation.[8]

Accordingly, our study of what outstanding philosophers and educators have observed about education has a two-fold purpose. The study supplies historical continuity and at the same time provides classic examples of critical thinking. Our discussion of language analysis is admittedly little more than a survey, but it should be sufficient to assist the student to clarify his thinking and to evaluate the ideas of others. Assuming that most college students have some knowledge of the basic principles of formal logic, our consideration in that regard is limited to the reading at the end of the chapter. The selection on formal logic from Harold Larrabee's *Reliable Knowledge* provides an excellent grounding for those who have not studied introduction to logic and a superb refresher for those who have. Even the keenest thinker will benefit by knowledge of easily applied methods for testing the correctness of his own reasoning and the reasoning of others. The third avenue to critical thinking, practice, must depend largely upon the diligence of each individual.

The Uses of Language

There have been many suggestive accounts about the origin of spoken language. One of the most comprehensive works is that of Jacquetta Hawkes and Sir Leonard Woolley in their volume in the *History of Man-*

---

[8] Report of the Harvard Committee, *General Education in a Free Society* (Cambridge, Massachusetts: Harvard University Press, 1945), p. 110.

kind.[9] They suggest that the spoken word may have risen out of the symbolic sounds that accompanied gestures, usually hand gestures; but, while there is much to recommend the position, the precise origin of spoken language must remain a mystery. Regardless of the source one posits, it seems reasonable that language at least developed out of a stage of pantomiming and babbling until signs and words assumed an individual relationship. The problems of use and clarification of language are intimately related to the concepts of *symbol* and *sign.*

Briefly, signs are indications of other things. Signs point, direct, stop, lead to inference, or to some physical response. A symbol is a contrived or conventional sign, but not all signs are symbols. For instance, words can serve both as signs and symbols to man but only as signs or cues to other animal species. Signs and symbols only *represent* things, and they should not be mistaken for things in themselves. Harold Larrabee says that one of man's greatest achievements is in detaching the symbol from its original context. He writes: "To realize, however, that there is no necessary connection between the symbol and the symbolized, that words are independent of things, takes a certain degree of sophistication that not everyone possesses. If we stop to think about the matter, we shall recognize that the structure of language does not necessarily duplicate the structure of the world about which we wish to write or talk."[10]

The overall purpose of language is communication of ideas, feelings, desires, descriptions, directions, warnings—the listing could continue for pages. At the risk of oversimplification, we shall consider the use of language in three very general categories: 1) informative; 2) expressive; and 3) directive. It should be emphasized that a clear-cut distinction is no more desirable in practice than it is possible in theory, for in both cases there is always a good deal of overlap.

Informative language is intimately related with instruction which is essentially verbal. The teacher-student interaction depends more than anything else upon how language operates in the classroom, and the importance of giving proper attention to the use of language by teacher and student cannot be overemphasized. The primary function of informative language is to communicate information, which is ordinarily accomplished by formulating and affirming or denying propositions. Truth and falsity play an important role, and in many cases information can be misinformation. Informative discourse is factual and is used to describe the world about us and to reason about it. It is used in journals, reports, and textbooks, and science provides us with prime examples of informative language.

Expressive language is used to communicate and to elicit emotions, and it relies heavily on emotive words, on connotative, rather than on denotative language. Although the best examples are found in poetry, ex-

9 Jacquetta Hawkes and Sir Leonard Woolley, *History of Mankind, Volume I, Prehistory and the Beginnings of Civilization* (New York: Harper & Row, Publishers, 1963), pp. 108–9.
10 Harold Larrabee, *Reliable Knowledge,* Revised Edition (Boston: Houghton Mifflin Company, 1964), p. 166.

pressive language is by no means limited to that medium, for we use it frequently in day-to-day conversation. It is used for worship, love-making, oratory, and football games. It is used whenever the speaker gives vent to feeling, or attempts to evoke feelings from others.

Directive language is used primarily for the purpose of causing or preventing some overt action. It commands, demands, requests, directs, prevents. It leans sometimes toward the informative, and at other times it veers toward the expressive. It is perhaps the least pure of the categories, for a command can wear the soft cloak of a smile and be masked with a "please" in order to pass as a request. There can be no question of truth or falsity in the strictest sense of the word, for in its naked imperative form a command such as, "Leave your papers on my desk," is neither true nor false. Questions are classified as directive, for ordinarily a question calls for a response from the one who is questioned. But at the same time, we have repeatedly seen how skillful questioning can also be highly instructive, and almost everyone has experienced questions that are most revealing.

The point is not to strive for a mechanical application of language according to the categories we have mentioned but to be aware of the special uses in order to blend the categories most effectively according to a particular objective. Tools are meant to be used, and language properly used is one of our most effective tools for communication. What could be more dull and less effective than a sermon with the predominant purpose of directing when the language is limited to one category? An effective sermon will not merely direct. Ideally, it will contain factual, instructive material, and it will certainly evoke feelings. Real finesse in the use of language blends the elements of communication much as a fine French chef blends his ingredients and chooses his spices to concoct a *pièce de résistance,* a salad, or a sweet.

We have seen that the language categories of function are informative, expressive, and directive. The grammatical categories of language, or the categories of form, are the declarative, interrogative, imperative, and exclamatory. Although the latter do sometimes provide a cue about the categories of function, there is no necessary connection between the two. There is no strict relation between *intended function* and *content,* but *context* is an important element of function. Words take on a different coloration and even a different meaning according to the context in which they are used. Although there is no mechanical method for determining function, when we speak of the *meaning* of language it becomes important to disentangle the informative function of a given passage from the nuances of language and from the other functions it may also be serving.

The Meaning of Language

We have noted that there is no *necessary* connection between a symbol and its referent; but at the same time, the study of words (semantics) is not separate from the things the words stand for and from the concepts they suggest. Although a word is an arbitrary symbol, there is a definite relationship between the word, the referent, and the concept. It has been suggested that we think of the word and the referent as forming the base of a triangle and the concept as being the apex. A study of the meaning of language is complicated by the fact that no word possesses a specific meaning of its own. Meaning varies according to the particular context, and according to the experiential background of different individuals with each word and referent. Whenever ideas are exchanged through the medium of language, written or spoken, the choice of words can either enhance or impede the exchange. We have all experienced the different coloration the use of language can import to identical data. Harold Larrabee has said that "Language is at least as capable of a variety of uses as gunpowder."[11]

We are threatened daily to be entrapped or misled by the words used for advertisements on television and in other media, by the words used by politicians, news reporters, and salesmen. History provides prime examples of the different coloration the use of language can impart to identical data. It is an historical problem to determine what actually occurred at a particular time and place in history, but it is a semantic problem to determine which words should be used to describe the event. John Dewey wrote in *How We Think:*

> A constant source of misunderstanding and mistake is indefiniteness of meaning. Because of vagueness of meaning we misunderstand people, things, ourselves; because of ambiguity we distort and pervert. Conscious distortion of meaning many be enjoyed as nonsense; erroneous meanings, if clear-cut, may be followed up and got rid of. But vague meanings are too gelatinous to offer matter for analysis and too pulpy to afford support to other beliefs. They evade testing and responsibility. Vagueness disguises the unconscious mixing together of different meanings, and facilitates the substitution of one meaning for another, and covers up failure to have any precise meaning at all. It is the aboriginal logical sin—the source from which flow most bad intellectual consequences. Totally to eliminate indefiniteness is impossible; to reduce it in extent and in force requires sincerity and vigor.[12]

Certainly we must all strive to determine meaning as exactly as possible, and it is a task that has special significance for teaching.

Words are an integral part of our lives, and a working vocabulary is the kind of wealth that anyone can acquire. One way to build a vocabulary is through paying close attention to the definition of terms, but this is only one reason for the importance of definition. It is important in order that we be able to make our use of a word, our particular meaning, clear to others. Exact definition helps eliminate the ambiguity that can arise when

---

[11] *Ibid.,* p. 171.
[12] John Dewey, *How We Think,* Revised Edition (Boston: D. C. Heath & Company, 1933), pp. 159–160.

there is some doubt as to which sense of a given word is intended. Ambiguous language leads to fallacious arguments and verbal disputes which cloud issues but that are dispelled as soon as the different definitions of a term are given and the different meanings distinguished.

There is also occasion for a definition of terms when the term is vague and it appears that clarification is in order. Vagueness is distinct from ambiguity, as the former occurs as a result of borderline cases, rather than from a term having two distinct meanings. Again, terms are sometimes defined to serve a theoretical purpose, to attach some property to the word. Finally, there are times when we define a term in order to influence attitudes by means of the definition we give. Thus we see that definitions can also have an expressive as well as an informative function.

There are five general types of definitions which relate to the reasons we have given for definition. They are: 1) stipulative definitions which are given to introduce a brand new term; 2) lexical definitions which are reportings of meanings already associated with a term; 3) precise definitions which transcend ordinary usage and are used to reduce the vagueness of a term; 4) theoretical definitions which strive to formulate a theoretically adequate characterization of the objects to which they are applied; and 5) persuasive definitions which relate to the corresponding purposes.

The techniques for defining can be divided into two main groups. The first group centers on denotation or extension and includes the following techniques: 1) giving examples of objects denoted by the term being defined; 2) definition by subclasses; and 3) ostensive (demonstrative) definitions. Denotative definitions can be either stipulative or lexical. The second group of techniques centers on connotation or intention and includes the following techniques: 1) operational definitions; and 2) definition by genus and difference—sometimes called "definition by division" or "analytical definition."

There are five rules for definition by genus and difference which apply primarily to lexical definitions. These are: 1) a definition should state the essential attributes of the species; 2) a definition must not be circular; 3) a definition must be neither too broad nor too narrow; 4) a definition must not be expressed in ambiguous, obscure, or figurative language; and 5) a definition should not be negative where it can be affirmative.[13]

Clarification of Language

A fallacy is a deceptive argument, one that appears to be correct but upon examination proves to be otherwise. Fallacies are divided into two main groups—formal fallacies and informal fallacies. The formal fallacy is a flaw which vitiates a syllogism, and the informal fallacy is a misuse of language out of carelessness, inattention to the subject, or occasionally through deliberation. Our concern in connection with clarification of lan-

---

[13] Irving Copi, *Introduction to Logic,* Second Edition (New York: The Macmillan Company, 1961), pp. 123–127.

guage is informal fallacies which are also sometimes called "material fallacies of reasoning." These fallacies can be grouped according to fallacies of relevance and fallacies of ambiguity.

Arguments that commit fallacies of relevance have premises that do not have a logical relevance to the conclusion of the argument. Some of the particular types have been given Latin names which in some cases— "ad hominem," for example—are so common that the Latin term has become a part of the English language. We shall mention only a few of these to illustrate the nature of the fallacies that beguile the unwary.

1. *Argumentum ad Baculum* (appeal to force). As the name suggests, this fallacy is committed when rational arguments fail, and force, or the threat of force, is used to persuade the opposition to agree with a proposal. It is often used by lobbyists who are trying to influence some legislation by reminding the representative of the thousands of voters the lobbyist represents.

2. *Argumentum ad Hominem* (abusive). If we suggested that since Bacon was removed from his chancellorship for dishonesty his philosophy should not be trusted, we should be committing this fallacy. Often when there is no case against a proposal, the character of the person making the proposal is attacked instead.

3. *Argumentum ad Ignorantiam* (argument from ignorance). This is the sort of fallacy that is committed when one argues that a proposition must be true since it has never been proven false or vice versa.

4. *Argumentum ad Misericordiam* (appeal to pity). As the name suggests, this fallacy is committed when an appeal is made to the sense of pity in the listeners in order to get them to agree to a proposition.

5. *Argumentum ad Populum* (appeal to the people). This is a fallacy that is committed by directing an emotional appeal to the people or to the gallery, in order to get them to agree to an unsupported conclusion. That is, a propagandist may use invidious terms in place of rational argument in order to mobilize public sentiment. It is a fallacy favored by hucksters and advertisers.

6. *Argumentum ad Verecundiam* (appeal to authority). The fallacy is committed when the speaker takes advantage of public respect for a figure or institution in order to win an argument. It is frequently used in advertising testimonials.

7. *Accident*. When a statement that in some connection is true is treated as though it were always true without qualification, the fallacy of accident has been committed.

8. *False Cause*. This fallacy occurs when an event is assumed to be the cause of another simply because the one occurred earlier than the second, or when anything that is *not* the cause of a given event is offered as the real cause for the sake of argument.

9. *Complex Question*. A complex question consists of two or more questions that are phrased as one. A straightforward "yes" or "no" answer

is impossible without affirming or denying the unstated question or questions. For instance, if you respond positively to the question, "Have you stopped cheating?" there is an admission (by implication) that you used to cheat.

10. *Ignoratio Elenchi* (irrelevant conclusion). The fallacy is committed when an argument for a particular conclusion is offered in support of an entirely different one.

The above listing is far from complete, but it should at least indicate the kind of irrelevancies that can persuade the unwary to error. Generalization is always risky, but it does seem reasonable to suggest that fallacies of relevance, as compared to fallacies of ambiguity, are more likely to be used with deliberation. Doubtless there are many instances when unclear thinking and/or faulty reasoning can be blamed for such fallacies, but the preponderance of evidence in advertising, news reporting, politics, and salesmanship leads one to suspect otherwise.

Fallacies of ambiguity, on the other hand, seem to result largely from carelessness, or ignorance. There is, of course, some deliberate use of fallacies in this grouping for the sake of entertainment. Ambiguities can be divided into five general types.

1. *Equivocation*. Most words have more than one literal meaning, and we equivocate if we use such a word in different senses in the same context; or if the word is used in one sense and taken in another. For instance, the following statement could be taken in either of two ways: "The professor failed his entire class."

2. *Amphiboly*. An amphibolous statement is one in which the meaning is unclear because of faulty grammatical construction. For instance, "She went to the dance with Tom wearing a sweater and skirt."

3. *Accent*. The fallacy of accent occurs when the meaning of a statement is changed, depending upon what part of it is emphasized. "Oh, no! You'd never lie to anybody!" is given a meaning opposite to the literal one by a sarcastic tone of voice.

4. *Composition*. Reasoning about the parts of a whole to the conclusion that the sum of the parts has the same distinction. An example would be to assume that because all of the individual members on a particular team are good athletes, it must be an outstanding team.

5. *Division*. The fallacy of division is the reverse of the fallacy of composition. An example would be the assumption that since a certain firm is a distinguished one, every person connected with the firm is also distinguished.

Teachers who are knowledgeable about the tools of critical thinking and who use the techniques of analysis in their classes will be able to communicate their subject matter effectively, for knowledge transmitted in a logical manner is apt to be handled by the student in a like manner. The treatment of a subject will be more searching and complete if the logical implications of the topic are brought out, and there is likely to be greater comprehension on the part of the student. When the student is drawn into the process of instruction by means of leading questions, teaching becomes a sort of guided conversation where all of the participants seek the kinds of evidence needed for valid and reliable conclusions. There can be little doubt but that successful teaching and learning are insured by the kinds of logical procedures that occur in classroom discourse.

HAROLD LARRABEE

Formal Logic: What Follows from Premises*

According to the view taken here, some knowledge of formal logic is essential to critical thinking. Since the place of logic in teacher preparation programs has not yet been finally determined, it is doubtful that all who are involved in the present study will be familiar with the basic principles of traditional logic. For that reason, the chapter, "Formal Logic," from Harold Larrabee's book, Reliable Knowledge, *has been selected for the reading to supplement the material in Chapter I. A careful study of the following pages, while by no means intended as a substitute for a course in logic, would go far toward helping a neophyte recognize the differences between correct and incorrect reasoning. Not only is Larrabee's presentation such that little doubt is left as to the importance of logic for ascertaining if one's knowledge is indeed reliable, it is a remarkable vignette of an introduction to logic.*

1. Short Cuts to Certainty?
No one can survey the long history of man's failures and successes as a knower without being struck by the discrepancy between the pretentiousness of most human knowledge-claims and the small amount of evidence actually available with which to back them up. Not only are most men, as we have seen, credulous by nature and inclined to accept whatever beliefs are first urged upon them strongly, clearly, and repeatedly; they are also dogmatic and assertive—that is, their affirmations about what they know with certainty are continually outrunning any proof that they are inclined or able to offer. This appetite for certainty tempts them to take the nearest short cut to the goal of apparently reliable knowledge. This is especially true of men who are constantly being called upon for decisive action: the intense conviction that they are absolutely right in their beliefs enables them to adopt and to pursue bold policies with vigor and per-

---
* From *Reliable Knowledge* by Harold Larrabee. Reprinted by permission of Houghton Mifflin Company, Boston, 1964.

sistence, where doubts and a divided mind might lead only to delay and confusion.

Humility about one's knowledge, or the admission of one's ignorance, is then a late lesson which man learns only at the cost of innumerable blunders. We begin life in the deepest ignorance, which is ignorance of our ignorance. Yet knowing little or nothing is seldom any obstacle to being confident in everything. It took an extraordinary individual named Socrates to boast, as early as the fifth century B.C., that he was the wisest of the Greeks, because he alone knew that he knew nothing. Even modern scientists have been slow to acknowledge that the true measure of their knowledge is their awareness of how much remains to be known. Says Dr. Abraham Flexner: "No scientist, fifty years ago, could have realized that he was as ignorant as all first-rate scientists now know themselves to be."[1]

Nothing is more dangerous than generalizing about the thinking of men who lived many centuries ago; yet it seems safe to say that primitive peoples the world over have tended to accept as reliable knowledge whatever has been handed down from their ancestors as tribal customs or folkways. Customs are ready-made generalizations about conduct: they "lay down the law" with or without supporting "reasons" for their observance. They are beliefs which are lived by; the tribe has survived, presumably, by following them; therefore they must be right. Thus, man's first formulated "universals," such as "All flesh of a certain sort must be avoided," or "Repeating this prayer correctly will bring rain," were practical imperatives which were strongly believed and implicitly followed by virtually all the members of a community. Just as habit-forming aided the individual, these fixed rules about what "was done" and what "was not done" lent stability and order to communal living. Whenever it was necessary for the group to act as a unit, such unwritten laws backed by irresistible sanctions could be used to coerce any recalcitrant objector.

Of course, we are inclined to be contemptuous of the "reasons" which were usually given for conforming to the accepted practices, regarding them as circular ("It's done because it's done") or grossly superstitious; but the important thing to note is that, in the atmosphere of authority, no reasons were really necessary. Anthropologists who have studied so-called "primitive" peoples have often called attention to the apparent spontaneity and sureness of their group decisions, as in the administration of justice, in spite of the absence of any legal machinery. The group's swift verdict is the practicing of a concrete habit, and not the deducing of the consequences of an abstract legal principle. Their behavior is dominated by a tacitly understood and firmly accepted pattern or premise, from which it "follows" inevitably. The particular case is seen to fall under an unquestionable generalization which does not need to be explicitly formulated, much less to be precisely defined. All that comes later.

This may help us to understand why the history of man's conscious quest for reliable knowledge in the Western world began as it did, and why it took so long for what we call scientific method to develop. Sometimes we may wonder why men were not more patient and humble in acquiring and claiming knowledge, and why they did not begin by adding fact to fact in order to confirm a few modest generalizations, and by cautiously labeling as knowledge only what their carefully tested evidence could support. What we forget is that, for

---

[1] *Universities* (New York, 1930), p. 17.

thousands of years, man was schooled under heavy pressures and penalties in a very different method of knowing. Where fixation of belief for confident group action was most important, he could hardly be blamed for taking what seemed to be the most promising routes to it. Thus for uncounted generations men grew up in communities which took it for granted that they already possessed a great deal of reliable knowledge in the generalized form of customs, rules-of-thumb, proverbs, laws, and commandments about the things that mattered most in life. People who are absolutely sure of such general truths come naturally to think of reliability in details as chiefly depending upon what follows from what they already assuredly know. If everyone regards it as self-evident and unquestionable that blasphemers against the gods ought to be put to death, then the correct disposition of an individual case hinges merely upon whether or not "this man is a blasphemer."

This dogmatic approach or habit of thought, once formed, is difficult to break, since it possesses the great advantage of complete assurance about a few highly economical "fundamental" convictions or principles on which a strong character may be based. The unswerving consistency of a man's actions with his announced beliefs is regarded as a sign of the highest virtue, and those of his actions which cannot actually be fitted in have to be rationalized. Doubt, hesitation, tentativeness, attention to exceptions—all these are denounced as subversive and reprehensible. Everything in a society of this sort seems to conspire to make men dogmatic and cocksure about the broad knowledge-claims which provide them, when challenged, with the premises of their actions.

The atmosphere of the periods of the history of Western Europe known as ancient and medieval may be fairly characterized as permeated by authority and the dogmatic approach to knowledge. Always remembering that there were shining exceptions, we may say that men on the whole were convinced that they possessed a supply of absolutely reliable principles or axiomatic truths upon which firm structures of detailed knowledge about the world could be built. The main outlines or "plot" of the cosmic story being already known, it remained only to fill in the gaps, where necessary, by speculative elaboration. It was not strange, then, that men were first attracted to tests of knowledge which concerned the processes of deduction from already accepted general principles, rather than to those which dealt with induction from particular instances. Thus it came about that, until well into the modern period, logic was almost universally understood to consist of the rules of valid deductive reasoning from premises that were already known to be reliable.

2. The Ancient Greeks and Abstract Generalizing

Professor F. J. E. Woodbridge of Columbia used to remark that "the ancient Greeks taught themselves how to think, and have taught all the rest of us in the Western world." What he referred to, of course, was the "miraculous" advance which was made by a few gifted Greeks of the fifth and fourth centuries B.C. in the art of formulating in language abstract general principles covering many concrete particular instances, such as: "All gods are immortal," or "No slave can be a citizen." These thinkers set the fashions and coined the vocabulary of logic for a good two thousand years; and it is mainly to them that we owe the technique of conceptual thinking that underlies all our Western science and technology. So accustomed are we to thinking in abstract "ideas" or class-concepts rather than in individual items or cases, that it is almost impossible for us to realize that things might have been very different in Western Europe if the Greeks had not happened to perfect this particular mathematical type of logic. But a glance at Oriental habits of thinking in fluid allegories and rhythmic patterns like the figures of a dance, as in Hindu and Chinese logics, should be enough to convince anyone of the immense debt which we, as thinkers, owe to the Greeks.[2]

The pre-Greek civilizations, notably the Egyptian and Babylonian, accumulated a certain amount of detailed knowledge in the fields of geometry (earth measurement) and astronomy (star classification), but their learned men seemed for the most part to be content with their specific measurements and tabulations without generalizing from them to form what we call theories about natural events. A famous example was the discovery by the Egyptian rope-stretchers, who measured land boundaries and the deposits of Nile mud, that a triangle with two sides measuring three and four units had a third side measuring five units. But the Greek Pythagoras (580–500 B.C.) went on to make that discovery into a theorem expressing the abstract relationship of the sides of *any* right triangle whatever: the famous statement of the equality of the square of the hypotenuse and the combined squares of the two sides.

Once begun, Greek philosophizing, or the critical cultivation of the love of wisdom through both scientific and humanistic inquiries, swiftly reached the heights in the work of three giants of the intellect: Socrates, Plato, and Aristotle. The first of the three, Socrates (470–399 B.C.) spurred men on to seek underlying forms or concepts by his tireless questionings concerning commonly used words and their meanings. Plato (427–347 B.C.) carried this tendency further in his Academy, exalting the study of pure mathematics as a theoretical discipline of the mind without reference to its application to buying and selling, trading and building.[3] Plato and his pupils also aided in the clarification of terms by arranging ideas in chains of decreasing generality, subdividing at each step, such as: beings are corporeal and incorporeal; corporeal beings are animal and nonanimal; animal beings are rational and nonrational; and so on. By this method, working down one side of the ladder of subdivisions, they were able to define a man as a rational, animal, corporeal being.

Aristotle (384–322 B.C.) sought not only to organize all the knowledge of his day which had been gained by observation, but also to connect it with the speculative achievements of his famous master, Plato. Accepting the prevailing view that all knowledge arises out of pre-existing knowledge, he strove to demonstrate how we are justified in placing the various classes of things in such descending orders as Plato had sketched. This, he believed, could be done by relating the two classes of things in question to a third class: animals are organisms having sensation and the power of independent locomotion; and so are men; therefore, men belong under the wider class, animals. This view took it for granted that every individual thing in Nature had its proper place in

---

[2] Cf., part II, chap. II, "Comparative Logic" in Paul Masson-Oursel, *Comparative Philosophy* (New York, 1926).

[3] "It was to be a study of abstract forms and not of objects embodying these forms." Raphael Demos, *The Philosophy of Plato* (New York, 1939), p. 287. Greek mathematics reached formulation as a purely deductive science, given certain axioms and postulates, in Euclid's famous *Elements* (about 290 B.C.). So incomparably superior was Euclid's system to any other product of human thinking up to that time that, as Professor C. J. Keyser points out, "men were dazzled by it, blinded by its very brilliance, so much so that . . . they failed to see its chief significance was, not geometric, but methodological." *Thinking About Thinking* (New York, 1926), pp. 26–27.

some species, which was included in some wider genus, which was in turn included as a species in some still higher genus. The task of the scientist was to see that everything was put in its proper place in the gigantic system of pigeonholes within pigeonholes which Nature was assumed to be.

In addition, Aristotle wanted to supply the pupils of his school, the Lyceum, with a series of handbooks of the art of public disputation or dialectic, in which they, as politically ambitious young Athenians, desired to excel. In the dialogues of Plato are many examples of the kind of public argument which was then in fashion, in which Socrates is made to play the part of the questioner who skillfully elicits from his fellow disputants a series of yes-or-no answers which eventually entangle them in logical contradictions. Aristotle endeavored to place this art on a solid basis by showing how a reasoner could both avoid the fallacies of his opponents and oblige them to accept his own valid conclusions.

What he and his later pupils provided was an *Organon* (or instrument) for the speedy testing of the deductive consequences of possibly damaging admissions when clearly stated in terms of classes and put together in pairs. It was a logic of deductive consistency in the use of language, designed to make the prospective disputant aware of the traps and pitfalls to which an apparently harmless verbal admission might lead. Its primary aim, says Minto, "was as practical as a treatise on navigation or 'Cavendish on Whist.' "[4] One began with already admitted assumptions, and then, by following the rules, one demonstrated their inescapable consequences in the realm of discourse for every rational human being.

The close connection of this kind of logic with man's increasing use of and dependence upon language is obvious. As long as he was relatively inarticulate, man's acts were checked for the most part by their immediate consequences. If the primitive hunter made an erroneous inference, he generally paid for it on the spot. But as human beings came to put a larger and larger proportion of their ideas into thoughts and words rather than into physical practice, they found, as John Dewey has pointed out, that "where there is no directly appreciable reaction of the inference upon the security and prosperity of life, there are no natural checks to the acceptance of wrong beliefs." In the absence of natural checks, artificial ones had to be devised, unless erroneous beliefs were to multiply unchecked. Greek logic was, in part at least, the new freedom of abstract thought and language trying to police itself.

Thanks to Aristotle's genius, his testing instrument was remarkably mature and complete. The Wise Men of Greece had hardly begun their first gropings toward the free use of abstract thinking before the beginning of the sixth century B.C., and yet, by the third century B.C., the technique of deduction by the relating of fixed class-concepts had apparently been worked out so comprehensively that it stood with only minor changes for over two thousand years. It was this seemingly finished character of the Aristotelian and Euclidean systems which induced men to believe that such verbal and mathematical theories must be identical with the patterns of physical Nature, a belief which retarded the development of science for centuries.

3. The Categorical Syllogism

Generations of students have begun their study of deduction with the classic example:

---

[4] William Minto, *Logic Inductive and Deductive* (New York, 1899), p. 3.

All men are mortal

Socrates is a man

Socrates is a mortal

Our first reaction to this is likely to be that plainly *if* the first two statements or premises are accepted as reliable, *then* any reasonable being will have to accept the third statement or conclusion, since it necessarily follows; but that actually all three are rather obvious and bring us little in the way of new knowledge. We assume that some such statement as "All men who are known to have lived are known to have died before reaching the age of two hundred years" is accepted as reliable knowledge to begin with; and also some such proposition as "Socrates is a being who may rightly be classified as a man."

But presumably we made the two statements for the purpose of determining Socrates' status with respect to mortality. We proceeded by connecting both Socrates and the state of being mortal with a third class, men, which disappeared in our conclusion. This is a familiar operation of the human mind, although generally not so systematically performed. It is useful in connecting hitherto scattered bits of our knowledge in such a way that the result can be tested. This is especially true when we are called upon to "prove our point" in an argument that does not win immediate assent. For example, let it be supposed that a question arose concerning the status of a male American Indian with respect to military service. One participant argues that American Indians are not citizens but wards of the Federal government, and hence are not subject to call for military service. Another arguer produces the act of June 2, 1924, by which American Indians were declared to be citizens, hence:

All male citizens are subject to call for military service.

All native-born male American Indians are male citizens.

All native-born male American Indians are subject to call for military service.

In such instances we are making it possible to test a conclusion by exhibiting it as the logical result of putting together either two supposedly reliable general principles, or one general principle and another particular proposition. One of the general principles happened to be lying dormant in the memory, unconnected with the other, or with particular instances which arose. It is the bringing together of the two which yields the conclusion; and that is sometimes surprisingly difficult. Looking back upon any chain of deductive reasoning, such as the final solution of a detective story, we are likely to say to ourselves: "How stupid of us not to have seen the answer all the time! It was right there in front of us: we knew perfectly well a number of separate truths that, properly fitted together, would have given us the correct result. But we failed to 'put two and two together' in such a way as to arrive at it." The skilled reasoner takes the same lot of queer, incoherent, and apparently unrelated clues, sifts out those which are irrelevant and misleading, and arranges the remainder in an unbreakable and convincing pattern. This ability to combine hitherto isolated propositions in such a way as to arrive at new, sound, and hitherto unsuspected conclusions is the mark of the keen-witted detective, the skillful lawyer, the adroit military strategist, and the far-sighted business man. Yet even the cleverest deducer cannot get his results accepted unless other equally astute reasoners can be convinced that his conclusions follow inevitably from acceptable premises. To do this, he must be capable of displaying his reasoning in terms of the class relationships which enable all who understand the rules of logic to test his conclusions for themselves.

Inference and Implication

So far, our discussion has been mainly about the process of deductive inference, which is a human activity of thinking by which we pass from one proposition to another, accepting or rejecting the latter on the basis of the former. Inferring is a temporal, psychological matter; it is something which people may either do or fail to do, and which can be done well or badly, depending upon the logical capacity of the one who does the inferring. In the presence of the same abundant evidence at the scene of a crime, for example, a layman might make no inferences at all; an untrained officer might make several incorrect ones; while an expert criminologist might make a great many correct inferences leading to the conviction of the guilty party.

In determining the reliability of knowledge that apparently follows from accepted premises, however, logicians are concerned with the rules for testing our inferences to see which ones are and which ones are not justified. Their concern is with the consistency of the reasoning. What they want to know is whether or not a given inference is valid or invalid—that is, whether or not it can be shown to follow necessarily or inescapably from the premises upon which it purports to be based. Now an inference, to be accepted as valid, must be rigorously demonstrated to rest upon an implication or necessary connection between the premises and the conclusion. If we assume that all A is included in B, and all B is included in C, that *implies* that all A is included in C, no matter what A, B, and C may happen to be, and no matter whether anyone ever happens to make that particular inference. The formal necessity is in the relations of the classes; and, once the premises are accepted, the conclusion is no longer a matter of opinion if you make any claim to being logical in your thinking. For you simply cannot accept the premises, reject the conclusion, and pretend to follow the rules of logic, all at the same time. But, if someone tries to convince you that all A is included in C on the grounds that all A is included in B, and *some* B is included in C, it can be pointed out that the conclusion is not implied by the premises. You can accept the premises, and yet escape the conclusion.

Implications are thus structural relationships between propositions; they are just there, whether or not we bring them to light and use them in the making of valid inferences. If in the heat of an argument I state that "All owners of firearms ought to register them," then I imply that Mr. X, who owns a shotgun, ought to register it, although neither I nor anyone else may ever have occasion to draw that particular inference. "We make," say Professors Lewis and Langford, "an inference upon observation of a certain relation between facts. Whether the facts have that relation or not we do not determine. But whether we shall *be observant of* just this particular relation of the facts and whether we shall *make that relation the basis of our inferences* are things which we do determine."[5] Once we have made our selection from the "extraordinarily large number" of alternative relations, and have established the precise meanings of

---

[5] C. I. Lewis and C. H. Langford, *Symbolic Logic* (New York, 1932), p. 258. (Italics theirs, H. A. L.) See also M. R. Cohen and E. Nagel, *op. cit.*, chap. I, 1–3.

the ones we have chosen to use as the premises of our inference, then their implications follow, and can no more be disputed, if correctly deduced, than the corollaries in a system of mathematics. We have all had the experience of admitting the truth of certain premises in a dispute without realizing, at the moment, their logical implications, and then discovering, too late, that we had inadvertently committed ourselves to the acceptance of some unwelcome conclusions. Men may and do quarrel endlessly about what relations shall be selected in the first place, and about the initial reliability and exact meaning of those which they choose as premises; but, once they have come to an agreement upon those points, the validity of their subsequent deductions can be checked with entire accuracy by anyone who is able to make a thorough analysis of the implications involved. Formal logic in its many branches deals with this analysis of implications. It is not concerned, as logic, with anything but the relations of the classes or propositions, the formal structure of the reasoning. It cares nothing about the material contents of the propositions, even though the reasoner may care a great deal about them.

Hence formal logic can examine seriously an argument which is completely absurd, such as:

> Some boneless turnips are square-wheeled bicycles
> All boneless turnips are drunken hyenas
> _____
> Some drunken hyenas are square-wheeled bicycles

> All sniks are murps
> Some worgs are not murps
> _____
> Some worgs are not sniks

In both of these examples, the meanings, if any, are hilariously at odds with existence; and yet the relationships of the classes, if there were such things, are perfectly clear and the conclusions are formally valid.

In order to test our reasoning by the rules of logic, it is therefore necessary in most cases, as Reichenbach has pointed out, to "reconstruct" our actual thought in the form of premises and conclusion. Men seldom think consciously by the rules of logic, which, strictly speaking, usually apply only to reconstructions of their thoughts. Like mathematics, which turns observations and measurements into numbers, and then manipulates the symbols to reach a result, formal logic takes instances of everyday thinking, and, where possible, turns them into sentences called propositions, and then into symbols for the purpose of demonstrating the validity or invalidity of the conclusion.

Analysis of the Categorical Syllogism

The kind of deductive argument considered to this point, consisting of two related premises and a conclusion, is called the categorical syllogism. The word syllogism comes from the Greek "discourses together," while categorical means here "directly asserted," and not relative or hypothetical. Since this type of syllogism has been studied for centuries, a complete elaboration of its rules and exceptions fills many pages in the elementary deductive logic textbooks, to which the interested reader is referred. We shall be concerned only with the main outlines of deduction in order to show how, in general, it is possible to test

formally any argument that is capable of being expressed in syllogistic terms.
If we examine a typical syllogism, such as:

All unearned income is taxable	M	P
All dividends are unearned income	S	M
All dividends are taxable	S	P

it is apparent that our argument yields a valid conclusion about the relation of the subject term of the conclusion (S), the class "All dividends" to the predicate term (P), the class "taxable things" by means of a third term (M), the class "unearned income," which does not appear in the conclusion. "Unearned income" in this example is what is called the *middle term* of the syllogism, since it is the mediating factor which brings the *minor term* (always the subject of the conclusion) into the asserted relationship to the *major term* (always the predicate of the conclusion). It is called *major* because the class of things mentioned in the predicate is ordinarily wider and more inclusive than the class in the subject, called *minor*.

Note that all three terms are classes of things, and that the reasoning proceeds by relating two of the classes to one another by means of a third. Each class is treated as homogeneous throughout on the assumption (known as the *dictum de omni et nullo*) that whatever can be asserted or denied of the whole of a class can be asserted or denied of a part of it. That is what distinguishes the logical class from the statistical group. "All students are athletes" does not mean in logic that all who are more-or-less students are more-or-less athletes; it means that all who satisfy the definition "students" also satisfy the definition "athletes." It becomes evident that if we are dealing with defined classes of things and their relations of inclusion and exclusion, it becomes of supreme importance to know whether, in a given instance, we are talking about *all* of a class or only *some* of it. In everyday speech we seldom bother to make that point wholly clear ("Englishmen are stolid"; "Wise men smoke Chokies"); but in logic we must always specify whether we are talking about all of a class (if so, the term is said to be *distributed*) or merely some of it, meaning "at least some" (when the term is said to be *undistributed*). It must also be borne in mind that the assertion "Some politicians are honest" does not carry with it, in logic, either any affirmation or any denial that "All politicians are honest." On the basis of "some," we know only that "at least some" are honest, and nothing either way about the rest. Propositions about a single individual: "George Washington was a general," may be treated logically as "all" or universal propositions, since the one man comprises the whole of the subject class.

Our first task in analyzing any argument syllogistically is therefore to state the meaning of each of the premises and of the conclusion in correct logical form—that is, as a relation between two classes which do or do not overlap. Not all the statements of which language is capable can be squeezed into this formula without doing violence to some of their shades of meaning. But if reasoning is to be tested in the syllogistic manner, its terms must be exhibited as related in one of four (and only four) possible ways: by total inclusion, partial inclusion, total exclusion, or partial exclusion. These are known respectively as A, universal affirmative; I, particular affirmative; E, universal negative; and O, particular negative propositions. Using the classes "students" and

A: Universal affirmative

> *All* students *are* players. (All S is P)
> The class of students who are not
> players is empty.

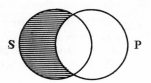

I: Particular affirmative

> *Some* students *are* players. (Some S
> is P)
> The class of students who are
> players is not empty.

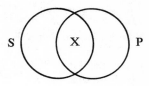

E: Universal negative

> *No* students *are* players. (No S is P)
> (Or, *All . . . are not . . .*)
> The class of those who are both
> students and players is empty.

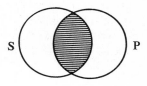

O: Particular negative

> *Some* students *are not* players.
> (Some S is not P)
> The class of students who are not
> players is not empty.

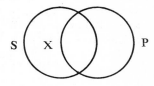

Fig. 2

"players," and representing their relationships by circles in the manner originated by John Venn,[6] we have the possibilities shown in Figure 2.[7]

In the diagrams (Figure 2), the shaded areas indicate complete absence or emptiness (as in A, there are no students who are not players); the presence of the cross indicates that there are at least some instances in that area (as in I, there are at least some students who are players); while the unmarked areas both inside and outside the circles indicate that the given data tell us nothing about the subclasses which they represent (as in O, we do not know whether or not there are some students who are players, or whether or not there are some players who are not students).

From the point of view of distribution, the four types of propositions arrange themselves as follows:

[6] *Symbolic Logic,* 2d ed. (London, 1894), chap. V.
[7] Identical classes, such as: "All sons of the king are princes," and "All princes are sons of the king," may be treated as a special perfectly reciprocal variety of A, total inclusion.

	Subject	Predicate
A: All students are players	Distributed	Undistributed
I: Some students are players	Undistributed	Undistributed
E: No students are players	Distributed	Distributed
O: Some students are not players	Undistributed	Distributed

It is perhaps easier to remember that the only terms which are distributed are the subject terms of universal propositions (A and E) and the predicate terms of negative propositions (E and O).

Moods, Figures, and Rules of the Syllogism

With these four kinds of propositions at our disposal, we may now begin to put them together in threes to make syllogisms; and a quick calculation will show that there are sixty-four different possible combinations, or moods, from AAA, AAE, AAI, etc., to OOE, OOI, OOO. But this is only the beginning, since the three terms (major, minor, and middle) may be arranged in four different orders, or figures, for each of the sixty-four combinations, or a total of two hundred and fifty-six moods in all. Happily only nineteen of the traditional two hundred and fifty-six are both valid and important. Using "students" as subject term, S; "members" as middle term, M; and "players" as predicate term, P;[8] the following are examples of the moods which yield valid conclusions:

In the first figure (4)

M   P
S   M
S   P

A—All members are players
A—All students are members
———————————————
A—All students are players

E—No members are players
A—All students are members
———————————————
E—No students are players

A—All members are players
I—Some students are members
———————————————
I—Some students are players

E—No members are players
I—Some students are members
———————————————
O—Some students are not players

In the second figure (4)

P   M
S   M
S   P

E—No players are members
A—All students are members
———————————————
E—No students are players

A—All players are members
E—No students are members
———————————————
E—No students are players

E—No players are members
I—Some students are members
———————————————
O—Some students are not players

A—All players are members
O—Some students are not members
———————————————
O—Some students are not players

In the third figure (6)

M   P
M   S
S   P

A—All members are players
A—All members are students
———————————————
I—Some students are players

I—Some members are players
A—All members are students
———————————————
I—Some students are players

---

[8] For convenience in identifying the terms, classes with names commencing with "s," "p," and "m" are used, but that is merely coincidental.

A—All members are players
I—Some members are students
———————————————
I—Some students are players

E—No members are players
A—All members are students
———————————————
O—Some students are not
players

O—Some members are not
players
A—All members are students
———————————————
O—Some students are not
players

E—No members are players
I—Some members are
students
———————————————
O—Some students are not
players

In the fourth
figure (5)

P	M
M	S

———————————————
| S | P |

A—All players are members
A—All members are students
———————————————
I—Some students are players

A—All players are members
E—No members are students
———————————————
E—No students are players

I—Some players are members
A—All members are students
———————————————
I—Some students are players

E—No players are members
A—All members are students
———————————————
O—Some students are not
players

E—No players are members
I—Some members are students
———————————————
O—Some students are not players

Total (19)

There are five other possible combinations that are valid, but which yield "weakened" conclusions in comparison with some of the above nineteen, and so are usually neglected. In the first figure, for example, AAI is a weakened form of AAA:

A——All members are players
A——All students are members
———————————————
I——Some students are players

That is, it seems trivial to conclude that *some* students are players, when we are warranted in concluding that *all* are. Similarly EAO in the first and second figures is a weakened form of EAE:

E——No members are players
A——All students are members
———————————————
O——Some students are not players

E——No players are members
A——All students are members
———————————————
O——Some students are not players

and AEO in the second and fourth figures is a weakened form of AEE:

A——All players are members
E——No students are members
———————————————
O——Some students are not players

A——All players are members
E——No members are students
———————————————
O——Some students are not players

We have now a positive although rather cumbersome method of testing the validity of any syllogistic argument: (1) state each of the three propositions in logical form; (2) determine from the position of the major, minor, and middle terms which figure of the syllogism is being employed; and (3) see whether or not the argument in question comes under any one of the valid moods.

In practice, however, not many persons are likely to take the trouble to master and to apply so complicated a method of checking. It is usually easier to resort to one or both of two negative tests to determine whether or not a given syllogism is invalid. The first of these is the Venn diagram method applied to three classes instead of two, as previously. This can be done by drawing three overlapping circles representing the three terms of the syllogism, S, P, and M (Figure 3). Using the minus sign to indicate "no," and reading across from left to right, there will then be seven enclosed areas or subclasses, as follows:

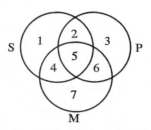

FIG. 3

1.	S, ——— M, ——— P	Students who are not members and not players
2.	S, P, ——— M	Students who are players and not members
3.	P, ——— S, ——— M	Players who are not students and not members
4.	S, M, ——— P	Students who are members and not players
5.	S, M, P	Students who are members and players
6.	P, M, ——— S	Players who are members and not students
7.	M, ——— S, ——— P	Members who are not students and not players

Proceeding as before, any syllogistic argument can be plotted on the diagram by shading the areas which are stated in the premises to be empty, placing a cross in those which are stated to be occupied by at least some instances, and leaving unmarked the areas which are left unspecified. Three rules, however, must be observed:

    1. In diagramming an argument consisting of one universal and one particular premise, the universal premise must be diagrammed first.

    2. In order that there may be no uncertainty as to what area a cross applies, whenever that area is cut by a line, the cross is placed on the line.

    3. The Venn diagram test does not apply to the nine valid moods of the syllogism in which a particular conclusion is drawn from two universal premises (the five weakened moods and AAI, EAO in the third and fourth figures).

The following examples show how the test operates when the reasoning is valid:

1st figure A —— All members are players   All M is P
            A —— All students are members   All S is M
            ————————————————————————————   ———————
            A —— All students are players   All S is P

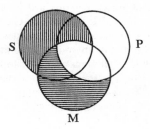

FIG. 4

We begin by shading all the area of M that is not P, in accordance with the major premise (Figure 4). Then we do the same for the minor premise, shading all the area of S that is not M. The conclusion, which can be diagrammed separately if desired, is plainly seen to follow from the premises (there is no area of S which is not included in P).

3d figure I —— Some members are players   Some M is P
           A —— All members are students   All   M is S
           ————————————————————————————   ————————
           I —— Some students are players   Some S is P

By Rule 1 above, the minor premise, since it is universal and the major premise is particular, must be diagrammed first (Figure 5). This is done by shading the area of M that is not S. A cross is then placed in the area of M that is P to indicate that it contains at least some instances. The conclusion, that at least some S is P, is seen to follow validly.

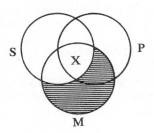

FIG. 5

The second negative method consists in applying the seven rules of the syllogism. They apply to all the moods; and if any one of the rules is violated, the syllogism is invalid.

Three Terms Rule
   Rule 1. A syllogism must include three and only three terms, used throughout in the same sense.

Distribution Rules
Rule 2. The middle term must be distributed at least once in the premises.

Rule 3. No term may have a greater distribution in the conclusion than
it had in the premises.

Negative Premises Rules
Rule 4. From two negative premises, no valid conclusion can be inferred.

Rule 5. If one premise is negative, the conclusion must be negative.

Particular Premises Rules
Rule 6. If one premise is particular, the conclusion must be particular.

Rule 7. From two particular premises, no valid conclusion can be drawn.

Common Rule Violations
The most frequent transgression of the rules concerns Rule 2, and is called
the Undistributed Middle. Political campaigns are especially rich in examples
of it, such as: All Communists favor peaceful coexistence; My opponent favors
peaceful coexistence; hence my opponent is a Communist. What has quietly
been inserted is the very different premise: *Only* Communists favor peaceful
coexistence.

Almost as dangerous is the violation of Rule 3, known as Illicit Process,
said by Jevons to be easier to commit and more difficult to detect than any
other syllogistic fallacy. If we argue that: All Buddhists are pacifists; No
Methodists are Buddhists; thus No Methodists are pacifists; we distribute (that
is, use in its widest sense) in the conclusion a term, "pacifists," which was
not distributed in the premises. We have taken out in our conclusion more
than we put into our premises. Nothing, perhaps, is more characteristically
human than this tendency to try to extract more than one puts in; and nothing
does more violence to the first principle of deduction.

Students are often puzzled about applying the rules to arguments employing assumed or unstated premises. Normal human talk is full of what Justice
Holmes called "inarticulate major premises." "I do not say that my opponent
has been wrong about every issue," says the campaign orator, leaving it to his
audience to reach the conclusion through innuendo. The technical name for
this incomplete form of reasoning is *enthymeme*.

Caution must constantly be observed in interpreting both "All" and "Some"
when either is accented. To say: *"All* you fellows are not cowards," indicates
that some are not, and suggests that some are. To say that in an accident:
"Some of the passengers were injured" conveys the notion that some, *but not
all,* were injured, whereas in logic "some" does not exclude the possibility that
all were injured. To assert that *"Some* hippogriffs are poisonous" seems to say
that "Some hippogriffs, *and there are some,* are poisonous." It requires an
effort to remember that in formal logic, as in mathematics, the question of
the existence of what is being talked about is always left unsettled.

Another source of confusion is any sentence beginning with the words
"Only" or "None but." "Only males are fathers" does not say that "All males
are fathers," but only that some are, and furthermore, it excludes the non-
males. Hence it is simpler to avoid the awkwardness of two propositions by
transposing the subject and predicate to read: "All fathers are males."

4. The "Laws of Thought"

The traditional syllogism does not represent the way men normally think, but rather a means of testing, retrospectively, whether they have thought validly. It is a formulation of the rules of deductive thinking of the Aristotelian variety which must be found to have been observed, intentionally or not, if the conclusion is warranted by the premises. This whole process of testing rests upon three famous assumptions known as "The Laws of Thought," which are:

The Law of Identity: A is A; or, a thing is what it is throughout a given argument. Meanings are not subject to change without notice.

The Law of Contradiction: A is not not–A; or, one cannot consistently assert and deny the same thing at the same time.

The Law of Excluded Middle: A is either B or not–B; or, of two contradictory judgments exhausting the possibilities, if one is false, the other must be true.

It will be seen at once that these "laws" are taken for granted by men who argue in the framework of our Western intellectual tradition. The poet, however, can ignore the Law of Contradiction with impunity, as Walt Whitman did. "His allegiance," says Professor Loewenberg, "is not primarily to the rules of thought."[9] Many Oriental thinkers reject either-or thinking on the ground that ultimate reality is both-and. Ever since Hegel, and especially since the rise of Existentialism, the Law of the Excluded Middle has been almost continuously under attack in Western thought.

5. Modern Logic of Propositions

In spite of the great historical importance of the syllogism, and its potential usefulness today for legal and business reasoning about the stable classes of things, logicians no longer regard it as constituting the whole of deductive logic, or even as possessing prime importance. Some of them look upon it with positive disdain as dealing with too narrowly restricted an area of thought: the categorical relations of classes. Under the influence of the new mathematics of Georg Cantor (1845–1918) and others, school children are beginning to do their formal thinking in terms of the Theory of Sets instead of classes. "A set is a collection of definite objects of our perception or of our thought," and is composed of elements.[10] All sets whose elements can be put into one-to-one correspondence with each other's elements are said to be equivalent and have the same cardinal number, such as five fingers, five toes, and five men on a basketball team.

Modern logic and mathematics, which take turns trying to swallow one another, embrace many varieties of deductive inference. One of the most important is the truth-value calculus of sentences or propositions which are either true or false. The truth or falsity of any statement which has meaning is considered to be its truth-value.

To move from the syllogism toward the logic of propositions, one changes the ordinary class-relation proposition A: "All students are players," to read: "If X is a student, then X is a player." It was the English mathematician George Boole (1815–1864) who paved the way for this advance by devising an algebra for logic in his *The Laws of Thought* (1854). He used the symbol zero, *0,* for

---

[9] J. Loewenberg, *Reason and the Nature of Things* (La Salle, Ill., 1959), pp. 29–30.
[10] Breuer, Joseph, *Introduction to the Theory of Sets* (Englewood Cliffs, N.J., 1958), p. 4.

the concept of an empty class. This enabled him to write down such a proposition as "There are no ghosts" (using *G* for the class "ghosts") as $G = 0$. Then the proposition: "There are men" (using *M* for the class "men") became $M \neq 0$. By adding the notion of the complementary class (for example, *G'* stands for "All the things in the universe which are not ghosts" and *M'* for "All that are not men"), Boole was able to express the four fundamental propositions of the syllogism as follows:

A	All students are players	$SP' = 0$
E	No students are players	$SP = 0$
I	Some students are players	$SP \neq 0$
O	Some students are not players	$SP' \neq 0$

The Boolean two-valued algebra has been supplemented and enlarged by a logic capable of dealing with more complex relations among propositions.[11] Truth-tables, some of them very elaborate, have been drawn up to deal with them. Among the simpler varieties is that which states the truth-values for the two propositions *p* and *q*, assuming that for each of them only two truth-values are possible: either true or false. It should be noted that in this form of logic there is no allowance whatever for propositions which are ambiguous, doubtful, or debatable.

If *p* is	and *q* is	Then *p* and *q* are	And *p* or *q* are
True	True	True	True
True	False	False	True
False	True	False	True
False	False	False	False

This two-valued truth-table and its further extensions have gained enormously in importance from the fact that they lend themselves to electronic handling by a modern computer. It is only necessary to assign the symbol *1* to truth, and *0* to falsity, in order to correspond with the binary notation used in digital computers.[12] In the electronic device, when a switch is closed, the current is on; when it is open, the current is off. These states correspond to the truth and falsity of any proposition; and a circuit can be designed for any desired truth-table.

Deduction by Machinery

The formal relationships of the syllogism were bound sooner or later to be first diagrammed and then "mechanized." The first man "to use a mechanical device as an aid to reasoning" may well have been Ramon Lull (1236?–1315). But the first logic machine, strictly speaking, was probably the "Demonstrator" built by Charles, third Earl Stanhope (1753–1816), British statesman and scientist.[13] The pioneer in suggesting a wedding of electricity

---

11 For a much fuller treatment, see Irving Adler, *Thinking Machines* (New York, paper, 1961), chap. 8, "Algebra of Classes," and chap. 9, "Algebra of Propositions."

12 *Digital* computers are fundamentally arithmetical, using only information coded in terms of *0* and *1*. *Analog* computers, often called "electronic slide rules," introduce physical distances, amounts of turning of a wheel, or of voltages which are analogous to the numerical magnitudes to be represented. There are also *hybrid* computers employing both sorts of elements.

13 See Martin Gardner, *Logic Machines* (New York, paper, 1958), to which this account is indebted, for the history of the subject.

and logic was the American Allan Marquand about 1885; but the first actual construction of an electrical logic machine was by Benjamin Burack about 1936. It was designed to test the forms of the syllogism; and many other similar devices have been constructed by both teachers and students of the traditional logic.

The leader in electrifying the propositional calculus by computer was Claude E. Shannon of the Massachusetts Institute of Technology in 1937. His work laid the foundations for the many types of modern truth-value logic machines, including digital computers adapted for the purpose. The devices so far constructed operate mainly as follows: premises are fed into the machine, whereupon it scans the programmed truth-table lines one at a time. The operator notes whenever the lights (those which are on) indicate "true." In time it is believed that machines specially designed to solve problems in propositional logic will be able to operate directly without scanning. There are no theoretical obstacles to the building of machines to handle multi-valued logics. In Gardner's words, "There is no reason why any formal logic that can be manipulated with symbols on paper cannot also be manipulated by properly designed electric circuits."

Much confusion has been created in the public mind by such book titles as *Intelligent Machines, Giant Brains,* or *Machines That Think,* since many persons have concluded that computers can now undertake nearly all the tasks of human thought, including original or creative thinking. This is very far from being the case, so far that some authorities have begun to define "real thinking" as "what a computer can*not* do." A machine has no curiosity; it can "think," that is to say, only in the terms previously fed into it. It is "an organized collection of hardware," which must be instructed (programmed) by a human being, ultimately, regarding what it is to think, and what it is to think about. Once it has had its function predetermined, it can carry out its programmed operations, such as following an involved process of deductive logic, far more rapidly and reliably than human beings can accomplish them. This is "thinking" only in the sense of "fixed-rule" calculation. "A problem," says Bruce W. Arden, "is computable for which the execution of an explicit, unambiguous, terminating sequence of instructions produces a solution."[14] Machines, that is, are utterly incapable of "free decisions" or original thought. A computer "specializes in deriving conclusions (logical or mathematical) without regard to the objective truth of the starting data."[15] In the course of exploring such consequences or implications, which it can accomplish with fantastic speeds (doing work that would take a man fifty years in about ten minutes), the machine may disclose hitherto unnoticed alternatives, and so may make "discoveries" possible. But it may also spew out vast numbers of irrelevant or unimportant conclusions known as GIGO ("Garbage in, garbage out").

Where the computer excels the human brain is in its virtually infallible stored-up memory and rapidity of recall. That is why "it has been predicted that during the next twenty years the world's champion chess-player will be an automatic computer program."[16] Even the keenest human memory, that is, will hardly be able to cope with an electronic memory stocked with the correct deductive inference for every possible situation in the game of chess. The com-

---

[14] Bruce W. Arden, *An Introduction to Digital Computing* (Reading, Mass., 1963), p. 1.
[15] Edmund C. Berkeley, *The Computer Revolution* (New York, 1962), p. 13.
[16] *Idem*, p. 172.

puter, of course, does not "know" what the right moves "mean"; only the programmer is aware of that.

The performance of such intricate deductions, as anyone can see, requires extremely complicated and expensive hardware. Current costs of computers range from $25,000 to over $10,000,000. As a result, their use is not warranted in dealing with small-scale operations. As Irving Adler remarks: "It is no routine matter to design a machine that can do routine thinking."[17]

Many uses have been suggested for electronic logic machines where large masses of data are available: in checking the consistency of title deeds and other involved legal documents; in the interpretation of complicated rule books; in the solution of crimes involving fingerprints and other sorts of evidence; in the unraveling of insurance tangles; in the elimination of conflicts in plane landings, train dispatching, and college class schedules; and in the logistical computations of military and industrial operations research. There is every prospect that computers will be more and more extensively employed by lawyers in searching for precedents and by physicians in the diagnosis of disease. The deductive consequences of a patient's symptoms might conceivably be worked out in the light of perhaps millions of cases.[18] Nevertheless it must be granted that most of the suggested uses of logic-machines are likely to be severely restricted by the lack of a sufficient volume of data to justify computer treatment. It may be expected, however, that some of the so-called "third generation" computers will be reduced in size and cost for the use of smaller organizations in solving their problems.

6. Formal Validity and Reliable Knowledge

The question that concerns us as knowers about all forms of deduction: Aristotelian, modern and electronic, is: what part has valid reasoning to play in the attainment of reliable knowledge? All we have established, so far, is the certainty that, given reliable premises and valid reasoning, we are obliged, if we value consistency, to accept the conclusion as reliable.

But what about our initial premises? What if they are unreliable, or "materially false" to begin with? Can the formal validity of the conclusion in any way assure that our premises are true of the world in which we live? Consider the syllogism:

> All Presidents of the United States have been married men
> James Buchanan was a President of the United States
> _____
> James Buchanan was a married man

We recognize at once a valid AAA syllogism in the first figure; and our major premise is *almost* materially true. But, unfortunately for our argument, James Buchanan never married. Our formal reasoning is valid enough, but one of our premises is false, and our conclusion is false.

At this point the reader is likely to leap to a dangerous conclusion, namely, that since true premises and valid reasoning are bound to yield true conclusions, any other combination automatically results in falsity. Using "true" and

---

17 Irving Adler, *op. cit.*, p. 12.
18 *Idem*, pp. 112–15 for an example. Russian doctors have suggested a nation-wide punch-card system for keeping a computer inventory of the country's state of health.

"false" in this context as convenient equivalents of "reliable" and "unreliable" in our world, there are four possible combinations:

	Premises	Reasoning	Conclusion
1.	True	Valid	True
2.	True	Invalid	?
3.	False	Valid	?
4.	False	Invalid	?

Exploring these alternatives, the second (True-Invalid) is extremely likely, of course, to yield a false conclusion. But, since the conclusion does not have to follow validly from the premises, it *can* be true, thus:

2d figure   A —— All Japanese are Orientals   True
             E —— No Caucasians are Orientals   True
             ——————————————————————
             E —— No Caucasians are Negroes   True

The reasoning is patently invalid, and yet the conclusion is true. False premises and valid reasoning, as in the third alternative, are also likely to produce false conclusions, but not necessarily so. For example:

1st figure   A —— All Mexicans are U.S. citizens   False
             A —— All native-born Iowans are Mexicans   False
             ——————————————————————————————
             A —— All native-born Iowans are U.S. citizens True

Given the premises, which are false, the conclusion, which is true, nevertheless follows validly. The same happy accident of material truth can even overtake invalid reasoning from false premises, such as:

4th figure   A —— All alligators are ostriches   False
             I —— Some ostriches are shellfish   False
             ——————————————————————
             A —— All squirrels are rodents   True

By this time it should be apparent that the fact that valid reasoning from true premises is the only way that we can be *sure* of reaching true deductive conclusions is no proof whatever that it is the *only* way to do so. Any one of the other three combinations can yield material truth, in spite of the fact that they are overwhelmingly likely to result in falsehoods. This should enable us to separate, once and for all, our thinking about formal logic, which deals wholly with consistency or validity, from that about the material truth or reliability of our premises.

It would be the height of folly to interpret all this as an argument against the value of validity in our deductive reasoning. For unless our reasoning *is* valid, our chances of getting reliable knowledge deductively are very small indeed. Nevertheless, the fact that our reasoning is valid is no guarantee whatever of the truth of the premises we have chosen. We must not confuse the question of the reliability of our procedure with that of the reliability of our premises. When the latter issue is raised, the formal logician is silent. It is his task to display the exact consequences of given assumptions, irrespective of their material truth or falsity. The necessity of accepting the consequences hinges upon our previous acceptance of the premises; and, if we reject the premises, no amount of formal logic can oblige us to accept their consequences. Premises must stand on their own feet. *If* they are materially true, certain valid and true conclusions can be shown to follow inexorably in accordance with the rules of formal logic. But other valid and true conclusions, and sometimes some of the same ones, can be shown to follow just as inexorably from premises which are materially false. To be sure that we have reasoned validly is not enough. The final verdict concerning the reliability of knowledge that is claimed to have been established by deduction must always be primarily a question of the reliability of the premises, and only secondarily, after the former has been established, a matter of the formal validity of the reasoning.

7. Deduction Then and Now

Looking back over the long history of the human quest for dependable knowledge, we can see why the deductive method has become associated with the working out of the consequences of finished or pre-existing knowledge, rather than with the discovery of new truths. For centuries, men felt no lack of apparently reliable premises in the form of customs and folkways. When, at the hands of a few precocious Greeks, the accepted social habits began to be questioned and reasoned about verbally, more and more people had to be convinced by argument rather than merely overawed by authority. Argument that is not emotional browbeating is discourse directed toward the making of inferences. To win a rational argument is to secure the assent of others by bringing about admissions which lead to other admissions. Among the disputatious Greeks, this usually meant in practice that one's hearers had to be shown that the particular case under discussion fell within a general principle which had been admitted by all the parties to the debate. What won the argument was the demonstration:—you have admitted these premises, therefore you are obliged to admit this conclusion. Aristotle codified the rules for checking the relations of such conclusions to their premises, and thereby supplied the arguers of his day with a means of avoiding some of the rhetorical tricks of their opponents. He was not furnishing them with the rules of the art of thinking or with the language of debate, but rather with artificial devices for testing "what admissions lead to." By mastering his technique of checking logical consequences, and by applying it to the scrutiny of whatever purported to be rational argument, they could at least avoid being coerced into accepting invalid conclusions.

The Scholastic Attitude

It is impossible to overemphasize the difference between Aristotle's own intentions and those of some of his admirers in the later Middle Ages, by whom he was idolized as "the philosopher" in spite of his pagan beliefs. Although he became famous as the formulator of the canons of deduction, Aristotle himself was probably the most *in*ductively, though not experimentally, minded of the Greek philosophers. Unhappily his medieval successors did not share his insatiable thirst for every variety of facts as well as for all-inclusive theories. To them, his philosophical system, embracing both the methods of thought and most of the scientific knowledge available in his era (and theirs also), seemed so complete that it could be accepted as authoritative in all matters not settled by Holy Writ.

Aristotle is not to be blamed for the blind dogmatism of many of those who came after him, whose purposes and demands were very different from his, and who misused his deductive logic to silence doubters and to prevent any serious attention to concrete facts. What they were seeking was an error-proof method of settling the only really important controversies, which were theological, in the light of the incontestably true premises which their religion supplied. They thought that they had found the final rules of "the grammar of thinking" in the syllogism, which dealt with rigid relations among fixed concepts, thus affording a handy guide to the fixed system of classes in nature. The ironical result was that what originated as a handbook for the guidance of eager Greek inquirers became, in medieval hands, a mighty engine for the coercion of heretics. Using some of the worst of Aristotle's blunders in the physical and biological sciences as authoritative, these wordy doctors retarded further advances in those subjects by applying the rules of his logic to the deduction of the consequences of old errors.

Aristotle's "instrument," in fact, reached its greatest prestige and popularity in the thirteenth century A.D. The Scholastic theologians of that period, led by Saint Thomas Aquinas, were in search of knowledge leading to salvation, and they were convinced that they were already in possession of an ample supply of it in the form of premises drawn from such unimpeachable authorities as the Bible, the Church Fathers, and such writings of Aristotle as did not conflict with the divine decrees. There were truths of revelation beyond all argument, which human reason was incapable either of discovering or demonstrating.

Since all the knowledge essential for salvation was already available, the chief task of human learning was application. The believer, already in the possession of the Truth with a capital "T," was simply concerned to deduce its consequences correctly. Today we marvel at the lack of interest shown by medieval thinkers generally in scientific facts. We forget that for them Nature was, in Whitehead's phrase, "overwhelmingly dramatic." Having, as they firmly believed, "inside information" of utter reliability regarding the plot of the cosmic drama and the ultimate purpose of things, the particular processes by which the ends were to be reached seemed to them to be comparatively unimportant.

This deductive approach to human problems also had important social consequences in an age when ardent believers sought to make their religion universal. Deductive logic in the hands of authoritarians bent upon religious or political uniformity, or both, became a powerful instrument of coercion to be wielded against dissenters. For reason was confined to one side of the argument. It could not be used against the premises, which were declared to be beyond its scope. But it could be used to crush, in the name of logic, any deviation from the accepted dogmas. Ecclesiastical and civil judges took their premises from the books of law, and applied them syllogistically to individual cases. Think how many hundreds of thousands of wretched epileptics and insane persons were hung or burned to death with good conscience and perfect logic because it is written in Exodus XXII:18: "Thou shalt not suffer a witch to live." If that premise is accepted as unassailably true, then in an individual instance it is only necessary to determine, by deductions from other equally certain premises, that "this old woman is a witch." The logic, once the premises were granted, was impossible to challenge without upsetting the whole notion of human rationality; while the premises could not be questioned without overthrowing the whole social fabric of Christendom. Small wonder that so potent a means of insuring social conformity was abused to the point where men began to rebel at the consequences, and thus to question the reliability of the premises.

Modern Views of Deduction

From our point of view, the mistake of the thinkers was not in developing and refining the traditional syllogism, but in cutting it off from induction, and in harnessing it exclusively to the task of filling in the details of a single system of religious dogma, the main outlines of which were already known by revelation. Yet by insisting upon the ultimate rationality of the universe, although veiled in part to the mind of man, the medieval Schoolmen paved the way for a different kind of deductive system based upon measurement rather than upon Aristotelian classes of things. When, at the Renaissance, thinkers began to turn their attention to physical Nature for worldly purposes, they retained the Scholastic standard of reliability in knowledge—inclusion in a unified rational system. But the axioms of the system were now mathematical instead of theological; and there was a new insistence upon checking their consequences against the concrete nature of things as discovered by observation and experiment. To the old coercion of men's beliefs by what must follow from accepted premises, there was added the new coercion of the stubborn facts. Besides the inescapable order in the ways conclusions could be shown to be related to premises in rational thinking, there was the newly discovered regularity in the nature of things. How were the two orders related? Modern science has had the difficult task of adjusting the claims of the rival systems and their methods of assaying knowledge: the deductive habit of using tight chains of abstract logical reasoning, and the inductive demand for fidelity to concrete observed fact.

Only the outline of the combined method which moves from induction through deduction to induction need be foreshadowed here. Deduction has been demoted from its high position as handmaiden of dogma, and has assumed the lowlier task of assisting in the development of hypotheses. Yet without deduction, most of our present scientific preoccupation with facts would be fruitless, since we should be unable to fit them into systems. To realize how powerful a tool deduction can be for the revelation of structures hidden beneath the surface of things, it is only necessary to mention the immense part played by mathematics in all our technical thought. The planning of rockets, missiles, satellites and space vehicles and the vastly complicated machinery for their guidance and detection requires a volume of mathematical calculation in advance which only computers can supply in time for effective use.

A powerful factor in changing the role of deductive systems in modern thought has been the discovery that the world of these formal relations between meanings, thoughts, or sentences is enormously larger than the traditional logic had led us to suppose. We know now that the syllogism represents only one choice among many possible alternative ways of drawing conclusions. We are aware that there is an endless array of logics and mathematics, each one a timelessly valid partial account of the possibilities, and each one completely consistent throughout in its own terms, but not all of them equally useful for our intellectual purposes. Far from there being any single cosmic standard of what constitutes valid inference, there are, instead, an indefinitely large number of relations which can be arranged in many deductive systems.

The traditional logicians were right in maintaining the absolute and unchanging rigidity of many of the formal relationships which they had discovered, once their premises had been accepted as reliable. But they were fatally wrong in supposing that the same absolute lack of choice prevailed in selecting the original premises of their arguments, or in deciding which of their implications should be explored. Modern man has some choice in these matters, among an immense wealth of implication-relations set forth with a refinement far beyond the dreams of an Aristotle or an Aquinas. Contemporary logic is prepared to demonstrate "all the things you can say in a language if you know the syntax and not a single word of the vocabulary." Thus it places at our disposal a constantly expanding science of consistent forms enabling us to manipulate an endless number of related possibilities.

But the greatest shift of all has been away from treating premises as dogma to regarding them as hypotheses to be tested. By assuming that his initial premises are no longer established certainties, but tentative postulates, the modern scientist is furnished by deductive logic with an extensive repertory of their valid implications to be checked against the observed facts. The resulting systems of knowledge upon which modern man places the greatest reliance, the exact sciences, are indeed those which are the most closely knit deductively. But this is not because of any absolute conviction that their initial premises are rocklike or beyond dispute. On the contrary, it is the deductive cross-buttressing of the entire system that gives us confidence in its original premises.

This hypothetical or postulational use of deduction has won its way with great difficulty, however, in those fields, like the social studies, where the store of finished knowledge is still commonly supposed to be large, and where many minds still work according to the dogmatic deductive pattern. In the so-called routine occupations, thousands of people do little more than apply deductively the rules, formulas, recipes and prescriptions worked out by others. This policy affords a mental economy which saves them the effort of treating each individual case in the light of a large number of systematically connected possibilities, as tentativeness in deducing would require. If such a person's premises happen to be false, he will merely be practicing what Joseph Wood Krutch calls "the art of going wrong with confidence."

If, on the other hand, we are humble about the reliability of our already acquired knowledge, we shall not try to build solid proofs by means of formal logic upon the shaky foundations of self-assumed or self-proclaimed authority. We shall refuse to make consistency an instrument of coercion and confinement of human thought to orthodox and conventional pathways which must not be questioned. We shall stop insisting that the patterns of our theory-making must necessarily constitute eternal laws of the nature of things.

Pre-modern logicians erred in mistaking the validity of their instrument, the syllogism, for the reliability of its premises; and we may even be obliged to guard ourselves against a similar fallacy which might be called "computer scholasticism." Deductive conclusions obtained at great cost from vast masses of data are likely to take on an imperative air. We must never fail to recall that most ancient and prevalent of all the pitfalls of deduction: the belief that it is possible to get more out in the conclusion that we put into the premises.

No doubt deductions by logic-machines will acquire prestige as they become more common. But it must constantly be pointed out that what goes into them in the way of premises must first be made "computable," that is, it must be transformed into a set of symbols which are the result of analysis and simplification. They are parts, not wholes. They represent binary alternatives entering into combinations with other symbolic abstractions. The machine that receives the symbol registers its presence only in ways it has been instructed to do. But when a human being is made aware of what the same symbol stands for, his whole mind may reach out in many unpredictable (and original) directions. A logic-machine has no awareness of meanings; it "thinks" only along narrow and predetermined pathways. That is why it is so difficult to get "ideas" out of a computer.

It must also be remembered that the alternatives with which a digital computer deals are true-false only. But the humanities and social studies are full of ambivalent and ambiguous situations which do not lend themselves to that sort of either-or, black-or-white reasoning. They abound instead in nuances, in shades of gray. The analog computer can deal with some of them, but its analogies are purely quantitative, and may be misleading. There should be, then, no abject surrender to the authority of the machine-made deduction until its premises have been carefully scrutinized. We must still avoid the tyranny of the logical instrument. It would be ironical indeed for twentieth century science to have escaped the bonds of religious dogmatism, only to fall into the clutches of tyrannically manipulated logic-machines.

In fleeing the evils of deductive dogmatism, however, we should not deprive ourselves of the virtues of deductive reasoning. That the two things, dogmatism and deduction, have been historically associated for centuries is unfortunate, because a revulsion from dogmatism about premises has often been accompanied by a complete disdain for logical rigor. The attempt is made to excuse sloppy thinking on the ground that one must not be dogmatic. Such a policy can be disastrous, for one does not avoid implications by ignoring or misreading them.

We should not make the mistake of asking too little of formal logic, just because we are determined, and rightly, not to ask too much. Instead, we should strive to develop free conceptualizing in new directions in the hope of producing novel patterns of possibilities (hypotheses) which may be elaborated, in some cases by computers, and then brought to bear experimentally upon ever-widening ranges of facts. In this way, deduction can be made an essential part of the inductive-deductive-inductive method of free inquiry. Thus we may be able to combine its rightful rigidity of form, once its assumptions are determined, with the needed flexibility of postulational thinking.

CHAPTER II

Values and Educational Choices

As late as 1944, John Dewey expressed concern and discouragement over discussions about value. His concern was not that he doubted his own conclusions about value, but that there seemed to be little headway toward a consensus among philosophers about such a fundamental issue. The problems recognized by Dewey had been a part of philosophic discourse before him, but the evidence today still shows little progress in philosophical circles toward finding workable solutions for these problems. One of the basic difficulties seems to be that we can never be sure that "value" has the same meaning for all involved in a particular discussion. In the first part of this chapter we shall try to supply the necessary background for a consideration of this difficulty by presenting an analysis of the concepts of "value," "valuing," and "theory of value," as well as some of the problems usually associated with the study of value. Next, we shall relate the concerns of three different philosophical views—Plato's, Augustine's, and Dewey's—about problems of value, with the view that such concerns have educational implications. The analysis of the three views will be followed by a discussion of values in connection with the individual and with contemporary society. The chapter will conclude with a consideration of the significance of value theory for current education. Plato's *Meno* has been selected as a reading for this chapter because of the ideas it generates about the possibility of teaching virtue. By extension of meaning, Plato's dialogue offers a useful commentary on the possibility of teaching values in the school.

Value, Valuing, and Theory of Value

Philosophers generally agree that the problems associated with theory of value are not only extremely important but are some of the most difficult ones man has faced in his history. Even the most elementary aspects of the concern with value remain ambiguous. The problem of meaning, a starting place in any study, is so thorny with ambiguity and vagueness that at any point investigations threaten to break down under the sheer weight of the alternatives. The first step toward clarification should be an attempt to delineate the terms "value," "valuing," and "theory of value." W. K. Frankena proposes that discussions of value theory must deal with several questions. He writes:

> Now value-theory is concerned both with the property of value and with the process of valuing. About the former it asks various questions. What is its nature? Is it a quality or a relation? Is it objective or subjective? Is it a single property, or is it several properties, value being an ambiguous term? Is its presence in a thing dependent on or reducible to the fact that the thing is valued by someone? About the latter it also has various questions. Is it a mere feeling or desire? Or does it involve judgment and cognition? And if so, is this a cognition of a value already there independently of the act of valuing or of knowing?[1]

Frankena distinguishes among the three terms by showing that "value" may be thought of as some sort of an existent with a particular property or properties; an existent that can be discussed in terms of its nature, and its relationship to other existents. The term is especially difficult to pinpoint, as it can be used as a concrete noun designating those things which have value, as an abstract noun which indicates the property of being valuable, or more rarely as being intermediate between these two. Further, "to value" can be used as a verb indicating a mental act or attitude.

The term "valuing" is somewhat less complicated, and according to Frankena it indicates a process that can be discussed in terms of whether or not it stems from feelings or from reason, whether it is irrational or rational. Finally, "value theory" is concerned with questions about the existent ("value"), and about the process ("valuing"). A theory of value makes a statement about those things which are held to be true, about the laws and principles of values and valuing.

There appears to be considerable agreement that the term "value" refers to an existent, whether or not the existent is dependent upon sentient beings. Harold Lee states in *Value: A Cooperative Inquiry,* that "there is no such thing as value that is not the value of some particular thing, event or situation."[2] Others writing in the same volume support the view. C. E. Ayres suggests that discussions of value have reference to some sort of existence which is a pattern in human behavior,[3] and H. D. Aiken refers to value as a "property or relation of persons or situations which may well

---

[1] D. D. Runes, ed., *The Dictionary of Philosophy* (New York: Philosophical Library, Inc., 1958), p. 330.
[2] Harold Lee, "Methodology of Value Theory," in *Value: A Cooperative Inquiry,* ed., Ray Lepley (New York: Columbia University Press, 1957), p. 154.
[3] C. E. Ayres, "The Value Economy," in *Value: A Cooperative Inquiry, op. cit.,* p. 44.

continue to exist without it."[4] Let us consider some typical statements that reflect value judgments.

"I don't like that picture."
"That's a beautiful landscape."
"We should teach moral and spiritual values in the schools."
"One should never commit adultery."
"He is a good man."
"You own a valuable piece of property there."
"Democracy is the best form of government."
"I value your friendship."
"Mrs. Brown is a good teacher."
"What is the value of this stock?"
"He is a valuable man to the company."

These statements are illustrative of the traditional categories of values, sometimes referred to as *types of values,* and they depict the types of meanings that have held man's attention in his search for values. We recognize judgments about art (aesthetic), morals (ethical), property (economic), people (social), and teaching (educational). A complete theory of value has something to say about each of these categories, although operationally discussions of values may involve only ethics or ethics and aesthetics. We note that some of the foregoing statements make judgments about transitory situations and that if the circumstances were changed the statement should be altered. Others of the statements are about fixed situations in that regardless of time, place, or circumstance, the meaning of the statement would remain constant.

One of the most pertinent questions about value is whether it is viewed as an actual existent or as a potential existent. According to the former view, man merely observes and grasps what is already there, and we have a strong case for the objectivity of value. On the other hand, if value is only potential, man must be instrumental in the actualizing of value, and it must be either subjective, or dependent upon a knowing mind if it is objective. A further distinction may be drawn between two kinds of value—intrinsic value which is valuable for itself and extrinsic value which is valuable as a means to something.

We have seen that Frankena raises the question as to whether valuing (the process) stems from feelings or desires or whether it involves judgment and cognition. He also raises the question as to whether cognition of a value is independent of the act of valuing. P. B. Rice writes in *Value: A Cooperative Inquiry* that:

Affective theories treat the basic sense of good in terms of pleasure (pleasantness, enjoyment, joy, satisfaction, consummatory quality,

---

4 H. D. Aiken, "Reflections on Dewey's 'Question on Values,'" in *Value: A Cooperative Inquiry, op. cit.,* p. 22.

hedonic tone), and evaluate striving by its issue in feeling. Conative theories take striving (Eros, desire, interest, goal-seeking) as fundamental, and treat feeling as its by-product. In general, those who come into value theory from a preoccupation with the "humanities" are predisposed toward an affective theory; and those who take their cues from the biological and social sciences favor a conative definition of elementary value. This alignment is probably unfortunate, but it is historically and psychologically intelligible.[5]

E. T. Mitchell,[6] another contributor to the same volume, favors a conative definition of elementary value. He contends that value and evaluation must be traced to the biological process of selectivity. Much as those things which are suitable or fitting to the organism play a role in its continued existence, biological response (which he calls valuing) precedes an evaluation. Valuing, according to Mitchell, is conditioned by habit, use, and custom. The impact of the social environment upon choices made by adolescents is stressed by Muzafer Sherif and Carolyn W. Sherif in *Problems of Youth: Transition to Adulthood in a Changing World*. They write:

> For a particular adolescent, the values and goals of other youth in his ken are salient aspects of his environment. Whether his personal radius for achievement and his potentialities are in line with theirs or not, he knows full well that his actions are gauged relative to their standards, which are revealed to him time and again in episodes of action, appraisal, approval, disapproval, notice and notoriety, or, worst of all, ignominity and personal oblivion.[7]

Psychologists are not primarily concerned with value theory, certainly not in the same sense that the philosopher is concerned, but their findings have been highly significant for many value theorists. A large number of theorists, for instance, are influenced by the investigations of social psychologists that indicate an unconscious internalization of external standards and values by the individual, and they temper their questions about the objectivity-subjectivity of values accordingly. There are those who believe that the emotions, desires, or interests of the individual prompt the valuing process. They maintain that the process begins as nonrational but may become rational during the process somewhere before choices are made. These theorists rely heavily upon information supplied by psychologists and social psychologists.

There are other value theorists, such as G. E. Moore, who claim access

---

[5] Philip B. Rice, "Science, Humanism and the Good," in *Value: A Cooperative Inquiry, op. cit.*, pp. 265–266.
[6] E. T. Mitchell, "Values, Valuing and Evaluation," in *Value: A Cooperative Inquiry, op. cit.*, pp. 193–194.
[7] Muzafer Sherif and Carolyn W. Sherif, *Problems of Youth: Transition to Adulthood in a Changing World* (Chicago: Aldine Publishing Company, 1965), p. 300.

to a different kind of information about values. Moore and others of his persuasion describe this source as "intuition" or as "immediate intellectual intuition." They claim that the information is immediate, all-encompassing, and *a priori*. They maintain that there is no intellectual process involved, for the propositions are unanalyzable and nonrational, and that since the unique propositions are infallible they ought to be accepted. Such views that eliminate the process of valuing are cast in the realm of faith, which may be (but does not have to be) supported by knowledge of an inductive-deductive nature.

There are still other value theorists who believe that man's intelligence or his reason is the source of the valuing process. But even here the theorists are divided according to their views about the nature of reason. One view is that reason has an individual character, one that differs with each person according to his particular experiences with others and with his particular environment. There is no evidence to suggest that when men face a problem they will all reason through to the same conclusion, even though they begin with the same facts. This lack of evidence indicates a relativism that those who believe in the individualistic nature of reason explain in much the same way as do the psychologists who say that the process of evaluating stems from the emotions. Aristotle wrote along these lines that "moral virtue comes about as a result of habit," and that "it is also plain that none of the moral virtues arise in us by nature; for nothing that exists by nature can form a habit contrary to its nature." Aristotle believed that man is by nature capable of receiving virtues but that not all men fulfill the capability.

A second view about the character of reason is that it is universal, that it is part of the original nature of man and has the quality of innateness. Even here there is a lack of consensus among those who posit the universal character of reason, for some insist upon a supernatural origin of reason, while others hold to a natural origin which is restricted to man. In either case, however, any relativity of values is automatically ruled out, and the process of valuing becomes a simple matter of recognizing universals since values are absolute.

Our analysis of "value" and "valuing" has shown that the terms are used to describe an existent (product) and a process (or in the case of intuition, a nonprocess) that involves the existent. We have learned that a theory of value attempts to answer certain questions about value and valuing. Is value subjective, objective, or is it a relation? Does valuing well up from the emotions? Does it originate in man's reason? Or is it intuitive? We have reason to suspect that the answers to these questions will fall into three general groupings, and this is indeed the case. There are, of course, certain variations and exceptions, but generally speaking there are three mainstreams of thought about theory of value.

Various labels have been used to describe the dominant views, but most contemporary discussions of value theory avoid the contrivance of forcing one set of labels to serve all of the philosophic divisions. Recent discussions of ethics describe fundamentally valid points of view with the terms *cognitivism,* which is subdivided into *naturalism* and *nonnaturalism* (or intuitionism) and *noncognitivism* (or various forms of *emotivism*). These terms are equally descriptive of the views of value theorists, and we shall use them here in preference to older, more traditional philosophical categories.

The traditional use of the term "naturalism" is in contrast to supernaturalism, but we use it in this context to refer to natural modes of inquiry in contrast to nonnatural modes of inquiry such as intuition. Those value theorists who believe that value statements can be verified empirically through observation and experimentation are called naturalists. Any disagreement that naturalists have among themselves regarding the meaning of value terms can usually be resolved by a definition of terms, for they maintain that there is no specific meaning that must necessarily be attached to particular value terms. Naturalists are inclined to the position that the value choices we make are a reflection of our natural feelings and that there are no absolute values that would be universally binding on all people.

Ralph Barton Perry represents a slight variation of the naturalistic theme, as he holds that individual feelings are merely clues to the interests and desires that condition our choices. He goes further to maintain that our value choices are made or ought to be made out of consideration for the interests of others as well as out of self-interest. Thus, according to Perry, certain actions can be labeled as "right" and ought to be performed by all. Although this is an absolutist position, in the final analysis, the choices are utilitarian and contribute to the well-being of the individuals who are members of a community.

The nonnaturalists agree with G. E. Moore's notions of *good* being a nonnatural property and of intuition being a nonnatural mode of knowing. The nonnaturalist insists that value names do refer to properties which cannot be verified by empirical means. Although the nonnaturalist will admit to a definition of some value terms, he claims that other terms such as *good, right,* and *duty* are simple and therefore unanalyzable. A unique characteristic of the nonnaturalist position is revealed in the response to the question, "How is one able to recognize the simple, absolute property of value names?" Osborne states that:

> When the philosophy of Value first emerged as distinct from theoretical philosophy it was assumed, as we have seen, by Kant that we have immediate intellectual intuition of principles of Right and Value which form the primordial warp of ultimate Reality, and by his immediate successors that in certain feelings we have immediate knowledge, of a non-theoretical kind, of the ultimate and eternal nature of Reality, which in sense perception and theoretical knowledge we know only imperfectly and as it were in images.[8]

---

[8] H. Osborne, *Foundations of the Philosophy of Value* (London: Cambridge University Press, 1933), pp. xx–xxi.

Recent suggestions from nonnaturalists as to how we recognize value are: by way of intuition, or by way of rational insight. The two suggestions have a common base, because in both cases an explanation depends upon sensitivity, nonperceptual awareness, or a simple assertion that the human mind has a capacity for the necessary knowledge. The quality of ineffability is unmistakable in any case.

The dominant noncognitivistic theory of value is called the *emotive theory* and is a view that denies that value terms (specifically ethical terms) have reference to properties of an observable nature. Generally, emotivists assert that expressions of value are only expressions of opinions and attitudes and that they are uttered for the purpose of influencing the attitudes of others. According to the emotivist, value statements are not intended to be factual but to have persuasive intent. The emotivist does not recognize a "higher" law that dictates value choices, nor does he rely upon empirical or scientific procedures. The emotivist claims that value decisions depend upon deliberation about how the individual reacts to all aspects of a theoretical problem. According to R. B. Brandt:

> The emotivist says that what we do when we deliberate about what is right or best is quite different from what we do when solving a theoretical problem. We are not thinking about proofs or evidence. When we are first faced with an ethical problem, we think over all its aspects, registering a reaction to them. At the end, we seem to sum it up, to see how we feel about the thing as a whole. If it isn't clear how we feel or if we have conflicting impulses and don't know what we want to support, we re-examine the facts, trying to see more facts or relationships that will release the indecision or remove the conflict.[9]

The emotivist's position requires that attitudes be clearly delineated so that there is no internal conflict. Only at the point where one arrives at a decision based upon individual emotions is it proper to make a value choice and to act in accordance with the choice.

Linguistic Problems

We have discovered that there is not only a lack of unanimity among theorists concerning the nature and the properties of value and valuing but even as to the best ways to approach the basic value problems. Some of the problems that confront the value theorist are so complex and so highly involved that to discuss them in the context of this study would be meaningless. Other problems, especially those which occur in everyday language, should be noted early in any discussion about values, in order that unnecessary linguistic complications may be avoided.

Our discussion in Chapter I about the clarification of language delineated the importance of correct usage for the communication of ideas. We

---

[9] Richard B. Brandt, *Ethical Theory: The Problems of Normative and Critical Ethics.* © 1959. Reprinted by permission of Prentice-Hall, Inc., Englewood Cliffs, New Jersey.

touched briefly upon the relationship between concept, sign, and referent, but in the context of value theory the problem of "language referent" takes on special significance. Whenever a value statement is made, the question of language referent is raised. Does a statement signifying approval or disapproval of some action refer to individual feelings, to private likes and dislikes? Or does it refer to some standard which exists apart from personal desires? If the referent is subjective, the value statement merely expresses agreement or disagreement of feelings, and nothing is demanded by the statement. On the other hand, if the referent is objective, if it is some external standard, the statement involves an obligation which is imposed upon the speaker or upon some other self. Perhaps in the final analysis the problem is a metaphysical one, for the points to be decided involve relations between a mind, language, and some sort of reality—whether it is objective, subjective, or a relation. But in any event, the nature of the response demanded by a value statement is determined by the nature of the referent.

We have seen that each of the dominant value theories involves an attempt to deal with the problem of value which in a most general sense is a concern about those things which we actually value and those things which we ought to value. The two parts of the larger concern suggest one of the most perplexing value problems, that which is generally referred to as the "is-ought" dichotomy. Simply put, this is a distinction between what is *actually* the case and what we might *wish* were the case.

The distinction is obviously useful, but theorists today claim that an attempt to move logically from description to prescription forces the distinction beyond the limits of its usefulness. Philosophers in the past have explored the relation of an *is* to an *ought,* and there are those who have maintained that the "isness" can validate the "oughtness." However, none has been able to demonstrate satisfactorily that a move from one kind of reality to another kind can be logically justified. Most value theorists agree that *is* and *ought* are simply expressions used to point up what is at issue in a particular context and that there is not a true dichotomy between the two designations.

In order to examine the "is-ought" dichotomy and to explore the limits of its usefulness let us consider the following statements:

1. This is the assignment for tomorrow.
2. You ought not to cheat.

The first statement is clearly an *is* statement, and the second one is an *ought* statement. Granting a true dichotomy between *is* and *ought,* each declarative statement will be one or the other, and we should have no reason to expect any middle ground. But supposing that I say to you, "You ought to study the assignment." The statement contains an *ought,* but yet it does not have the same value-laden imperative as our second statement. There seems, then, to be no alternative other than to place it somewhere in between the *is* statement and the *categorical ought* statement. The suggestion has been made that we label such a statement "a prudential ought statement." We now have the following statements:

1. This is the assignment for tomorrow. —— An *is* statement.
2. You ought to study the assignment. —— A *prudential ought* statement.
3. You ought not to cheat. —— A *categorical ought* statement.

At this point we have reason to wonder if there is some middle ground between the first and the second statement and between the second and the third statement. Supposing I say to you, "The assignment is material for our final exam." This appears to be another type of *is* statement, but it actually performs a mild *ought* function, as its intent is to inform you that you ought to realize the importance of the assignment. We can call this use of *ought* a "characterizing ought statement." Finally, supposing I announce to the class that "You ought to let me deal with any cheating." My statement suggests more than simple prudence and something less than the categorical quality of the final statement that made a moral judgment. We will call this a "judicial ought statement." We now have the following statements:

1. This is the assignment for tomorrow. —— An *is* statement.
2. The assignment is material for our final exam. —— A *characterizing ought* statement.
3. You ought to study the assignment. —— A *prudential ought* statement.
4. You ought to let me deal with any cheating. —— A *judicial ought* statement.
5. You ought not to cheat. —— A *categorical ought* statement.

In effect, we have one simple *is* statement, and four *ought* statements of varying degrees. Statement number 1 merely asserts the "isness" of an assignment. Statement number 2 describes or characterizes the assignment. Statement number 3 presents no particular problem, for you are merely being advised that it would be prudent for you to study the assignment. I can give a practical response to the anticipated "Why?" by pointing out that you must know the material in order to pass the exam. The acceptance or rejection of my *ought* can be successfully argued without deserting the realm of natural inquiry. The same thing can be said of the use of *ought* in statement 4, as the intent is to inform you that cheating on the exam should be dealt with through the proper channel, in this case by myself.

Statement number 5 illustrates the point that the use of *ought* is apt to become a problem when moral issues are involved. The realm of inquiry is considerably broadened, for there are responses other than those in the practical realm that can be given to the anticipated "Why?" in this case. After I exhaust all of the utilitarian reasons for not cheating, I face the task of explaining why it is *morally* wrong to cheat. Until this point the assertions have been in the practical realm, and the justification for the assertions has been from the same realm. The poser of the "is-ought" dichotomy is that there is no bridge from this point to the existence of *universal* normative standards that can be logically justified. To assert otherwise is to force the limits of the "is-ought" dichotomy past its usefulness.

The statements that we have used to illustrate the artificiality of an "is-ought" dichotomy may also be useful for a consideration of another value problem—the distinction that is so frequently made between "fact" language and "value" language. Here too, we have a useful distinction but one which can also be troublesome unless we are aware of the problems that may be engendered by an inflexible position. Again, we must remain clear about how language is used and resist the urge to push beyond the limits of its usefulness.

There have been many articles, essays, and books on language clarification with particular reference to values. Analyses of valuational terms such as *bad, good, better, right,* and *wrong* figure prominently in these, and invariably the question is raised about a distinction between "fact" and "value" language. Many theorists, especially those of a naturalistic persuasion, seem to feel that the distinction is man-made, and that there is no real breach between the two. Others maintain a hard-and-fast line between the two, asserting that "fact" words are descriptive and factual and that "value" words stand for attitudes, states of being, principles, and ideas. The implication is a distinction between the rational or intellectual, and the emotional or nonrational. According to such a view, even though a range of extrinsic or instrumental values are admitted to be cognitive, the only way to avoid *absolute* instrumentalism is, in the final analysis, to admit to a cognitive-noncognitive dichotomy which places intellectual judgments in sharp contrast to value choices.

We saw earlier that our division of the "is-ought" class into subclasses was not really a division of the class statements but rather was a division according to the *intent* of the statements. This suggests the possibility of a similar division of the "fact language-value language" class, for common usage shows that all kinds of conventional sentences are capable of making evaluations. We also see the difficulty of separating "fact" language from "value" language when a value claim is made about a fact or when statements that express feelings or attitudes have a factual content. Clearly, we are no more prompted to action by valueless facts than we are by factless values, which a cognitive-noncognitive dichotomy would appear to deny. An even more critical point is that such a dichotomy precludes the possibility of an empirical investigation of values and an intellectual assessment of our value choices.

The Problem of Verification

One of the issues that complicates the problem of value is the verification of our value choices. Our discussion of value theories has shown that the naturalist, the nonnaturalist, and the emotivist each have a different base for assuming the warrantability of value choices. In spite of any dissatisfaction with each of the three points of view, the obligation to verify individual value choices is fairly obvious. Each choice that we make gives preference to one value over another, and each choice is translated into action. Thus an act is a mark of value, and a life may be judged by the values it sustains.

Since no one has been able to set forth any standards of value that are binding on all men at all times, it appears that each of us must conduct our own search for the values we sustain. We need to ask, then, if we act merely as a reflection of our environment, following the values of others without question, or if we act freely at our own direction, according to our own values. This being the case, it depends upon each of us to determine how we can most effectively deal with the problem of verification of our present values and how we can test the efficacy of our future value choices.

Our delineation of naturalism, nonnaturalism, and emotivism has not been a detailed one, but it is sufficient to indicate the sort of proof that would be required by each view for the verification of value statements. The naturalist, who believes that values are objective and who arrives at truth by reason, grants the same status to moral law that he does to laws discovered by science. The naturalist claims that any value statement can be translated without any change of meaning into the language of empirical science, and his method for dealing with value problems relies heavily upon experimentation and observation and upon the sort of inductive reasoning used by science to confirm empirical statements. While it would not be feasible, in this context, to consider all of the methods that have been suggested, it may be helpful to give an example of the sort of proof that a majority of naturalists could accept. *The appeal to nature* is a method which involves checking our value statements to determine whether or not they assert or prescribe that which is *natural*. This is based on the assumption that those things which are in accordance with the natural law are *right* and those things which do not conform with the "ideal nature" are *wrong*. This method has been criticized for "begging the question." That is, we still have no criteria for determining what things constitute "ideal nature," and we have no justification for denying that some things occur that are not natural.

We have seen that the nonnaturalist agrees with the naturalist about the affinity between value statements and statements of science only to a point. The nonnaturalist agrees that value statements are like statements of science only in so far as they are either true or false, according to how accurately they describe the facts. But the nonnaturalists say that since value statements do not refer to *observable* properties, the truth of the statements can only be verified by intuition, or by rational insight. There are some nonnaturalists who verify statements according to a *theological rule*. They believe that if the statements coincide with the will of God, they are justifiable. The method has been criticized because there are no uniform criteria as to how the will of God may be determined. There are, of course, extensions of this rule which equate God with "the moral law" or with "those principles to which we ought to give our moral allegiance," but in any case, a nonnatural dimension, whether it is God, intuition, or rational insight, is the measure of verification.

The emotivist disagrees with the naturalistic view that statements can be confirmed through observation and inductive reasoning and with the nonnaturalistic view that we can "know" by intuition. As we have noted, the emotivist contends that value statements are merely expressions of individual attitudes. Other noncognitivists say that value statements declare policy, or that they are prescriptions, or that they are commands or directions. They say that, since scientific statements are made primarily to state that something is the case, reasoning about values is quite different from reasoning about science. At the same time, the noncognitivist does not deny that it is important to reason about values, for such reasoning draws attention to facts that will influence attitudes, and attitudes have causal relations among themselves. They do deny that there is the same sort of logic to value reasoning as there is to science reasoning, and any procedure that convinces someone is acceptable to them. The emotivists say that we do not ask value questions for the purpose of information, but that we request some sort of influence to help make up our minds, and we would expect their method of verification to have a utilitarian base. The most widely accepted form is called *rule-utilitarianism.* Briefly, an action is acceptable if it is not prohibited by the ideal rules of a given society. Again, we have the problem of determining which are the "ideal" rules.

All of these methods, and others like them, have been severely criticized, and in recent years theorists have approached the problem from a different view. One of these is Richard B. Brandt who has proposed a method for testing value statements that is comparable to a scientific rule of induction. At the same time, his method is flexible enough so that it should be acceptable to those who maintain the subjectivity of values. Brandt's method, which he calls *the qualified attitude method,* is based on the procedure that thoughtful people generally use to determine whether or not an ethical statement is justified. He writes:

> In summary, our proposal about the "standard" method of ethical thinking is this. (1) We decide particular problems both by appeal to principles that we already have more or less explicitly in mind and by appeal to our preferences, feelings of obligations, and so forth (which kind of attitude depending on whether the question is one about what is desirable, or what is obligatory, and so on). (2) We correct our principles if they are incompatible with our criticized (undiscounted) attitudes (feelings of obligations and so forth), and we rely on our criticized attitudes in filling out and weighing our principles. (3) Judgments, as noted in Chapter 2, must be consistent, and particular ones must be generalizable. (4) Attitudes are discounted if they are not impartial, informed, the product of a normal state of

mind, or compatible with having a consistent set of general principles not excessively complex. Ethical thinking, then, is a complex interplay of attitudes, principles, formal requirements for principles, and rules for discounting. None of these can be submerged in the other three.[10]

Brandt supports the method he has suggested in a number of ways. First, he demonstrates that most people, even though they may not be consciously aware of it, follow much the same procedure in dealing with questions of an ethical nature in their daily routine. Secondly, he shows that there is no systematic alternative to the Qualified Attitude Method that would be acceptable to most people. Finally, he gives positive defense for the method that is clear, concise, and reasonable. His support makes an excellent case for the universal appeal of the Qualified Attitude Method, and it is certainly one that must be given serious consideration by those who seek a way to deal with the problem of justification.

Value and Reality

Ultimately, both value choices and the way they are verified are matters for individual consideration. There are no "right answers" to valuational problems that can be gleaned from text-books or taught in a class, and it depends upon the individual to acquire methods of orderly inquiry and to develop the considered judgment that facilitates a reconstruction of individual patterns of meaning. Attention to philosophic theory can help tremendously toward the clarification of our own ideas and toward an understanding of the sort of reasoning that is necessary for making rational decisions. Indeed, it would be a serious mistake to assume that the value theories men have developed since the time of Socrates are unrelated to the practical decisions we are called upon to make every day, for the models of the past provide excellent example of how man has tried to structure his moral experiences. So far our discussion about value has been generalized as we have attempted to clarify some of the basic terminology and have considered the various sources of valuing and the ways of verifying our values. At this point we are ready to investigate some of the valuational ideas that wise men of the past have advanced and to consider their methods of developing moral judgments.

We shall consider three examples of how value and valuing function within the context of a philosophical system. We shall begin with Plato, who is a classic example of the systematic philosopher. St. Augustine is a philosophical descendant of Plato, but his philosophy reveals a different type of reality and we shall give some attention to the similarities and contrasts between the two thinkers. Finally, John Dewey represents a view that recognizes value discussions as independent of prior metaphysical considerations, and we shall attempt to show significant differences that exist as a result of the view. These examples will prepare the way for a discussion of

---

[10] *Ibid.*, pp. 250–251.

contemporary views about the relevance of value for the future of the individual, society, and education.

Plato (427?–347? B.C.)

Those who are interested in value theory invariably begin with a study of Plato, even though his discussion of the Good presupposes a prior analysis of metaphysics and epistemology. Plato, born an aristocrat and regarded by some scholars as an enemy of democracy, has represented "Philosophy" to people of all societies. Emerson wrote that "Plato is Philosophy and Philosophy Plato," and even those least sympathetic with Plato's flight from the world of senses recognize that he wrestled with most of the important problems that have plagued mankind. Our discussions will concentrate only upon those aspects of Plato's philosophical system which are necessary to see "value" in its proper setting.

We shall refer to a number of the Platonic dialogues during the following discussion, but for several reasons we have elected to use *The Republic* as a primary source. *The Republic* is generally considered to be one of the most complete and systematic of Plato's dialogues and might very well serve as a single textbook for an introductory course to the basic problems of philosophy. Other dialogues such as *Laches, Charmides,* and the *Euthyphro,* are discussions of a particular problem—courage, self-control, or piety—whereas a study of *The Republic* can lead to an understanding of major philosophical views about reality, knowledge, and value. Finally, *The Republic* is Plato's best expression of the connections among education, the individual, and the role of the individual in society.

Scholars agree that the main theme of *The Republic* is an attempt to analyze the concept of Justice in order to determine if it is a universal principle which can operate in the lives of men and in society. *The Republic* is composed of ten books. It begins with some current views about justice that Socrates attacks for being either inadequate or false and concludes with a discussion of the rewards of justice in this life and after death. It is systematically demonstrated, not only that a just state of just men is the ideal situation, but that it is a possible goal in this world, and the only reasonable one. Our present concern is primarily the analysis of the Platonic soul which is found in Book IV, the two worlds of Form and appearance as described in Book V, the demonstration of the four stages of cognition by means of the line in Book VI, and finally the famous allegory of the cave which is found in Book VII. The discussions reveal that the Good has relevance for the individual and that it is the pinnacle of value in Plato's philosophy.

According to Plato, to refer to the individual is to speak about the soul of the individual. Preceding the analysis of the soul it has been demonstrated that there are three distinct social functions in the just state—deliberative and governing, executive, and productive. It follows, according to Plato, that since the state is a composite of individuals, we will find the three corresponding elements in each soul. The three parts of the soul are the rational which is the higher part of man, and the spirit and the appetitive which represent the sexual and other biological desires.

Plato has described the soul in the *Timaeus* with his myth of creation. When the souls were created—enough for all time—the three parts of each soul were associated with the head, the chest or the heart, and the stomach or the generative organs. Although the rational soul is conceived to be immortal and able to move freely between the world of the living and the world of the dead, it would be a mistake to think of the soul as a material thing that can be broken up into components. The soul can have its reason dimmed if it is smothered by material desires, but it cannot be corrupted nor destroyed. The impurities, man's material desires, will be thrown off when the body dies if the soul is able to remain devoted to the purity of reason. Then the soul will seek "to apprehend and hold converse with the divine, immortal, and everlasting world to which she is akin."[11] For this reason the rational part of the soul is the crucial element and may be spoken of as "divine."

It is an arduous task to be rational, and Plato has described the difficulties mythically in the *Phaedrus*. Here we have a chariot drawn by two steeds which is the representation of a single living whole. One of the steeds represents the noble, or the rational part of the whole, and the other represents the ignoble, or the appetite. The charioteer represents judgment or the spirit, and it is his task to manage the horses of different strain so that they will pull together as a matched pair. There is no real problem in the case of the gods, for each of the three parts are as good as they can possibly be, but if the horses lose their wings and fall to the earth, the soul acquires an earthly body, and the spirit is the mediator between reason and appetite. The problem is illustrated further in *The Republic* by the analogy of a thirsty man driven by his appetite, yet held in check by his reason which tells him that to drink would be bad for him. A third factor, spirit, or what has been called "judgment" or "sense of honor," may take the side of reason, but yet may not be identified with reason. On the other hand, spirit may fall away from reason, in which case the soul falls away from the highest Good.

Probably the most difficult barriers to a complete understanding of Plato's concept of the soul are his belief in the transmigration of the soul and his doctrine of reminiscence (recollection), for these two doctrines have not formed a part of Western thought since about the time of St. Augustine. The doctrine of reminiscence holds that knowledge is a matter of remembering what was known by the soul before it came into the body. When the soul chooses a new life and leaves Hades to return to the earth (transmigration of the soul), the journey takes it across the River of Lethe (river of forgetfulness). Here all are required to drink, but some drink more than others, and, accordingly, forget more. All knowledge, then, is

11 Francis MacDonald Cornford, *The Republic of Plato* (New York: Oxford University Press, 1945), p. 346.

contained within the soul and flows outward from it in the manner of an overflowing vessel.

According to Plato's doctrine of transmigration it is possible for a soul to use any number of lifetimes before the cycle of successive lives is completed. The knowledge contained within the soul unfolds throughout the lifetime of the individual it inhabits. The idea is necessary to Plato because of his rejection of the "empirical world," the world of senses which he calls the world of appearance. The view is alien to most twentieth century thinking, but there are still those who are fascinated by the Platonic explanation of individual differences and abilities as they are related to the completeness of individual remembrance. Plato was a thinker who kept returning to questions, rethinking them, and raising additional problems, and perhaps his life is one of the best examples of a complete remembrance.

One of the foundation stones of Plato's philosophy is his metaphysical postulation of two worlds, the world of Form, or what some scholars call the world of Idea, and a world of appearance. The world of Forms represents the realm of universals, essences, absolute perfection. The Forms are not things in the ordinary sense, nor yet ideas in the mind—infinite or finite. They are quite outside of time and space, are self-caused, and are completely rational. Plato was in no way propounding a mystical doctrine for the occult, for it is one of the purest rationality. Only through rational processes could one apprehend the Forms, especially the highest Form, the Good.

Plato's encounter with the world of appearances was intolerable, for there was no constancy about the visible and tangible things which are commonly called real. Change and process quite destroyed any chance for man to recognize the essence of a thing, and there was no perfect manifestation of the ideal. His alternative was a flight to the world of Forms where stability and perfection could be found and which could explain the various degrees of approximation of the ideal in the world of appearances. The two worlds, the world of appearance and the world of Forms, are separate but connected in a manner described by the terms participation, imitation, transcendence, and immanence. The connection is that the world of appearance is an imitation of the world of Forms but participates in the Form world in such a manner that there is an element of the real in the imitation. The Forms are immanent within the world of appearance but are transcendent and exist apart. Accordingly, it is possible to speak of appearance as having reality, but a reality that can be lost by a separation of the Form and the appearance. As we have seen, this is a necessary arrangement for the metaphysical position of Plato.

The concept of two worlds is manifest in Plato's discussion of the four stages of cognition where he uses the device of a divided line in order to illustrate his point. First, a perpendicular line is divided into two unequal parts. The lower part represents the visible order, or the world of appearance. The upper part of the line represents the intelligible order. Next, each of the parts is again divided in the same proportion in order to symbolize the "degrees of comparative clearness or obscurity." The lowest segment of the line stands for images, shadows, or reflections, and the second segment stands for the actual things that are reflected. The third segment stands for those things which had images in the visible world, and the final segment stands for the world of Forms. A movement up the line represents the ascent of the mind from images, to visible things, into the intelligible world where a study of mathematics is necessary but not sufficient for true understanding of the Forms, and finally into the world of Forms where no use is made of the images that were used in the other segments and where inquiry is made only by the means of Forms. Assumptions are treated by the dialectic "not as first principles, but as hypotheses in the literal sense, things 'laid down' like a flight of steps up which it (reason) may mount all the way to something that is not hypothetical."[12]

Plato's idea of the two worlds is even more explicit in his allegory of the cave which Socrates relates to Glaucon in order to illustrate how the nature of man is enlightened or unenlightened. (See illustration.) Socrates tells Glaucon to imagine human beings living in an underground cavern which has a wide mouth, the width of the cavern, reaching up to the light. The inhabitants of the cavern are all seated facing the back wall, chained so that they are unable to move and can only look straight ahead. Behind and above the inhabitants is a flaming fire and in front of the fire is a raised platform extending like a wall along the width of the cave. Men, who carry vases, statues, and all manner of figures fashioned from a variety of materials parade in a continuous file along the wall-like walk before the burning fire. Some of the men speak, and others are silent.

The inhabitants of the cave, chained as they are, can only see the shadows of the figures as they are cast on the back wall of the cave by the light from the fire. The voices of the men carrying the figures resound against the walls of the cave, and it seems to the chained inhabitants that the voices come from the shadows which they take to be real. At this point the inhabitants of the cave represent man in the first stage of cognition—images. It is easy for Glaucon to see how the prisoners take the shadows for the truth, and Socrates continues the allegory to illustrate the pain and confusion the prisoners suffer when their chains are removed and they are forced to turn around and walk towards the light. At first the prisoners insist that the shadows are more real than the objects that caused the images or shadows. At this point they represent man in the second stage of cognition, visible things. We can imagine their increased agony when they are forced up the steep incline out of the cave and into the intelligible world, the third stage of cognition. When they first look directly at the sun, which represents the Forms, they are blinded by its brightness. In this manner, Socrates makes the point that the cave is the world of appearance where the fire is the only source of light. The climb out of the dark cavern repre-

---

12 *Ibid.*, p. 226.

STATES OF MIND

Intelligence or Knowledge

Thinking

Belief

Imagining

THE LINE

OBJECTS

The Good

Forms

Mathematical Objects

Visible Things

Images

Sun

Intelligible World

World of Appearances

Fire

Figure

Shadow of the Figure

Chained Prisoner

THE CAVE

sents the ascent of the soul into the intellectual world where the sun represents the source of all Good.

Thus, according to Plato, in the world of knowledge the idea of Good
appears last of all and with the greatest effort. Good is the highest Form
and is the pinnacle of the intelligible world. The allegory is a classic, not
only for the magnificence of the language, but because the simple analogy
can be extended to clarify much of the complexity of Platonism. It is illustrative, according to the level of interpretation, of a variety of Platonic
concepts, such as knowledge, Virtue, reason, and the Good, which is the
ultimate goal for Plato.

> Once it (Good) is perceived, the conclusion must follow that, for all
> things, this is the cause of whatever is right and good; in the visible
> world it gives birth to light and to the lord of light, while it is itself
> sovereign in the intelligible world and the parent of intelligence and
> truth. Without having had a vision of this Form no one can act with
> wisdom, either in his own life or in matters of state.[13]

The popular belief had been that pleasure was the most important
object of knowledge, but, according to Plato, the world is made intelligible
only by the supreme Good. The well-being of man and of society depend
upon how man acts. If he acts out of belief or disbelief, which can be
either true or false, the goals may be misconceived and his actions mis-
directed. But apprehension of the Good enables man to act rationally and
provides him with certain knowledge of the values which all life should
realize. Therefore, Good, the highest Form, is the most important object
of knowledge. Apprehension of the Good is the culmination of arduous
intellectual training, a necessary condition for the immediate *intellectual*
intuition which gives certain and immediate knowledge of the Good. Plato's
analysis makes the process totally rational, yet the ultimate goal—the Good
—is unanalyzable. It can only be described allegorically as the source of all
light in the world.

> It was the Sun, then, that I meant when I spoke of that offspring
> which the Good has created in the visible world, to stand there in the
> same relation to vision and visible things as that which the Good
> itself bears in the intelligible world to intelligence and to intelligible
> objects.[14]

Saint Augustine (354–430)

Saint Augustine, the second philosopher to be presented in our discussion of theories of value, is a complex figure. His early life was decidedly
unlike the ideals expressed by the Christian faith of his mother. He relates
many of his early experiences in his *Confessions,* and as we read them we

---

[13] *Ibid.,* p. 231.
[14] *Ibid.,* p. 219.

can easily identify ourselves with Augustine and even suffer with him. We are caught up by his inner strivings and his efforts to seek the good and the true. We agonize with Augustine as he shifts from paganism to skepticism to Manichaeanism to Christianity. After his conversion, Christianity became his way of life, and his religious views provide the base for his ideas about value and education.

Saint Augustine was able, for the most part, to synthesize the traditions of paganism as exemplified by Plato and the Neoplatonists, with the early medieval views which tended to suspect the use of reason in matters of truth. His synthesis was weighted toward Christianity, however, for he accepted only those ideas and ideals that were in accord with the principles of Christianity. For example, he was critical of the doctrine of the transmigration of the soul because the view was incompatible with Christian doctrine. He also opposed the concept of recollection of knowledge, for his religious principles told him that ". . . we ought rather to believe that the intellectual mind is so formed in its nature as to see those things, which by the disposition of the Creator are subjoined to things intelligible in a natural order, by a sort of incorporeal light of a unique kind."[15] Such a belief unquestionably conditioned Augustine's ideas about theory of value, and while we expect to find notable differences, it is clear that Augustine relied heavily on Platonic thinking.

Both Plato and Augustine believed in a supernatural creation of the soul, but where Plato credited this creation to one of the several gods—a Demiurge (creative god), Augustine believed in the one supreme God, the creator of all things. We have seen that Plato thought all of the souls were created at one time and that each soul could inhabit a number of different bodies in this world. Augustine's view about the manner in which the soul was created is not as precise. On the one hand, he was inclined to favor the idea of Traducianism, where all souls were created in Adam's soul so that each would be handed down by the parent. He was inclined to this view philosophically, for it would explain the concept of original sin as a transmitted stain on the soul, but he could not accept the materialistic view of the soul that was logically involved. Augustine was adamant on the point that the soul is an immaterial principle which gives life to the body. He was also firm in his refusal to allow that the soul is punished for its preearthly errors by being placed into an earthly body.

Plato made no distinction between the individual and the soul, but Augustine implies a difference when he says that, since the soul is superior to the body it inhabits, it cannot be acted upon nor altered by the body. According to Augustine, the soul is aware of bodily changes caused by external stimuli and can use the body as an instrument. Augustine's terminology is similar to Plato's when he describes the rational and the irrational parts of the soul, but Augustine is credited with positing five parts to the soul, rather than three. Intelligence and will, Augustine says, are rational

---

[15] Whitney J. Oates, ed. *Basic Writings of Saint Augustine* (New York: Random House, Inc., 1948), Vol. II, p. 824.

aspects of the soul, and memory, sense, and appetite are irrational aspects of the soul. Augustine uses methods similar to Plato's to prove the immortality of the soul but he does it without affirming the preexistence of the soul. Augustine says that the soul is an immaterial principle and is therefore assured of immortality and that, since it apprehends indestructible truth, it is also indestructible. He also argues from the soul's desire of beatitude and perfect happiness.

The Augustinian theory of knowledge also relies heavily upon Platonic thought, but again there are distinct differences. Rather than four levels of cognition, Augustine speaks in terms of the levels of: 1) sensing; 2) judgments about sense objects; and 3) the ability to contemplate eternal things. The first level is common to all animals, but only man is endowed with the reason that enables him to judge or question sense objects, and only man has the ability to contemplate eternal things. Augustine's prime concern is the soul's orientation to God, but he does not deny that we do learn by the bodily senses, even though corporeal things are not the proper objects of human intellect.

De Magistro, a dialogue between Augustine and his son Adeodatus, is primarily concerned with questions of knowledge as focused on the origin of ideas in man. Although true ideas are in the soul of man and do not come from an external source, Augustine does not desert the sense world entirely, for he recognizes that the senses are necessary for man to learn about the world in which he lives. Words and sense objects, according to *De Magistro,* function as cues or prompts that remind rather than teach. Augustine states that ". . . it is the truest reasoning and most correctly said that when words are uttered we either know already what they signify or we do not know; if we know, then we remember rather than learn, but if we do not know, then we do not even remember, though perhaps we are prompted to ask."[16] Both Plato and Augustine deprecate sense objects in comparison with immaterial realities, but the Augustinian goal is the achievement of a personal God rather than of an impersonal Good.

The eternal truths that Augustine speaks of are similar to the Forms in Plato's thought, but for Augustine they exist as exemplars, or ideas in the divine mind, and serve as patterns for the creation of the earth and the heavens. They are beyond our understanding and thus are in the realm of faith. The distinction that Augustine made between understanding and believing was that we believe what we understand, but we are not able to understand all that we believe. We may not understand the eternal truths, but they are made visible to the mind by divine illumination. The ultimate purpose of knowledge and faith is a supernatural vision and possession of God.

Augustine's *The City of God* contains the best description of his views about the two worlds, the "Godly" and the "earthly." Those who choose to love God and shun the earthly pleasures of self have chosen religion and merit

---

16 *Ibid.,* Vol. I, p. 389.

residence in the City of God. Those who choose to love self have turned away from God and will probably merit punishment. The choice is an important one, for without the true religion there can be no justice or virtue among men. A just society depends upon religion, for knowledge without faith does not assure justice. Augustine writes that ". . . the highest good, than which there is no higher, is God, and consequently He is unchangeable good, hence truly eternal and truly immortal."[17] We see that the Augustinian value (good) is infused with religious meanings. The standard is still an absolute one, unchanging, and eternal, and man can look to it and use it to insure personal goodness and a good society. Since religion should be dominant in the life of an individual, education must be religiously oriented. "Education does not consist in the accumulation of facts. It is an illumination of the soul, a turning of the eyes of the mind towards the light."[18] This is not too far removed from Plato, yet sufficiently removed to demarcate the classical mind from the theological. It is a giant step from this point to the thinking of John Dewey.

John Dewey (1859–1952)

A legend in his own time, John Dewey lived to see his philosophical writings become the battleground for liberal social reformers and conservative subject matter specialists. In a very real sense, Dewey was the great disturber of his age. Dewey was born in the same year that Horace Mann died, and it is a curiosity that he succeeded Mann as the leading theorist in matters pertaining to public schools. From an early adherence to idealism, Dewey went on to accept principles of pragmatism and Darwinian evolution (*Origin of Species* was published in the year of Dewey's birth) as the pillars of a developing philosophy which he called instrumentalism.

Dewey's philosophy may properly be called a living philosophy, for it is primarily concerned with man in relation to society. It is concerned with the ability of man to realize his potential and to develop as fully as possible within the framework of his society. It is a philosophy that does not lead man on a flight from experience into the aura of either a metaphysical Good or a theological God. Platonic metaphysics becomes anathema for men of Dewey's persuasion. Dewey had studied the history of man's struggle and had witnessed his survival through crusades, holy wars, inquisitions, and scientific and commercial revolutions. Through it all, man had been able to transform his world from a simple primitive one to the complexities of the metropolis. Dewey believed such a transformation had come about through men working together in this world.

We can readily see that Dewey's views will differ markedly from those of Plato and Augustine, and we expect a rejection of the beliefs previously expressed by these men. This is indeed the case. When we read Dewey we must keep in mind his belief in the principles of naturalism, process, and

---

17 *Ibid.*, Vol. I, p. 431.
18 S. J. Curtis and M. E. A. Boultwood, *A Short History of Educational Ideas* (London: University Tutorial Press, 1958), p. 86.

continuity, and his belief that there is no hierarchy leading to an unexperienceable value. To Dewey, ". . . values of some sort or other are not traits of rare and festal occasions; they occur whenever any object is welcomed and lingered over, whenever it arouses aversion and protest; even though the lingering be but momentary and the aversion a passing glance toward something else."[19]

In one of Dewey's major writings, *Experience and Nature,* he discusses his attitudes concerning the meaning of the term soul.[20] The term is interpreted naturally and is stripped of any mysterious meaning, for it refers simply to the ". . . properties of sensitivity and of marvelously comprehensive and delicate participative response characterizing living bodies." Such a description of the term reveals Dewey's attachment to the ordinary life-experiences of man, the ". . . realities designated in idiomatic speech . . .", and to his refusal to desert naturalistic phenomena. Here the soul is no longer the source of knowledge, nor is it caught up in a split between the purity of the soul and the impurity of the body. Simply put, when the ". . . soul is free, moving and operative, initial as well as terminal, it is Spirit." In the same place Dewey admits that possibly the words "soul" and "spirit" may have to be given up because of the traditional mythology attached to them.

"One world," a phrase borrowed from the political campaign of Wendell Willkie, although not a happy political doctrine, aptly describes Dewey's view of existence, for he rejects the division of existence into the natural and the supernatural. Dewey believed that the search for absolutes takes man away from the booming world of experience and reduces his chances of fulfilling the needs and the desires of the finite being. The infinite should be left to the infinite mind, whatever that might be. Dewey stated that:

> A philosophy which accepts the denotative or empirical method accepts at full value the fact that reflective thinking transforms confusion, ambiguity and discrepancy into illumination, definiteness and consistency. But it also points to the contextual situation in which thinking occurs. It notes that the starting point is the actually *problematic,* and that the problematic phrase resides in some actual and specifiable situation.[21]

The problem of knowledge is naturally raised by the above quotation. Dewey's world is one of continuity, and knowledge is of the world and continuous with the world. Dewey saw knowledge as being limited to the phenomenal world and felt that any other realm was the province of the individual and must be contacted through faith. Knowledge is not a matter of divine illumination or of recalling or remembering things already known but is the ordering of sense data that can be tested. Knowledge involves

---

[19] John Dewey, *Experience and Nature* (Chicago: Open Court Publishing Co., 1925), p. 400.
[20] *Ibid.,* pp. 293–297.
[21] *Ibid.,* p. 67.

the scientific task of verifying relations, facts, and events within a natural order. What is known must be understood. The "doer" in this natural order is an individual mind reconstructing its own experience. There is nothing mystical about it, and mind is not postulated as an entity but as process.

We conclude that Dewey relates existence and value. He deplores a situation in which philosophers create a realm of values and then set about trying to relate that realm to the one of experience. Dewey felt that such an exercise missed the point of value discussions entirely. A means of discriminating among the possibilities of experiences and actions on the basis of their consequences seemed far more relevant, and the scientific method functioned for Dewey even in value determination. It cannot be overemphasized that there is nothing metaphysical or mystical in his view.

Dewey affirmed an immediacy of experience, a liking or disliking, an approval or disapproval, of things that either are or are not. Values can be reflected upon as a basis for forming judgments, but the judgments, like the values, must continually undergo change. We must constantly reconstruct our judgment about values in order to deal with issues of value as they develop. Value judgments require the highest degree of intelligence, for values are created by man and cannot act as a standard above man. Society will disintegrate if individual desires, strivings, loves, and hates proceed haphazardly, and intelligence is the only guide that will assure value choices that are effective for the betterment of our conditions.

Values and Society

The Individual and Society

We have seen that value refers to something that has either fixed or relative existence; that values represent certain social or absolute ideals; that valuing is the process of judgment about values; and that the source of valuing may be emotional, intuitive, or intellectual. In terms of theory of value, whether one is a naturalist, a nonnaturalist, or a noncognitivist, one must nevertheless deal with the experiences in this world which sustain and enhance life, for such experiences indicate those things which are *valued* by the individual. The point at issue is that there is a distinction between our values and the valued.

Webster's Seventh New Collegiate Dictionary defines valuable as ". . . something having monetary value; something that is highly useful or serviceable; a precious possession; those things which are valued." Granted that one's theory of value may be *related* to the things he deems valuable, it would be a mistake to confuse our worldly possessions with our value structure, and we must be wary of the danger of equivocation when we speak in terms of value. For instance, we recognize the fact that primitive man, who was primarily concerned with personal survival, must have valued things which he could use as weapons for his own protection, implements for obtaining food, and fire for his protection and comfort. But it could scarcely be posited that primitive man subscribed to any theory of value. Rather it would seem that value theories are an outgrowth of societies and have experienced an evolution similar to that of mankind.

To illustrate the point, imagine yourself shipwrecked on a remote island, cut off from civilization forever with no hope of rescue. Survival would become paramount. If you had dry matches, or some other means of making fire, your chances for survival would be greatly enhanced, and you would place a high value on fire. Other things that would help make life on an island bearable would also be valued, but apart from some sort of societal context, a value structure would not seem particularly significant.

It is said that man is a social animal, but whether he began to band together with others of his own kind for companionship or for protection is not too important in this context. The important thing here is that individual members of any group are subject to all manner of disagreements and differences, and out of these differences individual theories become articulated. If it were not for the differences, the individual would be engulfed by a society operating as one collective organism with little change or progress. In the final analysis, the responsibility for the continuance of human society resides in the individual. If a society is composed of reluctant individuals, it is most likely that the social structure will not survive, for a reluctant member of a group is apt to feel resentment. His activities may therefore tend to destroy rather than to enhance and promote the continuance of the social structure which he feels holds him captive. On the other hand, individuals who band together for their mutual benefit strive for the same reason to preserve their unity. They recognize that in order to achieve this end there must be allowance for individual differences and that issues must be resolved by consensus.

Historically, the attempts to weld societies by gaining the allegiance of individuals have been varied, but the attempts which placed primary emphasis on the group to the exclusion of individual human rights have been doomed to failure. Hitler's plan was to fashion the individual desires and aspirations of all men to conform with the ideals of a mythical super-race for the glory of the state. Stalin tried to foster the supremacy of the state in a different way. If the state were prosperous, the citizens would realize individual economic prosperity. In both cases the state was supreme. The primary function of the individual was to serve the state, and individual values were measured only in terms of such service. Actually, Plato's ideas for a just state as expressed in *The Republic* are not as far removed from these concepts as one might think. There are obviously many differences, but in each case the individual would be educated to love and respect the state, and all men would therefore work together for the common ideal of a just state. There have been societies, and there are groups and individuals within our own society, who have a high regard for the worth of the individual but who feel that society would be far better if all individuals felt allegiance to a higher order. According to Augustine's thinking, all values should be uniformly derived from absolutes, in which case any inequalities or injustices would be solved in eternity. Dewey, whose attitudes were shaped by evolutionary and democratic principles, encouraged the free play of the individual value system, as he recognized a vast difference between conformity and harmony.

Musically, harmony is the structure of a piece of music according to the composition, progression, and modulation of its chords, and it would seem that the definition readily leads itself to the idea of a harmonious society wherein individual differences enter into harmonic relations. The choice of a musical analogy is deliberate, for it provides a vivid illustration of the necessity for, and the resolution of, differences within a democratic framework. We may even carry the analogy far enough to suggest that each member of a society, as each note of a composition, performs a particular function that contributes to the total composition. The character of a tone is distinguished by the regularity or consistency of vibration, and the character of an individual may be distinguished by a consistency of value orientation. A schizophrenic value orientation of an individual, or a group of individuals, destroys the harmony of the composition—society.

One of the most outstanding examples that I have seen of such a split in value orientation was during the time I taught philosophy in a state penitentiary.[22] An analysis of the ideas and opinions expressed by a number of the men in the class led to the conclusion that they held many beliefs which could be labeled as moral but that they had not allowed their beliefs to motivate their actions. The amazing thing was that they were completely unaware of any inconsistency and failed to see the irony of their contempt for one of the members of the group who planned to become an evangelist upon his release because it would be an easy way to earn a living. Most of the class were highly indignant at the dishonesty of his motives and had nothing but disgust for one who could sink so low.

The men insisted that it was consistent with moral attitudes to view armed robbery as a "status" crime, for did it not demand the qualities of courage, daring, initiative, and planning? And who could question that these are virtues to be admired by all? Imprisonment was simply one of the hazards of an occupation which was honest as long as only "decent" crimes were committed. Crimes of rape and murder were considered immoral, and the distinct demarcation that they made between "immoral" and "honest" crimes was reflected in the social structure within the prison.

There are those who blame crime and other social ills on the failure of the home and schools to inculcate moral and spiritual restraints in the individual. They believe that only a firm commitment to the heritages of authority can provide the necessary moorings and guidelines for making right decisions. Others are apt to place the blame for moral turpitude on the ineffectuality of spiritual values to cope with existence in a materialistic world, and prefer the empirical and the scientific to any sort of absolutes.

22 Carlton H. Bowyer, "Philosophy as an Aid to Correctional Education," *Journal of Correctional Education*, XII, No. 1.

But to insist on an either-or solution for societal problems is to lose sight of the democratic principles that permit both views. John Dewey stated that:

> The answer is that improved valuation must grow out of existing valuations, subjected to critical methods of investigation that bring them into systematic relations with one another.[23]

This is a demand for an intelligent use of means that are related to the desired ends, and these means-ends are values that must be viewed as operational and developmental. They must be seen in the context of a democratic heritage that fosters the freedoms and responsibilities necessary to the continued existence of the democracy. A society can grow and improve only in relation to individual growth, and by definition it would not be individual growth if there should be only one purpose, one goal, one means of achieving the desired ends. Many things contribute to individual growth, and it is far more to the point to recognize the variety of influences than it is to attach an untoward amount of blame for our failures to any one of them. Perhaps education is most often the scapegoat, because it plays a major part in individual development.

Society and Education

Throughout history man has recognized the importance of education both for the individual and for the dominant role it plays in society. If there should be any doubt of this, we need only consider the philosophers, theologians, and politicians who have concerned themselves with the problems of education. Historically, educational systems have developed in accordance with particular societies, for each member of a society is educated both formally and informally within the framework of his societal structure.

The formal aspects of education are prescribed by society, take place in institutions provided by society, and are implemented by teachers employed by society. It would be strange, indeed, if educational goals did not reflect the values held by a society, and if subjects were not taught that would assist young people to acquire the goods valued by their parents. Although each school is a complete society within a larger social structure, each school with its own culture, groupings, and values, the overriding purpose of education for the young is superimposed by the larger group. The view that schools should be walled off from the community has not prevailed since the nineteenth century, and the interaction between the schools and society is such that it would be an impossible and fruitless task to assess which wields the greater influence on the other. Suffice it to say that the salient feature of the society-education relationship is that, when a major change occurs in one, the other will surely be affected.

We have noted that there are those individuals in a society who look

---

[23] John Dewey "Theory of Valuation," *International Encyclopedia of Unified Science* (Chicago: The University of Chicago Press, 1939), II, No. 4, p. 60.

to absolutes to maintain the equilibrium of a *status quo,* and there are others who emphasize the importance of the experimental over the doctrinaire, the flexible over the rigid, and who share the hope of a reconstruction of society for the continuing good of all. It is no wonder, then, that the educational system reflects such a dilemma, and that schools are both stabilizers and disturbers; or that our educational system reflects what is in society, and at the same time is the agent for change in society. In both respects the values and the value structures of society play vital parts in education.

Education and Values

At this point we realize that values may exist independently of any formalized education. We have seen that the Platonist and the Augustinian look to a metaphysical good, or to God for their imperatives, and that they deal in terms of absolutes. Both views hold that values are independent of man and that they would remain the same without man to apprehend them. The pragmatist looks to man for values that are constantly changing and believes that there would be no values without man to do the valuing. Regardless of what value source is posited, formal education is not essential to the value structure. But, lacking some sort of value orientation, there should be no felt need for formal education. Values are the mainspring of education, and in this chapter the background has been sketched to point up the differences we might expect to find between educational programs that are based on metaphysical or religious or pragmatic value orientations.

As we make the following comparisons we should keep in mind the fact that they are extreme positions, and the actual implementation of any one view would be somewhat modified in practice. As we have previously indicated, it would be quite impossible to determine once and for all whether the different educational systems that have existed throughout history are reflections of changing values or if the different systems are responsible for value changes. What we subscribe to here is a definite correlation between education and values, and the purpose of our comparisons is to bring about a better understanding of such a correlation.

We have seen that the values held by Plato, Augustine, and Dewey are clear-cut and distinct. Logically, we should expect to find marked differences between the educational directives of the three. Such is the case, although there are fewer differences between the views of Plato and Augustine, both of whom looked to absolutes for their source of values. The primary difference between the Platonic and the Augustinian views about education is a matter of emphasis, which is governed by the difference between the ultimate goals.

The purpose of education for Plato was to achieve and maintain a state of justice. Ideally, each person would be educated according to his particular function in the ideal state. But where Plato would educate for the love and the good of the state, Augustine would educate for the love of

God in all things. In both cases, the system would be authoritarian. Conflicting opinions would be excluded through rigid censorship, and there would be no vacillation of aim, no confusion of purpose. In each case, the purpose of education would be to implement the truth.

The Platonic method would emphasize the dialectic in order to recall knowledge from the soul, and the Augustinian method would stress catechism for the moral and spiritual regeneration of the individual. Plato believed in educating the whole child and realized the importance of a healthy body, but Augustine, believing that the flesh is the source of evil, placed no special emphasis on physical fitness. Plato stressed mathematical subjects as a way to gain entrée to the Forms, but, although Augustine made numerous references to the power of numbers, he emphasized those subjects in the liberal arts which he thought provided the means by which God's works could be known and appreciated. In both cases, there would be no critics to disturb the *status quo* of the educational systems that would be founded on an authoritarian value structure. Critics persist only when there is freedom of learning and inquiry, and there would certainly be no justifiable reason for disagreement with an absolute truth such as Plato and Augustine maintained.

The basis for Dewey's value structure, as we have seen, was neither metaphysical nor religious, for he referred to experience and to the knowledge gained from that experience for his source of values. Value thus becomes a matter of choosing among experienceable alternatives, and the ground for choices is an intelligence developed through the processes of education which continue as long as one lives. Value has no single reference for Dewey but refers to all things which are valuable for the continued existence and growth of the individual. There are no final ends to such an evolutionary view. Any life has the possibility of being called moral, and the best life is the one which makes the fullest use of man's intelligence. Any society has the potential to become a good society, but a democratic society with its shared ideals and realities has the best possibility for continuing development.

A philosophy that denies absolutes does not exhibit any rigidity in the curriculum. According to Dewey, flexibility of subject matter leads to the development of self-concept and self-discipline. The child becomes central in the educational process, and through the development of his intelligence it is assumed he will choose to promote the good of the society.

Dewey's progressive educational theories have been described by many as being chaotic, for if there are no absolute values, the critics say, there can be no specific and set aims for education. There are those who feel we should return to a subject-matter curriculum with rigid controls that will foster discipline and respect for authority. But there will always be critics in a democratic situation, and this is as it should be. It would be impossible to fashion an educational system within the framework of democracy that would be pleasing to all. Our aims and goals develop out of a value structure, and it is evident that there is little valuational uniformity amongst the people of contemporary society. Thus far, valuations remain beyond scientific control, and it depends upon philosophy and education to unite the worlds of fact and value. American educators must attempt to fashion the sort of educational programs that will aid individuals to attain a wide variety of goals. Their task is rendered even more difficult by the view that education is one of the strongest implements for improving valuation. At the same time, our democratic system does not allow that specific values ought to be imposed upon all. However, a well-rounded program may help students gain a measure of control over their experiences, and can encourage the development of the systematic inquiry and considered judgment that leads to improved valuations.

PLATO

Meno*

The exact date of Plato's Meno *is not known, but it is thought to have been written about 403* B.C. *The* Meno *has been selected as the reading for Chapter II, because it illustrates the belief that value, knowledge, and metaphysics are related in such a way that the exploration of any one of the concepts requires similar investigations into the others. The major concern of Chapter II has been in the area of values, and we have noted how values are influenced by commitments about the nature of knowledge and by commitments to certain metaphysical concepts. We have also noted the importance of these commitments in regard to educational choices. A careful study of the* Meno *will provide further insights into the problem of meaning (in this case, the meaning of virtue); the nature of knowledge and learning, Plato's metaphysics; and finally, into one method of teaching, the Socratic method.*

The theme of the dialogue is revealed at the beginning by the questions of Meno who asks if virtue can be taught or if it comes in some other way. Such a direct approach at the beginning of a dialogue is a departure for Plato, but the Meno *quickly settles into the Platonic pattern of investigation by means of questions and analyses with careful consideration of language and meaning. The dialogue ends, as is most often the case, on an inconclusive note about the definition of virtue being a necessary condition to any conclusion about whether or not virtue can be taught. The dialogue suggests many questions which*

* From *The Dialogues of Plato,* trans. Benjamin Jowett, 4th ed., 1953, Vol. 1. Reprinted by permission of the Clarendon Press, Oxford.

provide avenues for discussions about value, teaching, and teaching about values. The following are examples of the kinds of questions that are raised: What is the meaning of the word virtue? How does virtue arise in the individual? Does virtue provide a relationship to beings other than man? Must Plato's metaphysics be accepted in order to benefit from the dialogue form? Can an analysis of the Meno *be fruitful for assessing modern problems associated with moral and spiritual values and for determining their relation to public school teaching?*

PERSONS OF THE DIALOGUE
MENO, SOCRATES, ANYTUS, *a slave of Meno*

MENO: Can you tell me, Socrates, whether virtue is acquired by teaching or by practice; or if neither by teaching nor practice, then whether it comes to man by nature, or in what other way?

SOCRATES: O Meno, there was a time when the Thessalians were famous among the other Hellenes only for their riches and their riding; but now, if I am not mistaken, they are equally famous for their wisdom, especially at Larisa, which is the native city of your friend Aristippus. And this is Gorgias' doing; for when he came there, the flower of the Aleuadae, among them your admirer Aristippus, and the other chiefs of the Thessalians, fell in love with his wisdom. And he has taught you the habit of answering questions in a grand and bold style, which becomes those who know, and is the style in which he himself answers all comers; and any Hellene who likes may ask him anything. How different is our lot! my dear Meno. Here at Athens there is a dearth of the commodity, and all wisdom seems to have emigrated from us to you. I am certain that if you were to ask any Athenian whether virtue was natural or acquired, he would laugh in your face, and say: "Stranger, you have far too good an opinion of me, if you think that I can answer your question. For I literally do not know what virtue is, and much less whether it is acquired by teaching or not." And I myself, Meno, living as I do in this region of poverty, am as poor as the rest of the world; and I confess with shame that I know literally nothing about virtue; and when I do not know the "quid" of anything how can I know the "quale"? How, if I knew nothing at all of Meno, could I tell if he was fair, or the opposite of fair; rich and noble, or the reverse of rich and noble? Do you think that I could?

MENO: No, indeed. But are you in earnest, Socrates, in saying that you do not know what virtue is? And am I to carry back this report of you to Thessaly?

SOCRATES: Not only that, my dear boy, but you may say further that I have never known of any one else who did, in my judgment.

MENO: Then you have never met Gorgias when he was at Athens?

SOCRATES: Yes, I have.

MENO: And did you not think that he knew?

SOCRATES: I have not a good memory, Meno, and therefore I cannot now tell what I thought of him at the time. And I dare say that he did know, and that you know what he said: please, therefore, to remind me of what he said; or, if you would rather, tell me your own view; for I suspect that you and he think much alike.

MENO: Very true.

SOCRATES: Then as he is not here, never mind him, and do you tell me: By the gods, Meno, be generous, and tell me what you say that virtue is; for I shall be truly delighted to find that I have been mistaken, and that you and Gorgias do really have this knowledge; although I have been just saying that I have never found anybody who had.

MENO: There will be no difficulty, Socrates, in answering your question. Let us take first the virtue of a man—he should know how to administer the state, and in the administration of it to benefit his friends and harm his enemies; and he must also be careful not to suffer harm himself. A woman's virtue, if you wish to know about that, may also be easily described: her duty is to order her house, and keep what is indoors, and obey her husband. Every age, every condition of life, young or old, male or female, bond or free, has a different virtue: there are virtues numberless, and no lack of definitions of them; for virtue is relative to the actions and ages of each of us in all that we do. And the same may be said of vice, Socrates.[1]

SOCRATES: How fortunate I am, Meno! When I ask you for one virtue, you present me with a swarm of them,[2] which are in your keeping. Suppose that I carry on the figure of the swarm, and ask of you, What is the nature of the bee? and you answer that there are many kinds of bees, and I reply: But do bees differ as bees, because there are many and different kinds of them; or are they not rather to be distinguished by some other quality, as for example beauty, size, or shape? How would you answer me?

MENO: I should answer that bees do not differ from one another, as bees.

SOCRATES: And if I went on to say: That is what I desire to know, Meno; tell me what is the quality in which they do not differ, but are all alike;—would you be able to answer?

MENO: I should.

SOCRATES: And so of the virtues, however many and different they may be, they have all a common nature which makes them virtues; and on this he who would answer the question, "What is virtue?" would do well to have his eye fixed: Do you understand?

MENO: I am beginning to understand; but I do not as yet take hold of the question as I could wish.

SOCRATES: When you say, Meno, that there is one virtue of a man, another of a woman, another of a child, and so on, does this apply only to virtue, or would you say the same of health, and size, and strength? Or is the nature of health always the same, whether in man or woman?

MENO: I should say that health is the same, both in man and woman.

SOCRATES: And is not this true of size and strength? If a woman is strong, she will be strong by reason of the same form and of the same strength subsisting in her which there is in the man. I mean to say that strength, as strength, whether of man or woman, is the same. Is there any difference?

MENO: I think not.

SOCRATES: And will not virtue, as virtue, be the same, whether in a child or in a grown-up person, in a woman or in a man?

MENO: I cannot help feeling, Socrates, that this case is different from the others.

SOCRATES: But why? Were you not saying that the virtue of a man was to order a state, and the virtue of a woman was to order a house?

---

[1] Cp. Arist. Pol. i. 13, § 10.
[2] Cp. Theaet. 146 D.

MENO: I did say so.

SOCRATES: And can either house or state or anything be well-ordered without temperance and without justice?

MENO: Certainly not.

SOCRATES: Then they who order a state or a house temperately or justly order them with temperance and justice?

MENO: Certainly.

SOCRATES: Then both men and women, if they are to be good men and women, must have the same virtues of temperance and justice?

MENO: True.

SOCRATES: And can either a young man or an elder one be good, if they are intemperate and unjust?

MENO: They cannot.

SOCRATES: They must be temperate and just?

MENO: Yes.

SOCRATES: Then all men are good in the same way, and by participation in the same virtues?

MENO: Such is the inference.

SOCRATES: And they surely would not have been good in the same way, unless their virtue had been the same?

MENO: They would not.

SOCRATES: Then now that the sameness of all virtue has been proven, try and remember what you and Gorgias say that virtue is.

MENO: Will you have one definition of them all?

SOCRATES: That is what I am seeking.

MENO: If you want to have one definition of them all, I know not what to say, but that virtue is the power of governing mankind.

SOCRATES: And does this definition of virtue include all virtue? Is virtue the same in a child and in a slave, Meno? Can the child govern his father, or the slave his master; and would he who governed be any longer a slave?

MENO: I think not, Socrates.

SOCRATES: No, indeed; there would be small reason in that. Yet once more, fair friend; according to you, virtue is "the power of governing"; but do you not add "justly and not unjustly"?

MENO: Yes, Socrates; I agree there; for justice is virtue.

SOCRATES: Would you say "virtue," Meno, or "a virtue"?

MENO: What do you mean?

SOCRATES: I mean as I might say about anything; that a round, for example, is "a figure" and not simply "figure," and I should adopt this mode of speaking, because there are other figures.

MENO: Quite right; and that is just what I am saying about virtue—that there are other virtues as well as justice.

SOCRATES: What are they? tell me the names of them, as I would tell you the names of the other figures if you asked me.

MENO: Courage and temperance and wisdom and magnanimity are virtues; and there are many others.

SOCRATES: Yes, Meno; and again we are in the same case: in searching after one virtue we have found many, though not in the same way as before; but we have been unable to find the common virtue which runs through them all.

MENO: Why, Socrates, even now I am not able to follow you in the attempt to get at one common notion of virtue as of other things.

SOCRATES: No wonder; but I will try to get nearer if I can, for you know that all things have a common notion. Suppose now that some one asked you the question which I asked before: Meno, he would say, what is figure? And if you answered "roundness," he would reply to you, in my way of speaking, by asking whether you would say that roundness is "figure" or "a figure"; and you would answer "a figure."

MENO: Certainly.

SOCRATES: And for this reason—that there are other figures?

MENO: Yes.

SOCRATES: And if he proceeded to ask, What other figures are there? you would have told him.

MENO: I should.

SOCRATES: And if he similarly asked what color is, and you answered whiteness, and the questioner rejoined, Would you say that whiteness is color or a color? you would reply, A color, because there are other colors as well.

MENO: I should.

SOCRATES: And if he had said, Tell me what they are?—you would have told him of other colors which are colors just as much as whiteness.

MENO: Yes.

SOCRATES: And suppose that he were to pursue the matter in my way, he would say: Ever and anon we are landed in particulars, but this is not what I want; tell me then, since you call them by a common name, and say that they are all figures, even when opposed to one another, what is that common nature which you designate as figure—which contains straight as well as round, and is no more one than the other—that would be your mode of speaking?

MENO: Yes.

SOCRATES: And in speaking thus, you do not mean to say that the round is round any more than straight, or the straight any more straight than round?

MENO: Certainly not.

SOCRATES: You only assert that the round figure is not more a figure than the straight, or the straight than the round?

MENO: Very true.

SOCRATES: To what then do we give the name of figure? Try and answer. Suppose that when a person asked you this question either about figure or color, you were to reply, Man, I do not understand what you want, or know what you are saying; he would look rather astonished and say: Do you not understand that I am looking for the "simile in multis"? And then he might put the question in another form: Meno, he might say, what is that "simile in multis" which you call figure, and which includes not only round and straight figures, but all? Could you not answer that question, Meno? I wish that you would try; the attempt will be good practice with a view to the answer about virtue.

MENO: I would rather that you should answer, Socrates.

SOCRATES: Shall I indulge you?

MENO: By all means.

SOCRATES: And then you will tell me about virtue?

MENO: I will.

SOCRATES: Then I must do my best, for there is a prize to be won.

MENO: Certainly.

SOCRATES: Well, I will try and explain to you what figure is. What do you say to this answer?—Figure is the only thing which always follows color. Will you be satisfied with it, as I am sure that I should be, if you would let me have a similar definition of virtue?

MENO: But, Socrates, it is such a simple answer.

SOCRATES: Why simple?

MENO: Because, according to you, figure is that which always follows color.

(SOCRATES: Granted.)

MENO: But if a person were to say that he does not know what color is, any more than what figure is—what sort of answer would you have given him?

SOCRATES: I should have told him the truth. And if he were a philosopher of the eristic and antagonistic sort, I should say to him: You have my answer, and if I am wrong, your business is to take up the argument and refute me. But if we were friends, and were talking as you and I are now, I should reply in a milder strain and more in the dialectician's vein; that is to say, I should not only speak the truth, but I should make use of premises which the person interrogated would be willing to admit. And this is the way in which I shall endeavour to approach you. You will acknowledge, will you not, that there is such a thing as an end, or termination, or extremity?—all which words I use in the same sense, although I am aware that Prodicus might draw distinctions about them: but still you, I am sure, would speak of a thing as ended or terminated—that is all which I am saying—not anything very difficult.

MENO: Yes, I should; and I believe that I understand your meaning.

SOCRATES: And you would speak of a surface and also of a solid, as for example in geometry.

MENO: Yes.

SOCRATES: Well then, you are now in a condition to understand my definition of figure. I define figure to be that in which the solid ends; or, more concisely, the limit of solid.

MENO: And now, Socrates, what is color?

SOCRATES: You are outrageous, Meno, in thus plaguing a poor old man to give you an answer, when you will not take the trouble of remembering what is Gorgias' definition of virtue.

MENO: When you have told me what I ask, I will tell you, Socrates.

SOCRATES: A man who was blindfolded has only to hear you talking, and he would know that you are a fair creature and have still many lovers.

MENO: Why do you think so?

SOCRATES: Why, because you always speak in imperatives: like all beauties when they are in their prime, you are tyrannical; and also, as I suspect, you have found out that I have a weakness for the fair, and therefore to humor you I must answer.

MENO: Please do.

SOCRATES: Would you like me to answer you after the manner of Gorgias, which is familiar to you?

MENO: I should like nothing better.

SOCRATES: Do not he and you and Empedocles say that there are certain effluences of existence?

MENO: Certainly.

SOCRATES: And passages into which and through which the effluences pass?

MENO: Exactly.

SOCRATES: And some of the effluences fit into the passages, and some of them are too small or too large?

MENO: True.

SOCRATES: And there is such a thing as sight?

MENO: Yes.

SOCRATES: And now, as Pindar says, "read my meaning":—color is an effluence of form, commensurate with sight, and palpable to sense.

MENO: That, Socrates, appears to me to be an admirable answer.

SOCRATES: Why, yes, because it happens to be one which you have been in the habit of hearing: and your wit will have discovered, I suspect, that you may explain in the same way the nature of sound and smell, and of many other similar phenomena.

MENO: Quite true.

SOCRATES: The answer, Meno, was in the orthodox solemn vein, and therefore was more acceptable to you than the other answer about figure.

MENO: Yes.

SOCRATES: And yet, O son of Alexidemus, I cannot help thinking that the other was the better; and I am sure that you would be of the same opinion, if you would only stay and be initiated, and were not compelled, as you said yesterday, to go away before the mysteries.

MENO: But I will stay, Socrates, if you will give me many such answers.

SOCRATES: Well then, for my own sake as well as for yours, I will do my very best; but I am afraid that I shall not be able to give you very many as good: and now, in your turn, you are to fulfill your promise, and tell me what virtue is in the universal; and do not make a singular into a plural, as the facetious say of those who break a thing, but deliver virtue to me whole and sound, and not broken into a number of pieces: I have given you the pattern.

MENO: Well then, Socrates, virtue, as I take it, is when he, who desires the honorable, is able to provide it for himself; so the poet says, and I say too—

Virtue is the desire of things honorable and the power of attaining them.

SOCRATES: And does he who desires the honorable also desire the good?

MENO: Certainly.

SOCRATES: Then are there some who desire the evil and others who desire the good? Do not all men, my dear sir, desire good?

MENO: I think not.

SOCRATES: There are some who desire evil?

MENO: Yes.

SOCRATES: Do you mean that they think the evils which they desire, to be good; or do they know that they are evil and yet desire them?

MENO: Both, I think.

SOCRATES: And do you really imagine, Meno, that a man knows evils to be evils and desires them notwithstanding?

MENO: Certainly I do.

SOCRATES: And desire is of possession?

MENO: Yes, of possession.

SOCRATES: And does he think that the evils will do good to him who possesses them, or does he know that they will do him harm?

MENO: There are some who think that the evils will do them good, and others who know that they will do them harm.

SOCRATES: And, in your opinion, do those who think that they will do them good know that they are evils?

MENO: Certainly not.

SOCRATES: Is it not obvious that those who are ignorant of their nature do not desire them; but they desire what they suppose to be goods although they are really evils; and if they are mistaken and suppose the evils to be goods they really desire goods?

MENO: Yes, in that case.

SOCRATES: Well, and do those who, as you say, desire evils, and think that evils are hurtful to the possessor of them, know that they will be hurt by them?

MENO: They must know it.

SOCRATES: And must they not suppose that those who are hurt are miserable in proportion to the hurt which is inflicted upon them?

MENO: How can it be otherwise?

SOCRATES: But are not the miserable ill-fated?

MENO: Yes, indeed.

SOCRATES: And does any one desire to be miserable and ill-fated?

MENO: I should say not, Socrates.

SOCRATES: But if there is no one who desires to be miserable, there is no one, Meno, who desires evil; for what is misery but the desire and possession of evil?

MENO: That appears to be the truth, Socrates, and I admit that nobody desires evil.

SOCRATES: And yet, were you not saying just now that virtue is the desire and power of attaining good?

MENO: Yes, I did say so.

SOCRATES: But if this be affirmed, then the desire of good is common to all, and one man is no better than another in that respect?

MENO: True.

SOCRATES: And if one man is not better than another in desiring good, he must be better in the power of attaining it?

MENO: Exactly.

SOCRATES: Then, according to your definition, virtue would appear to be the power of attaining good?

MENO: I entirely approve, Socrates, of the manner in which you now view this matter.

SOCRATES: Then let us see whether what you say is true from another point of view; for very likely you may be right:—You affirm virtue to be the power of attaining goods?

MENO: Yes.

SOCRATES: And the goods which you mean are such as health and wealth and the possession of gold and silver, and having office and honor in the state—those are what you would call goods?

MENO: Yes, I should include all those.

SOCRATES: Then, according to Meno, who is the hereditary friend of the great king, virtue is the power of getting silver and gold; and would you add that they must be gained piously, justly, or do you deem this to be of no consequence? And is any mode of acquisition, even if unjust and dishonest, equally to be deemed virtue?

MENO: Not virtue, Socrates, but vice.

SOCRATES: Then justice or temperance or holiness, or some other part of virtue, as would appear, must accompany the acquisition, and without them the mere acquisition of good will not be virtue.

MENO: Why, how can there be virtue without these?

SOCRATES: And the non-acquisition of gold and silver in a dishonest manner for oneself or another, or in other words the want of them, may be equally virtue?

MENO: True.

SOCRATES: Then the acquisition of such goods is no more virtue than the non-acquisition and want of them, but whatever is accompanied by justice or honesty is virtue, and whatever is devoid of justice is vice.

MENO: It cannot be otherwise, in my judgment.

SOCRATES: And were we not saying just now that justice, temperance, and the like, were each of them a part of virtue?

MENO: Yes.

SOCRATES: And so, Meno, this is the way in which you mock me.

MENO: Why do you say that, Socrates?

SOCRATES: Why, because I asked you to deliver virtue into my hands whole and unbroken, and I gave you a pattern according to which you were to frame your answer; and you have forgotten already, and tell me that virtue is the power of attaining good justly, or with justice; and justice you acknowledge to be a part of virtue.

MENO: Yes.

SOCRATES: Then it follows from your own admissions, that virtue is doing what you do with a part of virtue; for justice and the like are said by you to be parts of virtue.

MENO: What of that?

SOCRATES: What of that! Why, did not I ask you to tell me the nature of virtue as a whole? And you are very far from telling me this; but declare every action to be virtue which is done with a part of virtue; as though you had told me and I must already know the whole of virtue, and this too when frittered away into little pieces. And, therefore, my dear Meno, I fear that I must begin again and repeat the same question: What is virtue? for otherwise, I can only say, that every action done with a part of virtue is virtue; what else is the meaning of saying that every action done with justice is virtue? Ought I not to ask the question over again; for can any one who does not know virtue know a part of virtue?

MENO: No; I do not say that he can.

SOCRATES: Do you remember how, in the example of figure, we rejected any answer given in terms which were as yet unexplained or unadmitted?

MENO: Yes, Socrates; and we were quite right in doing so.

SOCRATES: But then, my friend, do not suppose that we can explain to any one the nature of virtue as a whole through some unexplained portion of virtue, or anything at all in that fashion; we should only have to ask over again the old question, What is virtue? Am I not right?

MENO: I believe that you are.

SOCRATES: Then begin again, and answer me, What, according to you and your friend Gorgias, is the definition of virtue?

MENO: O Socrates, I used to be told, before I knew you, that you were always doubting yourself and making others doubt; and now you are casting your spells over me, and I am simply getting bewitched and enchanted, and am at my wits' end. And if I may venture to make a jest upon you, you seem to me both in your appearance and in your power over others to be very like the flat torpedo fish, who torpifies those who come near him and touch him, as you have now torpified me, I think. For my soul and my tongue are really torpid, and I do not know how to answer you; and though I have been delivered of an infinite variety of speeches about virtue before now, and to many persons —and very good ones they were, as I thought— at this moment I cannot even say what virtue is. And I think that you are very wise in not voyaging and going away from home, for if you did in other places as you do in Athens, you would be cast into prison as a magician.

SOCRATES: You are a rogue, Meno, and had all but caught me.

MENO: What do you mean, Socrates?

SOCRATES: I can tell why you made a simile about me.

MENO: Why?

SOCRATES: In order that I might make another simile about you. For I know that all pretty young gentlemen like to have pretty similes made about them —as well they may—but I shall not return the compliment. As to my being a torpedo, if the torpedo is torpid as well as the cause of torpidity in others, then indeed I am a torpedo, but not otherwise; for I perplex others, not because I am clear, but because I am utterly perplexed myself. And now I know not what virtue is, and you seem to be in the same case, although you did once perhaps know before you touched me. However, I have no objection to join with you in the enquiry.

MENO: And how will you enquire, Socrates, into that which you do not know? What will you put forth as the subject of enquiry? And if you find what you want, how will you ever know that this is the thing which you did not know?

SOCRATES: I know, Meno, what you mean; but just see what a tiresome dispute you are introducing. You argue that a man cannot enquire either about that which he knows, or about that which he does not know; for if he knows, he has no need to enquire; and if not, he cannot; for he does not know the very subject about which he is to enquire.[1]

MENO: Well, Socrates, and is not the argument sound?

SOCRATES: I think not.

MENO: Why not?

SOCRATES: I will tell you why: I have heard from certain wise men and women who spoke of things divine that—

MENO: What did they say?

SOCRATES: They spoke of a glorious truth, as I conceive.

MENO: What was it? and who were they?

SOCRATES: Some of them were priests and priestesses, who had studied how they might be able to give a reason of their profession: there have been poets also, who spoke of these things by inspiration, like Pindar, and many others who were inspired. And they say—mark, now, and see whether their words are true—they say that the soul of man is immortal, and at one time has an end, which is termed dying, and at another time is born again, but is never destroyed. And the moral is, that a man ought to live always in perfect holi-

---

[1] Cp. Aristot. Post. Anal. I. i. 6.

ness. *"For in the ninth year Persephone sends the souls of those from whom she has received the penalty of ancient crime back again from beneath into the light of the sun above, and these are they who become noble kings and mighty men and great in wisdom and are called saintly heroes in after ages."* The soul, then, as being immortal, and having been born again many times, and having seen all things that exist, whether in this world or in the world below, has knowledge of them all; and it is no wonder that she should be able to call to remembrance all that she ever knew about virtue, and about everything; for as all nature is akin, and the soul has learned all things, there is no difficulty in her eliciting or as men say learning, out of a single recollection all the rest, if a man is strenuous and does not faint; for all enquiry and all learning is but recollection. And therefore we ought not to listen to this sophistical argument about the impossibility of enquiry: for it will make us idle and is sweet only to the sluggard; but the other saying will make us active and inquisitive. In that confiding, I will gladly enquire with you into the nature of virtue.

MENO: Yes, Socrates; but what do you mean by saying that we do not learn, and that what we call learning is only a process of recollection? Can you teach me how this is?

SOCRATES: I told you, Meno, just now that you were a rogue, and now you ask whether I can teach you, when I am saying that there is no teaching, but only recollection; and thus you imagine that you will involve me in a contradiction.

MENO: Indeed, Socrates, I protest that I had no such intention. I only asked the question from habit; but if you can prove to me that what you say is true, I wish that you would.

SOCRATES: It will be no easy matter, but I will try to please you to the utmost of my power. Suppose that you call one of your numerous attendants, that I may demonstrate on him.

MENO: Certainly. Come hither, boy.

SOCRATES: He is Greek, and speaks Greek, does he not?

MENO: Yes, indeed; he was born in the house.

SOCRATES: Attend now to the questions which I ask him, and observe whether he learns of me or only remembers.

MENO: I will.

SOCRATES: Tell me, boy, do you know that a figure like this is a square?

BOY: I do.

SOCRATES: And you know that a square figure has these four lines equal?

BOY: Certainly.

SOCRATES: And these lines which I have drawn through the middle of the square are also equal?

BOY: Yes.

SOCRATES: A square may be of any size?

BOY: Certainly.

SOCRATES: And if one side of the figure be of two feet, and the other side be of two feet, how much will the whole be? Let me explain: if in one direction the space was of two feet, and in the other direction of one foot, the whole would be of two feet taken once?

BOY: Yes.

SOCRATES: But since this side is also of two feet, there are twice two feet?

BOY: There are.

SOCRATES: Then the square is of twice two feet?

BOY: Yes.

SOCRATES: And how many are twice two feet? count and tell me.

BOY: Four, Socrates.

SOCRATES: And might there not be another square twice as large as this, and having like this the lines equal?

BOY: Yes.

SOCRATES: And of how many feet will that be?

BOY: Of eight feet.

SOCRATES: And now try and tell me the length of the line which forms the side of that double square: this is two feet—what will that be?

BOY: Clearly, Socrates, it will be double.

SOCRATES: Do you observe, Meno, that I am not teaching the boy anything, but only asking him questions; and now he fancies that he knows how long a line is necessary in order to produce a figure of eight square feet; does he not?

MENO: Yes.

SOCRATES: And does he really know?

MENO: Certainly not.

SOCRATES: He only guesses that because the square is double, the line is double.

MENO: True.

SOCRATES: Observe him while he recalls the steps in regular order. (*To the Boy.*) Tell me, boy, do you assert that a double space comes from a double line? Remember that I am not speaking of an oblong, but of a figure equal every way, and twice the size of this—that is to say of eight feet; and I want to know whether you still say that a double square comes from a double line?

BOY: Yes.

SOCRATES: But does not this line become doubled if we add another such line here?

BOY: Certainly.

SOCRATES: And four such lines will make a space containing eight feet?

BOY: Yes.

SOCRATES: Let us describe such a figure: Would you not say that this is the figure of eight feet?

BOY: Yes.

SOCRATES: And are there not these four divisions in the figure, each of which is equal to the figure of four feet?

BOY: True.

SOCRATES: And is not that four times four?

BOY: Certainly.

SOCRATES: And four times is not double?

BOY: No, indeed.

SOCRATES: But how much?

BOY: Four times as much.

SOCRATES: Therefore the double line, boy, has given a space, not twice, but four times as much.

BOY: True.

SOCRATES: Four times four are sixteen—are they not?

BOY: Yes.

SOCRATES: What line would give you a space of eight feet, as this gives one of sixteen feet;—do you see?

BOY: Yes.

SOCRATES: And the space of four feet is made from this half line?

BOY: Yes.

SOCRATES: Good; and is not a space of eight feet twice the size of this, and half the size of the other?

BOY: Certainly.

SOCRATES: Such a space, then, will be made out of a line greater than this one, and less than that one?

BOY: Yes; I think so.

SOCRATES: Very good; I like to hear you say what you think. And now tell me, is not this a line of two feet and that of four?

BOY: Yes.

SOCRATES: Then the line which forms the side of eight feet ought to be more than this line of two feet, and less than the other of four feet?

BOY: It ought.

SOCRATES: Try and see if you can tell me how much it will be.

BOY: Three feet.

SOCRATES: Then if we add a half to this line of two, that will be the line of three. Here are two and there is one; and on the other side, here are two also and there is one: and that makes the figure of which you speak?

BOY: Yes.

SOCRATES: But if there are three feet this way and three feet that way, the whole space will be three times three feet?

BOY: That is evident.

SOCRATES: And how much are three times three feet?

BOY: Nine.

SOCRATES: And how much is the double of four?

BOY: Eight.

SOCRATES: Then the figure of eight is not made out of a line of three?

BOY: No.

SOCRATES: But from what line?—tell me exactly; and if you would rather not reckon, try and show me the line.

BOY: Indeed, Socrates, I do not know.

SOCRATES: Do you see, Meno, what advances he has made in his power of recollection? He did not know at first, and he does not know now, what is the side of a figure of eight feet: but then he thought that he knew, and answered confidently as if he knew, and had no difficulty; now he has a difficulty, and neither knows nor fancies that he knows.

MENO: True.

SOCRATES: Is he not better off in knowing his ignorance?

MENO: I think that he is.

SOCRATES: If we have made him doubt, and given him the "torpedo's shock," have we done him any harm?

MENO: I think not.

SOCRATES: We have certainly, as would seem, assisted him in some degree to the discovery of the truth; and now he will wish to remedy his ignorance, but then he would have been ready to tell all the world again and again that the double space should have a double side.

MENO: True.

SOCRATES: But do you suppose that he would ever have enquired into or learned what he fancied that he knew, though he was really ignorant of it, until he had fallen into perplexity under the idea that he did not know, and had desired to know?

MENO: I think not, Socrates.

SOCRATES: Then he was the better for the torpedo's touch?

MENO: I think so.

SOCRATES: Mark now the farther development. I shall only ask him, and not teach him, and he shall share the enquiry with me: and do you watch and see if you find me telling or explaining anything to him, instead of eliciting his opinion. Tell me, boy, is not this a square of four feet which I have drawn?

BOY: Yes.

SOCRATES: And now I add another square equal to the former one?

BOY: Yes.

SOCRATES: And a third, which is equal to either of them?

BOY: Yes.

SOCRATES: Suppose that we fill up the vacant corner?

BOY: Very good.

SOCRATES: Here, then, there are four equal spaces?

BOY: Yes.

SOCRATES: And how many times larger is this space than this other?

BOY: Four times.

SOCRATES: But it ought to have been twice only, as you will remember.

BOY: True.

SOCRATES: And does not this line, reaching from corner to corner, bisect each of these spaces?

BOY: Yes.

SOCRATES: And are there not here four equal lines which contain this space?

BOY: There are.

SOCRATES: Look and see how much this space is.

BOY: I do not understand.

SOCRATES: Has not each interior line cut off half of the four spaces?

BOY: Yes.

SOCRATES: And how many spaces are there in this section?

BOY: Four.

SOCRATES: And how many in this?

BOY: Two.

SOCRATES: And four is how many times two?

BOY: Twice.

SOCRATES: And this space is of how many feet?

BOY: Of eight feet.

SOCRATES: And from what line do you get this figure?

BOY: From this.

SOCRATES: That is, from the line which extends from corner to corner of the figure of four feet?

BOY: Yes.

SOCRATES: And that is the line which the learned call the diagonal. And if this is the proper name, then you, Meno's slave, are prepared to affirm that the double space is the square of the diagonal?

BOY: Certainly, Socrates.

SOCRATES: What do you say of him, Meno? Were not all these answers given out of his own head?

MENO: Yes, they were all his own.

SOCRATES: And yet, as we were just now saying, he did not know?

MENO: True.

SOCRATES: But still he had in him those notions of his—had he not?

MENO: Yes.

SOCRATES: Then he who does not know may still have true notions of that which he does not know?

MENO: He has.

SOCRATES: And at present these notions have just been stirred up in him, as in a dream; but if he were frequently asked the same questions, in different forms, he would know as well as any one at last?

MENO: I dare say.

SOCRATES: Without any one teaching him he will recover his knowledge for himself, if he is only asked questions?

MENO: Yes.

SOCRATES: And this spontaneous recovery of knowledge in him is recollection?

MENO: True.

SOCRATES: And this knowledge which he now has must he not either have acquired or always possessed?

MENO: Yes.

SOCRATES: But if he always possessed this knowledge he would always have known; or if he has acquired the knowledge he could not have acquired it in this life, unless he has been taught geometry; for he may be made to do the same with all geometry and every other branch of knowledge. Now, has any one ever taught him all this? You must know about him, if, as you say, he was born and bred in your house.

MENO: And I am certain that no one ever did teach him.

SOCRATES: And yet he has the knowledge?

MENO: The fact, Socrates, is undeniable.

SOCRATES: But if he did not acquire the knowledge in this life, then he must have had and learned it at some other time?

MENO: Clearly he must.

SOCRATES: Which must have been the time when he was not a man?

MENO: Yes.

SOCRATES: And if there have been always true thoughts in him, both at the time when he was and was not a man, which only need to be awakened into knowledge by putting questions to him, his soul must have always possessed this knowledge, for he always either was or was not a man?

MENO: Obviously.

SOCRATES: And if the truth of all things always existed in the soul, then the soul is immortal. Wherefore be of good cheer, and try to recollect what you do not know, or rather what you do not remember.

MENO: I feel, somehow, that I like what you are saying.

SOCRATES: And I, Meno, like what I am saying. Some things I have said of which I am not altogether confident. But that we shall be better and braver and less helpless if we think that we ought to enquire, than we should have been if we indulged in the idle fancy that there was no knowing and no use in seeking to know what we do not know;—that is a theme upon which I am ready to fight, in word and deed, to the utmost of my power.

MENO: There again, Socrates, your words seem to me excellent.

SOCRATES: Then, as we are agreed that a man should enquire about that which he does not know, shall you and I make an effort to enquire together into the nature of virtue?

MENO: By all means, Socrates. And yet I would much rather return to my original question, Whether in seeking to acquire virtue we should regard it as a thing to be taught, or as a gift of nature, or as coming to men in some other way?

SOCRATES: Had I the command of you as well as of myself, Meno, I would not have enquired whether virtue is given by instruction or not, until we had first ascertained "what it is." But as you think only of controlling me who am your slave, and never of controlling yourself,—such being your notion of freedom, I must yield to you, for you are irresistible. And therefore I have now to enquire into the qualities of a thing of which I do not as yet know the nature. At any rate, will you condescend a little, and allow the question "Whether virtue is given by instruction, or in any other way," to be argued upon hypothesis? As the geometrician, when he is asked [1]whether a certain triangle is capable of being inscribed in a certain circle,[1] will reply: "I cannot tell you as yet; but I will offer a hypothesis which may assist us in forming a conclusion: If the figure be such that [2]when you have produced a given side of it,[2] the given area of the triangle falls short by an area [3]corresponding to the part produced,[3] then one consequence follows, and if this is impossible then some other; and therefore I wish to assume a hypothesis before I tell you whether this triangle is capable of being inscribed in the circle:"—that is a geometrical hypothesis. And we too, as we know not the nature and qualities of virtue, must ask, whether virtue is or is not taught, under a hypothesis: as thus, if virtue is of such a class of mental goods, will it be taught or not? Let the first hypothesis be that virtue is or is not knowledge,—in that case will it be taught or not? or, as we were just now saying, "remembered"? For there is no use in disputing about the name. But is virtue taught or not? or rather, does not every one see that knowledge alone is taught?

MENO: I agree.

SOCRATES: Then if virtue is knowledge, virtue will be taught?

MENO: Certainly.

SOCRATES: Then now we have made a quick end of this question: if virtue is of such a nature, it will be taught; and if not, not.

MENO: Certainly.

SOCRATES: The next question is, whether virtue is knowledge or of another species?

MENO: Yes, that appears to be the question which comes next in order.

SOCRATES: Do we not say that virtue is a good?—This is a hypothesis which is not set aside.

MENO: Certainly.

SOCRATES: Now, if there be any sort of good which is distinct from knowledge,

---

[1] Or, whether a certain area is capable of being inscribed as a triangle in a certain circle.
[2] Or, when you apply it to the given line, i.e. the diameter of the circle (αὐτοῦ).
[3] Or, similar to the area so applied.

virtue may be that good; but if knowledge embraces all good, then we shall be right in thinking that virtue is knowledge?

MENO: True.

SOCRATES: And virtue makes us good?

MENO: Yes.

SOCRATES: And if we are good, then we are profitable; for all good things are profitable?

MENO: Yes.

SOCRATES: Then virtue is profitable?

MENO: That is the only inference.

SOCRATES: Then now let us see what are the things which severally profit us. Health and strength, and beauty and wealth—these, and the like of these, we call profitable?

MENO: True.

SOCRATES: And yet these things may also sometimes do us harm: would you not think so?

MENO: Yes.

SOCRATES: And what is the guiding principle which makes them profitable or the reverse? Are they not profitable when they are rightly used, and hurtful when they are not rightly used?

MENO: Certainly.

SOCRATES: Next, let us consider the goods of the soul: they are temperance, justice, courage, quickness of apprehension, memory, magnanimity, and the like?

MENO: Surely.

SOCRATES: And such of these as are not knowledge, but of another sort, are sometimes profitable and sometimes hurtful; as, for example, courage wanting prudence, which is only a sort of confidence? When a man has no sense he is harmed by courage, but when he has sense he is profited?

MENO: True.

SOCRATES: And the same may be said of temperance and quickness of apprehension; whatever things are learned or done with sense are profitable, but when done without sense they are hurtful?

MENO: Very true.

SOCRATES: And in general, all that the soul attempts or endures, when under the guidance of wisdom, ends in happiness; but when she is under the guidance of folly, in the opposite?

MENO: That appears to be true.

SOCRATES: If then virtue is a quality of the soul, and is admitted to be profitable, it must be wisdom or prudence, since none of the things of the soul are either profitable or hurtful in themselves, but they are all made profitable or hurtful by the addition of wisdom or of folly; and therefore if virtue is profitable, virtue must be a sort of wisdom or prudence?

MENO: I quite agree.

SOCRATES: And the other goods, such as wealth and the like, of which we were just now saying that they are sometimes good and sometimes evil, do not they also become profitable or hurtful, accordingly as the soul guides and uses them rightly or wrongly; just as the things of the soul herself are benefited when under the guidance of wisdom and harmed by folly?

MENO: True.

SOCRATES: And the wise soul guides them rightly, and the foolish soul wrongly.

MENO: Yes.

SOCRATES: And is not this universally true of human nature? All other things hang upon the soul, and the things of the soul herself hang upon wisdom, if they are to be good; and so wisdom is inferred to be that which profits—and virtue, as we say, is profitable?

MENO: Certainly.

SOCRATES: And thus we arrive at the conclusion that virtue is either wholly or partly wisdom?

MENO: I think that what you are saying, Socrates, is very true.

SOCRATES: But if this is true, then the good are not by nature good?

MENO: I think not.

SOCRATES: If they had been, there would assuredly have been discerners of characters among us who would have known our future great men; and on their showing we should have adopted them, and when we had got them, we should have kept them in the citadel out of the way of harm, and set a stamp upon them far rather than upon a piece of gold, in order that no one might tamper with them; and when they grew up they would have been useful to the state?

MENO: Yes, Socrates, that would have been the right way.

SOCRATES: But if the good are not by nature good, are they made good by instruction?

MENO: There appears to be no other alternative, Socrates. On the supposition that virtue is knowledge, there can be no doubt that virtue is taught.

SOCRATES: Yes, indeed; but what if the supposition is erroneous?

MENO: I certainly thought just now that we were right.

SOCRATES: Yes, Meno; but a principle which has any soundness should stand firm not only just now, but always.

MENO: Well; and why are you so slow of heart to believe that knowledge is virtue?

SOCRATES: I will try and tell you why, Meno. I do not retract the assertion that if virtue is knowledge it may be taught; but I fear that I have some reason in doubting whether virtue is knowledge: for consider now and say whether virtue, and not only virtue but anything that is taught, must not have teachers and disciples?

MENO: Surely.

SOCRATES: And conversely, may not the art of which neither teachers nor disciples exist be assumed to be incapable of being taught?

MENO: True; but do you think that there are no teachers of virtue?

SOCRATES: I have certainly often enquired whether there were any, and taken great pains to find them, and have never succeeded; and many have assisted me in the search, and they were the persons whom I thought the most likely to know. Here at the moment when he is wanted we fortunately have sitting by us Anytus, the very person of whom we should make enquiry; to him then let us repair. In the first place, he is the son of a wealthy and wise father, Anthemion, who acquired his wealth, not by accident or gift, like Ismenias the Theban (who has recently made himself as rich as Polycrates), but by his own skill and industry, and who is a well-conditioned, modest man, not insolent, or over-bearing, or annoying; moreover, this son of his has received a good education, as the Athenian people certainly appear to think, for they choose him to fill the highest offices. And these are the sort of men from whom you are likely to learn whether there are any teachers of virtue, and who they are. Please, Anytus, to help me and your friend Meno in answering our question, Who are the teachers? Consider the matter thus: If we wanted Meno to be a good physician, to whom should we send him? Should we not send him to the physicians?

ANYTUS: Certainly.

SOCRATES: Or if we wanted him to be a good cobbler, should we not send him to the cobblers?

ANYTUS: Yes.

SOCRATES: And so forth?

ANYTUS: Yes.

SOCRATES: Let me trouble you with one more question. When we say that we should be right in sending him to the physicians if we wanted him to be a physician, do we mean that we should be right in sending him to those who profess the art, rather than to those who do not, and to those who demand payment for teaching the art, and profess to teach it to any one who will come and learn? And if these were our reasons, should we not be right in sending him?

ANYTUS: Yes.

SOCRATES: And might not the same be said of flute-playing, and of the other arts? Would a man who wanted to make another a flute-player refuse to send him to those who profess to teach the art for money, and be plaguing other persons to give him instruction, who are not professed teachers and who never had a single disciple in that branch of knowledge which he wishes him to acquire—would not such conduct be the height of folly?

ANYTUS: Yes, by Zeus, and of ignorance too.

SOCRATES: Very good. And now you are in a position to advise with me about my friend Meno. He has been telling me, Anytus, that he desires to attain that kind of wisdom and virtue by which men order the state or the house, and honor their parents, and know when to receive and when to send away citizens and strangers, as a good man should. Now, to whom should he go in order that he may learn this virtue? Does not the previous argument imply clearly that we should send him to those who profess and avouch that they are the common teachers of all Hellas, and are ready to impart instruction to any one who likes, at a fixed price?

ANYTUS: Whom do you mean, Socrates?

SOCRATES: You surely know, do you not, Anytus, that these are the people whom mankind call Sophists?

ANYTUS: By Heracles, Socrates, forbear! I only hope that no friend or kinsman or acquaintance of mine, whether citizen or stranger, will ever be so mad as to allow himself to be corrupted by them; for they are a manifest pest and corrupting influences to those who have to do with them.

SOCRATES: What, Anytus? Of all the people who profess that they know how to do men good, do you mean to say that these are the only ones who not only do them no good, but positively corrupt those who are entrusted to them, and in return for this disservice have the face to demand money? Indeed, I cannot believe you; for I know of a single man, Protagoras, who made more out of his craft than the illustrious Pheidias, who created such noble works, or any ten other statuaries. How could that be? A mender of old shoes, or patcher up of clothes, who made the shoes or clothes worse than he received them, could not have remained thirty days undetected, and would very soon have starved; whereas during more than forty years, Protagoras was corrupting all Hellas, and sending his disciples from him worse than he received them, and he was never found out. For, if I am not mistaken, he was about seventy years old at his death, forty of which were spent in the practice of his profession; and during all that time he had a good reputation, which to this day he retains: and not only Protagoras, but many others are well spoken of; some who lived before him, and others who are still living. Now, when you say that they deceived and corrupted the youth, are they to be supposed to have corrupted them consciously or unconsciously? Can those who were deemed by many to be the wisest men of Hellas have been out of their minds?

ANYTUS: Out of their minds! No, Socrates; the young men who gave their money to them were out of their minds, and their relations and guardians who entrusted their youth to the care of these men were still more out of their minds, and most of all, the cities who allowed them to come in, and did not drive them out, citizen and stranger alike.

SOCRATES: Has any of the Sophists wronged you, Anytus? What makes you so angry with them?

ANYTUS: No, indeed, neither I nor any of my belongings has ever had, nor would I suffer them to have, anything to do with them.

SOCRATES: Then you are entirely unacquainted with them?

ANYTUS: And I have no wish to be acquainted.

SOCRATES: Then, my dear friend, how can you know whether a thing is good or bad of which you are wholly ignorant?

ANYTUS: Quite well; I am sure that I know what manner of men these are, whether I am acquainted with them or not.

SOCRATES: You must be a diviner, Anytus, for I really cannot make out, judging from your own words, how, if you are not acquainted with them, you know about them. But I am not enquiring of you who are the teachers who will corrupt Meno (let them be, if you please, the Sophists); I only ask you to tell him who there is in this great city who will teach him how to become eminent in the virtues which I was just now describing. He is the friend of your family, and you will oblige him.

ANYTUS: Why do you not tell him yourself?

SOCRATES: I have told him whom I supposed to be the teachers of these things; but I learn from you that I am utterly at fault, and I dare say that you are right. And now I wish that you, on your part, would tell me to whom among the Athenians he should go. Whom would you name?

ANYTUS: Why single out individuals? Any Athenian gentleman, taken at random, if he will mind him, will do far more good to him than the Sophists.

SOCRATES: And did those gentlemen grow of themselves; and without having been taught by any one, were they nevertheless able to teach others that which they had never learned themselves?

ANYTUS: I imagine that they learned of the previous generation of gentlemen. Have there not been many good men in this city?

SOCRATES: Yes, certainly, Anytus; and many good statesmen also there always have been and there are still, in the city of Athens. But the question is whether they were also good teachers of their own virtue;—not whether there are, or have been, good men in this part of the world, but whether virtue can be taught, is the question which we have been discussing. Now, do we mean to say that the good men of our own and of other times knew how to impart to others that virtue which they had themselves; or is virtue a thing incapable of being communicated or imparted by one man to another? That is the question which I and Meno have been arguing. Look at the matter in your own way: Would you not admit that Themistocles was a good man?

ANYTUS: Certainly; no man better.

SOCRATES: And must not he then have been a good teacher, if any man ever was a good teacher, of his own virtue?

ANYTUS: Yes, certainly,—if he wanted to be so.

SOCRATES: But would he not have wanted? He would, at any rate, have desired to make his own son a good man and a gentleman; he could not have been jealous of him, or have intentionally abstained from imparting to him his own virtue. Did you never hear that he made his son Cleophantus a famous horseman; and had him taught to stand upright on horseback and hurl a javelin, and to do many other marvellous things; and in anything which could be learned from a master he was well-trained? Have you not heard from our elders of him?

ANYTUS: I have.

SOCRATES: Then no one could say that his son showed any want of capacity?

ANYTUS: Very likely not.

SOCRATES: But did any one, old or young, ever say in your hearing that Cleophantus, son of Themistocles, was a wise or good man, as his father was?

ANYTUS: I have certainly never heard any one say so.

SOCRATES: And if virtue could have been taught, would his father Themistocles have sought to train him in these minor accomplishments, and allowed him who, as you must remember, was his own son, to be no better than his neighbors in those qualities in which he himself excelled?

ANYTUS: Indeed, indeed, I think not.

SOCRATES: Here was a teacher of virtue whom you admit to be among the best men of the past. Let us take another,—Aristides, the son of Lysimachus: would you not acknowledge that he was a good man?

ANYTUS: To be sure I should.

SOCRATES: And did not he train his son Lysimachus better than any other Athenian in all that could be done for him by the help of masters? But what has been the result? Is he a bit better than any other mortal? He is an acquaintance of yours, and you see what he is like. There is Pericles, again, magnificent in his wisdom; and he, as you are aware, had two sons, Paralus and Xanthippus.

ANYTUS: I know.

SOCRATES: And you know, also, that he taught them to be unrivalled horsemen, and had them trained in music and gymnastics and all sorts of arts—in these respects they were on a level with the best—and had he no wish to make good men of them? Nay, he must have wished it. But virtue, as I suspect, could not be taught. And that you may not suppose the incompetent teachers to be only the meaner sort of Athenians and few in number, remember again that Thucydides had two sons, Melesias and Stephanus, whom, besides giving them a good education in other things, he trained in wrestling, and they were the best wrestlers in Athens: one of them he committed to the care of Xanthias, and the other of Eudorus, who had the reputation of being the most celebrated wrestlers of that day. Do you remember them?

ANYTUS: I have heard of them.

SOCRATES: Now, can there be a doubt that Thucydides, whose children were taught things for which he had to spend money, would have taught them to be good men, which would have cost him nothing, if virtue could have been taught? Will you reply that he was a mean man, and had not many friends among the Athenians and allies? Nay, but he was of a great family, and a man of influence at Athens and in all Hellas, and, if virtue could have been taught, he would have found out some Athenian or foreigner who would have made good men of his sons, if he could not himself spare the time from cares of state. Once more, I suspect, friend Anytus, that virtue is not a thing which can be taught?

ANYTUS: Socrates, I think that you are too ready to speak evil of men: and, if you will take my advice, I would recommend you to be careful. Perhaps there is no city in which it is not easier to do men harm than to do them good, and this is certainly the case at Athens, as I believe that you know.

SOCRATES: O Meno, I think that Anytus is in a rage. And he may well be in a rage, for he thinks, in the first place, that I am defaming these gentlemen; and in the second place, he is of opinion that he is one of them himself. But some day he will know what is the meaning of defamation, and if he ever does, he will forgive me. Meanwhile I will return to you, Meno; for I suppose that there are gentlemen in your region too?

MENO: Certainly there are.

SOCRATES: And are they willing to teach the young? and do they profess to be teachers? and do they agree that virtue is taught?

MENO: No indeed, Socrates, they are anything but agreed; you may hear them saying at one time that virtue can be taught, and then again the reverse.

SOCRATES: Can we call those teachers who do not acknowledge the possibility of their own vocation?

MENO: I think not, Socrates.

SOCRATES: And what do you think of these Sophists, who are the only professors? Do they seem to you to be teachers of virtue?

MENO: I often wonder, Socrates, that Gorgias is never heard promising to teach virtue: and when he hears others promising he only laughs at them; but he thinks that men should be taught to speak.

SOCRATES: Then do you not think that the Sophists are teachers?

MENO: I cannot tell you, Socrates; like the rest of the world, I am in doubt, and sometimes I think that they are teachers and sometimes not.

SOCRATES: And are you aware that not you only and other politicians have doubts whether virtue can be taught or not, but that Theognis the poet says the very same thing?

MENO: Where does he say so?

SOCRATES: In these elegiac verses[1]:—

Eat and drink and sit with the mighty, and make yourself agreeable to them; for from the good you will learn what is good, but if you mix with the bad you will lose the intelligence which you already have.

---

[1] Theog. 33 ff.

Do you observe that here he seems to imply that virtue can be taught?

MENO: Clearly.

SOCRATES: But in some other verses he shifts about and says[2]:—

> If understanding could be created and put into a man, then they [who were able to perform this feat] would have obtained great rewards.

And again:—

> Never would a bad son have sprung from a good sire, for he would have heard the voice of instruction; but not by teaching will you ever make a bad man into a good one.

And this, as you may remark, is a contradiction of the other.

MENO: Clearly.

SOCRATES: And is there anything else of which the professors are affirmed not only not to be teachers of others, but to be ignorant themselves, and bad at the knowledge of that which they are professing to teach? or is there anything about which even the acknowledged "gentlemen" are sometimes saying that "this thing can be taught," and sometimes the opposite? Can you say that they are teachers in any true sense whose ideas are in such confusion?

MENO: I should say, certainly not.

SOCRATES: But if neither the Sophists nor the gentlemen are teachers, clearly there can be no other teachers?

MENO: No.

SOCRATES: And if there are no teachers, neither are there disciples?

MENO: Agreed.

SOCRATES: And we have admitted that a thing cannot be taught of which there are neither teachers nor disciples?

MENO: We have.

SOCRATES: And there are no teachers of virtue to be found anywhere?

MENO: There are not.

SOCRATES: And if there are no teachers, neither are there scholars?

MENO: That, I think, is true.

SOCRATES: Then virtue cannot be taught?

MENO: Not if we are right in our view. But I cannot believe, Socrates, that there are no good men: And if there are, how did they come into existence?

SOCRATES: I am afraid, Meno, that you and I are not good for much, and that Gorgias has been as poor an educator of you as Prodicus has been of me. Certainly we shall have to look to ourselves, and try to find some one who will help in some way or other to improve us. This I say, because I observe that in the previous discussion none of us remarked that right and good action is possible to man under other guidance than that of knowledge ($\epsilon\pi\iota\sigma\tau\eta\mu\eta$);— and indeed if this be denied, there is no seeing how there can be any good men at all.

MENO: How do you mean, Socrates?

SOCRATES: I mean that good men are necessarily useful or profitable. Were we not right in admitting this? It must be so.

---

2 Theog. 435 ff.

MENO: Yes.

SOCRATES: And in supposing that they will be useful only if they are true guides to us of action—there we were also right?

MENO: Yes.

SOCRATES: But when we said that a man cannot be a good guide unless he have knowledge ($\phi\rho\acute{o}\nu\eta\sigma\iota\varsigma$), in this we were wrong.

MENO: What do you mean by the word "right"?

SOCRATES: I will explain. If a man knew the way to Larisa, or anywhere else, and went to the place and led others thither, would he not be a right and good guide?

MENO: Certainly.

SOCRATES: And a person who had a right opinion about the way, but had never been and did not know, might be a good guide also, might he not?

MENO: Certainly.

SOCRATES: And while he has true opinion about that which the other knows, he will be just as good a guide if he thinks the truth, as he who knows the truth?

MENO: Exactly.

SOCRATES: Then true opinion is as good a guide to correct action as knowledge; and that was the point which we omitted in our speculation about the nature of virtue, when we said that knowledge only is the guide of right action; whereas there is also right opinion.

MENO: True.

SOCRATES: Then right opinion is not less useful than knowledge?

MENO: The difference, Socrates, is only that he who has knowledge will always be right; but he who has right opinion will sometimes be right, and sometimes not.

SOCRATES: What do you mean? Can he be wrong who has right opinion, so long as he has right opinion?

MENO: I admit the cogency of your argument, and therefore, Socrates, I wonder that knowledge should be preferred to right opinion—or why they should ever differ.

SOCRATES: And shall I explain this wonder to you?

MENO: Do tell me.

SOCRATES: You would not wonder if you had ever observed the images of Daedalus;[1] but perhaps you have not got them in your country?

MENO: What have they to do with the question?

SOCRATES: Because they require to be fastened in order to keep them, and if they are not fastened they will play truant and run away.

MENO: Well, what of that?

SOCRATES: I mean to say that they are not very valuable possessions if they are at liberty, for they will walk off like runaway slaves; but when fastened, they are of great value, for they are really beautiful works of art. Now this is an illustration of the nature of true opinions: while they abide with us they are beautiful and fruitful, but they run away out of the human soul, and do not remain long, and therefore they are not of much value until they are fastened by the tie of the cause; and this fastening of them, friend Meno, is recollection, as you and I have agreed to call it. But when they are bound, in the first place, they have the nature of knowledge; and, in the second place, they are

---

[1] Cp. Euthyphro 11 B.

abiding. And this is why knowledge is more honorable and excellent than true opinion, because fastened by a chain.

MENO: What you are saying, Socrates, seems to be very like the truth.

SOCRATES: I too speak rather in ignorance; I only conjecture. And yet that knowledge differs from true opinion is no matter of conjecture with me. There are not many things which I profess to know, but this is most certainly one of them.

MENO: Yes, Socrates; and you are quite right in saying so.

SOCRATES: And am I not also right in saying that true opinion leading the way perfects action quite as well as knowledge?

MENO: There again, Socrates, I think you are right.

SOCRATES: Then right opinion is not a whit inferior to knowledge, or less useful in action; nor is the man who has right opinion inferior to him who has knowledge?

MENO: True.

SOCRATES: And surely the good man has been acknowledged by us to be useful?

MENO: Yes.

SOCRATES: Seeing then that men become good and useful to states, not only because they have knowledge, but because they have right opinion, and that neither knowledge nor right opinion is given to man by nature or acquired by him—(do you imagine either of them to be given by nature?

MENO: Not I.)

SOCRATES: Then if they are not given by nature, neither are the good by nature good?

MENO: Certainly not.

SOCRATES: And nature being excluded, then came the question whether virtue is acquired by teaching?

MENO: Yes.

SOCRATES: If virtue was wisdom [or knowledge], then, as we thought, it was taught?

MENO: Yes.

SOCRATES: And if it was taught it was wisdom?

MENO: Certainly.

SOCRATES: And if there were teachers, it might be taught; and if there were no teachers, not?

MENO: True.

SOCRATES: But surely we acknowledged that there were no teachers of virtue?

MENO: Yes.

SOCRATES: Then we acknowledged that it was not taught, and was not wisdom?

MENO: Certainly.

SOCRATES: And yet we admitted that it was a good?

MENO: Yes.

SOCRATES: And the right guide is useful and good?

MENO: Certainly.

SOCRATES: And the only right guides are knowledge and true opinion—these are the guides of man; for things which happen by chance are not under the guidance of man: but the guides of man are true opinion and knowledge.

MENO: I think so too.

SOCRATES: But if virtue is not taught, neither is virtue knowledge.

MENO: Clearly not.

SOCRATES: Then of two good and useful things, one, which is knowledge, has been set aside, and cannot be supposed to be our guide in political life.

MENO: I think not.

SOCRATES: And therefore not by any wisdom, and not because they were wise, did Themistocles and those others of whom Anytus spoke govern states. This was the reason why they were unable to make others like themselves—because their virtue was not grounded on knowledge.

MENO: That is probably true, Socrates.

SOCRATES: But if not by knowledge, the only alternative which remains is that statesmen must have guided states by right opinion, which is in politics what divination is in religion; for diviners and also prophets say many things truly, but they know not what they say.

MENO: So I believe.

SOCRATES: And may we not, Meno, truly call those men "divine" who, having no understanding, yet succeed in many a grand deed and word?

MENO: Certainly.

SOCRATES: Then we shall also be right in calling divine those whom we were just now speaking of as diviners and prophets, including the whole tribe of poets. Yes, and statesmen above all may be said to be divine and illumined, being inspired and possessed of God, in which condition they say many grand things, not knowing what they say.

MENO: Yes.

SOCRATES: And the women too, Meno, call good men divine—do they not? and the Spartans, when they praise a good man, say "that he is a divine man."

MENO: And I think, Socrates, that they are right; although very likely our friend Anytus may take offense at the word.

SOCRATES: I do not care; as for Anytus, there will be another opportunity of talking with him. To sum up our enquiry—the result seems to be, if we are at all right in our view, that virtue is neither natural nor acquired, but an instinct given by God to the virtuous. Nor is the instinct accompanied by reason, unless there may be supposed to be among statesmen some one who is capable of educating statesmen. And if there be such an one, he may be said to be among the living what Homer says that Tiresias was among the dead, "he alone has understanding; but the rest are flitting shades"; and he and his virtue in like manner will be a reality among shadows.

MENO: That is excellent, Socrates.

SOCRATES: Then, Meno, the conclusion is that virtue comes to the virtuous by the gift of God. But we shall never know the certain truth until, before asking how virtue is given, we enquire into the actual nature of virtue. I fear that I must go away, but do you, now that you are persuaded yourself, persuade our friend Anytus. And do not let him be so exasperated; if you can conciliate him, you will have done good service to the Athenian people.

CHAPTER III
Education
and Intelligent Action

The main concern of the present chapter is the relation between the rational process, education, and intelligent action in society. The discussion will be based upon a summary of ideas about the nature, origin, and purpose of rationality. The historical aspect places the greatest stress upon Aristotelian views and refers briefly to the views held by Aquinas, Dewey, and other pertinent figures. In each case, the philosopher is considered within the particular conceptual framework, and our immediate concern is with the aspects of a philosophical view which are important to the concept of rationality.

There are different basic attitudes about the rational in man. One attitude is that there is something innate and immutable about rationality and that the primary purpose of education should be to "draw out" the internal material. We have seen that Plato is one who believed that knowledge could be recollected, and there are still those who hold this view. A different interpretation of the same basic idea is that the structures of man's rationality can be exercised so as to organize the external world. Aristotle and Aquinas both thought in terms of the structures of man's intelligence. Still another basic attitude is that rationality is a developmental process which results from individual experiences. John Dewey is one who held this view.

We noted in Chapter II that if a discussion is to be fruitful we must first agree about a definition of terms and that the choice of terminology for a particular discussion may even be arbitrary if the definitions are mutually acceptable and if the usage is consistent. We find that there are many different terms used to describe the rational aspect of man. For instance, different philosophers who attempt to describe the *thinking* and the *thinking apparatus* of man refer variously to the rational soul, the intellect, the mind, reason, thinking, and intelligence. The choice of the term is often crucial to the point of view expressed and in that case to substitute one term for another is to lose some of the meaning which the philosopher wished to relate. Many current authors agree that knowing, understanding, and apprehending are common elements of the rational process but differ as to whether the process should be described by the word mind, intelligence, intellect, or reason. In our present discussion we shall use the term *intelligence* to describe the rational process, and the terms may be used interchangeably.

The Nature, Origin, and Purpose of Intelligence

The words intelligence and intellect come from the same Latin verb, *intellego*. Intelligence is a derivative of the infinitive, *intellegere,* which means "to know." Intellect is a derivative of the participle, *intellectus,* which means "having been known." The implication is one of activity versus passivity, and this is substantiated by one definition of intelligence found in the *Dictionary of Philosophy*.[1] According to Ledger Wood, intelligence refers to "the capacity of the mind to meet effectively—through the employment of memory, imagination, and conceptual thinking—the practical and theoretical problems with which it is confronted." Such a definition is based on the concept that mind is a natural substance. The term intelligence is more broadly conceived than the term intellect, which is primarily conceptual, and is merely one aspect of intelligence.

The 39th Yearbook of the National Society for the Study of Education was devoted to a study of the nature and nurture of intelligence.[2] In that work (Chapter I), Frank Freeman distinguishes three ideas about the nature of intelligence as the organic, the social, and the psychological. The organic refers to the bodily aspects, the social to the factors in social situations, and the psychological to behavior measured by different types of tests. Freeman suggests that confusion about intelligence develops when a clear distinction is not made between the three concepts.

The following definition of intelligence is given by George D. Stoddard in *The Meaning of Intelligence*[3]: *The ability to undertake activities that are characterized by (1) difficulty, (2) complexity, (3) abstractness, (4) economy, (5) adaptiveness to a goal, (6) social value, and (7) the emergence of originals, and to maintain such activities under conditions that demand a concentration of energy and a resistance to emotional forces.* The definition is in keeping with the psychological approach to an explanation of intelligence.[4] Stoddard suggests a separation between the emotional forces and the mental abilities in his description of intelligent behavior, and

---

[1] D. D. Runes, ed., *Dictionary of Philosophy* (New York: Philosophical Library, Inc.), p. 147.
[2] G. M. Whipple, ed., *Intelligence: Its Nature and Nurture,* 39th Yearbook of the National Society for the Study of Education (Bloomington, Ill.: Public School Publishing Co., 1940).
[3] George D. Stoddard, *The Meaning of Intelligence* (New York: The Macmillan Company, 1943), p. 4. (*Psychological Review,* 1941, 1948, pp. 250–260).
[4] For instance, see L. L. Thurstone, *Primary Mental Abilities* (Chicago: University of Chicago Press, 1938); E. L. Thorndike, "Intelligence and Its Uses," *Harper's Magazine,* 1920, 140: 227–235; and Charles Spearmen, *Abilities of Man* (New York: The Macmillan Company, 1927). Also, see any recent textbook in psychology or educational psychology for various definitions: L. J. Cronbach, *Educational Psychology* (New York: Harcourt, Brace, & Co., 1963); Bigge, *Learning Theories for Teachers* (New York: Harper & Row, Publishers, 1964); Clayton, *Teaching and Learning: A Psychological Perspective* (Englewood Cliffs, New Jersey: Prentice-Hall, Inc., 1965).

presumably these characteristics are open to measurement through different sorts of psychological tests.

Generally speaking, it seems that intelligence refers to the behavior of those who understand and cope successfully with their environment. The inclusion of the word understand draws the distinction between animals who manage to survive because of instinctual responses to their environment and those who surpass the level of mere survival to one of reflection which enables them to exercise a measure of control over the environment. Many animals seem to exhibit intelligence in eluding enemies, but the ability to understand one's environment and actions seems to be a function of intelligence that is restricted to man. The distinction leads us to speculate about the origin of intelligence. As we explore the possibilities we are intrigued by the grandeur and the simplicity of an Aristotle who states that "All men by nature desire to know," a Genesis with its "forbidden fruit," and a Prometheus with a metaphysical flight into the *a priori*.

It is highly unlikely that we could ever arrive at a consensus, but as we examine the alternatives we may discover views which are new to us, views which open the way to fresh ideas. Or we may find that our own views reflect a bias that is untenable in the light of analysis. Or it may be that we will simply discover means to articulate and strengthen our own position, or that we will be able to make it more defensible by making certain modifications. In any event, our investigation will lead toward a better understanding of the intellectual development of man. What is the origin of intelligence, and why is it limited to man? The alternatives are three. First, intelligence may have a supernatural origin. Second, intelligence may be a natural part of man which may or may not suggest the metaphysical. Finally, intelligence may be an aspect of the evolutionary process.

The early Greeks believed that intelligence had a supernatural origin. They believed that intelligence is either a gift of the gods or that it is a power that was stolen from the gods. Our Judaeo-Christian tradition tells us that God created man in His own image, and for this reason only man is endowed with intelligence. The same tradition allows the possibility that intelligence may be "forbidden fruit," that it is the result of man's inability to resist temptation. According to the particular metaphysical emphasis, man is either ennobled by the relation with a superbeing, or he is derogated to the position of a sinner because of his illicit possession of intelligence. On the one hand, intelligence is an instrument for the glorification of a supreme being or beings. On the other hand, the proper use of intelligence is for religious salvation. The supernatural or religious view of intelligence is founded on an affirmation of faith and militates against any sort of empirical proof which makes the position untenable for the empiricist.

An alternative to such an extreme position is to posit intelligence as a part of the original nature of man. Thus man is thought to be the favorite child of nature. Here again, despite the naturalistic overtones, are supernatural leanings. A belief in an overall purpose of nature implies that the rational process is directed to the realization of certain entelechies, and queries about the nature of intelligence lead to metaphysical speculation. A second alternative to the supernatural origin of intelligence is the idea of development in an evolutionary sense. Numerous empirical investigations show that only man can understand his environment to the point of being able to make tools and to build a culture. It may be that the actual birth of intelligence, apart from mere survival, came about when a creature recognized an "I" which was distinct from the surrounding world. Some investigators call this self-consciousness, or awareness of self. Certainly a perceptual separation of an "I" and a "Thou" would lead to a conceptualizing that would otherwise be impossible and would result in a more highly developed mental process. This stage of evolution can never be pinpointed, but it seems likely that there may have been some relation between the phenomenon and the enlargement of the brain which had occurred by the Late Pleistocene Age (40,000 to 8000 B.C.).[5]

H. J. Muller writes in *Freedom in the Ancient World* that:

> For 450,000 years, Carl Becker observed, the Dawn Man lived like "anachronistic disciples of Walter Pater," burning with a hard gem-like flame. They kept chipping flints, quite unaware that they were contributing to the progress of the human race, aware only that they were chipping flints. Actually, of course, we can never know just what went on in their heads. Nevertheless, we can be sure that they were not living simply for the moment: unlike the apes, they were making tools. In so doing they were taking thought of the morrow, thinking of things that were not, acting on premeditated instead of merely instinctive purposes—choosing as well as carrying out their purposes. They were already monkeying systematically with the world around them.[6]

Certainly the action of chipping flints could be called purposeful, since the reason for the action exists prior to the action, but it is not purposeful in a teleological sense. For instance, if I could imagine myself in the place of a Dawn Man and you should ask, "Why do you chip flint?" I should reply, "To make arrows." "Why do you make arrows?" "To kill birds and animals." "Why do you kill birds and animals?" "I kill them for food and for covering." The questions could continue indefinitely, in a cause and effect progression, as I give the *reasons* for my actions. But if your questions were to invoke responses which surpass a matter of survival, our dialogue would move to a different level.

Clearly, there is an intimate relation between one's view of the source and the purpose of intelligence. Those who posit a supernatural origin to intelligence will avow a purpose with a metaphysical base, one that exists

[5] Jacquetta Hawkes and Sir Leonard Woolley, *History of Mankind, Pre-history and the Beginnings of Civilization* (New York: Harper & Row, Publishers, 1963), Vol. I, p. 54.
[6] H. J. Muller, *Freedom in the Ancient World* (New York: Harper & Bros., 1961), pp. 3–4.

independent of mankind. Those who believe that man is intelligent by nature will hold that design is evident, and purpose is immanent in nature. Those who are inclined toward a developmental theory will maintain that it is the purpose of intelligence to control one's environment for the benefit of man. The preceding excerpt from Muller illustrates the beginning of this purpose, and according to such a view we would expect a correlation between a developing intelligence and a complexity of purpose.

Philosophers on Intelligence

There should be no question, especially in the mind of the student preparing to devote the major part of his life to teaching, that an investigation of the rational process is important. It has been stated earlier that man is distinct from other animals because of his ability to think, to make relationships, to hold concepts, and to reason. A discussion of the nature, origin, and purpose of intelligence makes it increasingly clear that man's attitudes in this regard will be reflected in the character of the education that he provides for his children. This has been the case throughout the history of education, and it will continue to be so. An historical approach to education shows that beliefs, attitudes, ideals, and values—all facets of the rational process—are not static but are undergoing constant modification and alteration.

At the same time, there have always been those who fight any change, those who are disturbed by new ideas, and those who are most comfortable with a *status quo*. Such reactionaries threaten man's progress but perhaps no more so than the extremists who discard the uses of the past and who sneer at tradition. There is little advantage to a forward look if we fail to glance over our shoulders to see what has brought us to our present condition. Both extremes are foolhardy and dangerous, and each bears the seeds of intellectual destruction. Surely no investigation of the rational process will be complete without a backward glance. We familiarize ourselves with what others before us have had to say about intelligence—not in the spirit of passive acceptance of ideas, but in the spirit of exploring all possibilities —gleaning a little here, a little there, separating and discarding what is no longer pertinent, and using the remainder as a foundation for the articulation of our own ideas.

Aristotle (384–322 B.C.)[7]

Aristotle, born in Stageira in Thrace, lived much of his life in Athens where he studied in the Academy of Plato until Plato's death in 347. Disagreements with Plato's nephew and successor, Speusippus, caused Aristotle to go to Assos in the Troad where he established a school similar to the Academy of Athens. His fame began to grow, and he interested himself in politics. In 343, he was invited to become tutor to Alexander, who was to rule later as Alexander the Great. In 335, Aristotle returned to Athens and established the Lyceum which quickly surpassed the Academy as the source

---

[7] The present analysis leans heavily upon *De Anima, Parva Naturalia,* and the *Metaphysics.*

of intellectual fare for Athenians. Again, Aristotle became involved in political affairs with disastrous results. In 323, he was rebuked much as Socrates had been, but Aristotle chose to leave Athens. He went to the island of Euboea where he lived only a short time before he died of a stomach illness.[8]

Even the most superficial survey of Aristotle's philosophical views would require many times the time and space that can be allotted here. The complexities of his philosophy also defy any rigid categorization such as realism, idealism, or empiricism, for to do so would necessarily exclude some things from consideration, as Aristotle's philosophy is larger than any one category. Aristotle developed his philosophical thinking from two main traditions, the naturalism of men such as Heraclitus, and the metaphysical realism of men such as Plato. Aristotle spent his life in the attempt to synthesize his own natural scientific persuasion with the traditions which he had inherited. A brief look at the traditions that were the wellspring of Aristotle's thought should be helpful toward an understanding of his philosophy.

One of the fundamental problems in Greek society involved man and nature and the relation of one to the other.[9] The naturalists were caught up with attempted explanations of the change they could observe in these natural processes. Harris states:

> It seems to me, however, that the most characteristic feature of the Greek conception of nature, and one most important for the problem of the relation to it of the human mind, is that, apart from their idea of nature as a living organism, they regarded it as the realm of perpetual change.[10]

Aristotle was never willing to dismiss the idea of perpetual change for the attitude which maintained that change could not logically occur, an idea that was epitomized around 450 B.C. in the writing of Zeno by his paradoxes of motion.

Plato, however, emphatically denied that change is real. He systematized the realist tradition where the Real is eternal and unchanging and where changing events can be known only through their participation in the unchanging. We have seen that Plato solved the dilemma between the changing and the unchanging by dualizing the soul, making the rational part akin to the eternal, and the irrational part akin to the material or the changeable. This was a solution that Aristotle could not accept, and he attempted to reconcile the changeable and the eternal.

---

[8] One of the most interesting accounts of the life and works of Aristotle is contained in the introduction, by J. A. K. Thomson, *The Ethics of Aristotle* (London: Penguin Books, Ltd., 1953). See also B. A. G. Fuller, *History of Philosophy* (New York: Holt, Rinehart & Winston, Inc., 1955), Vol. I and F. Copleston, *A History of Philosophy* (Westminster, Maryland: The Newman Press, 1957), Vol. I.

[9] E. E. Harris, *Nature, Mind and Modern Science* (London: George Allen & Unwin Ltd., 1954), p. 63.

[10] *Ibid.*, p. 56.

Aristotle's view of the soul provides a key to his philosophical thinking. Book I of *De Anima,* Aristotle's definitive study of the soul, is concerned with an historical analysis of what earlier philosophers believed, and Book II delineates Aristotle's own view of the soul. The components of the soul, as recognized by Aristotle, are material substance, form substance, and a combination of the two. This combination of matter and form is a fundamental aspect of the Aristotelian view of nature and constitutes the basis of Aristotle's metaphysical position. The soul is not body but is mingled with the body and informs it of its potentiality of life. The soul is the essence of the body and is the vital principle within nature. Aristotle says that "the soul must be a substance in the sense of the form of a natural body having life potentially within it."[11]

Aristotle characterizes the aspects of the body-soul relation as the vegetative, the sensitive, and the rational. The vegetative soul refers to those necessary bodily functions of nutrition and reproduction. The sensitive soul has reference to the special senses of vision, hearing, smelling, taste, and touch. Further analysis of the sensitive soul makes reference to the qualities of memory, motion, desires, and dreams. The vegetative and the sensitive souls are important, but the rational soul is most crucial in Aristotle's philosophy and to his concept of the nature and purpose of intelligence.

E. E. Spicer's *Aristotle's Conception of the Soul* states that:

> In speaking of the parts of the soul or of different souls, it must be remembered that this is only a mode of expression and that the soul is one. Thus the soul of a plant is one, a nutritive soul; the soul in an animal is one, but functions in various aspects under two main activities, nutrition and perception. Lastly man's soul is one, but functions under three main heads—nutritive, perceptive, and mind.[12]

But despite this claim, Aristotle obviously believes that the higher soul, the thinking, is separable from the lower soul. He states that the power to think ". . . seems to be a widely different kind of soul,"[13] and is capable of separate existence after the other kinds of soul perish at death. The perishable are the sensitive and vegetative which are both passive functions. The active soul is a nonmaterial, independent existence, a metaphysical substance which is eternal.

The rational soul appears to be the unifying principle between the changeable and the eternal. It is the vitalizer of the world. Aristotle's criticism of the Platonic Forms was because of the necessary separation of Form and appearance which sundered the world and called for the invocation of artificial principles (immanence and transcendence) to bring them

---

11 R. McKeon, *The Basic Works of Aristotle* (New York: Random House, Inc., 1941), p. 555 (*De Anima,* Book II, Chapter 1, 412a).

12 E. E. Spicer, *Aristotle's Conception of the Soul* (London: University of London Press, 1934), p. 55.

13 R. McKeon, *op. cit.,* p. 558 (Book II, Chapter II, 413b; Book III, Chapter V, 430a).

into some sort of relation. Aristotle felt this to be an unnecessary complication, one which tended to denigrate the sensible or changeable world. Aristotle's solution to the dichotomy was to place form *within* matter, but, in spite of the brilliance of the solution, certain problems are raised. They need not be considered in this particular context, however, other than to suggest Copleston's *History of Philosophy* for a thorough discussion of some of the problems.[14]

But it is pertinent to this discussion to note that certain crucial issues have been resolved by Aristotle's solution. Namely, one need not postulate a skepticism of nonknowledge about the physical, nor need one say that matter itself can be known. To deny knowledge of matter is not to deny change but is actually a recognition that matter is the individuating aspect of the form-matter hypothesis. The apparent necessity of the hypothesis lies in the dilemma of unity and diversity, the one and the many. Individuals come and go, but the species persists because of the universal that informs the particular matter. The species is immutable (a source of conflict between the nineteenth century Darwinians and religionists), for its designation as species is based upon an essence which is eternal and knowable. Knowledge is concerned with the universal rather than the variable, so one must look to form for intelligence. Because of Aristotle's form-in-matter hypothesis, intelligence comes into the sensible world in the complex of form and matter. When Plato looks to Form for intelligence it is a thing apart from the material world, but according to Aristotle, intelligence is the means by which one copes with the sensible world.

Aristotle introduced the additional concepts of actuality and potentiality which help clarify the relation between form and matter. The distinction between actuality and potentiality is an important one, for such a distinction makes possible a principle of development in the natural world. Potency refers to that which is already actual. The actuality is that which is in existence. Thus movement comes about through an actual acting upon a potential. A *thing* must not be thought of as being actual and potential simultaneously with respect to the same object. For example, wood may be actual now and at the same time be potentially a desk, but it cannot be actual wood and potential wood at one and the same time. The actual is prior in time and is principle to the potential.

Aristotle explains how change is initiated in his *Metaphysics* (Book VIII, Chapter 4). He speaks of the material cause, the moving cause (efficient), the formal cause, and the final cause. For example, if I am going to build a desk I will need wood (material cause), and I must have a plan (formal cause). There must also be a moving force (efficient cause), but the moving force must have a goal in mind prior to the actual construction of the desk (final cause). Thus we can see that the final cause is the first

---

[14] F. Copleston, *History of Philosophy* (Westminster: The Newman Press, 1957), Vol. I, pp. 301–306.

cause. The mental is prior to the material, and so it is the rational part of the soul which is the determining factor in change. Aristotle states in *De Anima:*

> The soul is the cause or source of the living body. The terms cause and source have many senses. But the soul is the cause of its body alike in all three senses which we explicitly recognize. It is (a) the source or origin of movement, it is (b) the end, it is (c) the essence of the whole living body.[15]

Aristotle makes two main divisions of the rational soul. The scientific is concerned with the invariable, and the calculative is concerned with the variable. The scientific faculty which investigates truth *qua* truth is characterized by three states of the soul: 1) scientific knowledge; 2) intuitive reason; and 3) philosophic wisdom. The calculative faculty which investigates practical truth is characterized by two states of the soul: 1) art; and 2) practical wisdom. These five kinds of activity constitute the intellectual virtues. If we examine each of these different types of wisdom we see that scientific knowledge concerns demonstration and proof and confines itself to the observable. "The object of scientific knowledge is of necessity. Therefore it is eternal; for things that are of necessity in the unqualified sense are all eternal; and things that are eternal are ungenerated and imperishable."[16] Aristotle says that scientific knowledge follows from first principles or the apprehension of the rational ground.

Aristotelian Soul

Rational soul	Scientific Faculty–Truth as Truth (invariable)	
	Calculative Faculty–Practical Truth (variable)	Active Intellect
Sensitive soul	Sense Perception Desire Local Motion Imagination Memory	Passive Intellect
Vegetative soul . . .	Nutrition Reproduction	

The soul is made up of material substance, form substance, and a combination of the two. The vegetative soul is found in plants, animals, and men; the sensitive soul is found in animals and men; but only men have all three aspects, the vegetative, the sensitive, and the rational.

15 McKeon, *op. cit.*, p. 561 (*De Anima*, Book II, Chapter 4, 415b).
16 *Ibid.*, pp. 1024–1025. (*N. Ethics*, Book VI, Chapter 3, 1139b).

Since scientific knowledge cannot investigate the grounds of its own first principles, it must turn to another state of the soul for such an investigation. This is the function of the intuitive reason. The combination of the words intuitive and reason furnish a clue to the understanding of this function which is to reason about certain experiences that are of an intuitive nature. Philosophic wisdom, also concerned with the invariable, ". . . must be intuitive reason combined with scientific knowledge—scientific knowledge of the highest objects which has received as it were its proper completion."[17] Wisdom becomes the knowledge of many remarkable and divine things which are removed from the practical quest for human goods.

The calculative faculty, characterized by two states of the soul, art and practical wisdom, includes the activities of making and doing. Making things involves art—bringing into being those things which can be brought into being. Doing things involves practical wisdom, a concern for human goods. This state of the soul must act with reason and truth in order to attain the happiness that Aristotle says is the aim of human nature.[18]

Aristotle says that there are three types of lives open to man: the sensuous, the political, and the contemplative. The three are by no means mutually exclusive, but as the contemplative is the surest way to happiness, it is the highest type of life. The activity of reason is loved for its own sake and expresses the divine in man. Aristotle states:

> If reason is divine, then, in comparison with man, the life according to it is divine in comparison with human life. But we must not follow those who advise us, being men, to think of human things, and, being mortal, of mortal things, but must, so far as we can, make ourselves immortal, and strain every nerve to live in accordance with the best thing in us; for even if it be small in bulk, much more does it in power and worth surpass everything.[19]

No clearer statement could be made about how Aristotle views the nature and the purpose of intelligence in man's endeavors.

St. Thomas Aquinas (1225–1274)

There is considerable disagreement over the biographical data of Aquinas—the year of his birth, the specifics of his entry into the Dominican Order, the dates and time sequences of his travels, degrees, and writings. But interpreters do agree that Aquinas became the intellectual giant of the Catholic Church in spite of a good deal of opposition.

The opposition to Aquinas was not personal. Rather, it resulted from a genuine academic quarrel with his idea that the writings of Aristotle could serve as a basis for a philosophical and theological synthesis.[20] Aristote-

---

17 Ibid., pp. 1027–1028. (N. Ethics, Book VI, Chapter 7, 1141a).
18 Ibid., p. 1102. (N. Ethics, Book X, Chapter 5, 1176a).
19 Ibid., p. 1105. (N. Ethics, Book X, Chapter 7, 1177b).
20 F. Copleston, op. cit., Vol. II, p. 423.

lianism suffered distortions at the hands of Arabian philosophers such as Averrhoës and Avicenna, and the theological authorities within the Church were offended by the interpretations which pointed to a universe and matter that were eternal, but which were uncreated, and to views that ruled out personal immortality. Such doctrines were looked upon as heresy and were unacceptable to the Church. It followed that Aquinas as an Aristotelian was equally unacceptable to Church leaders.[21]

The genius of Aquinas lies in his synthesis of the disparate worlds of Christian faith and Greek rationalism. There is much drama in the meeting of these two worlds and it has been well expressed by Pegis:

> Such was the problem that took shape in the thirteenth century. It called for the establishment of a universal Christian synthesis which would receive all the truths that the philosophers had to teach, which would know how to reject and refute their errors, and which could defend the cause of reason on its own ground and with the tools of philosophy.[22]

This was Aquinas' place in history, and the difficulty of his position was complicated by the fact that men are always slow to change their attitudes. From Justinian's prohibition against the teaching of philosophy in Athens (529 A.D.) to approximately the fifteenth century, there was a negativism toward the general state of learning, and the light of reason was dimmed in favor of the mystical and the occult. But it is, nonetheless, a mistake to view those centuries as the dark ages completely devoid of any sort of meaningful intellectual activity or progress.

Aquinas was a dedicated theologian, but his commitment did not blind him to the realities of his environment, and his philosophy was not aimed toward the complete derogation of the natural world. At the same time, an emphasis upon the supernatural and the immortal, on Church over state, and the linking of God, ethics, and the intellectual prowess of man, are to be expected.[23] Nor is it surprising to find God's existence proven from a starting point of 1) motion, 2) efficient cause, 3) possibility and necessity, 4) more and less, and 5) purpose.[24] In keeping with an investigation of the nature and purpose of intelligence, our discussion will be primarily concerned with the Aquinian view of the soul, the intellectual process, reason, and faith.

Aquinas saw the soul, not as a body, but as the act of the body, the form of the human body. Like Aristotle, Aquinas felt the necessity of a union between the intellectual soul and the body in order that we might

---

21 A. C. Pegis, *Introduction to Saint Thomas Aquinas* (New York: The Modern Library, Inc., 1948), p. xvi.
22 A. C. Pegis, *Basic Writings of Saint Thomas Aquinas* (New York: Random House, Inc., 1945), Vol. I, p. xxix.
23 F. Copleston, *op. cit.*, Vol. II, p. 428. For a succinct and provocative discussion of Aquinas and Aristotle consult Chapter XLI.
24 A. C. Pegis, *op. cit.*, Vol. I, pp. 22–23.

have an understanding of the sensible (nourishment, sensation, and local movement). Aquinas comes to a position similar to that of Aristotle in regard to powers in the soul—the vegetative, the sensitive, and the intellectual.[25] Each of these three powers has the several aspects ascribed to them that are shown in the following diagram.

Aquinian Soul

Intellectual soul	Active Intellect Passive Intellect Volition (will)
Sensitive soul	5 Exterior Senses 4 Interior Senses Locomotion Appetition
Vegetative soul	Nutrition Growth Reproduction

The different aspects are self-explanatory, with the possible exception of the four interior senses which are aspects of the sensitive soul. These are clarified when we label them imagination, memory, general sense, and estimative function which judges the utility of an object or of an idea. The intellectual soul is the source of the intellectual virtues. Aquinas states:

> But the human intellect, which is the lowest in the order of intellects and most remote from the perfection of the divine intellect, is in potentiality with regard to things intelligible, and is at first *like a clean tablet on which nothing is written,* as the Philosopher says. This is made clear from the fact that at first we are only potentially towards understanding, and afterwards we are made to understand actually.[26]

Several implications can be drawn from the foregoing. We see that there is an order of intellects and that even the lowest order has the potentiality of understanding. We can assume that since the intellect is like a clean tablet in its potentiality, all that comes into the intellect must come through the senses. Finally, we can assume that there must be some other power, probably one within the intelligible soul that is capable of actualizing the potential. Aquinas designates this power, the Active Intellect. According to Aquinas, the human soul receives the intellectual light from God. The power of the intellect in man is the same thing as reason, and Aquinas

---

[25] *Ibid.*, Vol. I (Q. 75–89, Articles 1–10). (One can note volition in Aquinas which appears to be an addition to Aristotelian concepts. Aristotle had no specific concept of will. See *N. Ethics,* 1113a; also Copleston, *op. cit.,* Vol. I, pp. 339–40.)

[26] *Ibid.*, Vol. I, pp. 747–748 (Q. 79, Article 2). The reference to Aristotle is *De Anima,* III, 4, 4302.

says that ". . . this term *Intelligence* properly signifies the very act of the intellect, which is to understand."[27] Hence, the three terms, intellect, reason, and intelligence, can be used interchangeably.

The intellect, beginning as a clean tablet, must be directed toward some object for its knowledge. Although such knowledge may be caused by phantasms originating from sense stimuli, sensible knowledge, the apparent object of the human intellect is not the material object itself but the essence of the object. The active intellect realizes the universal by extracting the intelligible from the particular material object and testing it for the order that is sought. Finally, the intellect makes a judgment which becomes the object of the intellect and is called self-knowledge. Ultimately, the process of judgment is no longer a percept but has become a concept. The senses are not necessary to God, the highest order of intellect capable of self-knowledge, but they are necessary to the intellectual action of man, the lowest order. Man moves from the particular object or objects, by way of the complex process we have described, to the universal—from sensible knowledge to intellectual knowledge.

We have seen that the religious attitudes and beliefs of Aquinas were responsible for certain dictates of his philosophical orientation. A fundamental distinction between theology and philosophy is that the theologian begins with the acceptance of authority, while the philosopher starts with principles that can be known through human reason. In other words, theological investigations begin with God and move toward the individual, and philosophical investigations begin with the natural and move toward the supernatural. Both use the process of reason, but they begin at opposite ends of the reason-faith spectrum. Thus Aquinas began his investigations secure in the belief that knowledge of God is the ultimate goal of man's rational activities. He knew that the imperfections of the lowest order of rational process would prevent the achievement of the goal without the assistance of theology, and he looked upon theology as the highest wisdom. He believed human philosophy to be the handmaiden to theology. Aquinas believed the human mind to be a curious and restless thing, always desiring to know more about the cause and source of all things, which is God. He says, ". . . the final aim of rational creatures is nothing short of the vision of God, the seeing of his very self."[28]

Aquinas posited an affinity between the separate provinces of reason and faith that neither contradict each other, nor come into conflict with one another. Real conflict could never exist between things which come from God. Intelligence that is put to good use leads man to know that God exists, but the essence and the power of God are truths which lie far beyond the limits of reason and must be taken on faith. Even certain truths which are theoretically within the grasp of reason must be initially taken on faith.

---

27 *Ibid.*, p. 762 (Q. 79, Article 10).
28 T. Gilby, *St. Thomas Aquinas, Theological Texts* (London: Oxford University Press, 1955), p. 5 (Compendium Theologiae, 104).

Aquinas, whose philosophical attitude was infused with the light of Aristotelian reason and the light of faith in a revealed religion, stands on the threshold of the modern world. His views were a reflection of a classical heritage which, tempered by his theological training, led him to see a harmony between reason and religious faith. Like Aristotle, Aquinas recognized the necessity for a practical intellect which can serve man in the temporal world. But Aquinas believed that man's best moments are those directed from the natural toward the goal of beatitude, rather than as Aristotle had believed, toward the goal of contemplation.

Both men believed the soul, the unifying principle within man and nature, to be capable of a separate existence, and they recognized similar divisions of the soul. Both recognized, in the union of body and soul, that sense knowledge is a way toward intellectual knowledge. Aristotle emphasized a balance in all things, a harmony leading to happiness which is the result of activity in accordance with reason. Aquinas emphasized those things which lead to beatific vision, to knowledge of God. He believed man's purpose to be the glorification of God in all things.

John Dewey's philosophical position which reflects the scientific-empirical temper that has developed since the Renaissance is a world apart from that of Aquinas. But there are points of similarity between Dewey and Aristotle. Dewey's efforts to relate the problems of metaphysics to philosophy as a whole (*Experience and Nature*) certainly reflect an Aristotelian flavor. Dewey's search for an effective method of inquiry led him toward an amelioration of the speculative and the practical aspects of philosophy. However, as we shall see, Dewey's approach to intelligence, which relies upon terms such as *unity, behavior, continuity,* and *interaction,* differs radically from the approaches of Aristotle and Aquinas.

John Dewey (1859–1952)

Much of modern philosophy has been concerned with the mind-body dichotomy delineated by Descartes in the seventeenth century. Those who have stressed mind over body have been accused of mentalism. Those who have stressed body over mind have been accused of materialism. From the vantage point of the twentieth century Dewey could look back and see little chance of a workable solution to the problem. His approach was a mediating one ignoring the metaphysical problem and starting with the fact of man's existence where there are no sharp lines between man and the surrounding world of nature. Any presumed dichotomy is merely an artificial creation. The stricture against dualism carries through all levels of existence but especially in regard to mind-body. Dewey chose to hyphenate the two words in order to emphasize the continuity.

According to Dewey, thinking involves intention of a practical nature, rather than of a metaphysical one. In *Democracy and Education,* he wrote that when one faces a task that cannot be performed from habit, one must consider the circumstances of the task, the facts, the resources, and the difficulties in order to forecast the results. "This foresight and this survey with reference to what is foreseen constitute mind."[29] He elaborates on his interpretation of mind as follows:

> . . . mind is not a name for something complete by itself; it is a name for a course of action in so far as that is intelligently directed; in so far, that is to say, as aims, ends, enter into it, with selection of means to further the attainment of aims. Intelligence is not a peculiar possession which a person owns; but a person is intelligent in so far as the activities in which he plays a part have the qualities mentioned. Nor are the activities in which a person engages, whether intelligently or not, exclusive properties of himself; they are something in which he *engages and partakes*. Other things, the independent changes of other things and persons, cooperate and hinder. The individual's act may be initial in a course of events, but the outcome depends upon the inter-action of his response with energies supplied by other agencies. Conceive mind as anything but one factor partaking along with others in the production of consequences, and it becomes meaningless.[30]

Man must discover particular connections between his actions and their consequences, and this implies doing things and having things done to the subject. One experiences the immediate environment as it is, and there is no substratum of substance which holds together the immediacy of experience. Whatever may be said about continuity of experience comes ultimately to be a matter of intelligence. In *Art as Experience*, Dewey wrote:

> Mind as background is formed out of modifications of the self that have occurred in the process of prior interactions with environment. Its animus is toward further interactions. Since it is formed out of commerce with the world and is set toward that world nothing can be further from the truth than the idea which treats it as something self-contained and self-enclosed.[31]

One can recognize reminiscences of Hume's Laws of Association, and Thorndike's Laws of Exercise and Effect, but there is more to it than the mechanism of connections. Certainly there is an activity inherent in the individual, but it is nonrational, an activity of an impulsive nature, blind, and seeking no end, for no end is possible for blind impulse. Intelligence, which is a response to impulse, clarifies and directs these impulses. In this way, the individual can be in control of the confusing push of his passions, sympathies, and desires.[32] Dewey believed that intelligent behavior is a re-

---

29 John Dewey, *Democracy and Education* (New York: The Macmillan Company, 1916), p. 154.
30 *Ibid.*, p. 155.
31 J. Dewey, *Art as Experience* (New York: Minton Balch & Co., 1934), p. 264.
32 J. Dewey, *Intelligence in the Modern World*, ed., J. Ratner (New York: The Modern Library, Inc., 1939), p. 760.

sult of meeting and solving immediate problems successfully and using the learned information to meet new problems. The process, according to Dewey, must be continuous throughout the life of an individual in order that continued existence may be insured.

Since intelligence refers to natural process, it would be a fruitless adventure to search for the higher in man or for what Aristotle and Aquinas called soul. Dewey denied that what men have called intelligence, mind, or soul has a separate existence, for he believed in a unity called the human being. He did not believe that man is a rational animal by nature, merely fulfilling a predetermined function. He believed that man is an animal with the natural *capability* of intelligence. He saw no guarantee that man would become intelligent out of necessity or predetermination. Dewey also denied an *a priori* purpose in man and in nature preferring an intention that is natural and related to the derived outcomes of man. He did not believe that intelligence could achieve any sort of metaphysical flight to the truth but that it could discover truths in various situations and could use these truths to construct a sensible society. One must look to the experience of man in order to come to an understanding of intelligence in the philosophy of Dewey. It is possible to distinguish intelligent behavior from unintelligent behavior in terms of how one or the other action copes with the particular environment. One looks to problematical situations in order to discover how man thinks, rather than to an analysis of the active and passive intellects.

Intelligence and Education

Lord James of Rusholme writes in *Challenges to Democracy,* that "the nation that does not value trained intelligence is doomed."[33] One could hardly disagree with the statement, but it is evident from the preceding discussions that not all people will agree about educational goals. Nor do we expect to find a consensus about the particulars of an educational system. A view of intelligence that states its purpose in terms of discovering a logical but transcendent order in the universe will result in a curriculum which stresses those subjects which discipline the logical and deductive. On the other hand, a view of intelligence that states its purpose in terms of understanding man and his relations to other men will result in a system which bears heavily upon the psychological and sociological motivations of individuals. Democracy is a melting pot of ideas, and in a democratic situation the educational system will reflect aspects of a variety of views. Let us consider what educational ideas we might glean from the philosophical positions held by Aristotle, Aquinas, and Dewey.

Aristotle

Since Aristotle failed to supply scholars with writings which detail his ideas about education, we are forced to speculate about them from what we

---

[33] Edward Reed, ed., *Challenges to Democracy* (New York: Frederick A. Praeger, Inc., 1963), p. 201.

know of his philosophical position. We can also speculate on the basis of Aristotle's description of a truly wise man who reaches the divine state through the very activity of his striving. A wise man, according to Aristotle, is one who exercises control over his passions and who directs his entire being toward the rational understanding of the universal. Discipline and habit are words that Aristotle used a great deal, but he makes a distinction between liberal and freeing endeavors and illiberal and mechanistic endeavors. He believed that a free man must be disciplined but not externally and vulgarly.

Aristotle did make it clear that he thought education should be a public matter. He thought that the educator should receive his direction from the statesman who would consider the individuals to be educated. Although there is little in the way of definitive material about Aristotle's educational views, he did offer suggestions in the *Politics* for the education of the body.

> And as the body is prior in order of generation to the soul, so the irrational is prior to the rational. The proof is that anger and wishing and desire are implanted in children from their very birth, but reason and understanding are developed as they grow older. Wherefore, the care of the body ought to precede that of the soul, and the training of the appetitive part should follow: none the less our care of it must be for the sake of the reason, and our care of the body for the sake of the soul.[34]

Believing that happiness is the goal of life and that happiness and speculative wisdom are related, it is clear that Aristotle would construe education in such a manner that the rational soul will be uppermost. That he had more to say about training the irrational than he did about educating the rational soul does not alter the fact that Aristotle placed greatest stress upon the contemplative activity of the rational soul. Several ideas come to mind as to how this might be accomplished. These are: 1) logical discourse with special emphasis upon the syllogism; 2) the study of metaphysics which would contribute to the search for theoretical knowledge and a certainty about principles and causes; and 3) the natural and social sciences which would contribute order and system to the developing mind.

St. Thomas Aquinas

During the span of years between Aristotle and Aquinas, education reflected the ancient and classical ideals. Aquinas devoted most of his energies to combat religious heresies, and even though he is considered to have been an educator for the Catholic clergy, his writings are basically theological. We can speculate from these writings, particularly the *Summa Theologica,* about educational ideals which flow from the Aquinian view

---

[34] R. McKeon, *op. cit.,* pp. 1300–1301 (*Politics,* Book VII; Chapter 15, 1334b). Also see *Politics,* Books VII, VIII for further analysis.

of man and the active intellect. However, there is at least one major writing of his which is concerned with teaching and the teacher. This is *De Magistro,* translated variously as *On the Teacher, Concerning the Teacher,* or simply as *The Teacher.*

The first thing to be noted about *De Magistro,* which appears as Question Eleven in Aquinas' investigations into the matters of Truth,[35] is the form of the writing. Each of the four articles begins with a statement of the thesis, usually in the form of a question. This is followed by objections, contraries, the Master's answer, and finally, the replies to the objections. In this manner, all points of view are presented and disputed so that the student can see the truth for himself. There is a prior commitment to the Truth on the part of the Master, and the method is authority which relies upon the use of logical argument and rebuttal. The following is illustrative of the method:

> Objection 11. Further, knowledge is a representation of things in the mind, since knowledge is said to be an assimilation of the knower to the thing known. But one man cannot represent in another's mind the likeness of things, for thus he would operate interiorly in him, which belongs to God alone. Therefore, one man cannot teach another.[36]

> Reply to Objection 11. The intelligible forms, of which knowledge received from teaching is composed, are impressed in the pupil immediately through the active intellect but mediately through the teacher; for the teacher proposes the symbols of intelligible things from which the intellect takes the abstractions and impresses them on the passive intellect. Hence, the words of the teacher, heard or seen in writing, have the same relation to causing knowledge in the intellect as anything outside the mind has, because from both, the intellect takes the intelligible content (meaning); yet the words of the teacher have a closer relation to causing knowledge than have the mere perceivable things outside the mind, inasmuch as words are symbols of intelligible content.[37]

According to the foregoing, the mind is formed by God. The teacher, like sense data, is only a stimulant for knowledge. The educative process is a highly symbolic one which depends primarily upon words. Mayer states that: "For the Scholastics, the intellect of man was equipped to deal with abstractions, and in dealing with them it was essentially logical."[38] This is in keeping with the generally accepted position that the *lectio* and the *disputatio* were basic to the Scholastic Method of teaching-learning. The

---

[35] Thomas Aquinas, *Truth,* James V. McGlynn S.J. trans. (Chicago: Henry Regnery Co., 1953), Vol. II, pp. 77–101.
[36] M. D. Mayer, *The Philosophy of Teaching of St. Thomas Aquinas.* Photocopy by University Microfilms of Original (Milwaukee: The Bruce Publishing Co., 1929), p. 45.
[37] *Ibid.,* pp. 57–58.
[38] *Ibid.,* p. 96.

Thomist places the curriculum antecedent to the individual, for knowledge of God is universal and *a priori,* and to suggest that the reconstruction of experience might be a factor in searching for truth would be totally foreign to the Aquinian view. A Thomist does not learn from experience, for the vagaries of everyday experience are ordered in accordance to the preconceptions received by way of the active intellect.

The Thomist philosophical views are not merely background to the present but constitute theory and practice for many educators today. Jacques Maritain, a leading Catholic theologian, shows his dependence upon St. Thomas as he centers his attention upon a liberal education where the purpose is ". . . essentially to cultivate and liberate, form and equip intelligence, and to prepare for the development of intellectual virtues, but that this development itself, once the threshold of virtue has been crossed, is necessarily particularized to a given branch of knowledge."[39] The writings of both Aquinas and Maritain suggest an educative process that is based upon logical discourse, that is highly intellectualist, that assumes intellectual virtues which are merely capacities to be *developed.*

John Dewey

In contrast to Aristotle and Aquinas, Dewey's writings abound with ideas about educational ideals and goals. *The Child and the Curriculum, The School and Society, My Pedagogic Creed,* and *Democracy and Education* are all works devoted solely to educational theory. Again, in contrast to Aristotle and Aquinas, Dewey's philosophical thinking turned more and more to problems and methods of educating the child. He writes in *School and Society* about children and the wide variety of things that interest them (inquiry, talking, communicating, constructing things, working on different kinds of art projects), and how these interests should be used in constructing the curriculum. Dewey has no preconceptions about the child's active intellect or his rationality. He emphasizes the notion of individuality and freedom in a very literal sense, and his outlook for education involves activity that is directed toward the reconstruction of experience.

Since the development of intelligence comes about through man's interaction with his environment, all of the environment constitutes subject matter. The child is not confined to a stationary desk in a formal classroom, for the educative process extends into all areas of the child's activity. A view of intelligence that is based on process and continuity emphasizes the contributions of the present social aspects to the natural future of the child, and learning continues throughout a lifetime.

Individual Intelligence and Intelligent Action in Society

We have seen that one of the concerns of philosophy is speculation about the nature, origin, and purpose of intelligence. We have also seen

---

[39] John Brubacher, ed. *Modern Philosophies and Education,* The 54th Yearbook of the National Society for the Study of Education (Chicago: University of Chicago Press, 1955), Chapter III, Jacques Maritain, "Thomist Views of Education," p. 61.

that historically man has posited the origin of intelligence to be either divine, supernatural, or natural; and it has been demonstrated that the philosophical view of intelligence stems from a particular philosophical position; and further, we have seen that the view one has of intelligence plays an important role in educational choices. The fact that much of this chapter has been devoted to philosophical background is not intended, however, to indicate that philosophy is thought to be the determining, or even the dominant factor, but rather that it provides a sound base for a study of intelligence and education. Perhaps we can most aptly place the philosophical view of intelligence in proper perspective by means of an analogy.

Let us think for a moment of education, both formal and informal, as being a journey through life. This is in keeping with John Dewey's view that education is a continuous process that is essential to existence. There are those who wander aimlessly through life with no particular concern for tomorrow and those who live from day to day subject to their particular environment, motivated only by basic needs that barely surpass those of a creature level. But even the most experienced traveler would be reluctant to undertake a world tour without an itinerary, without some sort of overall plan based upon all available information. Even if one had unlimited resources and could be sure of any amount of time, such a journey would require more thought and detailed planning than many accord to their journey through life.

A successful journey, one that takes us to strange and exotic places, one that affords the riches of varied and exciting experiences, one that expands the imagination and opens the way to new insights, does not just happen. By the same token, a journey through life stands to have more meaning if it is shaped by guiding principles, by attitudes and beliefs that are systematized to form a philosophical view that delineates purpose, direction, and goals. Such guide lines are a product of intelligence. We can see the importance of learning as much as can be known about the means to a successful trip.

All analogies have their attendant dangers, and in order to avoid the hazard of regarding intelligence as a "thing," it will be well at this point to restate the definition that we have accepted here. We speak of intelligence in this context in terms of behavior that includes such activities as perceiving, comprehending, remembering, relating, abstracting, manipulating, and expressing. An individual is considered to be more or less intelligent, depending upon his functioning in these areas. Accordingly, intelligence refers to behavior patterns that can be isolated and measured apart from what is believed about the source of rationality. A concern of the concluding part of this chapter is a survey of what is currently known about testing and measuring intelligence. The reporting will be brief, not because the subject does not merit more consideration, but because it is a study in its own right, a study that is requisite for those who choose teaching as a career. The purpose here is to demonstrate that learning theories depend upon scientific investigation as well as they do upon philosophical theory. In *Learning Theories for Teachers,* Morris L. Bigge writes:

> Although psychologists have tried during the past century to divorce psychology and philosophy, it is doubtful that this is possible. There is no science so "pure" that it lacks philosophical implications. Even physicists find it helpful to make assumptions about the basic nature of their materials and processes; they too become involved in philosophical formulations.[40]

Measuring Intelligence

It has become the special province of psychology and more recently of biochemistry to add to philosophical speculation about intelligence by way of laboratory testing and scientific research. The psychologist is interested in what *is,* in the ways that intelligence is manifest in our actions and behavior, and many tests have been devised for measuring and testing individual intelligence. These serve as a description of the present behavior of an individual. Based on the assumption that once a rate of development has been established, a like rate of development will be maintained, these tests also serve as a statement about past development and prediction of future development. Biochemists experimenting with drugs to control and combat mental disturbances have produced strong evidence that body chemistry, especially the chemistry of the brain, may be a crucial factor of intelligence. Some claim that the chemical breakthrough of the past few years may very well point the way to an enhancement of human intelligence. Neither psychologists nor biochemists claim to have all of the answers, but there is every indication that the results of current research could revolutionize our present thinking about intelligence and the learning process.

Briefly, the main line of psychological testing of intelligence extends to the late eighteen and early nineteen hundreds with the work of Alfred Binet who was commissioned by the French government to devise a way for early detection of retardation in children. Binet collaborated with T. Simon to publish scales of typical performance tests in 1905, 1908, and 1911. Later, in 1916, this scale was revised and adopted for American use by Lewis Terman at Stanford University, and since then the Stanford-Binet scale has become a standard for assessing and measuring intelligence.

Most of the intelligence tests that are commonly used are devices to determine the relationship or ratio between the mental and the chronological age of an individual, and they are based on the assumption that the contents of the tests are representative of situations that all children have the equal chance to encounter. For instance, although not all children would have reason to know that a ferryboat is a vessel for conveying passengers, equipment, and cars across a river or other narrow water, all chil-

---

[40] Morris L. Bigge, *Learning Theories For Teachers* (New York: Harper & Row, Publishers, 1964), p. 64.

dren would be apt to know that boats are for traveling on water. In this connection, psychologists recognize that it is impossible to devise tests that are not culture-bound, but they use every means to make them as culture-free as possible. Effort is also made to select items that will be of real interest to the ones who are being tested, in order to insure complete cooperation of the subject.

The variety of tests for measuring intelligence that have been devised during the past decades include the following: 1) verbal tests which deal primarily with highly abstract material; 2) performance tests which deal primarily with concrete materials; 3) group tests which can be administered to large groups of individuals at one time; 4) achievement tests; 5) aptitude tests; and 6) tests that combine the verbal and the performance items. But even though psychology has contributed significantly to the educative process with these tests, much remains to be accomplished in the area. Certain conclusions about the creative aspect of intelligence can be drawn from existing tests, but such conclusions still remain in a speculative realm. It is most likely that continued research in the area of measuring creativity could result in considerable change in both intelligence testing and teaching methods. In any event, proper use and understanding of the implications of intelligence testing is not only an invaluable aid in the teaching-learning process, it also provides empirical data for learning theorists.

The attempts of the biochemist to measure intelligence takes quite a different approach than that of the psychologist. It is prompted by a theory which is based on the experiments of a Swedish scientist, Holger Hyden, that intelligence is related to a living chemical inside the nerve cell, RNA. The chemical is closely related to DNA which carries the code of heredity. Dr. Hyden, after training rats to balance on a wire, discovered significant changes in the molecular structure of their RNA. More recently he has discovered that after training left-handed rats to extract food from a tube with the right paw, and right-handed rats to extract the food with the left paw, not only were the RNA molecules altered, but new forms of protein which became part of the memory trace had been manufactured. It seems reasonable to speculate that learning may depend upon chemical changes of the RNA inside the nerve cells.

One of the early and better-known experiments was conducted on flatworms by James V. McConnell at the University of Michigan. These worms, after being taught to escape a shock signaled by a flashing light, were chopped up and fed to other flatworms. The "cannibal" worms were as unusually quick to solve the same problem as the first group, almost as though they had absorbed knowledge along with their food. Other experiments with rats and hamsters indicate that an injection of RNA extracted from the brains of trained animals and injected into a new group result in a significant tendency in the injected group to respond in a similar manner to the trained group.

Dr. James L. McGaugh of the University of California has discovered that injections of strychnine or metrazol improve the ability of a mouse to learn a maze, and drug companies are testing a pill of chemicals less lethal that will produce the same effects in human beings. Dr. Sidney Cohen of the UCLA Medical School posits that intelligence, or learning ability, depends upon three different skills: 1) concentration on the problem, 2) a lasting memory trace, and 3) a retrieval system—a method of scanning memory traces and focusing on the right one. Since all of these processes can possibly be improved upon by the use of chemicals, it leads to the speculation about chemicals that could improve our thinking ability.

Learning Theories

Man's concern about *how* man learns has been responsible for the development of systematic theories of learning, and in the twentieth century a study of learning theories has become a discipline in its own right. Insofar as all purposeful actions are governed by theories, it can be said that all who teach have a learning theory. However, there are those teachers who have not thought through the principles that serve as a base for their actions and who operate in a haphazard manner. In such cases, teaching will most likely reflect the lack of theoretical orientation by being tenuous, casual, and generally ineffectual.

The problem, although it may be complicated by the fact, is made more interesting because there is no one correct view, no one learning theory that is superior in every way over all others. It would seem that those who are knowledgeable of the various approaches to learning, and who have either adopted one of the competing theories, or who have constructed their own theory, are better equipped to be successful teachers. It is not possible here to delve as deeply into a study of learning theories as those who plan to enter the teaching profession ought to do, but it would be an oversight to neglect any reference to them. It is suggested that the student refer to Ernest R. Hilgard's *Theories of Learning*[41] for a detailed study of the eight most prominent current learning theories in the United States. For our present purpose we shall sketch the development of learning theories and characterize the two main groups of current theories.

Of the three learning theories that developed previous to the twentieth century and still have considerable influence on contemporary education, the first, *mental discipline,* has its beginning in the traditional philosophies of Plato and Aristotle. *Mental discipline* is associated with rationalism which posits reason as the source of knowledge. According to this theory of learning, education is thought of as the process of disciplining or training minds. The philosophical view assigns the mind substance a position that is dominant in the mind-body dualism. It should be noted that there are at least two versions of mental discipline—*classicism,* and *faculty psychology*.

The second major position that developed before the twentieth century is called *natural unfoldment*. According to this theory, education is

---

[41] Ernest R. Hilgard, *Theories of Learning* (New York: Appleton-Century-Crofts, 1956).

thought to be the developing of man's nature in a corruption-free environment, as all men are thought to be naturally good. This view is associated with Jean J. Rousseau (1712–1778), and later with Heinrich Pestalozzi (1746–1827), and Friedrich Froebel (1782–1852). The overall philosophical position is called romantic naturalism, and it is akin to rationalism in that both positions maintain an inborn human nature.

A third position, which is a good deal more complicated than the other two, is called *apperception*. *Apperception* is idea-centered, and education is thought of as the process of associating new ideas with old ones. It is based on the premise that there are no innate ideas, and that everything an individual knows comes from outside of the individual. We will see in the next chapter that it was John Locke who challenged the idea of innate faculties or ideas and that it was he who developed the *tabula rasa* (blank tablet) theory which gave rise to the learning theory developed by Johann Friedrich Herbart (1776–1841).

All of the early learning theories can be identified with nonexperimental psychologies of learning, but the theories that have developed in the twentieth century are well supported by experimentation. For our present purpose, we have noted that we can classify the contemporary learning theories into two families, each being related to a particular school of psychology. These are the S-R associationistic family and the cognitive-field family. The S-R associationists focus upon observable and measurable behavior, both external and internal, as a means of changing behavior. They view man as being a passive creature in a determining environment, and they embrace a mechanistic theory of learning. Reality and existence are treated as being identical. The physical world that is experienced by the individual is thought to be more or less what it appears to be and independent of an observer to give it character. It is further assumed that the world is governed by natural laws and that the basic principle of the universe is cause and effect. Teaching practices recommend that chosen subject matter reflects those things which will be useful in contemporary society.

The other group of learning theories comes under the general heading of the *cognitive-field* family. Theorists in this grouping view learning as a process of reorganizing perceptual or cognitive fields. They see man as a purposive being, interacting with a psychological environment, and view education as the process of changing our understanding of problems and situations. The *cognitive-field* family is associated with systematic relativism, that is with pragmatism, experimentalism, and instrumentalism. It is thought that a thing derives its qualities from its relationship with other things, and in this manner the distinction is made between reality and existence.

While this brief characterization of the primary differences between the two major groups of learning theories may appear to be an over-simplification, it does indicate the variety of suggested approaches to the learning process. Even though no one of the theories claims to solve all practical learning problems, each merits the consideration of the prospective teacher for a number of reasons. First, the various learning theories can provide the neophyte with a vocabulary and with a conceptual framework for understanding those things that are observable. Second, they can lead to a consideration of the variables that are important for finding solutions. Finally, they can serve as a base for one's learning theory that will be instrumental for the educational goal of intelligent action in society.

Intelligent Action

If we think of intelligence as being the effectiveness with which one operates in various life situations, it would seem that intelligent action is the ultimate goal of all education, regardless of one's philosophical view or psychological orientation. Although we would expect to find as many different views of the particulars that constitute intelligent action as we do of the best ways in which to achieve educational goals, it is generally agreed that there are two principal ways of knowing something and that both are essential to adjustment in the social, economic, and intellectual spheres of everyday life. These different mental operations have been called "knowing that" and "knowing how" by Gilbert Ryle,[42] one of the group of philosophers, such as R. M. Hare, A. J. Ayer, and Israel Scheffler, who have been concerned in one way or another with the distinction.

When we speak of "knowing that," we are talking about propositional knowledge, or having knowledge of something that is actually the case. This sort of knowledge can be, but is not necessarily, obtained on a memory-level. Ideally, it proceeds from the memory-level through the understanding-level to the reflection-level, which leads to further understanding or independent insights. Even though a certain amount of memory work is essential to additional knowledge, knowledge that stops at the memory-level has far less relation to intelligent action than it does to habitual or mechanical action.

The second category of knowledge, according to Ryle, is "knowing how," which is a skill knowledge, the knowledge of how to do something. There are those who argue that the two are not distinct categories, as they claim that "knowing that" is only a special case of the category of "knowing how." There are also those who maintain that "knowing how" is the key to intelligent action, but it seems far more reasonable that both categories are essential, as it is the category of "knowing that" which gives supportive reasons for one's actions which is one of the qualifications of intelligent action. If, in addition to this qualification, we think of intelligent action as that conscious behavior which follows a logically thought out process toward goals that are desirable, it seems fairly obvious that it is necessary for the individual to "know how" and to "know that" in order to act intelligently in society.

---

[42] Gilbert Ryle, *The Concept of Mind* (London: Hutchinson House, 1949).

ARISTOTLE

Ethics and Politics (Selections)*

Since Aristotle left no definitive work on education and teaching, we must look to several of his writings in order to glean his views about education. According to Aristotle, the goal of education should be to produce virtuous citizens, for the individual must necessarily function in relation to others within the context of the entire society. Therefore, education should be a function of the state and in consonance with the political system of the state. The following selections from the Ethics and Politics *provide insights into the structure of man's intelligence, according to Aristotle, and particular note should be made of his discussion of the calculative and scientific faculties of the individual. Although Aristotle believed pure reasoning and intuition to be the only avenues to absolute truth, he differed from Plato in his emphasis upon sense perception. He also had a greater concern than Plato for the actual conditions of man and for what man* ought *to do in the "Community of Man," and we see that philosophy is more practical for Aristotle than it was for Plato. The selections that we have chosen from* Ethics and Politics *raise questions about the purpose in man, education, and the universe. Questions of good, character, and conduct all figure prominently in the selections, and it can be fruitful to explore the relation of these to educational aims and purposes. Other points of interest might be to compare Aristotle's description of intelligence with that of modern psychologists or to pursue the meaning of "liberal education," curriculum choices, and the nature of critical thinking.*

Ethics

Book VI

1   Since we have previously said that one ought to choose that which is intermediate, not the excess nor the defect,[1] and that the intermediate is determined by the dictates of the right rule,[2] let us discuss the nature of these dictates. In all the states of character we have mentioned,[3] as in all other matters, there is a mark to which the man who has the rule looks, and heightens or relaxes his activity accordingly, and there is a standard which determines the mean states which we say are intermediate between excess and defect, being in accordance with the right rule. But such a statement, though true, is by no means clear; for not only here but in all other pursuits which are objects of knowledge it is indeed true to say that we must not exert ourselves nor relax our efforts too much nor too little, but to an intermediate extent and as the right rule dictates;

* From *The Basic Works of Aristotle* (New York: Random House, Inc., 1941). By permission of Oxford University Press. Original source: Oxford University Press translation of Aristotle, ed. W. D. Ross.
1 1104ᵃ 11–27, 1106ᵃ 26–1107ᵃ 27.
2 1107ᵃ 1, Cf. 1103ᵇ 31, 1114ᵇ 29.
3 In iii. 6–v. 11.

but if a man had only this knowledge he would be none the wiser—e.g. we should not know what sort of medicines to apply to our body if some one were to say "all those which the medical art prescribes, and which agree with the practice of one who possesses the art." Hence it is necessary with regard to the states of the soul also not only that this true statement should be made, but also that it should be determined what is the right rule and what is the standard that fixes it.

We divided the virtues of the soul and said that some are virtues of character and others of intellect.[4] Now we have discussed in detail the moral virtues; with regard to the others let us express our view as follows, beginning with some remarks about the soul. We said before[5] that there are two parts of the soul—that which grasps a rule or rational principle, and the irrational; let us now draw a similar distinction within the part which grasps a rational principle. And let it be assumed that there are two parts which grasp a rational principle—one by which we contemplate the kind of things whose originative causes are invariable, and one by which we contemplate variable things; for where objects differ in kind the part of the soul answering to each of the two is different in kind, since it is in virtue of a certain likeness and kinship with their objects that they have the knowledge they have. Let one of these parts be called the scientific and the other the calculative; for to deliberate and to calculate are the same thing, but no one deliberates about the invariable. Therefore the calculative is one part of the faculty which grasps a rational principle. We must, then, learn what is the best state of each of these two parts; for this is the virtue of each.

2   The virtue of a thing is relative to its proper work. Now there are three things in the soul which control action and truth—sensation, reason, desire.

Of these sensation originates no action; this is plain from the fact that the lower animals have sensation but no share in action.

What affirmation and negation are in thinking, pursuit and avoidance are in desire; so that since moral virtue is a state of character concerned with choice, and choice is deliberate desire, therefore both the reasoning must be true and the desire right, if the choice is to be good, and the latter must pursue just what the former asserts. Now this kind of intellect and of truth is practical; of the intellect which is contemplative, not practical nor productive, the good and the bad state are truth and falsity respectively (for this is the work of everything intellectual); while of the part which is practical and intellectual the good state is truth in agreement with right desire.

The origin of action—its efficient, not its final cause—is choice, and that of choice is desire and reasoning with a view to an end. This is why choice cannot exist either without reason and intellect or without a moral state; for good action and its opposite cannot exist without a combination of intellect and character. Intellect itself, however, moves nothing, but only the intellect which aims at an end and is practical; for this rules the productive intellect as well, since every one who makes makes for an end, and that which is made is not an end in the unqualified sense (but only an end in a particular relation, and the end of a particular operation)—only that which is *done* is that; for good action is an end, and desire aims at this. Hence choice is either desiderative reason or ratiocinative desire, and such an origin of action is a man. (It is to be noted that

---

[4] 1103[a] 3–7.
[5] 1102[a] 26–8.

nothing that is past is an object of choice, e.g. no one chooses to have sacked Troy; for no one *deliberates* about the past, but about what is future and capable of being otherwise, while what is past is not capable of not having taken place; hence Agathon is right in saying

> For this alone is lacking even to God,
> To make undone things that have once been done.)

The work of both the intellectual parts, then, is truth. Therefore the states that are most strictly those in respect of which each of these parts will reach truth are the virtues of the two parts.

3   Let us begin, then, from the beginning, and discuss these states once more. Let it be assumed that the states by virtue of which the soul possesses truth by way of affirmation or denial are five in number, i.e. art, scientific knowledge, practical wisdom, philosophic wisdom, intuitive reason; we do not include judgment and opinion because in these we may be mistaken.

Now what *scientific knowledge* is, if we are to speak exactly and not follow mere similarities, is plain from what follows. We all suppose that what we know is not even capable of being otherwise; of things capable of being otherwise we do not know, when they have passed outside our observation, whether they exist or not. Therefore the object of scientific knowledge is of necessity. Therefore it is eternal: for things that are of necessity in the unqualified sense are all eternal; and things that are eternal are ungenerated and imperishable. Again, every science is thought to be capable of being taught, and its object of being learned. And all teaching starts from what is already known, as we maintain in the *Analytics*[6] also; for it proceeds sometimes through induction and sometimes by syllogism. Now induction is the starting-point which knowledge even of the universal presupposes, while syllogism proceeds *from* universals. There are therefore starting-points from which syllogism proceeds, which are not reached by syllogism; it is therefore by induction that they are acquired. Scientific knowledge is, then, a state of capacity to demonstrate, and has the other limiting characteristics which we specify in the *Analytics*;[7] for it is when a man believes in a certain way and the starting-points are known to him that he has scientific knowledge, since if they are not better known to him than the conclusion, he will have his knowledge only incidentally.

Let this, then, be taken as our account of scientific knowledge.

4   In the variable are included both things made and things done; making and acting are different (for their nature we treat even the discussions outside our school as reliable); so that the reasoned state of capacity to act is different from the reasoned state of capacity to make. Hence too they are not included one in the other; for neither is acting making nor is making acting. Now since architecture is an art and is essentially a reasoned state of capacity to make, and there is neither any art that is not such a state nor any such state that is not an art, *art* is identical with a state of capacity to make, involving a true course of reasoning. All art is concerned with coming into being, i.e. with contriving and considering how something may come into being which is capable of either

---

[6] *An. Post.* 71ª 1.
[7] Ib.ᵇ 9–23.

being or not being, and whose origin is in the maker and not in the thing made; for art is concerned neither with things that are, or come into being, by necessity, nor with things that do so in accordance with nature (since these have their origin in themselves). Making and acting being different, art must be a matter of making, not of acting. And in a sense chance and art are concerned with the same objects; as Agathon says, "art loves chance and chance loves art." Art, then, as has been said,[8] is a state concerned with making, involving a true course of reasoning, and lack of art on the contrary is a state concerned with making, involving a false course of reasoning; both are concerned with the variable.

5   Regarding *practical wisdom* we shall get at the truth by considering who are the persons we credit with it. Now it is thought to be the mark of a man of practical wisdom to be able to deliberate well about what is good and expedient for himself, not in some particular respect, e.g. about what sorts of thing conduce to health or to strength, but about what sorts of thing conduce to the good life in general. This is shown by the fact that we credit men with practical wisdom in some particular respect when they have calculated well with a view to some good end which is one of those that are not the object of any art. It follows that in the general sense also the man who is capable of deliberating has practical wisdom. Now no one deliberates about things that are invariable, nor about things that it is impossible for him to do. Therefore, since scientific knowledge involves demonstration, but there is no demonstration of things whose first principles are variable (for all such things might actually be otherwise), and since it is impossible to deliberate about things that are of necessity, practical wisdom cannot be scientific knowledge nor art; not science because that which can be done is capable of being otherwise, not art because action and making are different kinds of thing. The remaining alternative, then, is that it is a true and reasoned state of capacity to act with regard to the things that are good or bad for man. For while making has an end other than itself, action cannot; for good action itself is its end. It is for this reason that we think Pericles and men like him have practical wisdom, viz. because they can see what is good for themselves and what is good for men in general; we consider that those can do this who are good at managing households or states. (This is why we call temperance (*sophrosyne*) by this name; we imply that it preserves one's practical wisdom (*sodsousa ten phronesin*). Now what it preserves is a judgment of the kind we have described. For it is not any and every judgment that pleasant and painful objects destroy and pervert, e.g. the judgment that the triangle has or has not its angles equal to two right angles, but only judgments about what is to be done. For the originating causes of the things that are done consist in the end at which they are aimed; but the man who has been ruined by pleasure or pain forthwith fails to see any such originating cause—to see that for the sake of this or because of this he ought to choose and do whatever he chooses and does; for vice is destructive of the originating cause of action.)

Practical wisdom, then, must be a reasoned and true state of capacity to act with regard to human goods. But further, while there is such a thing as excellence in art, there is no such thing as excellence in practical wisdom; and in art he who errs willingly is preferable, but in practical wisdom, as in the virtues, he is the reverse. Plainly, then, practical wisdom is a virtue and not an

---

[8] I. 9.

art. There being two parts of the soul that can follow a course of reasoning, it must be the virtue of one of the two, i.e. of that part which forms opinions; for opinion is about the variable and so is practical wisdom. But yet it is not only a reasoned state; this is shown by the fact that a state of that sort may be forgotten but practical wisdom cannot.

6   Scientific knowledge is judgment about things that are universal and necessary, and the conclusions of demonstration, and all scientific knowledge, follow from first principles (for scientific knowledge involves apprehension of a rational ground). This being so, the first principle from which what is scientifically known follows cannot be an object of scientific knowledge, of art, or of practical wisdom; for that which can be scientifically known can be demonstrated, and art and practical wisdom deal with things that are variable. Nor are these first principles the objects of philosophic wisdom, for it is a mark of the philosopher to have *demonstration* about some things. If, then, the states of mind by which we have truth and are never deceived about things invariable or even variable are scientific knowledge, practical wisdom, philosophic wisdom, and intuitive reason, and it cannot be any of the three (i.e. practical wisdom, scientific knowledge, or philosophic wisdom), the remaining alternative is that it is *intuitive reason* that grasps the first principles.

7   *Wisdom* (1) in the arts we ascribe to their most finished exponents, e.g. to Phidias as a sculptor and to Polyclitus as a maker of portrait-statues, and here we mean nothing by wisdom except excellence in art; but (2) we think that some people are wise in general, not in some particular field or in any other limited respect, as Homer says in the *Margites,*

> Him did the gods make neither a digger nor yet a ploughman
> Nor wise in anything else.

Therefore wisdom must plainly be the most finished of the forms of knowledge. It follows that the wise man must not only know what follows from the first principles, but must also possess truth about the first principles. Therefore wisdom must be intuitive reason combined with scientific knowledge—scientific knowledge of the highest objects which has received as it were its proper completion.
   Of the highest objects, we say; for it would be strange to think that the art of politics, or practical wisdom, is the best knowledge, since man is not the best thing in the world. Now if what is healthy or good is different for men and for fishes, but what is white or straight is always the same, any one would say that what is wise is the same but what is practically wise is different; for it is to that which observes well the various matters concerning itself that one ascribes practical wisdom, and it is to this that one will entrust such matters. This is why we say that some even of the lower animals have practical wisdom, viz. those which are found to have a power of foresight with regard to their own life. It is evident also that philosophic wisdom and the art of politics cannot be the same; for if the state of mind concerned with a man's own interests is to be called philosophic wisdom, there will be many philosophic wisdoms; there will not be one concerned with the good of all animals (any more than there is one

art of medicine for all existing things), but a different philosophic wisdom about the good of each species.

But if the argument be that man is the best of the animals, this makes no difference; for there are other things much more divine in their nature even than man, e.g., most conspicuously, the bodies of which the heavens are framed. From what has been said it is plain, then, that philosophic wisdom is scientific knowledge, combined with intuitive reason, of the things that are highest by nature. This is why we say Anaxagoras, Thales, and men like them have philosophic but not practical wisdom, when we see them ignorant of what is to their own advantage, and why we say that they know things that are remarkable, admirable, difficult, and divine, but useless; viz. because it is not human goods that they seek.

Practical wisdom on the other hand is concerned with things human and things about which it is possible to deliberate; for we say this is above all the work of the man of practical wisdom, to deliberate well, but no one deliberates about things invariable, nor about things which have not an end, and that a good that can be brought about by action. The man who is without qualification good at deliberating is the man who is capable of aiming in accordance with calculation at the best for man of things attainable by action. Nor is practical wisdom concerned with universals only—it must also recognize the particulars; for it is practical, and practice is concerned with particulars. This is why some who do not know, and especially those who have experience, are more practical than others who know; for if a man knew that light meats are digestible and wholesome, but did not know which sorts of meat are light, he would not produce health, but the man who knows that chicken is wholesome is more likely to produce health.

Now practical wisdom is concerned with action; therefore one should have both forms of it, or the latter in preference to the former. But of practical as of philosophic wisdom there must be a controlling kind.

8 Political wisdom and practical wisdom are the same state of mind, but their essence is not the same. Of the wisdom concerned with the city, the practical wisdom which plays a controlling part is legislative wisdom, while that which is related to this as particulars to their universal is known by the general name "political wisdom"; this has to do with action and deliberation, for a decree is a thing to be carried out in the form of an individual act. This is why the exponents of this art are alone said to "take part in politics"; for these alone "do things" as manual labourers "do things."

Practical wisdom also is identified especially with that form of it which is concerned with a man himself—with the individual; and this is known by the general name "practical wisdom"; of the other kinds one is called household management, another legislation, the third politics, and of the latter one part is called deliberative and the other judicial. Now knowing what is good for oneself will be one kind of knowledge, but it is very different from the other kinds; and the man who knows and concerns himself with his own interests is thought to have practical wisdom, while politicians are thought to be busybodies; hence the words of Euripides,

> But how could I be wise, who might at ease,
> Numbered among the army's multitude,

Have had an equal share? . . .
For those who aim too high and do too much . . . .

Those who think thus seek their own good, and consider that one ought to do so. From this opinion, then, has come the view that such men have practical wisdom; yet perhaps one's own good cannot exist without household management, nor without a form of government. Further, how one should order one's own affairs is not clear and needs inquiry.

What has been said is confirmed by the fact that while young men become geometricians and mathematicians and wise in matters like these, it is thought that a young man of practical wisdom cannot be found. The cause is that such wisdom is concerned not only with universals but with particulars, which become familiar from experience, but a young man has no experience, for it is length of time that gives experience; indeed one might ask this question too, why a boy may become a mathematician, but not a philosopher or a physicist. Is it because the objects of mathematics exist by abstraction, while the first principles of these other subjects come from experience, and because young men have no conviction about the latter but merely use the proper language, while the essence of mathematical objects is plain enough to them?

Further, error in deliberation may be either about the universal or about the particular; we may fail to know either that all water that weighs heavy is bad, or that this particular water weighs heavy.

That practical wisdom is not scientific knowledge is evident; for it is, as has been said,[9] concerned with the ultimate particular fact, since the thing to be done is of this nature. It is opposed, then, to intuitive reason; for intuitive reason is of the limiting premises, for which no reason can be given, while practical wisdom is concerned with the ultimate particular, which is the object not of scientific knowledge but of perception—not the perception of qualities peculiar to one sense but a perception akin to that by which we perceive that the particular figure before us is a triangle; for in that direction as well as in that of the major premise there will be a limit. But this is rather perception than practical wisdom, though it is another kind of perception than that of the qualities peculiar to each sense.

9 There is a difference between inquiry and deliberation; for deliberation is inquiry into a particular kind of thing. We must grasp the nature of excellence in deliberation as well—whether it is a form of scientific knowledge, or opinion, or skill in conjecture, or some other kind of thing. *Scientific knowledge* it is not; for men do not inquire about the things they know about, but good deliberation is a kind of deliberation, and he who deliberates inquires and calculates. Nor is it *skill in conjecture;* for this both involves no reasoning and is something that is quick in its operation, while men deliberate a long time, and they say that one should carry out quickly the conclusions of one's deliberation, but should deliberate slowly. Again, *readiness of mind* is different from excellence in deliberation; it is a sort of skill in conjecture. Nor again is excellence in deliberation *opinion* of any sort. But since the man who deliberates badly makes a mistake, while he who deliberates well does so correctly, excellence in deliberation is clearly a kind of correctness, but neither of knowledge nor of opinion; for

<hr>

[9] 1141[b] 14–22.

there is no such thing as correctness of knowledge (since there is no such thing as error of knowledge), and correctness of opinion is truth; and at the same time everything that is an object of opinion is already determined. But again excellence in deliberation involves reasoning. The remaining alternative, then, is that it is *correctness of thinking;* for this is not yet assertion, since, while even opinion is not inquiry but has reached the stage of assertion, the man who is deliberating, whether he does so well or ill, is searching for something and calculating.

But excellence in deliberation is a certain correctness of deliberation; hence we must first inquire what deliberation is and what it is about. And, there being more than one kind of correctness, plainly excellence in deliberation is not any and every kind; for (1) the incontinent man and the bad man, if he is clever, will reach as a result of his calculation what he sets before himself, so that he will have deliberated correctly, but he will have got for himself a great evil. Now to have deliberated well is thought to be a good thing; for it is this kind of correctness of deliberation that is excellence in deliberation, viz. that which tends to attain what is good. But (2) it is possible to attain even good by a false syllogism, and to attain what one ought to do but not by the right means, the middle term being false; so that this too is not yet excellence in deliberation— this state in virtue of which one attains what one ought but not by the right means. Again (3) it is possible to attain it by long deliberation while another man attains it quickly. Therefore in the former case we have not yet got excellence in deliberation, which is rightness with regard to the expedient—rightness in respect both of the end, the manner, and the time. (4) Further it is possible to have deliberated well either in the unqualified sense or with reference to a particular end. Excellence in deliberation in the unqualified sense, then, is that which succeeds with reference to what is the end in the unqualified sense, and excellence in deliberation in a particular sense is that which succeeds relatively to a particular end. If, then, it is characteristic of men of practical wisdom to have deliberated well, excellence in deliberation will be correctness with regard to what conduces to the end of which practical wisdom is the true apprehension.

10   Understanding, also, and goodness of understanding, in virtue of which men are said to be men of understanding or of good understanding, are neither entirely the same as opinion or scientific knowledge (for at that rate all men would have been men of understanding), nor are they one of the particular sciences, such as medicine, the science of things connected with health, or geometry, the science of spatial magnitudes. For understanding is neither about things that are always and are unchangeable, nor about any and every one of the things that come into being, but about things which may become subjects of questioning and deliberation. Hence it is about the same objects as practical wisdom; but understanding and practical wisdom are not the same. For practical wisdom issues commands, since its end is what ought to be done or not to be done; but understanding only judges. (Understanding is identical with goodness of understanding, men of understanding with men of good understanding.) Now understanding is neither the having nor the acquiring of practical wisdom; but as learning is called understanding when it means the exercise of the faculty of knowledge, so "understanding" is applicable to the exercise of the faculty of opinion for the purpose of judging of what some one else says about matters with which practical wisdom is concerned—and of judging soundly; for "well"

and "soundly" are the same thing. And from this has come the use of the name "understanding" in virtue of which men are said to be "of good understanding," viz. from the application of the word to the grasping of scientific truth; for we often call such grasping understanding.

Politics

Book VIII

1   No one will doubt that the legislator should direct his attention above all to the education of youth; for the neglect of education does harm to the constitution. The citizen should be moulded to suit the form of government under which he lives.[1] For each government has a peculiar character which originally formed and which continues to preserve it. The character of democracy creates democracy, and the character of oligarchy creates oligarchy; and always the better the character, the better the government.

Again, for the exercise of any faculty or art a previous training and habituation are required; clearly therefore for the practice of virtue. And since the whole city has one end, it is manifest that education should be one and the same for all, and that it should be public, and not private—not as at present, when every one looks after his own children separately, and gives them separate instruction of the sort which he thinks best; the training in things which are of common interest should be the same for all. Neither must we suppose that any one of the citizens belongs to himself, for they all belong to the state, and are each of them a part of the state, and the care of each part is inseparable from the care of the whole. In this particular as in some others the Lacedaemonians are to be praised, for they take the greatest pains about their children, and make education the business of the state.[2]

2   That education should be regulated by law and should be an affair of state is not to be denied, but what should be the character of this public education, and how young persons should be educated, are questions which remain to be considered. As things are, there is disagreement about the subjects. For mankind are by no means agreed about the things to be taught, whether we look to virtue or the best life. Neither is it clear whether education is more concerned with intellectual or with moral virtue. The existing practice is perplexing; no one knows on what principle we should proceed—should the useful in life, or should virtue, or should the higher knowledge, be the aim of our training; all three opinions have been entertained. Again, about the means there is no agreement; for different persons, starting with different ideas about the nature of virtue, naturally disagree about the practice of it. There can be no doubt that children should be taught those useful things which are really necessary, but not all useful things; for occupations are divided into liberal and illiberal; and to young children should be imparted only such kinds of knowledge as will be useful to them without vulgarizing them. And any occupation, art, or science, which makes the body or soul or mind of the freeman less fit for the practice or exercise of virtue, is vulgar; wherefore we call those arts vulgar which tend to deform the body, and likewise all paid employments, for they absorb and degrade the mind. There are also some liberal arts quite proper for a freeman to

[1] Cp. v. 1310ᵃ 12–36.
[2] Cp. *Nic. Eth.* x. 1180ᵃ 24.

acquire, but only in a certain degree, and if he attend to them too closely, in order to attain perfection in them, the same evil effects will follow. The object also which a man sets before him makes a great difference; if he does or learns anything for his own sake[3] or for the sake of his friends, or with a view to excellence, the action will not appear illiberal; but if done for the sake of others, the very same action will be thought menial and servile. The received subjects of instruction, as I have already remarked,[4] are partly of a liberal and partly of an illiberal character.

3   The customary branches of education are in number four; they are—(1) reading and writing, (2) gymnastic exercises, (3) music, to which is sometimes added (4) drawing. Of these, reading and writing and drawing are regarded as useful for the purposes of life in a variety of ways, and gymnastic exercises are thought to infuse courage. Concerning music a doubt may be raised—in our own day most men cultivate it for the sake of pleasure, but originally it was included in education, because nature herself, as has been often said,[5] requires that we should be able, not only to work well, but to use leisure well; for, as I must repeat once again, the first principle of all action is leisure. Both are required, but leisure is better than occupation and is its end; and therefore the question must be asked, what ought we to do when at leisure? Clearly we ought not to be amusing ourselves, for then amusement would be the end of life. But if this is inconceivable, and amusement is needed more amid serious occupations than at other times (for he who is hard at work has need of relaxation, and amusement gives relaxation, whereas occupation is always accompanied with exertion and effort) we should introduce amusements only at suitable times, and they should be our medicines, for the emotion which they create in the soul is a relaxation, and from the pleasure we obtain rest. But leisure of itself gives pleasure and happiness and enjoyment of life, which are experienced, not by the busy man, but by those who have leisure. For he who is occupied has in view some end which he has not attained; but happiness is an end, since all men deem it to be accompanied with pleasure and not with pain. This pleasure, however, is regarded differently by different persons, and varies according to the habit of individuals; the pleasure of the best man is the best, and springs from the noblest sources. It is clear then that there are branches of learning and education which we must study merely with a view to leisure spent in intellectual activity, and these are to be valued for their own sake; whereas those kinds of knowledge which are useful in business are to be deemed necessary, and exist for the sake of other things. And therefore our fathers admitted music into education, not on the ground either of its necessity or utility, for it is not necessary, nor indeed useful in the same manner as reading and writing, which are useful in money-making, in the management of a household, in the acquisition of knowledge and in political life, nor like drawing, useful for a more correct judgment of the works of artists, nor again like gymnastic, which gives health and strength; for neither of these is to be gained from music. There remains, then, the use of music for intellectual enjoyment in leisure; which is in fact evidently the reason of its introduction, this being one of the ways in which it is thought that a freeman should pass his leisure; as Homer says—

---

3 Cp. iii. 1277[b] 3.
4 [a]39–[b]3.
5 ii. 1271[a] 41 sqq., vii. 1333[a] 16–1334[b] 3; *N. Eth.* x 6.

But he who alone should be called[6] to the pleasant feast,

and afterwards he speaks of others whom he describes as inviting

The bard who would delight them all.[7]

And in another place Odysseus says there is no better way of passing life than when men's hearts are merry and

The banqueters in the hall, sitting in order, hear the voice of the minstrel.[8]

It is evident, then, that there is a sort of education in which parents should train their sons; not as being useful or necessary, but because it is liberal or noble. Whether this is of one kind only, or of more than one, and if so, what they are, and how they are to be imparted, must hereafter be determined.[9] Thus much we are now in a position to say, that the ancients witness to us; for their opinion may be gathered from the fact that music is one of the received and traditional branches of education. Further, it is clear that children should be instructed in some useful things—for example, in reading and writing—not only for their usefulness, but also because many other sorts of knowledge are acquired through them. With a like view they may be taught drawing, not to prevent their making mistakes in their own purchases, or in order that they may not be imposed upon in the buying or selling of articles, but perhaps rather because it makes them judges of the beauty of the human form. To be always seeking after the useful does not become free and exalted souls.[10] Now it is clear that in education practice must be used before theory, and the body be trained before the mind; and therefore boys should be handed over to the trainer, who creates in them the proper habit of body, and to the wrestling-master, who teaches them their exercises.

4 Of those states which in our own day seem to take the greatest care of children, some aim at producing in them an athletic habit, but they only injure their forms and stunt their growth. Although the Lacedaemonians have not fallen into this mistake, yet they brutalize their children by laborious exercises which they think will make them courageous. But in truth, as we have often repeated,[11] education should not be exclusively, or principally, directed to this end. And even if we suppose the Lacedaemonians to be right in their end, they do not attain it. For among barbarians and among animals courage is found associated, not with the greatest ferocity, but with a gentle and lion-like temper. There are many races who are ready enough to kill and eat men, such as the Achaeans and Heniochi, who both live about the Black Sea;[12] and there are other mainland tribes, as bad or worse, who all live by plunder, but have no courage. It is notorious that the Lacedaemonians themselves, while they alone

---

6 The line does not occur in our text of Homer, but in Aristotle's text it probably came instead of, or after, *Od.* xvii. 383.
7 *Od.* xvii. 385.
8 *Od.* ix. 7.
9 An unfulfilled promise.
10 Cp. Plato, *Rep.* vii. 525 ff.
11 ii. 1271ᵃ 41–ᵇ10, vii. 1333ᵇ 5 sqq., 1334ᵃ 40 sqq.
12 Cp. *N. Eth.* vii. 1148ᵇ 21.

were assiduous in their laborious drill, were superior to others, but now they are beaten both in war and gymnastic exercises. For their ancient superiority did not depend on their mode of training their youth, but only on the circumstance that they trained them when their only rivals did not. Hence we may infer that what is noble, not what is brutal, should have the first place; no wolf or other wild animal will face a really noble danger; such dangers are for the brave man.[13] And parents who devote their children to gymnastics while they neglect their necessary education, in reality vulgarize them; for they make them useful to the art of statesmanship in one quality only, and even in this the argument proves them to be inferior to others. We should judge the Lacedaemonians not from what they have been, but from what they are; for now they have rivals who compete with their education; formerly they had none.

It is an admitted principle, that gymnastic exercises should be employed in education, and that for children they should be of a lighter kind, avoiding severe diet or painful toil, lest the growth of the body be impaired. The evil of excessive training in early years is strikingly proved by the example of the Olympic victors; for not more than two or three of them have gained a prize both as boys and as men; their early training and severe gymnastic exercises exhausted their constitutions. When boyhood is over, three years should be spent in other studies; the period of life which follows may then be devoted to hard exercise and strict diet. Men ought not to labor at the same time with their minds and with their bodies;[14] for the two kinds of labor are opposed to one another; the labor of the body impedes the mind, and the labor of the mind the body.

5   Concerning music there are some questions which we have already raised;[15] these we may now resume and carry further; and our remarks will serve as a prelude to this or any other discussion of the subject. It is not easy to determine the nature of music, or why any one should have a knowledge of it. Shall we say, for the sake of amusement and relaxation, like sleep or drinking, which are not good in themselves, but are pleasant, and at the same time "make care to cease," as Euripides says? And for this end men also appoint music, and make use of all three alike—sleep, drinking, music—to which some add dancing. Or shall we argue that music conduces to virtue, on the ground that it can form our minds and habituate us to true pleasures as our bodies are made by gymnastic to be of a certain character? Or shall we say that it contributes to the enjoyment of leisure and mental cultivation, which is a third alternative? Now obviously youths are not to be instructed with a view to their amusement, for learning is no amusement, but is accompanied with pain. Neither is intellectual enjoyment suitable to boys of that age, for it is the end, and that which is imperfect cannot attain the perfect or end. But perhaps it may be said that boys learn music for the sake of the amusement which they will have when they are grown up. If so, why should they learn themselves, and not, like the Persian and Median kings, enjoy the pleasure and instruction which is derived from hearing others? (for surely persons who have made music the business and profession of their lives will be better performers than those who practice only long enough to learn). If they must learn music, on the same principle they should learn cook-

---

13 Cp. *N. Eth.* iii. 1115ᵃ 20.
14 Cp. Plato, *Rep.* vii. 537 ʙ.
15 1337ᵇ 27–1338ᵃ 30.

ery, which is absurd. And even granting that music may form the character, the objection still holds: why should we learn ourselves? Why cannot we attain true pleasure and form a correct judgment from hearing others, like the Lacedaemonians?—for they, without learning music, nevertheless can correctly judge, as they say, of good and bad melodies. Or again, if music should be used to promote cheerfulness and refined intellectual enjoyment, the objection still remains —why should we learn ourselves instead of enjoying the performances of others? We may illustrate what we are saying by our conception of the Gods; for in the poets Zeus does not himself sing or play on the lyre. Nay, we call professional performers vulgar; no freeman would play or sing unless he were intoxicated or in jest. But these matters may be left for the present.[16]

The first question is whether music is or is not to be a part of education. Of the three things mentioned in our discussion, which does it produce?—education or amusement or intellectual enjoyment, for it may be reckoned under all three, and seems to share in the nature of all of them. Amusement is for the sake of relaxation, and relaxation is of necessity sweet, for it is the remedy of pain caused by toil: and intellectual enjoyment is universally acknowledged to contain an element not only of the noble but of the pleasant, for happiness is made up of both. All men agree that music is one of the pleasantest things, whether with or without song; as Musaeus says,

Song is to mortals of all things the sweetest.

Hence and with good reason it is introduced into social gatherings and entertainments, because it makes the hearts of men glad: so that on this ground alone we may assume that the young ought to be trained in it. For innocent pleasures are not only in harmony with the perfect end of life, but they also provide relaxation. And whereas men rarely attain the end, but often rest by the way and amuse themselves, not only with a view to a further end, but also for the pleasure's sake, it may be well at times to let them find a refreshment in music. It sometimes happens that men make amusement the end, for the end probably contains some element of pleasure, though not any ordinary or lower pleasure; but they mistake the lower for the higher, and in seeking for the one find the other, since every pleasure has a likeness to the end of action.[17] For the end is not eligible for the sake of any future good, nor do the pleasures which we have described exist for the sake of any future good but of the past, that is to say, they are the alleviation of past toils and pains. And we may infer this to be the reason why men seek happiness from these pleasures.

But music is pursued, not only as an alleviation of past toil, but also as providing recreation. And who can say whether, having this use, it may not also have a nobler one? In addition to this common pleasure, felt and shared in by all (for the pleasure given by music is natural, and therefore adapted to all ages and characters), may it not have also some influence over the character and the soul? It must have such an influence if characters are affected by it. And that they are so affected is proved in many ways, and not least by the power which the songs of Olympus exercise; for beyond question they inspire enthusiasm; and enthusiasm is an emotion of the ethical part of the soul. Besides, when men hear imitations, even apart from the rhythms and tunes them-

---

[16] Cp. c. 6.
[17] Cp. *N. Eth.* vii. 1153[b] 33.

selves, their feelings move in sympathy. Since then music is a pleasure, and virtue consists in rejoicing and loving and hating aright, there is clearly nothing which we are so much concerned to acquire and to cultivate as the power of forming right judgments, and of taking delight in good dispositions and noble actions.[18] Rhythm and melody supply imitations of anger and gentleness, and also of courage and temperance, and of all the qualities contrary to these, and of the other qualities of character, which hardly fall short of the actual affections, as we know from our own experience, for in listening to such strains our souls undergo a change. The habit of feeling pleasure or pain at mere representations is not far removed from the same feeling about realities;[19] for example, if any one delights in the sight of a statue for its beauty only, it necessarily follows that the sight of the original will be pleasant to him. The objects of no other sense, such as taste or touch, have any resemblance to moral qualities; in visible objects there is only a little, for there are figures which are of a moral character, but only to a slight extent, and all do not participate in the feeling about them. Again, figures and colors are not imitations, but signs, of moral habits, indications which the body gives of states of feeling. The connection of them with morals is slight, but in so far as there is any, young men should be taught to look, not at the works of Pauson, but at those of Polygnotus,[20] or any other painter or sculptor who expresses moral ideas. On the other hand, even in mere melodies there is an imitation of character, for the musical modes differ essentially from one another, and those who hear them are differently affected by each. Some of them make men sad and grave, like the so-called Mixolydian, others enfeeble the mind, like the relaxed modes, another, again, produces a moderate and settled temper, which appears to be the peculiar effect of the Dorian; the Phrygian inspires enthusiasm. The whole subject has been well treated by philosophical writers[21] on this branch of education, and they confirm their arguments by facts. The same principles apply to rhythms;[22] some have a character of rest, others of motion, and of these latter again, some have a more vulgar, others a nobler movement. Enough has been said to show that music has a power of forming the character, and should therefore be introduced into the education of the young. The study is suited to the stage of youth, for young persons will not, if they can help, endure anything which is not sweetened by pleasure, and music has a natural sweetness. There seems to be in us a sort of affinity to musical modes and rhythms, which makes some philosophers say that the soul is a tuning, others, that it possesses tuning. . . .

[18] Cp. Plato, *Rep.* iii. 401, 402; *Laws,* ii. 659 C–E.
[19] Cp. Plato, *Rep.* iii. 395.
[20] Cp. *Poet.* 1448ª 5, 1450ª 26.
[21] Cp. *Rep.* 398 E sqq.
[22] *Rep.* iii. 399 E, 400.

/

CHAPTER IV
Empiricism and the Problem of Knowledge

Scientific advancements of the fifteenth and sixteenth centuries brought about the kinds of experimental investigations that frequently seemed to be in conflict with the metaphysical commitments and the religious orthodoxy of the ancient and medieval scholars. Among other changes, the scientific spirit which could not be suppressed, was responsible for quite a different approach to the problem of knowledge than had been possible according to the views of men such as Plato, Aristotle, St. Augustine, and Aquinas. Although there had been an intimate relation between reality and epistemological problems in the philosophical systems of these thinkers, their metaphysical commitments had conditioned the nature of their questions about knowledge. It was the scientific temper of the sixteenth century that prompted men to ask questions about *how* we know, and much of the twentieth century concern about the problems of knowledge stems from the searching analyses of men such as Francis Bacon (1561–1626), René Descartes (1596–1650), and John Locke (1632–1704).

Origins of a Philosophy of Empiricism

When, after the collapse of the Hellenic civilization, and the long "dark night of the soul" that followed, men finally gathered their forces in the sixteenth and seventeenth centuries for a new enterprise of thought at a new level of understanding, it was to the world of physical fact that they turned, casting off with a gesture of impatience the last lingering remnants of Greek rationalism that had survived in the systems of the medieval Schoolmen.[1]

Although there are elements of a scientific-empirical attitude in Aristotelianism, the philosophies of Descartes, Bacon, and Locke represent a new spirit in the history of philosophy. It is a spirit of freedom which rejects

[1] J. P. McKinney, *The Challenge of Reason* (Brisbane, Australia: The Mountain Press, 1950), p. 53.

155

155

such authoritarianism as Aquinas' attempt to harmonize reason and revelation by insisting that they both emanate from God. The medieval scholars had maintained that the intervention of God was necessary to imbue the discrete experiences of man with meaning, for without divine help man would be lost in a series of meaningless physical ordeals.

René Descartes, who has been credited with setting most of the philosophic problems of the modern period, replaced such extreme rationalism with the concept of innate ideas as a legitimate source of knowledge. However, the empiricism of Bacon and Locke was as opposed to this Cartesian concept as it was to early Greek and medieval rationalism. The empirical attitude that developed out of the scientific heritage which included Copernicus, Vesalius, Cardan, Galileo, and Newton, denied *a priori* knowledge and denied that man can reason beyond the natural world of sense perception to some other-world source of knowledge. The denial was shocking to those who believed implicitly in *a priori* universals, and who reasoned from self-evident principles without depending upon perceptual experiences. They could not reject a *transcendental* concept of knowledge for a *functional* concept which refers to things of this world for the prediction of future occurrences.

Thus, during the period in philosophical history that begins with Francis Bacon and René Descartes and continues into the eighteenth century, a period that is most often called the Age of Rationalism, both methods—rationalism and empiricism—flourished. Both had their beginnings in a reaction against medieval views, but the most influential views in contemporary philosophy are largely dependent for their beginnings upon the inductive methods developed by Bacon and Locke and upon the concept of knowledge that emphasizes sense experiences as legitimate avenues to understanding.

Francis Bacon (1561–1626)

Few men in history have left such an ambiguous portrait as the one left by Francis Bacon. Of noble birth, he was learned and witty. He held a number of high offices of the state—Solicitor General, Attorney General, Lord Keeper of the Great Seal, and Lord Chancellor. He received a number of high titles but, coincidental to his being created Viscount St. Albans in 1621, he was accused of bribery and was prohibited from ever again holding public office. (Bacon admitted that he had received gifts from parties whose cases were before him, which was a common practice at that time, but he insisted that his judgment was never influenced by the gifts.) Bacon was a scientific philosopher whose training was in the law and who lacked the credentials of either a scientist or a philosopher. In spite of his real contribution to modern philosophy he is most often ignored by historians in this regard. He has received far more attention from literary critics who speculate about the possibility that he may have authored some of the plays that are commonly credited to Shakespeare.

Bacon was dissatisfied with the scholastic systems. He deplored the preoccupation of the Schoolmen with traditional texts and clever rhetoric, to the exclusion of a direct study of the physical universe. He was especially firm in his disagreement with the Aquinian concept that the mind is at first like a clean tablet. Quite to the contrary, Bacon insisted that as a prerequisite to real learning, the mind must be cleansed of faulty impressions and traditional prejudices. He delineates these false opinions by dividing them into four groups: 1) the *idols of the tribe* which are those superstitions which we hold by nature; 2) the *idols of the cave* which are idiosyncrasies that arise from our personal history; 3) the *idols of the marketplace* which are the individual interpretations that come from education, from intercourse with others, and from reading; and 4) the *idols of the theatre* which are artificial fallacies that can be completely dispelled by sound logic. Bacon believed that the first three idols are a part of the human condition. Since they are natural faults, it is impossible to eradicate them completely from man's mind, but their hold can be loosened by calling attention to them. According to Bacon, the prevalent philosophical systems were like stage plays, and all belonged to the theatrical realm. He said that the three main schools of philosophy were the superstitious, the empirical, and the rational or sophistical. Bacon suggested that the way to *correct* reasoning is to reason from particulars to general principles, using an inductive form of reasoning.

Bacon firmly believed that he was ordained to inaugurate his reform of knowledge. He called his project the *Great Instauration of Human Control in the Universe*. There were to be six phases of the program, but Bacon was only able to complete the first part, "The Division of the Sciences," and to make some contribution to the next two parts. Probably the most far-reaching contribution that Bacon made was his idea that philosophy should be restricted to the study of nature which he believed to be the only legitimate source of knowledge. Bacon not only pointed the way to a view of the supernatural in terms of sensible appearances, but his method for the study and metaphysical interpretation of material nature was gradually expanded to be used, in principle, for the study of psychology and ethics. His empirical approach perhaps reached its fullest expression in the work of John Locke.

John Locke (1632–1704)

This, therefore, being my purpose, to inquire into the original, certainty, and extent of human knowledge; together with the grounds and degrees of belief, opinion, and assent; I shall not at present meddle with the physical consideration of the mind;[2]

---

[2] Sterling P. Lamprecht, ed., *Locke Selections* (New York: Charles Scribner's Sons, 1956), p. 90. From "Essay Concerning Human Understanding."

The above is a statement of purpose from Locke's *Essay Concerning Human Understanding,* a culmination of much of his thinking for a twenty-year period. His reputation would have been secure on the basis of this essay, but he did not rest until he had written the equally important *Two Treatises of Civil Government, On Toleration,* and *Some Thoughts Concerning Education.* There were other essays, but they are of relatively minor significance.

As we read about Locke's life, we can sympathize with his distaste for the regular school routine to which he was subjected, for the dullness of the scholastic method would certainly tend to stifle the creativity of such a student. Locke attended a grammar school in Bristol, then went to Westminster School in London. He finished his undergraduate work on a scholarship at Christ Church, Oxford. After his graduation he received a tutorship at Christ Church and later the post of lecturer in Greek and Rhetoric. Locke was first attracted to theology but turned to medicine and even practiced for a short time as an assistant to an Oxford M.D. He also exhibited an interest in physics, chemistry, and political problems, but was forced to limit his activities because of poor health and political difficulties which caused him to live for a time in Holland under an assumed name.

Locke's voluntary exile did not hinder his literary activity, and many of his ideas were shocking to his peers. *The Essay* was even condemned by Oxford authorities for its skepticism, and his polemic against innate ideas and principles disturbed all who accepted them as authority for their beliefs. It was left to history to judge *The Essay* as an outstanding contribution to man's knowledge and to recognize Locke as the inaugurator of the modern epistemological era which culminated in the philosophical system of Kant. Locke's repudiation of innate ideas was the first step in that direction.

The concept of innate ideas, the last resort of a dying authoritarianism, was one used to support all manner of belief. The concept was anathema to John Locke's philosophical views, and he set about to clear away all vestiges of a nonsensuous source of knowledge by a broadly conceived attack that centered upon no one thinker and on no one particular form of innatism. Kant later delivered the fatal blow to innatism with his discussion of the *a priori,* and the concept has not been held in any serious way since the late eighteenth century.

Locke began his attack by devoting the first book of *The Essay* to a delineation and analysis of the concept of innatism. The current belief was that there were certain principles, characteristics, and ideas that are inherent in the understanding of man. The belief was supported in a circular manner by the contention that the evidence of general agreement about certain principles substantiated their common origin. This sort of proof was utter nonsense to Locke, and he refuted it by showing that the principles did not exist in children, savages, or idiots. He did agree that the mind has a capacity for ideas and principles but insisted that the principles had to be learned.

Those who persisted in resorting to innate ideas countered by the claim that all men know and assent to the principles when they come to the use of reason. Locke agreed that people seem to exhibit an implicit knowledge of certain principles but insisted that such agreement was no more than an admission that the mind does have the capacity for comprehending and understanding. It seemed that the opposing views had reached an impasse, but Locke delivered the telling blow to the concept of innate ideas by making a distinction between universal feelings of appetite and innate principles of knowledge. Not being able to deny that all people do seem to exhibit similar feelings of hunger, love, hate, and fear, he allowed the possibility of universal feelings of appetite, but he maintained that if there were innate *cognitive* principles, all men would hold the same beliefs regarding matters of morality, virtue, and contracts. Obviously this was not the case, and Locke felt that his arguments against these principles of innateness cleared the way for his investigation and analysis in a properly structured manner, and on firm ground.

According to Locke, there are only two legitimate sources of ideas, the senses and reflection upon the material of the senses and reflection itself. The greatest source of ideas is sensation which conveys distinct perceptions of things into the mind. In this manner, sensible qualities such as color, softness, bitterness, and sweetness are produced. Reflection, the perception of the way our mind operates with the ideas it has received from the senses, can be called an internal sense. The ideas furnished by reflection are things such as thinking, doubting, believing, reasoning, and willing. Thus, there is no reason to believe that the soul could possibly think before it receives impressions by way of the senses. Locke suggests that doubters search their own thinking to discover, as he is sure they will, that all of their ideas have come either from their senses or from reflections upon material that has been provided by the senses. Again, Locke refers to the child to prove the point that ideas grow in proportion to sense experiences and that as reflection upon sensible ideas increases, the faculties of judging and reasoning are developed.

The foregoing also tells something about how the mind gains ideas from experience. As we have seen, Locke posited the mind to be a blank sheet on which perceptions are imprinted. Some impressions fade away almost as soon as they are received, and others leave their mark and are remembered. The remembered perceptions are material for reflection, for contrasting and comparing, for composing and arranging, and for abstracting which Locke says is unique to man. The senses are presented with simple ideas and complex ideas which are either *substances, modes,* or *relations.* Finally, recording all images in a passive manner, the mind cannot refuse ideas. A matter of preference comes into play during the mental activity of reflection after the initial impressions have been made. According to Locke, freedom of the will is not the power to choose but is the power to act according to choice which recognizes preferences. In other words, it is more accurate to speak of free *men* than it is to speak of free *wills.*

In order to avoid unnecessary confusion, it should be noted that Locke uses the word *idea* to signify the object of thought as well as thought itself. Quite early in *The Essay* he makes two statements regarding his use of the word. First, he uses *idea* to mean whatsoever is the object of the understanding when a man thinks. Second, *idea* expresses whatever is meant by *phantasm, notion, species* or whatever the mind is employed about in thinking. On the surface, this might appear to be a contradiction of terms, but it is rather that Locke makes *idea* a heavily-laden word. Once this is understood, we are ready to proceed to a consideration of Locke's intricate analysis of the various kinds of ideas which he uses as proof of his contention that all ideas originate in sensation and reflection. The analysis is basic to a consideration of Locke's view of the nature of knowledge.

The diagram on page 161 illustrates the complexity of ideas, and the epistemological dualism of Locke. This dualism will play an important role later in our discussion, but at this point it will suffice to indicate that the rectangular shape at the top of the sketch represents the materialistic— the things of this world—and the triangle that fans out from the base represents the mind where ideas are formed. Germane to the present discussion is the graphic example that all ideas, simple and complex, stem from substances and experiences in the physical world, and are dependent upon sensation and reflection. The most simple ideas are those that are dependent on only one of the senses, such as the idea of color which comes through the eye. When several senses function together, the ideas become less simple. One example is the idea of a flower which depends upon a combination of the sensations of sight, touch, smell, and resistance. The progression of ideas approaching the complex continues as mind reflects upon sensible ideas through the powers of perception and volition. The combination of sensation and reflection brings forth ideas such as pleasure, pain, and power. These are increasingly complex but are still in the realm of simple ideas.

Complex ideas depend upon the power of abstraction. The mind has the ability to combine, relate, separate, compare, and contrast simple ideas to form complex ones. It is this ability that allows man to rise above the level of the sensate and still remain in the sensate realm. Even the most abstract ideas, such as those of cause and effect, space, infinity and duration, are sensation bound. The question may be raised as to how this can be if we do not actually experience the substances in themselves. The answer lies in the fact that Locke divided the qualities of substance into the three different categories that are noted in the diagram. We gain an idea of the substance by experiencing the *qualities* of the substance. Still referring to the diagram, we see that all complex ideas come under one of the following headings: 1) things subsisting by themselves are termed *substances;* 2) those things which are dependent on substances are cate-

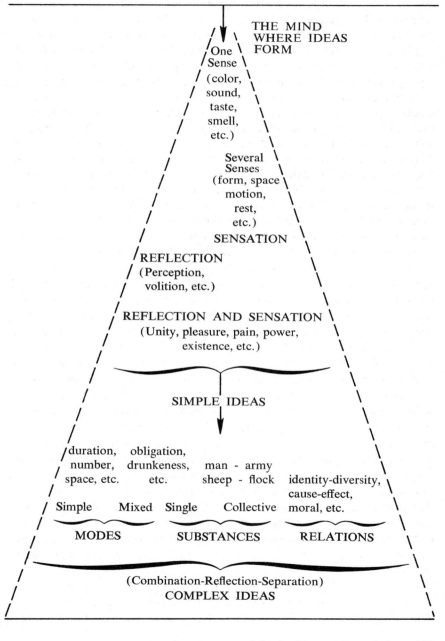

THE MATERIALISTIC THINGS OF THE WORLD

THE MIND
WHERE IDEAS
FORM

One
Sense
(color,
sound,
taste,
smell,
etc.)

Several
Senses
(form, space
motion,
rest,
etc.)

SENSATION

REFLECTION
(Perception,
volition, etc.)

REFLECTION AND SENSATION
(Unity, pleasure, pain, power,
existence, etc.)

SIMPLE IDEAS

duration,   obligation,
number,   drunkeness,   man - army
space, etc.   etc.   sheep - flock   identity-diversity,
                                              cause-effect,
Simple   Mixed   Single   Collective   moral, etc.

MODES   SUBSTANCES   RELATIONS

(Combination-Reflection-Separation)
COMPLEX IDEAS

gorized as *modes;* and 3) relations of various sorts are called *relations.*

All ideas are formed in the mind, and they remain private until an attempt is made to express them or to communicate them to others. At that time we are confronted with the ambiguity of the words that we use as symbols for our ideas. Words play such a significant role in our thinking that Locke devoted all of the third book of his *Essay* to this problem. His concern with these symbols is crucial to his theory of knowledge, and it foreshadows the twentieth century linguistic analysts. Locke's discussion of words revolves around the main point that, since they only stand for the ideas in the mind of the user, they have no metaphysical meaning. He makes a distinction between *nominal* essences, which rest upon experienced resemblances, and *real* essences, which stand for real groupings that are independent of our experience. Since the latter are purely hypothetical, Locke felt that they have no bearing upon knowledge. Locke stressed the point that understanding depends largely upon our use of language, and that so far as possible we should strive to eliminate imperfections and abuses of words. The meanings we ascribe to words should not vary unless we are certain to explain our change in usage. Whenever possible, we should illustrate what we mean by the words we use, we should mean something when we speak, and we should speak what we mean. These ideas are discussed in the first three books of the *Essay* and provide the background material for Locke's discussion of knowledge.

Locke defines knowledge as "the perception of the connection of and agreement, or disagreement and repugnancy of any of our ideas." According to the definition, perception is a requisite for all knowledge, and knowledge can extend no further than our ideas or previous connection among ideas. The perception of agreement or disagreement of ideas can occur in four different areas. The first area of such perception is that of *identity* or *diversity.* Perception in this area accompanies the mental possession of any idea by accepting it either precisely as it is (identity) or as being distinct from every other idea (diversity). Thus, in the order of knowing, the first act of the mind takes place in the area of identity or diversity. The second area of agreement or disagreement is that of *relations* between ideas; the third area, *coexistence,* is in the broadest sense of the word another instance of *relation.* It is to be expected that, since Locke makes a sharp epistemological distinction between mental connections and concrete connections, he would make the same sort of distinction between the relation of ideas only (relations), and the mutual presence of qualities in the same real subject (coexistence). The fourth area of perception of agreement or disagreement is that of *real existence* where the mind gains knowledge from an examination of certain ideas that are verified by checking them against the actual object.

Locke describes three degrees of knowledge: 1) intuition; 2) demonstration; and 3) sensation. Intuition means simply an immediate perception of agreement or disagreement among ideas with no intervention of another idea. For example, the difference between a cone and a ball is evident at once, and no intermediate connection or inference is needed for the perception of disagreement. Demonstration, on the other hand, is the sort of reasoning process that depends on the intervention of other ideas for the perception of agreement or disagreement. Since each stage of this process depends upon intuitive perceptions which must be remembered throughout the demonstration, the connections are apt to be less clear and distinct than they are with intuitive knowledge. The third degree of knowledge, sensation, refers to the perception of the mind about the existence of particular beings that are presumed outside of the mind. This knowledge does not pretend to achieve the sort of certainty that is given by intuition and demonstration, but it still is more than bare probability. Locke states that the evidence here rests upon the obvious "difference between dreaming of being in the fire, and being actually in it."

In summary, the various degrees of knowledge give us *intuitive* knowledge of self, *demonstrative* knowledge of God (both are the most reliable sources of knowledge), and finally *sensitive* knowledge of the external world which is only probable. Since most of our knowledge is in the realm of probability, we must expect the wide diversity of opinion on all subjects that we do experience. We must make every effort to understand the reasons for such diversity.

Locke: Empiricism and Education

It can hardly be said that Locke's contributions to education were highly original, but the forcefulness of his writing and thinking, coupled with his high repute as a philosopher, provided Locke with a wide and appreciative reading audience. He is quoted in almost every eighteenth century treatise on education from his essays on educational topics. Our discussion to this point suggests something about the general trend of his educational directives. There was an immense gulf between classes in Locke's day, which undoubtedly played a large part in limiting his acquaintances to those of his own class, and helps to account for the fact that Locke's educational writings are predominantly concerned about the education of young gentlemen.

We have noted that Locke deplored the futility of his own education and that he rebelled against the intellectual ruts of tradition and pedantry. He reacted by insisting on training that would capture the interest of the child and equip him for a life of vitality in a practical world. Locke's stress on individuality is borne out in his emphasis on training that considers the uniqueness of the individual and his particular goals. Locke's medical interests, his knowledge of Greek ideas on education, and his own scientific and philosophic bent, all contributed to the general outlines of the sort of educational training that Locke urged for young gentlemen. Finally, Locke's firm belief in the three essentials of Christian faith helped shape his ideas about education. Locke believed that two essentials, the existence of God and the principles of morality, are demonstrable doctrines. The third essential, the messiahship of Christ, he believed could be proven by judicious use of the Scriptures which is an important factor in Locke's proposals about proper education.

Locke's rejection of innatism and his promotion of the empirical origin of ideas indicate a belief that the experiences of men are the legitimate content for education in a society that is constructed for man's well-being. This attitude may have prompted one of his minor essays, *Working Schools*, where he proposes that such schools be established by law. Education in these working schools would be limited to instruction in an industrial skill or craft and to training in religion and morality. The teachers would have the responsibility of assuring church attendance on Sunday. Locke suggested that some of the boys might serve as apprentices to master craftsmen and farmers. These would take the boys at whatever age they thought advisable, and bind them—without pay—until the age of twenty-three. Boys who remained in the schools until they were fourteen would be taken as apprentices by gentlemen, yeomen, or farmers.

Locke emphasized the practicality of his plan. If the children of the working class were required to attend the schools after they were three years old, it would be a great saving of public funds by eliminating relief payments. Also, a profit could be realized from the sale of the various goods that the children would produce. The schools would not be expensive to maintain, because the children would be accustomed to a bread-and-warm-water gruel. But practical as Locke's ideas about education for poverty may have been, they are hardly worthy of the grandeur of his democratic ideas in his *Treatise on Civil Government* and are even disappointing from one who elsewhere gives evidence of believing that all men have the right to an equal educational opportunity.

Some Thoughts on Education, which was written as advice for a friend who had questioned Locke about how his son should be educated, more accurately reflects Locke's views. The essay was widely read during Locke's time, and it is most likely the basis for his reputation during the eighteenth century as an educator. The essay begins with instructions for parents about how to insure a healthy constitution for the child. Locke's description of happiness and well-being in this world is encompassed in his phrase, "a sound mind and a sound body." Locke does not rank physical conditioning on a par with morality and knowledge, but it is the first step in the education of young gentlemen. Locke encouraged simplicity in food and dress, plenty of exercise and sleep, and restraint, moderation, and regularity in physical habits.

Parents should keep a firm control over their children, and they should be taught by example and reason, rather than by rules. A child should experience simple reasoning as early as possible so that he may build toward the goal of reasoning from remote principles. Locke maintained that children understand reasoning as early as they do language and that, if a child is treated as a rational being, it will please the child and ensure that he gets practice in reasoning within the limits of his capabilities.

Locke did not believe that schools are able to give adequate supervision to each child, and he directs his remarks to the parents and tutors. Nevertheless, much of his pedagogy has relevancy for contemporary teachers. His approach to character building, his ideas about teaching by example, making use of individual interests, moods, and inclinations, treating a pupil as a reasoning individual, habit forming through practice instead of rules, developing intellectual self-control through experience and practice, are only a few of the principles he sets forth in his *Thoughts* that foreshadow progressive education. A little more than two hundred years later John Dewey wrote that:

> Everything the teacher does, as well as the manner in which he does it, incites the child to respond in some way or other, and each response tends to set the child's attitude in some way or other.[3]

After dealing with the general methods of education Locke devotes his attention to a consideration of what he believes to be the four aspects of education: virtue, wisdom, breeding, and learning. He stresses their importance in that order. The first three are acquired from example rather than from precept. Virtue is founded in a true notion of God, and the virtuous man is one who has piety toward God and religion untainted by superstitions. Consistent with this view is Locke's insistence that although the Lord's prayer, the creed, and the Ten Commandments should be learned perfectly by heart even before the child has learned to read, the child must be protected from fear of the unknown and from ideas which would haunt them with myths stamped upon their minds. This recalls Bacon's *idol of the theatre,* which could be dispelled by sound logic, but Locke's peers placed a different interpretation upon his demand that reason function in all areas. Many felt that it was heresy for Locke to say that unless it was carefully restricted, Bible reading by children is apt to result in an odd jumble of harmful thoughts.

The second aspect to education, wisdom, is above the reach of children but should be a goal of education. The child can be directed along the lines of wisdom by being discouraged from becoming crafty, cunning, or sly, qualities mocking wisdom. The best preparation for wisdom is to keep the child from falsehood and direct him to true notions of all things. The third aspect, good breeding, is twofold. It consists of the desire not to offend others and of expressing the desire in the most agreeable and acceptable manner. The gentleman who is well-bred respects himself and others without being fawning or neglectful.

The last aspect to education is learning, and Locke admits that it may seem strange for a bookish man to place it last in the ranks, but he feels

---

[3] John Dewey, *How We Think* (Boston: D. C. Heath & Company, 1910), p. 47.

that reading and writing are subservient to the greater qualities in man. If the young gentleman is properly schooled, he will achieve a love of knowledge and the ability to pursue knowledge on his own. When the child begins to read, it should be from some easy, pleasant book, suited to his capacity and styled to reward his pains in reading so as to make it a delight. Locke suggested *Aesop's Fables* and *Reynard the Fox*. As soon as the child can read English, he is ready to learn to write and to learn some other living language, such as French. Latin is necessary to a gentleman, but it should not be imposed on all children. The child should be instructed in both Latin and grammar only as they will be useful and necessary for the sort of activities he will engage in as he grows into manhood. The study of Greek should be limited to those engaged in scholarship. The child should be instructed in arithmetic, geography, chronology, history, geometry, and civil law. Rhetoric and logic should be avoided, as they are governed by the sort of rules that Locke believed are debilitating to reason.

Locke's curricular ideas are shaped by the idea that education must be styled to suit individual position and needs and that there must be no wasted time, for there is no end to the things to be learned. Locke writes about other accomplishments which are necessary for a gentleman, such as dancing and music, but stresses the importance of not wasting too much time on gaining more than a moderate skill in such things.

The last part of education is travel which should wait until the young man has become suited through careful training to avoid the dangers of temptation. He will have something to exchange with those abroad if he has first acquired the accomplishments of reason, foresight, and knowledge of his own country. Locke overlooks very little for the well-rounded education of a young man. He suggests that, when the young gentleman has finished his travels and approaches the time to think of matrimony, he should be left to his mistress. He concludes his advice with the statement that:

> ". . . yet it may give some small light to those, whose concern for their dear little ones makes them so irregularly bold, that they dare venture to consult their own reason, in the education of their children, rather than wholly to rely upon old custom."[4]

Today Locke's curricular ideas are commonplace, if not naive, but they were revolutionary for his time. The common-sense approach to learning, the idea that subjects should be chosen for their practical contribution to a particular way of life, and the idea that promiscuous Bible reading should be prohibited were in opposition to the educational views that were generally accepted during Locke's time. But in many respects, the new

---

[4] Peter Gay, ed., *John Locke on Education* (New York: Bureau of Publications, Teachers College, Columbia University, 1964), p. 176.

philosophy of empiricism showed man a different world, and Locke's educational ideas reflect the difference. His emphasis upon the natural and the practical, upon the knowledge man gains from his experiences in an ever-changing world, was only the beginning of a reaction against the humanism and the religious attitudes that continued to define educational goals into the nineteenth century. Locke was not an extremist, but there is no doubt that the changing view about education during the next several decades dates from his moderate empiricism.

Problems of Knowledge

Man's search for knowledge can be placed along a continuum between the "I doubt," of the skeptic, and the "I know," of the dogmatist. The points along the way include, "I have some doubt," "I believe," "I have an opinion," "I think," and "I have some knowledge." During his conscious life man passes from doubt to belief, to opinion, to knowledge, and back again. There is no evidence that suggests a regular pattern or universal design to the shiftings, and the individual may experience any number of these positions at any moment of time. It is not surprising to find ideas in conflict when men attempt to come together at a time of decision. We have arrived at a point in history where, unless reason prevails at such a time, the whole of mankind may be in mortal danger. Man must be able to state his "I know," with confidence, and he must be able to verify his source of knowledge to the satisfaction of others. The firm "I know" cannot be structured on the shifting sands of unsupported beliefs and opinions, but must be grounded on the bedrock of empirical evidence. It has become essential to human survival that man learn to function with a high degree of correctness, and the whole issue of epistemology (the problem of knowledge) is of vital importance.

The word knowledge is so commonly used that ordinary conversational exchange requires no explicit definition of the term. But as we consider the historical views of the problem of knowledge—the nature, the sources, and the various methods of arriving at knowledge—we will begin to realize that the different positions tend to alter the nuances and overtones. In one case knowledge may infer universal or ultimate truths, and in another simply a body of information. As we read what various scholars have written about the problem of knowledge, we discover that one source may use the term *believing* to designate what another calls *knowing;* others may equate *knowing* with *knowledge;* and still others distinguish between *knowing that* as being propositional and *knowing how* as being procedural.

Traditional Philosophic Attitudes

Traditionally, the problem of knowledge has been overshadowed by the metaphysical. The crux of the problem—what is the nature of knowledge, and where does it originate?—is intimately related to the appearance versus reality dualism. Is the nature of knowledge mental, spiritual, materialistic, or some combination of these? According to the views of Plato, Aristotle, and Aquinas, the answer had to be in the realm of the mental or the spiritual. But beginning with the empirical ideas of Bacon and Locke, men began to turn to the materialistic or to a combination of the mental and the materialistic for the answers they sought.

The range of philosophic attitudes about the nature of knowledge can be classified as having either a monistic or a dualistic view of the world. Monism is the assertion that the world is one substance, either mentalistic, materialistic, or spiritualistic which is universal and is variously termed Being, God, or nature. There are three monistic views of the mind-body relation: 1) *psychical monism;* 2) *epiphenomenalism;* 3) *double aspect.* Dualism posits a combination of either the materialistic and the mentalistic or of the materialistic and spiritualistic. There are two dualistic views of the mind-body relation: 1) *parallelism;* and 2) *interactionism.*

We shall see that each of these five answers to the mind-body question is associated with one or another of the three major divisions of epistemological concern. These are called *subjectivism, epistemological dualism,* and *objectivism.* They are pure categories in theory only, for there are variations of each which depend upon other philosophical commitments, and there is also considerable overlapping. We will describe each main division in a very general manner but one sufficient to suggest a rationale for the conflicting views about the nature of knowledge and to provide the necessary background for an understanding of the current emphasis on the verification and the structures of knowledge.

Subjectivism is the attitude that is probably most alien to the empirical orientation of contemporary Western society. It states that nothing exists independent of a consciousness that is variously thought to be the mind of man, God, Being, nature, or some other unknown substance. In any event, the only reality is thought to be a knowing mind. The position is best represented by George Berkeley (1685–1753), who described subjectivism economically and precisely with the terse statement that: "To be, is to be perceived." Berkeley argued that all of the qualities attributed to material substance are actually mental constructions, and, therefore, there can be no material substance. According to such a view we can never go beyond, nor get outside of our own experiences, as the position is "self-bound." If the subjectivity is extended to include space and time and laws of nature, we are only a step from solipsism which is the view that only the individual self exists. Although the view has never been held seriously, the possibility of such an extension of subjectivism is enough to cause many to question its tenability.

Subjectivism asserts a monistic position in regard to the mind-body problem, and subjectivists look to the mental or to the spiritual for the nature of knowledge. For the most part, subjectivists hold the view of *psychical monism,* where the causal series is confined to the mental. What is thought of as matter is only appearance or shadows cast by the mental. This position is illustrated by the following diagram. In this diagram, as in the succeeding mind-body diagrams, the symbol X represents the mental; the symbol O represents the material; the symbol U represents the Unknown; and the straight lines are the causal connections.

Psychical Monism and the Denial of Matter

```
    O     O     O     O
   /     /     /     /
  X —— X —— X —— X
```

A different solution to the mind-body problem is asserted by the subjectivist who views all of reality as being God, or nature, or an unknown substance. The double-aspect theory states that both mind and matter are underlying expressions of God, nature, or an unknown substance, and both are different aspects of the same reality.

The Double Aspect of Identity Theory

```
    O     O     O     O     O
   /     /     /     /     /
  U —— U —— U —— U —— U
   \     \     \     \     \
    X     X     X     X     X
```

Epistemological dualism is a dualistic position which depends upon the acceptance of two orders of reality. One order of reality is the sense data within our consciousness, and the other is the external order of nature which is inferred from the sense data. Epistemological dualism takes several different forms. One of the areas may be physical and the other mental, both may be physical, or both may be mental. In any case, the sense data exist apart and are distinct from the cause of the data. This position is an intermediate one between subjectivism and objectivism, and it recognizes two separate areas that are involved in the knowing process.

The view of the mind-body problem held by the epistemological dualist is one where the mental and the physical processes are thought to be equally real, but they disagree about the causal connections between the two realities. The most commonly held view is called interactionism, or sometimes the common-sense view. The diagram illustrates the physical and psychical causal sequence and shows that the mind may cause bodily changes and that bodily changes may also have a mental effect.

Interactionism

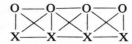

The other dualistic view is called parallelism. According to this view, there is no causal connection or interaction between the mental and the physical. Those who object to the view say that it splits the universe and does not really solve the mind-body problem. The position appears to deny that reflective thinking can make any difference in our experiential world.

Parallelism

O——O——O——O

X——X——X——X

Objectivism is based on the belief that there is a reality apart from mind, an external world of physical objects that exist independently of our knowing them. Usually, those who hold this view accept the world for what it appears to be, and differences of opinion about the essential nature of the external world are explained as resulting from differences in location and from differences in physical abilities. There is thought to be a physical reality that excites a response in the brain by means of the sensory apparatus. This results in a copy, image, or reproduction of the external reality. The evidence from different sense organs comes together to form a unified picture of our world.

Contrary to subjectivism, the fact that things cannot be known until they are experienced does not mean that there cannot be unexperienced things. Objectivism distinguishes between ideas of things, which is the act of thought, and the things themselves, which is the object of an act of thought. The ideas of things are in the mind of the individual, and the things have an independent existence outside of the mind of the individual. There is also a distinction made between the experiences that we create, such as imagination, thinking, dreams, and the sense perceptions from the external world. Knowledge is thought to be the direct experiencing of things.

The view of the mind-body problem accepted by the objectivist is called epiphenomenalism. The consciousness, or mind, is thought to be a secondary phenomenon which accompanies some bodily processes. Matter is primary, the one real substance, and what has been called mind is a shadow that appears under some conditions. Our conscious experiences are thought to be caused by certain processes in the brain and in the nervous system.

Epiphenomenalism

```
X    X    X    X
/    /    /    /
O —— O —— O —— O
```

There is another approach to the mind-body problem that was not included with the other mind-body theories, as it does not fit into any one of the three main divisions we have been considering. Emergence, or what is sometimes called emergent evolution, is an interpretation of mind that is based on evolution. Matter, life, and mind are considered to be equally real, although each is a distinct level of reality. Mind, the last level of reality to emerge or evolve, has new qualities of its own which require different standards from those of the previous levels for adequate interpretation. Science, art, philosophy, religion, and moral distinctions are realized because of mind. The self is not the mind but is the living individual who experiences, reasons, and feels.

The theory of emergence does not follow the established precepts of a monism or of a dualism. Possibly a case could be made to place it in one category or the other, but there would be small profit, other than the intellectual exercise involved. Those who affirm the emergence theory of the mind-body position take a naturalistic view of knowledge and look to the world about them for experiential information. The theory is the most compatible with the scientific-empirical outlook, and any definition of knowledge that can be generally accepted today must at least take the emergence theory into consideration.

The Sources of Knowledge

We have been considering the problem of knowledge in a theoretical sense. We have seen that the nature of knowledge is thought to be mentalistic, materialistic, spiritualistic, naturalistic, or perhaps a combination of any two. As long as we were discussing knowledge in the abstract there was no urgency for the kind of definition that is required as we move from the general to the particular. When we talk in terms of individual knowledge and how it may be acquired, we find that we must be explicit about our use of the term. This is important, not only for reasons of communication, but because the way in which we define knowledge does make a difference in educational directives. For instance, if knowledge is thought of as a body of information or as an accumulation of facts, teachers become dispensers of knowledge, and teacher preparation will place the greater stress upon a good liberal arts and subject-matter background. In order that we may fully utilize the suggestions for the source or sources of knowledge that are generally considered, we will preface the discussion with a definition of the terms we will be using. As we consider each suggestion, we should be able to move from the universal to the particular without undue ambiguity.

The pragmatist says that knowledge is experience which is organized by the self or mind, and this is essentially the same statement made by the definition that will be suggested here. The primary difference is that the following definition is broader in scope and is more explicit so that it may also serve as a basis for the definition of related terms. We shall define knowledge here as: *an acquaintance with or an awareness of ideas, things, facts, or feelings, combined with the activities of separating, categorizing, relating, structuring, and testing which results in an instrument that may be used for inquiry and prediction.* Knowledge defined in this way is threefold. The first part of the definition concerns the range of data or the *knowable,* and the particular data which become the *known,* when apprehended or experienced by a subject (implied), the *knower.* The possibility of sources can be inferred from the categories of ideas, things, facts, and feelings. Our investigations into the sources of knowledge will reveal that the definition accepts them as being complementary. The second part of the definition deals with the treatment of the data, a process that we will call *knowing.* Note especially the activity of testing, as it is important to distinctions we will make shortly and is also the main concern of the next section, verification for knowledge.

The first two parts of the definition constitute a clear statement about the meaning of knowledge without any additional explication, and the third part is purposely stated in such a way (by the use of the phrase "that *may* be used" which implies choice) so that the use of knowledge for inquiry and prediction is not an imperative or necessary qualification. The addition of a third part which attributes teleological overtones and implications of utility to knowledge is more descriptive than definitive. The definition accomplishes a number of things that should be noted. First, it asserts the reliability of knowledge by virtue of the way knowledge is defined. That is, information must be tested for reliability before it is properly called knowledge. Second, the definition is not restrictive, because no source is excluded. Further, although for the most part the definition takes a *functional* view of knowledge, the possibility of a *transcendental* knowledge, where the *known* is something other than sense data, is not disallowed.

We will refer to the definition from time to time during the rest of our probing into the problem of knowledge, but at this point we are ready to give attention to the sources of knowledge. Different scholars throughout history have variously believed the source of knowledge to be the soul, revelation, divine or natural authority, mysticism, intuition, the senses, imagination, memory, reason, and others. Contemporary discussions usually recognize four main categories—authority, sense perception, reason, and intuition.

There are two kinds of authority that have been considered as sources of knowledge. First, divine authority which has traditionally been viewed as a primary source by way of revelation or by direct apprehension of God. The empirical attitude could not accept a supernatural source for justification in matters of fact, and generally speaking, those in contemporary society who do appeal to the supernatural in this respect are considered to be other-worldly. They exhibit an attitude that the natural environment is either a place of punishment or a testing ground for a better life.

The authority moderns are more apt to accept as a source of knowledge is called human or natural authority. Although a secondary source, it would be pointless to deny this sort of authority as a legitimate source of knowledge, for without it each generation would be forced to make a new start in all areas of human endeavor. If we were not able to rely on the testimony (authority) of others for that body of knowledge that has been amassed since the time when man first began to record his experiences and discoveries, for knowledge about the thoughts of other men, and for knowledge of areas of specialization, life should be different and difficult beyond all imagination. However, when we accept authority as a source of knowledge, it is essential to recognize the difference between authority and authoritarianism. The primary difference is that authoritarianism is the uncritical assertion of authority, whether it has to do with custom, tradition, the family, the church, or any of the mass media of communication. Authoritarianism demands a blind acceptance of authority that precludes all elements of reason and judgment. Such uncritical acceptance carries the belief that knowledge is automatically guaranteed or validated. Scholars during the Middle Ages who accepted the teachings of the church and the writings of such men as Aristotle without any questions or doubts exhibited such a belief.

Locke viewed the mind as being comparable to a piece of wax capable of receiving impressions from the external world through the senses. David Hume adopted an extreme form of empiricism, a narrow sensationalism that viewed experiences as merely discrete impressions. Later empiricists, under the influence of William James, accepted the idea that the mind is an essential element of knowledge getting. According to this position, the mind organizes the sense data, making experience a continuous structure, without reference to any sort of transempirical support. The position relies primarily upon the senses for knowledge, yet does not imply that sensational experiences alone are sufficient for knowledge. The scientific-empirical method views the senses and reason as being complementary. Generally, the modern temper of empiricism admits that sense data without an intellect is blind, even though the senses are the primary source of knowledge.

Those who posit reason as the central factor of knowledge are called rationalists. An extreme form of rationalism has an all-cognitive approach to reality and is inclined toward the absolute, the universal, and the innate, claiming the self-evidence of their universal principles. Mathematics and logic are given a dominant role by the rationalist, who asserts that we know what we have thought out and that mind by itself can discover truth. Knowledge is thought to be the result of comparing ideas with other ideas. A moderate form of rationalism views sense data as the material of knowledge that must be organized into a meaningful system to become knowledge but does not go so far as to admit that intellect depends upon the senses. Generally, the contemporary attitude is similar to that of the empiricist in that both see reason and sense perception as being complementary. The difference is a matter of stress, for the rationalist says that reason is dominant, and the empiricist says that the senses are dominant.

Traditionally, intuitionism is closely related to the supernatural and to mysticism and is thought to be the power of knowing without recourse to inference or reasoning. The rationalist believes that there are self-evident truths which form the basis of human knowledge; one who affirms innatism views reason as the process or activity of coming to know; but the intuitionist scorns the idea of a process and claims that intuition gives direct apprehension of knowledge. According to the extreme traditional view, intuitionism has religious implications, and knowledge is restricted to ultimate reality. There are those such as Henri Bergson, who recognize knowledge revealed by the senses or reason, but who maintain that intuition points in the opposite direction from intelligence, and that it is the way to a different, higher kind of knowledge. Others view intuition as being the total of all our past experiences and thinking—as short cuts to the knowledge that would ordinarily be revealed by the senses or by reasoning.

Today, partly because of twentieth century parapsychological studies that recognize the legitimacy of scientific investigations into the areas of telepathy, clairvoyance, thought transference, and extrasensory perception, people have quite a different view of intuitionism than the traditional one. Those who bring it into the laboratory as subject matter for experimentation represent the opposite extreme of the mystical view. Contemporary thinkers generally consider intuition to be an extraordinary power of invention or a sudden flash of insightful (subconscious) relating. The creativity of the scientist, as well as that of the poet or the artist, relies on this sort of insight.

The foregoing characterizations show that while there are extreme positions that have been held in each case, positions that would be untenable to contemporary thinking, there is something in each category that is accepted in a matter-of-fact way by the so-called common-sense view (sometimes equated with good sense). We all depend upon authority in our daily living in too many ways to enumerate. We rely upon our senses for information about our physical environment, for empirical data, but we realize that at times the senses do deceive us, and that we should have no more than a hodgepodge of unrelated items without reason or intellect to organize and relate the sense data. We recognize an element of intuition in all knowledge, rely upon it for what we call self-knowledge, and often as a short cut to the sort of knowledge that ordinarily would come by way of the senses and reflective thinking.

Common sense also tells us that a reliance upon one way of knowledge getting to the exclusion of all others would be limiting and dangerous. If authority is our only source of knowledge, it degenerates to authoritarianism. If we rely entirely upon our sensational experiences we should deny the ability to reason that sets man apart from other animals. Exclusive reliance on reason would inhibit relating with our physical environment and rule out the sort of empirical observation that has relevance for the world in which we live. We realize that unless intuition is checked by the senses and controlled by reason it is apt to lead us into impossible situations. Clear support for the intimacy of the four methods based on these sources is given by Montague in the following statement:

> Rationalism and authoritarianism might be described as methods of justifying beliefs by making them conform either to testimony or to axioms already established in the *past*. Empiricism and mysticism could analogously be described as methods of testing beliefs by their agreement with immediate *present* experiences, either external or internal.[5]

Verification for Knowledge

What do we mean by verification for knowledge? The definition of knowledge that we accepted earlier includes the stipulation that testing is a step in the knowing process which may result in knowledge. Obviously, when we speak of verification for knowledge, we are referring to some sort of testing. But do we mean just any sort of testing? Are there different kinds of testing, and if so, how do they differ? Is there a special test for knowledge? Do we attribute special qualities to verification for knowledge that may not be requisite for the sort of common-sense testing that we do every day? These questions and others that grow out of the attempt to answer them provoke the following discussion.

History shows us that there is a connection between what a man believes and the things that he does, the choices that he makes and the way that he acts. Each of us learns that the self can be related to the surrounding world in a variety of ways, and, as experience teaches us that some ways work better than others, we are apt to rely heavily upon belief. In many instances, belief may simply signify a willingness to act. It may indicate an opinion, or it may result from habit. In the latter case, we can see that there is a distinction we need to make between conditions or experiences that *cause* belief and grounds which *warrant* belief. Frequently the words believe and know are used interchangeably, but, if we have any

---

[5] W. P. Montague, *The Ways of Knowing* (New York: The Macmillan Company, 1958), p. 138.

doubts about a position we are stating, we are more apt to say, "I *believe* this to be the case," than we are to say, "I *know* this to be true." If we are to move from an "I believe," to a firm "I know," we need to explore the ways to verify our position.

Almost everything we do in daily living, whether or not we are conscious of the fact, involves some sort of testing. Every action, from striking a match to driving a car, from brushing our teeth to deciding on a career, involves a testing of information that we have heard, assumed, read, reasoned, experienced, or perhaps intuited. For the most part, we are unaware that we are actually testing, and we are even ignorant of the basic belief, theory, or data that we test. We simply act in accordance with what we have come to believe, and routine, unconscious testing is more apt to condition than it is to enlighten. Some common-sense testing, however, is deliberate and purposeful. For instance, we may try a number of different brands of a product in order to determine which one we prefer. Experience tells us that not all people are going to prefer the same brand, and we wonder if some tests are more objective than others. This may, of course, be the case, but we do need to clarify our meaning of objective.

Beginning in the thirteenth century with Duns Scotus' appeal to the superior order of revealed truth and extending into the eighteenth century, objective referred to anything that does not have an independent existence, but that exists only in the mind as an idea. Since Brumgarten (1714–1762), who was largely responsible for the altered view, objective has come to signify real objects that exist independently of a knowing mind. There are a number of standard meanings for the objective-subjective distinction, but it is not important for the purpose of this discussion to detail all of the different meanings. We need only to make it clear that in this particular context, unless otherwise stated, objective is used to mean an impartial, unprejudiced, and unbiased attitude. The term subjective is used here to indicate attitudes which exhibit personal bias, attitudes which are conditioned by personal characteristics or particular states of mind. This brings us to make a further distinction between the personal in us, and the state of subjectivity. It is the personal in us which determines individual preference and which motivates discovery. In his book, *Personal Knowledge*, Michael Polanyi writes that:

> . . . I think we may distinguish between the personal in us, which actively enters into our commitments, and our subjective states, in which we merely endure our feelings. This distinction establishes the conception of the *personal*, which is neither subjective nor objective. In so far as the personal submits to requirements acknowledged by itself as independent of itself, it is not subjective; but in so far as it is an action guided by individual passions, it is not objective either. It transcends the disjunction between subjective and objective.[6]

---

[6] Michael Polanyi, *Personal Knowledge* (Chicago: University of Chicago Press, 1958), p. 300.

We have seen thus far that common sense testing may be an unconscious act, or that it may be done purposefully, with deliberation. We have seen that if we hope to substantiate a belief, to verify its authenticity, we must deal objectively with related facts. It is fairly commonplace to hear someone speak of "the true facts," or to say that "your facts are false," and we may wonder if there is some way to determine whether or not our facts are "true." Actually, a fact can no more be false than a shoe can be happy. We may be mistaken or misinformed about a fact; we may have false ideas about a fact; but nonetheless, a fact is simply a fact. We must make a distinction, however, between *genuine* facts and *pseudo*-facts, and we are confronted with the problem of how to avoid the error of mistaking one for the other. But there appears to be no particular method, nor fixed rules that govern common-sense testing, and we wonder if the exactness of science might suggest guidelines for our task of describing verification for knowledge.

It has been said that science is a refinement of common sense, and that facts are the starting point for scientific investigations. While it is the task of science to discover and manipulate facts in order to produce more facts, it would be a grave error to equate science with a collection of facts. The scientist acquires facts by observation and experimentation and works toward a systematic organization of knowledge by classifying, associating, ordering, and measuring his facts. A. Cornelius Benjamin, in *Science, Technology, and Human Values,* gives the following working definition of science:

> . . . we shall now define "science" as *that mode of inquiry which attempts to arrive at knowledge of the world by the method of observation and by the method of confirmed hypotheses based on what is given in observation.*[7]

Dr. Benjamin points out that the definition does not include mathematics and the descriptive sciences, but he accounts for these by postulating three distinct forms of science. These are: 1) descriptive sciences, such as geography, geology, astronomy, archaeology, and some of the behavioral sciences; 2) explanatory sciences which include the laboratory and experimental sciences such as physics, chemistry, and the like; and 3) formal science which is best exemplified by pure mathematics. According to this distinction, there is obviously more than one scientific method, but the method of "confirmed hypotheses" seems most appropriate for our task of moving from belief to knowledge. Admittedly, it is an oversimplification, but in brief, this method consists of three stages. It involves a movement from the first stage which is hypothesis or conjecture (belief), to the second stage of theory or credibility, which is achieved by observing and collecting

---

[7] A. Cornelius Benjamin, *Science, Technology, and Human Values* (Columbia, Mo.: University of Missouri Press, 1965), p. 20.

data to check the hypothesis, to the final stage of practical certainty (knowledge).

Several methods for confirming hypotheses have been suggested by philosophy. One of these is the *coherence theory of truth* where belief is treated as an idea rather than as an overt action or as a willingness to act. Objects and relations are also treated as ideas and may be represented by artificial symbols. Thus, if a statement of a belief (idea) coheres with a statement about known objects, qualities, activities, or relations (known ideas), the new idea that is being tested may be immediately accepted as being true. One does not have to deal with the objects themselves but only with the symbols that represent them. The theory does not automatically rule out the acceptance of new ideas which do not immediately cohere with what is already known to be true, as some critics have claimed, for if the new concept is sufficiently impressive, a reevaluation of an entire system of thought may be in order. There is the possibility, in such an event, that a reconstruction of the system will result in an even larger degree of coherence and make additional explanations possible.

Critics of the theory claim that there is no way to distinguish between consistent truth and consistent error, and that, accordingly, coherent systems which are false may be constructed. The theory is criticized by others who feel it is too rationalistic to be an adequate test for everyday experience. These critics are apt to prefer the *correspondence theory of truth,* as it follows the maxims of common sense and the familiar. According to this theory, truth is agreement between a hypothesis (statement of fact), and the experiential reality. Truth and falsity depend only upon the conditions which are being confirmed. If the expression of a belief is an accurate representation of objective reality (the view of objects that exist independently of a knowing mind), if it corresponds with those things which are perceivable and experiential, the belief must be true. Critics of the theory of correspondence insist that the mind tends to alter the view of the perceptual world, and that one cannot get outside of one's own experience to know how reality *really* is. They also criticize the theory for making no provision to test ideas that do not have objects outside of human thought.

A third test for truth is the *pragmatic theory of truth* (see chapter VII), where beliefs are considered in terms of the actions they indicate. The truth of the belief (hypothesis) is tested by prediction of the success of the future action predicated by the belief. The pragmatic principle is directly related to man and his experimentally verifiable experiences and to man's struggle for continued existence. It includes all aspects of human living as part of the truth but refuses any absolutistic and metaphysical scheme for truth. The theory denies the universalization of fact into an "ought" that serves as a guide for all men. William James expresses the pragmatic concept of truth as follows:

> The truth of an idea is not a stagnant property inherent in it. Truth *happens* to an idea. It *becomes* true, is made true by events. Its verity

is in fact an event, a process; the process namely of its verifying itself, its veri-*fication*. Its validity is the process of its valid-*ation*.[8]

There are many critics of the pragmatic test for truth, and a main concern is that it is an expedient doctrine without constant standards for judging decisions. Critics maintain that the pragmatic criterion is ultimately reducible to personal desire, and may be self-defeating. However, the pragmatic criterion has been accepted by a great many scholars, and the view does appear to be in the mainstream of contemporary investigations into the issue of verification. Close in spirit to the pragmatic view is one which is related to the movement of logical empiricism.

The analytic philosophers of the twentieth century try to approach all philosophical questions with the rigor of the established natural sciences, and the attempt is especially notable in the area of verification. A. J. Ayer states the basic attitude of the analytic philosopher regarding verification.

> We say that a sentence is factually significant to any given person, if, and only if, he knows how to verify the proposition which it purports to express—that is, if he knows what observations would lead him, under certain conditions, to accept the proposition as being true, or reject it as being false.[9]

According to this principle of verification, a meaningful statement is one that can be tested, directly or indirectly, by reference to experiences. These experiences may be those of immediate perceptions or deductions from past verified perceptions. Some modification has taken place in the principle of verification as a result of recent analytical philosophical development. The principle has been broadened to one of confirmability, rather than simply testability, and refers to the idea of suggesting conditions which would confirm the proposition. To test means to discover some method whereby the confirming conditions could actually be produced.

These tests for truth seem to have more to offer if they are viewed as being complementary, for each has its particular value. No one of the tests directly contradicts the validity of the others, and it seems reasonable to the common-sense view that all may be combined into tests which consider the complete range of possible situations that may be tested according to the particulars of each. There are times when we deal in complicated, abstract areas, such as mathematics, that coherence seems to be the only possible way of testing. On the other hand, everyday experiences and many of the sciences call for a different sort of testing. There are some areas in our lives which are important for the fulfillment and completeness of self, that cannot be subjected to laboratory or empirical testing, and if they were to be discredited because of this factor, man would lead a sterile sort of life.

---

8 William James, *Pragmatism* (New York: Longmans, Green and Co., 1907), p. 196.
9 A. J. Ayer, *Language, Truth and Logic* (New York: Dover Publications, Inc., 1936), p. 35.

In this regard we need a theory that recognizes the relevancy of the *personal* in man.

One final point should be made before we leave the question of verification for knowledge. The definition of knowledge that we accepted earlier made a distinction between the known and knowledge. That is, the known are the data that are the material of the knowing process which results in knowledge. At what point then, may we say an "I know," with complete conviction? Must we wait until the knowing process has been completed, or is knowledge, as we have defined it, a requisite for the firm "I know"? In other words, is there a difference between knowledge, and the things, concepts, or feelings that can be tested for truth, before they have been separated, categorized, related, and structured for knowledge? Since our definition stipulates that testing is only one part of the knowing process, we may draw the conclusion that while all knowledge is true (by definition), not all that is known to be true can be called knowledge.

It follows, then, that at any point where the known can be tested for truth, we have the legitimate basis for a confident "I know." By the same token, a belief that can be tested for truth, even though it has not taken the shape of knowledge, allows the same conviction. It should not be necessary to elaborate on the fact that while truth alone is sufficient for an "I know," intelligent choices and actions rely on related truths that have been structured into a body of knowledge, the proper goal of educational directives.

JOHN LOCKE

Some Thoughts Concerning Education *

Excerpts from John Locke's Some Thoughts Concerning Education *have been selected as the reading for Chapter IV. The work, published in 1693, had considerable influence in changing our conception of the nature of the child, and our ideas about the most appropriate sort of education for children. Locke borrowed the idea of "a sound mind in a sound body" from Juvenal* (Satires —X) *in order to express his belief in the importance of considering the total organism as it experiences the surrounding world. Locke's confidence in the*

* From *John Locke on Education*, ed. Peter Gay. © 1964 by Peter Gay.

changeability of the organism was a revolutionary idea in his time, and his insistence upon using the present and total environment of the child as a basis for learning pushed the classics into the background of education. Locke's views on education were practical, humane, and utilitarian. Above all, he insisted that learning can be a relevant activity only if the needs and the desires of the individual child are the prime consideration. Locke's fundamental empiricism, which is exemplified in Some Thoughts Concerning Education, *raises many questions about learning and teaching, and about the purposes and outcomes of education. The selections also raise questions about the rights, duties, and responsibilities of students which are especially pertinent considerations today.*

§ 1.   "A sound mind in a sound body," is a short but full description of a happy state in this world: he that has these two, has little more to wish for; and he that wants either of them, will be but little the better for any thing else. Men's happiness or misery is most part of their own making. He whose mind directs not wisely, will never take the right way; and he whose body is crazy and feeble, will never be able to advance in it. I confess, there are some men's constitutions of body and mind so vigorous, and well framed by nature, that they need not much assistance from others; but, by the strength of their natural genius, they are, from their cradles, carried towards what is excellent; and, by the privilege of their happy constitutions, are able to do wonders. But examples of this kind are but few; and I think I may say, that, of all the men we meet with, nine parts of ten are what they are, good or evil, useful or not, by their education. It is that which makes the great difference in mankind. . . .

§ 2.   I imagine the minds of children as easily turned, this or that way, as water itself; and though this be the principal part, and our main care should be about the inside, yet the clay cottage is not to be neglected. I shall therefore begin with the case, and consider first the health of the body. . . .

§ 3.   How necessary health is to our business and happiness, and how requisite a strong constitution, able to endure hardships and fatigue, is to one that will make any figure in the world, is too obvious to need any proof.

§ 31.   Due care being had to keep the body in strength and vigor, so that it may be able to obey and execute the orders of the mind; the next and principal business is, to set the mind right, that on all occasions it may be disposed to consent to nothing but what may be suitable to the dignity and excellency of a rational creature. . . .

§ 33.   As the strength of the body lies chiefly in being able to endure hardships, so also does that of the mind. And the great principle and foundation of all virtue and worth is placed in this, that a man is able to deny himself his own desires, cross his own inclinations, and purely follow what reason directs as best, though the appetite lean the other way. . . .

§ 43.   For I am very apt to think, that great severity of punishment does but very little good; nay, great harm in education: and I believe it will be found, that, cæteris paribus, those children who have been most chastised, seldom make the best men. . . .

§ 52.   Beating then, and all other sorts of slavish and corporal punishments, are not the discipline fit to be used in the education of those who would have wise, good, and ingenuous men; and therefore very rarely to be applied, and that only on great occasions, and cases of extremity. On the other side, to flatter children by rewards of things that are pleasant to them, is as carefully to be avoided. . . . Thus people, to prevail with children to be industrious about their grammar, dancing, or some other such matter, of no great moment to the happiness or usefulness of their lives, by misapplied rewards and punishments, sacrifice their virtue, invert the order of their education, and teach them luxury, pride, or covetousness, &c. For in this way, flattering those wrong inclinations, which they should restrain and suppress, they lay the foundations of those future vices, which cannot be avoided, but by curbing our desires, and accustoming them early to submit to reason. . . .

§ 56. The rewards and punishments then whereby we should keep children in order are quite of another kind; and of that force, that when we can get them once to work, the business, I think, is done, and the difficulty is over. Esteem and disgrace are, of all others, the most powerful incentives to the mind, when once it is brought to relish them. If you can once get into children a love of credit, and an apprehension of shame and disgrace, you have put into them the true principle, which will constantly work, and incline them to the right. But it will be asked, How shall this be done?

I confess, it does not, at first appearance, want some difficulty; but yet I think it worth our while to seek the ways (and practice them when found) to attain this, which I look on as the great secret of education. . . .

§ 64. And here give me leave to take notice of one thing I think a fault in the ordinary method of education; and that is, the charging of children's memories, upon all occasions, with rules and precepts, which they often do not understand, and are constantly as soon forgot as given. . . .

§ 65. Let therefore your rules to your son be as few as is possible, and rather fewer than more than seem absolutely necessary. For if you burden him with many rules, one of these two things must necessarily follow, that either he must be very often punished, which will be of ill consequence, by making punishment too frequent and familiar; or else you must let the transgressions of some of your rules go unpunished, whereby they will of course grow contemptible, and your authority become cheap to him. Make but few laws, but see they be well observed, when once made. Few years require but few laws; and as his age increases, when one rule is by practice well established, you may add another. . . .

§ 66. But pray remember, children are not to be taught by rules, which will be always slipping out of their memories. What you think necessary for them to do, settle in them by an indispensable practice, as often as the occasion returns; and, if it be possible, make occasions. This will beget habits in them, which, being once established, operate of themselves easily and naturally, without the assistance of the memory. . . .

This method of teaching children by a repeated practice, and the same action done over and over again, under the eye and direction of the tutor, till they have got the habit of doing it well, and not by relying on rules trusted to their memories; has so many advantages, which way soever we consider it, that I cannot but wonder (if ill customs could be wondered at in any thing) how it could possibly be so much neglected. I shall name one more that comes now in my way. By this method we shall see, whether what is required of him be adapted to his capacity, and any way suited to the child's natural genius and constitution: for that too must be considered in a right education. We must not hope wholly to change their original tempers, nor make the gay pensive and grave, nor the melancholy sportive, without spoiling them. God has stamped certain characters upon men's minds, which, like their shapes, may perhaps be a little mended; but can hardly be totally altered and transformed into the contrary.

He therefore, that is about children, should well study their natures and aptitudes, and see, by often trials, what turn they easily take, and what becomes them; observe what their native stock is, how it may be improved, and what it is fit for: he should consider what they want, whether they be capable of having it wrought into them by industry, and incorporated there by practice; and whether it be worth while to endeavor it. For, in many cases, all that we can do, or should aim at, is, to make the best of what nature has given, to prevent the vices and faults to which such a constitution is most inclined, and give it all the advantages it is capable of. Every one's natural genius should be carried as far as it could; but to attempt the putting another upon him, will be but labor in vain; and what is so plastered on will at best sit but untowardly, and have always hanging to it the ungracefulness of constraint and affectation. . . .

§ 73.   1. None of the things they are to learn should ever be made a burden to them, or imposed on them as a task. Whatever is so proposed presently becomes irksome: the mind takes an aversion to it, though before it were a thing of delight or indifferency. Let a child be but ordered to whip his top at a certain time every day, whether he has or has not a mind to it; let this be but required of him as a duty, wherein he must spend so many hours morning and afternoon, and see whether he will not soon be weary of any play at this rate. Is it not so with grown men? What they do cheerfully of themselves, do they not presently grow sick of, and can no more endure, as soon as they find it is expected of them as a duty? Children have as much a mind to show that they are free, that their own good actions come from themselves, that they are absolute and independent, as any of the proudest of you grown men, think of them as you please. . . .

§ 74.   . . . a child will learn three times as much when he is in tune, as he will with double the time and pains, when he goes awkwardly, or is dragged unwillingly to it. If this were minded as it should, children might be permitted to weary themselves with play, and yet have time enough to learn what is suited to the capacity of each age. . . .

. . . were matters ordered right, learning any thing they should be taught might be made as much a recreation to their play, as their play is to their learning. The pains are equal on both sides: nor is it that which troubles them; for they love to be busy, and the change and variety is that which naturally delights them. The only odds is, in that which we call play they act at liberty, and employ their pains (whereof you may observe them never sparing) freely; but what they are to learn, is forced upon them: they are called, compelled, and driven to it. This is that which at first entrance balks and cools them; they want their liberty: get them but to ask their tutor to teach them, as they do often their playfellows, instead of his calling upon them to learn; and they being satisfied that they act as freely in this as they do in other things, they will go on with as much pleasure in it, and it will not differ from their other sports and play. By these ways, carefully pursued, a child may be brought to desire to be taught any thing you have a mind he should learn. The hardest part, I confess, is with the first or eldest; but when once he is set aright, it is easy by him to lead the rest whither one will. . . .

§ 81.   It will perhaps be wondered, that I mention reasoning with children: and yet I cannot but think that the true way of dealing with them. They understand it as early as they do language; and, if I misobserve not, they love to be treated as rational creatures sooner than is imagined. It is a pride should be cherished in them, and, as much as can be, made the greatest instrument to turn them by.

But when I talk of reasoning, I do not intend any other but such as is suited to the child's capacity and apprehension. Nobody can think a boy of three or seven years old should be argued with as a grown man. Long discourses, and philosophical reasonings, at best amaze and confound, but do not instruct, children. When I say, therefore, that they must be treated as rational creatures, I mean, that you should make them sensible, by the mildness of your carriage, and the composure, even in your correction of them, that what you do is reasonable in you, and useful and necessary for them; and that it is not out of caprice, passion, or fancy, that you command or forbid them any thing. This they are capable of understanding; and there is no virtue they should be excited to, nor fault they should be kept from, which I do not think they may be convinced of: but it must be by such reasons as their age and understanding are capable of, and those proposed always in very few and plain words. . . .

§ 82.   But, of all the ways whereby children are to be instructed, and their manners formed, the plainest, easiest, and most efficacious, is to set before their eyes the examples of those things you would have them do or avoid. . . .

§ 108.   . . . Recreation is as necessary as labor or food: but because there can be no recreation without delight, which depends not always on reason, but oftener on fancy, it must be permitted children not only to divert themselves, but to do it after their own fashion, provided it be innocently, and without prejudice to their health; and therefore in this case they should not be denied, if they proposed any particular kind of recreation; though I think, in a well-ordered education, they will seldom be brought to the necessity of asking any such liberty. Care should be taken, that what is of advantage to them, they should always do with delight; and, before they are wearied with one, they should be timely diverted to some other useful employment. . . .

§ 118.   Curiosity in children (which I had occasion just to mention, § 108) is but an appetite after knowledge, and therefore ought to be encouraged in them, not only as a good sign, but as the great instrument nature has provided, to remove that ignorance they were born with, and which without this busy inquisitiveness will make them dull and useless creatures. The ways to encourage it, and keep it active and busy, are, I suppose, these following:

1. Not to check or discountenance any inquiries he shall make, nor suffer them to be laughed at; but to answer all his questions, and explain the matters he desires to know, so as to make them as much intelligible to him, as suits the capacity of his age and knowledge. But confound not his understanding with explications or notions that are above it, or with the variety or number of things that are not to his present purpose. Mark what it is his mind aims at in the question, and not what words he expresses it in: and, when you have informed and satisfied him in that, you shall see how his thoughts will enlarge themselves, and how by fit answers he may be led on farther than perhaps you could imagine. For knowledge is grateful to the understanding, as light to the eyes: children are pleased and delighted with it exceedingly, especially if they see that their inquiries are regarded, and that their desire of knowing is encouraged and commended. And I doubt not but one great reason, why many children

abandon themselves wholly to silly sports, and trifle away all their time insipidly, is, because they have found their curiosity balked, and their inquiries neglected. But had they been treated with more kindness and respect, and their questions answered, as they should, to their satisfaction, I doubt not but they would have taken more pleasure in learning, and improving their knowledge, wherein there would be still newness and variety, which is what they are delighted with, than in returning over and over to the same play and playthings. . . .

§ 119. 2. To this serious answering their questions, and informing their understandings in what they desire, as if it were a matter that needed it, should be added some peculiar ways of commendation. Let others, whom they esteem, be told before their faces of the knowledge they have in such and such things; and since we are all, even from our cradles, vain and proud creatures, let their vanity be flattered with things that will do them good; and let their pride set them on work on something which may turn to their advantage. Upon this ground you shall find, that there cannot be a greater spur to the attaining what you would have the elder learn and know himself, than to set him upon teaching it his younger brothers and sisters.

§ 120. 3. As children's inquiries are not to be slighted, so also great care is to be taken, that they never receive deceitful and illuding answers. They easily perceive when they are slighted or deceived, and quickly learn the trick of neglect, dissimulation, and falsehood, which they observe others to make use of. We are not to intrench upon truth in any conversation, but least of all with children; since, if we play false with them, we not only deceive their expectation, and hinder their knowledge, but corrupt their innocence, and teach them the worst of vices. They are travellers newly arrived in a strange country, of which they know nothing: we should therefore make conscience not to mislead them. And though their questions seem sometimes not very material, yet they should be seriously answered; for however they may appear to us (to whom they are long since known) inquiries not worth the making, they are of moment to those who are wholly ignorant. Children are strangers to all we are acquainted with; and all the things they meet with, are at first unknown to them, as they once were to us: and happy are they who meet with civil people, that will comply with their ignorance, and help them to get out of it.

If you or I now should be set down in Japan, with all our prudence and knowledge about us, a conceit whereof makes us perhaps so apt to slight the thoughts and inquiries of children; should we, I say, be set down in Japan, we should, no doubt, (if we would inform ourselves of what is there to be known) ask a thousand questions, which, to a supercilious or inconsiderate Japanese, would seem very idle and impertinent; though to us they would be very material, and of importance to be resolved; and we should be glad to find a man so complaisant and courteous, as to satisfy our demands, and instruct our ignorance.

When any new thing comes in their way, children usually ask the common question of a stranger, What is it? whereby they ordinarily mean nothing but the name; and therefore to tell them how it is called, is usually the proper answer to that demand. The next question usually is, What is it for? And to this it should be answered truly and directly: the use of the thing should be told, and the way explained, how it serves to such a purpose, as far as their capacities can comprehend it; and so of any other circumstances they shall ask about it; not turning them going, till you have given them all the satisfaction they are capable of, and so leading them by your answers into farther questions. And perhaps to a grown man such conversation will not be altogether so idle and insignificant, as we are apt to imagine. The native and untaught suggestions of inquisitive children do often offer things that may set a considering man's thoughts on work. And I think there is frequently more to be learned from the unexpected questions of a child, than the discourses of men, who talk in a road, according to the notions they have borrowed, and the prejudices of their education.

§ 121. 4. Perhaps it may not sometimes be amiss to excite their curiosity, by bringing strange and new things in their way, on purpose to engage their inquiry, and give them occasion to inform themselves about them; and if by chance their curiosity leads them to ask what they should not know, it is a great deal better to tell them plainly, that it is a thing that belongs not to them to know, than to pop them off with a falsehood, or a frivolous answer. . . .

§ 129. This, I think, is sufficiently evident, that children generally hate to be idle: all the care then is that their busy humor should be constantly employed in something of use to them; which if you will attain, you must make what you would have them do, a recreation to them, and not a business. The way to do this, so that they may not perceive you have any hand in it, is this proposed here, viz. to make them weary of that which you would not have them do, by enjoining and making them, under some pretence or other, do it till they are surfeited. . . .

§ 133. This is what I have thought concerning the general method of educating a young gentleman; which, though I am apt to suppose may have some influence on the whole course of his education, yet I am far from imagining it contains all those particulars which his growing years, or peculiar temper, may require. But this being premised in general, we shall, in the next place, descend to a more particular consideration of the several parts of his education. . . .

§ 134. That which every gentleman (that takes any care of his education) desires for his son, besides the estate he leaves him, is contained (I suppose) in these four things, virtue, wisdom, breeding, and learning. I will not trouble myself whether these names do not some of them sometimes stand for the same thing, or really include one another. It serves my turn here to follow the popular use of these words, which, I presume, is clear enough to make me be understood, and I hope there will be no difficulty to comprehend my meaning.

§ 135. I place virtue as the first and most necessary of those endowments that belong to a man or a gentleman, as absolutely requisite to make him valued and beloved by others, acceptable or tolerable to himself. Without that, I think, he will be happy neither in this, nor the other world.

§ 136. As the foundation of this, there ought very early to be imprinted on his mind a true notion of God, as of the independent Supreme Being, Author and Maker of all things, from whom we receive all our good, who loves us, and gives us all things: and, consequent to this, instil into him a love and reverence of this Supreme Being. This is enough to begin with, without going to explain this matter any farther, for fear, lest by talking too early to him of spirits, and being unseasonably forward to make him understand the incomprehensible nature of that infinite Being, his head be either filled with false, or perplexed with unintelligible notions of him. . . .

§ 140. Wisdom I take, in the popular acceptation, for a man's managing his business ably, and with foresight, in this world. This is the product of a good natural temper, application of mind and experience together, and so above the reach of children. The greatest thing that in them can be done towards it, is to hinder them, as much as may be, from being cunning; which, being the ape of wisdom, is the most distant from it that can be. . . .

§ 141.   The next good quality belonging to a gentleman, is good-breeding. There are two sorts of ill-breeding; the one, a sheepish bashfulness; and the other, a misbecoming negligence and disrespect in our carriage; both which are avoided, by duly observing this one rule, Not to think meanly of ourselves, and not to think meanly of others. . . .

§ 147.   You will wonder, perhaps, that I put learning last, especially if I tell you I think it the least part. This may seem strange in the mouth of a bookish man: and this making usually the chief, if not only bustle and stir about children, this being almost that alone which is thought on, when people talk of education, makes it the greater paradox. When I consider what ado is made about a little Latin and Greek, how many years are spent in it, and what a noise and business it makes to no purpose, I can hardly forbear thinking, that the parents of children still live in fear of the schoolmaster's rod, which they look on as the only instrument of education; as if a language or two were its whole business. How else is it possible, that a child should be chained to the oar seven, eight, or ten of the best years of his life, to get a language or two, which I think might be had at a great deal cheaper rate of pains and time, and be learned almost in playing?

Forgive me, therefore, if I say, I cannot with patience think, that a young gentleman should be put into the herd, and be driven with a whip and scourge, as if he were to run the gantlet through the several classes. "What then, say you, would you not have him write and read?" Not so, not so fast, I beseech you. Reading, and writing, and learning, I allow to be necessary, but yet not the chief business.

§ 148.   . . . There may be dice, and playthings, with the letters on them, to teach children the alphabet by playing; and twenty other ways may be found, suitable to their particular tempers, to make this kind of learning a sport to them.

§ 149.   Thus children may be cozened into a knowledge of the letters; be taught to read, without perceiving it to be any thing but a sport, and play themselves into that which others are whipped for. Children should not have any thing like work, or serious, laid on them; neither their minds nor bodies will bear it. It injures their healths; and their being forced and tied down to their books, in an age at enmity with all such restraint, has, I doubt not, been the reason why a great many have hated books and learning all their lives after: it is like a surfeit, that leaves an aversion behind, not to be removed.

§ 150.   I have therefore thought, that if playthings were fitted to this purpose, as they are usually to none, contrivances might be made to teach children to read, whilst they thought they were only playing. For example: What if an ivory-ball were made like that of the royal oak lottery, with thirty-two sides, or one rather of twenty-four or twenty-five sides; and upon several of those sides pasted on an A, upon several others B, on others C, and on others D? I would have you begin with but these four letters, or perhaps only two at first; and when he is perfect in them, then add another; and so on, till each side having one letter, there be on it the whole alphabet. This I would have others play with before him, it being as good a sort of play to lay a stake who shall first throw an A or B, as who upon dice shall throw six or seven. This being a play amongst you, tempt him not to it, lest you make it business; for I would not have him understand it is any thing but a play of older people, and I doubt not but he will take to it of himself. And that he may have the more reason to think it is a play, that he is sometimes in favor admitted to; when the play is done, the ball should be laid up safe out of his reach, that so it may not, by his having it in his keeping at any time, grow stale to him. . . .

§ 195.   To conclude this part, which concerns a young gentleman's studies; his tutor should remember, that his business is not so much to teach him all that is knowable, as to raise in him a love and esteem of knowledge; and to put him in the right way of knowing and improving himself, when he has a mind to it. . . .

§ 216.   Though I am now come to a conclusion of what obvious remarks have suggested to me concerning education, I would not have it thought, that I look on it as a just treatise on this subject. There are a thousand other things that may need consideration; especially if one should take in the various tempers, different inclinations, and particular defaults, that are to be found in children; and prescribe proper remedies. The variety is so great, that it would require a volume; nor would that reach it. Each man's mind has some peculiarity, as well as his face, that distinguishes him from all others; and there are possibly scarce two children, who can be conducted by exactly the same method. Besides that, I think a prince, a nobleman, and an ordinary gentleman's son, should have different ways of breeding. But having had here only some general views, in reference to the main end and aims in education, and those designed for a gentleman's son, whom, being then very little, I considered only as white paper, or wax, to be molded and fashioned as one pleases; I have touched little more than those heads, which I judged necessary for the breeding of a young gentleman of his condition in general; and have now published these my occasional thoughts, with this hope, that, though this be far from being a complete treatise on this subject, or such as that every one may find what will just fit his child in it; yet it may give some small light to those, whose concern for their dear little ones makes them so irregularly bold, that they dare venture to consult their own reason, in the education of their children, rather than wholly to rely upon old custom. . . .

CHAPTER V

Eighteenth Century Revolution In Philosophical and Educational Thought

A study of history may very well help us to avoid mistakes of the past, but more importantly, it provides us with intellectual models that may be suggestive for our own time. There are many different ways to approach intellectual history—as a warfare between science and theology, as a struggle between certain dualisms such as mind and matter, or as a chronology of art, music, or social and political structures, to name only a few. But whatever the approach, the underlying rationale is to achieve some understanding of how men have ordered their lives in the context of their particular environment. Thoughtful men of each generation have come to grips with the attitudes that constitute their intellectual heritage, and the speculations and conclusions that they make in light of their own times have an impact on succeeding generations.

During the eighteenth century, concepts about the nature of man, man's place in the universe, and the nature and limits of man's knowledge underwent significant changes. Sometimes labeled the *Age of Reason,* sometimes called the *Enlightenment,* the eighteenth century was a scene of intellectual and physical conflict. Many ideas and institutions were overthrown or modified beyond recognition, and the central purpose of this chapter is to examine the implications for education. Jean Jacques Rousseau (1712–1778), and Immanuel Kant (1724–1804), are pivotal figures in the history of man's intellectual development. As Rousseau's doctrines contributed significantly to altered views of government, religion, social structure, and education, Kant's thoughtful criticisms provided new insights to philosophical concepts and implemented the reconstruction of philosophy demanded by the changing concepts. The interaction between the educational and philosophical thought of these men was significant during their lives, and it has left its mark on succeeding generations.

The stage for the contributions of Rousseau and Kant was set by two fundamental concepts of the eighteenth century—nature and reason. Rousseau's democratic and humanitarian ideas were an attack upon the growth of an extreme rationalism that expressed religious ideals scientifically and made Deism the religion of intellectuals. He contributed the concept of "the natural goodness of man" to the intellectual world, and his idea that teaching should consider the individual interests of the child over a prescribed subject matter is an educational milestone.

Kant's contribution was a synthesis of the rational and the empirical into a critical philosophy which depends upon the view that man is a combination of the rational and the religious. Kant, although separated from Plato by more than two thousand years, reacted philosophically to a similar stimulus. As Plato had reacted to the skeptical conclusions introduced into Greek society by the Sophists, Kant reacted to the skepticism of David Hume. But while Plato's reaction was to construct a world view based on abstruse metaphysical principles, Kant's was to plunge into an exhaustive investigation of the limits of man's knowledge in order to ascertain the possibility of a science of metaphysics. The diverse reactions to a debilitating skepticism can surely be explained, in part, by the position each occupied in history. Certainly the philosophical contributions of both men, as well as the educational offerings of Rousseau, would have taken a different turn if these thinkers had lived in a time other than their own. It is important, therefore, to consider the intellectual bequests of Rousseau and Kant in the light of the philosophical attitudes and educational ideals that were the heritage of eighteenth century thinkers.

Philosophical Views and Educational Ideals

We have seen that philosophy is systematic when there is an attempt to find a consistency among the solutions to metaphysical, epistemological, and axiological problems. It follows that the answers made by philosophers throughout history to any one of the so-called "large questions" should characterize the general philosophical attitude of each. A characterization of the development of Western philosophical attitudes from the early Greeks through the eighteenth century, in even the broadest sense, exceeds the scope of this study. But it should serve the purpose of relating the mainstream of philosophical views to educational ideals to settle upon one of the recurrent philosophical problems for the theme of this investigation.

Throughout the history of philosophy, man's major concern about the nature of reality has been the primary issue which has traditionally divided philosophers. It can be said that the resolution to this problem determines the character of the particular philosophical system. This seems to be sufficient justification for the assumption that a brief historical sketch of man's search for reality will be an efficient and effective method for tracing his intellectual development, and that it may also serve as a basis to depict the relationship between man's philosophical attitudes and his educational ideals. An extensive study of man's intellectual development would include an investigation of the social, the religious, the scientific, and the artistic aspects of his life; but it must suffice our purpose to note that the development among these areas is so interwoven that they are as strands of a single cord and that in the event of any choice among them, the theme should remain the same.

A Search for Reality

Although an investigation into the nature of reality is considered to be a metaphysical problem, strictly speaking, the word metaphysics was not included in the philosophical vocabulary until sometime during the first century B.C. It was Andronicus of Rhodes who, assembling the rediscovered works of Aristotle, placed the writings about first principles after the writings on physics, or meta-physics. Until then, investigations into the nature of things, their causes and their purposes, were referred to as investigations into first principles, and it is merely a technicality that we do not speak of Platonic and Aristotelian metaphysics.

The concern about primary causes and the nature of reality is as old as philosophy. Basically, there are two answers to the question regarding the nature of reality. Naturalists believe that some type of universal substance is found in the physical aspects of our world. Realists believe that the real or the universal is in some supersensible realm. Modifications and variations of the two extremes are found throughout the history of philosophy, sometimes one dominating the general attitudes of scholars, sometimes the other. It should be noted that during the eighteenth century the term realism began to take on quite a different meaning, and in modern philosophical parlance, those who believe that reality is in the supersensible are called idealists.

Most of the early Greeks were occupied with a search for primary causes, and they were spectacularly successful in systematizing their world views. For the most part, these early Greeks posited the character of the real to be in one of the elements of nature. Thales believed water to be the ultimate substance, and Anaximenes believed it to be air. Anaximander, who represents a more sophisticated form of naturalism, posited the real to be the material cause or an indeterminate "stuff." Later emphasis upon the elements of earth, air, fire, and water by Empedocles is something of a regression but is probably closer to the spirit of naturalism.

Early Greek educational ideals were rationalistic in thinking there was no authority higher than reason. As a result, free inquiry flourished. The laws of nature were thought to be the basis for morality, and life was to be enjoyed to the fullest. The Sophists, who believed in the relativity of truth and that man is the measure of all things, naturally encouraged the sort of learning that directly benefits man in his social and physical environment. They emphasized the humanities and considered public speaking to be the highest art form. Socrates, however, believed that truth is absolute and that the dialectic method can achieve an absolute definition of truth. He considered intellectual growth to be far more important than the material aspects of life and believed that education is a spontaneous process that should be enjoyed by all people. It was impossible for him to accept a mechanistic interpretation of life, as he ascribed purpose and moral order to the universe, and believed that intellect and morality are synonymous. When the real is thought to be in the individual, as Socrates believed it to be, the primary purpose of education must be self-knowledge, the method reason, and the ultimate goal the creation of rational individuals.

Although Plato, like Socrates, could not accept a mechanistic reality, he did not believe that reality is in the individual. As we have noted earlier, Plato epitomizes the realist who views the physical as a barrier to a realization of the universal. The Platonic view, which posits reality to be in the realm of the eternal, unchanging, and completely perfect, immaterial Forms, implies knowledge that is not concerned with the individual. Knowledge cannot be relative as the Forms are the ideal standard of evaluation, and the highest type of knowledge is philosophy which strives for a complete view of reality.

Aristotle also rejected a mechanistic philosophy, but he was far more concerned with specific things than he was with the reality of universals. His view of reality extended into all substances, as his belief in the unity of matter and form precluded formless matter and matterless form in all things but pure actuality or God who is pure form. Aristotle argued that the changing relationship between form and matter accounts for changes in the phenomenal world in a way that Plato's static Forms were unable to do. Aristotle's view that man's intellect is able to achieve knowledge of the universal by natural means is a synthesis of realism and naturalism, and along with his idea of the immortality of the active reason is the base of his ideal for education. He stressed the importance of man and his ability to reason, moderation in all things, and the development of all of man's capacities. The idea that there is a correlation between where reality is posited and educational ideals is particularly clear-cut in the ideas of Plato and Aristotle, and their different views of art are illustrative of the point. Plato, maintaining that art has a secondary reality, thought it should be strictly regulated in the state; but Aristotle, who posited reality in all things, believed that art is a catharsis which expands the vision and enables man to see life on a cosmic plane.

After the death of Aristotle in 322 B.C., scholars began to place a greater emphasis on the ethical than they did on the nature of reality. A conflict developed between faith and reason and between skepticism and religion. Knowledge became more specialized, and the idea of practicality reigned supreme. One might expect a wane of creativity, refinement, and freedom under such circumstances. It was indeed the case, and education came to be valued less for its own good than for the good it could achieve. By the time the glory of Greece faded into the glory of the Roman Empire, the period of system-building had come to a standstill. Roman education was limited. The primary emphasis was on the utilitarian, and there was no interest in speculation about the large questions. Philosophers were thought to be inferior to statesmen, and professional education achieved a new high. It is not surprising that many historians ascribe the decline of the Roman Empire as much to the system of education as to any one other cause.

Before the philosophical world could recover, the advent of Christianity brought the teachings of Jesus with an influence on Western education that should not be minimized. The influence is so diverse that it has been felt by deists, pietists, orthodox believers, and liberals. Like Socrates, Jesus believed in the identity of knowledge and virtue and that real education and true religion are both ways of life. The emphasis was on the individual as an intellectual and emotional being who desires something more than knowledge. Early Christian education equated teaching with preaching, and the fundamentals of doctrine were taught in catechumenal schools. The search for reality had a religious character, and the writings of Plato and Aristotle were thought to be pagan until St. Augustine began to view Plato's spiritualism to be well suited to a Christian who seeks salvation in another realm. Augustine's philosophy, although relying on the authority of the Church, reflects the Platonic influence which also colors his educational ideas. Augustine believed that only a few are capable of grasping the truth, which is absolute; that subjects should be mastered not for their own sake but as background for the study of Church doctrines; and that all learning should have a religious purpose.

The Council of Nicea and the Union of State and Church contributed further to the emphasis on the religious in philosophical and educational thinking. Revelation and divine authority held sway in such a fashion that any system-building was merely the elaboration of certain beliefs, or faiths. The year 529 A.D. stands as a further monument to the ascendency of faith and mysticism, for in that year the Emperor Justinian forbade the teaching of philosophy at Athens, and the pagan university which had its beginnings in Plato's Academy of 388 B.C. was closed to any formal scholarly endeavor.

The light of reason was dimmed until sometime during the eleventh and twelfth centuries. This is not to say that there was no intellectual activity during the middle ages, but the goal of the medievalist was salvation in a heavenly world. It was believed that the physical was a deterrent to the attainment of the goal, and intellectual ferment was tempered by the gradual formalizing of Church dogma. The Greek ideals of literary excellence through intellectual and physical education and the Roman ideal of the orator and rhetorician were replaced by a curriculum rigidly oriented to an unliberal view of the seven liberal arts—grammar, rhetoric, dialectic, arithmetic, geometry, music, and astronomy. The method, based upon disciplining human nature viewed in moral and religious terms, resulted in a highly verbal and formal education, and views remained static until Peter Abelard, who was born in 1079.

Although Abelard is perhaps better remembered for his love of Heloise than for his contributions to philosophy, his position in philosophical controversy is secure, for he symbolizes the resurgence of reason as critic of all beliefs. His philosophy, conceptualism, or moderate realism, is one of mediation between the extreme individualism of Roscelin (c. 1050–c.1120), and the universalism of William of Champeaux (1070–1121). The theological implications of this nominalist-realist controversy were to question the nature and the existence of God. The problem was simple. The definition of substance implied possession of attributes, and attributes implied finitude. This was paradoxical, of course, but little more than the Platonic one and many an inquiry in another time. Abelard entered the fray, insisting that "Universals exist at the same time *ante res* (as Ideas in the divine intellect), *in rebus* (as the common natures shared by individual substances) and *post res* (as the general concepts formed by human minds)."[1]

In more familiar terms, the nominalist-realist debate was over the question of whether particular things in the world are merely imperfect copies of actually existing universals, or if particular things in the world are simply, as a matter of convenience, given names that arise out of habit or accidental usage and do not refer in any way to universals. Abelard attempted to mediate the debate in much the same way that Aristotle had resolved the naturalism-realism problem some fourteen hundred years earlier. But the medieval world was not quite ready for Abelard's attempt to harmonize revelation and reason, and he found himself in constant difficulty. It was more than a century later before St. Thomas Aquinas successfully modified the positions of Aristotle and Abelard to coincide with certain doctrines of the Church.

Eleven centuries of belief in the reality of the super-sensible, and the tenuousness of the physical, prohibited questions about how man knows the real and about the nature and the limits of man's knowledge. But the development of science during the sixteenth century contributed immeasurably to an increasing emphasis on epistemological concerns. As early as 1543, with Copernicus' *De Revolutionibus Orbium Celestium* and Vesalius' *Concerning the Fabric of the Human Body,* the vision of the scientist began to emerge. The new group of scholars who were primarily interested in natural matters began to supplant the scholastics, and new concepts began to replace the traditional ones. Scientific progress, facilitated by an expanding universe, the invention of printing, the invention of better scientific instruments, the establishment of scientific societies, and cooperative research, left no room for old logic. The new knowledge was based on observation and experimentation—induction motivated by doubt, rather than deduction motivated by faith—and the difference is descriptive of the new attitudes of the early moderns.

The new scientific perspective infected both philosophic and educational attitudes. Awe at the miracles of the Old Testament gave way to a new regard for astronomy, mathematics, and the order of nature. The *Idols*

---

[1] B. A. G. Fuller, revised by Sterling M. McMurrin, *A History of Philosophy, Ancient and Medieval* (New York: Henry Holt & Co., 1955), Vol. I, p. 376.

of Sir Francis Bacon contributed the idea that the beliefs of others should be respected but ought not to be blindly accepted. God should be worshiped in a rational manner, and real knowledge would lead to religion by demonstrating the order and providence of the universe. The modern period of philosophy can be dated from René Descartes' use of mathematical knowledge to demonstrate the existence of God. Descartes and later philosophers, who also depended upon reason to determine the nature of reality, had a greater concern for the epistemological than for the metaphysical, and the metaphysical categories of naturalism and realism were replaced by the categories of rationalism and empiricism.

John Amos Comenius (1592–1670), a product of the reformation, made greater educational contributions than any of his peers. His educational ideals are closely related to his religious views, which grew out of a deep mystical faith, and are colored by his conviction that in life's struggle good will triumphs over evil. Comenius believed in the greatness of man and in every man's ability to learn all things. He agreed with his contemporaries about faculties of the mind but placed greater stress than most on the importance of sense experience for knowledge. Comenius' belief in progress through science and in power through knowledge led him to place greater emphasis on the useful subjects than on the humanities. He reacted against Church control of education even though he felt that the primary goal of education should be to promulgate the teachings of Christ. He firmly believed that learning is an unending process of education by experiencing and doing.

The beginning of the eighteenth century marks a distinct break with medieval traditions. There was an intellectual, social, religious, and political turning point in the tides of time that is characterized by protest against all authority, class disinctions, and emotionalism. It was an age of optimism when the articles of faith were reason, progress, and peace; an age of optimism which predicted an end to the evils of ignorance, immorality, bondage, poverty, and crime; an age of optimism which extended to the view of nature. According to a description by Crane Brinton in *Ideas & Man,* "Nature, to the man of the Enlightenment, was the external world he lived in, a world that clearly existed but in which by no means everything that happened was 'natural'."[2] The base for such a cheerful acceptance of the natural world is found in the writings of Descartes, Newton, and Locke. Newton's *Mathematical Principles of Natural Philosophy* (1687), which formulated laws of gravitation and cause and effect, led man to see the cosmos and the natural environment as orderly, simple, and uniform. The idea of a world machine was popular, and the mathematical and scientific laws influenced many areas of man's thinking. Natural law became the final arbiter of opinion, and the appeal to nature in matters from governmental to moral was the rule.

There is no better expression of the concept of orderliness than the

---

2 Crane Brinton, *Ideas & Men* (New York: Prentice-Hall, Inc., 1950), p. 370.

religious view called Deism, which became popular during the eighteenth century. The view of a mechanical universe, with clocklike works that had been wound up and set in motion by a detached sort of God with urgent business in some other realm, left man to fend for himself as best he could among the workings of nature. Reason became the prime factor in man's struggle for survival and progress and was the key to all of the mysteries of this world and of the one beyond. Reason would open the doors to the most abstruse mathematical and scientific phenomena, and reason would bring man closer to perfection, the goal of all human endeavor. Such an idyllic view of man and his environs was the perfect foil for the natural cynicism of Jean Jacques Rousseau.

Jean Jacques Rousseau (1712–1778)

In spite of the tremendous influence Rousseau had on the course of modern civilization, he is personally one of the sorriest figures in history. Explanations of his excessive behavior pattern make a fascinating psychological study, but they are scant justification for his record of self-indulgence, arrogance, irritability, irresponsibility, lasciviousness and outrageous actions. The chronicle of his sixty-six years is such a shoddy one that it would be pointless to repeat it, were it not for the intriguing possibilities that his doctrines may have grown out of an intense psychological need for self-justification. This is not to decry the significance of his views, for in making an assessment of their worth, historians are far less inclined to make a value correlation between source and concept than Rousseau himself did in regard to the arts and sciences. Rousseau wrote that:

> Astronomy was born of superstition; eloquence of ambition, hatred, falsehood and flattery; geometry of avarice; physics of an idle curiosity; and even moral philosophy of human pride. Thus the arts and sciences owe their birth to our vices; we should be less doubtful of their advantages if they sprang from our virtues.[3]

Jean Jacques Rousseau's birth in 1712, at Geneva, resulted in his mother's death, and for ten years the child was cared for by his father. When the father deserted Rousseau, leaving him to the guidance of relatives, the boy was sent to a village school in Bossey for the next few years which was the extent of his formal education. The facts attest that Rousseau must have been an obnoxious child—undisciplined, irritable and indolent. He admits in his *Confessions* that he was a liar, a cheat, and a thief. It is hard to say if his father did him a favor, or a disservice, when he taught the six-year-old to read romantic novels and such works as Plutarch's *Lives*, and Bossuet's *Discourse on Universal History*. The literary diet was far too rich and overstimulating for a child, but it left him with an insatiable appetite for reading.

---

[3] J. J. Rousseau, "Discourse on the Arts and Sciences," *The Social Contract and Discourse* (New York: Everyman's Library, E. P. Dutton & Co., Inc., 1914), pp. 139–140.

The young Rousseau was incapable of adjusting to the give and take of childhood play and as a young man he was no more successful in holding a job. He tried everything from studying for the priesthood, clerical work, music, and secretarial work, to teaching, but for the first half of his life his only productivity was to sire five children. All were illegitimate (he finally married his mistress after living with her for twenty-three years), and each was immediately dispatched to an orphanage by the father who was later to become famous for his views about educating a child according to nature. At thirty-seven, Rousseau was a bitter and unhappy man who had as much trouble keeping his friends as he did holding a job. He was unable to win the acceptance of the intellectuals of his time, nor, in spite of his efforts, was he accepted by the patrons of the arts and letters who were the protectors of the intellectuals. As a result, he hated himself and all of society which he blamed for his notably undistinguished record.

The turning point of Rousseau's life came in his thirty-seventh year when he happened to see a notice of an essay contest sponsored by the Academy of Dijon. The essay was to answer the question: *"Did the restoration of Sciences and Arts contribute to purify morality?"* There are some accounts that when Rousseau read about the contest he was suddenly caught up in an experience akin to intellectual drunkenness; others say that genius settled on his shoulders like a mantle; and still others imply a sort of mystical experience. There are elements of all three in Rousseau's own recounting of how he was affected by the announcement of the contest. In any case, Rousseau decided to enter, and his essay, the *Discours sur les sciences et les arts* is the result of his decision. Before writing it Rousseau asked a friend to predict how he would respond to the question, but the only prediction the friend would make was that he was sure Rousseau's answer would be different from any other. That this was the case may have had some bearing on the decision of the members of the academy to award the prize to Rousseau, or they could have been influenced by his elaborate prose and elegant rhetoric. Whatever the reason, Rousseau's scathing denunciation of civilization (which did not actually answer the question but broadened it by replying that *ever since the origins of mankind* the arts and sciences had been a cause of moral decadence) won the prize, and Rousseau was seized by a holy mission to restyle all aspects of society.

The prize-winning essay was the first of a series of severe criticisms of society and its corrupting influence upon the manners and morals of the individual—a polemic that did little to disguise Rousseau's plea for understanding of his own actions. It has been said that Rousseau spent the last half of his life rationalizing about his earlier misspent years, and one biographer has said that his works were actually all novels. The same biographer reasoned that since Rousseau detested things as they were, he made them over to suit his own liking. Thus, he reasoned, *Inequality* was Rousseau's novel of humanity; the *Contract* his novel of sociology; *Émile* his novel of education; the *New Heloise* his novel of sentiment; and the

Confessions a novel of his own life. But regardless of the label attached to the works, Rousseau's doctrines have unquestionably had a tremendous influence on the thinking of others about government, religion, social life, and education. In spite of the fact that Rousseau died in exile, a victim of his own recalcitrant temperament, he looms large in the annals of education.

One of the most severe criticisms that Rousseau made of contemporary society was what he considered to be the debilitating effect of the prevailing emphasis on the rational aspect of human nature. Rousseau voiced the opinion that reason is not a part of man's nature, which is essentially emotional, but is a contrivance, a development. He agreed that one of the goals of education should be to *develop* the rational in man but insisted that it was erroneous to place a greater emphasis on reason than on emotion, particularly in the educative process. This doctrine serves as the base for his educational ideas, which are for the most part delineated in his *Émile*.

Rousseau's New Education: Émile

The eighteenth century mathematical interpretation of the universe, remote from the strivings of the individual, was untenable for one who believed that a forced emphasis upon the artificialities of the arts and sciences tends to smother the natural goodness of man. Rousseau's contention that such extreme rationalism was a destructive force colored all of his thinking, which is admittedly more remarkable for its originality and abundance, than for any real greatness. But unlike many critics, Rousseau was never at a loss for alternatives to the concepts and institutions under attack, a quality, which coupled with his facility for literary self-expression, gives *Émile* a position in the order of classics. The study, with its emphasis on the education of the individual in accordance with nature, has had more influence on the course of education than any other comparable writing, and it continues to have significance for us today when the complexities of twentieth century living often threaten to engulf the individual.

The excitement and stimulation, engendered by the story Rousseau tells to illustrate his argument for a natural education, is not dependent upon whether one agrees or disagrees with the thesis. Nor does the merit of the work rely upon the practicability of the course of study that Rousseau outlines for Émile. Rousseau recognized in his Preface to the work that the practicability of the educational program would depend upon the conditions under which it was attempted, and that these would vary according to nationality, class, and other such considerations. He stated that he was far less concerned with the *particular* applications than he was with the plan's *capability* of application. Émile's education obviously could not be accomplished in public schools, as a literal interpretation of the program would present difficulties, even for tutors in private schoolrooms. The work is most effectively viewed as an illustration of certain principles which may be adapted to methods suitable for a variety of conditions.

The plan for Rousseau's new education was prompted by the interest of a mother who was concerned about the best possible education for her son. It grew from a small collection of memoirs and reflections into a large book which presents an alternative to the kind of education Rousseau thought to be more destructive than constructive. The proposal was a bold one, spectacular not only for its unorthodoxy, but exciting by virtue of Rousseau's clever device of highlighting abstract propositions with the story of Émile, a healthy, attractive lad of ordinary abilities. The child, sired by Rousseau's active imagination, was far more real and enduring than any of his natural children who were lost to their parents and to history. Unlike the other five, Émile is secure in the annals of education as the first to receive full benefit of a natural education constructed with the child himself as the center of the educational concern.

The first drafts of *Émile* began with a general discussion and proceeded directly to the education of the young boy, but so many who read these asked for particulars about the training of infants that Rousseau set about gathering what information he could about babies from mothers of his acquaintance. He must have regretted many times having given away his five children—if for no other reason than that they could have provided him with excellent source material. At the same time, they would surely have been corrupted by the evils of a man-made society and could not have provided the same sort of enduring satisfaction that Rousseau realized from his brainchild.

The work, revised to include instructions for the care of infants and finally published in 1762, consists of five books, each dealing with one of the five progressive stages of Rousseau's new education.

Book One (Infancy). Book One begins with a general statement concerning the dichotomy between the natural man and the man who lives in society, and the contrast between the natural goodness in man and the unnatural evils of a corrupting society. Based on the premise that we must therefore choose between educating a man and educating a citizen, Rousseau attempts to demonstrate a possible reconciliation by means of a controlled environment during the educational process so that the original nature of the child may be preserved while he is being educated to take his place in society.

Locke had emphasized the importance of reasoning with children, but Rousseau observed that such a technique resulted in the most stupid children who merely imitated their elders. He maintained that since reason is compounded of all of the other faculties, it is the last to develop and is ideally the *result* of a good education. If children appreciated reason there would be no need for their education, and it struck Rousseau as being utter nonsense to assume that the ends could be used as a means towards itself. The error was in the accepted but unnatural view of the child as a small adult.

The gardener does not expect a miniature plant, a small copy of the fully developed flower or shrub, to spring all at once from his planting. The good gardener knows that the ways of nature are set, and that each shoot must be nourished and cultivated and carefully tended until it reaches maturity and fulfills the promise of the bud. Rousseau maintained that the child is no less a creature of nature and should be encouraged in the same manner to grow and develop into manhood according to the laws of nature. The function of the teacher becomes similar to that of the gardener and to carry the analogy a little further, better an untended plant—or child—left to grow wild in nature, than one forced too soon into some preconceived, imposed pattern.

Rousseau's discussion in Book One is general, in that his instructions for the care of infants are not related to any particular child. The natural educators at this stage are the parents, and it is not until Rousseau takes over the tutelage of the young Émile that his educational directives become particularized. The stage of infancy begins at birth, or even before and lasts until the child is weaned—which should not be hurried but should come naturally at about the same time that the child begins to speak and to take his first steps. The purpose of this earliest stage should be to allow the infant to develop into a good healthy animal. He should be carefully tended, but not restrained, forced, or coddled. He should be given opportunities for as wide a variety of experiences as his vague feelings of pleasure and pain will allow.

Book Two (Boyhood). The primary emphasis in Book Two is on "negative education" and points out the dangers of premature instruction. As Rousseau likened the infant to a healthy animal, he likens the young boy to a noble savage who learns best through direct experience and who is motivated only by an interest, or curiosity, and a *need* to learn. Rousseau, basing his educational directives on the idea of emerging faculties, maintains that a boy does not yet have the ability to compare and relate facts and can only make sensual judgments where information gained from one sense is checked by information gained from the others. Thus a very young boy is only capable of concrete thinking, and it would be going against nature to introduce him to subjects that require abstraction. The boy cannot be expected to have correct understanding, and unless he is withdrawn from the artificial life of society he will be at the mercy of his social environment. Since the child must be protected from vice and error until the age of reason when he can acquire virtue and truth on his own, his boyhood education must be more negative than otherwise.

Any positive education during this stage would come through the training of the senses, the first of our faculties to mature. Such training would include the natural activities of sports and all sorts of exercises that engage the senses. Other kinds of educational activities would be postponed until about the age of twelve after the senses are fully developed.

Book Three (Approach to Adolescence). Up until the years approaching adolescence, bodily activity has provided sufficient expression for Émile's urge to activity, but as his powers develop past the point of utility the energy must find another outlet. This is nature's way, according to Rousseau, of telling us that the time has come for labor, instruction, and studies. Thinking is still based on sense data, but from the years of twelve to fifteen a boy begins to develop a capacity for sustained attention and thus begins to make comparisons and predictions. During these years the boy commences to see the use of things and the underlying reasons for them. The concept of utility forms a part of his intelligence.

Émile is a Robinson Crusoe on the island of the world using his intelligence for personal survival and for his own well-being. He is curious and adventuresome, but his urges come from nature where the drive for knowledge is a utilitarian one, rather than from society where the drive is the desire to be well thought of by others. Because of his mental limitations (a natural limitation at this stage of development), his explorations are still confined to science and handcrafts. His knowledge is not memorized but that which he has gained through his own efforts and experiences.

Book Four (Adolescence). According to Rousseau, each individual is born twice; the first time into existence, or as a human being, and the second time as a man or a woman, or into self-awareness. The second birth, or the rebirth, occurs at adolescence when the boy is preparing to cross the threshold of manhood and enter into a moral sphere. His awakened sex drive brings the realization of new needs that become more and more insistent as he reaches the end of adolescence and full entry into community life.

The need for a mate manifests itself first in an interest in other people and Émile's self-love gradually changes to a concern for all human relationships. The first sentiment to affect a young man is friendship, and the first social sentiment that affects the heart is pity. The second stage of adolescence begins in the eighteenth year when it becomes time to study human differences in order to achieve an idea of the whole social order. This is the time to read the facts of history as a basis for forming judgments about them. It is the time for the study of literature, languages, and social studies. On the whole, at this stage there is little difference between Émile's course of study and that of other young men of his day, the crucial difference being that Émile's education is to prepare him for an ideal marriage, rather than for a career, which is the usual motivation for the education of young men.

The final years of adolescence mean that manhood is near and it is time for the student to enter into society, for his taste to be developed, for him to become aware of agreeable or disagreeable things. Social groups, good books, theatre, a study of the classics and of Latin (Rousseau finds the ancients to be closer to nature than the modern writers) are necessary to the full development of taste. It is also time to begin thinking about the ideal mate for Émile. She must be sought, but not found too soon, and it is with this in mind that Rousseau guides Émile on the search in the places where she is least likely to be. Throughout all of the stages of Émile's education, Rousseau insists on the right time and place for all things, with nature always the determining factor.

Book Five (*Marriage*). The final stage of Émile's education culminates in his marriage to the ideal woman, which gives Rousseau the opportunity to embellish his story and to extend his educational theories to include a discussion of the natural education for girls. Émile's story is interrupted long enough for Rousseau to delineate the essential differences between the sexes which go deep in human nature and which determine the educational differences between the two sexes. When Émile finally meets his ideal mate, Sophie, they are still too young for marriage and Émile and his tutor depart on further journeys that will prepare the youth for citizenship by allowing him to study at firsthand the problems of government. Finally, at the conclusion of these travels, again when the time is right, the last task of the tutor is to instruct the young people in their marital rights and duties. The story ends with Émile's announcement that he and Sophie are to have a child and that their need for the aid and advice of the beloved tutor will be even greater as the young parents undertake the tutelage of their own children.

We gain a number of educational principles from Rousseau's new education that were revolutionary during his time and that are still significant. Some of these are: 1) the point of view of the child as a creature of nature who grows according to the laws of nature; 2) an emphasis on the importance of the individual which results in a child-centered educational process; 3) an emphasis on stages of development and grading of experiences; 4) the study of the child for the formulation of educational directives, such as readiness for learning and motivational techniques.

Émile is generally recognized as Rousseau's masterwork, which is one of the reasons for its being the best known of his educational writings, but it is by no means a complete statement of his educational views. A study limited to the one work is apt to result in a one-sided view of his doctrines as well as a misinterpretation of *Émile*. The fact that the views in this work are concretely put often leads to the wrong assumption that Rousseau limited his directives to the sort of education he outlined for Émile, but the broader and more accurate educational idea is one that would result in individual perfection and civic devotion in a natural society. Rousseau had developed a scheme for such national education in his article on political economy which appeared in the *Encyclopédie* in 1755, and where the Platonic influence is especially strong. Rousseau made the statement in *Émile* that Plato's *Republic* was the finest treatise ever written on education, and his discipleship to Plato which indicates an interest in national education is evident in many of his works. A complete picture of Rousseau's educational doctrines should include a study of minor educational writings, such as the *Project for the Education of M. de Sainte-Marie,* which was drawn up after teaching two young sons of M. de Mably for several months; the *Memoir on the Education of the Prince of Wirtemberg's Infant Daughter, Sophie,* which is only one of a number of letters that Rousseau wrote after the publication of *Émile* in response to questions by parents who wished to follow the methods in *Émile; Extracts from Three Letters to the Abbé M.;* Chapters III and IV from the *Considerations on the Government of Poland* (1773), which was written at the suggestion of Count de Wielhorski; Rousseau's own boyhood from *The Confessions,* Books I and II; Part V of *The New Heloise;* and finally, the article, "Political Economy."

Immanuel Kant (1724–1804)

Immanuel Kant is one of the most important of all the philosophers who have engaged in the monumental task of constructing world views, for no other system in the history of philosophy has had such an immediate and profound effect on the thoughts and lives of intellectuals. On the other hand, his influence on education, while of great significance, has not been as obvious or as direct as Rousseau's. There was nothing abstruse nor highly intellectual about the ideas Rousseau articulated so skillfully, so their effect on education was instantaneous. Also, his natural education caught the fancy of many of the nobility who could afford tutors to implement the techniques, which helped to popularize the new education during Rousseau's lifetime. Kant's contributions were of such a nature that while their effects on education have been far reaching and of considerable consequence, the general public is not apt to relate them to the philosopher. It was Kant's *Critique of Pure Reason* that revolutionized ideas about how man comes to know, and these ideas form the substructure for the variety of educational theories that have developed since the eighteenth century. His thinking is the highly intellectual sort that takes a good deal of time to sift down to a practical level that can be understood by the masses, and in any event, there is always a considerable gap between educational theories and educational practices.

Unfortunately, even many histories of educational thought neglect the significance of Kant's contributions to educational method and educational philosophy. Some historians recognize his educational influence but fail to do more than touch lightly upon the relationship between his philosophical attitudes and educational directives. Others limit their discussions to the *Critique* or to Kant's theory of ethics, and still others deny his contribution of original ideas about pedagogy, mentioning him only because of the important role Rousseau played in his development by demonstrating in *Émile* and the *Social Contract* the importance of a vital, moral philosophy.

Certainly Kant's "notes" on pedagogy are overshadowed by the magnitude of his methodical and systematic philosophical works, and by themselves, cannot be considered as being especially noteworthy. But the "notes" take on added dimension when considered as a continuation of Kant's general philosophy. This is the rationale for the more detailed discussion of the Kantian synthesis in this text than is the general rule.

Kant was born in Königsberg to parents of meagre circumstances. His entire life, the very antithesis of the excitement engendered by his thinking, was spent in the seclusion of the small-town atmosphere. Although he was raised in a home filled with human warmth, he was a methodic pedant, and his personal life was a combination of Rousseauistic piety and Prussian rigidity. His early religious training was pietistic, and the stress upon a personal inner religion left its mark long after Kant ceased formal association with the pietists.

During his entire lifetime Kant ventured less than forty miles from his native Königsberg, but his exceptionally wide range of reading compensated for the limitation, and contributed towards making him a brilliant conversationalist and a highly successful teacher. Although for the most part Kant's friendships were limited to the Prussian officials he knew in Königsberg, he was by no means a recluse. His social contacts provided him with personal pleasure and with a kind of extension into the larger world. Kant studied the Leibniz-Wolffian philosophy under Martin Knutzen, who was a critical young man of only twenty-one when he began teaching in Königsberg. Knutzen never doubted the rationalist tenet that the human mind is capable of discovering the necessary principles of reality, but he felt that Newton had been successful in integrating observational data into a necessary conceptual scheme. Kant, Knutzen's favorite student, was greatly concerned to understand the success of Newtonian physics in terms of method, and the influence of Newton's physics and Lockean psychology was at odds with his Leibnizian training. Long before he thought of writing the *Critique of Pure Reason,* Kant came to feel that modern physics worked where Leibnizian metaphysics did not.

Kant's early writings indicated a wide range of interests including science, metaphysics, and religion—and the scope of his abilities was recognized by offers of the Chair of Poetry at the Universities of Königsberg and Jena. He refused both offers, and in 1755 he became tutor in the family of Count Kayserling; in 1766 he was made under-librarian; and in 1770 he accepted the chair of logic and metaphysics at the University of Königsberg. He gave his *Dissertation on the Form and Principles of the Sensible and Intelligible World,* on assumption of the chair.

Kantian Synthesis

During the years following his appointment, Kant set about a systematic analysis of his thinking which is variously referred to as the critical philosophy, criticism, transcendentalism, or transcendental idealism. We have made brief mention of some of the influences that led Kant to feel keenly the frustration of metaphysics. But it was the impact of David Hume's skeptical conclusions which wakened Kant from his "dogmatic slumbers." Hume and Leibniz were in complete opposition, and Kant, feeling the influence and merits of both, sought to find a way between them. The results of Kant's mature investigations began appearing in 1781 when he published the *Critique of Pure Reason*. The more important works that followed are: *Prolegomena to Any Future Metaphysics* (1783); *Fundamental Principles of the Metaphysics of Morals* (1785); *Critique of Pure Reason* (Second Edition, 1787); *Critique of Practical Reason* (1787); *Critique of Judgment* (1790); *Religion Within the Limits of Reason Alone* (1793); *Perpetual Peace* (1795); *Metaphysics of Ethics* (1797). There were other publications, but they were of less importance in the determination of Kant's contribution to man's conceptualizing processes.

Kant recognized three distinct stages in his own philosophical thought, and it is interesting to note that these have counterparts in the broad outlines of the history of philosophical thinking. They are dogmatism, skepticism, and criticism. The first stage, dogmatism, represents that time when man accepts assumptions without any sort of examination or question regarding their truth or validity. As we noted, Kant was shaken out of this stage by Hume's extreme empiricism, and he progressed to the second stage, skepticism, where all things are cautiously rejected. But the belief that a philosopher must make a positive contribution impelled Kant to a reevaluation leading to the third stage, criticism, which is a stage of searching analyses based upon sound principles of judgment. Once again a certainty about truth is attained, but now it is an empirical certainty and one that is open to further questioning. Kant exemplified the true philosopher in that as late as 1802 he began a reevaluation of his whole philosophy. His notes in this regard were published as *Opus Postumum*.

The publication of John Locke's *Essay Concerning Human Understanding* (1690) marks the beginning of the full impact of theory of knowledge as the dominant concern of philosophers. The drive for truth and certainty had led men in many directions and to questionable ends. The last resort of Descartes, the innate idea, had been effectively destroyed and man's knowledge about reality seemed to be caught between a degree of subjectivism and crass materialism. Many thinkers began to accept Hume's assertion that reason had no *a priori* knowledge, and that any sort of knowledge regarding a necessary connection between cause and effect was impossible. Hume states:

> We have sought in vain for an idea of power or necessary connection in all the sources from which we could suppose it to be derived. It appears that, in single instances of the operation of bodies, we never can, by our utmost scrutiny, discover any thing but one event following another, without being able to comprehend any force or power by which the cause operates, or any connection between it and its supposed effect.[4]

---

[4] David Hume, "An Inquiry Concerning Human Understanding," Walter Kaufmann, ed., *Philosophic Classics* (Englewood Cliffs, N.J.: Prentice-Hall, Inc., 1962), p. 359.

According to this, there can be no necessary connection between ideas, and man is more or less a pawn of his environment, affected in a random sort of way by external events over which he has no control. Kant was unable to accept an extreme empiricism that reduced man to a mechanism, nor could he choose the rationalistic way that was likely to end in the supersensuous regions where the physical became anchorless. The alternative seemed to be a transcendental bridging of the two positions so that both the physical and man's unique contribution to the knowledge dilemma could be recognized. Kant emphasized that a *transcendental* use must not be confused with a *transcendent* use. By transcendent, Kant meant the attempt to go beyond man's finite rational powers into a supersensible realm.

The *Critique of Pure Reason* and the *Prolegomena to any Future Metaphysics,* a shorter statement primarily designed to explicate the more difficult *Critique,* are basic to the understanding of Kant's analysis of the knowing powers of man. A study of these two works shows that Kant presents the knowledge-getting faculties under three fundamental headings: sensibility; understanding; and reason. The *Critique* presents them under the following topics: transcendental aesthetic (sensibility); transcendental analytic (understanding); and transcendental dialectic (reason).

Kant begins his analysis by discussing the two main features of the aesthetic (sensibility): 1) matter; and 2) form. Matter refers to the intuitions or to the immediate affecting of the sensibility by sensations. The intuitions are distinguished first, as the intellectual—a pure, creative act, limited to a divine being and not any part of man's makeup—and second, as the sensuous—those peculiar to man. Man's intuitions would be presented to him in a formless and indeterminate manner if it were not for their organization by the forms of the sensibility. These forms are space and time, and they are the *a priori* conditions for the organization of the manifold of sensations of our experience. These forms (Kant does not wish to call them concepts or ideas) are necessary for things to be sensed in their appearances. Kant writes that "space is the subjective condition of our sensibility, without which no external intuition is possible for us." He states that "time is nothing but the form of the internal sense, that is, of our intuition of ourselves, and of our internal state." He concludes that without time man could not "predicate anything of external objects *a priori* and synthetically."

There seems to be an element of passivity in the forms of the sensibility, as though space and time receive the matter of sensation automatically and order it mechanically, but an accurate assessment is difficult, as the way in which the forms function is not clearly defined. Kant is precise, however, in the purpose of the *Critique,* an attempt to provide a basis for the *a priori* organizing principles that does not make the supersensuous (thing-in-itself) necessary to knowledge. Kant felt that Locke's claim that the mind was composed of capacities with no formal structure was hedging, and Kant described the structure of these capacities of the mind in his analytic by establishing the necessity for *a priori* elements or categories in the knowledge process and by listing or naming these categories.[5] The familiar mind-body dilemma is discernible in Kant's insistence that an *a priori* condition of knowledge must not extend into a supersensuous realm but must be capable of correlation with obvious physicosensuous data. The necessity for this close relationship is expressed by Kant in his statement that, "Without sensibility objects would not be given to us, without understanding they would not be thought by us. *Thoughts without contents are empty, intuitions without concepts are blind.*"

The statement that knowledge is achieved only when sensibility and understanding function cooperatively is only preliminary to the question of how these function and how intuitions and categories are matched. Kant asserted that the synthesizing power within the understanding, the means by which a sensation becomes knowledge, is the transcendental unity of apperception. The gap between sensibility and understanding must be bridged by something which is "homogeneous on the one side with the category, and on the other with the phenomenon, to render the application of the former to the latter possible." This something is the imagination which functions through schema that are distinguishable from the imagination. The schema, which are *a priori,* and the *image,* which is empirical, combine in the imagination to bridge the gap between the sensibility and the understanding. Time seems to play a crucial role in the process, as Kant states:

> We have thus seen that the schematism of the understanding, by means of a transcendental synthesis of imagination, amounts to nothing else but to the unity of the manifold in the intuition of the internal sense, and therefore indirectly to the unity of apperception, as an active function corresponding to the internal sense (as receptive).[6]

The structure of man's conceptualizing processes gradually becomes clearer as Kant presses to those elements which provide the *a priori* conditions for knowledge. One should be aware that the categories are the goal of this analysis, for in them rests the salvation of the universal element of man's knowledge. The way to these is suggested by the kinds of mental activities, specifically making judgments. In essence, the sensibility intuits while the understanding judges. Kant grants that judging is a process of synthesizing, but such a process is certainly organized rather than haphazard. A sorting out of the types of judgments leads to the categories, and

---

[5] This reverses the discussion of *Critique* itself and follows the suggestion by A. C. Ewing, *A Short Commentary on Kant's Critique of Pure Reason* (London: Methuen & Co. Ltd., 1961), p. 66.
[6] Immanuel Kant, *Critique of Pure Reason,* trans. F. Max Müller (New York: The Macmillan Co., 1911), p. 119.

the correlation between the two suggests a side-by-side arrangement. Various scholars have presented them in the following manner:[7]

Judgments	Categories
1. Quantity.	1. Quantity.
Universal.	Unity.
Particular.	Plurality.
Singular.	Totality.
2. Quality.	2. Quality.
Affirmative.	Reality.
Negative.	Negation.
Infinite.	Limitation.
3. Relation.	3. Relation.
Categorical.	Inherence and subsistence (substance and accident).
Hypothetical.	Causality and dependence (cause and effect).
Disjunctive.	Community (reciprocity between agent and patient).
4. Modality.	4. Modality.
Problematic.	Possibility—impossibility.
Assertoric.	Existence—nonexistence.
Apodictic.	Necessity—contingency.

One of the most difficult problems facing Kant was to determine something about the categories. According to Wolff[8] the material on the Transcendental Deduction was completely rewritten for the Second Edition of the *Critique,* but the result was still vague and ambiguous. There are conflicting opinions about Kant's meaning, but it should serve our purpose simply to outline the problem. The problem was not merely to establish means for obtaining knowledge, ways of interpreting it, and ways of unifying or synthesizing it, but to determine how all of these can work together yet remain separate. It is crucial to the problem that there can be a contribution to knowledge which is not materialistically based but is pure; a nonempirical contribution that can work with the materialistic yet be no part of it. Some have suggested that the purity is merely fanciful, but Kant believed that the purity of the categories was necessary in order that all of knowledge should not be reduced to sensibility. The statement that knowledge is that which comes about when a sensation is taken into the understanding through the unity of apperception is a direct reversal of the Lockean conformity of idea to object. In keeping with the Kantian concept of knowledge, determinations of truth are made through the conformity of external objects to the

---

7 Notably James Collins, *A History of Modern European Philosophy* (Milwaukee: The Bruce Publishing Co., 1954), p. 488; F. Copleston, *op. cit.,* pp. 250–251; and Ewing, *op. cit.,* pp. 134–135. See Muller, *op. cit.,* pp. 58, 66–67 for originals.
8 Robert Paul Wolff, *Kant's Theory of Mental Activity* (Cambridge, Mass.: Harvard University Press, 1963), pp. 183–223 *et passim.*

a priori categories of the understanding. This new theory of conformity is the basis for what Kant terms as his intellectual revolution.

Judgments and the new theory of conformity form the fundamental basis of Kant's first *Critique*.[9] The overriding purpose is again the security of a universal element in knowledge. Kant's own statement concerns the fact that metaphysical knowledge must find its source in the *a priori* which necessitates synthetical *a priori* judgments.

> But whatever be their origin or their logical form, there is a distinction in judgments, as to their content, according to which they are either merely *explicative,* adding nothing to the content of knowledge, or *expansive,* increasing the given knowledge. The former may be called *analytical,* the latter *synthetical,* judgments.[10]

Admittedly, Kant's analysis of judgments is far from satisfying, and his discussion has been subjected to a variety of attacks. Again, the issues should be viewed in light of the demands envisioned by Kant: any addition to knowledge must come from an *a priori* source, such as the understanding of man, for resorting to the empirical brings forth the criticism of being *a posteriori* or analytic. At the same time, the supersensible must be excluded as a source of additions to man's knowledge. A. C. Ewing's *Commentary* on the *Critique* states that it "may be said to have had two main aims, (1) in the *Aesthetic* and the *Analytic,* to provide a philosophical basis for physical science, which assumed an *a priori* knowledge that was necessary for its very existence, yet hard to defend, (2) chiefly in the *Dialectic,* 'to deny knowledge in order to make room for faith.' "[11] One could hardly reconcile the denial of knowledge as stated in the above quotation with Kant's lengthy and detailed analysis of knowledge as presented in the *Aesthetic* and the *Analytic.* The resolution of the *apparent* contradiction comes in the *Dialectic* and rests upon several points. First, the twofold nature of the categories; second, the distinction between phenomena and noumena; and, third, the nature of man's reason.

The categories of the understanding were presented by Kant as "absolutely or in themselves, and relatively or in reference to sensuous intuitions."[12] Viewing the categories as absolute, Kant states that they have meaning or significance apart from the sensuous even though such meaning would not lead to real objects. The alternative to *real* possibility is that of *logical* possibility, and the pure categories taken in themselves open the way for a *possible* object. One should be clear on this point, for a logically *possible* object does not at all imply a *real* object. Logically, mermaids could exist, but actual existence does not appear to be the case. The projection

---

9 Muller, *op. cit.,* pp. 5–10; Immanuel Kant, *Prolegomena to any Future Metaphysics,* L. W. Beck, trans., (New York: The Liberal Arts Press, 1950), p. 42–56.
10 Beck, *op. cit.,* p. 14.
11 Ewing, *op. cit.,* p. 9.
12 Collins, *op. cit.,* p. 491.

into real existence would have established a realm of absolutes comparable to Plato's World of Forms.

The foregoing distinction leads into the phenomenal-noumenal relationship. The phenomenal realm is the world of objects, that is, the appearance of things to our sensibility and the schematizing of them by the categories into knowledge. The noumenal brings us to the pure categories in their absolute status. As expected, the noumenal is a *possible* realm only and is designated by Kant as things-in-themselves. The *Prolegomena* states:

> Not only are our concepts of substance, of power, of action, of reality, and others, quite independent of experience, containing nothing of sense appearance, and so apparently applicable to things in themselves (noumena), but, what strengthens this conjecture, they contain a necessity of determination in themselves, which experience never attains.[13]

The logical possibility of noumena is the source of difficulty, since there is an inherent quality in man that leads him to error. Man's reason tends toward the transcendent, that which is beyond the limits of man as envisioned by Kant. Since "All our knowledge begins with the senses, proceeds thence to the understanding, and ends with reason," the function of reason is to unify the categories of the understanding under several principles. "If the understanding is a faculty for producing unity among phenomena, according to rules, reason is the faculty for producing unity among the rules of the understanding, according to principles."

There are three organizing principles and they correspond to certain relations, which in turn lead to three transcendental sciences. The relations are to a subject, to the object, and to things in general. The transcendental sciences are psychology, cosmology, and theology. Out of these, Kant frames the unifying ideas of soul, world, and God. Through the medium of these principles or ideas, man is able to synthesize his knowledge and Kant, criticizing traditional metaphysics for its illegitimate, transcendent use of reason, establishes metaphysics as a science.[14] He concludes that when man uses the ideas or principles of pure reason as regulative or as guides, rather than as constitutive or real, it is possible for metaphysics to be a transcendental science. At this stage, Kant has carefully delimited the rational capacities of man, with reason playing a unique and necessary role in obtaining knowledge. He has also established faith as a very real and vital part of man's life, and this culmination is important for Kant's moral philosophy which sought to delineate the meaning of human experience and the value of human life. The connection between Kant's theory of knowledge and his attention to questions of morality is clear with the point of

---

13 Immanuel Kant, *Prolegomena to any Future Metaphysics, op. cit.,* p. 62.
14 These criticisms come under the headings of Paralogisms, antinomies, and Ideals of Pure Reason. It is sufficient for our present purposes to state that what Kant does is to show how illusion and contradiction result from the transcendent use of reason. For those interested, see histories of philosophy already noted in this chapter.

contact being between ideas of reason—the world, the soul and God, and the postulates of practical reason—freedom, immortality, and God. That is, man's actions should follow from principles; and the belief in freedom, immortality of the soul, and God is necessary for actions to be intelligible and good. These postulates are not established as actual existences but rather as regulative ideas that guide action and that must have their ultimate justification in faith.

Even a brief discussion of these postulates requires attention to Kant's statements on the moral law. The moral law imposes itself on man as a fact: Men may have different interpretations of the moral law, but it must be applicable to all. The source of this unconditioned *ought* is located in the conceptions of pure reason, rather than in any empirical part, and man must act because of a sense of duty rather than because he desires rewards. An act motivated by reward, or one that leads to some other action, is called a hypothetical imperative. A categorical imperative, on the other hand, is an absolute command which man's reason recognizes. The categorical imperative is a subjective condition for action which Kant formulates as: *"act only on that maxim whereby thou canst at the same time will that it should become a universal law."* A maxim is a subjective principle of volition and appears to be the formal conditions of action. Simply, the *impulse* to act is distinct from the action itself and from the consequences of the action. Kant suggests that desire and inclination often replace duty and this must be avoided. A further formulation of the categorical imperative is: *"So act as to treat humanity, whether in thine own person or in that of any other, in every case as an end withal, never as means only."*

The issue of choice and responsibility clearly points to freedom. Kant says we must be free to choose, since we are *commanded* (categorical imperative) to act in accordance with the moral law and are responsible for our actions. Even though determinism functions within the realm of physical nature, man's will must be a law in itself such that man *is presumed* free. Since the highest good for man is the achievement of a will which is in perfect accord with an infinite being (Holy Will), endless existence (immortality of the soul) is demanded. The point seems to be that one lifetime is not sufficient to the task, and therefore extended existence is demanded. Finally, if the happy and moral life of man is to have any meaning, the existence of God must be assumed. Although Kant continues to deny that God actually exists, he postulates God subjectively. Collins states that:

> The postulate of God gives more unity and consistency to Kant's moral doctrine than he acknowledges. It brings together the loose threads of morality, happiness, freedom, and continued existence, which had been kept rigidly apart in the discussion of the motive of morality.[15]

---

15 Collins, *op. cit.*, p. 533.

Kant's Educational Theory

One way to approach an understanding of Kant's educational theory is to compare his ideas about education with Rousseau's, for Kant was probably one of Rousseau's greatest admirers, and Rousseau's influence on Kant is evidenced in many regards. Kant maintained that no work ever stirred him as deeply as *Émile,* and he credited Rousseau for relieving him of prejudice against the uneducated, common man and for inspiring him with a deep respect for all of mankind. Rousseau's influence in this regard, according to Kant, cleared the way for wider intellectual vistas. It should be noted, however, that in spite of Kant's avowed discipleship to Rousseau, the points of agreement between the two men are only brief contacts between lines of thought which are by no means parallel. Too often we make the mistake of assuming that discipleship implies sameness of thought, when in reality, the most profound influences are more likely to be points of departure for additional creativity. Kant's reaction to *Émile* illustrates the point admirably.

Kant was persuaded to Rousseau's view that man is good by nature, but at the same time he maintained that man must be free to choose to be good. The point of agreement, coupled with the difference, inspired Kant to the sort of creative thinking that produced his phenomenon-noumenon concept. As a part of nature, man is phenomenon, and as a member of the realm of freedom, man is noumenon. As phenomenon, man has a predisposition to animality, humanity, and moral perfection. Animality and humanity (natural perfection) can be altered by evil and vice, but moral perfection cannot be altered. As noumenon, man is either all good, or all bad, and the choice is his. Man (phenomenon) has only the predisposition to good, and man (noumenon) chooses to be virtuous or vicious, but is neither by *natural* necessity. Thus man is naturally good, even though he chooses to be otherwise.

The view of the nature of man is only one instance where the ideas of the two men coincide at the point of influence and then diverge to different conclusions. Generally speaking, this is the pattern of their educational views. There is a similarity between the stress each places on the importance of the individual, the idea of a child-centered, as opposed to a subject-centered, education, and on the dangers of beginning formal education too soon, but the points of agreement are developed in different ways. For instance, Kant accepted the idea of the unfolding of human nature, of predispositions, but he maintained that the process must not be left entirely to nature. The child will never develop further than animality without the guidance of skilled teachers, according to Kant. Left to follow his own inclinations and natural desires without any opposition, control, or direction, the child will develop the sort of lawlessness that makes adjustment to community living impossible.

Kant's educational theory is related to his idea of humanity and to his hopes for the future of mankind. The following statement by Kant stresses this point and serves as an expression of a fundamental principle which motivates teacher education. "Each generation, provided with the knowledge of the preceding one, can more and more bring about an education, which will develop man's natural gifts in due proportion and relation to their end, and thus advance the whole human race towards its destiny." We have seen that Kant viewed the natural goodness of man in terms of capabilities without any moral distinction. He believed that the moral sense must be developed and that moral training should be one of the most important aspects of education.

Kant did not agree with the tutorial techniques Rousseau stressed, for tutors, he felt, are prone to leave the moral training of their charges to the Church, while it should be the backbone of all instruction. Children need to be taught from youth that vice must be despised, not merely for religious reasons, but because vice is detestable in itself. The moral distinctions learned through proper education are the seeds of societal good, Kant thought, and, therefore, society should be concerned and involved in education.

The far-reaching effects of education demand keen attention to all of its aspects which Kant divided into two main categories, the physical and the practical. Rousseau's influence is manifest in Kant's approach to the physical, as he too was concerned with the feeding and clothing of infants. He also emphasized a progressive program in physical activities according to the maturation of the child and exercises to help in the development of the senses. He agreed with Rousseau that there should be opportunities for experiences and that the child should be protected from harmful situations.

Kant's practical category includes all of the learned skills, such as reading, writing, and numbers. The category also emphasized teacher training, as Kant believed that teaching is one of the most significant activities of man. The learned skills should be taught with a sense of moral culture, according to Kant, and thinking and reasoning should be stressed. Both categories implied constant growth and development to Kant, not only in the individual, but in the broader historical sense, for he firmly believed that the practice of education by succeeding generations is the only way to the kind of perfection that man strives to attain.

Kant was by no means systematic in his attempts to construct a philosophy of education, but he was one of the few great philosophers who have concerned themselves with theory of education in any detail. Kant was far more occupied with theory than he was with the particulars of educational practices and was convinced that the mechanism of education should be changed into a science. It is important to keep in mind Kant's rather unique interpretation of science, for he paid little attention to the techniques of scientific procedure, and his statements about a science of education do not have the same implications as if they were made within the framework of modern scientific methods. Kant had observed that in nature, each happening is always accompanied by another happening and that there is a uniformity to the events. The science of nature is derived from the rules that can be formulated about these uniformities, and Kant extended this theory to include education. He maintained that if we search for the first principles that are inherent in human nature, we will discover the attendant happening in each case and be able to derive rules that will make the cultivation of character and intellect more certain. The statement of relevant uniformities in this regard is Kant's definition of the science of education. His science of education stresses the processes of judgment, and the concept that the natural goodness in man will be freed by education that is properly directed toward the physical, intellectual, and moral aspects of mankind. Kant thought it highly unlikely that any one generation might discover a complete system of education, for, since it is impossible to predict accurately by reason alone, we must be guided in our educational efforts by constant experimentation. He urged, therefore, that schools be used for experimentation as well as for instruction.

Rousseauian and Kantian influences emanated from eighteenth century enlightenment in different ways and with varying degrees of intensity. Rousseau, a pioneer in many fields, disturbed by the conflicting principles and tendencies he found in nature, society, and institutions, plotted the way to a new, child-centered education designed to preserve the natural goodness in man. Such of his followers as J. B. Basedow (1723–1790), J. H. Pestalozzi (1746–1827), Friedrich Froebel (1782–1852), and Johann Friedrich Herbart (1776–1841), carried his reforms into the nineteenth century. For a time, Rousseau's ideas that had been so revolutionary came to be thought of as romantic sentimentality. But the twentieth century renaissance of the new education shifted attention back to Rousseau with a different emphasis. He is credited with fathering modern child psychology and for laying the foundation for a new curriculum.

Kant, writing at a time when there was a greater concern for education than there had been since the Greeks, agreed with Rousseau that the art of education was far from perfect. But he did feel that with so many exhibiting an interest in what really belongs in a good education, the turning point might well be at hand. Kant's greatest influence has come about because of his philosophical thinking, especially in the areas of ethics and epistemology, but his theories of education attracted a good deal of attention in Germany, and consequently in Latin America and Japan. His successor, J. F. Herbart, adopted Kant's view that the primary goal of an education should be to produce a good man. Kant's influence in America was first felt during the period of transcendentalism and again through Hegelian idealism. His thinking was especially influential on W. T. Harris, a United States Commissioner of Education, and on John Dewey.

The crux of the educational differences between Rousseau and Kant is not entirely philosophical, for it rests at least in part on the contrariety of their societal views. As we have seen, Rousseau had never been able to adjust to the pressures of society which he made the scapegoat for all of his

214   *Philosophical Perspectives for Education*

trials and difficulties. Kant, on the other hand, thoroughly enjoyed the limited sort of social intercourse that was an important part of his existence. Each viewed the world about him through the lens ground by his own experience, and they appeared to be entirely different worlds. Rousseau, because of his own flagrancy and emotional instability, saw little but the evil and corruption in society, and Kant, because of his limited experience, had no firsthand acquaintance with the social ills that Rousseau deplored. So, throughout history, the thinking of those who contribute to our intellectual foundations has been forged by individual passions and tempered by particular biases. Our intellectual heritage would be far less abundant were this not the case.

IMMANUEL KANT

Education (Chapter 1)*

According to E. F. Buchner, a rule at the University of Königsberg required that some one professor from the philosophical faculty should lecture for two hours each week on pedagogy. During the years of 1776–1777 and 1786–1787, Kant complied with the rule on four different occasions, and the reading for Chapter V is the first part of these lectures. Ideally, Kant's lectures should be read in conjunction with Rousseau's Émile, *but since an inclusion of the latter is not possible here, the similarities and differences between Kant and Rousseau which were noted in Chapter V will have to suffice.*

The Lecture Notes on Pedagogy (*translated by Annette Churton as* Education) *constitutes a quite different approach to education than that of John Locke. Although like Locke, Kant concentrates upon the development of the individual, he approaches educational problems by way of the philosophical categories of morality, freedom, and humanity. According to Kant, man should remain no more than an animal without the sort of education required to develop the qualities of morality, freedom, and humanity. Kant believes that a child must be disciplined and that his experiences must be regulated, but he emphasizes the distinction between* training *a child and teaching a child to* think. *The distinction is a crucial factor in Kant's pedagogy and can serve admirably as a point of departure for discussions about the relation between the purposes of education and methods of teaching.*

* From *The Lecture Notes on Pedagogy* by Immanuel Kant, tr. Annette Churton, 1960. By permission of the University of Michigan Press.

Introduction

1   Man is the only being who needs education. For by education we must understand nurture (the tending and feeding of the child), discipline (*Zucht*), and teaching, together with culture.[1] According to this, man is in succession infant (requiring nursing), child (requiring discipline), and scholar (requiring teaching).

2   Animals use their powers, as soon as they are possessed of them, according to a regular plan—that is, in a way not harmful to themselves.

It is indeed wonderful, for instance, that young swallows, when newly hatched and still blind, are careful not to defile their nests.

Animals therefore need no nurture, but at the most, food, warmth, and guidance, or a kind of protection. It is true, most animals need feeding, but they do not require nurture. For by nurture we mean the tender care and attention which parents must bestow upon their children, so as to prevent them from using their powers in a way which would be harmful to themselves. For instance, should an animal cry when it comes into the world, as children do, it would surely become a prey to wolves and other wild animals, which would gather round, attracted by its cry.

3   Discipline changes animal nature into human nature. Animals are by their instinct all that they ever can be; some other reason has provided everything for them at the outset. But man needs a reason of his own. Having no instinct, he has to work out a plan of conduct for himself. Since, however, he is not able to do this all at once, but comes into the world undeveloped, others have to do it for him.

4   All the natural endowments of mankind must be developed little by little out of man himself, through his own effort.

One generation educates the next. The first beginnings of this process of educating may be looked for either in a rude and unformed, or in a fully developed condition of man. If we assume the latter to have come first, man must at all events afterwards have degenerated and lapsed into barbarism.

It is discipline, which prevents man from being turned aside by his animal impulses from humanity, his appointed end. Discipline, for instance, must restrain him from venturing wildly and rashly into danger. Discipline, thus, is merely negative, its action being to counteract man's natural unruliness. The positive part of education is instruction.

Unruliness consists in independence of law. By discipline men are placed in subjection to the laws of mankind, and brought to feel their constraint. This, however, must be accomplished early. Children, for instance, are first sent to school, not so much with the object of their learning something, but rather that they may become used to sitting still and doing exactly as they are told. And this to the end that in later life they should not wish to put actually and instantly into practice anything that strikes them.

5   The love of freedom is naturally so strong in man, that when once he has grown accustomed to freedom, he will sacrifice everything for its sake. For this very reason discipline must be brought into play very early; for when this has not been done, it is difficult to alter character later in life. Undisciplined men are apt to follow every caprice.

We see this also among savage nations, who, though they may discharge

---

1 Culture *(Bildung)* is used here in the sense of moral training.—(Tr.)

functions for some time like Europeans, yet can never become accustomed to European manners. With them, however, it is not the noble love of freedom which Rousseau and others imagine, but a kind of barbarism—the animal, so to speak, not having yet developed its human nature. Men should therefore accustom themselves early to yield to the commands of reason, for, if a man be allowed to follow his own will in his youth, without opposition, a certain lawlessness will cling to him throughout his life. And it is no advantage to such a man that in his youth he has been spared through an overabundance of motherly tenderness, for later on all the more will he have to face opposition from all sides, and constantly receive rebuffs, as soon as he enters into the business of the world.

It is a common mistake made in the education of those of high rank, that because they are hereafter to become rulers they must on that account receive no opposition in their youth. Owing to his natural love of freedom it is necessary that man should have his natural roughness smoothed down; with animals, their instinct renders this unnecessary.

6   Man needs nurture and culture. Culture includes discipline and *instruction*. These, as far as we know, no animal needs, for none of them learn anything from their elders, except birds, who are taught by them to sing; and it is a touching sight to watch the mother bird singing with all her might to her young ones, who, like children at school, stand round and try to produce the same tones out of their tiny throats. In order to convince ourselves that birds do not sing by instinct, but that they are actually taught to sing, it is worthwhile to make an experiment. Suppose we take away half the eggs from a canary, and put sparrow's eggs in their place, or exchange young sparrows for young canaries; if the young birds are then brought into a room where they cannot hear the sparrows outside, they will learn the canary's song, and we thus get singing sparrows. It is, indeed, very wonderful that each species of bird has its own peculiar song, which is preserved unchanged through all its generations; and the tradition of the song is probably the most faithful in the world.

7   Man can only become man by education. He is merely what education makes of him. It is noticeable that man is only educated by man—that is, by men who have themselves been educated. Hence with some people it is want of discipline and instruction on their own part, which makes them in turn unfit educators of their pupils. Were some being of higher nature than man to undertake our education, we should then be able to see what man might become. It is, however, difficult for us accurately to estimate man's natural capabilities, since some things are imparted to man by education, while other things are only developed by education. Were it possible, by the help of those in high rank, and through the united forces of many people, to make an experiment on this question, we might even by this means be able to gain some information as to the degree of eminence which it is possible for man to attain. But it is as important to the speculative mind, as it is sad to one who loves his fellow-men, to see how those in high rank generally care only for their own concerns, and take no part in the important experiments of education, which bring our nature one step nearer to perfection.

There is no one who, having been neglected in his youth, can come to years of discretion without knowing whether the defect lies in discipline or culture (for so we may call instruction). The uncultivated man is crude, the undisciplined is unruly. Neglect of discipline is a greater evil than neglect of culture, for this last can be remedied later in life, but unruliness cannot be done away with, and a mistake in discipline can never be repaired. It may be that education will be constantly improved, and that each succeeding generation will advance one step towards the perfecting of mankind; for with education is involved the great secret of the perfection of human nature. It is only now that something may be done in this direction, since for the first time people have begun to judge rightly, and understand clearly, what actually belongs to a good education. It is delightful to realize that through education human nature will be continually improved, and brought to such a condition as is worthy of the nature of man. This opens out to us the prospect of a happier human race in the future.

8   The prospect of a *theory of education* is a glorious ideal, and it matters little if we are not able to realize it at once. Only we must not look upon the idea as chimerical, nor decry it as a beautiful dream, notwithstanding the difficulties that stand in the way of its realization.

An idea is nothing else than the conception of a perfection which has not yet been experienced. For instance, the idea of a perfect republic governed by principles of justice—is such an idea impossible, because it has not yet been experienced?

Our idea must in the first place be correct, and then, notwithstanding all the hindrances that still stand in the way of its realization, it is not at all impossible. Suppose, for instance, lying to become universal, would truth-speaking on that account become nothing but a whim? And the idea of an education which will develop all man's natural gifts is certainly a true one.

9   Under the present educational system man does not fully attain to the object of his being; for in what various ways men live! Uniformity can only result when all men act according to the same principles, which principles would have to become with them a second nature. What we can do is to work out a scheme of education better suited to further its objects, and hand down to posterity directions as to how this scheme may be carried into practice, so that they might be able to realize it gradually. Take the auricula as an example. When raised from a root, this plant bears flowers of one color only; when raised from seed, the flowers are of the most varied colors. Nature has placed these manifold germs in the plant, and their development is only a question of proper sowing and planting. Thus it is with man.

10   There are many germs lying undeveloped in man. It is for us to make these germs grow, by *developing his natural gifts* in their due proportion, and to see that he fulfils his destiny. Animals accomplish this for themselves unconsciously. Man must strive to attain it, but this he cannot do if he has not even a conception as to the object of his existence. For the individual it is absolutely impossible to attain this object. Let us suppose the first parents to have been fully developed, and see how they educate their children. These first parents set their children an example, which the children imitate and in this way develop some of their own natural gifts. All their gifts cannot, however, be developed in this way, for it all depends on occasional circumstances what examples children see. In times past men had no conception of the perfection to which human nature might attain—even now we have not a very clear idea of the matter. This much, however, is certain: that no individual man, no matter what degree of culture may be reached by his pupils, can insure their attaining their destiny.

To succeed in this, not the work of a few individuals only is necessary, but that of the whole human race.

11   Education is an *art* which can only become perfect through the practice of many generations. Each generation, provided with the knowledge of the fore-going one, is able more and more to bring about an education which shall develop man's natural gifts in their due proportion and in relation to their end, and thus advance the whole human race towards its destiny. Providence has willed, that man shall bring forth for himself the good that lies hidden in his nature, and has spoken, as it were, thus to man: "Go forth into the world! I have equipped thee with every tendency towards the good. Thy part let it be to develop those tendencies. Thy happiness and unhappiness depend upon thy-self alone."

12   Man must develop his tendency towards *the good*. Providence has not placed goodness ready formed in him, but merely as a tendency and without the distinction of moral law. Man's duty is to improve himself; to cultivate his mind; and, when he finds himself going astray, to bring the moral law to bear upon himself. Upon reflection we shall find this very difficult. Hence the greatest and most difficult problem to which man can devote himself is the problem of education. For insight depends on education, and education in its turn depends on insight. It follows therefore that education can only advance by slow de-grees, and a true conception of the method of education can only arise when one generation transmits to the next its stores of experience and knowledge, each generation adding something of its own before transmitting them to the follow-ing. What vast culture and experience does not this conception presuppose? It could only be arrived at at a late stage, and we ourselves have not fully realized this conception. The question arises, Should we in the education of the individ-ual imitate the course followed by the education of the human race through its successive generations?

There are two human inventions which may be considered more difficult than any others—the art of government, and the art of education; and people still contend as to their very meaning.

13   But in developing human talents *where are we to take our stand?* Shall we begin with a rude, or with an already developed state of society?

It is difficult to conceive a development from a state of rudeness (hence it is so difficult to understand what the first man was like), and we see that in a development out of such a condition man has invariably fallen back again into that condition, and has raised himself out of it. In the earliest records of even very civilized nations we still find a distinct taint of barbarism, and yet how much culture is presupposed for mere writing to be possible! So much so that, with regard to civilized people, the beginning of the art of writing might be called the beginning of the world.

14   Since the development of man's natural gifts does not take place of itself, all education is an art. Nature has placed no instinct in him for that purpose. The *origin* as well as the *carrying out* of this art is either *mechanical* and with-out plan, ruled by given circumstances, or it involves the exercise of *judgment*. The art of education is only then mechanical, when on chance occasions we learn by experience whether anything is useful or harmful to man. All education which is merely mechanical must carry with it many mistakes and deficiencies, because it has no sure principle to work upon. If education is to develop human nature so that it may attain the object of its being, it must involve the exercise

of judgment. Educated parents are examples which children use for their guidance. If, however, the children are to progress beyond their parents, education must become a study, otherwise we can hope for nothing from it, and one man whose education has been spoilt will only repeat his own mistakes in trying to educate others. The mechanism of education must be changed into a science,[1] and one generation may have to pull down what another had built up.

15 One *principle of education* which those men especially who form educational schemes should keep before their eyes is this—children ought to be educated, not for the present, but for a possibly improved condition of man in the future; that is, in a manner which is adapted to the *idea of humanity* and the whole destiny of man. This principle is of great importance. Parents usually educate their children merely in such a manner that, however bad the world may be, they may adapt themselves to its present conditions. But they ought to give them an education so much better than this, that a better condition of things may thereby be brought about in the future.

16 Here, however, we are met by two difficulties—(*a*) parents usually care that their children *make their way* in the world, and (*b*) sovereigns look upon their subjects merely as *tools* for their own purposes.

Parents care for the home, rulers for the state. Neither have as their aim the universal good and the perfection to which man is destined, and for which he has also a natural disposition. But the basis of a scheme of education must be cosmopolitan. And is, then, the idea of the universal good harmful to us as individuals? Never! for though it may appear that something must be sacrificed by this idea, an advance is also made towards what is the best even for the individual under his present conditions. And then what glorious consequences follow! It is through good education that all the good in the world arises. For this the germs which lie hidden in man need only to be more and more developed; for the rudiments of evil are not to be found in the natural disposition of man. Evil is only the result of nature not being brought under control. In man there are only germs of good.

17 But by whom is the better condition of the world to be brought about? By rulers or by their subjects? Is it by the latter, who shall so improve themselves that they meet halfway the measures for their good which the government might establish? Were it to depend upon rulers, their own education will first have to be improved, for this has for a long time suffered, owing to the great mistake that they have been allowed to meet with no opposition in their youth.

A tree which stands in a field alone grows crooked and spreads wide its branches; while a tree which stands in the middle of a forest, with the pressure of other trees around, grows tall and straight, seeking air and sunshine from above. It is the same with rulers. In any case it is always better that they should be educated by some one among their subjects, rather than by one of themselves. We can therefore only expect progress to be brought about by rulers if their education has been of a higher kind than that of their subjects.

It depends, then, mainly upon private effort, and not so much on the help of rulers, as Basedow and others supposed; for we find by experience that they have not the universal good so much in view, as the well-being of the state, whereby they may attain their own ends. If, however, they provide funds for

---

[1] Rink and Schubert add here: "otherwise it will never be a consistent pursuit."—(Tr.)

this object, the drawing up of the scheme must be deferred to them. So it is with everything which concerns the perfection of man's intellect and the widening of his knowledge. Influence and money alone cannot do it; they can only lighten the task. They might do it, if only the financial authorities of the state were not so anxious to calculate beforehand the interests which any sums spent for this purpose might bear for the treasury. Even academic bodies hitherto have not undertaken the task, and the likelihood that they will do so in the future is now as small as ever.

The management of schools ought, then, to depend entirely upon the judgment of the most enlightened experts. All culture begins with the individual, one man gradually influencing others. It is only through the efforts of people of broader views, who take an interest in the universal good, and who are capable of entertaining the idea of a better condition of things in the future, that the gradual progress of human nature towards its goal is possible. Do we not still meet, now and then, with a ruler who looks upon his people merely as forming part of the animal kingdom, and whose aim it is merely to propagate the human species? If he considers the subject of training the intellect at all, it is merely in order that his people may be of more use to him in working out his own ends. It is, of course, necessary for private individuals to keep this natural end in view, but they must also bear in mind more particularly the development of mankind, and see to it that men become not only clever, but good; and, what is most difficult, they must seek to bring posterity nearer to a state of perfection than they have themselves attained.

18   Through education, then, man must be made—

First, subject to *discipline;* by which we must understand that influence which is always restraining our animal nature from getting the better of our manhood, either in the individual as such, or in man as a member of society. Discipline, then, is merely restraining unruliness.

Secondly, education must also supply men with *culture.* This includes information and instruction. It is culture which brings out ability. Ability is the possession of a faculty which is capable of being adapted to various ends. Ability, therefore, does not determine any ends, but leaves that to circumstances as they arise afterwards.

Some accomplishments are essentially good for everybody—reading and writing, for instance; others, merely in the pursuit of certain objects, such as music, which we pursue in order to make ourselves liked. Indeed, the various purposes to which ability may be put are almost endless.

Thirdly, education must also supply a person with *discretion* (*Klugheit*), so that he may be able to conduct himself in society, that he may be liked, and that he may gain influence. For this, a kind of culture is necessary which we call *refinement* (*Civilisierung*). The latter requires manners, courtesy, and a kind of discretion which will enable him to use all men for his own ends. This refinement changes according to the ever-changing tastes of different ages. Thus some twenty or thirty years ago ceremonies in social intercourse were still the fashion.

Fourthly, *moral training* must form a part of education. It is not enough that a man shall be fitted for any end, but his disposition must be so trained that he shall choose none but good ends—good ends being those which are necessarily approved by everyone, and which may at the same time be the aim of everyone.

19   Man may be either broken in, trained, and mechanically taught, or he may be really enlightened. Horses and dogs are broken in; and man, too, may be broken in.

It is, however, not enough that children should be merely broken in; for it is of greater importance that they shall learn to *think*. By learning to think, man comes to act according to fixed principles and not at random. Thus we see that a real education implies a great deal. But as a rule, in our private education *the fourth and most important point is still too much neglected,* children being for the most part educated in such a way that moral training is left to the Church. And yet how important it is that children should learn from their youth up to detest vice;—not merely on the ground that God has forbidden it, but because vice is detestable in itself. If children do not learn this early, they are very likely to think that, if only God had not forbidden it, there would be no harm in practicing wickedness, and that it would otherwise be allowed, and that therefore He would probably make an exception now and then. But God is the most holy being, and wills only what is good, and desires that we may love virtue for its own sake, and not merely because He requires it.

We live in an age of discipline, culture, and refinement, but we are still a long way off from the age of moral training. According to the present conditions of mankind, one might say that the prosperity of the state grows side by side with the misery of the people. Indeed, it is still a question whether we should not be happier in an uncivilized condition, where all the culture of the present time would find no place, than we are in the present state of society; for how can man be made happy, unless he is first made wise and good? And until this is made our first aim the amount of evil will not be lessened.

20   *Experimental schools* must first be established before we can establish *normal schools.* Education and instruction must not be merely mechanical; they must be founded upon fixed principles; although at the same time education must not merely proceed by way of reasoning, but must be, in a certain sense, mechanical.

In Austria the greater number of schools used to be normal schools, and these were founded and carried on after a fixed plan, against which much has been said, not without reason. The chief complaint against them was this, that the teaching in them was merely mechanical. But all other schools were obliged to form themselves after the pattern of these normal schools, because government even refused to promote persons who had not been educated in these schools. This is an example of how government might interfere in the education of subjects, and how much evil might arise from compulsion.

People imagine, indeed, that experiments in education are unnecessary, and that we can judge from our reason whether anything is good or not. This is a great mistake, and experience teaches us that the results of an experiment are often entirely different from what we expected.

Thus we see that, since we must be guided by experiments, no one generation can set forth a complete scheme of education. The only experimental school which had in a measure made a beginning to clear the way was the Dessau Institute. This must be said in its praise, in spite of the many mistakes with which we might reproach it—mistakes which attend all conclusions made from experiments—namely, that still more experiments are required.

This school was in a certain way the only one in which the teachers were free to work out their own methods and plans, and in which the teachers were in communication with each other and with all the learned men of Germany.[1]

21   Education includes the *nurture* of the child and, as it grows, its *culture.* The latter is firstly *negative,* consisting of discipline; that is, merely the correcting of faults. Secondly, culture is *positive,* consisting of instruction and guidance (and thus forming part of education). *Guidance* means directing the pupil in putting into practice what he has been taught. Hence the difference between a *private teacher* who merely instructs, and a *tutor* or *governor* who guides and directs his pupil. The one trains for school only, the other for life.

22   Education is either *private* or *public.* The latter is concerned only with instruction, and this can always remain public. The carrying out of what is taught is left to private education. A complete public education is one which unites instruction and moral culture. Its aim is to promote a good private education. A school which does this is called an educational institute. There cannot be many such institutions, and the number of children in them can be but small, since the fees must of necessity be high, for the institutions require elaborate management, which entails a good deal of expense. It is the same as with almshouses and hospitals. The buildings required for them, and the salaries of directors, overseers, and servants, take away at once half of the funds, so that there can be no doubt that the poor would be better provided for, if all that money were sent direct to their houses. For this reason it is also difficult to provide that any but the children of rich people should share in these institutions.

23   The object of such *public institutions* as these is the improvement of home education. If only parents, or those who are their fellow-helpers in the work of education, were well educated themselves, the expense of public institutions might be avoided. The purpose of these institutions is to make experiments, and to educate individuals, so that in time a good private education may arise out of these public institutions.

24   *Home education* is carried on either by the parents themselves, or, should the parents not have the time, aptitude, or inclination for it, by others who are paid to assist them in it. But in education which is carried on by these assistants one very great difficulty arises—namely, the division of authority between parent and teacher. The child is called upon to obey the teacher's rule, and at the same time to follow his parents' whims. The only way out of this difficulty is for the parents to surrender the whole of their authority to the tutor.

25   How far, then, has home education an advantage over public education, or *vice versâ?* Regarded not only from the point of view of developing ability, but also as a preparation for the duties of a citizen, it must, I am inclined to think, be allowed that, on the whole, public education is the best. Home education frequently not only fosters family failings, but tends to continue these failings in the new generation.

26   *How long,* then, should education *last?* Till the youth has reached that

---

[1] In the editions of Rink and Schubert § 27 follows here.—(Tr.)

period of his life when nature has ordained that he shall be capable of guiding his own conduct; when the instinct of sex has developed in him, and he can become a father himself, and have to educate his own children. This period is generally reached about the sixteenth year. After this we may still make use of some means of culture, and secretly exercise some discipline; but of education in the ordinary sense of the word we shall have no further need.

27 In the first period of childhood the child must learn submission and positive[1] obedience. In the next stage he should be allowed to think for himself, and to enjoy a certain amount of freedom, although still obliged to follow certain rules. In the first period there is a mechanical, in the second a moral constraint.

28 The child's submission is either *positive* or *negative*. *Positive* in that he is obliged to do what he is told, because he cannot judge for himself, and the faculty of imitation is still strong in him; or *negative,* in that he is obliged to do what others wish him to do, if he wishes others to do him a good turn.[2] In the former case, the consequence of not obeying is punishment; in the latter, the fact that people do not comply with his wishes. He is in this case, though capable of thinking for himself, dependent on others with regard to his own pleasure.

29 One of the greatest problems of education is how to unite submission to the necessary *restraint* with the child's capability of exercising his *freewill*—for restraint is necessary. How am I to develop the sense of freedom in spite of the restraint? I am to accustom my pupil to endure a restraint of his freedom, and at the same time I am to guide him to use his freedom aright. Without this all education is merely mechanical, and the child, when his education is over, will never be able to make a proper use of his freedom. He should be made to feel early the inevitable opposition of society, that he may learn how difficult it is to support himself, to endure privation, and to acquire those things which are necessary to make him independent.

30 Here we must observe the following:—

First, we must allow the child from his earliest childhood perfect liberty in every respect (except on those occasions when he might hurt himself—as, for instance, when he clutches at a knife), provided that in acting so he does not interfere with the liberty of others. For instance, as soon as he screams or is too boisterously happy, he annoys others.

Secondly, he must be shown that he can only attain his own ends by allowing others to attain theirs. For instance, should he be disobedient, or refuse to learn his lessons, he ought to be refused any treat he may have been looking forward to.

Thirdly, we must prove to him that restraint is only laid upon him that he may learn in time to use his liberty aright, and that his mind is being cultivated so that one day he may be free; that is, independent of the help of others. This is the last thing a child will come to understand. It is much later in life that children realize such facts as that they will afterwards have to support themselves; for they imagine that they can always go on as they are in their parents' house, and that food and drink will always be provided for them without any trouble on their part. Indeed, unless children, and especially the chil-

---

[1] Rink and Schubert read: "passive."—(Tr.)
[2] Vogt's text is here obviously corrupt. The reading given is taken from the editions of Rink and Schubert.—(Tr.)

dren of rich parents and princes, are made to realize this, they are like the inhabitants of Otaheiti, who remain children all their lives.

Again, we see the advantage of public education in that under such a system, we learn to measure our powers with those of others, and to know the limits imposed upon us by the rights of others. Thus we can have no preference shown us, because we meet with opposition everywhere, and we can only make our mark and obtain an advantage over others by real merit. Public education is the best school for future citizens.

There is yet another difficulty to be mentioned here—that is, the difficulty of anticipating the knowledge of sexual matters in such a manner as to prevent vice at the very outset of manhood. This, however, will be discussed later on.
31   Education is either *physical* or "practical." One part of physical education is that which man has in common with animals, namely, feeding and tending. *"Practical"* or *moral* training is that which teaches a man how to live as a free being. (We call anything *"practical"* which has reference to freedom.) This is the education of a personal character, of a free being, who is able to maintain himself, and to take his proper place in society, keeping at the same time a proper sense of his own individuality.
32   This *"practical"* education consists, then, of three parts:—

(*a*) The *ordinary curriculum of the school,* where the child's general ability is developed—the work of the schoolmaster.

(*b*) Instruction in the practical matters of life—to act with wisdom and discretion—the work of the private tutor or governess.

(*c*) The training of moral character.

Men need the training of school-teaching or instruction to develop the ability necessary to success in the various vocations of life. School-teaching bestows upon each member an individual value of his own.

Next, by learning the lesson of discretion in the practical matters of life, he is educated as a citizen, and becomes of value to his fellow-citizens, learning both how to accommodate himself to their society and also how to profit by it.

Lastly, moral training imparts to man a value with regard to the whole human race.
33   Of these three divisions of education school-teaching comes *first* in order of time; for a child's abilities must first be developed and trained, otherwise he is incapable of gaining knowledge in the practical matters of life. Discretion is the faculty of using our abilities aright.

Moral training, in as far as it is based upon fundamental principles which a man must himself comprehend, comes last in order of time. In so far, however, as it is based on common sense merely, it must be taken into account from the beginning, at the same time with physical training; for if moral training be omitted, many faults will take root in the child, against which all influences of education at a later stage will be powerless. As to ability and the general knowledge of life, everything must depend entirely upon the age of the pupil. Let a child be clever after the manner of children; let him be shrewd and good-natured in a childish way, but not cunning (*listig*) like a man. The latter is as unsuitable for a child as a childish mind is for a grown-up person.

CHAPTER VI
Structures of Social, Historical, and Educational Theories

Chapter VI is concerned with the educational implications of a social reality, a philosophical vista that stems from ideological, rather than from cosmological or epistemological commitments. An understanding of such a philosophical outlook entails a conceptual structure which recognizes the developmental role of men such as Georg Hegel, Karl Marx, Auguste Comte, Søren Kierkegaard, and John Stuart Mill. The meaning for education is best illustrated by the educational philosophies of Johann Herbart and Friedrich Froebel.

The nineteenth century was turbulent, a scene of change and reform, activated by the ascendancy of the middle class. The emerging, united mass of humanity was able in 1828 to elect Andrew Jackson—the first "common man" to hold the high office—as President of the United States. During the following two decades the middle class grew into a force that considerably altered the character of the nation. The increased spending power of the people affected the national economy. The labor movement which grew out of the workingman's need for group action was another significant factor of the change. The Mechanics Union of Trade Association in Philadelphia, formed in 1827, was only one of the organizations that helped the workers to protect their rights and to achieve better working conditions. The urban communities that grew rapidly around industrial centers in haphazard fashion became breeding grounds for crime and corruption, and the resulting slum conditions focused public attention on social reform to control the evils that accompany an overrapid growth. The interest extended to academic areas, giving rise to a scholarly interest in societal problems and their impact on the individual. There was an increasing emphasis on the scientific approach to sociology, and scholars began to look to philosophy for different sorts of answers than they had formerly sought. There was less interest in the deliberate and dispassionate philosophizing of a Descartes, for the nineteenth century scholar cared more about finding

227

ways to change society than he did about finding ways to understand it. The emphasis on scientific investigations and scientific standards in all areas tended away from the earlier romanticizing of individual goodness and caused thinkers to search for a rationale more sound than individual feelings or faith to serve as a base for societal good.

The claim has been made by many historians that one must be acquainted with Hegel's Absolute Idealism in order to approach an understanding of the nineteenth century, and there is no doubt but that his thinking set the stage for much of the philosophical enterprise of that century and the following one. Two aspects of his thought—*the dialectic,* and *Absolute Spirit*—are the basis for the writings of Comte, Marx, and Kierkegaard.

Auguste Comte modified the Hegelian dialectic by replacing Hegel's idealism with scientific principles which he applied to the sequence of events in history. His organization of knowledge is used today by some curriculum theorists who stress subject matter as the basis for intellectual structuring. Karl Marx's revision of the Hegelian dialectic, substituting materialism for idealism, illustrates another reaction against absolute idealism and was concurrent with Kierkegaard's complete rejection of all Hegelianism. Kierkegaard felt that the reduction of all things to reason was a monstrous attack on the subjective aspect of man, which was unthinkable to one of his passions. John Stuart Mill completes this quartet of nineteenth century philosophers whose thinking contributed immeasurably to the new discipline, social philosophy. We shall see that, while all four were concerned with societal goods, each placed a different emphasis on the individuals who constitute a society. Comte contributed the idea of a religion of humanity and made no separation between the many and the one. According to his view, a society is composed of its members, and the individual is important as a vital part of the whole. Marx, on the other hand, placed little importance on the individual, for ideally, all personal identity is submerged in the society. Kierkegaard stressed the individual who is thought to retain his identity in the society, which is important only as it serves individual needs. Finally, Mill, who provided an intellectual rationale for the maintenance of individual rights and freedom within a democratic system, can be viewed as a synthesizer of the other attitudes.

The most notable nineteenth century philosophers of education whose educational ideas reflect the import of the new social philosophies are Johann Herbart and Friedrich Froebel. Both men saw education as a means for directing and controlling the future of the individual and society, but Herbart's view of the individual drew primarily on the idea of Comte, and his approach to education was that of an analytical scientist. Froebel, however, was more of a poet—a man of intense feeling—admittedly vague and indefinite on specific points. Perhaps his greatest contribution was the development of the kindergarten which found immediate favor in the United States as a socializing force. These two educational philosophers represent the extremes of the science-oriented and the art-oriented. We shall see in this chapter that the combination or interweaving of a view which stresses the importance of discipline, tradition, and classicism, with the view of a man such as Froebel, who advocates a moral interpretation of education which transcends intellectual analysis and who emphasizes individual creative development, can result in an educational system that is a full expression of our democratic hope.

Philosophical Background to Nineteeth Century Social Theories

G. W. F. Hegel (1770–1831)

Hegel did not leave a systematic educational treatise, and we find no place in his writings where he made any attempt to define or summarize his educational views. His contributions to education are, for the most part, the ideas emanating from his general philosophical position. They come to us through the medium of those social theorists and educational philosophers who reacted in one way or another to Hegelian absolute idealism. Hegel's philosophical contribution was distinguished, for he achieved what Kant previously insisted was impossible, with brilliance and systematic thoroughness. Kant believed that man cannot have knowledge in the metaphysical (noumenal) realm, but Hegel provided a new rationale for the nature of reality. From the general proposition that "what is rational is real and what is real is rational," Hegel concluded that all things can be known through reason. There were a variety of reactions against Hegelianism, and most of twentieth century philosophy—including Marxism, existentialism, and fascism—represent the range of reactions. Our purpose here will be to concentrate on the philosophical aspects of Hegelianism which were influential in the development of nineteenth and twentieth century intellectual thought.

Hegel, born at Stuttgart in 1770, during Germany's most outstanding intellectual period, was not an exceptional student. When he was eighteen he enrolled in the theological school at the University of Tübingen where his interest began to turn toward the relationship between philosophy and theology. He was influenced by the Greek writers and believed that Plato and Aristotle were the sources of all modern philosophy. After he left the university, Hegel became a family tutor for six years, and also began writing —mostly minor works, but some of them containing the nucleus of problems which eventually became the theme of his major works. During the remainder of his life, Hegel was personally involved with education, for he was appointed to the faculty of the University of Jena in 1801. He became rector of the secondary school at Nürenberg in 1807 where he remained until 1816 when he joined the faculty at Heidelberg. Two years later he was given the chair of philosophy at the University of Berlin and was still teaching there when he died of cholera in 1831.

A Synopsis of the Hegelian Dialectic

As we remember from Chapter V, Kant, believing that the human mind is constructed so that it could not go beyond sense data—the realm of phenomena or appearances—posited another world beyond or behind phenomena which he called the noumenal world. This is the world of things as they really are. The human mind can only grasp the appearance of the things; man cannot know the thing-in-itself, because the categories of the mind (cause and effect, existence and negation, and others) apply only to the phenomenal world. Ultimate reality, for Kant, is the thing-in-itself, so obviously, we can have no knowledge about that reality.

The idealists saw the contradiction in Kant's argument. If we say the thing-in-itself exists, but we can know nothing about it, we have already stated that we know at least one thing about it—that it exists. Further, when Kant said that the thing-in-itself is the cause of our sensations, he contradicted his own rule which limits the use of the categories to our judgments about the objects of sense experience. The idealists insisted that whatever is, is knowable, and transferred Kant's theory into a metaphysical idealism where all objects—the entire universe—is thought to be a product of mind. Idealists translate the basic theory in different ways, but all agree that there is no such thing as an unknowable thing-in-itself.

This rejection of the unknowable thing-in-itself is the first of two major points in Hegel's argument. The second point is that the nature of reality is thought, rationality, and ultimate reality is the *Absolute Idea*. Although Hegel died when Charles Darwin was only twenty-two, long before the publication of Darwin's *The Origin of Species* (1859), the trend toward evolutionary thinking was already under way, and it was manifest in Hegel's suggestion of a *cosmic* evolution which he called *world idea*. This process of idea, culminating in the *Absolute Idea*, is what we mean by Hegelian dialectic. The dialectic has a triadic structure which moves from *thesis,* to *antithesis,* to *synthesis.* The *thesis* is opposed by its opposite, the *antithesis,* which in Hegelian logic is always contained in, and therefore deduced from, the *thesis.* Out of the conflict of these two idea forms, a single, higher form emerges—the *synthesis.* The *synthesis* then becomes the *thesis* of a new triadic structure and the process is repeated, the *thesis* and *antithesis* finding unity in a higher *synthesis* until finally the dialectic terminates in the *Absolute Idea*—all of reality, which is ultimately knowable.

Hegelian dialectic, then, is the triadic process from an idea form which generates its opposite idea form, uniting with it into a higher form which generates its opposite to unite in a still higher form, until eventually the highest idea form—*Absolute Idea*—is attained. However, in order to describe the outline of the whole structure, it is most efficacious to start at the apex of the large triad—*Absolute Idea*—which is actually the ultimate goal.

The final triad culminating in *Absolute Idea* is made up of three distinct aspects of reality: 1) *Logical Idea* (the idea in itself) which is the thesis; 2) *Nature* (the idea outside of itself) which is the antithesis; and 3 *Mind (Spirit)*[1] (the idea in and for itself) which is the synthesis. This triad is representative of the complete triadic nature of Hegel's dialectic. For example: *Logical Idea* (thesis) is composed of *being, essence,* and *concept; being* (the thesis of that triad) is composed of *quality, quantity,* and *measure; essence* (the antithesis of the triad) is composed of *ground of existence, appearance,* and *actuality; concept* (the synthesis of the triad) is composed of *subjective concept, objective concept,* and *idea.* Each of these idea forms is arrived at by way of a triad of lesser idea forms, and this structuring is consistent throughout all of the Hegelian system.[2]

Returning to the final triad that culminates in *Absolute Idea,* the antithesis, *Nature* (the not-idea) is composed of *mechanics, physics,* and *organics; Mind (Spirit),* the synthesis, is composed of *subjective spirit, objective spirit,* and *absolute spirit.* Each of these has a triadic composition, and so on. There is reason to make a more detailed analysis of *Mind (Spirit)* in order to facilitate an understanding of Kierkegaard's rejection of Hegel's absolute idealism.

In order to discover the implied nature of *Mind (Spirit),* we use the same process we have sketched to explain the dialectic, each idea form uniting with its opposite, or not-idea form, to a synthesis of a higher idea form, and so on. The thesis of the triad which reveals the nature of *Mind (Spirit)* is *subjective mind (spirit),* which is arrived at by way of the triad, *anthropology* (where spirit is found in nature), phenomenology of mind (or consciousness), and *psychology* (mind as independent spirit). As we have indicated, each of this triad, like the other, is arrived at by a lesser triad, and so on.

The antithesis of the *Mind (Spirit)* triad is *objective mind (spirit)* which Hegel presents as a concern for certain rights—legal, moral, and social—and a concern for the human race, the organization of societies, and an investigation of the underlying principles of social behavior. *Objective mind (spirit)* is reached by the triad of *formal, abstract right* (which is external), united with *right of an individual conscience* (which is internal), to form the synthesis, *social ethics.* This is a clear statement of Hegel's belief that the individual can only achieve morality in the social realm, and only through the state can man achieve freedom by way of social morality and responsibility.

The synthesis of the *Mind (Spirit)* triad is *absolute mind (spirit)* which is reached by the triad of *art* (thesis), *religion* (antithesis), and *philosophy* (synthesis). It is particularly at this point that Kierkegaard disagreed with Hegel. Kierkegaard's faith would not permit him to agree to the reduction of all things to reason, and he especially quarreled with the

---

[1] There could be confusion because of the various translations of the word *Geist.* Some interpreters use the term *Mind,* others the term *Spirit.* In this context we shall follow the lead of William Wallace, translator, *Hegel's Philosophy of Mind* (Oxford: Clarendon Press, 1894), using the term *Mind,* followed by *Spirit* in parentheses.
[2] W. T. Stace, *The Philosophy of Hegel* (New York: Dover Publications, Inc., 1955). See end piece for complete diagrammatic structure.

concept that made religion subordinate to philosophy, which Hegel equated with *Absolute Idea.*

We have seen that Hegel believed the universe to be governed by logical laws that make all of reality knowable. The Absolute, Hegel's principle of reality, can be identified with the world structure, for he posited a cosmic evolution, a dynamic principle of reality in a constant state of flux, always seeking perfection. His system tended to deify the state, as it is only in the service of the state, which exemplifies the ideals of God, that men can realize true freedom. Hegel further believed that education is the process leading to the freedom—not of self-direction—but of an identification with a Universal Idea. It is interesting to note that even Hegel's ideas about the educational process fall into the triadic structure of his dialectic. The thesis of the triad is the external process, which is parental control; and the synthesis, self-development, leads to an appreciation of universal concepts. The teacher serves as a synthesizer, and the life of scholarship combines the objectivity and the subjectivity in subordination to a universal cause. The emphasis on universal concepts as an educational goal and on the teacher as a synthesizer, rather than as an information dispenser or a disciplinarian, foreshadows contemporary educational views that will be discussed in Chapter IX.

Within the totality of Hegel's philosophical system, the foregoing analysis of the dialectic is admittedly sketchy. But at the same time, it is definitive enough to provide a base for understanding nineteenth century intellectual climate and the various reactions against complete idealism. If no more, Hegel was certainly an intellectual catalyst, for Hegelian thought was responsible for the generation of much antagonism among those who succeeded him. Equating God and the Absolute Spirit, as he did in his essay *Theory of Right, Duties and Religion,* resulted in attacks from both extremes of the philosophical spectrum. It is easy to picture Karl Marx, fascinated by the Hegelian dialectic, yet rejecting out of hand the idealistic view of the universe as being "God intoxicated." The idealistic metaphysic which leaves no room for the obvious material structure was unthinkable to him, and Marx substituted an economically based development that claims the mental is merely a residual of the material. He contended that the consciousness of men should not be a primary concern, for the environment, especially the social and economic relationships of men, is far more important.

At the other end of the philosophical spectrum, Søren Kierkegaard reacted against Hegelianism with understandable vehemence. The suggestion of pantheism, a view conjoining God and nature, was certainly reasonable in the light of Hegel's system, but an orthodox Christian could not accept the loss of an infinite Being, author of the universe. Such a loss would mean a lack of purpose and meaning for man. Kierkegaard and others of his persuasion had no desire to replace a personal God with the neutralism of a rational principle working itself to self-actualization. Nor would they accept Hegel's subjugation of religion by philosophy which made religion understandable at its base by means of reason and logic and robbed the individual of a grace beyond understanding. Kierkegaard would not tolerate the loss of individual uniqueness and emotionalism. In this manner, the Hegelian synthesis of the subjective and the objective was split asunder, and dialectical materialism and Christian existentialism became two of the significant nineteenth century themes. On the one hand, there was a concern for man involved in social relations—a cipher in the social structure, which was of paramount importance—and on the other hand, a real concern for the uniqueness and the importance of the individual.

Hegel's influence was understandably slight in the area of the natural sciences, but his thinking gave impetus to the development of the social sciences, to some extent the philosophy of history, and contributed considerably to the development of educational theories. Herbart's theory that the mind is the means by which empirical presentations are brought into interaction with information or knowledge that is already held, so that the conflict between the two results in a synthesis that is knowledge, is reminiscent of the dialectic. The Hegelian influence is also evidenced in Froebel's thoughts about education, based on the assumption of organic development where the function of education is to mediate the contrasts between individual activities and social relations.

Social Theory—Society and the Individual Social Philosophy

Auguste Comte (1798–1857)

Auguste Comte was born at Montpellier in 1798 into a century of intellectual confusion and social instability. He was born to a Catholic family who were ardent royalists, but by his early teens Comte was a religious and political free thinker. He was educated at the École Polytechnique where he was influenced by reading philosophy and keeping abreast with all of the scientific developments of the day. French philosophy during the nineteenth century was considerably influenced by internal political events, and a number of antirevolutionary philosophies began to appear. There were many who saw the French Revolution as an attempt to destroy not only the legitimate power of the church and the state, but all institutions, including the family. Comte found the mental anarchy of his time and the general breakdown of old standards most disturbing.

Comte became secretary in 1818 to Saint-Simon, the most prominent French socialist of the time, and held the post for a number of years. During this time, Comte wrote a series of books, including his first *Système de politique positive* (1824) which was a sketch of a later major work. After recovering from a mental breakdown in 1826, Comte taught mathematics at the Polytechnique but devoted the greatest part of his time to writing. He was considerably affected by his romantic involvement with Clotilde de Vaux which was terminated after two years by her tragic death. There can be no doubt but that the affair was responsible for the great stress he placed on love in his "Religion of Humanity," an emphasis contrary to his strict views about the scientific understanding of humanity.

Comte was a prolific writer, and the voluntary contributions of his friends and supporters of his positivism enabled him to devote the greater part of his time to his writing. His major works include: *Cours de philosophie positive* which was written in several volumes between the years of 1830 and 1842; his second *Le système de politique positive* written from 1851 to 1854; *Catéchisme positiviste* (1852); and the *Synthèse subjective* (1856). He was working on a projected series on ethics, the positive industrial organization, and other philosophical projects when he died at the age of fifty-nine in 1857. Our particular interest here in Comte is his philosophy of positivism, his law of the three stages, and his classification of the sciences (reminiscent of Hegel, and the heart of positivism), his creation of sociology, and his "Religion of Humanity." These topics will be considered in that order.

According to John Stuart Mill, positivism was "the general property of the age," and although Comte may not have discovered the mode of thought, he was nonetheless the originator of *positive philosophy*. Briefly, positivism is a curiosity about, and a way of searching for, the facts of human existence. This science of human behavior rejects any teleology in nature, and there is no interest in seeking the so-called "essence" of things. As Newton described the phenomena of physics without inquiring into the essential nature of things, positivism seeks the constant relations between things in order to discover the facts and describe scientific laws in terms of these constant relations. There is the assumption that knowledge derived from science can be used in all areas, including social relations. Positivism claims to deal effectively, by the same methods, with both physical and political reality and is an attempt to eliminate conflict between science and religion. Comte believed that unless a statement can be reduced to a simple fact, it has no real meaning or sense. All knowledge is relative, because we know facts only as they are related to other facts, and this applies equally to science, society, and religion. Comte saw the brain as a mirror to the external order, the medium for checking new facts against known facts and relating them for new knowledge. He posited the law of the three stages to point up the validity of positivism.

Comte maintained that the development of the scientific point of view has undergone three stages or what he calls a law of growth. The stages, which hold good for the evolution of intellectual activity in both the individual and the race, are: 1) the theological; 2) the metaphysical; and 3) the positivist. The theological stage of intellectual thought, where all phenomena are explained as resulting from supernatural or divine powers, is the starting point of all intellectual activity. The second stage, the metaphysical, is one of intellectual transition, where the individual or the racial mind goes beyond the anthropocentric explanations, to impersonal or abstract forces. Finally, the positivist stage can be equated with the scientific. The final stage is realized through criticism and evaluation of the other stages, which is a kind of a synthesis. As the mind progresses, it passes through stages of accepting all sorts of mystical and imaginary explanations for phenomenal events. It is finally satisfied by laws which do not explain the causes or whys of things but merely describe *how* phenomena do behave. This law of evolution from one stage to another is thought to be effective in each particular science, including political science. According to the law, slavery and the military state coincide with the theological stage; liberal democracy, where the equality of men is held to be true, is an outgrowth of the metaphysical; and only with the realization that men are not equal, that they have different capacities and abilities, and therefore different societal functions, has the positivist stage been achieved. Comte's classification of the sciences is also evolutionary and is intimately related to his law of three stages.

Comte asserted that mathematics is the first science to have arisen from the theological stage, and evolved through the metaphysical to the positivist stage. The next to follow this order was astronomy, then physics, and finally, chemistry. He believed biology to be in the process of evolving to the highest stage and saw no reason why ethics and the most complex sciences—the social sciences—could not follow. Comte pointed out that the parts of the advanced sciences are better known than the whole. Since science progresses by building up general concepts from an observation of the particular, or inductively, these advanced sciences would most naturally be the first to evolve to the highest stage. On the other hand, the subject matter of biology and the social sciences is more readily first observed as a whole, and the descriptive process moves from the group to the individual, or deductively. This progression from the universal to the particular is the base for Comte's creation of the new science, sociology.

Sociology, the necessary outcome of biology, is concerned with social phenomena rather than natural phenomena and deals with the relations of human being to human being in society. Mathematics and astronomy developed in the ancient world; physics as a true science began with Isaac Newton (1642–1727); chemistry began with Antoine Lavoisier (1743–1794); and biology with Bichat (1711–1802). Now Comte saw that it was dependent on him to introduce sociology, the queen of science, to the intellectual world.

Two points dominate Comte's sociology, the *static* and the *dynamic* components of social existence. The static is the stable aspect of society— the family, private property, language, and religion—and since these elements are permanent, there is no need for any revolutionary change in them. The dynamic component is the force of progress and has to do with a refinement of our understanding about how existing social elements can be used to best advantage. Since progress is by way of understanding, there is no more need for the structures of society to change as we move from one stage to another, than there was for the stars and the constellations to change as our understanding of them increased. One outcome of the achievement of the positivist stage in sociology would be to confer an enlightened status on women. Another would be the utilization of property in such a way as to promote altruism, instead of greed and envy. Comte measures all progress in terms of the methods of involving reason and science that are used to deal with ethical and social problems. He believed that moral progress is historically identical with intellectual progress, which brings us to Comte's "Religion of Humanity."

Comte's law of three stages automatically rules out any idea of God, for an object of worship acceptable to positivism would have to be drawn from an objectively real source. Believing as he did that we draw our intellectual, spiritual, and moral resources from humanity, Comte termed humanity *Grand-Être,* the Supreme Being, and offered it as a substitute for God. Along the lines of a secularized version of Catholicism, he became his own High Priest, with the most renowned scientists his calendar of Saints. Comte posited love to be the supreme moral principle, with all thoughts of the intellect subordinate to love. Living for others brings feeling, reason, and activity into complete harmony, Comte maintained, and makes life "a continuous and intense act of worship." It seemed to Comte that all people could accept the principles of this new religion built on ideas and reality and that it would serve as a unifying force between people and between their thoughts and their actions.

Karl Marx (1818–1883)

The close collaboration of Karl Marx with Friedrich Engels (1820–1895) is often overlooked, in spite of the fact that it is difficult to separate their writings. Nor shall we attempt to make the separation here, other than to acknowledge the possibility, for their thinking follows the same course. As is so often the case with the "great disturbers" of their age, Marx is both venerated and vilified. There are those who have a philosophical appreciation of his scientific socialism, those who exhibit an emotional commitment to his political and economic theories, and those who blame him for all of the evils of a communism that would bury the free world. Our discussion of Marx will be undertaken in the spirit of inquiry about the ideas of a man whose main concern seems to have been to effect social change for the good of all individuals and who was eminently successful in structuring his political, economical, and social ideas.

Karl Heinrich Marx was born in Trier, Germany, in 1818. Although his father was a Jewish lawyer, he had become a Lutheran and raised his family as Protestants, very likely more out of expediency than religious convictions. Marx attended the University of Bonn after he finished high school in Trier and for a year studied the law. When he was eighteen he transferred to the University of Berlin to study philosophy and was tremendously impressed with Hegelianism, the dominant influence at that time. Hegel had not intended his philosophy to undermine the foundations of religion, but it was a simple matter for Marx—a meticulous and thorough student—to go a step further, and use the Hegelian dialectic to arrive at philosophical atheism.

Karl Marx received his doctoral degree from Jena when he was only twenty-three, and went when he was twenty-five to Paris to join with his friends in the publication of a radical periodical, *Deutsch-Französiche Jahrbücher*. It was here that Marx and Engels met and their long and intimate association began. After a year, Marx was expelled from Paris, and he spent the next three years in Brussels where he helped to organize a German Worker's Union which later became, in conjunction with similar European groups, an international Communist League. Engels was the first secretary and Marx formulated the statement of principles in the form of *The Manifesto of the Communist Party*. After being expelled once more from Paris, Marx moved to London in 1849 where he spent the rest of his life. He became an isolated figure, spending most of each day in the reading room at the British Museum, studying and writing, poring over texts in economics, history, and philosophy. He derived some meagre income from articles written for the *New York Tribune* but was forced to depend upon the beneficence of Engels for most of his sustenance. Though a gentle family man, Marx could be merciless with those who disagreed with his philosophy and often directed bitter attacks against them, as well as against those who lacked sufficient understanding and dedication to join his efforts. He was a complex figure—bitter, arrogant, kindly, pathetic—but with it all, a man whose vision was responsible for dialectical materialism and whose thinking was responsible for much of the turmoil of the modern age.

Karl Marx's philosophy has been variously labeled. Engels called it *historical materialism;* G. V. Pleknanov used the term *dialectical materialism,* which has persisted; and Marx himself seems to have preferred *scientific socialism.* All of the terms are descriptive but especially the terminology Marx preferred as he incorporated ideas from both Hegel and Comte into his system. Actually, there was very little intellectual activity in the nineteenth century that did not stem, either directly or indirectly, from the various interpretations of Hegelianism which made a tremendous stir in metaphysics, theology, and politics. Hegel was attacked for his *a priori* method of philosophizing, for depending too much on logic to determine the nature of the real, and for his determinism. He was accused of being godless, berated for his latent pantheism and condemned for his dualistic conception of the Creator and the created—of mind and matter. It is small wonder that in no time at all, the Hegelians were split into left, right, and center parties. The most important development to come from the Hegelian left is the theory developed by Marx and Engels, dialectical materialism.

One way to an understanding of dialectical materialism is to approach it in terms of the debt Marx owed to Hegelianism. There are a number of points where Marx agreed with Hegel's philosophy, especially with his dialectic. Marx accepted the idea of reality being an intelligible, logical process, and he also accepted the dialectical law of thesis, antithesis, and synthesis. Further, he accepted the Kantian and Hegelian category of *reciprocity,* whereby causes produce effects that react on the causes in such a way that the character of the causes may be modified or determined; whereby wholes are built up of parts and react on the parts so that the character of the constituents may be altered. In other words, the law of reciprocity states that a given set of conditions depends upon its antecedents and also upon the resulting set of conditions.

The concept is important for dialectical materialism, as when the law is applied to the thesis, antithesis, synthesis triad, the thesis and antithesis are mutually interactive—each the cause and the effect of the other. The synthesis is a new situation, created by and in the process of creating, the interplay of thesis and antithesis. In this manner, the materialism of Marx is not mechanistic and deterministic but develops in a dynamic manner. For instance, a transition from capitalism to communism is characterized by the tension of opposites within the process. There is a tension within capitalism between the material forces of technology and the individualism associated with private property. The cooperative effort demanded by industrial production is in conflict with individualism, resulting in a breakdown of the capitalistic system and the necessary synthesis of a classless society where the proletariat controls production and utilizes the products for a societal benefit. Clearly, Marx borrowed heavily from the Hegelian dialectic, but his dialectical materialism was also shaped by his rejection of many of the concepts expressed in Hegel's philosophy.

Some of the points of disagreement between Hegelianism and Marxism are already evident. We have seen that the Hegelian leftists rejected all idealistic interpretations of the universe. Marx held that a belief in any supernatural, immaterial, and theological entity was superstitious. By the same token, although accepting the dialectic, Marx emphatically rejected the view of a purposeful design or master plan to the world-process or any implied moral guidance. According to Marx, material aspects cannot be reduced to the mental, as matter exists in time and space, independent of any mental awareness, and therefore is not the content of mind. Marx asserted that the Hegelian statement that laws of being are an expression of laws of thought and can be discovered by analyses of thinking processes is based on a false assumption. Human thinking, he said, is the adaptation of the human mind to the movement of the universe, and therefore the logic of events must be discovered by observation of external operations in the entire course of human history. Here is the rationale for the Marxian materialistic concept of history.

Hegel made the world-process a closed circle, but Marx insisted that, although the process is indeed circular, it is not a closed circle. He saw that humanity and human institutions are constantly evolving and posited a circular movement that spirals. He criticized Hegel for identifying final syntheses in all departments of life with conditions that existed in his own lifetime. While Marx accepted the Hegelian proposal of the general theory of the dialectical movement of history, he was primarily interested in discovering history's law of motion in order to explain the *whys* of history, so that the future could be predicted. He distinguished five historic phases, which he called: 1) the primitive communal; 2) slave; 3) feudal; 4) capitalist; and 5) (a prediction of things to come) the socialist and communist phase. He looked upon each of the epochs as the result of conflict between the material order (the substructure of society) and the order of human thought (the superstructure of society). History is movement caused by material conflicts, the process of change from one epoch to the next. The Marxian view of change is not one of growth or maturation but the emergence of new institutions and forms.

The Hegelian dialectic would terminate when the idea of freedom was finally realized, but for Marx the dialectic process would cease only with the emergence of socialism and communism—when the inner contradictions between classes are resolved. Only then would the cause of the movement be eliminated and all forces and interests be in perfect and perpetual balance.

In sum, dialectical materialism is a repudiation of all nonmaterialistic interpretations of appearance and behavior of world-process. Marx felt that any philosophy worthy of its name must be a way of life, and an important aspect of dialectical materialism is the application of the knowledge man gains of the universe. Understanding alone is meaningless to Marx, for he believed that theory and practice cannot be separated and that the only value of science is in applied science. Dialectical materialism, then, is *active, creative,* and *applied* knowledge and contains an element of prediction which can only be applied by society pulling together as one. Contrary to Hegel, who exalted the individual at the expense of society and viewed society as a means to individual self-expression, Marx believed the individual to be a means to the self-realization of a society of which the individual is an integral part. Individuals stand in a relation of reciprocity to each other and to the community, all for one and one for all. Thus society is the real human unit which prevents slavery and enables man to be the master of his destiny.

Whether or not scientific socialism is indeed scientific, Marx is certainly the epitome of the social scientist wishing to understand the workings of human endeavors and relations in order to promote a change in human affairs and conditions. His belief that the point of philosophy should be to change society, and his own analysis of how the change can be accomplished, is a landmark in social science. Marx claimed that the inexorable flow of economic forces makes it clear that man must be nonmetaphysical, scientific, and concerned with history and the social sciences. The social turmoil of the Western world in the past century attests to the fact that the central problem of philosophy has indeed become the social environment of man, and it is clear that the explanation of historical events is important to the future of man. The search for such an explanation continues, and we turn to Søren Kierkegaard for an interpretation that places primary emphasis on the individual.

Søren Kierkegaard (1813–1855)

Historically, Kierkegaard represents an *in toto* rejection of Hegelianism, a lonely attack against the destructive factors of intellectualism and absolutism. The solo onslaught of this intense individualist against everything that militates against the full expression of individualism—industrialized society, institutionalism, and the established Church—was more or less ineffectual in his own time. But most scholars credit Kierkegaard for the inception of the movement called existentialism, a philosophy which has received considerable attention from educational philosophers in the past two decades. Kierkegaard's philosophy of the human situation, emphasizing individualism, subjectivity, introspection, and feeling, is usually termed Christian existentialism. It is a philosophy of life, as opposed to logic, of individual freedom, as opposed to mechanism and determinism. Contrary to the expectations of its lonely, agonized beginnings, existentialism eventually invaded almost every form of human expression, and has received a wider response in the arts, education, and theology than any other mode of philosophy in current times. A partial explanation of this fact is the many different forms that existentialism has taken among writers and thinkers of widely diverse philosophical orientations. The common core is a real concern about human existence and about the quality and condition of the individual. The theme of Christian existentialism, first expressed in the writings of Søren Kierkegaard, is readily understandable in light of the biographical details of his own tortured forty-two years.

Søren Kierkegaard, the youngest of seven children, was born May 5, 1813, in Copenhagen, Denmark. His early training was in accordance with strict Lutheran doctrine, but at an early age he began to question the authenticity of the Christianity that seemed powerless to comfort the elder Kierkegaard, who practiced it so stringently. Søren Kierkegaard attended the university where he studied the Hegelian Logic, which he thought to be merely comic. It seemed comic to Kierkegaard for one to attempt to capture all of reality in his system of thought, yet to ignore the most important element—existence.

Doubtless there was a connection between Kierkegaard's ponderings about individual existence and his own physical handicap. He was born with a slight curvature of the spine, a condition which must have predisposed his mind toward melancholia. Certainly he doubted that his life would be a long one, as he wrote in his journal that he was surprised to celebrate his thirty-fourth birthday. He was also obsessed by a feeling of guilt which he thought to be a family legacy brought about by his father.

As a young boy, the elder Kierkegaard had cursed God for the extreme poverty and misery he suffered, and it seemed to Søren Kierkegaard that God continued to vent His anger on the entire family. When Kierkegaard was still in his early twenties, the feeling must have been strengthened by the death of his mother and all but one of his brothers within a few years. Certainly Kierkegaard's concern for individual existence, his melancholia, his deep feelings of inherited guilt, all contributed to the formulation of his intense and foreboding philosophical attitude—an attitude characterized by fear, alienation, dread, and agony. Kierkegaard's philosophy was not systematic in the traditional sense of the word. He was interested in what he called ethical action and religiousness, but he developed no system of ethics or religious dogma, which is understandable in view of his belief that value and morality can only be derived from man's existential situation.

According to Kierkegaard, truth is not some prefabricated absolute that can be found outside of the individual. Truth, he believed, can be attained only by an existing individual, for truth *is* subjectivity. A description of man's existential situation involves a distinction between man's present state—the way he is—and his potential state—the way he ought to be. There is a movement in the life of the individual from what he is *essentially* to his *existential* condition, from essence to existence. Kierkegaard translated the theological doctrine of original sin into a psychological analysis where man's anxiety over his own finitude is the cause of his estrangement from his essential being, which entails his relation to God. Until the individual can realize his essential self in God, his life is filled with anxiety caused by this alienation. The feeling of alienation creates a dynamic drive for man to recover his essential self, and Kierkegaard calls this movement the "stages on life's way."

Kierkegaard's dialectic process, consisting of three stages, is markedly different from Hegel's theory of the gradual development of individual self-consciousness. According to Hegel, the individual mind moves through the stages of *intellectual* awareness by means of the thinking process toward a knowledge of the universal. Kierkegaard describes the self moving through the stages of existence by an act of will, by choice, to individual actualization. He calls the three stages: 1) the aesthetic stage; 2) the ethical stage; and 3) the religious stage.

An individual is directed in the first stage, the aesthetic, by his impulses and his emotions. He is somewhat more than merely sensual, but he is ruled by his senses. While existence *can* be achieved at this level if the person makes the deliberate choice to be an aesthetic man, the quality of the existence is inferior. Man can make a deliberate choice to live in a sewer, but the lure of the spirit (the antithesis) produces a conflict which results in agony and despair, and man is faced with an either-or choice. Either he wallows in sensuality, accepting its limitations, or he moves to the next stage, the ethical.

Man in the ethical stage accepts certain rules of conduct that are dictated by reason. No longer is he governed strictly by his senses, for he sees that moral evil is the result of ignorance, and he assumes a moral responsibility, taking a stand on questions of good conduct and moral actions. At the same time, he begins to realize that his knowledge of moral law is insufficient for him to fulfill the law, and he feels the guilt of his own inadequacy. Again, guilt is the dialectic element, the antithesis that places man once more in an either-or position. He must choose either to remain at the ethical level and try to fulfill the moral law, so far as he is able, agonizing with the guilt of his own inadequacy, or he must respond to his new awareness of his own finitude and estrangement from God. If he makes the latter choice, man can only achieve the final stage, the religious, by a leap of faith.

The movement from the aesthetic stage to the ethical stage required an act of choice of commitment to bring man into the presence of reason. The leap of faith brings man—not into the presence of a God or the Knowable (objective) Truth, but into a subjective, personal, and unique relationship with God. Obviously this dialectic process must be subjective, and it cannot be accomplished if man tries to lose himself in a crowd. Any kind of collectivity, according to Kierkegaard, weakens the individual sense of responsibility through a dilution of the self. Thus Kierkegaard's central theme is that each person possesses an essential self which he *ought* to actualize. The process of such actualization is not one of reason or intellect but is a matter of commitment and faith—a continuous process of choice.

John Stuart Mill (1806–1873)

John Stuart Mill, born in 1806, knew every intellectual advantage of inheritance, environment, and training. His father, James Mill, had been a close associate of Jeremy Bentham (1748–1832) whose general views of ethics, government, and law had a tremendous influence on the boy. Through his father's ideas and associations, John Stuart Mill was introduced at an early age to the thinking of the leading men of the time. He was subjected to the most rigorous sort of education beginning at the age of three with a study of Greek. By the time he was fourteen, Mill had studied logic, natural science, economics, and Greek and Latin literature in the original. He was tutored by his father in the classics, language, and history, and the intense study was distinguished by an emphasis on critical and analytical thinking.

Mill felt that his habit of analysis tended to wear away the feelings, and it was only after a breakdown at the age of twenty that he turned to writers such as Coleridge, Carlyle, and Wordsworth, who affected his thoughts so that the cultivation of the feelings became central in his ethical and philosophical creed. He was further persuaded of the importance of the role of feeling by his long romance with Mrs. Harriet Taylor. She was married when they first met and became friends at a time when Mill was suffering from a melancholia over a lack of purpose in his life. Her influence was instrumental in Mill's attempt to restore balance to his life, and they maintained a close relationship for over twenty years. They were finally able to marry after her husband's death in 1849, and for seven years until her death in 1858, lived in complete emotional and intellectual harmony. Mill often referred to their "joint productions" in the scholarly world. After Harriet's death, Mill retired to a life of study and writing that was interrupted only once, beginning in 1865, by a three-year service in the House of Commons. Mill died in 1873 at the age of sixty-seven.

All of Mill's writings are characterized by the premium he placed on maintaining a balance among the range of human faculties. His *Principles of Political Economy* published in 1848, the same year as Marx's *Communist Manifesto,* was in direct contrast to the latter, as the theme of Mill's work is progress through peaceful and orderly change. Another of his monumental works, his *System of Logic* (1843) contributed to inductive methods. His brilliant essay, *On Liberty,* was published in the same year, 1859, as Darwin's *The Origin of the Species.* His much admired *Utilitarianism,* which began as a defense of Bentham's *principle of utility* but broadened into a version of utilitarianism somewhat different in several respects, was first published in *Fraser's Magazine* in 1861, and two years later set forth in a separate volume. His other literary achievements include *Considerations on Representative Government* (1861), his *Autobiography,* and *Three Essays on Religion,* which were published after his death. The present discussion will center on the basic ideas about freedom, individualism, and social philosophy that are found in his essay, *On Liberty,* and in his *Utilitarianism.*

Mill makes an entirely different sort of plea for individual liberty than the impassioned cry of Søren Kierkegaard. The subject of his essay is not a liberty of the will but a civil or social liberty, a concern about the extent and limitations of the controls that a society can legitimately impose on the individual. Bentham had placed his faith on democracy as a cure for social evils, but while Mill believed democracy to be the best form of government, he was keenly aware of the inherent dangers. He wanted people to be aware of the fact that the tyranny of opinion can be another sort of oppression. He wanted them to be alert to the need to guard against forces that have the potential of denying man his right to self-development. And he wanted people to feel the urgency of preserving liberty by setting limits to governmental control.

Mill believed that the only reason governmental control should be imposed on any member of a community against his will is to prevent harm to other members of the community. He stated that the government should not interfere when action can be effected by individuals or when governmental action might result in too much central power. Each individual should pursue his happiness in his own way and should be free to express his thoughts and beliefs in his own way without fear of reprisal. At the same time, while an individual has certain rights, he also has duties and responsibilities to others and to the society which protects his rights. The interests of others must not be injured, and each must bear his share of supporting and defending the social order from internal and external enemies.

When Mill considers the ideal goal of man as each achieving the best state or condition possible for him, he is faced with the question of what is to be done about those individuals who do not appreciate the higher values, who have no desire to achieve their highest potential. Too much governmental help can surely weaken the stamina of individual initiative, but is it not interfering to suggest that the government should be granted the right to make education compulsory? Indeed, Mill's advocacy of compulsory education, prohibitions against self-enslavement, compelling parents to educate children, and forbidding marriage by those unable to support a family are surely a reversal of his earlier contention that men must not interfere with the liberty of others, even for their own good. However, the fact that Mill is not able to put forward a single principle that can determine the question of infringement in all instances does not lessen the merit or the relevance of what he does have to say about liberty and individual freedom. The fact that there is no generally accepted solution to a given problem does not make it right to ignore the problem, and Mill's ideas on liberty open the way to the sort of speculation that is the best assurance of individual freedom.

Mill's version of utilitarianism started with essentially the same base that Bentham had established. That is, that actions are right in proportion to the happiness they produce; that happiness is equated with pleasure; and that the absence of pleasure is pain. But after making the same sort of relationship between happiness and pleasure as Bentham had, Mill adds another dimension to Bentham's idea that pleasures differ only in degree or quantity. Bentham posited the *amount* of pleasure an act produces as the only measurement of good, which led to the accusation of moral relativity. Through his attempt to defend utilitarianism against this charge, Mill was led to the refinement of substituting a qualitative approach for Bentham's quantitative measure. Actually, Mill stood with the ancient Epicureans who, crediting man with faculties far above mere animal appetites, rated pleasures of the intellect, feeling, and moral sensations far superior to the physical pleasures of sensation. According to Mill, if pleasures are graded for quality rather than for quantity, pleasure is no longer the standard of morality. The standard becomes a measure of the degree of the fulfillment of our human faculties, which is consistent with the ideas about the highest good of man that Mill had expressed earlier in his essay *On Liberty*.

The difference in approaches—the qualitative versus the quantitative—results in a further distinction between the utilitarianism of the two men, which has to do with the pleasure-pain calculus. Bentham's pleasure-pain calculus had a simple quantitative base, where the duration, extent, and intensity of pleasure and pain could be measured and compared. But Mill's qualitative base rules out this kind of measurement, and indeed, Mill insisted that neither quantity nor quality can be measured. A choice cannot be made between two pleasures, Mill said, unless we have experienced both choices. According to this, we can express a preference for one over another, but the subjectivity of the choice makes it unsuitable for any kind of calculus.

Mill accepted Bentham's greatest happiness principle, that we ought to choose the acts that give us the greatest pleasure, but he added the quality of altruism to the principle. That is, the standard of utilitarian happiness should be the happiness of *all* concerned—not just the happiness of the agent. Thus Mill's greatest happiness principle is the greatest happiness for the greatest number, which is often equated with the golden rule of Jesus of Nazareth. It is in this manner that Mill defends utilitarianism against the charge of egoism. In many ways it seems that the greater Mill's defense of utilitarianism, the further he departs from it. An emphasis on the quality of pleasures and on the good of the whole suggests some other ground of obligation than happiness. If one maintains, as Mill did, that happiness is the center of the moral life and the most desirable goal of man, the question of why we ought to seek happiness needs to be answered. Mill's answer was that we just naturally do strive to be happy; but this is not a satisfactory answer for those who see a fallacy in the idea of basing a moral structure on what man already does, rather than on what he ought to do.

There are other logical difficulties in Mill's utilitarianism. For instance, his defense of the desirable forces the conclusion that, if a thing is desired, it is worthy of the desire. Actually, Mill's defense of utilitarianism results in quite different principles from those he set out to defend. Mill ends by a complete departure from Bentham's external standard of goodness, as he finally turns inward to "a subjective feeling in our own minds" for the basis of morality. Nonetheless, in spite of the many difficulties, Mill's efforts did result in a social philosophy that explains change in a way that most men can readily understand and one that still holds a good deal of appeal for many.

Philosophy of History

A commonly held view of history is that it deals with individual facts about the past which become the material of social science. According to this view, the historian discovers the things that have happened, and the social scientist explains the happenings. But what historian is satisfied to know that certain things happened, without exhibiting some curiosity about why they happened? Most historians, bent on an intelligent and an intelligible reconstruction of the human past, are not content merely to discover, order, and record past events. They are interested in questions about the meaning of history and about the kinds of changes in history. They attempt to discover if there is any relationship between specific events and the general course of history and are concerned with an interpretation of the development of man in relation to ends, values, and progress. Most historians exhibit an overriding interest in patterns, order, plot, theme, and discernible development. The idea thus emerges that there is a distinct difference between history and historiography, or historical research.

Erich Kahler writes in *The Meaning of History,*[3] that "History is happening, a particular kind of happening, and the attendant whirl it generates. Where there is no happening, there is no history." He points out that all events are related, and that there is a necessary "substratum or focus" for the connection of happenings. History, then, can be said to be comparable to a good story or a novel, which is never a series of isolated episodes but is the orderly development of a complex situation with a unity of plot or theme. Just as there can be no story without meaning, there can be no history without meaning. It seems a reasonable assumption that the nature of the meaning of history is the special province of the philosopher of history.

There are, however, many who even today do not recognize the legitimacy of philosophy of history. One reason for this could stem from a narrow, metaphysical interpretation of the word *meaning.* Such an interpretation limits philosophy of history, as it was traditionally conceived, to a speculative endeavor aimed at understanding the course of history as a whole in terms of "purpose." Such an interpretation clearly implies the assumption of an overall plan that, once grasped, would lay bare the secret of history. But Kahler[4] posits two modes of meaning: 1) *meaning as purpose or goal;* and 2) *meaning as form.* Accordingly, philosophy of history is twofold. One part, the speculative, is concerned with questions of historical principles, causes, underlying laws, and overall purpose. We call this part the metaphysics of history. The second part, the cognitive, is concerned with historic understanding or with the logic of history, and the approach is analytical or critical. Thus, similar in this respect to scientific thinking which is concerned on the one hand with the activity itself and on the other hand with its objects, historical thinking has come to have both a speculative and an analytical part. Even the most anti-metaphysically minded, who reject the first grouping of problems, are inclined to accept the legitimacy of the other grouping. We shall see that prior to the twentieth century historical thinking was predominantly speculative.

Philosophy of History Prior to the Twentieth Century

The exact origin of the phrase, philosophy of history, is a matter of debate. R. G. Collingwood,[5] a noted philosopher whose opinion is highly regarded by scholars, gives credit to Voltaire (1694–1778). Others credit Giambatista Vico (1668–1744), who contended that historical events, like natural events, follow each other according to unswerving natural laws. He assumed the three stages of development of fantasy, of will, and of science. Some writers go back even further to the writings of St. Augustine, who

---

[3] Erich Kahler, *The Meaning of History* (New York: George Braziller, Inc., 1964), p. 17.
[4] *Ibid.,* p. 19.
[5] R. G. Collingwood, *The Idea of History* (London: Oxford University Press, 1946), p. 1.

gave the oldest theological interpretation, that all historic events have a bearing on the redemption of mankind through Christ and will find completion at the end of this world. W. H. Walsh[6] states that the first recognition of philosophy of history as a separate subject was during the period that began with J. G. Herder's (1744–1803) *Ideas for a Philosophical History of Mankind*. The exponents of the study as it was conceived during this period were, for the most part, speculative metaphysicians who were not averse to distorting fact for the sake of the unity they sought. In many cases there was little to distinguish speculation from guesswork, and it is small wonder that it is only in the past few decades that philosophy of history has achieved its present degree of respectability.

All of the various interpretations of history can be grouped according to one of four general historical attitudes. First, *historical nihilism* which denies any meaning, pattern, or purpose to history. Second, *historical skepticism* which says that we cannot really know if there is a pattern or purpose. Third, *historical subjectivism* which posits that any seeming patterns are merely creations of the human mind. And finally, *historical objectivism* which detects certain patterns and connections and which may, or may not, ascribe some overall purpose. The first three attitudes reject both modes of meaning and thus limit historical research to a factual recounting. The fourth attitude, however, includes a variety of interpretations which, chronologically speaking, coincide with the changing points of view in the Western world as we have noted them elsewhere in our study. It is important to note here that when we speak of philosophy of history prior to the twentieth century, it is not to say that all of the historical interpretations were abandoned at the turn of the century. On the contrary, some of the earlier views are still held by many, and others have been revived, redefined in a different context, or adopted with a different emphasis.

Strictly speaking, we do not credit the ancients with having a philosophy of history, but the development of a concept of history coincides with the development of man's awareness of self. A sense of change was crucial to the early Greeks whose dominant theme came to be an attempt to reconcile the actuality of change with a permanent cosmic order. This is illustrated by the claim of Heraclitus that we step and do not step into the same river. Thus, change in itself is constant. The Greek themes of fate and recurrence give rise to an historical attitude that we now call the world-cycles theory where societies are thought to rise and fall in eternally recurring cycles through the world year. The Greeks saw the workings of fate in recurring cycles of construction and destruction, full of import and sense, yet with no discernible purpose in the sense of being directed to an ultimate end. The cyclical view, accepted by the Stoics and later reflected in the writings of such Roman historians as Marcus Aurelius and Seneca, was rejected at the advent of Christianity. However, the cyclical view was revived in the nineteenth century by Friedrich Nietzsche (1844–1900) and

---

[6] W. H. Walsh, *Philosophy of History* (New York: Harper & Row, Publishers, Harper Torchbooks, 1960), p. 11.

by Oswald Spengler (1880–1936). Spengler's philosophy of history is a modern example of the theory of cycles.

The view of purpose in history has its origin in metaphysical and religious beliefs. It carries the idea that the individual derives meaning from the larger scheme; that events in the world are no more than small pieces of a master plan; and it suggests a rationale or some type of determinism. The Christianizing of the Western world brought the view of history as being the scene of promise with a purpose beyond any human purpose, and the idea of a world cycle was replaced by the idea of a line of advance, a line representing the power of God. Variations of the providential theory see God as being manifest through processes of the human mind and nature, the individual soul, or the spiritual geniuses of a race in order that the divine purpose may be worked out in world history. The providential view of history was held by the early Hebrews and Christians and is traditional to the West. St. Augustine set forth the providential view in his *City of God,* where God's purpose is revealed to man by history and the church is the visible representation of the City of God on earth.

As the scientific temper began to take over and the power of knowledge and natural explanations made God remote to history, the idea of history as progress persisted with the power of knowledge replacing the universal purpose. Progress was seen in terms of the individual and through the individual in terms of a society. Such a view of history, where progress is in terms of the natural understanding of the world, is called the progress theory. There are many variations of the progress theory that have been formulated in different countries and at different times, but they all have points of general agreement. All agree that progress is a natural product of history, necessary because all human evils are due to ignorance. The increase of human knowledge moves man in the direction of perfect happiness, and, although the possibility of regression is admitted, it may be overcome by man's initiative. Education is most often perceived as the key factor to progress, an attitude that has strong support in twentieth century American rationale. The view is essentially optimistic with its movement towards the good society.

Kant's philosophical interpretation of history is a variation of the eighteenth century theory of progress, as he saw a continuous, though not necessarily straightforward, progression towards a better world. Kant argued the necessity of our accepting the idea of a long-term plan that may be incoherent to the individual yet turn out to be orderly and intelligible from the viewpoint of the species.

The social philosophies of the eighteenth century, especially ideas such as Rousseau's rights of revolution, contributed to the idea of history as conflict and development. The most noteworthy of such an attitude are the dialectics of Hegel and Marx. The Hegelian view of history, a mingling of fate, purpose, and progress, is called the endless dialectic theory. As we have noted, Hegel regarded his philosophy as a synthesis of the scientific outlook of the Enlightenment and the opposing romantic philosophies. Hegel viewed history as having a direction and a goal, with progress occurring in the world through conflict. According to Hegel, world history belongs to the realm of spirit whose essence is rational freedom, and the historical process moves from one level to the next by means of the dialectic movement from thesis to antithesis to synthesis. The pattern of development moves on a triadic pattern rather than along a straight line, and there is no stopping point. Each resolution of the dialectic leads toward the goal of history, but the goal can never be realized in the material world.

On the other hand, if the goal of other eighteenth century philosophers who believed that peace and happiness in an ideal society could be realized by all men, a dialectic which could attain a world goal would be possible. For instance, Karl Marx's economic interpretation of history involves a terminating dialectic which centers around class struggle, with revolution as the natural means of resolving class conflicts. According to Marxian dialectical materialism, there are five stages of history. The first four, primitive communism, the slave system, military and feudal groups, and the bourgeois or capitalist system, have already appeared in human society. The final stage, the classless society, is presently taking form. Once the final stage is realized, the dialectic will cease to operate, and we will have reached the end of history.

Another view of history that occurred prior to the twentieth century stemmed from Comte's social dynamics and is called the positivist theory. Believing history to be unintelligible, Comte turned to his law of three stages to make some sense out of it. Even though he believed his method to be empirical, his construction actually involved a great deal more *a priori* theorizing than it did scientific data, and historians find it as unsatisfactory as the most metaphysical of the speculative philosophies of history. Nevertheless, the positivist method did have an effect on the development of nineteenth century historical studies by way of an emphasis on the accumulation and examination of historical records and data, and the positivist movement in history foreshadowed twentieth century analytical philosophy of history.

Twentieth Century Philosophy of History

We have seen that through the nineteenth century, problems concerning the philosophy of history were, for the most part, those of a speculative or metaphysical nature. A wholly irrational course of history was unthinkable to the traditional philosopher who sought to discover the purpose of the historical process. Even the Marxian economic interpretation of history, by positing the *necessity* of a classless society, leaned heavily on what many feel is closer to an *a priori* truth than it is to an empirical hypothesis. The attempts of the positivists to base metaphysical speculation on a sound scientific basis, although having a substantial influence on the development of historical studies, were unsuccessful, because the facts of history would not comply to the same sorts of natural laws that explain the facts of science. The realization that physical laws cannot be formed about data that occurs in a singular space and at a particular time—impossible to repeat under the same circumstances—posed different sorts of questions for the twentieth century, empirically oriented philosopher of history. The twentieth century emphasis on critical analysis resulted in a search for an epistemological meaning of history, rather than a teleological one, and twentieth century philosophy of history added another dimension, analytical or critical thinking.

Analytical philosophers of history are concerned with the differences between historical thinking and other kinds of thinking, and they raise questions about the differences and similarities between history and other forms of knowledge. Since history deals largely with facts of the past which only extend into the present by way of artifacts, documents, buildings, institutions, and so forth, they are not open to the same sort of testing that is possible for the directly accessible facts of science. Hence, the analytical philosopher must attempt to deal with the problem of truth and fact in history, as well as with questions about historical objectivity. The twentieth century philosopher of history views history as a living thing that man creates both as a concept and as a reality. Kahler[7] says:

> For as soon as a concept forms, it starts influencing and changing the actual world. It fuses with actuality, becomes part of it. People gradually come to act in awareness of the new concept. The concept continues effective, and out of conceptually changed reality an ever more elaborate comprehension of coherence, i.e. more and more consciousness, develops which, in turn, further transforms reality. History, then, appears to be an ever widening process of intercreation between conscious comprehension and material reality.

Philosophers of Education

The philosophers we have studied thus far have all been more or less concerned about educational ideals, but, with the possible exception of Rousseau, the concern was a minor part of a grand philosophical construct. The foregoing statement is by no means intended to minimize the significant contributions that philosophers have made to education, but rather to point out the distinction between philosophers who philosophize about education and philosophers of education. Although, strictly speaking, philosophy of education was not generally recognized as a distinct discipline until the twentieth century, Rousseau, Herbart, and Froebel are generally placed in the latter category. Herbart marks the beginning of a science of psychology, and both he and Froebel pioneered in the use of motivational psychology in their educational directives. Both are examples of philosophers whose first concern was education and whose major efforts were in that regard. As we discuss the educational contributions of these men who prepared the

---

[7] Erich Kahler, *op. cit.,* p. 22.

way for the recognition of philosophy of education as a distinct discipline, some of the significant factors that contribute to the distinction will begin to emerge.

Johann Herbart (1776–1841)

Johann Herbart is frequently bypassed in philosophy courses, in spite of the fact that he occupied one of the most important chairs of philosophy in Europe, the one that had been held by Kant. Perhaps one reason may be that he is still overshadowed by Hegel, as he was for the better part of his lifetime. It was a crushing blow that he did not succeed Hegel to the chair of philosophy at the University of Berlin after Hegel's death in 1831. However, Herbart ranks high in the annals of history for his significant contributions to education. He was one of the earliest writers to make a clear demarcation between a science of psychology and a psychology based upon metaphysical speculation. He was also one of the first to ascribe a socially oriented moral aim to instruction, and his attention to methods of teaching is remarkable for the emphasis he places on process and outcome in a practical way.

When he was only five, Herbart fell into a tub of boiling water and narrowly escaped death. Because of the accident it was necessary for the boy to have a tutor, and the choice was a fortunate one. The emphasis he placed on clarity, definiteness, and continuity of thought was a significant influence on Herbart's later ideas about education and contributed immeasurably to his outstanding scholarship. At the age of eighteen, Herbart entered the University of Jena where he was influenced by some of the greatest minds in Europe, particularly Fichte's and Schiller's. At the age of twenty-one, Herbart left the university to accept the post of tutor to the three sons of the governor of Interlaken. He had come to the decision to give up the study of law at Jena, partly because he had little taste for it, and partly because of the influence of Schiller who was writing his *Letters on the Aesthetic Education of Man*. Herbart made the decision to devote his life to the study of education and philosophy, and his tutoring experience, which had a decisive influence upon his psychological and ethical theories, helped to determine his pedagogical theory. Herbart taught at Göttingen from 1802 until 1809, and during that period he wrote his chief works on education. He was called to the University of Königsberg in 1809 where, in connection with his lectures on education, he conducted a pedagogical seminar and also established an important teacher-training institution in which he emphasized the development of character, his fundamental idea of education. Herbart returned to the University of Göttingen in 1833 where he remained until his death in 1841.

In addition to being a skilled teacher, Herbart was a profound philosopher; but, unlike other philosophers whose educational contributions are noteworthy, Herbart was an accomplished educator before he became a philosopher. Rather than growing out of a philosophical position, Herbart's educational ideals led to the construction of his speculative theories. Herbart recognized that teaching is both an art and a science, and his approach to the science of education was direct. The first task, he believed, was to determine the educational goal, which he summed up in the concept of morality with five basic ideas: 1) freedom; 2) perfection; 3) goodwill, which must be constant and unwavering; 4) right; and 5) retribution. Once he had established the ultimate goal of education, Herbart used the deductive method to discover how it could be realized. His practical observations culminated in the ideas about the principles of psychology, ethics, and metaphysics that have contributed greatly to pedagogical theory.

Herbart's Science of Education

As we have noted, according to Herbart who was one of the first to base the end of instruction on ethics, the aim of instruction is morality. He states in the *Aesthetic Revelation of the World as the Chief Work of Education* that the "one and the whole work of education may be summed up in the concept—morality."[8] Later, in *The Science of Education,* he elaborated on the statement to explain that morality is based on the circle of thought.

> The circle of thought contains the store of that which by degrees can mount by the steps of interest to desire, and then by means of action to volition. . . . The whole inner activity, indeed, has its abode in the circle of thought.[9]

The circle of thought is built up as the teacher directs attention to objects, ideas, concepts, and the like, working directly with what Herbart calls "presentations." It is built up by manipulations of the ideas that are brought to the attention of the child. Finally, it is built up by the interweaving of new ideas into the texture of the mind. Herbart saw three levels in the development of the mind: 1) the stage of sensations and perceptions; 2) the level of imagination and memory; and 3) conceptual thinking and judgment.

One of the most important and lasting contributions that Herbart made to pedagogical theory is his doctrine of interest. Interest, according to Herbart, is some inner tendency, an active power residing in the mind that urges the retention of a concept (an object of thought) in the consciousness or a return of the concept to consciousness. The tendency is increased by the law of frequency and by the law of association. The primary task of the educator is to present the best ideas constantly and consistently to the attention of the child. In this way, the teacher is able to control the experiences of the child, and to provide him with the sorts of insights that will mature his judgment.

---

[8] Johann F. Herbart, trans. by H. M. and E. Felkin, *The Science of Education* (Boston: D. C. Heath & Co., 1896), p. 57.
[9] *Ibid.,* p. 213.

A recognition of the moral law is acted out by an exhibition of good judgment, decisiveness, warmth, and self-restraint in all regards, and children should be educated to will the good so freely and so constantly that it becomes second nature. Since it is impossible to foresee what the choices and the goals of the man will be, it depends upon the teacher to prepare the child with principles that should guide the normal man to good choices and with the abilities and qualifications that will enable the man to attain his goals. Therefore, it is highly essential for instruction to cover a wide range of subjects.

Herbart's discussion of curriculum is in very general terms, but there are a number of indications that he would place equal stress on the humanistic, scientific, and mathematical studies. Herbart wrote that "since the moral order of life takes its direction from circumstances, a many-sided culture gives a priceless facility and pleasure in passing on to every new kind of activity and mode of life that may at any time be the best. The more individuality is blended with many-sidedness, the more easily will the character assert its sway over the individual."[10]

We have noted Herbart's use of the term "presentations," and his analysis of the kinds of presentations has a bearing on curriculum decisions. The first kind of presentations are those which arise from experiences of things, the empirical knowledge of the objects, laws, and forces of nature. The child will have acquired some knowledge of this sort before he comes to school. Often it is faulty and inaccurate, and it will certainly lack system and will be limited in scope. It depends upon the teacher to make the necessary corrections and to move the child's mind from the sensory level to the higher level of scientific knowledge—from the particular to the universal. The necessary presentations will be found in nature and the sciences. The second kind of presentations are what Herbart calls sympathy with humanity, with society, and with the relation of man and society to the Highest Being. The presentations in this group come from social intercourse and personal relations and are the base for all higher intellectual and moral development. Such presentations are found in history, literature, languages, religion, and art.

Others before Herbart had urged that learning be made easy and painless, that it should be more a game than a task. But Herbart thought that discipline should be an integral part of instruction in order to provide a base for the whole of education. Discipline is not only necessary for instruction, but it helps to form a deep and firm desire for right action. Instruction had a profound and special meaning for Herbart. He did not confine instruction, as had been done before him, to developing the intellect but believed that it must actually create intellect. The only method of educating that he recognized was that which would cause the growth of ideas in the child's mind. Instruction must create and develop interests by: 1) *clearness* —starting with clear presentations; 2) *association*—associations of ideas

---

[10] *Ibid.*, p. 120.

that are already in the mind of the student; 3) *system*—organizing the old and new ideas into a new system or concept; and 4) *method*—developing latent powers in new material by applying and using it.

Herbart distinguished three modes of instruction, each serving a necessary function in any plan. The first mode is *presentational instruction,* which is merely accurate and informative description delivered in a convincing manner. The second mode is *analytical instruction,* which separates the environment into components. The third mode is *synthetic instruction,* whereby structures of thought are built. The three modes have the object of supplying the elements of education and synthesizing them so that the empirical and the sympathy presentations will be developed together. The new duties that Herbart's science of education imposed on teaching demanded a clear-cut psychology for his educational methodology. Accordingly, Herbart developed psychological foundations which played an important part in shifting educational emphasis from mind training to acquiring knowledge through sense data.

Herbart's Psychology

Herbart made any number of outstanding contributions to psychology. He transformed it from the speculative, philosophical method, into a science in its own right. He was the first to insist on the unity of the mind in all of its operations, and his attempts to apply mathematics to psychology led to the development of experimental psychology. His psychology which grew out of his practical teaching experiences, contributed to the beginnings of association psychology and to the beginning of physiological psychology.

Herbart agreed with Locke that the infant is born without knowledge and maintained that primary sense data, which he called *percepts,* begin to accumulate almost as soon as the child is born. The acquisition persists, regardless of education. Herbart called the entire process of gathering and assimilating percepts *apperception,* and it is the function of education to select from the accumulation of percepts and organize them into apperceptual masses that enable the student to make intelligent decisions.

Herbart recognized three basic functions of the mental life—intellect, feeling, and will—which are all aspects of ideas. That is, an ethical idea must be known, and it must also be agreeable or acceptable—adjusted to previously acquired ideas. The will is not a separate faculty but underlies all mental processes and emotional reactions. It is small wonder that Herbart insisted teachers must have a psychological background in order to be aware of the plasticity of human behavior, and in order to understand and implement the educational process.

Friedrich Froebel (1782–1852)

It is not purely by chance that Herbart and Froebel are the two figures we have selected to illustrate the beginnings of philosophy of education as an autonomous discipline; nor were they chosen solely for obvious reasons of a commonality of generation, nationalism, intellectual and educational influences; nor yet for chronological purposes. We have seen that Herbart was not given to an expression of emotional feelings but was an analytical scientist primarily concerned with a science of education and with methodology. Froebel, on the other hand, wrote like a poet about philosophic attitudes that were an expression of his heart and extolled the transcendental function of an education that is the expression of man's ultimate hopes. In short, the views of the two men, as well as their different modes of expression, can be seen as thesis and antithesis, culminating in a synthesis that symbolizes the whole fabric of education—the subjective and the objective, the subject and the method, the art and the science.

A comparison of the childhood years of the two men gives rise to speculation about the underlying reasons for the differences in their philosophical views. We will remember that Rousseau placed considerable stress on the importance of parental attention and guidance during the formative years. He had persuaded mothers to devote themselves to their young children, to their care, their nurture, and above all, to their emotional needs. Herbart's mother had lavished attention on the boy, guided every step in his development, and had even participated in his studies. Fortunately, certainly for Herbart's sake and possibly for the sake of posterity, she had loved him both well and wisely. But imagine the differences in the man, if the boy, like Froebel, had been reared without benefit of parental love; had been left to his own devices by a father—engrossed in his own theological pursuits and devoid of parental instincts—who was persuaded by the stepmother that the child was stupid; had been the object of undisguised hostility, and denied the normal schooling for boys. It is small wonder that Froebel became moody and subjective and that his emotional needs turned him to a love of nature where he found his only companionship.

Froebel was born in the mountain village of Oberweisbach on April 21, 1782. His mother died when he was only nine months old, and for the next ten years, while he lived in the home of his maternal uncle, his only education was what he could pick up on his own at the school for older girls his father directed. When he was fifteen he was apprenticed to an expert forester but did not receive the training that had been promised. He was able to manage a few months study at the University of Jena when he was seventeen, although it was chiefly along elementary lines. His education had been so sketchy, it is doubtful if he was able to appreciate fully the profound intellectuality at Jena. It was purely by accident that Froebel was invited to teach drawing in the normal school of Herr Grüner in Frankfort and realized his *raison d'être*. At the age of twenty-five he undertook to train three young boys and attended classes with them at Pestalozzi's school in Yverdun. Froebel, like other students of Pestalozzi's, was inspired by the master's enthusiasm for a higher, nobler life but complained that Pestalozzi failed to indicate the means of attaining it. In order to supply what he found wanting in Pestalozzi's educational directives, Froebel was driven to discover principles that would explain the underlying laws of all phenomena. In spite of his inclination to subjectivity and introspection, Froebel began to form his philosophy by a study of the empirical sciences. He was already fairly proficient in mathematics, and he began to devote his time to a study of the other sciences, with an emphasis on mineralogy. He studied at the University of Göttingen and later at Berlin under the direction of Professor Christian S. Weiss, who was famous for his work in mineralogy and natural history, and rose to the position of assistant curator of the mineralogical museum under the directorship of Weiss. His work at Berlin was interrupted by his service during the Napoleonic wars, and when he was thirty-five he opened a school for boys at Keilhau, in Thuringia, similar to Pestalozzi's school at Yverdun. The school was not a great success, and he returned to Germany where he opened the first kindergarten. Until his death in 1852, he devoted his time to founding kindergartens, training kindergartners, and elaborating his methods, which included the creation of play-educational devices for the schools.

Froebel's evolutionistic philosophy is the result of a lifelong striving for an all-sided unity. He was too independent (his early years had taught him the necessity of self-reliance) to accept the views of others without question, and his creative genius was to select, supplement, question, and combine ideas of the past into a system in keeping with the single principle he believed to explain the organization of the entire universe. He admittedly borrowed from Rousseau, Bruno, Fichte, Schelling, Schiller, Krause, Hegel, Pestalozzi, and others, but his evolutionistic philosophy is unique. It is an arrangement of the process of a cosmic evolution which includes, yet goes beyond all that has gone before—the process of an individual development into a self-conscious being with all of its powers developed in accordance with nature and society.

Froebel's principle, "the law of contraries," is similar to the law of thesis, antithesis, and synthesis, with the difference that Froebel's is a dynamic principle. It is a law of action, reaction, and equilibrium and has a broader application than the other, which is only applicable to ideas. Some call Froebel's philosophical point of departure the Absolute, and others call it God. Froebel characterizes the source of all things as a self-conscious, active, energizing, creating, intelligent agent. The sum of Froebel's doctrine is the idea of unity where every object in the universe has the twofold aspect of being a unity and at the same time a part of a more complex unity. The "part-unity" progresses to the ultimate of the entire universe as a living organism, of which God, or the original source of all, is the ultimate unity. Conversely, the ultimate unity unfolds into the complex organism, much as an embryo unfolds into its parts, which unfold into their parts.

Froebel's view of man as a human plant is reminiscent of Rousseau's comparison of the child to a tender young plant that must be nurtured by the gardener. Froebel's analogy, however, is far more profound, for he extends the same gradual unfolding to all things in the universe, and posits man's distinguishing feature—self-awareness—as the greatest step in the cosmic evolution. Since the original source of all creative energy is spiritual, man, the last and perfect product of evolution is a combination of the physical and the mental. Man, partaking of the creative spiritual energizing of the Absolute, is essentially dynamic or productive. He is a self-generating source of spontaneous activities of self-expression and grows in self-realization through his self-expression.

There are a number of important implications here. First, man is clearly viewed as a unity where physical movements and mental processes function together, rather than dually. (See mind-body problem, Chapter IV.) Second, man can act in a scientific or rational way because of his knowledge of the laws of development and his knowledge of his own nature. Third, man is self-determined. Froebel believed that man was not determined from within by inner law, nor from without by physical forces. He is self-determined, because he can choose his own goals and to a measure can create the environment he needs to attain them. He can understand the best ways to educate his children. Finally, there is the strong implication that man is still in the evolutionary process, since Froebel was firmly convinced of man's ability for unlimited progress.

> Man, humanity in man, as an external manifestation, should, therefore, be looked upon not as perfectly developed, not as fixed and stationary, but as steadily and progressively growing, in a state of ever-living development, ever ascending from one stage of culture to another toward its aim, which partakes of the infinite and eternal. It is unspeakably pernicious to look upon the development of humanity as stationary and completed.[11]

Aquinas, St. Augustine, and others have explained the existence of evil in man by the doctrine of original sin. But Froebel, maintaining that the essence of being is divine energizing, could not accept such an explanation. Nor could he deny the existence of evil in man. His explanation of evil revolves around his concept of the order of virtues. The lowest order is related to the physical life and includes such traits as courage, industry, perseverance, and the like. The second order, the social virtues, are those of the heart, mind, and will, and include friendliness, self-control, moderation, and truthfulness. These are the virtues that Froebel believed could be developed by childhood games, which explains his emphasis on play activities for young children. The highest order of virtues include such traits as forebearance and compassion and are virtues of sympathy.

The chief evils, are the antithesis of the virtues. Each vice is a virtue that has been perverted in its unfolding, and evils are caused by: 1) neglecting the development of certain aspects of human life; or 2) by willful distortion of, or interference with originally good human powers or tendencies.

---

11 Friedrich Froebel, *The Education of Man* (New York: Appleton-Century, 1892), p. 17.

Thus all evils can be traced to faulty development, which in turn can be traced to faulty education.

Rousseau had loosely formulated the idea that the individual passes through stages comparable to stages of racial progression. Schiller believed the concept to be the fundamental principle of culture, and Herbart, using the theory as a psychological guide for understanding child development, also used it as a base for his curriculum. Herbart believed that the past was less complex than the present and was thus far more consistent with the experiences of the child. In this regard the theory is logically consistent with Froebel's cosmic evolution, and he posited that each individual develops or unfolds in the same way as the history of the creation and development of all things. He maintained that each individual can understand and appreciate his own stage of development by comparing it with the history of his racial development and that the individual can also see mankind as a whole and feel the unity of all humanity through his own development. The culture-epoch theory is a significant factor in Froebel's educational directives.

Froebel's Theory of Education

Froebel's educational directives constitute a protest against the idea that culture or learning can be imposed from without and are a reversal of the traditional idea of educational progress. The objectives and methods are an extension of his organismic evolution and rest on spiritual ideals that can only be experienced. His predominant interest in preschool education undoubtedly stems from his own childhood experiences of insecurity and lack of parental love and understanding, as well as from his later association with Pestalozzi at Yverdun. He came to feel that the most important stage of education was the most neglected one and in 1836 gave up the training of teachers to establish the first institution for the education of preschool children. Characteristically, he called his school *Kindergarten,* to designate his view of the child as a young plant to be cultivated by the teacher.

Generally speaking, Froebel's ideas about education for self-realization and individual freedom place a greater stress on instruction to build up habits, skills, and powers of will and character, than on instruction to build up knowledge. Froebel believed that the child learns through doing. His emphasis on creativity lead him to evaluate an educational object according to what the child can make of it for self-expression, rather than as Rousseau did for its usefulness, Pestalozzi for its function of training sense organs, and Herbart for its contribution to knowledge. Froebel urged that the activities of the child be directly related to his surrounding social life and that they follow a generic order of development unfolding from the child's basic nature. He observed that, since each new interest springs from some activity already functioning, it depends upon the educator to know when the time is right for another interest.

It is a mistake to assume that Froebel limited himself to an interest in preschool training, as much of what he professed has equal relevance for primary and secondary education. However, his contributions to preschool education are so unique that he is most generally recognized for them. Among these was the stress he placed on the use of language, drawing, and the use of symbols in the kindergarten. Froebel held that language is the earliest means of self-expression; that drawing is the language which stands between the perception of a thing and the written symbols; and that symbolism has played a significant part in man's becoming what he is. Froebel was also the first educator to recognize the value of play for self-expression, to recognize the significance of social education, and to invent graded, systematic play tools—apparatus of self-expression—for the child. Froebel looked upon education as the cultivation of awareness, love, and independence. As he put it, "Education should lead and guide man to clearness concerning himself and in himself, to peace with nature, and to unity with God."[12]

Summary

The men and events discussed in this chapter represent the range of social, historical, and educational theories that developed during the nineteenth century. Beginning with G. W. F. Hegel and his constructions of a metaphysical dialectical process, the century stretched into a turbulent panorama of intellectual change and social reform. Auguste Comte's scientific outlook led him to a religion of humanity, to develop the science of sociology, and to a positivistic philosophy. Karl Marx leaned heavily upon the Hegelian dialectic but chose to interpret the process as an economic materialism. Søren Kierkegaard rejected both dialectics and reacted against Hegelianism with an individualism that has since found expression in a variety of constructions, including Christian existentialism. John Stuart Mill's principle of utility was opposed to intuitionism in the traditional sense and led men to speculate about the liberties of individuals within a societal context.

Speculation about societal and individual relations underscores the importance of determining meaning in the course of human affairs. The problem of meaning has been a recurrent metaphysical concern for philosophers throughout the history of man, but nineteenth century empiricism altered the course of the search for meaning, and another dimension, the analytical, was added to teleological investigations. In a like manner, nineteenth century scientific, technological, and intellectual growth made heavy demands on other areas of philosophical investigations, which tended more and more toward specialization.

We noted at the beginning of our study that philosophy was originally viewed as the most general science, as both the seeking of wisdom and the wisdom sought. Reference was made in Chapter I to the analogy of René

---

[12] *Ibid.,* pp. 4–5.

Descartes, comparing philosophy to a tree that branched out into a variety of "sub-sciences." Pursuing the analogy, by the last decades of the nineteenth century, some of the branches had become so heavily laden that the burden of their own weight caused them to separate from the main trunk of the philosophy tree. As branches broken from a parent tree can put down roots and develop into separate trees, so did some of the offshoots of philosophy become firmly rooted in empirical ideas and begin to develop and flourish in the nineteenth century intellectual climate. The ultimate result was the development of a number of autonomous disciplines from what had been merely branches of the one, all-inclusive, science of philosophy. Among those that took root in the nineteenth century and have come into full bloom in recent decades are sociology, and the social sciences, philosophy of history, psychology, educational psychology, and philosophy of education.

Herbart and Froebel were among the first to make significant contributions to the autonomous development of educational psychology and educational philosophy. As we have noted, it was Herbart who turned psychology from the metaphysical to the empirical examination of mental processes. It was he who insisted on the unity of the mind in all of its operations, and whose emphasis on the internal changes that learning involves made the study of educational psychology paramount. His contributions to educational philosophy were by way of his emphasis on the intimate connection between education and ethics, speculation on the moral purpose of education as determined by historical experience and positing a science of education.

We have seen that Froebel, on the other hand, was primarily concerned with the other aspect of education, the problem of creativity. The questions he raised about whether creativity is an outward or an inward process; whether it demands discipline or spontaneity; and about the relationship between creativity and self-realization, are the kinds of questions that are the concern of educational philosophers. Froebel's belief that education points to man's social nature as well as his metaphysical ideals, led him to the development of the kindergarten as an important socializing force. Modern educational practices in the Western world incorporate many of Froebel's methods, and his principles receive full measure in educational philosophy. Certainly he was one of the most vital educational reformers of the nineteenth century, and his ideas about education contributed to the implementation of the twentieth century discipline, philosophy of education.

KARL POPPER

The Open Society and Its Enemies (Chapter 22)*

The Moral Theory of Historicism

This selection has been chosen as the reading for Chapter VI for several reasons. First, our own chapter has dealt with a number of men and with a variety of topics during a time of great social and philosophical upheaval, and the selection by Popper provides an historical perspective for that era. The economic and philosophical expressions of Karl Marx were substantial factors in bringing about changes in the nineteenth century, and Popper's discussion of the ideas and movements set in motion by Marx contributes to an understanding of these influences and their implications. Secondly, Popper's emphasis upon the morality of economic and social systems provides another dimension to our continuing concern about the moral nature of man and society. Finally, Popper's definitive analyses of terms, such as historical relativism, historicism, and sociologism, is in keeping with our emphasis on the clarification of language. Issues raised by the selection might center around the following philosophical questions: 1) What degree of freedom does man have in his actions? 2) Do concepts of morality extend into every aspect of man and society? and 3) Can man's reason truly function in the face of irrational forces?

The task which Marx set himself in *Capital* was to discover inexorable laws of social development. It was not the discovery of economic laws which would be useful to the social technologist. It was neither the analysis of the economic conditions which would permit the realization of such socialist aims as just prices, equal distribution of wealth, security, reasonable planning of production and above all, freedom, nor was it an attempt to analyze and to clarify these aims.

But although Marx was strongly opposed to Utopian technology as well as to any attempt at a moral justification of socialist aims, his writings contained, by implication, an ethical theory. This he expressed mainly by moral evaluations of social institutions. After all, Marx's condemnation of capitalism is fundamentally a moral condemnation. The *system is condemned,* for the cruel injustice inherent in it which is combined with full "formal" justice and righteousness. The system is condemned, because by forcing the exploiter to enslave the exploited it robs both of their freedom. Marx did not combat wealth, nor did he praise poverty. He hated capitalism, not for its accumulation of wealth,

* From "The Moral Theory of Historicism," in *The Open Society and Its Enemies,* by Karl Popper (Vol. II, Princeton University Press, 4th rev. edn., 1963; Routledge and Kegan Paul, 5th edn., 1966). Reprinted by permission of the author and the publishers.

but for its oligarchical character; he hated it because in this system wealth means political power in the sense of power over other men. Labor power is made a commodity; that means that men must sell themselves on the market. Marx hated the system because it resembled slavery.

By laying such stress on the moral aspect of social institutions, Marx emphasized our responsibility for the more remote social repercussions of our actions; for instance, of such actions as may help to prolong the life of socially unjust institutions.

But although *Capital* is, in fact, largely a treatise on social ethics, these ethical ideas are never represented as such. They are expressed only by implication, but not the less forcibly on that account, since the implications are very obvious. Marx, I believe, avoided an explicit moral theory, because he hated preaching. Deeply distrustful of the moralist who usually preaches water and drinks wine, Marx was reluctant to formulate his ethical convictions explicitly. The principles of humanity and decency were for him matters that needed no discussion, matters to be taken for granted. (In this field, too, he was an optimist.) He attacked the moralists because he saw them as the sycophantic apologists of a social order which he felt to be immoral; he attacked the eulogists of liberalism because of their self-satisfaction, because of their identification of freedom with the formal liberty then existing within a social system which destroyed freedom. Thus, by implication, he admitted his love for freedom; and in spite of his bias, as a philosopher, for holism, he was certainly not a collectivist, for he hoped that the state would "wither away." Marx's faith, I believe, was fundamentally a faith in the open society.

Marx's attitude towards Christianity is closely connected with these convictions, and with the fact that a hypocritical defence of capitalist exploitation was in his day characteristic of official Christianity. (His attitude was not unlike that of his contemporary Kierkegaard, the great reformer of Christian ethics who exposed the official Christian morality of his day as anti-Christian and antihumanitarian hypocrisy.) A typical representative of this kind of Christianity was the High Church priest J. Townsend, author of *A Dissertation on the Poor Laws, by a Well-wisher of Mankind,* an extremely crude apologist for exploitation whom Marx exposed. "Hunger," Townsend begins his eulogy, "is not only a peaceable, silent, unremitted pressure but, as the most natural motive of industry and labor, it calls forth the most powerful exertions." In Townsend's "Christian" world order, everything depends (as Marx observes) upon making hunger permanent among the working class; and Townsend believes that this is indeed the divine purpose of the principle of the growth of population; for he goes on: "It seems to be a law of nature that the poor should be to a certain degree improvident, so that there may always be some to fulfill the most servile, the most sordid, the most ignoble offices in the community. The stock of human happiness is thereby much increased, whilst the more delicate . . . are left at liberty without interruption to pursue those callings which are suited to their various dispositions." And the "delicate priestly sycophant," as Marx called him for this remark, adds that the Poor Law, by helping the hungry, "tends to destroy the harmony and beauty, the symmetry and order of that system which God and nature have established in the world."

If this kind of "Christianity" has disappeared today from the face of the better part of our globe, it is in no small degree due to the moral reformation brought about by Marx. I do not suggest that the reform of the Church's attitude towards the poor in England did not commence long before Marx had any influence in England; but he influenced this development especially on the continent, and the rise of socialism had the effect of strengthening it in England also. His influence on Christianity may be perhaps compared with Luther's influence on the Roman Church. Both were a challenge, both led to a counterreformation in the camps of their enemies, to a revision and revaluation of their ethical standards. Christianity owes not a little to Marx's influence if it is today on a different path from the one it was pursuing only thirty years ago. It is even partly due to Marx's influence that the Church has listened to the voice of Kierkegaard, who, in his *Book of the Judge,* described his own activity as follows: "He whose task it is to produce a corrective idea, has only to study, precisely and deeply, the rotten parts of the existing order—and then, in the most partial way possible, to stress the opposite of it." ("Since that is so," he adds, "an apparently clever man will easily raise the objection of partiality against the corrective idea—and he will make the public believe that this was the whole truth about it.") In this sense one might say that the early Marxism, with its ethical rigor, its emphasis on deeds instead of mere words, was perhaps the most important corrective idea of our time. This explains its tremendous moral influence.

The demand that men should prove themselves in deeds is especially marked in some of Marx's earlier writings. This attitude which might be described as his *activism,* is most clearly formulated in the last of his *Theses on Feuerbach:* "The philosophers have only interpreted the world in various ways; the point however is to *change* it." But there are many other passages which show the same "activist" tendency; especially those in which Marx speaks of socialism as the "kingdom of freedom," a kingdom in which man would become the "master of his own social environment." Marx conceived of socialism as a period in which we are largely free from the irrational forces that now determine our life, and in which human reason can actively control human affairs. Judging by all this, and by Marx's general moral and emotional attitude, I cannot doubt that, if faced with the alternative *"are we to be the makers of our fate, or shall we be content to be its prophets?"* he would have decided to be a maker and not merely a prophet.

But as we already know, these strong "activist" tendencies of Marx's are counteracted by his historicism. Under its influence, he became mainly a prophet. He decided that, at least under capitalism, we must submit to "inexorable laws" and to the fact that all we can do is "to shorten and lessen the birthpangs" of the "natural phases of its evolution." There is a wide gulf between Marx's activism and his historicism, and this gulf is further widened by his doctrine that we must submit to the purely irrational forces of history. For since he denounced as Utopian any attempt to make use of our reason in order to plan for the future, *reason can have no part in bringing about a more reasonable world*. I believe that such a view cannot be defended, and must lead to mysticism. But I must admit that there seems to be a theoretical possibility of bridging this gulf, although I do not consider the bridge to be sound. This bridge, of which there are only rough plans to be found in the writings of Marx and Engels, I call their *historicist moral theory*.

Unwilling to admit that their own ethical ideas were in any sense ultimate and self-justifying, Marx and Engels preferred to look upon their humanitarian aims in the light of a theory which explains them as the product, or the reflection, of social circumstances. Their theory can be described as follows. If a social reformer, or a revolutionary, believes that he is inspired by a hatred of "injustice," and by a love for "justice," then he is largely a victim of illusion (like anybody else, for instance, the apologists of the old order). Or, to put it more precisely, his moral ideas of "justice" and "injustice" are by-products of the social and historical development. But they are by-products of an important kind, since they are part of the mechanism by which the development propels itself. To illustrate this point, there are always at least two ideas of "justice" (or of "freedom" or of "equality"), and these two ideas differ very widely indeed. The one is the idea of "justice" as the ruling class understands it, the other, the same idea as the oppressed class understands it. These ideas are, of course, products of the class situation, but at the same time they play an important part in the class struggle—they have to provide both sides with that good conscience which they need in order to carry on their fight.

This theory of morality may be characterized as historicist because it holds that all moral categories are dependent on the historical situation; it is usually described as *historical relativism* in the field of ethics. From this point of view, it is an incomplete question to ask: Is it right to act in such a way? The complete question would run like this: Is it right, in the sense of fifteenth century feudal morality, to act in such a way? Or perhaps: Is it right, in the sense of nineteenth century proletarian morality, to act in such a way? This historical relativism was formulated by Engels as follows: "What morality is preached to us today? There is first Christian-feudal morality, inherited from past centuries; and this again has two main subdivisions, Roman Catholic and Protestant moralities, each of which in turn has no further lack of subdivisions, from the Jesuit-Catholic and Orthodox-Protestant to loose 'advanced' morality. Alongside of these, we find the modern bourgeois morality, and with it, too, the proletarian morality of the future. . . ."

But this so-called "historical relativism" by no means exhausts the historicist character of the Marxist theory of morals. Let us imagine we could ask those who hold such a theory, for instance Marx himself: Why do you act in the way you do? Why would you consider it distasteful and repulsive, for instance, to accept a bribe from the bourgeoisie for stopping your revolutionary activities? I do not think that Marx would have liked to answer such a question; he would probably have tried to evade it, asserting perhaps that he just acted as he pleased, or as he felt compelled to. But all this does not touch our problem. It is certain that in the practical decisions of his life Marx followed a very rigorous moral code; it is also certain that he demanded from his collaborators a high moral standard. Whatever the terminology applied to these things may be, the problem which faces us is how to find a reply which he might have possibly made to the question: Why do you act in such a way? Why do you try, for instance, to help the oppressed? (Marx did not himself belong to this class, either by birth or by upbringing or by his way of living.)

If pressed in this way, Marx would, I think, have formulated his moral belief in the following terms, which form the core of what I call his historicist moral theory. As a social scientist (he might have said) I know that our moral ideas are weapons in the class struggle. As a scientist, I can consider them without adopting them. But as a scientist I find also that I cannot avoid taking sides in this struggle; that any attitude, even aloofness, means taking sides in some way or other. My problem thus assumes the form: Which side shall I take? When I have chosen a certain side, then I have, of course, also decided upon my morality. I shall have to adopt the moral system necessarily bound up with the interests of the class which I have decided to support. But before making this fundamental decision, I have not adopted any moral system at all, provided I can free myself from the moral tradition of my class; but this, of course, is a necessary prerequisite for making any conscious and rational decision regarding the competing moral systems. Now since a decision is "moral" only in relation to some previously accepted moral code, my fundamental decision can be no "moral" decision at all. But it can be a *scientific* decision. For as a social scientist, I am able to see what is going to happen. I am able to see that the bourgeoisie, and with it its system of morals, is bound to disappear, and that the proletariat, and with it a new system of morals, is bound to win. I see that this development is inevitable. It would be madness to attempt to resist it, just as it would be madness to attempt to resist the law of gravity. This is why my fundamental decision is in favor of the proletariat and of its morality. And this decision is based only on scientific foresight, on scientific historical prophecy. Although itself not a moral decision, since it is not based on any system of morality, it leads to the adoption of a certain system of morality. To sum up, my fundamental decision is not (as you suspected) the sentimental decision to help the oppressed, but the scientific and rational decision not to offer vain resistance to the developmental laws of society. Only after I have made this decision am I prepared to accept, and to make full use of, those moral sentiments which are necessary weapons in the fight for what is bound to come in any case. In this way, I adopt the facts of the coming period as the standards of my morality. And in this way, I solve the apparent paradox that a more reasonable world will come without being planned by reason; for according to my moral standards now adopted, the future world must be better, and therefore more reasonable. And I also bridge the gap between my activism and my historicism. For it is clear that even though I have discovered the natural law that determines the movement of society, I cannot shuffle the natural phases of its evolution out of the world by a stroke of the pen. But this much I can do. I can actively assist in shortening and lessening its birth-pangs.

This, I think, would have been Marx's reply, and it is this reply which to me represents the most important form of what I have called "historicist moral theory." It is this theory to which Engels alludes when he writes: "Certainly, that morality which contains the greatest number of elements that are going to last is the one which, within the present time, represents the overthrow of the present time; it is the one which represents the future; it is the proletarian morality. . . . According to this conception, the ultimate causes of all social changes and political revolutions are not increasing insight into justice; they are to be sought not in the *philosophy* but in the *economics* of the epoch concerned. The growing realization that existing social institutions are irrational and unjust is only a symptom. . . ." It is the theory of which a modern Marxist says: "In founding socialist aspirations on a rational economic law of social development, *instead of justifying them on moral grounds,* Marx and Engels proclaimed socialism a historical necessity." It is a theory which is very widely held; but it has rarely been formulated clearly and explicitly. Its criticism is therefore more important than might be realized at first sight.

First, it is clear enough that the theory depends largely on the possibility of correct historical prophecy. If this is questioned—and it certainly must be questioned—then the theory loses most of its force. But for the purpose of analyzing it, I shall assume at first that historical foreknowledge is an established fact; and I shall merely stipulate that this historical foreknowledge is limited; I shall stipulate that we have foreknowledge for, say, the next 500 years, a stipulation which should not restrict even the boldest claims of Marxist historicism.

Now let us first examine the claim of historicist moral theory that the fundamental decision in favor of, or against, one of the moral systems in question, is itself not a moral decision; that it is not based on any moral consideration or sentiment, but on a scientific historical prediction. This claim is, I think, untenable. In order to make this quite clear, it will suffice to make explicit the imperative, or principle of conduct, implied in this fundamental decision. It is the following principle: Adopt the moral system of the future! or: Adopt the moral system held by those whose actions are most useful for bringing about the future! Now it seems clear to me that even on the assumption that we know exactly what the next 500 years will be like, it is not at all necessary for us to adopt such a principle. It is, to give an example, at least conceivable that some humanitarian pupil of Voltaire who foresaw in 1764 the development of France down to, say, 1864, might have disliked the prospect; it is at least conceivable that he would have decided that this development was rather distasteful and that he was not going to adopt the moral standards of Napoleon III as his own. I shall be faithful to my humanitarian standards, he might have said, I shall teach them to my pupils; perhaps they will survive this period, perhaps some day they will be victorious. It is likewise at least conceivable (I do not assert more, at present) that a man who today foresees with certainty that we are heading for a period of slavery, that we are going to return to the cage of the arrested society, or even that we are about to return to the beasts, may nevertheless decide not to adopt the moral standards of this impending period but to contribute as well as he can to the survival of his humanitarian ideals, hoping perhaps for a resurrection of his morality in some dim future.

All that is, at least, conceivable. It may perhaps not be the "wisest" decision to make. But the fact that such a decision is excluded neither by foreknowledge nor by any sociological or psychological law shows that the first claim of historicist moral theory is untenable. Whether we should accept the morality of the future just because it is the morality of the future, this in itself is just a moral problem. The fundamental decision cannot be derived from any knowledge of the future.

In previous chapters I have mentioned *moral positivism* (especially that of Hegel), the theory that there is no moral standard but the one which exists; that what is, is reasonable and good; and therefore, that *might is right*. The practical aspect of this theory is this. A moral criticism of the existing state of affairs is impossible, since this state itself determines the moral standard of things. Now the historicist moral theory we are considering is nothing but another form of moral positivism. For it holds that coming *might is right*. The future is here substituted for the present—that is all. And the practical aspect of the theory is this. A moral criticism of the coming state of affairs is impossible, since this state determines the moral standard of things. The difference between "the present" and "the future" is here, of course, only a matter of degree. One can say that the future starts tomorrow, or in 500 years, or in 100. *In their theoretical structure there is no difference between moral conservatism, moral modernism, and moral futurism.* Nor is there much to choose between them in regard to moral sentiments. If the moral futurist criticizes the cowardice of the moral conservative who takes sides with the power that be, then the moral conservative can return the charge; he can say that the moral futurist is a coward since he takes sides with the powers that will be, with the rulers of tomorrow.

I feel sure that, had he considered these implications, Marx would have repudiated historicist moral theory. Numerous remarks and numerous actions prove that it was not a scientific judgment but a moral impulse, the wish to help the oppressed, the wish to free the shamelessly exploited and miserable workers, which led him to socialism. I do not doubt that it is this moral appeal that is the secret of the influence of his teaching. And the force of this appeal was tremendously strengthened by the fact that he did not preach morality in the abstract. He did not pretend to have any right to do so. Who, he seems to have asked himself, lives up to his own standard, provided it is not a very low one? It was this feeling which led him to rely, in ethical matters, on understatements, and which led him to the attempt to find in prophetic social science an authority in matters of morals more reliable than he felt himself to be.

Surely, in Marx's practical ethics such categories as freedom and equality played the major role. He was, after all, one of those who took the ideals of 1789 seriously. And he had seen how shamelessly a concept like "freedom" could be twisted. This is why he did not preach freedom in words—why he preached it in action. He wanted to improve society and improvement meant to him more freedom, more equality, more justice, more security, higher standards of living, and especially that shortening of the working day which at once gives the workers *some* freedom. It was his hatred of hypocrisy, his reluctance to speak about these "high ideals," together with his amazing optimism, his trust that all this would be realized in the near future, which led him to veil his moral beliefs behind historicist formulations.

Marx, I assert, would not seriously have defended moral positivism in the form of moral futurism if he had seen that it implies the recognition of future might as right. But there are others who do not possess his passionate love of humanity who are moral futurists just because of these implications, i.e. opportunists wishing to be on the winning side. Moral futurism is widespread today. Its deeper, nonopportunist basis is probably the belief that goodness must "ultimately" triumph over wickedness. But moral futurists forget that we are not going to live to witness the "ultimate" outcome of present events. "History will be our judge!" What does this mean? That *success* will judge. The worship of success and of future might is the highest standard of many who would never admit that present might is right. (They quite forget that the present is the future of the past.) The basis of all this is a half-hearted compromise between a moral optimism and a moral scepticism. It seems to be hard to believe in one's conscience. And it seems to be hard to resist the impulse to be on the winning side.

All these critical remarks are consistent with the assumption that we can predict the future for the next, say 500 years. But if we drop this entirely fictitious assumption, then historicist moral theory loses all its plausibility. And we must drop it. For there is no prophetic sociology to help us in selecting a moral system. We cannot shift our responsibility for such a selection on to anybody, not even on to "the future."

Marx's historicist moral theory is, of course, only the result of his view concerning the method of social science, of his *sociological determinism,* a view which has become rather fashionable in our day. All our opinions, it is said, including our moral standards, depend upon society and its historical state. They are the products of society or of a certain class situation. Education is defined as a special process by which the community attempts to "pass on" to its members "its culture including the standards by which it would have them to live," and the "relativity of educational theory and practice to a prevailing order" is emphasized. Science, too, is said to depend on the social stratum of the scientific worker, etc.

A theory of this kind which emphasizes the sociological dependence of our opinions is sometimes called *sociologism;* if the historical dependence is emphasized, it is called *historism.* (Historism must not, of course, be mixed up with historicism.) Both sociologism and historism, in so far as they maintain the determination of scientific knowledge by society or history, will be discussed in the next two chapters. In so far as sociologism bears upon moral theory, a few remarks may be added here. But before going into any detail, I wish to make quite clear my opinion concerning these Hegelianizing theories. I believe that they chatter trivialities clad in the jargon of oracular philosophy.

Let us examine this moral "sociologism." That man, and his aims, are *in a certain sense* a product of society is true enough. But it is also true that society is a product of man and of his aims and that it may become increasingly so. The main question is: Which of these two aspects of the relations between men and society is more important? Which is to be stressed?

We shall understand sociologism better if we compare it with the analogous "naturalistic" view that man and his aims are a product of heredity and environment. Again we must admit that this is true enough. But it is also quite certain that man's environment is to an increasing extent a product of him and his aims (to a limited extent, the same might be said even of his heredity). Again we must ask: which of the two aspects is more important, more fertile? The answer may be easier if we give the question the following more practical form. We, the generation now living, and our minds, our opinions, are largely the product of our parents, and of the way they have brought us up. But the next generation will be, to a similar extent, a product of ourselves, of our actions and of the way in which we bring them up. Which of the two aspects is the more important one for us today?

If we consider this question seriously, then we find that the decisive point is that our minds, our opinions, are only largely dependent on our upbringing—not totally. If they were totally dependent on our upbringing, if we were incapable of self-criticism, of learning from our own way of seeing things, from our experience, then, of course, the way we have been brought up by the last generation would determine the way in which we bring up the next. But it is quite certain that this is not so. Accordingly, we can concentrate our critical faculties on the difficult problem of bringing up the next generation in a way which we consider better than the way in which we have been brought up ourselves.

The situation stressed so much by sociologism can be dealt with in an exactly analogous way. That our minds, our views, are in a way a product of "society" is trivially true. The most important part of our environment is its social part; thought, in particular, is very largely dependent on social intercourse; language, the medium of thought, is a social phenomenon. But it simply cannot be denied that we can examine thoughts, that we can criticize them, improve them, and further that we can change and improve our physical environment according to our changed, improved thoughts. And the same is true of our social environment.

All these considerations are entirely independent of the metaphysical "problem of free will." Even the indeterminist admits a certain amount of dependence on heredity and on environmental, especially social, influence. On the other hand, the determinist must agree that our views and actions are not fully and solely determined by heredity, education, and social influences. He has to admit that there are other factors, for instance, the more "accidental" experiences accumulated during one's life, and that these also exert their influence. Determinism or indeterminism as long as they remain within their metaphysical boundaries, do not affect our problem. But the point is that they may trespass beyond these boundaries; that metaphysical determinism, for instance, may encourage sociological determinism or "sociologism." But in this form, the theory can be confronted with experience. And experience shows that it is certainly false.

Beethoven, to take an instance from the field of aesthetics, which has a certain similarity to that of ethics, is surely to some extent a *product* of musical education and tradition, and many who take an interest in him will be impressed by this aspect of his work. The more important aspect, however, is that he is also a *producer* of music, and thereby of musical tradition and education. I do not wish to quarrel with the metaphysical determinist who would insist that every bar Beethoven wrote was determined by some combination of hereditary and environmental influences. Such an assertion is empirically entirely insignificant, since no one could actually "explain" a single bar of his writing in this way. The important thing is that everyone admits that what he wrote can be explained neither by the musical works of his predecessors, nor by the social environment in which he lived, nor by his deafness, nor by the food which his housekeeper cooked for him; not, in other words, by any definite set of environmental influences or circumstances open to empirical investigation, or by anything we could possibly know of his heredity.

I do not deny that there are certain interesting sociological aspects of Beethoven's work. It is well known, for instance, that the transition from a small to a large symphonic orchestra is connected, in some way, with a socio-political development. Orchestras cease to be the private hobbies of princes, and are at least partly supported by a middle class whose interest in music greatly increases. I am willing to appreciate any sociological "explanation" of this sort, and I admit that such aspects may be worthy of scientific study. (After all, I myself have attempted similar things in this book, for instance, in my treatment of Plato.)

What then, more precisely, is the object of my attack? It is the exaggeration and generalization of any aspect of this kind. If we "explain" Beethoven's symphony orchestra in the way hinted above, we have explained very little. If we describe Beethoven as representing the bourgeoisie in the process of emancipating itself, we say very little, even if it is true. Such a function could most certainly be combined with the production of bad music (as we see from Wagner). We cannot attempt to explain Beethoven's genius in this way, or in any way at all.

I think that Marx's own views could likewise be used for an empirical refutation of sociological determinism. For if we consider in the light of this doctrine the two theories, activism and historicism, and their struggle for supremacy in Marx's system, then we will have to say that historicism would be a view more fitting for a conservative apologist than for a revolutionary or even a reformer. And, indeed, historicism was not used by Hegel with that tendency. The fact that Marx not only took it over from Hegel, but in the end permitted it to oust his own activism, may thus show that the side a man takes in the social struggle need not always determine his intellectual decisions. These may be determined, as in Marx's case, not so much by the true interest of the class he supported as by accidental factors, such as the influence of a predecessor, or perhaps by shortsightedness. Thus in this case, sociologism may further our understanding of Hegel, but the example of Marx himself exposes it as an unjustified generalization. A similar case is Marx's underrating of the significance of his own moral ideas; for it cannot be doubted that the secret of his religious influence was in its moral appeal, that his criticism of capitalism was effective mainly as a moral criticism. Marx showed that a social system can as such be unjust; that if the system is bad, then all the righteousness of the individuals who profit from it is a mere sham righteousness, is mere hypocrisy. For our responsibility extends to the system, to the institutions which we allow to persist.

It is this moral radicalism of Marx which explains his influence; and that is a hopeful fact in itself. This moral radicalism is still alive. It is our task to keep it alive, to prevent it from going the way which his political radicalism will have to go. "Scientific" Marxism is dead. Its feeling of social responsibility and its love for freedom must survive.

CHAPTER VII
Pragmatism, Dewey, and Educational Theory

Pragmatism, one of the five mainstream philosophic investigations, was sketched in broad outlines at the beginning of our study. We learned that pragmatism has an experimental and scientific outlook and a firm commitment to empirical data. Pragmatists, viewing change and process as fundamental aspects of reality, were characterized as relativists—those who reject absolutes and the transempirical, and so must look elsewhere for justification for moral and religious attitudes. The discussion of pragmatism in this chapter will be more detailed and will include the thinking of some of the major figures in the development of pragmatism, with special emphasis on John Dewey and the impact of his ideas on educational thought in America. The discussion will conclude with an analysis of educational theory with the purpose of examining the role of theory in education.

There are a number of reasons why pragmatism has been selected over the other systems of philosophy for a more detailed discussion. Among other reasons, pragmatism is America's unique contribution to the philosophical scene, and it is an apt description of the most prevailing attitude of contemporary Americans. Further, the pragmatism developed by John Dewey is the philosophical underpinning of progressivism, and therefore has a more intimate connection with education than any of the other systems of philosophy. Finally, it is important that teachers have a clear understanding of pragmatism, not only because of its intimacy with education, but because there have been so many misconceptions about it. Some of these arose from the rejection of progressivism in its extreme form, as many have erroneously assumed a total identity between pragmatism and the educational philosophy it spawned.

Philosophy of Pragmatism

Historical Outlines of Pragmatism

Fragmentary illustrations of key pragmatic concepts are found in all periods of history, for the present is built on the past, and there is nothing

271

entirely new. For example, we find the pragmatic idea of *process* in the writings of Heraclitus (c. 536–470 B.C.), the philosopher of flux, who wrote that "One cannot step twice in the same river." Another statement of the same time cannot be definitely proven to have been made by Heraclitus but is certainly expressive of the Heraclitean view, and the idea of process is that "All things flow; no thing abides." Starting with Protagoras (early fifth century B.C.), who said that man is the measure of all things, we find examples of the pragmatic view which focused on *man as the center of reality and value judgments*. Something of the concept is foreshadowed in Rousseau's child-centered education, and in Froebel's education for self-realization. We find the pragmatic *emphasis on the natural aspects of the world* as early as the Sophists' rejection of the Platonic Forms and all things that indicate any sort of transempirical reality. The pragmatic *method of induction* was used as early as Francis Bacon (1561–1626); and Auguste Comte (1798–1857) is only one example of those who anticipated the pragmatic emphasis on the *social relations of man* and demonstrated against metaphysical and religious controls. Numbers of such examples of pragmatic attitudes in history could be given here, but, as we discuss the development of pragmatism, many of these early anticipations will begin to surface.

We have seen that the nineteenth century was generally a period of tempestuous change and contrasts. The American scene was no exception, as there are evidences of dramatic contrasts in the artistic, the social, the political, and the philosophical aspects of society. American philosophic attitudes, like other facets of the national character and culture, although basically an admixture of inheritance, have been uniquely tempered in the fire of democratic experiences. Americans are traditionally free agents, certainly not people given to blind acceptance of doctrines, attitudes, or ways of life. An analysis of nineteenth century philosophic traditions in America shows some overlapping among categories such as transcendentalism, evolutionism, and idealism, but the most prevalent attitudes were in sharp contrast to each other, and there was a definite swing between religious, idealistic, or supernatural doctrines and scientific, secular, or naturalistic ones. It was against this sort of conglomerate background that pragmatism began to develop late in the nineteenth century with the Darwinianism of Chauncy Wright, the metaphysical realism of Charles Sanders Peirce, the moral-religious persuasiveness of William James; and pragmatism came into full flower during the twentieth century with the instrumentalism of John Dewey.

The movement grew out of the conviction that there is an intimate relationship between thinking and doing, a conviction which was shared by the New England contemporaries, Peirce, James, and Dewey. Each of these highly skilled academicians expressed a different aspect of pragmatism in a manner which certainly refutes the popular notion that the pragmatist is disdainful of theoretical thought and cares only for getting things done. Undoubtedly, no one of the three could see any value in modes of thinking that do not make a difference in everyday living, but they all believed that meaningful behavior rests on thought. It should be kept in mind that these original pragmatists used the term *practical* to mean *the way thought works in action*. Charles S. Peirce, initially interested in logic and science, gave pragmatism its first theoretical formulation, and William James converted the theory into a theory of truth. James, who did not confine himself to any one discipline, was a brilliant essayist and a wonderfully stimulating lecturer and gave pragmatism a wide and popular circulation. John Dewey, absorbed with problems of ethical and social thought which he expressed through his philosophy of education, did much to implement pragmatism into the daily affairs of American institutions.

Chauncy Wright (1830–1875), is often neglected in brief critiques of pragmatism, but was nonetheless recognized by both Peirce and James as an important influence on their own thoughts.[1] Wright was born in Massachusetts and attended Harvard University where his major interests were physics, mathematics, and philosophy. He was employed by the *American Ephemeris and Nautical Almanac* as an astronomical computer, and one year before his death he was appointed to an instructorship at Harvard in physics. He was not a prolific writer, perhaps partly because of his brief life span, and partly because he believed that the best philosophizing was done in the manner of Socrates. Wright carried the Platonic spirit of inquiry, without Plato's metaphysical and epistemological commitments, into the nineteenth century. Wright said in one of his letters that:

The most profitable discussion is, after all, a study of other minds,— seeing how others see, rather than the dissection of mere propositions. The re-statement of fundamental doctrines in new connections affords a parallax of their philosophical standpoints (unless these be buried in the infinite depths), which adds much to our knowledge of one another's thought.[2]

Chauncy Wright's contributions to developments within pragmatism rest on his defense of Charles Darwin, and on his insistence that the scientific method be freed of metaphysical and ethical bonds, so that philosophy might question even the most fundamental and rigidly held ideas.

In the search for knowledge, Wright emphasized the spirit of Newton and Bacon but did not deny that generalizations are sometimes useful. He pointed out that the really great contribution of philosophers such as Socrates and Plato was not that they taught us *what* to think and believe but that they showed us the *how* of thinking and believing. Wright's spirit of inquiry, his empiricism directed toward outcomes, his insistence that the purpose of education is to provide the kind of knowledge that leads to

---

[1] Philip P. Wiener, *Evolution and the Founders of Pragmatism* (Cambridge, Mass.: Harvard University Press, 1949) devotes a portion of his book to the ideas of Chauncy Wright. It should be consulted for background to pragmatism.

[2] A letter to F. E. Abbot, Oct. 28, 1867. (Reported in Wiener, *op. cit.*, p. 30.)

wider ranges of knowledge and to mental discipline are all pragmatic leanings that had an impact on the thinking of Peirce and James.

Charles Sanders Peirce, the son of a noted Harvard mathematics professor, was born in Cambridge, Massachusetts on September 10, 1839. He studied mathematics, science, and philosophy—first under his father's tutelage, and later at Harvard, where he graduated without distinction. He worked at the Harvard astronomical observatory for three years after receiving his M.A. degree in mathematics and chemistry. He was never a full-time member of any university faculty but did lecture on philosophy at Harvard and was a lecturer in logic at the Johns Hopkins University. He accepted a post as a physicist with the United States Coast and Geodetic Survey in 1861 which he held for thirty years. *The Grand Logic,* had been completed by the time of his death in 1914 and was published posthumously, as were most of his works. His photometric researches, made during the three years that he worked at the Harvard astronomical observatory, were published in 1878; but probably because he did not hold an academic position, Peirce published very little during his lifetime, and it was long after his death that his complete works were collected, and organized into several volumes.

It has been said that Peirce's brilliance was overshadowed by his personal eccentricities which might help to account for the fact that publishers were indifferent to his works during his lifetime. Peirce received little of the fame one of his abilities might expect, but there are those who believe he may still emerge as the most original thinker in American philosophy. Since the Charles Hartshorne and Paul Weiss publication (1931–1935) of six volumes of his writings[3] there has been increased appreciation of Peirce's philosophic contributions, and future histories of American thought will most likely devote more space to the explication of his ideas.

Peirce described his philosophy as the attempt of a physicist, using methods of science and the aid of all previous philosophical contributions, to contemplate the makeup of the universe. He had an overriding interest in how words acquire their meanings and insisted that unless a word refers to an object or a quality about which practical effects can be conceived, the word has no meaning. Peirce coined the word *pragmatism* to describe his theory of logical analysis, or true definition. It comes from the Greek word, *pragma,* which means act or deed and underscores Peirce's theory that words and ideas derive their meanings from some sort of action. Peirce's philosophy is a reaction against authoritarian and deterministic thinking and revolves around his proposal of an operational technique for pinning down meanings.

Peirce's theory of inquiry is based on the idea that the concepts of doubt, habit, and belief provide a biological basis for inquiry. He looked

---

[3] Charles Hartshorne and Paul Weiss, eds., *Collected Papers of Charles Sanders Peirce* (Cambridge, Mass.: Harvard University Press, 1931–1935) Vols. I–VI. Two additional volumes appeared in 1958 edited by A. W. Burks.

upon belief as occupying the middle position between thought and action, for we attempt, by means of thought, to fix the belief that shapes our action. Peirce distinguished four different ways of fixing the beliefs that constitute the end of inquiry. These are: *tenacity, authority, a priori,* and *scientific.* Peirce rejected the first three for reasons inherent in each. He viewed *tenacity* and *authority* as forms of intellectual slavery, and the *a priori* as arbitrary and subjective. He maintained that the method of science is the most acceptable because it is an objective and self-corrective technique, and because its flexible and tentative character allows the investigator to retain integrity of belief.

Peirce delineated his pragmatic theory of meaning in an article, "How to Make Our Ideas Clear," which was published in 1878. The article was relatively unknown and had attracted scant attention until twenty years after its publication when William James referred to it in one of his speeches. However, Peirce was considerably upset by what he insisted was a misinterpretation of his attempt to apply criteria of meaning to metaphysical problems. What he had intended as a maxim for clearing up metaphysics, James had interpreted to mean a mere rule of action, which according to Peirce, carried the assumption that the end of man is action. Peirce held that his principle had been carried too far when James changed it from one of methodology to one of practicality, and he adopted the term *pragmaticism,* hoping that the addition of the suffix, *icism* would distinguish his more strictly defined acceptation of the doctrine from the extremes it was pushed to by James and others.

Peirce's definition of his doctrine was as follows: "In order to ascertain the meaning of an intellectual conception one should consider what practical consequences might conceivably result by necessity from the truth of that conception; and the sum of these consequences will constitute the entire meaning of the conception." Peirce maintained that he intended the doctrine as "a theory of logical analysis, or true definition," and held that "its merits are greatest in its application to the highest metaphysical conceptions." Simply, Peirce was saying that if ideas are regarded as plans of action and defined in terms of the consequences that would necessarily follow if the plans of action are put to work, most disagreements over terms would be avoided. His thesis was to give ideas *future* reference rather than *past* reference, by indicating the actions to be taken and the consequences to be anticipated. In this way, the meanings would become the same for everyone, and the validity of the ideas could be established in experience.

It is this simple doctrine of the meaning of concepts—Peirce's insistence that the "rational purpose of a word or other expression, lies exclusively in its conceivable bearing upon the conduct of life"—that James converted into the theory of truth which is the basis of his pragmatism. Dewey also enlarged on the original principle, and with James, is responsible for modern pragmatism which tests reality by immediacy, finds truth in the exigencies of practical life, and searches for practical principles that will bring the greatest good to the greatest number.

The Spirit of Pragmatism

Peirce's theory of meaning, expanded into a theory of truth, became the basis for a physiological science of mind and a philosophy of radical empiricism. According to William James, "The pragmatic rule is that the meaning of a concept may always be found, if not in some sensible particular which it directly designates, then in some particular difference in the course of human experience which its being true will make. . . . If two concepts lead you to infer the same particular consequence, then you may assume that they embody the same meaning under different names." Again, according to James, radical empiricism means that "the only things that should be debatable among philosophers shall be things definable in terms drawn from experience." These ideas are the cornerstone of the early pragmatic spirit delineated by James in his writing and his lectures at Columbia University and elsewhere.

William James was born in New York City in 1842, traveled extensively throughout Europe, and studied at Harvard where he received his M.D. degree in 1869. He was appointed to the faculty as an instructor in physiology in 1872. During the next thirty-seven years James, equally at home in the sciences and humanities, also taught courses in psychology and philosophy. By the time of his death in 1910, James had not only published his *Principles of Psychology,* a two volume classic, but many definitive essays which fashioned a new approach to philosophy and were read throughout the world. James' pragmatism was a practical, empirical, and flexible doctrine, maintaining that as the right is the only expedient in the way of our behaving, so is the truth the only expedient of our thinking.

The Pragmatic Method and Theory of Truth

James believed that the whole point of philosophy should be to determine the practical difference if one theory or another is assumed to be true. He proposed that if each idea is regarded basically as a plan of action, two different ideas—if they really are different—will be expected to produce different effects. As he says, "There can *be* no difference anywhere that doesn't *make* a difference elsewhere—no difference in abstract truth that doesn't express itself in a difference in concrete fact and in conduct consequent upon that fact, imposed on somebody, somehow, somewhere, and somewhen." The pragmatic method assumes a purpose to human life that can be tested against rival theories about man and the world. At the same time there is no single definition of man's purpose which derives its meaning from a sense of being at home in the universe. Pragmatism as a method has no dogma, and although it is oriented around results and consequences, it does not specify any particular results. James' illustration to point up the pragmatic method for settling philosophical disputes has become a classic.

He recalls the following experience when he was with friends on a camping party.*

> I returned from a solitary ramble to find every one engaged in a ferocious metaphysical dispute. The *corpus* of the dispute was a squirrel—a live squirrel supposed to be clinging to one side of a tree-trunk; while over against the tree's opposite side a human being was imagined to stand. This human witness tries to get sight of the squirrel by moving rapidly round the tree, but no matter how fast he goes, the squirrel moves as fast in the opposite direction, and always keeps the tree between himself and the man, so that never a glimpse of him is caught. The resultant metaphysical problem now is this: *Does the man go round the squirrel or not?* He goes round the tree, sure enough, and the squirrel is on the tree; but does he go round the squirrel? In the unlimited leisure of the wilderness, discussion had been worn threadbare. Every one had taken sides, and was obstinate; and the numbers on both sides were even. Each side, when I appeared therefore appealed to me to make it a majority. Mindful of the scholastic adage that whenever you meet a contradiction you must make a distinction, I immediately sought and found one, as follows: "Which party is right," I said, "depends on what you *practically mean* by 'going round' the squirrel." If you mean passing from the north of him to the east, then to the south, then to the west, and then to the north of him again, obviously the man does go round him, for he occupies these successive positions. But if on the contrary you mean being first in front of him, then on the right of him, then behind him, then on his left, and finally in front again, it is quite as obvious that the man fails to go round him; for by the compensating movements the squirrel makes, he keeps his belly turned toward the man all the time, and his back turned away. Make the distinction, and there is no occasion for any further dispute. You are both right and both wrong according as you conceive the verb "to go round" in one practical fashion or the other.[4]

James held that the seemingly interminable controversy between theism and materialism, and other metaphysical arguments may be settled as easily by considering the "practical difference" which it would make to the individual if one or the other alternative is true. The important outcome of the pragmatic method is that man is no longer engaged in looking to concepts of necessity and *a priori* categories, and a changed conception of truth emerges.

According to James, "Ideas (which themselves are but parts of our

---
* From *Pragmatism* by William James. Reprinted by permission of Alexander R. James, Literary Executor.
[4] *Lecture II, Pragmatism: A New Name for Some Old Ways of Thinking* (New York: Longmans Green and Co., 1907).

experience) become true just in so far as they help us to get into satisfactory relation with other parts of our experience." His statement that "The true is the name of whatever proves itself to be good in the way of belief, and good, too, for definite, assignable reasons," means that judgments about truth reflect the time, place, and circumstances in which the judgment was made. The tentative and precarious nature of the situations are part of the evolving scheme of things, and the truth of today is open to modification tomorrow, for there is a plurality of truths. James rejected the traditional correspondence theory of truth because of its static character and said that truth must be equated with the dynamic verification process.

The practical import, for James (and for pragmatism), is that true ideas can lead us to execute plans of action with success. False ideas terminate action, but in either case, the judgment of truth or falsity follows upon the action. Thus the pragmatist is more interested in where ideas lead than in their origin. The pragmatic answer to whether or not an idea is true is to reply that a true idea is one we can assimilate, validate, corroborate, and verify.

Pragmatic Reality, Knowledge and Value

James accepted a definition of reality that posits the real to be whatever we are obliged to take into account in any way, and he recognized three kinds of reality. These are: 1) the unexperienceable reality; 2) the reality of percepts and concepts; and 3) the reality of experience. In spite of the assertion that the "only things that should be subject to philosophic debate shall be in terms drawn from experience," James did admit the possibility of a transexperiential world. Although his belief in the reality of a finite God as a powerful moral force in the world was no more than a human ideal, he seemed to take it as a symbol of divine power that goes beyond the limits of experience. Concepts and percepts, according to James, are so interwoven that it is difficult to be sure how much of what we perceive comes through the senses, and how much through the apperceiving intellect. He wrote that "perception prompts our thought, and thought in turn enriches our perception." Both are important, but concepts, being secondary and derivative, are less so. He maintained that the "flux" of pure and direct experience is the only absolutely real.

James posited two kinds of knowledge. *Knowledge-by-acquaintance,* which is direct and immediate, comes through our feelings, the starting point of cognition. Knowledge-by-acquaintance causes us to know such things as colors when we see them or the flavor of fruits when we bite into them, but not anything about the inner nature of these things. Knowledge-by-acquaintance is prior to, more fundamental than the second type of knowledge—*knowledge-about,* which is indirect and mediate and is the foundation of intellectual operations. Meaningful knowledge-about, which consists of conceptions and judgments, must terminate in knowledge-by-acquaintance. James makes the statement that: "The pursuance of future ends and the choice of means for their attainment are thus the mark and criterion of the presence of mentality in a phenomenon." By mentality here, James simply means that the pursuit of ends is a primary function of all consciousness, rather than a criterion of cognition. James believed that knowledge of sensible realities comes about through experience. He says, "It is *made;* and made by relations that unroll themselves in time. Whenever certain intermediaries are given, such that, as they develop toward their terminus, there is experience from point to point of one direction followed, and finally of one process fulfilled, the result is that their starting-point thereby becomes a knower and their terminus an object meant or known."

The problem of value was of primary concern to James in most of his philosophical reflections. He believed that the principles of ethics are independent of the principles of science. He recognized three kinds of value experiences—the aesthetic, where feeling is dominant; the moral, where the will to action is dominant; and the religious, where the personal supporting presence of a more powerful superconsciousness is felt. James attached special implications to religious values. He did not believe that ethical terms could have any universal meaning or application, since the universe is filled with a diversity of private aims, and thus he maintained that moral obligation rests on the "demands" of existing individuals. In an attempt to determine whose claims should have priority, and whose claims ought to be binding on other persons, James concluded that the guide to answer these issues should be the principle of inclusiveness, "satisfying as many demands as we can." He did not believe that ethical treatises could ever be final, except in "their abstractest and vaguest features."

James' Pedagogy

James' ideas about educational theory have come to us by way of his pedagogical lectures which were later published in *Talks to Teachers on Psychology; and to Students on Some of Life's Ideals.* The talks were a combination of his thinking about philosophy, psychology, general theories of education, and the good life. Although it is not completely definitive, for want of a better name, his attitude toward education is called the habit-tendency theory. The lectures came at a time when the Herbartian Methodology (See Chapter VI) was directing the classroom activities of most teachers, and James' discussion of apperception foreshadows the rejection of Herbartian methodology by later scholars, such as John Dewey. While the lectures had the air of "practical hints to teachers," they are of value for the relationship that they delineate between psychology and teaching. The relation contributed to the movement known as the child-study group and furthered the belief that education could be a science.

James defines education as *"the organization of acquired habits of conduct and tendencies to behavior."* An additional factor is that education is *"little more than a mass of possibilities of reaction, acquired at home, at school, or in the training of* affairs. The teacher's task is that of supervising the acquiring process." James notes the biological nature of the organism, man, whose reactions are determined by the mind. When man is affected by the environment, the reaction modifies the life of the man in some way. The teacher must, therefore, have an intimate acquaintance with the native reactions of the child, which include fear, love, curiosity, imitation, emulation, ambition, pugnacity, pride, ownership, and constructiveness. There are others, but the teacher is supposed to use his own observational results and make note of them. "The acquired reactions must be made habitual whenever they are appropriate." The automatic responses are the material of behavior which is the reason for education. James admonishes teachers to be firm about the process of habituating responses, to allow no exceptions until the habit is firmly established.

The teacher's professional task is to train the pupil to behavior, "taking behavior, not in the narrow sense of his manners, but in the very widest possible sense, as including every possible sort of fit reaction on the circumstances into which he may find himself brought by the vicissitudes of life." The training should be based on the fact that man is a practical being with a mind that enables him to adapt to the world. Even granting regions beyond this world, the important task is the immediate one of coming to grips with the here and now. Another concern of the teacher is the problem of interest. James advised them to begin with the child's interest, and starting with objects that are related to the interest, move into the unfamiliar at a rate that will allow the child to assimilate all that the teacher wants him to learn. James states: "your pupils, whatever else they are, are at any rate little pieces of associating machinery. Their education consists in the organizing within them of determinate tendencies to associate one thing with another,—impressions with consequences, these with consequences, these with reactions, those with results, and so on indefinitely."

John Dewey's Instrumentalism

John Dewey's philosophic career was not only the longest of any philosopher in terms of life span but in terms of actual years of productivity. He was a little more than twenty at the time of his first publication, which dealt with metaphysical problems, and his vigorous mind produced some of his weightiest contributions during the last decade of his ninety-three years. He was a prolific writer whose interests ranged from logic, theory of value, methodology of the behavioral and physical sciences, and theory of knowledge to problems of psychology, ethics, political science, jurisprudence, religion, and topical issues. The magnitude of his writings is so great that just the bibliography, beginning with his first article in 1882 and including posthumous notes that appeared as late as 1960, is a one-hundred-and-fifty-three page listing in a volume that devotes another one-hundred-and-forty-three pages to the bibliography of dissertations, criticisms, and commentaries on his works.[5] Since the publication of M. Halsey Thomas'

[5] M. Halsey Thomas, *John Dewey, A Centennial Bibliography* (Chicago: The University of Chicago Press, 1962).

John Dewey, A Centennial Bibliography (1962), there has been no letup of publications about Dewey and his contributions to the variety of problems in American thought and education. In addition, Professor Thomas and others continue to discover unpublished writings, mostly short pieces, by Dewey himself.

The abundance of the available material that must somehow be capsulized into only a few pages of a textbook is overwhelming, and it is obvious that such a chronicle must be limited to a particular point by stringent guidelines. The theme for our discussion of John Dewey is established by two factors: first, by the character of our present study, which is primarily concerned with philosophic attitudes and modes of thinking that guide us in the search for solutions to problems of education; and second, by the outstanding characteristic of Dewey's philosophy—*continuity* and *process*—concepts that are antithetical to a factual chronicling and rote memorization of available material. The theme is illustrated by a comment that Dewey is said to have made about himself. The comment is found in one of the most engaging books that has been written about Dewey, *Dialogue on John Dewey*,[6] in which some of his friends recall snatches of conversation with him. Harold Taylor recalls, "I remember once a great fuss was being made over him as an educator, a social thinker, a man of his time, and so on. He said what he was fond of saying, 'Sorry, I'm just a philosopher; I'm just trying to think; that's all I'm doing.' "[7]

Biographical Sketch

Charles Frankel, professor of philosophy at Columbia University, made the following comment in an address he gave for the John Dewey Centenary held at the Johns Hopkins University. "Even during his lifetime John Dewey suffered the unfortunate fate which the gods seem to reserve for those who become too influential in philosophy. He disappeared as an individual and became a symbol. Plato, it will be remembered, fought in his letters to preserve the image of his poor singular self and insisted that what he had taught could not be condensed into a doctrine. Even Karl Marx felt the need to remind his friends wistfully that, after all, he himself was not a Marxist. And it is difficult now to remember that John Dewey was a man, not an institution, a philosopher and not a social movement."[8]

Because he became a symbol of progress, liberalism, reason, and enlightenment, we do not dwell on the particulars of Dewey's formative years that helped shape the courageous, shy, and pedantic man who loved children, marched in women's suffrage parades, championed the labor move-

---

6 Corliss Lamont, *Dialogue on John Dewey* (New York: Horizon Press, 1959). The participants are James T. Farrell, James Gutmann, Alvin Johnson, Horace M. Kallen, Harry W. Laidler, Corliss Lamont, Ernest Nagel, John H. Randall, Jr., Herbert W. Schneider, Harold Taylor, Milton Halsey Thomas.
7 *Ibid.*, p. 126.
8 Charles Frankel, "John Dewey: Where He Stands," *The Johns Hopkins Magazine*, December 1959, p. 7.

ment, and fought for a retrial of Sacco and Vanzetti. Because his ideas had the sort of vitality that makes them immortal, we are apt to forget that Dewey was born over a hundred years ago, and was raised in a world quite different from ours. Dewey was born in Burlington, Vermont, in 1859, the same year as the publication of Charles Darwin's *The Origin of Species,* and two years before Lincoln became president. Dewey's father was a shop keeper, and it is natural to suppose that the young boy may have been influenced by the shrewd and lively comments of the Vermont farmers who gathered round a pot-bellied stove in the general store and discussed the issues of their day. What better source for an awareness of the power and strength of group consciousness and a realization that schools, like politics, are a function of the society? What better source for the nineteenth century, New Englander respect for firsthand experience, the private dignity of the individual, and the sense of fair play that Dewey retained throughout his life?

Dewey was not an outstanding student, for there was nothing about his early schooling, where the key to education was strict discipline by the rod, to interest or to inspire the boy to excellence. He was a diligent student, however, and graduated from the University of Vermont when he was twenty. After a year's study of philosophy, and a short period of public school teaching, he entered Johns Hopkins as a graduate student in philosophy and received his doctor's degree in 1884. Dewey became a member of the faculty at Michigan that year and remained there until 1894 when he was appointed chairman of the Department of Philosophy, Psychology, and Pedagogy at the University of Chicago. During his ten years at Chicago, Dewey developed many of his educational principles, and assisted by his wife, Alice Freeman Dewey, he put them into practice in a "Laboratory School" in connection with the University. He moved to Columbia University in 1904 and taught there until his retirement in 1930.

Dewey had six children by his first wife, and their rearing stimulated his interest in the theory and practice of education and was an important influence on his development as a pragmatist. His observation of his own children, coupled with the insights derived from James about the importance of children's native impulses and interests, led Dewey to base education upon the interests, ideas, and activities of children. Dewey's second marriage, long after the death of his first wife in 1927, was to Roberta (Lowitz) Grant of New York City. Dewey, who was eighty-seven at the time of this marriage, and his wife adopted two war orphans, a brother and sister, and the happiest times during the last five years of his life was spent with his second family on the Dewey farm in Pennsylvania. Dewey died on June 1, 1952.

The Natural History of a Philosopher

The central idea that motivated and controlled Dewey's thinking was the crucial notion that he termed "the pattern of inquiry." He believed that the uniqueness of man is his ability to think and that the whole of experience and society has meaning in relation to the free participation of the individual in the activities of inquiry, imaginative hypothesizing, and enlightened critical perception. The pattern of inquiry, according to Dewey, is a structure of the ideas themselves—their origin and development and effects. Accordingly, the most effective way to trace individual philosophic development is to search out the primary influences that have shaped one's thinking. In the case of John Dewey, we are fortunate to have his own intellectual biography in his essay, "From Absolutism to Experimentalism,"[9] published in 1930.

The distance of time enabled Dewey to write about his early intellectual influences and development as objectively as though he were another person. Furthermore, as Dewey pointed out, since many things fade with the passing of time, the few points which did not have to be forced into the foreground, but stood out in his recollections, were undoubtedly the major influences on his early intellectual development. Dewey begins his recall of these influences by a description of the course of study he followed the last year of his undergraduate work at the University of Vermont. The course was designed to introduce the student who had spent three years of specialization in the languages and sciences into the world of ideas. Although Dewey doubted that the course achieved its purpose in most cases, he personally found it exciting and rewarding. He also mentions a course in his previous year at the university that was responsible for his interest in Darwinian evolution, and that was perhaps his first inclination toward the philosophic. The physiology course used T. H. Huxley's textbook which gave Dewey an appreciation for the unity of the living creature, and he dates his philosophic interest from that point. Another influence from that time was his reading of Auguste Comte's writings which stimulated his concern for political and social philosophy. Dewey writes that he could not remember exactly how he was affected by Comte's law of the three stages, but that he was deeply impressed by the idea of a synthesis of science as a method to regulate an organization of societal living.

Probably the greatest influence on Dewey's future career was the teaching of Professor H. A. P. Torrey. It was from him that Dewey learned about Scottish Common Sense, German Intuitionism, and Kantian *a priori* philosophy. Dewey writes that he was an excellent teacher and that it was he who turned Dewey's thoughts definitely to the study of philosophy. Dewey studied privately with Torrey for a year before he entered Johns Hopkins for "graduate work" which was a new thing at that time. Dewey was also encouraged in this direction by Dr. W. T. Harris, the well-known Hegelian, and editor of the only philosophic journal in America then, the *Journal of Speculative Philosophy*. Dewey sent him a number of articles and was urged by Dr. Harris to try philosophy as a professional career. At

---

[9] John Dewey, "From Absolutism to Experimentalism" in G. P. Adams and W. P. Montague, eds. *Contemporary American Philosophy: Personal Statements* (New York: The Macmillan Co., 1930), Vol. II.

Johns Hopkins, under the inspiration of George Sylvester Morris, Dewey became a neo-Hegelian. Dewey writes of Professor Morris, "I have never known a more single-hearted and whole-souled man—a man of a single piece all the way through; while I long since deviated from his philosophic faith, I should be happy to believe that the influence of the spirit of his teaching has been an enduring influence."[10] (It was Professor Morris who persuaded Dewey to become a member of the faculty at the University of Michigan, where he was teaching, after Dewey finished his Ph.D. at Johns Hopkins.) Dewey writes that Morris was not the only source of his own Hegelianism.*

> The eighties and nineties were a time of new ferment in English thought; the reaction against atomic individualism and sensationalistic empiricism was in full swing. It was the time of Thomas Hill Green, of the two Cairds, of Wallace, of the appearance of the *Essays in Philosophical Criticism,* cooperatively produced by a younger group under the leadership of the late Lord Haldane. This movement was at the time the vital and constructive one in philosophy. Naturally its influence fell in with and reinforced that of Professor Morris.[11]

Dewey tells us that although he drifted away from Hegelianism during the next fifteen years, he should not think of denying that Hegel left a permanent deposit in his thinking. He believed that Hegel had a greater variety of insight than any systematic philosopher other than Plato. He wrote of Plato that, "Nothing could be more helpful to present philosophizing than a 'Back to Plato' movement; but it would have to be back to the dramatic, restless, cooperatively inquiring Plato of the Dialogues, trying one mode of attack after another to see what it might yield; back to the Plato whose highest flight of metaphysics always terminated with a social and practical turn, and not to the artificial Plato constructed by unimaginative commentators who treat him as the original university professor."[12]

Like the poet, Dewey finds it difficult to write about the things and events that are not far enough removed as to be recollected in tranquility. His comments in this regard are illustrative of the idea of continuity and process that permeate his very being.

> The philosopher, if I may apply that word to myself, that I became as I moved away from German idealism, is too much the self that I still am and is still too much in process of change to lend itself to record. I envy, up to a certain point, those who can write their intellectual biography in a unified pattern, woven out of a few distinctly

---

10 *Ibid.,* p. 18.
* "From Absolutism to Experimentalism" by John Dewey from *Contemporary American Philosophy: Personal Statements,* eds. G. P. Adams and W. P. Montague, Vol. 2 (1930) New York: Russell & Russell, 1962.
11 *Ibid.,* p. 18.
12 *Ibid.,* p. 21.

discernible strands of interest and influence. By contrast, I seem to be unstable, chameleon-like, yielding one after another to many diverse and even incompatible influences; struggling to assimilate something from each and yet striving to carry it forward in a way that is logically consistent with what has been learned from its predecessors.[13]

Dewey points out that although he has learned a great deal from philosophic writing, it has been of a technical nature, and for the most part, the most significant influences on his own thinking came from persons and experiences. He mentions four realms of influence that are guidelines for his later philosophical wanderings. The first of these is the theory and practice of education for the young. He says that . . . "I have never been able to feel much optimism regarding the possibilities of 'higher' education when it is built upon warped and weak foundations."[14] He wonders if philosophers in general take education seriously enough, for it seems to Dewey that education is the supreme human interest where all other problems come to a head and therefore the one most worthy of philosophizing about.

The second area of Dewey's mature concern is the traditional dualism of scientific and moralistic method. He believed that one method of effective inquiry should apply to both of the areas. He says that "This belief has had much more to do with the development of what I termed, for lack of a better word, 'instrumentalism,' than have most of the reasons that have been assigned."[15] A third realm of influence on Dewey's thinking was William James' organic and dynamic psychology that recognizes life in terms of life in action and thus contributes to the problems of human existence. The final realm that Dewey mentions is that of distinctive social categories, especially participation and communication. Dewey was convinced that most of our philosophizing needs to be done over again to achieve a synthesis between modern science and social subjects. According to Dewey:

> Intellectual prophecy is dangerous; but if I read the cultural signs of the times aright, the next synthetic movement in philosophy will emerge when the significance of the social sciences and arts has become an object of reflective attention in the same way that mathematical and physical sciences have been made the objects of thought in the past, and when their full import is grasped.[16]

A philosophy based upon the qualities of process, continuity, and dynamics presents a difficult challenge for discussants. As Dewey recognized, his thought was a developing thing, and it was in a state of constant revision. Yet there are stable elements which can serve as guidelines for our discussion. These appear most significantly in two works—both mature

---

13 *Ibid.*, p. 22.
14 *Ibid.*, p. 22.
15 *Ibid.*, p. 23.
16 *Ibid.*, p. 26.

statements, for Dewey was past sixty-five years of age when they were published. *Experience and Nature* (1925) and *Logic, the Theory of Inquiry* (1938) represent long years of serious thought and writing about logic, metaphysics, value theory, and epistemology. These works, with special emphasis on Chapter X from *Experience and Nature* and Chapter VI from *Logic, the Theory of Inquiry,* will provide the nucleus for our discussion of Dewey's epistemology and logic which are *dominant* problems in his philosophy.

Naturalistic Epistemology

Dewey published two articles in 1884 which pointed up the struggle going on in his intellectual development. The first was "Kant and the Philosophic Method," which reflects Dewey's idealistic leanings, and the second was "The New Psychology," which grew out of his association with G. Stanley Hall and the newer developments in psychology. The contest, which it seemed to be, was between a transcendental and rationalistic soul-psychology, and a naturalistic and empirical sense-psychology, and the contest revolved around the problem of learning. The idealistic aspects of Dewey's thought led him to account for individual consciousness by referring to a universal consciousness.[17] It was his rejection of the implied absolute or absolutes which turned Dewey to a consideration of the sensory-based epistemology of the empiricist, but he found the empiricist view of mind as a passive receptacle for sense impressions equally unacceptable. Dewey recognized his debt to Jamesian psychology and to Darwinian evolutionary concepts for the resolution of his problem. His rejection of the dualisms of individual and universal consciousness led him to naturalize his psychology and accept the organism in an active role in nature. The specific point of his "conversion" occurred with his rejection of any relation with a mechanical interpretation of the organism in favor of viewing it as the unifying element for the perceptual and conceptual parts of the knowledge-getting process. The concepts of continuity and conflict culminated in an emphasis upon process and the sociality of man, and the gradual shift of emphasis in Dewey's philosophizing led him to the position which he called experimental idealism. According to Morton White, the elements that afforded the union of the idealistic and the experimental were "activism, organicism, and opposition to formalism and dualism."[18]

As the idealistic elements of Dewey's philosophy receded, the scientific and experimental aspects came to the fore. At the same time, his investigations did not lead him to a laboratory science, for the methods he promoted were always related to an organism and its environment, an aspect of his organismic psychology and its social orientation. The concept of *activity,* one that probably had its beginning in psychology, soon became

---

17 John Dewey, "The Psychological Standpoint." *Mind,* January 1886, XI, 7.
18 Morton White, *The Origins of Dewey's Instrumentalism* (New York: Columbia University Press, 1943), p. 111.

a key element in Dewey's logic which he viewed as a method of inquiry. He states:

> That which satisfactorily terminates inquiry is, by definition, knowledge; it is knowledge because it *is* the appropriate close of inquiry.[19]

According to Dewey, the older epistemological views which separate the knower from the known create a false dichotomy and lead the philosopher away from the experiental into a realm of concepts, thus sidetracking him from the genuine problem of knowledge. Dewey refused to separate the knower from the known, as he maintained that knowing and knowledge-getting are situational and involve the organism and its environment; that it is a natural phenomenon which may be described by terms such as transaction and interaction. The interaction of organism (knower) and environment (known) occurs by means of inquiry. When doubt arises, inquiry is brought to bear upon problems, and it is this activity that Dewey calls logic.

We have noted Dewey's rejection of traditional dualisms that posit different methods of investigation for the scientist and for the moralist. Dewey suggests that we observe what men do, see the ways in which they meet problems, and note how they hold to the solutions that work, sloughing off those that fail. We will note that men develop their ways of inquiring by building on these experiences. An indeterminate situation creates anxiety in men. When their automatic responses fail to meet the problem satisfactorily, they must begin to analyze it in order to know what is the exact difficulty. Since it is unlikely that any situation will be completely indeterminate, it is necessary to discover what elements of the problem are in doubt. The possible solutions suggested serve as stimuli for overt activity. One must reason hypothetically in order to predict where the overt activity will probably lead, and the activity that seems most likely to succeed is obviously the one to initiate. The results will determine the correctness of the prediction, and if the solution is a correct one, it will serve to reduce the number of future problematic situations. Ideas, then, are instruments by which an indeterminate present may be transformed into a fact for future determinations. Here is a basis for calling Dewey's particular type of pragmatism *instrumentalism*.

Intelligence and experience are key concepts in the theory of inquiry, and the following statement is a significant addendum here to the more lengthy discussion of Dewey's view of intelligence in Chapter III. Dewey delineates intelligence in the following manner. "For the holding an end in view and the selecting and organizing out of the natural flux, on the basis of this end, conditions that are means, *is* intelligence."[20] Dewey's definition

---

[19] John Dewey, *Logic, The Theory of Inquiry* (New York: Henry Holt and Company, 1938), p. 8.

[20] John Dewey, "Nature and Its Good: A Conversation," *Hibbert Journal*, VII, No. 4, July 1909 (Also in Dewey, *The Influence of Darwin on Philosophy*, New York: Henry Holt and Company, 1910), p. 43.

of truth as "a character which belongs to a meaning so far as tested through action that carries it to successful completion"[21] underscores the dominant characteristics of Dewey's theory of knowledge, continuity, and process. The view of workability supports the ideas that truth happens to an idea, that truth is not eternal, but is relative.

Dewey says that experience is *of* nature as well as it is *in* nature. He states: "It is not experience which is experienced, but nature—stones, plants, animals, diseases, health, temperature, electricity, and so on. Things interacting in certain ways *are* experience; they are what is experienced. Linked in certain other ways with another natural object—the human organism—they are *how* things are experienced as well. Experience thus reaches down into nature; it has depth. It also has breadth and to an indefinitely elastic extent. It stretches. That stretch constitutes inference."[22] Truth and intelligence that are limited to experience *in* and *of* nature pinpoints Dewey's altered concept of metaphysics. As a matter of fact, many scholars have suggested that Dewey's instrumentalism has no metaphysics. Actually, this is a false charge, for a type of reality structure that is termed naturalistic metaphysics can be delineated, and its intimate relationship with Dewey's naturalistic value theory is sufficient reason for discussing them jointly.

Naturalistic Metaphysics and Values

Our decision to discuss Dewey's metaphysics and his value theory conjointly is not meant to imply a value theory, such as Plato's, that is subordinate to prior metaphysical commitments. This is not the case, for the meanings associated with naturalism prevent such a subordination, and the relationship between Dewey's value and metaphysics is reciprocal. According to J. H. Randall, Jr.:

> Naturalism as a metaphysic is thus a protest, against views maintaining the supreme reality of certain aspects of Nature, that all experienced aspects are equally real. Naturalism as a theory of values is a protest, against the dominance of codes emphasizing certain goods to the exclusion of others, that immediately and in themselves all goods are on the same level.[23]

Professor Randall's remarks reflect Dewey's attempt to "ground" values and metaphysics in the natural world of man. Again we see that Dewey rejects all types of dualisms, since they tend to split the world into two distinct parts, usually the absolute, which is judged to be superior, and the relative, which is thought to be necessarily inferior. Such dualisms designate the absolute as the *real* and therefore the source of truth; and the relative

21 John Dewey, "The Intellectualist Criterion for Truth," *Mind*, XVI, N.S. July, 1907 (Reprinted in Dewey, *The Influence of Darwin on Philosophy,* pp. 112–153), p. 139.
22 John Dewey, *Experience and Nature* (Chicago: Open Court Publishing Co., 1925), pp. 4a–1.
23 John H. Randall, Jr., "Dualism in Metaphysics and Practical Philosophy," in *Essays in Honor of John Dewey* (New York: Henry Holt and Company, 1929), p. 311.

as *unreal* and the source of error. All such juxtapositions are rejected by Dewey, and the whole force of his philosophy is directed toward the acceptance of the natural world as the only province of man. This view has caused some commentators to label Dewey's metaphysics as "all foreground," and although the characterization may be apt, an epithet of "immediacy" which these same critics have applied to it is unjust. Dewey's statement about nature and the human condition leads to a rejection of the concept of immediacy and to an acceptance of a reality entirely composed of foreground. He writes that:

> While, therefore, philosophy has its source not in any special impulse or staked-off section of experience, but in the entire human predicament, this human situation falls wholly within nature. It reflects the traits of nature; it gives indisputable evidence that in nature itself qualities and relations, individualities and uniformities, finalities and efficacies, contingencies and necessities are inextricably bound together.[24]

The processes and continuities of existence are mediated by criticism (philosophy) and man's experience is *of* nature, *in* nature, and ultimately *for* nature. There is no supernature against which all experiences must be judged, and no transcendental realm of essences or even efficacious ideals which give meaning to the flow of natural phenomena. Nature includes uncertainty and incompleteness which constitute the problematic situation, and the continuity from one problematic situation to another comes through reflection. Knowledge and knowing, taking place in a "contextual situation,"[25] relate the parts of existence in an empirically intelligible manner and provide the base for value choices. Dewey states, "To pass beyond direct occurrence, even though the passage be restricted to an attempt to define value, is to begin a process of discrimination which implies a reflective criterion."[26]

Value, like existence, is a natural phenomenon for Dewey, a choosing from among a host of natural events, using consequences and origin as standards. The choice among the "possibles" reflects intelligent responses and has nothing transcendental or mysterious about it. Ends-in-view, a phrase used by Dewey in *Human Nature and Conduct,* describes the process of valuation, of liking some things and disliking others. Values are of infinite diversity and refer to temporal qualities that either exist or do not exist—are enjoyed or are not enjoyed. This reactive stage is preliminary to reflection upon value, which is a natural process, something that man learns as he grows. Dewey claims that the introduction of an is/ought dichotomy, the postulating of an ideal realm of norms, is debilitating and self-defeating.

---

[24] Dewey, *Experience and Nature, op. cit.,* p. 421.
[25] *Ibid.,* p. 67.
[26] *Ibid.,* p. 398.

He replaces artificially invoked standards with the method of criticism, the use of intelligence in value choices.

> What the method of intelligent, thoughtful valuation will accomplish, if once it be tried, is for the result of trial to determine. Since it is relative to the intersection in existence of hazard and rule, of contingency and order, faith in a wholesale and final triumph is fantastic. But some procedure has to be tried; for life is itself a sequence of trials.[27]

Dewey saw the school as a place for testing ideas, as a place for trial and error with a minimum of hazards, and he began to devote most of his energies to ideas about educational theory.

Educational Theory

John Dewey wrote a number of books and articles that reflect the development of his ideas about educational thought and practice, and throughout this educational saga his optimism about education, his *hopes* for education, remain constant. His essay, *My Pedagogic Creed,* is a moving and effective statement of these hopes which he spent the next several decades explaining, defending, and disseminating. While it is almost impossible to transmit to the printed page the aura of vigor and vitality that characterized Dewey's life, this essay and the next two which elaborated on the creed—*The School and Society* (1900) and *The Child and the Curriculum* (1902)—are imbued with the poignant quality of a man philosophizing, of a man struggling to formulate ideas that were important to him. Perhaps for this reason, these three essays have a dynamic quality that is wanting in his more famous book, *Democracy and Education* (1916), or in either of the other two books, *The Sources of a Science of Education* (1929), and *Experience and Education* (1938), which are generally included in a consideration of Dewey's educational theory.

My Pedagogic Creed consists of five "articles of faith": 1) What Education Is; 2) What the School Is; 3) The Subject Matter of Education; 4) The Nature of Method; and 5) The School and Social Progress. These five articles, written before he was forty, are the basis of Dewey's educational theory, the seeds of his reformist fervor, beliefs which he developed laboriously, sometimes painfully, but always confidently. Those who have not read the essay may well wonder that so brief a work could contain sufficient material to prompt much of Dewey's later educational writings, and to inspire, or antagonize, but always to stimulate others for three quarters of a century. However, the initial statement of the credo sufficiently illustrates the point, for these few sentences, so abundantly rich in ideas, typify the entire essay.

---

27 *Ibid.,* p. 437.

I believe that all education proceeds by the participation of the individual in the social consciousness of the race. This process begins unconsciously almost at birth, and is continually shaping the individual's powers, saturating his consciousness, forming his habits, training his ideas, and arousing his feelings and emotions. Through this unconscious education the individual gradually comes to share in the intellectual and moral resources which humanity has succeeded in getting together. He becomes an inheritor of the funded capital of civilization. The most formal and technical education in the world cannot safely depart from this general process. It can only organize it or differentiate it in some particular direction.[28]

The foregoing paragraph lends itself to the sort of exhaustive analysis that would lead into all areas of a philosophic investigation, but it is the last sentence that implies the *raison d'être* of educational theories. An educational theory is a complexity of ideas about the child, the teacher, and society that are in keeping with one's philosophy of education, and it involves the relationship between social aims and goals, the individuals who are to become contributors to the aims and goals, and the mediator—the educational program and the teacher. In a manner of speaking, the fully developed educational theory is a blueprint for the implementation of a philosophy of education. Consequently, the two are so intimately related that there is not always a clear line of demarcation between them. We should begin to see how a theory of education develops in all of its relationships by considering some of Dewey's thinking about the child in the educative process, the educative experiences of the teacher, and the relationship of education to the societal context.

Dewey presents contrasting views about education in his essay *The Child and the Curriculum*. Those who hold the first view are primarily concerned with the subject matter of the curriculum and emphasize the logical arrangement of topics for study. It is assumed that all children will progress in a uniform and orderly pattern from the most elementary subjects through set stages to the most difficult and in the same fashion from the simple beginning to the more complex end of each topic. At some predetermined point the child, having mastered the sequential material, will have completed his education. According to this view, when the child is attentive and passive, he is playing his proper role in a system where subject matter determines the method and furnishes the end. The subject matter centered school program is an established pattern that dispenses a uniformity of information and discipline to all children and at several predetermined periods in the program, each child is judged against his classmates and ranked accordingly. Such group ranking, Dewey maintains, not only becomes a

---

[28] John Dewey, *My Pedagogic Creed*, Article I, from *Dewey on Education*, ed. by Martin S. Dworkin (New York: Bureau of Publications, Teachers College, Columbia University, 1959), pp. 19–20.

permanent part of the child's external record, but is apt to be internalized by the child so that it is reflected in his self-image.

The contrasting view of education, one which Dewey affirms, sees the child as the starting point, the center, and the end of the educational process. Subject matter is merely the material for part of the educational experiences, which cover a far wider range than subject matter alone. Individual growth and development determine individual standards, and studies are valued only as they serve the needs of this growth. The greatest stress is placed on *present* experiences, for the future is an undetermined mystery. This evolutionary attitude accepts the child as an unformed organism capable of the sort of development that will enable him to adjust to his changing environment and to play a significant role in the future community, whatever it may be, for as Dewey says:

> With the advent of democracy and modern industrial conditions, it is impossible to foretell definitely just what civilization will be twenty years from now. Hence it is impossible to prepare the child for any precise set of conditions. To prepare him for the future life means to give him command of himself; it means so to train him that he will have the full and ready use of all his capacities.[29]

The purpose of a child-centered education is to assist the child in the development of his self-awareness and the realization of his individual capacities but always within the societal context, for as Dewey says, ". . . all activity takes place in a medium, in a situation, and with reference to its conditions."[30] Materials for the educational experiences, including subject matter, are not uniformly predetermined but are selected on the basis of individual interests, habits, and abilities. Thus, according to Dewey, the child begins in the feelings of his own excitement and is helped toward a consciousness of his interests and a broadening of the range of his experiences. It would be a mistake to conclude that because the learning experiences may resemble playful activity and be more pleasurable than not, the nature of this sort of education is not serious, for this is not the case. Dewey is not writing of the sort of willy-nilly, permissive and undirected activities that have sometimes been attributed to his instrumentalism; nor is the teacher a glorified baby-sitter whose role is simply to keep the children amused and happy. An understanding of Dewey's child-centered education makes it quite clear that the duties and responsibilities of the teacher are far greater than those of the "information dispenser" of the subject-centered curriculum. Dewey's essay, *The Child and the Curriculum*, elucidated the stress that the Laboratory School placed on the *present* experience of the child, as opposed to the "old" subject-centered curriculum, and he concludes the case of Child *vs.* Curriculum as follows:

---

29 *Ibid.,* pp. 21–22.
30 John Dewey, *The Child and the Curriculum* (Dworkin, p. 110).

The case is of Child. It is his present powers which are to assert themselves; his present capacities which are to be exercised; his present attitudes which are to be realized. But save as the teacher knows, knows wisely and thoroughly, the race-experience which is embodied in that thing we call the Curriculum, the teacher knows neither what the present power, capacity, or attitude is, nor yet how it is to be asserted, exercised, and realized.[31]

Dewey stated in his credo that the teacher, he believed, should be in the school as a *member of the community*. Aided by her larger wisdom, her greater experience, and a genuine interest in the child—the unformed organism—it should be her function to select the influences which shall affect the child and to assist him in his response to the influences. This is quite a different teacher from the one who teaches the subject-centered school and is, of necessity, impelled to impose certain ideas and behavior patterns on the child. Dewey pointed out that order and discipline, like other methods, are necessarily related to the ends. That is, if the end is a group of children learning certain set lessons, to be recited to the teacher, then the teacher must use disciplinary methods to secure those results. On the other hand, if the teacher is striving to achieve a spirit of social cooperation and community life, the disciplinary methods must be relative to that end, and Dewey believed that discipline should proceed from the life of the school as a whole, much as social discipline proceeds from the community at large.

Dewey saw the teacher-child relationship as one of "learners-together," where the teacher leads through suggestion. She shares her experiences in a way that they will contribute to the development of the child, and as the child learns, the teacher learns more about the child. Clearly, the teacher of the child-centered school needs a sound training, not only in race-experience (what Dewey says is embedded in the curriculum), but in the psychology of the child so that she may be sensitive to the child's interests and needs. She must have a knowledge of the school environment and the history of the society in order to be aware of societal aims and ideals. She is both a member of the school community, and of the community at large, and as a mediator, must know the goals and values of the one, as well as the means to help the members of the other to develop their potentialities and to contribute to societal goals. The task demands the dedication of a professional in the best sense of the word. Dewey made it clear in an address to the Progressive Education Association[32] in 1928, that while an experimental school may be tempted to improvise its subject matter, . . . "if it permits improvisation to dictate its course, the result is a jerky, dis-

---

[31] *Ibid.*, p. 111.

[32] Dewey had originally refused involvement with the Progressive Education Association, which was founded in 1919, as he was disturbed over some of the programs that had developed in the name of "progressivism." However, he reversed his decision in 1928 when he agreed to become an honorary president, using the occasion to warn against oversimplifications and exaggerations of the child-centered approach to education.

continuous movement which works against the possibility of making any important contribution to educational subject matter."[33]

Contrary to the charges made by some of his critics, Dewey never overlooked, or denied, the importance of subject matter as an essential aspect of education. The misunderstanding may have stemmed, in part, from Dewey's preference for the broader term, race-experience; or it may have stemmed from his insistence that a knowledge of subject matter alone, regardless of how thorough the knowledge might be, does not sufficiently qualify one to teach. Learning, Dewey said involves knowledge, skill, and character, and an effective teacher must have studied each factor in order to be able to select the most effective conditions of learning. The teacher needs the kind of training that will enable her to detect progress or lack of progress in learning and to be able to detect the causes or reasons for success or failure. She must be able to combine the science of education with the art of teaching, which Dewey thought to be not only the most difficult, but the most important of all of the human arts.

In 1897 Dewey stated in his credo that he believed the school to be a social institution and education a social process. He believed then that the school is a form of community life that functions to bring the child to share in a common cultural heritage and to develop his abilities for social ends. Two years later, Dewey gave a series of lectures on *The School and Society,* and in the first lecture he said that the school should not just be a place for learning lessons that may or may not have some remote reference to future living. The school, Dewey believed, should be given the chance to be a miniature community, "an embryonic society," where the child learns through directed living. In the same lecture Dewey said that since what the best and wisest parent wants for his child will be reflected in what the community at large want for their children, we must broaden our standards for judging the school. He believed that any ideals other than those of the community at large would destroy our democracy.

Almost two decades later, Dewey enlarged on this idea in his book *Democracy and Education.* He pointed out that a democratic society where all members have equal participation requires an educational system where individuals gain a sense of personal worth, a concern for the society at large, and habits of thought which allow for the orderly reconstruction of the society. He points out that the school is far more important in social progress than any enactment of law or imposition of penalties. He urged that the reconstruction of philosophy, education, and social ideals should, ideally, be so closely related that they seem to evolve in chorus.

The Role of Theory in Education

Marc Belth, writing on education as a discipline, says: "If education, especially teaching, is to be more than a craft, the role of theory therein must be identified and studied intensively. Otherwise we are committed to

---

[33] John Dewey, "Progressive Education and the Science of Education" (Dworkin pp. 120–121).

the belief that one need only look at teaching in order to know it fully."[34] Dewey, writing on the science of education, expressed somewhat the same idea when he pointed out that until we are quite confident that we know *exactly* what education is, what its goals and aims should be for all time, and can all agree about the best method of obtaining these goals, different sciences of education are not only possible but necessary. Dewey maintained that unless schools degenerate to a monotonous uniformity in all respects, there must be more than just one theory of education.

We note that Dewey uses the terms *science* of education and *theory* of education interchangeably, and there can be little doubt but that it was intentional. We saw earlier in the chapter that philosophy of education and theory of education are so intimately related that there are times when it is difficult to distinguish between the two. Indeed, Dewey made the statement in *Democracy and Education* that: "If we are willing to conceive education as the process of forming fundamental dispositions, intellectual and emotional, toward nature and fellow men, philosophy may even be defined *as the general theory of education.*"[35] The statement might be confusing to the distinction we have tried to make between philosophy and theory unless it is recognized as Dewey's way of stressing the importance of philosophy, by way of theory, for educational goals and ideals. On the other hand, Dewey's synonymous use of science of education and theory of education can be helpful to our understanding of theory when we view science with the latitude he suggests in *The Sources of a Science of Education.* He says that he takes science to signify . . . "the existence of systematic methods of inquiry, which, when they are brought to bear on a range of facts, enable us to understand them better and to control them more intelligently, less haphazardly, and with less routine."[36]

Much of the controversy about the role of theory in education can be traced to a confusion of terms, and it will be profitable to examine the concept of theory in order to clarify our meaning of theory in education. *Webster's New Collegiate Dictionary* gives several definitions of theory, but the most appropriate one seems to be the following: *"Theory is the general or abstract principles of any body of facts; pure, as distinguished from applied."* *Roget's Thesaurus* lists nineteen synonyms, including such unlikely terms as *guess, suspicion, inkling,* and the like. Both *Roget's* and *Webster's* offer the synonym, hypothesis, which is most frequently used to mean theory. A suggestion made by A. C. Benjamin in *Science, Technology and Human Values,*[37] serves admirably to eliminate the confusion that results when theory and hypothesis are used interchangeably. He suggests that we use the terms *hypothesis, theory,* and *confirmed belief* to designate dif-

---

34 Marc Belth, *Education as a Discipline* (Boston: Allyn & Bacon, Inc., 1965), p. 27.

35 John Dewey, *Democracy and Education* (New York: The Macmillan Company, 1916), p. 383.

36 John Dewey, *The Sources of a Science of Education* (New York: Horace Liveright, 1929), pp. 8–9.

37 A. Cornelius Benjamin, *Science, Technology, and Human Values* (Columbia: University of Missouri Press, 1965), p. 26.

ferent degrees of knowledge, a distinction which makes a three-fold contribution to our understanding of theory.

First, it establishes theory as a specific kind of knowledge. Theory serves education in much the same way that it serves science, art, music, medicine, and the like, but in each case the theory is necessarily bound to the particular discipline. That is, while education may borrow from other disciplines, such as psychology, biology, or sociology, it makes use of certain established facts, or data; but a theory may not be transferred from one discipline to another, and theory in education is distinct from the theory in any other area. It is also a unique *kind* of knowledge. Theory in education is concerned with the problems of knowledge, the character, production, and limitations of knowledge, and it produces knowledge *about* the tools or instruments of knowledge. According to our definition of theory, it sets up general principles from which inferences may be made about a particular discipline, and these principles allow us to ascribe meaning to certain events, to explain observable phenomena, and to interpret the events that we observe or postulate.

Secondly, the distinction we have made here between hypothesis and theory implied a relationship between the levels of knowledge and does away with the old dualistic notion of two worlds. It obviates the suggestion of a dichotomy between theory and practice which would relegate theory to a rarified, speculative realm and reduce it to a kind of ivory tower parlor game. Dewey emphasized the importance of a continuing relationship between the theory and the practice of education in his lecture to the Progressive Education Association in 1928. He pointed out that the contributions the progressive schools had made up until that time, although impressive, were merely a starting point for theory of education. Dewey saw the contributions not only in terms of the happiness and integrity of the individuals affected, but as the materials for a flexible and moving intellectual organization—for a theory of education that can determine objectives and select every discipline in the curriculum accordingly. Dewey believed that educational advances are made, as in other sciences, by a consideration of different points of view and by working on different theories, for there can be no single universal system of truth in a democratic society. Thus, theory in education does not present a fixed or closed orthodoxy; nor is it generated out of the ether; it depends both on philosophic attitudes and on empirical data drawn from practice. This brings us to the third point of clarification of what we mean by theory.

The distinction between hypothesis and theory as different levels of knowledge is graphic of the positional role of theory in a continuum of inquiry. It is the bridge between the purely speculative and the experimental, and it serves as both a check and a guide. Theory in education produces knowledge on a mediating level; theory in education enables us to deduce from actual practice, in order to arrive at theoretical decisions which are the material for new hypotheses; and theory in education is the context for predicting the probable outcome or development of new hypotheses with a minimum of effort. However, the study of theory in education is a good deal more than an exploration of different hypotheses. The role of theory in education is to construct a kind of "metaknowledge" that enables us to alter the observable conditions of learning—the curriculum, the tests and measurements, the methods, and the like—in order to increase the maximum effectiveness of education and to keep failure to a minimum.

PAUL H. HIRST

Philosophy and Educational Theory*

The reading selected for Chapter VII delineates several views of the relation between philosophy and educational theory and is an excellent supplement for our discussion of educational theory. Hirst represents a point of view regarding philosophy of education which has developed in recent years, and close study of his analysis can be especially meaningful to those in the formative stages of considering education in its theoretical aspects. The different views of philosophy and educational theory presented in the article provide a base for the exploration of significant concepts as they relate to education, and Hirst's statement that "philosophical agreement is no guarantee of educational agreement and fortunately many educational principles are acceptable to the holders of very diverse philosophical views . . . " is suggestive for additional explication of the meaning of philosophy and of education. Further, Hirst's comments about educational theory as an autonomous discipline set the stage for our discussion in Chapter IX of education as a discipline, as a unique study in its own right. Finally, Hirst's discussion of philosophical analysis raises questions about the relation between theory and practice which is a point of concern for the philosophical analyst.

Philosophers have not infrequently written on education and their ideas, until the recent spate of works by psychologists and sociologists, have exerted considerable influence in this field. The impact of empirical studies however, together with contemporary radical questionings about the nature of philosophy itself, has of late made educationists uncertain of the function of philosophy in educational discussion. Clarification here is urgently needed.

* From *British Journal of Educational Studies*, by Paul H. Hirst, XII, No. 1, November 1963. Reprinted by permission of Faber and Faber Ltd., London.

There are three particular views of the relationship between philosophy and education which I wish to discuss.

(a) The traditional view that from philosophy there follow directly certain implications for educational practice.

(b) The view that there is an autonomous discipline of education which draws to some extent on philosophical beliefs.

(c) The more analytical view that philosophy has a purely critical and clarificatory function for educational discussion.

I

It is often taken for granted, though rarely explicitly asserted, that from a set of philosophical beliefs there follow directly and necessarily certain clear explicit implications for educational practice.[1] After all, is it not rather obvious that if people differ about the nature of ultimate reality they must differ in judging what is important in the school curriculum? Must not a religious person think religious education absolutely essential and an atheist think it thoroughly undesirable? Must not a western liberal democrat, because he holds different ethical doctrines, necessarily disagree with a communist on at least some issues in moral education? And must it not therefore be true that philosophical beliefs do determine clear educational principles which must be put into practice if obvious inconsistencies are to be avoided?

Certainly few people would wish to deny that a system of metaphysical, epistemological and ethical beliefs that provides a theory of what is ultimately real and ultimately important in life must have some significant contribution to make to educational ideas and practice. But whilst it is perhaps obvious that there is *some* connection between philosophy and education, the traditional view takes this to be one of direct implication assuming that thoroughly valid principles for determining educational practice can be readily inferred straight from philosophical beliefs. Even if we accept the view that philosophy is a body of beliefs of this kind, what is here said about its connection with education seems to me not only far from obvious but in fact quite untenable for two major reasons.

First I would suggest that the account is far too simple and that it thereby gives a seriously misleading picture of what is involved in making judgments on educational issues. It is too simple because it implies that on philosophical grounds alone we can satisfactorily answer certain questions about educational practice. This, however, is not so. By their very nature all such questions are necessarily complex and any answers based on philosophical beliefs only must therefore be regarded as ill-considered. No matter what one's ethical views may be, to ignore in issues of moral education what is known of the psychological development of moral understanding is bound to result in irresponsible judgments. Similarly to decide matters of curriculum content without due regard to social and psychological as well as philosophical considerations is quite indefensible. Whether we are thinking about particular practical decisions made whilst teaching or, as here, about the formation of general principles that state what ought to be done in practice, there are many diverse aspects to the issues that must be taken into account. The philosophical alone can never be sufficient

---

[1] For a statement and criticism of this position, see H. W. Burns: "The Logic of the 'Educational Implication,'" in *Educational Theory,* Vol. XII, No. 1, 1962.

for the task. I am not wanting to deny that on the basis of certain philosophical beliefs alone some valuable general statements about education can be made and that these have an important place in educational discussion. But I am wanting to deny what the traditional view implies, that such statements are adequately formed principles that ought to be allowed to determine our educational practice.

If this is so, it means that responsible educational principles need to be formed by a serious attempt to build together whatever knowledge, values and beliefs are relevant to the practical issues. And further, it means that between philosophical beliefs themselves and educational practice we must envisage a domain of theoretical discussion and investigation concerned with forming these principles. To this domain, which I shall refer to as educational theory, philosophical beliefs make their own distinctive contribution alongside social theory, psychological theory and so on. The traditional view that there is a direct connection between philosophy and educational practice either totally ignores, or heavily underestimates, the significance of educational theory in this sense. It fails to recognize the important truth that unless philosophical beliefs are to influence educational practice in a distorting manner, they must influence it indirectly through the medium of educational theory where they are considered conjointly with many other elements before any particular principles for educational practice are explicitly formulated.

In reply to this a traditionalist might argue that if the term philosophical beliefs is interpreted broadly enough it will embrace all the considerations that could possibly be relevant to judgments of educational principle. In this case, it would be true to say, after all, that educational principles do follow directly from philosophical beliefs. But this reply simply covers up the problem by a blanketing use of the term "philosophy." If the term is to be used so as to include psychology, sociology, and all else that is significant for education, then by definition the traditionalist is right. One can only protest at the refusal to recognize important distinctions and point out that without them we must give up all hope of distinguishing the role of philosophy in educational affairs from that of psychology, sociology, etc. For a purely verbal victory one must pay a very high price.

But secondly the traditional view is not only too simple in that it fails to recognize the many different elements that must go into the making of educational principles. It also suggests that these principles can be and ought to be formally deduced from our beliefs. And even if it is granted that philosophical beliefs are not of themselves adequate to the task, it might still be maintained that given all the necessary understanding whatever its nature, educational principles ought to be derived in much the same way as we can derive the theorems in Euclidean geometry from the axioms. This I think mistaken.

The process of deduction depends entirely on the formal manipulation of statements, and the conclusions to which it leads are therefore based solely on what is actually and literally expressed in the premises. The process must begin with statements that cover quite explicitly all the considerations that are involved in the issues. What is more, all the concepts and terms that are used must be fully related to each other so that no gaps appear in the chains of argument. Deduction can never be used unless we can start with premises equal to the task, covering all the necessary facts and beliefs and relating these so that the conclusions are reached in a purely formal manner.

Can we then set out our beliefs and knowledge in series of statements so that from them we can work out deductively what our educational principles must be? There are several reasons why in general this is impossible. Sometimes when an issue is clear cut and the factors on which it depends are limited, deduction may be used, and small pieces of deduction may well occur too as part of some larger argument. But in general the complexity of practical issues is so great that it is quite impossible to set out explicitly all the facts and beliefs which must be taken into account. Nor is this difficulty simply one of time and space for the job. Many of the terms in which we express the knowledge and beliefs that are vital for educational issues are not exact and precise but vague and ill-defined. Terms expressing personal relations and moral values are notoriously lacking in the quite clear constant meaning that the deductive use of statements assumes. Again much of our relevant understanding is not expressible in literal terms but depends on metaphor, analogy and even paradox. Deductive arguments using, or rather misusing, such statements are quite valueless even when they make sense. In addition, to evolve educational principles by deduction certainly means using, amongst other statements, a set of moral principles, and whilst these can be used formally in this way, if they are, it means that morally speaking educational judgments are being produced by rule. Yet moral principles are never once for all rules whose formal implications should be invariably accepted. They need perpetual reconsideration and reinterpretation in the light of experience. If they are used formally to produce educational principles they are likely to be as destructive of what is good in educational practice as mechanical living is in everyday affairs. Finally, it is difficult to see how conclusions that depend on the putting together of considerations from practical experience, from psychology, social theory and philosophy, weighing them up, estimating their relative importance, could possibly be reached in an uninterrupted chain of deduction. The process that is employed generally is far removed from the formal manipulation of accepted statements, being rather a form of judgment based on as comprehensive a view of the issues as it is possible to get.

Once again I am not wishing to deny that from statements of our knowledge and beliefs we can by a process of deduction come to make some valuable statements for education. It is the adequacy of these as principles for practice that I am again questioning. For the reasons given above deduction seems to be a far too limited and in some respects far too dangerously perverting a method for us to work by it uncritically in this field. It follows from the nature of adequate educational principles that in general they cannot and ought not to be formed in this way. We need to think in terms of a much looser and much more open process of judgment to which philosophical beliefs, psychological and social theory, etc. contribute in their appropriate ways. Beliefs, knowledge of facts and values provide the grounds on which judgments of educational principle are made and it is by reference to these that we give the reasons for what we advocate. But this does not mean that there is some logically necessary connection between the knowledge and beliefs on the one hand and the educational principles on the other. It is not that we work out formally our conclusions from explicit statements which are the complete and necessary grounds for the resulting principles. It is rather that in the midst of a complex network of understanding which cannot be adequately and formally expressed, we form our judgments and in the statements which we use to express our reasons, draw attention to the major considerations which have influenced us. This being so, it is not at all surprising that people who agree to certain statements of their beliefs do often in fact advocate quite different educational principles. It is not at all uncommon, for instance, to find Christians who favor a secular school system and not a few atheists judge there to be good reasons for having universal religious instruction. Contrary to the crude assumption mentioned earlier, it appears on closer inspection that educational principles that are adequate for directing practice do not follow by simple deduction from philosophical beliefs. This is borne out by the fact that philosophical agreement is no guarantee of educational agreement and fortunately many educational principles are acceptable to the holders of very diverse philosophical views. This does not mean that philosophical beliefs are unimportant for educational theory, it means simply that the part they play is not that of axioms in a deductive system. Their role is highly influential but much more subtle than that envisaged by traditionalists, being part of a broad overall understanding that lies behind all educational judgments. A philosophical system of considerable generality may of course greatly determine a set of educational principles even when other factors have been taken into account. It is then tempting to speak loosely of the principles as derived or even deduced from the system. This is however most misleading, and it would be better to describe the principles as constructed so as to be consistent with the system. Consistency between beliefs and principles denotes nothing more than the absence of any contradiction between the two. This there must be, but it by no means follows that there must also be an explicit deductive chain that leads from one to the other.

From this brief discussion of the traditional view, I suggest that in seeking to be clear about the connection between philosophy and education we must

   (i) reject the idea of a direct relationship and instead recognize the importance of a field of educational theory concerned with the formation of educational principles, and
  (ii) reject the idea that philosophical beliefs form some of the premises for deducing educational principles and instead think of them as providing some of the reasons for the educational judgments we make.

II

If the traditionalist view underestimates the importance of what I have called educational theory, the second view I wish to comment on swings radically to the opposite extreme. There is here the impressive claim that the theory of education is an autonomous discipline. Philosophical beliefs and other branches of knowledge are said to contribute to this discipline but their contributions are assessed by criteria that arise within the theory itself. Educational principles are thus formed within a theoretical framework that is in some genuine sense free from, independent of, all other disciplines, including philosophy.[2]

But what are the features of an "autonomous discipline" and are these the features that characterize educational theory? Disciplines may be demarcated from one another in more than one way. Physics, for instance, may be demarcated from chemistry because it deals with a different range of related

---

2 See F. McMurray: Preface to an Autonomous Discipline of Education, in *Educational Theory*, Vol. V, No. 3, 1955. Quoted and discussed in G. F. Kneller: Philosophy, Education and Separatism, in *Educational Theory*, Vol. XII, No. 1, 1962.

physical properties and in so doing develops techniques peculiar to itself. The two studies have distinguishable subject matters. Yet they have many points of contact and are not in any final sense separable from each other. What is more they share the same theoretical or logical structure and both rest firmly on empirical tests. They cannot be distinguished from each other in terms of any particular types of judgment that they use, only in terms of the particular subjects with which they deal. On the other hand it is maintained by some that physics and history, though they too have many points of contact can be distinguished not only in their subject matters but also in terms of their logical forms. Historical explanation is said to involve a type of judgment which the natural sciences, including physics, do not employ.[3] To explain why Hitler invaded the U.S.S.R. in 1941 depends on the use of evidence and the putting together of many strands of knowledge and conjecture in a way that has no parallel in the explanation of why it is a stick looks bent when standing at an angle in water. It is in fact in terms of distinctive types of judgment that disciplines are usually said to be autonomous. It can be claimed that history is just such an autonomous discipline. It is not claimed that there is no use of other forms of knowledge and judgment here, indeed historical explanation usually depends on a great deal of scientific investigation. But historical knowledge is said to be not entirely dependent on the forms of judgment that are used elsewhere, in some important respects historical explanations are sui generis and unique in character. Perhaps the most frequent claim of this kind is made for the autonomous character of moral judgments. These may depend on many facts and much experience, but the judgments themselves are unique in kind, clearly distinguishable from all others, for instance, those of an aesthetic or factual kind.

What then about educational theory, does it contain any unique forms of judgment? As we cannot lay down a priori that this is or is not impossible the only way for the question to be decided is for those who claim there are such to produce examples of these judgments. As far as I am aware no judgments of quite this exclusive character have been shown to occur, and it is therefore difficult to accept the claim in this extreme form. The formation of educational principles does certainly involve particular acts of judgment and these do not seem to be of a kind that occurs in the pursuit of theoretical knowledge in say the sciences or history. These are in fact practical judgments as to what ought to be done in education made on the basis of much knowledge and experience. In this way educational theory draws on a great variety of specialist disciplines, but consists of much more than a collection of isolated pieces of knowledge. A building together of these elements occurs when in the judgments rational educational principles are formed. Practical judgments are, however, not unique to educational theory for in everyday affairs and in political and social theory, for example, the same process is to be found. I would suggest that educational theory is one of a group of related theories each concerned with making similar forms of judgment, much in the same way as the various physical sciences form a related group. It is their concern to answer questions about intentional practical activities by making practical judgments that distinguishes this group of theories from other groups. And within the group it is the particular constella-

---

[3] See W. Dray: Laws and Explanation in History, O.U.P. 1957 especially chapters II and V.

tion of activities we label "educational" that determines in the first place the scope of educational theory.

Because of the nature of the questions with which it deals, educational theory is dependent on a particularly wide range of knowledge and experience. It does not however seem to me correct to speak of the theory as developing criteria of its own for assessing the knowledge and beliefs on which it draws. These forms of understanding are valid in their own rights and must therefore be accepted into the theory as they are. As their function is to provide a wider knowledge of what is involved in educational practice and so promote more responsible judgments, it is difficult to see how the knowledge itself can be assessed by criteria within the theory. The theorist has to recognize or discover the relevance of other specialist studies for education, taking these into account when he forms his principles.

If then educational theory is not in the strictest sense an autonomous discipline, it is nevertheless a distinctive theoretical pursuit which

   (i) is distinguishable like all other disciplines by the particular questions which it seeks to answer, in this case questions about a certain group of practical activities, and

  (ii) is dependent on many branches of learning, including philosophy, the understanding thus drawn on being the basis of practical judgments.

III

Though both the views I have commented on are quite widely held in educational circles, neither of them has been expounded or criticized at any length in recent British writings. The third view I wish to discuss has, however, received fairly detailed treatment by Professor D. J. O'Connor in his book "An Introduction to the Philosophy of Education." Early in this volume the author makes it clear that in his view "philosophy is not in the ordinary sense of the phrase a body of knowledge, but rather an activity of criticism or clarification" that "can be exercised on any subject matter at all, including our present concern, the problems of educational theory." This analytical activity is not "a kind of superior science" which can "be expected to answer difficult and important questions about human life, and man's place and prospects in the universe" by using special techniques.[4] It is better understood as an attempt to answer questions where the meaning of terms and their relations to each other have produced complex and far-reaching difficulties in our understanding. Problems of this kind certainly arise when we are trying to formulate educational principles, and philosophy has thus a distinctive contribution to make to educational debate. Quite clearly O'Connor assumes the distinction between philosophy and educational theory that I have previously urged, but his elaboration of the relationship between the two is largely a consequence of his idea of educational theory. Whilst in general his view of the nature of philosophy seems to me acceptable as far as it goes (and to this I will return), his account of educational theory is, I think, open to serious criticism. Indeed there are good reasons for thinking his account unsatisfactory whatever one's attitude to his philosophical position may be.

---

[4] D. J. O'Connor: *An Introduction to the Philosophy of Education*, Routledge and Kegan Paul, 1957, p. 4.

Professing to look for the "job an educational theory is supposed to do,"[5] O'Connor first distinguishes four main senses of the word "theory," two of which seem to be important in educational contexts. In one of these, theory is contrasted with practice and here the word refers to "a set or system of rules or a collection of precepts which guide or control actions of various kinds. . . . Educational theory would then consist of those parts of psychology concerned with perception, learning, concept formation, motivation and so on which directly concern the work of the teacher."[6] In the other, the word "theory" is used as it occurs in the natural sciences where it refers to a single hypothesis or a logically interconnected set of hypotheses that have been confirmed by observation. It is this sense of the word that is said to provide us with "standards by which we can assess the value and use of any claimant to the title of 'theory.' In particular this sense of the word will enable us to judge the value of the various (and often conflicting) theories that are put forward by writers on education."[7]

Judged by these standards, a great deal of educational theory certainly comes off rather badly. For as O'Connor himself states, educational discussions are not usually entirely empirical in character but include as well value judgments and appeals to metaphysical beliefs. These other two elements differ quite radically from the first as his earlier analysis of them has shown. Of metaphysical statements it is said that we have no way of confirming what they assert and that we cannot even be sure that they have any cognitive meaning at all. Their contribution to educational theory is therefore of very doubtful value. The importance of value judgments in this field is not questioned and O'Connor's chief concern is that we should recognize them for what they are so that we do not get into muddles by confusing them with assertions of fact. Nevertheless he concludes:

> We can summarize this discussion by saying that the word "theory" as it is used in educational contexts is generally a courtesy title. It is justified only where we are applying well established experimental findings in psychology or sociology to the practice of education. And even here we should be aware that the conjectural gap between our theories and the facts on which they rest is sufficiently wide to make our logical consciences uneasy. We can hope that the future development of the social sciences will narrow this gap and this hope gives an incentive for developing these sciences.[8]

The first thing that must be said about this account is that O'Connor has singularly failed to do what he set out to do—to discover the job educational theory performs. If in fact he had begun to discover this a very different picture of the theory would certainly have emerged. In addition, because of his obsession with scientific theory as a paradigm for all theories, he totally misjudges the importance of the nonscientific elements that he himself diagnoses in educational discussions. In the last analysis metaphysical statements and value

---

[5] *Ibid.,* p. 74.
[6] *Ibid.,* p. 75.
[7] *Ibid.,* p. 76.
[8] *Ibid.,* p. 110.

judgments are dismissed as not being elements that fundamentally characterize this field of discourse.

If we accept O'Connor's classification of the two main senses of the word "theory" that are important for education, it is surely the first of these that gives the primary meaning here, not the second as he suggests. Educational theory is in the first place to be understood as the essential background to rational educational practice, not as a limited would-be scientific pursuit. Even when O'Connor momentarily recognizes this, he nevertheless fails to realize the complex kind of theory that is necessary to determine a whole range of practical activities. He therefore falls back on his scientific paradigm maintaining that the theory must be simply a collection of pieces of psychology.

Yet the theories of science and the theories of practical activities are radically different in character because they perform quite different functions; they are constructed to do different jobs. In the case of the empirical sciences, a theory is a body of statements that have been subjected to empirical tests and which express our understanding of certain aspects of the physical world. Such tested theories are the objects, the end products of scientific investigation, they are the conclusions of the pursuit of knowledge. Where, however, a practical activity like education is concerned, the place of the theory is totally different. It is not the end product of the pursuit, but rather is constructed to determine and guide the activity. The function of the theory is to determine precisely what shall and shall not be done, say in education. The distinction I am drawing between scientific theory and say educational theory is the traditional distinction between knowledge that is organized for the pursuit of knowledge and the understanding of our experience, and knowledge that is organized for determining some practical activity. To try to understand the nature and pattern of some practical discourse in terms of the nature and pattern of some purely theoretical discourse can only result in its being radically misconceived.

If the theories of theoretical knowledge must be clearly distinguished from the theories of practical knowledge because they fulfill quite different functions, we must also recognize that practical theories will differ considerably amongst themselves because of the very different kinds of practical activity with which they are concerned. In some cases, as for instance in engineering, the theory is largely a reorganization of scientific theory. In the case of medicine, other elements including certain moral values are involved. Education being the kind of activity it is, the theory must range right across and draw from many kinds of knowledge, value judgments and beliefs including the metaphysical, the epistemological and the religious. All these must contribute to the peculiar character of the theory.[9]

At the beginning of his book, O'Connor gives the impression that philosophy, even of the strictest analytical variety, has some genuine contribution to make to educational theory. As the work proceeds, greater and greater importance is attached to the scientific ideal for that theory, and the contribution that philosophy can make seems to grow less and less. The final impression that is left is that philosophy is no more than an accessory to the theory, useful only when difficulties of a logical or conceptual kind arise. If we reject the scientific model as thoroughly false and artificial, with it there can go too the idea that philosophy is of only peripheral significance, even if by philosophy we still mean an analytical activity.

9 For a fuller discussion see L. A. Reid: *Philosophy and Education*, Heinemann, 1962, ch. VI.

From this contemporary point of view, philosophy does not directly lead to knowledge about the world or about ourselves; it is in fact a study of the meanings of the terms in which such knowledge is formed. If the sciences and humanities are said to be first order subjects because they seek to describe and explain the world, philosophy can be said to be a second order subject because it seeks to describe and explain the way in which first order subjects do their job.[10] In this double-decker system, lower deck activities are concerned with understanding the world, upper deck activities with understanding what goes on on the lower deck. Seen in this way, philosophy has a contribution to make to educational theory wherever second order understanding is necessary, wherever we need to know about the nature of human knowledge, about the meaning of particular concepts and so on. If educational theory is thought of as scientific in character, then this kind of understanding may well seem of only fringe significance. If however the theory is as complex as has been suggested above, it may well be of quite central importance after all.

I suggest therefore,

(i) that to think of educational theory after the pattern of scientific theory is to fail to understand the function it performs as a background to educational practice and therefore to misconceive its nature, and

(ii) that if philosophy is understood as a second order activity, there is no a priori reason to think that it has little or no significance for education; what is needed is a thorough investigation of the ways in which understanding of this kind enters into a theory concerned with the making of practical judgments.

IV

On the basis of what has already been said about the nature of educational theory and about philosophy as a second order subject, I should like to add a few very tentative comments about the relationship between the two.

By the nature of the case, philosophy will be related to educational theory in the formal sense in which it is related to other fields of discourse. It is second order to this theory in the same way as it is second order to scientific theory, legal theory and so on. Because of this, philosophy is of value whenever difficulties arise about the meaning of terms in educational discussion. "Equality of opportunity," "subject-mindedness," "the education of character" are examples of phrases of uncertain meaning which cause genuine difficulties in educational debate. They are all in need of careful philosophical clarification. But clarification of this sort does not contribute to the basic first order knowledge that the theory draws on. The philosopher is doing a formal job, clearing the lines of understanding, helping to make plain what the fundamental issues are. In a similar way philosophy can be of use to the sciences, for though it can contribute nothing of substance to them, it can contribute in this formal way when problems of meaning arise. Yet the significance of philosophical work in these two fields is very different. Generally speaking the sciences depend little on this kind of clarification for it is part of the scientific pursuit itself to construct and refine the concepts used so that they clearly express what is understood about the world. This they do directly against the empirical evidence. As has been re-

---

10 See A. J. Ayer: Philosophy and Language, an Inaugural Lecture, O.U.P. 1960.

peatedly stated, educational theory is not developed in this monolithic manner, but depends upon the bringing together of many diverse elements of understanding to form a composite theory in which practical judgments are made. In such a complex activity, serious problems of meaning frequently occur and in particular a failure to understand the relations between different fields of discourse befogs many educational issues. Behind certain questions of planning there lies the difficulty of knowing what we mean by this concept "equality of opportunity" and how we are to reconcile it with an equally difficult notion, that of "the freedom of the individual." In dealing with questions of moral education we must be able to relate together all the relevant understanding that we have from moral insight, religious beliefs, and accounts of psychological development, etc. The formal contribution that philosophy makes to educational theory in cases of this sort is surely of major importance. If philosophy is an accessory to the theory, then it would seem to be rather like some crucial tool without which it is hard to see how the various bits of the machine can be put together.

But besides this formal contribution to educational theory, philosophy does also seem to contribute to its "substance." Philosophical analyses are themselves part of the basic evidence on which certain judgments of educational principle are made. They constitute one of the diverse elements that are brought together as the material out of which educational theory is built. To take again the example of moral education, it is not enough when dealing with questions in this area to have moral insight, psychological knowledge, and religious beliefs and be able to relate all this understanding. We must also know what moral judgments are, how they differ from other judgments and how they are justified. Only with knowledge of this kind can we be aware of a great deal of what moral education is about. Similarly in discussing the place of the physical sciences in education and the content of courses in them, an understanding of the nature and scope of these sciences is indispensable as well as much scientific knowledge, a grasp of the psychology of scientific understanding, an awareness of society's scientific needs and so on. Educational theory needs then the aid of philosophy in a "substantial" sense, for it needs understanding which only philosophical investigation can provide. It would seem that the analytical philosopher can after all be said to contribute philosophical beliefs to educational theory, but because of their particular second order character he would wish to distinguish them from other beliefs, say religious and moral, which the theory will include.

In an attempt to make out an exclusive field for philosophy of education, it might be maintained that only the formal function of philosophy for the theory is strictly speaking its concern, moral philosophy, philosophy of science and other branches being able to make the "substantial" contribution. Such a distinction is, I think, unfortunate. In practice the distinction between the two functions is almost impossible to draw, for the "substantial" contribution of some piece of philosophical analysis to the theory is likely to provide help in formal clarification too. In addition many of the problems of formal significance have been discussed by philosophers in other contexts so that philosophy of education in this sense would not be unique in its subject matter. What is important is not any dispute over labels, but a recognition of the distinctive character of the contribution that philosophy makes to the theory and an awareness of the extent to which it is necessary.

V

From this discussion the following conclusions about the relationship between philosophy and education can be drawn.

1. A satisfactory account of the relationship turns on
   (a) the recognition of a distinctive body of theory whose function is the determination of educational practice, and
   (b) the clarification of the distinctive contribution that philosophy makes to educational theory.

2. Educational theory is thoroughly composite in character and is not on the one hand describable after the pattern of some other theory, but neither is it on the other hand in a strict sense autonomous. Such misunderstandings of its nature only serve to distort any attempt to clarify its relationship to philosophy.

3. Educational theory is distinctive because of the particular questions with which it is concerned, questions about a range of intentional activities. It is the theory which in practical judgments determines what ought to be and what ought not to be done in educational practice.

4. Understood as a second order activity, philosophy contributes both formally and in a "substantial" sense to educational theory. This contribution is in part one of second order, or philosophical, beliefs.

5. Though educational theory must be built so as to be consistent with some set of philosophical and other beliefs, it is not in general deduced from these and there is no logically necessary relationship between the two. As in addition the theory is by no means entirely philosophical in character but radically complex, "educational theory" seems to me a much less misleading term for it than the more traditional phrase "a philosophy of education."

6. The term "philosophy of education" is perhaps best used to refer to the comprehensive contribution of distinctively philosophical methods of investigation to the discussion of problems that occur within educational theory.

These conclusions are of more than theoretical interest. There is a marked tendency for those involved in the work and teaching of philosophy of education to look at things from a firmly traditional angle, seeing educational theory as largely determined by philosophy. The result is frequently a very superficial consideration of the vast field of philosophy in general and an attempt to draw some educational principles from this without serious appeal to other fields of knowledge. It has here been contended that the function of philosophy for educational theory is more rightly understood and better exercised by working in the opposite direction. This means starting with questions about educational practice that occur within the theory, philosophical clarification and understanding being directly brought to bear on the principles that these involve. Educational theory is primarily concerned with making practical judgments in answer to practical questions and it looks to philosophy and other studies for the particular forms of help they can provide. But educational practice brooks no delay and it often seems that whilst philosophers are busy debating the possible implications of certain beliefs for education, the philosophical contribution that educational theory really needs goes by default. There is indeed a pressing need for the development of philosophically informed educational principles, but these can only be achieved if those engaged in the work and teaching of philosophy of education direct their attention to philosophical questions that arise from specific educational issues.

CHAPTER VIII
Educational Critics and Crucial Issues

The contemporary educational scene in America, where there is a greater reliance on process than there is on static knowledge and where the emphasis is on learning for all, is without precedence. Dr. Carl R. Rogers, resident fellow at Western Behavioral Sciences Institute, La Jolla, California, told conferees at the annual meeting (Spring–1967) of the Association for Supervision and Curriculum Development that: "We are . . . faced with an entirely new situation in education where the goal of education, if we are to survive, is the facilitation of change and learning." He went on to say that the only man who is educated is the one who has learned how to learn, how to adapt and change. That he is a man who realizes that since no knowledge is secure, the only basis for security is the process of seeking knowledge.

Dr. Clark Kerr, former President of the University of California, has said that we are entering an era where status is no longer determined by birth but depends largely upon learned skills and abilities. Certainly, we see fewer restrictions on individual opportunity for education and training, and on occupational choice because of membership in a minority group, or because of sex, race, place of birth, or residence than heretofore. Education has been an important factor in this regard, and continued progress places even greater demands on education, for individual civil obligations increase in proportion to the freedom to realize personal goals. The strengthening of the role and function of education calls for an enlightened citizenry conversant with the crucial issues in education and for professional educators who distinguish between valid and invalid criticism.

Historically, educational systems have been used to serve the church, the aristocracy, or some other institution. Today, although the various connections between education and government, technology, the military complex, and other special interest groups cannot be ignored, the idea prevails that education *can* be for all of the people, that it can be both the servant

309

of the people and an independent force in society. The realization that the individual role is largely dependent upon the kind and the degree of education that is available increases personal involvement with educational activities. In 1966 the United States Office of Education listed over 110,000 public educational institutions at all levels. The teachers within these schools and colleges numbered approximately 3,000,000, and the student enrollment was in the neighborhood of 56,000,000. It has been estimated that by 1970 there will be more than 7,500,000 college students in the United States. The number of teachers and administrators made up the largest single segment of our national work force, about 3,500,000 people, and nearly 115,000 citizens spent part of their time participating as school board members who exercise some measure of control over educational decisions.

Policy-making resides with the boards of education at state and local levels, and the citizen exercises his control through elections and by the way he votes on school bonds or increases in school taxes. Whether or not state law makes it mandatory that the school boards are insulated from partisan politics, the level of public expenditures for education is as much a political decision, and rightly so, as the level of expenditures for highways, medical care, or national defense. Legally, school boards have the power to enter into contracts, levy taxes, disperse school funds, acquire property, enter into bonded indebtedness, enact changes in the school curriculum, and establish procedure for hiring and firing school personnel.

As work has become more mental, the university has become more and more essential to the professions, agriculture, and industry, and the time is coming when the whole population may be served by university extension. However, the vastness and the inherent power of the educational enterprise is bound to generate negative as well as positive reactions. Those who fail to acquire advanced degrees are often disgruntled and prone to be suspicious of the so-called intellectuals. These are apt to place the blame for their own failure on the educational system and stand in opposition to the educators who consider intellectual goals to be more significant than nonintellectual ones. Adherents and critics alike keep the educational scene in turmoil. The tradition that education in the United States is the responsibility of the people results in a nation of educational critics who range from those who view education as a panacea to those who claim that it paves the way to total destruction. It is indeed a multifarious population that determines the kind of education that ought to be provided, the methods for financing education, and the improvement of curricular material. It is not surprising to find the intellectuals in conflict with the rest of society about goals and how they should be achieved.

During the 1930's and the 1940's there was at least a connection between the trade union movements and the intellectuals, but that has disappeared, and during the last few years the gap between the two seems to have widened. There is disagreement about Vietnam policy, about civil rights, and about questions of academic freedom. Students have become involved in demonstrations for student rights, participation in school policy decisions, and educational reforms such as those advocated by the Free Speech Movement. They set up their own committees to investigate a variety of areas which they believe have a direct bearing on their educational opportunities and demand a voice in administrative decisions. Many adults are disturbed by the political activities of students and demand discipline, control, and adherence to traditional values. They want youth to be controlled with a heavy hand and view the ivory towers of academia as havens for communists. Many feel that the universities which do not adhere to any rigid system of morality but merely teach that a fact is better than a rumor, that logic is better than confusion, are failing to meet the proper challenge.

All in all, false reports, distortions, and lack of real communication, accent the mutual suspicions between the educators, administrators, students, politicians, and the general public. The schools are constantly confronted with real or threatened conflict with the public, and a multiplicity of self-styled critics of education sometimes do more to impede educational progress and change than they do to facilitate it. Educators who are forced to some kind of response to such criticisms frequently dissipate efforts and talents which could be used to far better advantage, but it is important for teachers to be informed about the different kinds of critics and criticisms of education in order to recognize valid critiques and to concern themselves in a positive manner.

The immediate objective of Chapter VIII is twofold. Our first task is to become familiar with the different kinds of educational critiques in order to make an assessment of their impact on educational directives, and to be able to judge the validity of a critique. The second undertaking is a consideration of some of the crucial issues that shape contemporary educational practice and suggest future trends in American education. The overriding purpose of the chapter is to sketch the changing societal, political, and intellectual elements that make new demands on the educational philosopher and on the teacher. The redefinition of these roles will be the prime concern of the concluding chapter of our study.

Critics and Criticism

The American educational system is a good deal more than a "happening." It is the culmination of half a century of research and theoretical speculation in an attempt to discover how skills, attitudes, and understanding may best be learned. Schools, the most influential institutions in our society, are highly complex organizations which affect the lives of all individuals in one way or another. Perhaps it is because the school is generally viewed as the primary instrument for shaping the citizen that Americans are so ambivalent about education. Or perhaps it stems from the belief that neutrality in education is impossible, and therefore education must either be directed to maintain the *status quo,* or to implement changes in it. Whatever the reason, even as Americans place the highest value on education, they are traditionally suspicious of the educated.

George Wallace, former governor of Alabama, predicting "political upheaval" in the United States, said at a news conference in June of 1967, that "The people are tired of professors sitting in ivory towers looking down their noses at us." The idea seems to be that education that gets you something—a better job, power, money, or the like—is desirable. But education that intrigues with ideas, that suggests new horizons, that inspires creative thinking, and challenges old ideas, is automatically suspect.

Americans also have an intense suspicion of authority, and the power that is imputed to teachers makes them prime targets for criticism. The idea is that the most effective way to deal with those who threaten to become too powerful, if you cannot replace them or join them, is to cut them down to size. The media of the popular press contribute markedly in this regard. Teachers and teaching seem to evoke all sorts of emotional reactions, and one is not likely to pick up a magazine or a newspaper that does not supplement the controversy over the miseducation of teachers, or add to the volumes of educational criticisms which range from the ridiculous to the considered, from the vicious to the pontifical. Much of the popular criticism is prompted and furthered by fear of the future, by fear of the threat of war, or of automation, or by resistance to change and progress. When things are not going right in the larger societal context, it seems that Americans look first to the schools for a place to fix the blame.

Certainly, even though much of the popular criticism is unwarranted and therefore meaningless for constructive change, there is much about the schools that can and should be criticized. Whatever else it may be, American education is not static. Self-evaluation and self-criticism are essential to good growth. We have arrived at a crucial point in the history of education when it is time to review the theoretical ideas and tested propositions which are the base of our educational programs. The ideas and principles may be fundamentally sound, but in the face of widespread criticism, we must strive to respond constructively and turn criticism to intellectual advantage. This age of automation, this twentieth century space age, calls for a reappraisal of our educational concepts and beliefs in order that we may determine what is worth defending and what should be discarded for newer ideas. There is little doubt but that the new experiences and the changing conditions of the twentieth century call for corresponding changes in our educational thought, and we need to develop a theoretical framework wherein we may effect a synthesis of the best of the old with the best of the new.

One important step in this direction is the ability to recognize the validity or the invalidity of educational criticism and to be able to distinguish between the kinds of critiques. It would be as foolish to assert that all popular criticism·is trivial as it would be to maintain that all theoretical criticism is necessarily meaningful, for education may well profit from both the popular and the theoretical. The point is to clear away pseudo-problems and pseudo-questions, to recognize logical inconsistencies, to pinpoint erroneous lines of reasoning and conceptual blunders, and to explore the dimensions of educational terminology in order to have a firm base for meaningful educational theorizing. Toward this end, the following discussion will be concerned with various levels of educational criticism.

Theoretical Critics

The critics in this group are either professional educators, generally professors or administrators, or scholars who may or may not have had formal training in education but who have given serious thought to educational problems. These scholars tend to be more severely self-critical than those of any other professional group. The theoretical or philosophical critic bases his criticisms on a particular theory which is the achievement of abstract or general principles arrived at through the ordering of facts. To a degree, a theory evolves out of speculation, but it must be verifiable in order to explain satisfactorily the discrete elements of experience. A theoretical critic of education, therefore, is one who proposes clear, general principles for explaining educational phenomena. The explanations are offered as logically coherent guidelines for directing educational choices in respect to aims, methods, and curriculum. It is self-evident then that in order to deal effectively with an educational critique a recognition of the underlying theory is essential.

It is unfortunate that the public is seldom acquainted with these critics and their theories, but it is understandable, for their writing is usually highly technical and lacks the sensationalism that seems to appeal to the mass media. Most often the theoretical critic deals with an entire system, or with theory *per se,* which is proper material for educational journals but has little popular appeal. Theoretical critics may comment upon specific aspects of a school program by way of illustration, but their goals are generally more far reaching than any specifics. Alfred North Whitehead, whose *Aims of Education* is a landmark in critiques of education, is one of the most significant of all of the theoretical critics.

Alfred North Whitehead was born February 15, 1861 at Ramsgate in the Isle of Thanet, Kent. The members of his family were variously engaged in education, religion, and local administration. Both his father and his grandfather were successful schoolmasters until the father gave up his school for clerical duties when he was ordained as a clergyman of the Anglican Church. Whitehead's early education conformed to the normal standard of the time with Latin at the age of ten and Greek at twelve. His classical studies were interspersed with mathematics which became his major interest. He attended Trinity College, Cambridge from 1880 until the summer of 1910, first as a "scholar" and later as a "fellow." He was married in 1890 to Evelyn Willoughby Wade whose influence he credits as being an essential factor in his philosophic output. He writes in his autobiographical notes that "Her vivid life has taught me that beauty, moral and aesthetic, is the aim of existence; and that kindness, and love, and artistic satisfaction are among its modes of attainment. Logic and Science are the disclosure of relevant patterns and also procure the avoidance of irrelevancies."[1]

Whitehead's first book, *A Treatise on Universal Algebra,* was seven years in the writing, and led to his election to the Royal Society in 1903. For a year after Whitehead left Cambridge in 1910 he held no academic position but spent the time in London writing his *Introduction to Mathematics.* During the next three years Whitehead held various positions at University College, London, and from 1914 to the summer of 1924 he was a professor at the Imperial College of Science and Technology in Kensington where in the later years he was Dean of the Academic Council. He began his philosophic writings in London at the latter end of the war, and when he was sixty-three he joined the Faculty of Harvard University in the Philosophy Department, where he became Professor Emeritus in 1937. Whitehead concludes his autobiographical notes with the following statement:

> To-day in America, there is a zeal for knowledge which is reminiscent of the great periods of Greece and the Renaissance. But above all, there is in all sections of the population a warm-hearted kindness which is unsurpassed in any large social system.[2]

Many who approach Whitehead's philosophy are discouraged by his involved terminology and suggest that his thinking is obscure to the point of confusion. On the other hand, his writings on educational matters are noted for their clarity and conciseness. The bulk of his writings on education are found in *The Aims of Education and Other Essays* and in *Essays in Science and Philosophy.* They bear the mark of the philosophic critic, for throughout the works there is a consistent relationship between Whitehead's general philosophy of organismic development and his thoughts on education. The presentation of his ideas follows the pattern of aims, methods, and curriculum, and woven throughout are his comments about the students and the things that should occur for the intellectual and emotional growth of the individual.

The basic aim of education, according to Whitehead, is to provide for the development of a man of culture who has expert knowledge and who is capable of creative responses. Every caution should be taken to guard against presenting the child with what Whitehead calls "inert ideas," those ideas which are not tested nor used but are simply assimilated. The whole approach is a protest against dead knowledge which is anathema to Whitehead. Knowledge of the past is justifiable, Whitehead believes, only

---

[1] Alfred North Whitehead, *Science and Philosophy* (Patterson, N.J.: Littlefield, Adams & Co., 1964), p. 15.
[2] *Ibid.,* p. 21.

insofar as it serves the present, and unutilized ideas may actually be harmful.

Whitehead maintained that it is far better to teach a few subjects well and thoroughly than it is to present superficial information about many subjects. Ideas introduced into a child's education should be few, important, and connected. They should be presented in every possible combination until the child makes them his own, and all theoretical ideas should fit into a connected curriculum. Ideas, knowledge, and education are nothing unless they are useful, and the first thing to do with an idea in scientific training is to prove its worth. Since it is an essential part of the activity to prove the truth of the propositions, either by experiment or by logic, the two processes of proof should proceed concurrently.

Whitehead believed that education ought to impart "an intimate sense for the power of ideas, for the beauty of ideas, and for the structure of ideas, together with a particular body of knowledge which has peculiar reference to the life of the being possessing it."[3] The power of ideas, as we have noted, involves a rejection of inert ideas and an acceptance of the utility of knowledge. It implies that ideas should contribute to the self-development of the man of culture. The sense of beauty in ideas is movement toward the aesthetic appreciation of ideas and has special relevance when associated with the appreciation of the structure of ideas. The last and most useful acquirement of the educated mind is style which should pervade the whole being. Our power is increased by style which fashions and restrains the power. Style is the exclusive privilege of the expert, for it is the product of specialist study and the "ultimate morality of mind."[4] Whitehead concludes his essay on the aims of education by describing the essence of education as being religious. In response to his own question about the nature of education, he says:

> A religious education is an education which inculcates duty and reverence. Duty arises from our potential control over the course of events. Where attainable knowledge could have changed the issue, ignorance has the guilt of vice. And the foundation of reverence is this perception, that the present holds within itself the complete sum of existence, backwards and forwards, that whole amplitude of time, which is eternity.[5]

Whitehead is not concerned with an analysis of the lecture method versus the discussion method, as his approach to the problem is more in keeping with the philosophic method of Hegel. The specific terms Whitehead suggests are the stages of: 1) romance; 2) precision; and 3) generalization. The first stage of intellectual progress involves novelty and excitement, rather than system and precision. The preliminary stage is followed by

---

[3] Alfred North Whitehead, *The Aims of Education and Other Essays* (Toronto, Ontario: Collier-Macmillan Canada, Ltd., 1967, First Free Press Paperback Edition), p. 12.
[4] *Ibid.*, p. 12.
[5] *Ibid.*, p. 14.

precision, which represents exactness or analysis, and can only build upon the facts gained through romance. The second stage is characterized by order and system. In the final stage, generalization, the essence of romanticism comes into prominence with the added quality of "classified ideas and relevant technique."[6] The excitement of knowledge, coupled with the precision of learning, culminates in some type of control over the life of the individual, and there is the suggestion that what counts is the application or the use of knowledge. Properly handled, the stages of mental development will result in a life of order and symmetry. This cyclic view suggested by Whitehead implies a development from infancy to adulthood with the thread of a "self" running throughout. The rhythmic character of growth is a good description of the view. Whitehead states: "It is that the development of mentality exhibits itself as a rhythm involving an interweaving of cycles, the whole process being dominated by a greater cycle of the same general character as its minor eddies."[7]

Whitehead rejects two traditional approaches to method, giving short shrift to the dictum that claims knowledge should begin with the simplest and proceed to the most difficult. He points to the fact that, although one of the most difficult tasks is to acquire a language, it is a task readily achieved by small children. He also rejects the principle of necessary progression of subject matter, for an uncritical application of the principle will produce a barren education. The stages of mental development are crucial to Whitehead who believed that subjects and ideas must be attuned to the existing mental capacity of the child. We see an affinity in this regard between Whitehead and Dewey and also in the idea that complicated instruments and apparatus are not necessary for the best education of the child. The logical conclusion of the methods outlined by Whitehead is wisdom, which surpasses mere knowledge. As Whitehead says, ". . . wisdom is the way in which knowledge is held. It concerns the handling of knowledge, its selection for the determination of relevant issues, its employment to add value to our immediate experience."[8]

Whitehead believed that the only subject matter for education is life in all of its manifestations, and one of his main criticisms of current practice was that instead of this single unity, children were offered "Algebra, from which nothing follows; Geometry, from which nothing follows; Science, from which nothing follows; History, from which nothing follows; a Couple of Languages, never mastered; and lastly, most dreary of all, Literature, represented by plays of Shakespeare, with philological notes and short analyses of plot and character to be in substance committed to memory."[9] He viewed such an offering as little more than a table of contents, rather than a representation of the fullness of life. Whitehead elab-

---

[6] *Ibid.,* p. 19.
[7] *Ibid.,* p. 27.
[8] *Ibid.* (The Rhythmic Claims of Freedom and Discipline), p. 30.
[9] *Ibid.,* p. 7.

orates on the idea of "Life" forming the content of the curriculum in his *Essays on Science and Philosophy*. He states that:

> In the democracy of the future every man and every woman will be trained for a free intellectual life by an education which is directly related to their immediate lives as citizens and as workers, and thereby elicits speculations and curiosities and hopes which range through the whole universe.[10]

Synthesis of opposites plays an important role, and the curriculum must begin and end with content that has meaning and relevance for the lives of workers and citizens. A healthy speculation about life, society, and the cosmos should be promoted by means of the curriculum. Whitehead's suggestions are not idealistic in the sense that they are detached from the reality of school procedure, for he is well aware of the pressures of time. Rather than making additional demands on the already overloaded curriculum, Whitehead posited that his synthesis should arise from connections to be realized out of the existing content and by the individual student who must ultimately educate himself.

Whitehead's analysis of the processes of general education involves both a language-literary stage, and a scientific stage, after which the student must let one of the curricula pass into the stage of generalization. The outcome of the literary cycle has a humanistic orientation, where the mind is given the opportunity to develop logically, aesthetically, historically, and philosophically. The classics can play a role in this development, but their traditional claim of "necessity" cannot hold up for the modern world. The scientific curriculum is best illustrated by the abstractions and generalizations of mathematics and the manner in which they are applied to the concrete facts. Whitehead felt impelled to allow for specialism, although he admitted that it seemed contradictory to his design of a curriculum for broad culture. He maintained that man is naturally specialist, that one man sees a whole subject, while others realize only detached parts of it. It was his feeling that if specialism is excluded, life is destroyed.

Whitehead's educated man exhibits fellow-feeling interest and enjoyment in his chosen activities, but most of all he exhibits a sense of duty and responsibility. Religious feelings should predominate, but here Whitehead has reference to the spiritual attitude that results in a sense of value and importance of man to man and to the universe, rather than to any specific religion. In sum, the individual is primary in the educational scene, and self-development is the final goal of education. The essence of education is religious which implies a love of duty and a reverence for eternity. Education must be both abstract and applicable, and wisdom and understanding are the ultimate educational outcomes.

---

[10] Whitehead, *Science and Philosophy, op. cit.*, pp. 180–181.

Public Theoretical Critics

There are a number of theoretical critics who are distinct from scholars such as Whitehead in that they speak both to the layman and the educator. They, too, are scholars who are predominantly concerned about educational ideals and directives, but because of a conviction that in the final analysis the general public will have more control over education issues than educators are able to implement, they write with the layman in mind. Toward this end, they are more apt to write in terms of the particular and to stress specific suggestions that they feel should be followed. Scholars whose educational critiques are theoretically based and who have the attention and respect of their colleagues, as well as a following among the general public, are relatively few in the United States today. James Conant and Robert Hutchins are probably the best known of these. Both are highly qualified, experienced scholars and educators; both exhibit an earnest concern for the betterment of American education. But we shall see that their theoretical bases, their methods and their diagnoses, and the solutions they offer are widely divergent.

James Bryant Conant was born in Massachusetts in 1893. He received his education at Harvard where he became assistant professor of chemistry, then Head of the Chemistry Department, and in 1933 President of the University. He served in that capacity until 1953 when he became U.S. High Commissioner of Germany. He later was made Ambassador to Germany and held the post until 1957 when he returned to the United States to a full-time study of public education in America. He has authored over a dozen books and numerous articles for educational journals and popular magazines. The career of this educator, statesman, and scientist continues to be a distinguished one, as he probably has more influence on American education than any contemporary critic. Certainly he has done a remarkable job in presenting an objective picture of the educational situation to the general public. His assessments are based on extensive research, and he deals with facts rather than with sweeping generalities. For the most part, he is optimistic about the American educational situation, and his criticisms are considered and constructive.

Dr. Conant's two-year study of the American public high school was done under a grant from the Carnegie Corporation administered by the Educational Testing Service of Princeton, New Jersey. The focus of his study was the comprehensive high school, which is any school that provides secondary academic and vocational education for all of the high school age children of one area. Assisted by four experienced co-workers, Dr. Conant concentrated his attention on schools with a graduating class of at least one hundred, in twenty-six states. He personally visited fifty-five of these schools in eighteen of the most populous states.

Some educational critics overlook the rather obvious fact that there are reasons for the kind of public tax-supported educational system that we have in America. The system is not merely some horrible mistake that the so-called educationalists have foisted on an unsuspecting public. It is the logical development of the best of American traditions. Dr. Conant's report, *The American High School Today*,[11] begins with an excellent summary of the characteristics of American public education and the basic underlying assumptions that determine the pattern. Dr. Conant leaves no doubt in the reader's mind as to his belief in the significance of the comprehensive high school which is unique in America.

The report is not intended as a survey of the comprehensive high school, as Dr. Conant makes it clear that he does not believe it possible to realize the kind of information that might justify generalizations about the success or failure of the system. His positing that valid judgments about American secondary education can only be made school by school is one of the basic premises of the report. The one general conclusion that Dr. Conant feels is justified, is that there are three requisites for a good high school. These are: 1) a good school board which is devoted to policy making, rather than to administration; 2) a first-rate superintendent; and 3) good principal. He assumes that the development of the curriculum will be left to the administrative officers and the teaching staff but that the board members will reserve the right to ask searching questions about the details of the curriculum through the proper channels. Dr. Conant says:

> Given a good school board and strong leadership by the superintendent and principal, an excellent group of teachers will be recruited, and it is hardly necessary to emphasize that on the quality of the teachers (assuming wise leadership) the quality of the education must ultimately depend.[12]

The twenty-one recommendations of the report include only those features which Dr. Conant observed to be well-established in at least one of the schools that were visited. For this reason, some of the new departures whose merit has not yet been proven to Dr. Conant's satisfaction were not included in the recommendations. Dr. Conant admits that his recommendations are conservative but hopes that, because they are presented in what he believes to be necessarily a rather dogmatic form, it will not be assumed that he is among those who would like to freeze the development of the curriculum and maintain an organizational *status quo*. Whether or not one agrees with Dr. Conant's conclusions about the comprehensive high school and with his suggestions for its improvement is not the case at point. Whatever one's views, it must be admitted that Dr. Conant's report exemplifies the highest type of educational critique. The research is thorough, the reporting is objective and well documented, the premises are clearly stated, and the logical development of ideas leads to valid conclusions that are the

11 James B. Conant, *The American High School Today* (New York: McGraw-Hill Book Company, Inc., 1959).
12 *Ibid.*, pp. 38–39.

base for constructive suggestions. Dr. Conant concludes his report with this statement:

> As I have already stated, I am convinced American secondary education can be made satisfactory without any radical changes in the basic pattern. This can only be done, however, if the citizens in many localities display sufficient interest in their schools and are willing to support them. The improvements must come school by school and be made with due regard for the nature of the community. Therefore, I conclude by addressing this final word to citizens who are concerned with public education: avoid generalizations, recognize the necessity of diversity, get the facts about your local situation, elect a good school board, and support the efforts of the board to improve the schools.[13]

Conant's educational views are those of the realist who believes that man realizes faithful and direct knowledge of the world about him through the media of his senses. Realists vary according to the emphasis they place upon empiricism or rationalism, but most agree to the idea of balance, to a federation of the sources of knowledge. They see truth as the adherence of judgment to experience and would never agree to a separation between experience and learning. The realist is suspicious of generalizations, has a real respect for science, and recognizes the affinity between science and philosophy. The realist does not consider that a quiet contemplation of the so-called "eternal truths" is the most significant way to meet crucial issues in a changing society, for there is no one inevitable answer to questions about the mind, freedom, purpose, and the good. The view of the realist is one which is acceptable to most contemporary thinking.

On the other hand, theorists whose criticisms of contemporary education are inclined to be reactionary generally accept the view of the classical humanist. Classical humanism emphasizes a common nature to man that transcends any particular time or society and maintains that the power of reason can be most effectively cultivated by a study of the classics which are thought to provide an authoritative, universal, moral and intellectual tradition. Mind is thought to be composed of special faculties (an idea which has been discredited by experimental research done in recent years), which can be developed through discipline, with no reference to environment and experience.

Practicing educators of this persuasion include scholars such as Stringfellow Barr, Mark Van Doren, Mortimer Adler, and Robert Maynard Hutchins. Hutchins, although not as well equipped philosophically as others who share his views, will likely be recorded in history as the most influential member of the grouping. He is one of the most widely read of the educational theorists who insist that education should not be directed

---

[13] *Ibid.*, p. 96.

toward guiding social interpretation and action, and his pessimistic conclusions about American education appeal to those who fear the implications of twentieth century technological progress. His enthusiastic supporters among the lay public are not troubled by the fact that his educational theories are not based upon the sort of school research that makes Dr. Conant's suggestions meaningful to most educators.

Robert Hutchins became President of the University of Chicago at the age of thirty and served in the position until 1945 when he became Chancellor of that institution. He resigned from the Chancellorship in 1951 to become Associate Director of the Ford Foundation, and since 1954 he has served as President for the Fund for the Republic and as Director of the Center for the Study of Democratic Institutions. During this time his writings and criticisms of contemporary education have appeared in many journals and popular magazines, and his views have remained consistent to the point of rigidity throughout the years. As early as 1936 his book, *The Higher Learning in America,*[14] called for a uniform, liberal education that would transcend the provincialism of local societies, and thirty years later he reiterated the same theme in an article for the *Saturday Evening Post* entitled, "Colleges are Obsolete."

The primary target of Hutchins' educational critiques has long been the American system of higher education. He is prone to comparisons, and he finds the European "university" far superior to any spawning of American democracy. Hutchins believes that colleges of liberal arts are a conglomerate of trivia, that the degrees they offer merely signify that a student has broken no laws and has been able to regurgitate the inconsequential bits of anti-intellectualism he has been spoon-fed by his teachers. He maintains that the university is distinguished only by professional schools that are meaningless and by the Ph.D. degree which is no more than a badge or insignia of the university teacher. Hutchins peppers his comments about higher education in America with expressions such as "the magic parchment," students who "serve their time," a curriculum of "hilarious courses," and the takeover of "trivialities." He assumes a uniformity of character that makes one high school indistinguishable from all of the others and charges that all are confused, all offer the same course of study for all groups, and that the course of study is always geared for the few who are marked for higher learning. He says that the junior college is merely an extension of the high school curriculum which he so thoroughly discredits.

Critics who believe that our educational problems can be solved only after current theories and practices have been replaced by those of their own recommendation find it necessary to discredit existing systems and education directives. This Herculean task requires the sort of "intellectual legerdemain" that depends more upon sophisticated persuasiveness than it does upon empirical data, and it is important to be able to distinguish between the two approaches. Regardless of whether or not one approves

---

14 Robert M. Hutchins, *The Higher Learning in America* (New Haven: Yale University Press, 1936).

of the program proposed by the classical humanists, one should be alerted by the fact that they completely discredit the existing democratic educational ideals. Granting that American education is not without many flaws and shortcomings, the assumption that it has no merit and should be completely scrapped scarcely seems reasonable. However, according to Hutchins, once the "trivia" of the American system has been cleared away, little remains, and the way is clear for his alternative, "a return to the classics."

Hutchins' view that truth is always the same for all men prompts him to propose a careful reading of the most distinguished works of the leading minds in history for the best general education. An education such as he proposed, designed to draw out the elements of our common human nature, suggests that the classics be read for the "transcendental truths" they contain as well as for mental discipline. Ideally, Hutchins would relegate general education to the junior college, and higher learning for those students who have clearly demonstrated their superior ability would begin at about the age of twenty-one. Hutchins' reorganized university would have only three main divisions: 1) philosophy; 2) the natural sciences; and 3) the social sciences. He would set up "research institutes" on the fringe of the university, but the members would not have faculty status.

Although he recognizes the need of collecting certain facts and sense data, Hutchins believes that these are important only for illuminating the self-evident first principles. Finally, he would allow the establishment of "technical institutions" for training the lawyers, teachers, and doctors who had already received the bulk of their education at the universities. One can only speculate as to the efficacy of the program as the best possible preparation for democratic rule, for since Hutchins views the scientific method as an inferior way to acquire knowledge, his program is not open to scientific scrutiny. The point to be made here is that such speculation should not be based merely on particular points of agreement or disagreement but on the basis of the underlying theoretical structure and within the framework of our democratic rule.

Popular Critics

There is a sprinkling of scholars and educators among the popular critics of education, but for the most part the number consists of public figures, professional writers, and lay people who may or who may not have any direct connection with education. Professional writers, newspaper columnists, and magazine contributors include many well-informed and thoughtful critics of education, but not all have an understanding of the complexities of American education, and few of the popular critics have developed any sort of theoretical base. As we have noted, this does not necessarily invalidate their criticisms; but the categories are distinct and should be judged accordingly.

The bulk of popular criticism seems to be prompted by reaction to some social crisis, or it may occur in response to one of the crucial issues in society or a feeling of nostalgia for "the good old days." These criticisms are frequently on the emotional side and are often characterized by charges and counter charges, by particulars blown into generalizations or categorical imperatives, by an admixture of fact and fancy, documentation and myth, sense, and nonsense. The need for an alert, questioning attitude toward such critics is obvious, and if teachers hope to respond in a meaningful way to legitimate complaints they must develop the ability to discriminate, to analyze, to make accurate judgments, and to be objective.

The American public was stunned on October 4, 1957 when Russia put the first space satellite into orbit. It was only a short time before all were informed that the American schools were to blame because the Deweyites failed to emphasize science education. A report on Russian education released by the U.S. Office of Education five weeks after Sputnik I was one of the few such publications to be featured as a lead story in the *New York Times,* and for months almost every periodical featured articles and stories about Russian education or about the scientific disciplines being neglected in American schools for something called "life adjustment."

There could be little doubt but that the Russians were educating more and better scientists than Americans, and something must be done to rectify the mistake. Most of the critics completely overlooked the fact that the scientists responsible for Sputnik I could have been the products of the pre-Revolutionary schools, rather than of the contemporary Soviet education which they praised so highly. Never before have there been so many critics of education, or so many variations on the same theme, with the teacher always cast in the role of the villain. Chastened educators remained mute but managed to regroup their forces in time to leap on the band wagon in support of the Hill-Elliott (NDEA) bill. No one seems to think it the least bit strange that the passage of the bill brought forth another rash of education critiques by those who dolefully predict that Federal aid will result in Federal control of education and in a loss of academic freedom.

The majority of criticisms that were prompted by the fear that Russia would "outspace" America concentrate on a comparison of educational systems in terms of exaggerated praise of the one and condemnation of the other. Arthur Bestor, a professor of history and one of the most vocal of the popular critics, told a reporter for the *U.S. News & World Report* that American secondary education declined in quality because of the confusion of the professional educators. The teachers, according to Bestor, merely obeyed orders to push aside the fundamentals in favor of teaching students how to act on dates and how to select good radio programs. He pointed out that the Soviet secondary grades spend forty per cent of the time on science and mathematics and that they don't play at it. The implication is that for Americans education time is play time.

A report on education and professional employment in the U. S. S. R., prepared for the National Science Foundation in 1961, shows that the scientific and technical orientation of Soviet schooling has been and will probably continue to be considerably intensified since 1956, but that the general academic education, especially the social sciences and the humanities, have suffered by comparison. According to the report, ". . . political bias permeates every subject of instruction," and the subject matter of instruction is slanted to ". . . make sure that students consciously adopt a materialistic outlook and militant antireligious attitude." The report states that Soviet education is designed to perform ". . . certain tasks of political and moral indoctrination . . ." and demonstrates the price of the overdisciplined and overdirection of education by the following statement made by a Soviet statesman:

> The Soviet secondary school does not develop, but stifles all initiative. . . . Learning without direction does not exist. . . . Even such voluntary activities as Komsomol meetings can take place only when a school director or teacher-supervisor is present. . . . The quality of work of the teachers is measured by the percentage of students admitted to higher education. . . . The universities receive totally immature students. . . . Those who are graduated are persons totally incapable of creative ability. . . .

It is not the point here to defend nor to attack, but simply to indicate the availability of material for documentation of the weighted comparisons that many critics favor. Whether it is American, Russian, or British, each educational system is distinct and should be judged within a particular framework and according to specific goals. Otherwise, comparisons are as meaningless as an argument to determine the relative merits of poached and scrambled eggs.

There are, of course, many criticisms that need to be made of American education, and there can be little quarrel with some of the points that men such as Hyman G. Rickover and Arthur Bestor make about the shortcomings of public education. Certainly we do need much better training and stronger education if we are to cope with the increasing complexities of technology. At the same time, not all of their suggestions can be seriously considered by the professional educators. The reasons are many and diverse, but several can be noted here. For instance, recommendations that reflect a view of society that is more akin to an "elitism" than to a representative democracy are not tenable. One example which would certainly conflict with well-established ideals of American society is Hutchins' university programs which would cater to the top fifteen per cent of the academically talented.

Again, educational views that are "fact" oriented and memoriter based ignore the new frontiers of the behavioral sciences and the increasing amount of evidence that concept formation and critical thinking are essential for man to cope with twentieth century knowledge explosion. Nineteenth century rationale, which affirms the mental storehouse psychological doctrine that many popular critics espouse, is no more appropriate for the tasks of contemporary education than the horse and buggy is for cross-country travel. One aspect of our democratic rule is the right to dissent, to criticize, to suggest alternatives, and since the activity is not limited to any one group, there will naturally be many criticisms of educational programs from those who are not really qualified to speak with authority. These should by no means be denied the right to speak, but it is clear that the professional educator has a responsibility to go beyond the particular charges, to determine the basic premises or assumptions for an accurate assessment of the critique, and to respond in a meaningful way.

The popular critique of education is frequently characterized by some form of extremism, as a moderate position lacks the element of controversy that seems to appeal to the mass media. The discriminating reader must allow for a modicum of overstatement in a critique, but one should be alerted by a stark composition of black against white, with no shading or merging to the mediating tones of grey. For the most part, it is the exception that is all black or all white, for the facts about public education in America are more likely to be found in a blending of the two extremes.

A closely reasoned and well-documented view will not tend to overstatement and oversimplification but will rely upon a consideration and interpretation of the facts. The extremist, in lieu of scholarly research and documentation, depends upon emotive language, innuendo, and distortion, and will slide with the greatest of ease from "some" to "all" in an attempt to make the exception seem to be the rule, the unusual seem to be typical. A critique of this nature, whether it is in the form of an attack or a defense, is not only futile, but keeps us from the sort of positive leadership and action that can build a really superior system of public education. The American public wants the best, and there is no reason to believe that the professional educator wants to settle for less. Professional educators realize that we can learn a great deal from systems other than our own and from just criticism that is based on fact, for there are many errors that need illumination. But there is reason to suspect a critique when the weight of the evidence cited is all on one side.

Crucial Issues

The foregoing discussion about the educational critiques indicates that the field of education has been more or less in a constant state of ferment for the past many years. Almost every aspect of educational policy has been subject for controversy, and educators, academicians, professional writers, and laymen have been quite vocal in their concern about educational policy. The professional and public controversy reflects the diversity of attitudes, beliefs, and opinions that shape American education which in turn reflects significant social, economic, cultural, religious, and political trends of the people.

The school, the single most important institution in America, does not exist in a social vacuum. Each school setting is a significant factor in what goes on in the particular school. The neighborhood social system, in turn, functions within a community or a local political unit which functions within a geographical region with definite and distinct social characteristics. The character of the regional institutions will vary accordingly. Thus, in spite of the fact that all schools ultimately function in and for a nation with a common federal government and a common cultural heritage, we can expect each school to be distinct from the others of its kind. We have noted the problems that occur if educational critics fail to take this fact into consideration.

Clearly, crucial issues which affect society as a whole—issues such as the exploration of outer space, the separation of church and state, civil rights, individual freedom, and others—will affect all schools but in varying degrees. Other crucial issues, such as the problems engendered by the urban crisis, by migratory workers, and by poverty pockets, will directly affect only some of the schools. Further, since educational institutions play an important part in fostering change and innovation, crucial issues in education, such as the role of the teacher, control of educational policy, teacher certification, and so on, will affect the whole of society. The interplay of influence between the school system and the public eliminates the need to consider crucial issues in education apart from crucial issues in society.

It would constitute a study in its own right to consider just the implications of all of the crucial issues which complicate the task of educators, to say nothing of attempting to offer possible solutions. But the purpose here is merely to point out the significance of crucial issues for education and the need to view them in proper perspective. Therefore, we shall limit ourselves to a discussion of three different kinds of crucial issues: 1) the relationship between church and state, a crucial issue in society which affects all schools in varying degrees; 2) the control of school policy, a crucial issue in education, which ultimately affects all of society; and 3) the urban crisis, a crucial issue which affects only a part of our schools at the present time.

The Relationship Between Church and State

The United States Constitution is the supreme law of the land, and although no authority over education is given to it, the Federal Bill of Rights does have a number of provisions which have a bearing on educational policy. One of these is the guarantee of religious freedom in the First Amendment, which states that: "Congress shall make no law respecting an establishment of religion, or prohibiting the full exercise thereof." The exact phraseology of the amendment came only after a great deal of controversy over the meaning of the word, "establishment." The colonial heritage reflects several meanings, specifically whether there should be legal enforcement and moral support for religion or whether there should be actual financial support for all 660 forms of religion. Jefferson stated in 1776 that: "All persons shall have full and free liberty of religious opinion; nor shall any be compelled to frequent or maintain any religious institution." Madison's *Memorial and Remonstrance Against Religious Assessments* was of sufficient persuasion so that the movement for multiple establishment in Virginia was firmly rejected, and by 1787, Virginia had brought about a separation of church and state. Thus the principle was clear in the minds of the leaders and was incorporated as the first of ten amendments to the Constitution which were passed by Congress on September 25, 1789 and ratified by three-fourths of the states on December 15, 1791.

As is so often the case, the realization of the principle has been far more complex, and during the early decades of the nineteenth century there was a close association between religion and the common school. Ministers frequently performed the dual function of occupying the pulpit on Sundays and teaching in the school during the week.[15] This practice caused many to look upon the public school as a Protestant institution that was a defense against the threat of Catholicism.[16] Church publications in the 1840's, such as "The Watchman," were especially vitriolic in their defense of the Protestant nature of the public school. The intensity of the abuse leveled against the Catholics increased during the Bible controversies of the 1840's, primarily because the Catholics preferred their own Douay Bible to the King James version. A Supreme Court decision rendered in 1854 (*Donahoe v. Richards,* 38 Me. 379) decreed the constitutionality of the King James version. Children of all faiths were governed by school board regulation, as prior to the Civil War there was nothing in the Federal Constitution to limit states rights in the field of education. Any grievance about local educational directives or violation of religious freedom could be taken no further than the state's judicial system.

However, in 1868, one of the legal consequences of the Civil War, the Fourteenth Amendment, was ratified and imposed broadly phrased limitations on the states. The first of the three clauses of Section 1 of the Fourteenth Amendment says that: "No State shall make or enforce any law which shall abridge the privileges or immunities of citizens of the United States." The exact meaning of this sweeping phrase is a matter of interpretation and ultimately dependent upon the Supreme Court decisions. Educational policy frequently violates claims of religious conscience, and the Supreme Court decisions of 1962 on the New York Regents Prayer (*Engel v. Vitale,* 370 U.S. 421) and 1963 on Bible reading and Lord's Prayer recitation (*School District of Abington Township, Pennsylvania v. Schempp; Murray v. Curlett,* 374 U.S. 203) show that the issue is still only partially resolved. There have been changes in state laws and constitutional require-

---

[15] Franklin H. Littell, "From Persecution or Toleration to Liberty," *Theory Into Practice,* IV, No. I (Columbus, Ohio: Bureau of Educational Research and Service, The Ohio State University, February 1965), 4.

[16] Lloyd P. Jorgenson, "The Birth of a Tradition!" *Phi Delta Kappan,* XLIV, No. 9, June 1963, 412.

ments[17] as a result of the Supreme Court decisions, and some state attorneys have ruled against Bible reading and the recitation of the Lord's Prayer in public schools. But it will take more time for the issue to be completely resolved, for there is strong sentiment at the state and local level, and several states have enacted silent meditation laws to circumvent Supreme Court decisions.

R. B. Dierenfield's study, *Religion in American Public Schools* (1962), noted that twelve states and the District of Columbia had laws *requiring* Bible reading, and that another twelve had laws *permitting* the activity.[18] There are many other state decisions that avoid the letter of the law. For instance, several states issue free textbooks for religious schools, and others provide public transportation and direct aid to sectarian schools. Additional questionable practices are noted by Dierenfield, such as schools that display the Ten Commandments and those that prohibit the theory of evolution to be taught.[19] There is every indication that Texas school children, for example, have more exposure in the schools to religious activity than before the 1962 and 1963 Supreme Court rulings. A survey of 166 Texas public schools to determine what changes in opinion and practices resulted from the Supreme Court edict was made in 1965 for a thesis at the University of Texas. The survey showed that since the court decision there had been a three per cent increase in the number of religious hymns sung in school, a three per cent increase in announcements made about religious activities, a four per cent increase in assembly programs with religious themes, and a five per cent increase of invitations to ministers to participate in school assemblies. The following comment by one of the principals reflects the attitude shared by most of the 166 who were questioned. "If it is permissible and general practice for each session of Congress to open with a prayer . . . as provided by the Constitution, it is just as important that the child in the public schools be given an opportunity to participate or not participate in daily devotions."

Unfortunately, there has been no consistent pattern to the United States Supreme Court decisions which further complicates the problem. The United States Supreme Court ruled in 1940 that the Minerville School District in Pennsylvania (versus Gobitis) had the legal right to expel students who were Jehovah's Witnesses for not saluting the flag. The Court reversed itself in 1943 in the case of West Virginia State Board of Education versus Barnette where the defendants were also Jehovah's Witnesses. The United States Supreme Court has made it clear, however, on the issue of "released time," ruling that when children are let out of the school to leave the premises for religious instruction, the principle of separation of church and state is not violated.

---

17 August W. Steinhilber, "The U.S. Supreme Court and Religion in the Schools," *Theory Into Practice*, IV, No. I, February 1965, 8–13.

18 Richard B. Dierenfield, *Religion in American Public Schools* (Washington, D.C.: Public Affairs Press, 1962), p. 21.

19 *Ibid.*, p. 25.

The legal guarantee given to private and parochial schools by the 1925 United States Supreme Court decision (*Peirce* v. *Society of Sisters,* 268, U.S. 510) has been a major factor in creating problems for the schools and for legislatures in regard to the issue of finances. Those who advocate Federal aid to education have been plagued by the fact that the "establishment clause" prohibits such aid. Exceptions to the clause have been allowed through the child benefit theory, which is based upon the principle of general welfare, aid to individuals rather than to religious organizations. The United States Supreme Court has established the principle through two cases. The first case dealt with furnishing textbooks (*Cochran* v. *Louisiana,* 281 U.S. 370 [1928]). The second, in New Jersey, dealt with the use of tax money to reimburse parents for transportation costs (*Everson* v. *Board of Education,* 330 U.S. 1 [1947]). The implications of these decisions are becoming more troublesome, and the Elementary and Secondary Education Act of 1965 makes extensive use of the principle of child benefit.

The principle of separation of church and state, as we have seen, is a many-faceted one, and one can only guess what its future may be. Additional court cases will arise, cases that have to do with shared time, with the curriculum, with the child benefit theory, and others. The pattern of the past will not necessarily be the blueprint for the future, for the men who occupy the high court bench will change, and the philosophical makeup of the United States Supreme Court could undergo drastic revision. The principles of sociological jurisprudence could be discarded in favor of other principles. The variety of possibilities makes the matter of school policy control even more acute, for it is most likely that the educational future of the nation will be determined on this point.

Control of School Policy

As we have noted, the United States Constitution, although it has no authority over education, makes certain stipulations that relate to educational policy and control. The Tenth Amendment states that "the powers not delegated to the United States by the Constitution, nor prohibited by it to the states, are reserved to the states respectively, or to the people." One such power is the control of public schools and educational policy. Thus, traditionally, education in the United States is the function and the responsibility of the people. The law of 1642 in Massachusetts emphasized learning to read and training for profitable work, and in this law the ideal of compulsory, tax-supported education was embodied. The Kalamazoo Decision in 1872 which enabled a community to levy taxes for high school education was instrumental in assuring the future of secondary public education, and the present state of our schools is the accumulation of ideas and practices that have been approved by different groups of people and adopted by still other groups.

We have reached a point where many feel we need to examine the consequences of local control of schools—both on the debit and the credit side—where we need to decide whether or not we want to depart from the framework of values that has determined our status quo. There are many others who fear that the control of education and schooling is gradually slipping away from legally constituted authorities and who resist anything that might possibly be viewed as a threat to local control. These see the use of Federal, business, and philanthropic monies as a threat to local control of education, and they resist legislative requirements for certification of teachers or any attempt to standardize accreditation procedures and requirements for the same reason. They point out the devastating effects of education directed and controlled by Nazi ideology on a generation of German children and make dire predictions about similar consequences in America if we do not do anything to resist any sort of central control of education in the United States.

The forces in opposition to local control claim that our vigilance against the strawman of central control leaves our system prey to many insidious and subtle controls that are even more destructive than any extreme of what we fear might be. They cite instances of censorship of literature, textbooks, and subjects by uninformed individuals and reactionary pressure groups; politically expedient decisions made on the floor of some state legislatures; materials circulated for classroom use by groups such as the John Birch Society and the Legion of Decency; and local school boards that are unable to withstand pressures generated by powerful national organizations.

Certainly there is evidence that at least some of the shortcomings of our educational system can be traced to our myopia about educational controls. One example is the problem of certification of teachers, a problem which is becoming even more urgent with the increased mobility of teachers. Those who fear that any attempt to standardize accreditation procedures will lead to unreasonable control over education see no discrepancy when they complain about the "mis-education" of our teachers. *The Saturday Evening Post* carried an article, "They Wouldn't Let Beethoven Teach Music in Indiana,"[20] which obviously was intended to make certification procedures for teachers appear ridiculous if not authoritarian. The article cited the case of a fine musician who was an excellent college professor but who was not allowed to teach in the secondary schools without a teaching certificate. The fallacy in assuming that, since a good musician is a good university professor, all good musicians will be good elementary teachers who need no special training to teach youngsters is painfully obvious. It is small wonder that such reasoning confuses *national standards with federal control;* or that it fails to recognize the difference between refusing certification for teachers and insisting upon medical boards for doctors and bar examinations for lawyers.

The American public is so apprehensive about any form of dictatorship that there is an automatic assumption that good education cannot

---

20 *The Saturday Evening Post,* July 19, 1958.

exist without local control. Actually, we have evidence that much excellent education is produced in a state or federal system. The schools in Australia and New Zealand, where all phases of public education are state controlled and managed, are splendid examples of the success of uniformity among schools in the content and method of instruction and in the organization and administration of schools. At the same time, it does not follow that government participation necessarily leads to government control.

Federal participation in the areas of vocational education, agriculture, and the like has definitely upgraded the quality by setting minimum standards of achievements. The G.I. Bill following World War II had the effect of increasing the educational level of veterans as nothing else could have done. The role of the government in promulgating equal rights has done far more to assure equal educational opportunities than local control would ever have accomplished. As a matter of fact, the governmental role has been a positive one ever since the Northwest Ordinances of 1785 and 1787. A chronological report of the acts which have aided education reach from the Morrill Act in 1862, through the Smith-Hughes Act of 1917, the National Defense Education Act of 1958, to the Higher Education Bill of 1965.

Yet in spite of evidence on the credit side, and in spite of the fact that conflict in the school situation is inevitable so long as the roles of the public and the professional are not clearly defined, the people continue to resist any plan to permit the United States as a nation to enter into the local school situation. However, bigness promotes power, and as urban, suburban, and rural areas continue to merge, and the new frontier for education becomes the megalopolis, educators are bound to become involved in the politics of metropolitan change. The lack of correlation between fiscal resources and school needs will surely result in some shifting of control of education in the public schools. Hopefully, educators will be able to discover more enlightened solutions to the problem of the proper relationship between education and the government and will eventually find some way to involve the schools in "good" politics, yet keep them free from the "bad."

The Urban Crisis

Americans, who have created some of the great cities of the world in a relatively short time, are witnessing the metamorphosis of merging towns and cities as they spread to overlap state boundaries and unite to form giant urban complexes. Jean Gottman, a French geographer, has called such a complex a "megalopolis." Four of these complexes had evolved by 1962—one along the Northern Seaboard, one around Chicago, one on the Gulf Coast, and the fourth throughout the Pacific Coast area. To illustrate the size of the megalopolis, the Northern Seaboard complex extends 500 miles from Virginia to Massachusetts and includes thirty-two population centers with eighteen per cent of the total population of the United States. According to the 1960 census, more than sixty per cent of the 180 million people in the United States live in 212 metropolitan centers, an increase of 48.5 per cent over 1950, and predictions are that by 1980, 80 per cent of the people will live in urban areas. The megalopolis trend is clearly indicated by the fact that in nonmetropolitan areas the population increase from 1950 to 1960 was only 7.1 per cent.

Where once the city was the first home for most immigrants who would become Americanized and move out for other groups to take their place, today the megalopolis has become a rattrap for minority groups. Today's migrant, the Negro, the Puerto Rican, or the Mexican-American, can see no way out of the trap no matter how hard he may try, and the city is no longer a way station for changing ethnic groups. Nor is the city any longer an attractive place for middle-class and upper-class Americans who used to enjoy theaters, restaurants, and the other advantages of metropolitan living. No longer is it an attractive escape from the narrowness of rural and small-town life, for the city is rotting at the core, and the middle and upper classes are spilling into suburbia which spreads farther and farther from the center of the city. Suburban dwellers shun the city shops, preferring the shopping centers that cater to suburbia, and even big business finds that employees are happier if the firms are located in suburbia. The big cities are decaying; housing is more tightly restricted than ever before; public services are neglected; schools are unsupported; standards for police protection and sanitation are low; and slum living provides the only sense of community. It is small wonder that the problems of the schools in urban areas have become so intensified in recent years.

One of the problems is that the ideal model of the school we have come to accept has little relationship to the reality of slum living, and the tenement child cannot see himself in terms of this ideal school, the curriculum, or the educational materials. Also, city teachers are likely to be strangers to the community they serve and even to the children they teach. Whether the teacher is Negro or Caucasian, there is most often little understanding of the slum child who starts educationally from quite a different place than the middle-class child, and the learning goals the teacher uses are apt to be completely alien to the children he attempts to reach. The teacher knows that the school shapes young people and provides the bridge between their adolescence and their projected adult careers, but ordinary instruction that is integrated with and responsive to the ideals of the home and the community is not effective in the slum conditions of the urban areas. The schools that serve these areas, therefore, are apt to be scenes of disorder and even of violence, and the teachers are apt to be viewed with suspicion and lack of esteem. Obviously, such conditions cannot be conducive to the sort of education that is needed.

A related problem has to do with the matter of control that we have previously discussed. As we have noted, localism is engrained in the American tradition, but the increasing pressures on the urban schools are forcing them to seek outside help and support. Only through education can we achieve healthy, attractive metropolitan communities, and the necessary systems and programs of education for urban schools are so costly that they must be attempted within a larger frame of reference than a particular metropolitan area. The urban areas do not have the necessary tax resources for a number of reasons. For one thing, the federal government has removed from the tax rolls property that is needed for freeways, traffic arteries, and public housing. There is also a continuing decrease in property valuation because of the exodus of home owners to the suburbs, while the vacuum they leave is filled by slum and blight.

Clearly, the urban school must do more than provide the special educational experiences that are needed to assist children to adjust to urban life. The urban school must also accept the responsibility for helping to acculturate the members of the diverse groups that constitute the area, and it must provide support for social control mechanisms in the area. The prospect of our becoming a nation of cities need not be overwhelming if we look on the positive side toward the kinds of achievements that might not be possible in rural communities. The diversity of human talents, if properly developed and channeled, can add immeasurably to the strength and enrichment of city life, and the metropolitan complexes can be the most effective means of providing the greatest number of advantages of economic opportunities and cultural and educational resources to the largest numbers of people, if we learn how to develop and utilize our resources to the optimum. Mass purchasing, for instance, can be an advantage for urban school systems by enabling them to effect economies in purchase and production of materials and facilities and allowing a greater use of modern techniques such as radio, television, telemation, automatic computer instruments, and the like.

Already there are many positive signs in the urban school crisis. The March 1967 issue of *Phi Delta Kappan* is representative of a number of leading educational journals which point to practices that are being initiated in an effort to provide educational services to the big city. In many instances cooperative structures of a centralized nature are being tried. For example, the city of Nashville, Tennessee, and Davidson County, Tennessee, consolidated their efforts into a metropolitan government.[21] The results have been impressive, especially so far as the schools have been concerned, as they are receiving more support from the citizens, desegregation has proceeded with minimum interference, the purchase of food and supplies has been centralized, and transportation services have become more efficient.

The success of this consolidation may serve as a model that others will follow as we recognize the advantages of a central system of educational services that can accommodate many more students than would be possible otherwise. The response of teachers and administrators to new instructional methodologies, educational technologies, and organizational structures will doubtless be one of the determining factors in future educational goals. Ulti-

---

[21] John Egerton and Jim Leeson, "Nashville: Experiment in Urban School Consolidation," *Phi Delta Kappan,* XLVIII, No. 7, March 1967, 323.

mately, however, it is the beliefs of the people—their values, and therefore their aims—that will shape educational decisions in rural, suburban, or urban schools. Since there are a multitude of theories about how we may best achieve the desired goals and since there are a variety of legitimate avenues to a common destination, it depends upon teachers and administrators to guard against a separation of the means and the ends. Educators need to understand the philosophical principles of analysis, criticism, and evaluation in order to engage in the kind of philosophic enterprise that will enable them to make intelligent decisions about purposes, aspirations, wants, and needs; that will help them to make an accurate analysis of the impact of their judgments; and that eliminates dogmatism as a base for educational policy decisions.

WILLIAM K. FRANKENA

Philosophical Inquiry*

One of the prime concerns of Chapter VIII has been an assessment of a variety of criticisms about educational goals and practices, both from the standpoint of testing their validity and of determining the best ways in which to make intelligent and considered responses to such criticisms. William K. Frankena's article, "Philosophical Inquiry," in which he discusses the normative and the nonnormative (factual) premises upon which critics rest their conclusions, will assist the student to gain considerable insight into these problems. Frankena speaks primarily to educational philosophers, but he also points out ways in which those who administer and those who plan curricula may respond to recent philosophical ideas and developments. Frankena's determination of how philosophy may properly have a bearing on educational problems centers upon questions about educational goals and methods, and his development of the role of philosophy in the relation of the theory and practice of schools is concise and to the point. His discussion of recent philosophical developments which he terms as "recent non-Deweyan and non-Thomistic (and non-Marxist) philosophy" is excellent and will provide the student with a clear resume of au courant ideas which are relevant to educational theory and perhaps practice.

Introduction

What philosophical ideas or developments after World War II have implications for the schools and might or should have been responded to by them? What is there in "the new world of philosophy" that might or should have been taken as a basis for conclusions about education in our schools or about the schools

* From *The Changing American School* by William K. Frankena. Reprinted by permission of the author and the National Society for the Study of Education, The University of Chicago Press, 1966.

themselves? That is the question of this chapter. Thus stated, however, it is somewhat too broad and vague to permit a very profitable response.

Since I can write profitably only about the work of professional philosophers, and since, even in dealing with this, I can say little that is new about the work of Dewey and his followers or of the Thomists, I shall restate the question in a clearer and narrower form. What is there in recent professional non-Deweyan and non-Thomistic philosophy[1] to which the schools might well have responded in some positive way, at least experimentally, i.e., what is there that has implications which might well be taken seriously by those who philosophize about the schools and school education, by those who plan the curricula, and by those who administer or teach in schools? There are at least these three levels at which the schools might respond, and I shall try to keep them all in mind, although it will turn out, as might be expected, that I shall find a good deal more to say to educational philosophers than to teachers, curriculum-planners, or administrators.

In order to get a purchase on our question, we must first see just how and where philosophy *might* come to bear on questions about school education. Education was defined by Bertrand Russell as *"the formation, by means of instruction, of certain mental habits and a certain outlook on life and the world";* and by John Dewey as "the process of forming fundamental dispositions, intellectual and emotional, toward nature and fellow men."[2] The task of education, if we accept the definitions, is the formation of desirable abilities, dispositions, habits, and traits of character—of what the Greeks called excellences. If this is true, then the theory of school education must answer two questions. (*a*) Which abilities, dispositions, and habits are to be cultivated by the schools? (*b*) How are school educators to foster these abilities, dispositions, or habits and by what methods, through what curricula, and in what kind of an atmosphere?

Now, anyone who seeks to give reasoned answers to such questions must rest his conclusions on premises of two kinds:

(*a*) normative premises, ethical principles, or basic value judgments, i.e., premises about the ends, values, or principles to be pursued or acted on;

(*b*) nonnormative or factual premises about the nature of man, the results of certain methods of teaching, the kinds of knowledge, and so on.

A partial answer to the first question might read:

(1) We ought to promote the greatest general happiness.
(2) Honesty will promote the greatest general happiness.
(3) Therefore, we ought to foster honesty.

Another answer might be:

(4) The aim of education is the transmission of knowledge.
(5) Religion and theology are not forms of knowledge.
(6) Therefore, they should not be taught.

---

[1] Hereafter, by "recent philosophy" I shall mean "recent non-Deweyan and non-Thomistic (and non-Marxist) philosophy."

[2] Bertrand Russell, *Mysticism and Logic* (London: Allen & Unwin, Ltd., 1917), p. 37; John Dewey, *Democracy and Education* (New York: Macmillan Co., 1916), p. 383.

And a reply to the second question might run:

(7) Schools should foster honesty.
(8) The indirect method is more effective in cultivating honesty than the direct method.
(9) Therefore, schools should use the indirect method in fostering honesty.

In these examples, premises (1), (4), and (7) are normative, while (2), (5), and (8) are not.

Premises of both kinds may be supplied by philosophy. For instance, premises like (1) and (4) would be provided by ethics, value theory, or social philosophy, and premises like (5) by epistemology or metaphysics. Thus, one way in which philosophy may enter into our thinking about schools and their practices is by furnishing some of its *premises*, normative or nonnormative. However, philosophy may enter in another way. For all such thinking involves concepts or terms; in the examples given, there are the following: "happiness," "honesty," "teaching," "knowledge," "religion," "truth," "God," and "education" itself. None of these concepts or terms is entirely clear and unambiguous. They all need some kind of *analysis, clarification,* or *definition,* else our thinking about schools and education cannot have the accuracy, rigor, or certainty that it ought to have. It is just here that philosophy can make its second kind of contribution. For one of the main tasks of philosophy, especially as it is conceived today, is that of analyzing or clarifying the key concepts or terms of human thought, or the central phenomena of human experience, as phenomenologists prefer to say, including many of those that appear over and over in educational literature. Along the same line, philosophy can also make a contribution by analyzing and evaluating the logic of the slogans and arguments used in the discourse of education.

Philosophy might, then, influence the theory and practice of the schools in these ways:

1. It might supply its basic normative premises.
2. It might supply some of its other premises (still others would come from psychology, theology, anthropology, etc.).
3. It might provide analyses of concepts and slogans, evaluations of arguments, and clarification of terms.

Actually, there are two other ways in which philosophy might be related to the schools:

4. It might be made part of the curriculum of the high school.
5. It might be made part of the training of schoolteachers and administrators.

I shall take occasion later to say something about these last two possible responses of the schools to philosophy but shall devote most of this chapter to the first three.

Recent Philosophy and Normative Premises for the Schools

Analytical Philosophy and Existentialism
   Let us ask, then, whether recent philosophy offers the educator any normative (ethical or value) premises for answering the three questions formulated

earlier. In reply, it is necessary to observe, to begin with, that both of the newer movements in philosophy, analytical philosophy and existentialism, have tended to avoid laying down normative premises for human thought and action.

Analytical philosophers—those belonging to "the revolution in philosophy" stemming from G. E. Moore, Bertrand Russell, and Ludwig Wittgenstein—have tended to regard the making of normative or value judgments as not a proper part of philosophy and have sought to limit philosophy to the analysis of concepts and the elucidation of the logic of various kinds of terms, sentences, or reasoning. Some of them have written at length in ethics or value-theory, and even in social and educational philosophy, but even then their concern has not been with making and defending any basic ethical principles or value judgments, i.e., not with answering normative questions but with answering metaethical ones, such as "What is the meaning or use of expressions like 'good,' 'ought,' 'promise,' 'free will,' 'choice,' 'action,' 'teaching,' etc.?" and "What is the logic of justifying statements in which such expressions are used?" It can be plausibly argued that some analytical philosophers have been more normative than they claimed to be, but, at any rate, if they have, it was by inadvertence from their own point of view.

This tendency of analytical philosophers to avoid taking normative positions has, at least sometimes, the effect of leaving the normative premises of educational thought to be provided by others—psychologists, social scientists, or theologians—or by the prevailing mores or popular demand. This seems to me, for example, to be the net effect of Daniel J. O'Connor's approach to the philosophy of education and especially to his "tentative list of the aims of education."[3] On the other hand, while he dislikes "the endless talk about the aims of education," Richard S. Peters believes that it is possible to show by philosophical analysis that certain "pretty formal" principles, which he calls "procedural," are "presupposed by the very activity of giving reasons in practical discourse," namely, the principles "of impartiality, truth-telling, liberty, and the consideration of interests." For instance, the principle of impartiality tells us that people are to be treated equally unless treating them unequally is justified, i.e., that equality must be assumed and inequality justified. These principles he then offers us as providing very general criteria for justifying or ruling out more specific judgments and practices. He argues also (a) that in moral education it is particularly important to pass on these procedural rules, and (b) that the principle of the consideration of interests requires education to be concerned with the promotion of good or worth-while activities as well as with the maintenance of rules for social conduct.[4] Here, at least, we have an example of an analytical philosopher seeking in a novel way to establish social principles which might well be taken seriously as a basis for the theory and practice of the schools.

Another point may be made here. Even when they most completely avoid making normative commitments, analytical philosophers are still presupposing the desirability of certain abilities or traits of mind: clarity of thought, rigor of

---

[3] Daniel J. O'Connor, *An Introduction to the Philosophy of Education,* chap. i. London: Routledge & Kegan Paul, 1957.
[4] Richard S. Peters, "Reason and Habit: The Paradox of Moral Education," in *Moral Education in a Changing Society,* pp. 51–53. Edited by W. R. Niblett. London: Faber & Faber, Ltd., 1963.

reasoning, awareness of assumptions, a knowledge of the standards to be applied in each area, and an ability to judge intelligently by them (which Aristotle regarded as the marks of an educated man). The insistence on such abilities and traits is something—in my opinion, one of the main things—that school educators and their teachers could learn from recent philosophy. Here, surely, is a family of dispositions (not enough insisted upon by Dewey and his followers), which the schools ought to promote. Furthermore, teachers and educators can learn a great deal from the work of analytical philosophers about what it is like to be clear and rigorous and about the standards to be used in various fields of activity and thought, even if they cannot learn anything that they can take bodily into the classroom.

Existentialists reject the analytical philosopher's notion of neutral and objective analysis. They regard a philosopher as inevitably committed, engaged, and normative, and they call upon us all to choose an ethics, anxiously perhaps, but whole-heartedly and without self-deceit. Yet, paradoxically, they hesitate to help us by presenting us with substantive moral principles or ends which we might espouse and use as a basis of thought and action, whether in the field of education or elsewhere. They tend to stress the form or manner of our approach to life—it is to be authentic or existential rather than unauthentic and unanxious, et cetera—rather than its content or substance. In this respect, analytical philosophy and existentialism, temperamentally so hostile to one another, are curiously similar in outcome: both avoid laying out a normative ethics for us to go by.

Still, just as the practice of analytical philosophy involves a family of dispositions which may be taken as part of the goal of school education, just so does existentialism present a group of dispositions for us to foster. It is a very different family, including authenticity, decision, commitment, courage, autonomy, responsibility, devotion, and so on. These may be called moral dispositions as compared with the intellectual or logical ones emphasized by analytical philosophers, but they are moral dispositions that have to do with the *mode* of what we do in life rather than with its *content* (as do such dispositions as benevolence, justice, et cetera). They are dispositions which express themselves not so much in *what* we do, being compatible with doing all sorts of actions, good or bad by conventional standards, but in *how* we do it. To quote Wild:

> Value lies not so much in what we do as in how we exist and maintain ourselves in time. To express this new sense of existential value, a new terminology is required . . . words like *authentic, genuine, real,* and *really* . . . express those more basic "existential values" . . . which underlie all the valuable things we do or say. Since they characterize our ways of existing in the world, they . . . apply to every phase and region of our care. There is nothing . . . that may not be done either authentically . . . or unauthentically. . . . They are not "values" at all, in the traditional sense of this term. . . . They are patterns of our lived existence in the world.[5]

It is reasonable to argue that there is a place for a stress in education, both in and out of school, on such existential virtues, as well as on the analytical

[5] John D. Wild, *Existence and the World of Freedom,* pp. 164–165. Englewood Cliffs, New Jersey: Prentice-Hall, Inc., 1963.

ones mentioned before. The two families of dispositions are not incompatible, for all the opposition there may be between the two kinds of philosophy advocating them. Even the Hatfields and the McCoys have learned to live together. Indeed, if we were to add these two groups of excellences to those stressed earlier by Dewey—scientific method, regard for empirical fact and experimental verification, democracy, and benevolence—then we should have a list of most of the dispositions our schools could be expected to help in cultivating. In this perspective, Deweyan pragmatism, philosophical analysis, and existentialism present us with three complementary (and even overlapping) sets of attitudes or traits for the schools to aim at.

Other Recent Philosophers

Some recent philosophers, however, have sought to be more directly normative than the analysts and the existentialists and to lay down ends or principles for human conduct, social or individual. Like Dewey, they have, for the most part, been utilitarians in ethics, though not hedonists. In other words, they would hold that education should foster those abilities and dispositions which most promote the good life for all concerned. This group includes Ralph Barton Perry, Brand Blanshard, P. B. Rice, Arthur Campbell Garnett, A. C. Ewing, J. J. C. Smart, and probably Richard B. Brandt. (Some analytical philosophers are at least very close to utilitarianism, e.g., Stephen Toulmin, R. M. Hare, and P. H. Nowell-Smith.) In fact, such philosophers would probably say that education should foster (a) those abilities and dispositions which put the individual in a position to live the best life he is capable of, and (b) those which equip and dispose him to respect the lives of others and perhaps even to help make them as good as possible, too.

It should be observed in this connection that one must distinguish between the morally good life and the good life, even if they tend to coincide. On such views as we are discussing, the morally good life is one of seeking the good life for all concerned as far as possible, but the good life to be promoted is not simply the morally good life. What, then, do the philosophers in question regard as the good life? As indicated, they have usually not been hedonists. That is, they usually refuse to equate the good with pleasure, for reasons we cannot go into here. On the other hand, they have generally not gone to any antihedonist extreme. They might be thought of as quasi-hedonists; for most of them, the good or the good life consists in the end of what is desired, enjoyed, satisfying, or found worth while, either for its own sake or (as for Dewey) on a reflective consideration of everything involved. Some of them, e.g., Rice and Clarence Irving Lewis, take the affective tone of activities and experiences (not to be identified with pleasantness) as the criterion of their value; others, e.g., Perry and De Witt H. Parker, take as the criterion of their value the fact of their being desired or of satisfying desire; and still others, e.g., Blanshard and Garnett, argue that the criterion is a kind of synthesis of affective tone with being desired or satisfying desire. Perhaps there is nothing basically new in all this, but I do think that the discussions of these philosophers would at least be useful to those responsible for the philosophy of education in the schools.

There is one formal principle which has found much favor with both analytical philosophers and more normative ones—though not with the existentialists. This is a principle which is involved in the *golden rule* and in Kant's *categorical imperative* and is now usually referred to as the *principle of generalization* or *universalization.* The idea behind it is that, when one judges a particular action to be right, one is thereby committed to the general rule that an action of the same kind would be right for everyone in the same kind of situation, and that one cannot regard an action as morally right for one person in a certain situation unless he is ready to see it universally acted on by others in similar situations. "What is right for one person must be right for every similar person in similar circumstances." Sometimes this is regarded as a substantive moral principle, e.g., by Marcus George Singer; sometimes as a logical "feature of moral language" which, by itself, has no moral implications, e.g., by Hare, Nowell-Smith, Bernard Mayo, and possibly Lewis. In any case, however, it is insisted that, in determining whether or not one should do A, one must ask whether or not one is ready to see it become a universal law. If one is not, then one must judge A to be wrong, or at least admit that he is not trying to decide the question on moral grounds. The application of the principle may not be a sufficient condition for determining whether an action is right or whether one's approach is moral, but it is a necessary one.

However this may be, if the *principle of generalization* is correct, as it seems to me to be, this fact has an important implication for moral education which must be remembered in the schools. For it means that we must cultivate, among other things, a disposition to be consistent in our actions and judgments and to ask ourselves what maxims we are ready to see universally adopted—not ignorantly, but in the light of the facts.[6]

Recent Philosophy and Other (Nonnormative) Premises

Now, let us suppose that we have our axiological and ethical premises for answering our questions about the schools, whether we find them in recent philosophy or not. The next question is whether recent philosophy offers the school educator any nonnormative premises that bear on his problems—premises about the nature of man and the universe, or about the nature and limits of knowledge. It must be pointed out at once that no such premises can be regarded as having been established in any final way or even as agreed on by all contemporary philosophers. In a sense, then, it is not possible to say that there are any epistemological or metaphysical doctrines in recent philosophy to which the schools must respond by drawing out their implications and putting them into practice. It may be added, moreover, that public school educators must, in any case, be wary of presupposing any particular philosophical position, theistic or otherwise, as a basis for their conclusions about what is to be taught or how.

One could argue that recent philosophy is in a very broad sense empiristic in opposition to the various forms of rationalism prevailing in the past. It would require some temerity, therefore, for an educator to rest any of his theories or practices on rationalistic premises, e.g., on a rationalistic view of the nature of mathematics. On the other hand, it is not clear that the various empiricisms of today, except perhaps for existentialism, would require any very different responses on the part of the schools from those already made. Analytically minded philosophers are perhaps more insistent than ever before that scientific questions are to be answered by scientific methods, historical questions by historical methods, and so forth. They tend, however, to avoid seeking for

---

[6] For more about recent moral philosophy and moral education, see William K. Frankena, "Toward a Philosophy of Moral Education," *Harvard Educational Review,* XXVIII (Fall 1958), 300–313.

substantive epistemological or metaphysical doctrines from which educational conclusions can be drawn and to limit themselves to more purely analytical and methodological findings, such as we shall look at in the following section. As for existentialism—in its more extreme forms, at least—it seems to offer a view of man which makes it hard to see how education can play any important part in his formation. It is so antideterministic, so insistent that man is a creature of his own free unguided choice, that it even talks as if an individual chooses his nature and dispositions independently of experience and training or even of heredity. There are, as we saw, certain dispositions which it advocates, but its assertion of the priority of existence to essence is such as to render the role of education in their formation unclear. In any case, however, existentialism, in so far as it is wedded to the phenomenological method, is surprisingly like analytical philosophy in being averse to speculative metaphysics in the grand style. To quote Wild again, the function of philosophy is "not to establish an objective science of being" or "a great super-science of the universe" but to be "an expression of the basic, noetic freedom of man, refusing to be locked up permanently in any fixed frame . . ."[7]

Philosophical Analysis and the Schools

General Remarks: Hook's Critique

In the preceding section, I was looking, not very successfully, for sweeping substantive premises or "world-hypotheses," established by recent philosophy, which might well be taken as premises for deducing educational implications for the schools. Now we must look at the works of so-called analytical philosophers to see what relevant findings, if any, they may contain.

We must remember here that the purer analytical philosophers do not think of themselves as searching for or discovering any substantive insights or synthetic truths, factual or normative. This they leave to the empirical scientist, the historian, the theologian, the artist, and the moralist, though they are, of course, quite ready to try to analyze the nature of the various kinds of insights and truths at which these people may arrive. Rightly or wrongly, they typically think of themselves as seeking and gaining insights of a different sort, variously described as analytical, logical, methodological, formal, conceptual, or linguistic. To borrow an example from one of them: It is an empirical truth that human beings often dream at night, but it is a conceptual or linguistic truth that stones cannot dream. The validity of any such sharp distinction between two or more kinds of insights would be questioned by some Deweyans; it is, in fact, questioned by some analytical or near-analytical philosophers whose views may be thought of as pragmatic or even as "beyond pragmatism."[8] We cannot discuss this issue here, of course, anymore than we can discuss the question of whether analytical philosophers are merely descriptive and elucidatory in what they do or whether they are legislative and normative. Our job is to see what bearing their analyses have on the thinking and practice of the school educator, if any.

The importance of analytical philosophy for the school educator has been discussed and somewhat impugned by Hook in the second edition of *Education*

---

7 Wild, *op. cit.*, pp. 121, 131.
8 Morton Gabriel White, *Toward Reunion in Philosophy*, chap. viii (Cambridge, Massachusetts: Harvard University Press, 1956); Willard V. O. Quine, *From a Logical Point of View*, Essay 2 (Cambridge, Massachusetts: Harvard University Press, 1953).

for Modern Man.[9] In part, his complaint is that what is wanted is answers to educational problems of a normative sort about the aims, methods, and content of education and that analytical philosophy does not and cannot provide answers to such problems—even "analytical philosophy of education" cannot do so. He is right, in my opinion, in both parts of this complaint, but it does not follow that analytical philosophy of education is "misconceived." For analytical philosophers would be the first to say that analysis does not by itself answer normative educational problems. Neither does it follow that analysis is irrelevant to "the theory and practice of education," for, even if it is not *sufficient* to answer the questions of educational theory and practice, it may still be *helpful* in doing so or even *necessary*. Hook does not deny, in fact he admits, that conceptual and linguistic analysis may be very *helpful* in preventing confusion and looseness in educational thinking and writing and in enabling us "to express things in a way that leads to greater self-understanding or to readier inquiry and test." And this is most, if not all, of what an analytical philosopher would care to claim. All that needs to be added is that the analysts could confer an untold benefit along this line, at least in the area of educational theory, as anyone can see by looking at the quality of thought and expression that infects so much of our literature on education.

For the rest, Hook argues (*a*) that linguistic analysis is not needed for the solution of educational problems, and (*b*) that the findings of such analysis are sometimes bizarre and inept. On the latter point he is certainly right; but he does not cite the best examples of analytical work on slogans or on the concept of teaching. The analyses of Scheffler in *The Language of Education*[10] and of Komisar in *Language and Concepts in Education*[11] do not exhibit the faults Hook finds in others. These authors are no less analytical, but their analyses are more complete. As a contemporary Francis Bacon might put it, the remedy for a little analytical philosophy is not something else but greater depth in it. I also find it hard to believe that such analyses would not be *helpful* in the thinking of educators and teachers. It would, no doubt, be too much to claim that any teacher *needs* "the benefit of linguistic analysis to realize that a child may learn to answer questions on the duties of a good citizen correctly yet habitually disregard them . . . ," et cetera. But this is because he has already achieved some conceptual clarity, besides experiencing some empirical failure. Would it also be too much to claim that many teachers (and their teachers) need more conceptual and linguistic clarity than they show when they talk about what they do and why they do it? Or that linguistic analysis is sometimes necessary at the level of educational theory, if not of practice? On this last point, it may be enough to remark that Hook himself often finds it necessary to do what is actually a kind of conceptual analysis. Did he not, his thought would be much less clear and his arguments much less cogent.

Some Contributions, Actual or Possible

However this may be, there is at any rate a growing interest in analytical philosophy among educators, and it is by no means all negative, though a

---

9 Sidney Hook, *Education for Modern Man*, pp. 45–51. New York: Alfred A. Knopf, 1963.
10 Israel Scheffler, *The Language of Education*. Springfield, Illinois: Charles C Thomas, Publishers, 1960.
11 B. P. Komisar, "Need and the Needs-Curriculum," in *Language and Concepts in Education*, chap. ii. Edited by B. Othanel Smith and Robert H. Ennis. Chicago: Rand McNally & Co., 1961.

philosopher can only shudder at some of the forms it takes. In addition to the volume, *Language and Concepts in Education,* this interest is attested to in books edited by Joe Park, T. H. B. Hollins, Reginald D. Archambault, J. E. McClellan, and B. P. Komisar, as well as in papers by G. L. Newsome, C. D. Hardie, and others. As a matter of fact, it is not hard to find places in educational discussion where the analytical philosopher can make a contribution.

Consider, for example, Dewey's discussion of the criteria of an educative experience in *Experience and Education.*[12] He correctly points out that, although all education comes about through experience, not all experiences are educative. Then he states two general propositions about experiences, (*a*) the *principle of continuity,* which says that every experience is affected by previous experiences and affects the nature of subsequent experiences, and (*b*) the *principle of interaction,* which says that every experience is the result of an interaction between external and internal factors. But, even though he sees that these two principles are true of *all* experiences, Dewey persists in speaking as if they can also serve as criteria "by which to discriminate between experiences which are educative and those which are mis-educative." He does not notice that the two principles are purely factual, and that a normative principle is also needed if one is to be able to tell which experiences are educative and which are not; e.g., the principle that an experience must contribute to growth rather than to its opposite. An analytical philosopher might not be able to show that Dewey is mistaken here in any matter of substance, but he would have little trouble in showing that Dewey is confused about the form in which he puts what he is saying.

Consider, also, the following argument from Hutchins, one of Dewey's critics: "Education implies teaching. Teaching implies knowledge. Knowledge is truth. The truth is everywhere the same. Hence education should be everywhere the same."[13] It takes only a little logic to show that Hutchins needs at least one more premise to establish his conclusion, namely, the normative premise that everyone should be taught the same truths, which is just the question at issue. But a little more analytical philosophy—conceptual analyses of "education," "teaching," "knowledge," and "truth," and of their relations to one another—would be necessary to show whether or not the original four premises are true. It would then turn out, I think, that they are either false or in need of qualifications of such a kind as to render the argument quite inconclusive.

One hesitates, in a case like this, to mention one's own work, and I do so only because my article, "Public Education and the Good Life,"[14] has found some favor with educators. In it, I discuss a problem which is important for both "the theory and practice of education" in public schools, namely, the teaching of values and moral principles, and much, though not all, of what I do is analysis. I seek to show that even though the public schools cannot teach religion, they can still do something worth while toward promoting the good and the moral life, and the analysis I use seems to me not only helpful but necessary in making this point. There seem to me to be many more educational

12 John Dewey, *Experience and Education,* chaps. ii and iii. New York: Macmillan Co., 1938.
13 Robert M. Hutchins, *The Higher Learning in America,* p. 66. New Haven, Connecticut: Yale University Press, 1936, 1962.
14 William K. Frankena, "Public Education and the Good Life," *Harvard Educational Review,* XXXI (Fall 1961), 413–426.

questions in connection with which conceptual and linguistic analysis would be useful.

Another potential contribution of the analytical philosopher is indicated by the Educational Policies Commission's booklet, *Moral and Spiritual Values in the Public Schools*.[15] I skip over the vagueness of the word "spiritual" and the failure to distinguish between values proper like happiness and knowledge, moral virtues like honesty and cooperativeness, and ethical or political principles like "The individual personality is supreme," "Institutional arrangements are the servants of mankind," or "Mutual consent is better than violence." (These are three very different sorts of things, but they are all called "values" and are treated as if they were alike and as if they figure in education in the same ways.) What concerns me is the discussion of "sanctions" or reasons for conduct, e.g., for Johnny's returning a dime given to him by mistake. The use and teaching of sanctions or reasons is regarded as important in the schools. Seven different sanctions are distinguished:

1. Justice: "The dime doesn't belong to you. It isn't fair for you to keep it."
2. The Law: "Keeping the dime is stealing, and the law punishes stealing."
3. Property Rights: "What would you think if someone else kept something that belongs to you?"
4. Integrity: "You would lose respect for yourself."
5. Group Approval: "Others will feel that they can't trust you."
6. Authority: "It is wrong to keep it, and I shall punish you if you don't return it."
7. Guidance: "What do *you* think, Johnny [after full discussion]?"

It is recognized that religious sanctions cannot be appealed to in public schools, but it is not adequately noticed how different the above seven are or that some of them are much more appropriate in moral education than others. Effectiveness is said to be the test of the use of a "sanction," and it is deemed wise "to utilize a variety of sanctions" rather than to rely on one alone.

Now, it happens that the business of "sanctions" or reasons for action and moral judgment has been much discussed by recent moral philosophers, especially analytically minded ones like Charles L. Stevenson, R. M. Hare, W. D. Falk, Kurt Baier, and Bernard Mayo. They make or debate distinctions between telling and getting to; between guiding and goading; between reasons, motives, and causes; between justifying reasons and motivating ones; between moral and other reasons; between reason and authority. Both in this way and in others, they have much to say to those who write about the teaching of moral and spiritual values in the schools and, perhaps, also to those who do the teaching.

A related vexing question which has been agitating both educational theorists and practicing teachers is that of the extent to which education does, may, or may not involve the teacher "imposing" his values or ethical principles on the child. Here again there is much that the analytical philosopher could do to help the discussion along, e.g., by exploring the logic of terms like "teach,"

---

15 Educational Policies Commission, *Moral and Spiritual Values in the Public Schools.* Washington: Educational Policies Commission, 1951.

"impose," "authority," "guide," "autonomy," and so on. As a matter of fact, such authors as were just referred to have already done a good deal of work on some of these notions. Besides, the worry about imposition in the case of ethical and value judgments stems in part, I am convinced, from the fact that such judgments are widely assumed or feared to be mere subjective or relative expressions of attitude or preference. And, again, the writers mentioned, along with others, have done much to show that this assumption or fear is not correct, i.e., there are important ways in which ethical and value judgments are susceptible of rationality, if not of proof. No doubt O'Connor is right in saying that the problem of how to justify such judgments is still unsolved, but at least some progress has been made—along rather different lines from those taken earlier by Dewey or Perry.

Recent Methodological Discussions, e.g., History

I have been trying to indicate areas and ways in which analytical philosophers have done or might do work that is relevant to the theory and even to the practice of school education. Another such area may be pointed out as follows. One of the chief articles in the Deweyan pedagogic creed is "the centrality of method," meaning by "method" the method of intelligent or scientific inquiry conceived as consisting of five steps:[16]

1. The presence of a problem
2. Clarification and definition of the problem
3. Formulation of a hypothesis as to its solution
4. Deducing and envisaging the consequences of acting on the hypothesis
5. Acting on the hypothesis and observing whether the predicted consequences take place or not.

The notion is that the central point of education is to foster the ability and the disposition to use this method in all fields of belief and action. Now, whether one takes method as central or merely as important, one must have some conception of it. There has, however, been much discussion of method since Dewey's day—in science, mathematics, history, and so forth—some of it by followers of Dewey like Ernest Nagel and Abraham Kaplan; some by others like Karl Popper, Nelson Goodman, R. B. Braithwaite, Carl G. Hempel, Toulmin, and Scheffler. I have little competence in this field, but it strikes me that this recent discussion of method is better than Dewey's was and that it is educationally relevant—just as relevant as Dewey's own views were. Is Dewey's pattern of reflective inquiry correct even for science? Is "scientific method" the same for all sciences? Is the same pattern applicable in history, mathematics, the humanities, and the arts? In so far as method is important in education, it must also be imperative that school educators have some awareness of the most recent answers to these questions.

Recent debate on the nature of historical inquiry may be taken as an illustration here. Roughly speaking, the debate is between those who think that history is a science and those who think it is something different—with such writers as Hempel and Patrick Gardiner on one side, R. G. Collingwood, W. H. Walsh, and William H. Dray on the other.[17] Is the aim of history a knowledge of the particular events of the past? Does or should the historian seek to ex-

---

[16] Hook, *op. cit.*, chap. vii.
[17] E.g., William H. Dray, *Philosophy of History.* Englewood Cliffs, New Jersey: Prentice-Hall, Inc., 1964.

plain past events by exhibiting them as examples of general laws or in some other way? Is history objective or subjective? While the recent discussion of such questions has not brought about agreement, it has been acute and interesting and should be instructive both to those who wish to evaluate Dewey's views on history and to teachers of history.

Other Possibly Useful Analyses

Now I shall cite a few fairly specific examples of recent philosophical analysis which strike me as bearing on the theory and even the practice of education in the schools. Much of the activity of recent philosophers has been in the area of the philosophy of language—many of them even conceive of philosophy as in some sense a "linguistic" inquiry. Many of their studies are very interesting, and it seems to me that some of them may well be of use to school teachers and curriculum-planners. One of the objects of concern has been the possibility and manner of distinguishing between two or more types of discourse, e.g., between discourse that is descriptive, factual, cognitive, constative, scientific, and so on, and discourse that is nondescriptive, evaluative, normative, noncognitive, nonscientific, performative, et cetera. In one of the more elaborate studies, Charles W. Morris distinguishes five "modes of signifying."[18] These are identification, designation, appraising, prescription, and "formation," and are exemplified, respectively, by "there," "deer," "fine," "Run!" and "or." He then also distinguishes four kinds of sign uses: the informative, the valuative, the incitive, and the systemic; and, finally, combining the five modes and the four uses, defines sixteen "major types of discourse," e.g., scientific discourse, which is designative-informative, and poetic discourse, which is appraisive-valuative. Whatever one may think of this particular theory of signs—and I hold no brief for it—it does seem to me that some acquaintance with such recent work would be of use to teachers of, what used to be called, grammar and rhetoric.

As also of possible interest to such teachers, as well as to other educators, one might mention P. W. Taylor's attempt to work out a systematic account of normative discourse (evaluating according to standards, evaluating according to rules, and prescribing), its various "realms" (moral, aesthetic, intellectual, religious, economic, political, legal, and conventional), and eight corresponding kinds of education.[19] Along a somewhat different line, there is the sort of grammar or semantic analysis done by Zeno Vendler in his articles on verbs and on the words "each," "any," "every," and "all"; or by Ziff, as well as Vendler, in works on the word "good."[20]

Perhaps the most heralded of recent work in this area of "linguistic phenomenology," as he himself calls it, is that of the late J. L. Austin.[21] Among other things, Austin is famous for calling attention to "performative utterances," i.e., sentences in which we *do* something as contrasted with sentences in which

---

[18] Charles William Morris, *Signs, Language, and Behavior*. New York: Prentice-Hall, Inc., 1946.

[19] Paul Warren Taylor, *Normative Discourse*. Englewood Cliffs, New Jersey: Prentice-Hall, Inc., 1961.

[20] Zeno Vendler, "Verbs and Times," *Philosophical Review*, LXVI (1957), 143–160; "Each and Every, Any and All," *Mind*, LXXI (1962); "The Grammar of Goodness," *Philosophical Review*, LXXII (1963), 446–465; and Paul Ziff, *Semantic Analysis* (Ithaca, New York: Cornell University Press, 1960).

[21] John L. Austin, *How to Do Things with Words*. The William James Lecture delivered at Harvard University in 1955. Cambridge, Massachusetts: Harvard University Press, 1962.

we merely state a fact or describe something (which he calls "constative"). Kinds of performatives, with examples, are the following:

1. Verdictives, e.g., "We find him guilty," "I estimate. . . ."
2. Exercitives, e.g., "I appoint . . . ," "I bequeath. . . ."
3. Commissives, e.g., "I promise . . . ," "We swear. . . ."
4. Behabitives, e.g., "I apologize . . . ," "Congratulations!"
5. Expositives, e.g., "I assume . . . ," "We affirm. . . ."

In the course of seeking for a way of distinguishing constatives and performatives, Austin makes a very important division between three kinds of speech acts. When I utter a sentence like, "You can't do that," I am saying something or performing a *locutionary* act. *In* saying this, I am also performing an *illocutionary* act—that of forbidding you to do something or protesting against your doing it. *By* doing *this,* I may keep you from doing it, bring you to your senses, or annoy you; i.e., I bring about a certain effect, and Austin calls my doing so a *perlocutionary* act. Some illocutionary acts are: reporting, asking, promising, thanking; some perlocutionary acts: persuading, inspiring, impressing, amusing. Both may be done through the performance of a locutionary act, i.e., through uttering a sentence, but they may also be done through acts that do not involve speech, e.g., through gestures or movements of the body.

It would, no doubt, be too much to suggest that Austin's findings should be taken bodily and taught in the schools, nor would I go about it. But it does seem plausible to maintain that some of them might well be made part of the training of English teachers and perhaps even trickle into their classroom instruction. At any rate, Austin does have incidentally instructive things to say about indirect speech, about the difference between threatening and intimidating, and many other matters relating to how to do things with words, which is certainly one of the things we have to learn as we grow up. In general, if there is any value in our having some conscious understanding of our modes of speech, it would seem appropriate that we should be initiated into this understanding before we come to take philosophy courses in the university.

Phenix says, ". . . knowledge has a fundamental role in education. . . . It follows that . . . it is important to know what knowledge is. The ways and content of teaching and learning depend very much on what one understands knowledge to be."[22] This statement is not so wholly true as it might seem to be or as educators have often taken it to be, but perhaps we may assume that there is something in it. If so, then it may also be relevant here to call attention to some recent discussions of knowing. It may be well to point out at once that they do not all go on within the old idealism-realism-pragmatism triangle. Rather, these discussions are often motivated, at least in part, by a wish to undercut such "skeptical" conclusions as "One can never know what another person is feeling," "We cannot be certain that there is an external world," or "We cannot really know anything except what is true on analytical or logical grounds alone." They tend to take the form of studies of the use of expressions like "I know . . . ," "I am certain . . . ," and "I believe . . . ," and of cognate forms in other persons and tenses. The possible relevance of these discussions

---

[22] Philip H. Phenix, *Philosophy of Education*, pp. 297–298. New York: Henry Holt & Co., 1958.

to education in the schools is indicated by the fact that they sometimes include such questions as "How do we learn the use of the expression 'I know'?" or remarks like "When I say 'S is P,' I imply at least that I believe it and, if I have been strictly brought up, that I am (quite) sure of it."

One of the earliest and best-known contributions along this line is Austin's paper on "Other Minds."[23] Here Austin makes a number of points, among them the following: (a) When one says, "I know . . . ," one is not reporting or describing the state of one's mind or passing on a piece of information, as older views seem to assume. "I know" is not "a descriptive phrase." (b) Rather, it is a performative utterance of some kind. When I say, "I know," I am doing something. In fact, I am doing something similar to what I am doing when I say, "I promise." When I say, "I promise," I am not reporting or describing what I am doing; I am doing it—I am promising, binding myself, giving another my word. Likewise, "When I say, 'I know,' I give others my word: I give others my authority for saying that 'S is P.' " (c) Thus, "I know" is different from "He knows," much as "I promise" is different from "He promises." (d) It is also very different from "I believe," "I am sure," "I am absolutely sure," "I swear," and the like. (e) If I say, "I know p," someone may challenge me by asking "How do you know?" and, in reply, I may be expected to show that I am in a position to know and what my evidence is. (f) It is not strictly correct to say, as some do, that I can know p only if p is true. If I say, "I know p," I cannot also say, "But I may be mistaken." But I may be justified in saying, "I know p" in some cases in which it later turns out that p is false; and in those cases it is not always appropriate to round on me by saying, "You've been proved wrong, so you *didn't* know" anymore than it is to say "You haven't performed, so you didn't promise." (g) When someone has said to me "I know," I am entitled to say "*I* know" too, at second hand. "The right to say 'I know' is transmissible, in the sort of way that other authority is transmissible."

Some of these points and others like them are now common currency, but some of them have been challenged by later writers, especially (b), (f), (g), and even (a).[24] Austin himself later indicated doubt whether "I know" is a commissive or an expositive. However, what has been said will exhibit the terms in which the discussion is going on, besides showing that it may be instructive for educators who use terms like "believe" and "know" (and not only jargon like "cognitive response," "identify with," and the like).

Perhaps a further note about point (g) will be of interest here, since education is often conceived of as involving a transmission of knowledge. It seems, among other things, to bear on the question of the admissibility in education of second-hand knowledge, of learning by being told rather than by doing. It may, therefore, be worth noticing that Hintikka in *Knowledge and Belief* agrees with Austin that knowledge is transmissible and that belief is not.[25] "If I know that you know that p is true, I virtually know myself that p is true. Hence, if you tell me that you know that p is true, I cannot (defensibly) deny that I know myself whether p is true without indicating that I do not wholly trust you (your

[23] John L. Austin, "Other Minds," reprinted in his *Philosophical Papers*. Oxford: Clarendon Press, 1961.
[24] Cf., e.g., Alan R. White, "On Claiming to Know," *Philosophical Review*, LXVI (April 1957), 180–192; Winston H. F. Barnes, "Knowing," *Philosophical Review*, LXXII (January 1963), 3–16.
[25] Jaako Hintikka, *Knowledge and Belief*, pp. 61–64. Ithaca, New York: Cornell University Press, 1962.

judgment or your sincerity)." But Hintikka doubts that Austin is right on point (*b*) and offers a different account of the transmissibility of knowledge. The explanation is not that A, in saying "I know *p*," is passing on his *authority* or right to say it to B, but that B *trusts* A when A says it. If B does not trust A, then A's saying "I know *p*" does not justify B in saying it also, unless A gives B his evidence for *p*. If we substitute a teacher for A and a pupil for B, then it looks as if two different conceptions of education go with these two different explanations of the transmissibility of knowing.

Conclusion

With some trepidation, I offer the above as an attempt to review three of the ways in which recent philosophy might or even should have a bearing on the theory and practice of the schools: (1) by providing normative premises, (2) by providing premises of other sorts, (3) by providing conceptual or linguistic analyses, methodological elucidations, and so forth. There are, as I said in the first section of this chapter, two other ways in which philosophy may be connected with the schools: (4) by being made a part of their curriculum, and (5) by being included in the training of their teachers and administrators. Space does not permit me to take up these topics, which are in any case of a very different order from the others dealt with here. They have, however, been rather thoroughly canvassed by philosophers in the following works: *Philosophy in American Education,* by Brand Blanshard, *et al.;*[26] and two committee reports, "The Teaching of Philosophy in American High Schools"[27] and "Philosophy in the Education of Teachers."[28] As a philosopher, I cannot but approve, in connection with (5), Conant's recommendations[29] that our future teachers be required to take a general philosophy course taught by a "real philosopher," and that future courses in the philosophy of education be taught by people "well trained" in philosophy. What I have said may, in fact, be taken as part of an argument for these recommendations. It should not, however, be taken, in connection with (4), as part of an argument for teaching recent philosophy in the schools, for it shows at most that recent philosophy has something to say that may be of value to school educators both for their theory and perhaps even for their practice. Of course, if what I have said be error and upon me proved, I should like to claim that I never writ. But it is too late for that now.

---

26 Brand Blanshard, *et al., Philosophy in American Education.* New York: Harper & Bros., 1945.

27 Committee on Philosophy in Education of the American Philosophical Association, "The Teaching of Philosophy in American High Schools," *Proceedings of the American Philosophical Association, 1958–59,* pp. 91–137. (Published for the Association by Antioch Press, Yellow Springs, Ohio, 1959.)

28 Committee on Philosophy in Education of the American Philosophical Association and the Committee on Cooperation with the American Philosophical Association of the Philosophy of Education Society, "Philosophy in the Education of Teachers," in *ibid.,* pp. 139–156.

29 James B. Conant, *The Education of American Teachers,* pp. 127–131. New York: McGraw-Hill Book Co., 1963.

CHAPTER IX
The Philosophic and Educational Enterprises

The conjunctive treatment of the philosophic and educational enterprises is not meant to imply that the two are identical. Rather it is because of the interaction between philosophy and education and because the same basic elements are important to both activities. Both the philosopher and the good teacher are concerned with the problem of meaning or language clarification, and both philosophizing and teaching require the sort of critical thinking that is based on asking and responding to relevant questions, the kind of thinking that recognizes valid alternatives and that results in truthful evaluations. Finally, in each case, the successful outcome is a synthesis of these elements into meaningful patterns that determine choices and guide actions.

The choice of the word "enterprise" to describe the philosophic and educational activities, rather than some other term such as "undertaking," "endeavor," "task," or "pursuit," is deliberate. *Webster's Seventh New Collegiate Dictionary* defines enterprise as "a project or undertaking that is difficult, complicated, or risky." The definition is descriptive of the challenge that confronts both the philosopher of education and the educator who do not deny the new ways of teaching and learning but who attempt to relate mental concepts in their newer sense to educational theory and who accept the responsibility of grappling with the problems that are inherent in the American ideal of education for all people.

Throughout our study, as we have noted the intimate relation between philosophy and education, we have seen that methodology grows out of general principles which are formally organized analytical concepts. We are again reminded that the philosophic commitment to these logical procedures is an ancient one by a brief review of the major philosophic and educational attitudes which we have considered in our study. As we move into the last decades of the twentieth century, the idea of accelerated change predominates, and the new demands on education underscore the philosophic emphasis on the process of education, the structures of knowledge, and the use of logical operations in the classroom.

During the past two decades there has been a growing recognition of the importance of automation to our way of life, but we are just beginning, with mixed emotions, to appreciate the potential power of the computer in the field of education. There are those who believe that instructional technology is dangerous. Some think it trivial, and still others see the computer as a universal panacea for the task of education. Whether one views the situation with alarm or with hope, there is no doubt but that modern technology does indeed modify the concerns of the educational philosopher and that programed instruction and business concepts in education will surely alter the basic organizations and structures of the school and the role of the teacher. The concluding section of Chapter IX deals with the philosophic enterprise and the teacher in terms of new educational vistas.

Philosophy and Education

At the beginning of our study, we realized the difficulties of making a definitive analysis of philosophy, education, and philosophy of education, but we soon began to see the affinity between philosophy and education. We saw that the two have the same means and end, inquiry and wisdom. We saw that the problems of the one are the concern of the other and that philosophy and education are mutually reconstructive. It was only after we sketched, in broad outlines, the scope of philosophy and of education that we were ready to attempt a definition of philosophy of education. We saw that, while philosophy of education has become a distinct discipline, it is not separate from either philosophy or from education, for it uses philosophic methods to deal with educational problems. We saw that philosophy of education deals with the problems of education and with the problems of philosophy as they are expressed in education. Finally, we saw that philosophy of education brings together our beliefs about the problem of reality, the nature of man, the theory of knowledge, the theory of value, and countless philosophic attitudes and judgments into a consistent body of thought which directs our educational choices and that these choices are conditioned by our views.

Throughout our study, our concern for the patterns and for the relations of ideas, for the symbolic constructions that provide man with a background of knowledge, has shown the intimacy between philosophic concepts and educational method. Our study has also underscored the continuity of the development of intellectual thought in Western culture, and we have seen that each generation has been influenced by the aspirations of the preceding one and has in turn contributed to the intellectual development of the one that follows. Therefore, a quick glance at our philosophical and educational heritage will help us to assess what adjustments and improvements in our educational practices are needed to meet the challenge of new technological, social, and political developments.

Traditional Attitudes

Traditionally, philosophy has attempted to respond in a disciplined way to the "large issues," to answer formally the recurrently great questions about life. In sum, we have seen that historically philosophers have been concerned about: 1) the nature of reality, whether the sum of reality is one or many, and the substance of the one or the many; 2) the nature of the good, ethical and moral beliefs, and whether or not values are dependent upon mankind; and 3) the nature of truth and of knowledge—if we can know, how we can know, and what we can know. These concerns fall into one of the three large areas of metaphysics, axiology, and epistemology.

Prior to the end of the nineteenth century, philosophy of education was not a discipline in its own right. Philosophy dealt with education in the abstract, in terms of some abstruse definition of the nature of man and of moral excellences. If the philosopher exhibited a specific concern about education it was not over the immediate and practical problems, but in regards to what "ought to be," to "ultimate purpose," or to "outcomes." All educational problems were considered in relation to some moral, ethical, or metaphysical commitment, and in terms of abstractions about good and evil, truth and error, or reality and appearance. Thus, until the latter part of the nineteenth century, the problems of education were considered to be the problems of philosophy. Until the Normal School of the 1840's, the concept of method in education was not defined, and educational methods were not in themselves subjects of inquiry. Knowledge of subject matter was thought to be sufficient for teaching, and teachers did not approach the various disciplines as members of a separate one. However, we have seen that throughout history there has been a natural relation between educational concepts and modes of teaching.

For instance, Plato's view of the nature of reality told him that man is born with his full quotient of knowledge which is all contained in the rational soul. Accordingly, this latent knowledge must be drawn from the soul into the realm of individual awareness and what better way than by means of the searching questions of a Socrates? A student is not "taught" but is led to a personal insight as the dialogue between student and teacher progresses, and pertinent questions call for a careful examination of concepts. Inquiry is the prime consideration, and the assertion of any definite position is only incidental.

Augustine also made use of the dialogue but with a different emphasis. According to his view, words are the stimuli that can induce the discovery of realities which are not yet known by the student. Again the teacher does not actually "teach" or transmit knowledge, but his questions need not be probing, for the first consideration is a skillful use of words that will prompt a religious insight. Augustine speaks as follows to Adeomantus in *The Teacher:*

> But, referring now to all things which we understand, we consult, not the speaker who utters words, but the guardian truth within the

mind itself, because we have perhaps been reminded by words to do so. Moreover, He who is consulted teaches; for He who is said to reside in the interior man is Christ,[1] that is, the unchangeable excellence of God and His everlasting wisdom, which every rational soul does indeed consult. But there is revealed to each one as much as he can apprehend through his will according as it is more perfect or less perfect.[2]

Scholasticism also used the dialogue form but in a different pattern and for different goals. The Platonic dialogue was not based on the assumption that the discussants could arrive at any final and complete truth, and the underlying rationale was that the discussants might achieve an understanding as they are forced to refine ideas that are in conflict with each other. Scholasticism, on the other hand, presupposes absolute truths which are derived from truths and which lead to other truths. Each dialogical investigation, in which all truths are connected, concludes with final assertions. The works of St. Thomas Aquinas, with the general principle of opposing statements which are placed together in such a way that a method for further analysis is indicated, provide us with the finest examples of the scholastic form. Each of the works begins with an explanation in essay form of the nature of the problem and the need for its resolution. The resolution is presented in the beginning, and the important factor is the manner in which the resolution of the problem is supported. The form is highly persuasive and thoroughly rationalistic. It is interesting to note that, while modern analysis is far more sophisticated than the scholastic method, they both tend to reduce reality to a system of definitions.

We have said that educational method is derived, at least in part, from philosophic concept and that there is a close relation between the two. Yet we have seen that the dialogic form, which originated with Plato, was used by Socrates to lead a student to reliable knowledge through a comparison of meanings and ideas. We saw that churchmen such as Augustine used a slight variation of the same form to encourage the student to recognize the revealed truths of God and that scholastics such as St. Thomas Aquinas used the same general principle to direct the student to a system of absolute truths. We shall see presently that computerized instruction also relies upon the principle of question and answer, and it becomes apparent that the dialogue has been used by outstanding teachers throughout the history of Western education. On the surface, this seems sufficient reason to question our assertion about the intimacy between concept and method.

However, if one is careful to make a distinction between *method,* and the less inclusive term, *technique,* there is no problem. If the terms are used interchangeably, as is often the case in educational writings, it is difficult to be definitive about the concept of method. Method, a far broader

---

[1] Ephesians 3:16–17.
[2] St. Aurelius Augustine, *Concerning the Teacher* and *On the Immortality of the Soul,* George G. Leckie, trans. (New York: Appleton-Century-Crofts, Inc., 1938), pp. 47–48.

term than technique, is a general plan which is concerned with broad goals and consequences, and it is bound to a wide range of conditions. In order to determine a method, or a way of accomplishing certain goals, full use must be made of our reflective and explorative powers, as we reason, experiment, and analyze, in order that we may determine which acts or techniques will be the most effective for our purpose. Methods are affected by expectations, aspirations, and attitudes, and one method may include a number of techniques, the sum of which go beyond the consequences of the specific objective of each of the techniques.

For instance, upholstering requires a special skill. The manner in which the material is cut, fit, and applied to a frame is a matter of technique. But deciding upon the texture, pattern, color, and type of material that will be used are decisions that must be made within a particular context, which includes the type of article which is being upholstered, where and how it will be used, by how many, and other demands that need not be considered for the immediate task of upholstering. The technique of upholstering remains basically the same, whether or not the particular item is a club chair for a den, a couch for a formal salon, a chaise lounge for a bedroom, or seats for a Mercedes Benz. The same is true of the dialogic form, which is a *technique* employed to achieve a specific goal within the context of a particular *method,* which is concerned with the overall purpose. The dialogic form is an effective technique which can be used to teach almost any kind of subject matter, but clearly, it is better suited to some kinds of knowledge than it is to others. Specifically, it is an excellent technique to encourage the development of verbal skills, the process of logical analysis, deductive reasoning, and the exploration of a sequence of ideas. It is of far less value in a naturalistic or experimental context.

Aristotle, for example, was concerned with the world around him in ways that would have been completely foreign to Plato. We remember that, according to Aristotle, universal truths are attained only by pure reason and intuition (See Chapter III), but reality was revealed to him through sense perception and by the facts of experience. His methods could be called inductive, for he began with what was knowable, from the empirical, and moved to that which is knowable in-itself. This use of the scientific method was an early anticipation of the scientific-empirical outlook which makes use of the experiences of the child for the development of potential faculties. More recent expression of this attitude is found in the writings of John Locke whose ideas were a stimulus for views that have come to be known as faculty psychology.

The idea of broadening experience may have been instrumental in the development of Jean Jacques Rousseau's beliefs about letting nature teach the child. *Émile* is the classic example of the view that nature is discovered and used for purposes that are abstracted from nature. The emphasis upon discovery is a preliminary step for the development of symbolic process in reasoning. It is a short step from the idea of natural goodness to the idea of a rational order in man. As our discussions of Immanuel Kant and J. F.

Herbart have shown, the acceptance of a rational order followed upon the beliefs of Rousseau. Kant provided the philosophical base of the rationalistic view, and Herbart was largely responsible for the educational implications.

The aim of education as expressed by Herbart could best be described by the phrase, moral character. Moral character is developed by moral teachers and by the use of beautiful thoughts as they have been expressed in the literature of man. Although highly verbal and literary, the method depended upon a psychology of interest, practice, and apperception. Through the method of the formal steps of learning, the abstractions of theory could *direct* practice through the derivation of well-established rules. The rationalistic view of education assumes general rules or principles which are generative of other rules that serve as educational directives. In modern parlance, this view has been called a *rule model*.[3]

Modern Attitudes

Through the nineteenth century, philosophers were still confident that they could know the ultimate nature of the world through reason, but by the turn of the century science and common sense began to have their way. Once all of the sciences had been a part of philosophy, but astronomy, then physics, and finally psychology and sociology developed into independent disciplines. Philosophy, bereft and unable to compete with science as a way of studying the real world, became more and more introspective looking inward to its own problems rather than outward to man in society. Experience in the twentieth century world of advanced technology, space, and science contradicts the idealistic theory that material objects are not in themselves "real," and where formerly men had looked to the philosopher for guidance, they began to turn instead to those who were closer to the immediate concerns of humanity.

When philosophers turned from abstract metaphysics as the source of educational ideals, they did not completely desert philosophy in the "grand tradition," for they realized that questions about knowledge, value, and reality are important for the development of a philosophy of education. But the realization that the problems of education are distinct from the problems of philosophy was the impetus for the development of a philosophizing about education in terms of broad social issues. The development of educational psychology, the accumulation of psychological data about the learning process, measuring and testing general and special abilities, and other such studies, have had a great impact on contemporary educational philosophers. Dewey's view of education as a social process was compatible with the thinking of those interested in economics and social philosophy. During the first half of this century educational thought centered on a protest against systematized scientific knowledge, externally imposed tasks, subjects and subject matter, and personal and social distress. The emphasis, as we noted

---

[3] See reading at the end of the chapter.

in Chapter VII, was on experimentation, discovery, and observation and stressed freedom of individual choice and movement. The goals were technical and practical know-how, adjustment and happiness within a societal context.

Today the human environment is undergoing change at such a rate that our concern over the inadequacy of our educational programs to meet the demands of the next decades borders on anxiety. Our discussion of educational critics indicated the extent of the national concern that education is not keeping abreast with the times, much less looking ahead. Some insist that subjects need to be taught as ways of thinking about and explaining the world; they say that a generality of knowledge is far more needed than a specificity of learning. Others claim that salvation lies in a return to the classics and that we need to stress the rigor of instruction. We find ourselves in the midst of a ferment of claims and counterclaims and in dire need of philosophical direction.

At the same time, there are those critics who believe that the philosopher can no longer provide vision and direction for educational goals. These claim that the philosopher has revolted against traditional ways to become more concerned with the analysis of social, scientific, and political issues. Certainly it is true that contemporary philosophers and philosophers of education are logically and linguistically oriented in their approaches to the problems of man. This shift of focus is particularly noticeable in the writings of philosophers of education, for their efforts have been directed, for the most part, toward methods of a theoretical nature. According to W. K. Frankena:

> We must now take a look at education, in order to see how philosophy may come to bear upon it. At once a distinction must be made between education as a process and education as an academic discipline. In the former sense, education is the process by which society makes of its members what it is desirable that they should become (not merely what it desires them to become), either in general or in so far as this may be carried on by what are called "schools." In the second sense, education is the discipline which studies this process in one way or another, its findings being reported and passed on in professional courses in schools of education.[4]

The distinction made by Frankena has served as a stimulus for new approaches to educational theorizing. The idea that education is an academic discipline has been subjected to continuing analyses by educators and particularly by educational philosophers. Marc Belth, for one, insists that education is a discipline in its own right, with the act of thinking as its unique subject matter, that it is a discipline which studies not only all methods of thought but all of the ways to teach thought. He maintains that

---

[4] W. K. Frankena, "Toward a Philosophy of Education," *Harvard Educational Review,* XXVI, No. 2 (Spring 1956), 95.

it is a discipline, or branch of inquiry, which inquires into all other disciplines and is therefore the queen of disciplines. He doubts if there would be a psychologist, a biologist, or a sociologist in the world, were it not for the discipline of education which works at improving methods of inquiry and creativity. Certainly, whatever view one takes of education, whether it is thought to be a process or a discipline, recent searching analyses in this regard indicate new approaches to educational theory.

New Horizons in Educational Theorizing

Education and the Structures of Knowledge

Some of the leading philosophers of education who are concerned about the need for curriculum changes in the schools have become involved with analyses of the concept of knowledge structure, hoping to determine what bearing, if any, it has upon education and teaching. They believe that a theoretical approach to curriculum problems, one which places greater emphasis upon the basic elements of knowledge, will result in more useful and rigorous educational programs. Numbers of curriculum study groups, such as the Physical Science Study Committee, the School Mathematics Study Group, and the Biological Sciences Curriculum Study, were formed in the 1950's out of a growing concern for better science and mathematics programs. All of these emphasized the importance of the concept of structures of knowledge for curriculum revitalization.

The idea of structures of knowledge is not without historical precedent, as we recall Plato's description of the Divided Line and Aristotle's critique of knowledge. Each was an attempt to find structure in knowledge, and our discussions of the two men indicated their bent toward teaching fundamental structure. Later, Auguste Comte's analyses of organization served as models of the search for structure. Current investigations, however, have a scientific-empirical nature rather than a metaphysical sense of structure.

As we have noted, the basic idea of structure is one of relationships, of how things go together. The idea is that genuine knowledge of any subject matter discipline, such as physics, English, or history, can be claimed only when the interrelationships of elements within a total complex are known. The idea of structure of a particular discipline is really a cluster of problems. There seem to be at least three distinct questions about the determination of the structure of knowledge. First, there is the question of what it is about physics, chemistry, or English that is unique and fundamental to each. Assuming that there is a uniqueness to each subject, the second question seeks the answer to how these individual disciplines can be organized into some scheme for purposes of generalization. Finally, there is the question about what sorts of warrants or proofs will be acceptable to those who are concerned with these problems.

The structure of each discipline, in many instances, goes beyond the limits of common sense observation which creates certain problems. For example, the discussion of DNA and RNA, of genetic structure, of the atom, of an organic function, of light waves and particles is in each case a rather sophisticated attempt to delineate structure. This is not to deny that there are more obvious cases of structure that can be noted through simple observational schemes such as the stimulus-response actions of animals. Each discipline is so designated on the basis that there is a determinable structure. Many scholars, however, are not satisfied with the investigations that have been accomplished thus far and feel that a great deal more research in the area is mandatory.

The second question deals with the organization of the individual disciplines into a structure. There are traditional schemes which are readily recognizable, such as the natural sciences, mathematics, the humanities, and the social sciences. Other curricula arrangements which have been tried in the American public school system include the classical curriculum, the core curriculum, the integrated curriculum, team teaching, the needs of students, and programed learning, which we shall discuss in some detail later in the chapter. Qualities of intelligence and value have played a prominent part in all of the curricular organizations. The idea that the curriculum should be organized around cognitive functions has been suggested by Philip Phenix.[5] He lists the following categories: 1) symbolics—a concern for language use, mathematics, and non-discursive forms; 2) empirics—a concern for the physical, social, and life sciences; 3) aesthetics—a concern for the arts and literature of men; 4) synnoetics—a concern for the existential elements of philosophy, literature, psychology, and religion; 5) ethics —a concern for moral and ethical issues; and 6) synoptics—a synthesis of ideas through the medium of history, philosophy, and religion.

Joseph Tykociner,[6] who writes of the need to view knowledge as a whole, suggests an even more elaborate scheme for organizing the curriculum. He believes that a concept of unity and coherence must be in the foreground of all instructional procedures. His own organizational structure involves five fundamental zones of experience which are comprised of twelve areas of knowledge. The function of the first zone is to develop systems of symbolic representation of perceptual and cognitive activity for purposes of communication. The function of the second zone is to systematize knowledge of basic facts and their relations. The third zone has the function of systematizing knowledge of the past, of projecting future needs, and of regulating activities. The function of the fourth zone is to promote the growth of all of the arts and sciences, and that of the last zone is to create an all-embracing synthesis.

Those who are convinced that the concept of knowledge structure has a bearing upon education and teaching claim that teaching will be more effective if it is based on the ways that the elements of knowledge are

[5] Philip Phenix, "The Architectonics of Knowledge," Chapter II in B. O. Smith's, *Education and the Structure of Knowledge.* (Chicago: Rand McNally Co., 1964).
[6] Joseph T. Tykociner, "Zetetics and Areas of Knowledge," Chapter IV in B. O. Smith's, *Education and The Structure of Knowledge.* (Chicago: Rand McNally Co., 1964).

logically related. They say that a concern for structure will lead the teacher to a sensitivity about the processes of logical analysis and language clarity and help her to a genuine perspective of teaching-learning in the classroom.

Logical Operations for Critical Thinking

The most extensive of the investigations into logic and teaching has been done by Professor B. Othanel Smith, and his associates at the University of Illinois. Professor Smith has observed classroom teaching behavior of teachers over a period of years, and as a result of his observations, he has constructed a series of broad concepts to describe logical operations. These categories must be studied in the light of the following comment by Smith and Meux:

> Our observations indicate that teaching behavior seldom conforms to strict logical structures, such as those that are laid down in ideal forms of explanation, definition, and so forth. Of course, the question of whether or not teaching behavior should so conform is an empirical one, to be answered by reference to some criterion of effective teaching.[7]

The categories listed by Smith and Meux are: episodes, entries, defining, describing, designation, stating, reporting, substituting, evaluating, opining, classifying, comparing and contrasting, conditional inferring, and explaining. The first two categories, episodes and entries, are really the setting for the logical responses which are listed above. An episode is some type of interaction, usually verbal, between a number of individuals who are concerned about a common topic. The interaction would be best described as episodic, since one episode flows rather quickly into another which gives continuity to discussion. Entries are the means whereby episodes are brought to life. Perhaps the most common type of entry would be the questioning of the student by the teacher, which is reminiscent of the dialogic form. Certainly, the teacher who is conscious of the categories described by Smith and Meux has a good start toward developing the kind of environment that will stimulate critical thinking. The success of the teacher will be evident when the students are able to evaluate assumptions, evidence, form, and conclusions in a series of arguments. This means that the student will be sensitive to meaning, validity, and reliability of statements and arguments.

Robert Ennis has been a contributor to the idea that logic can be important to teaching. He has proposed twelve logical operations for directing classroom activities. They are the following:

1. Grasping the meaning of a statement.
2. Judging whether there is ambiguity in a chain of reasoning.

---

[7] B. O. Smith and Milton O. Meux, "Logical Dimensions of Teaching Behavior," in Bruce Biddle and William Ellena, eds., *Contemporary Research on Teacher Effectiveness* (New York: Holt, Rinehart & Winston, Inc., 1964), p. 152.

3. Judging whether statements contradict each other.
4. Judging whether a conclusion follows necessarily.
5. Judging whether a statement is specific enough.
6. Judging whether a principle establishes a statement claimed to be an application of it.
7. Judging whether an "observation statement" is reliable.
8. Judging whether an inductive inference is warranted.
9. Judging whether the problem has been identified.
10. Judging whether something is an assumption.
11. Judging whether a definition is adequate.
12. Judging whether a statement made by an alleged authority is acceptable.[8]

Logic is expressed in language, and the tendency during the past few decades to stress various forms of activity other than speech and writing as the preferred media of teaching has obscured the importance of logical operations. It has not been popular in the schools to think of problems as intellectual dilemmas, and the emphasis has been on the development of confidence and flexibility for the solution of difficulties that impede action. The primary concern has not been to teach correct reasoning or to teach the principles of logical thinking, and most often a student is not even made aware of the logical operations he just *happens* to perform.

Contemporary philosophical interest in language clarification, structures of knowledge, and logical operations will eventually be reflected in classroom procedures. Already educational philosophers point out that no matter how wide the range of knowledge a student accumulates, his intellectual development is neglected if he has not mastered the logical procedures which are designed to stimulate and guide intellectual powers. They urge that training in logic be required of all teachers so that teaching may be more intellectually oriented. They point out that, generally speaking, one set of logical procedures and standards for assessing thought can be used in different realms of knowledge and that if a student understands the principles of logical thinking he will be able to benefit in one area from the thinking he does in a different one. Concentration upon the logical order of subject matter, according to educational theorists, promotes sequential learning and critical thinking which, in turn, lead to implicative thinking and creative speculation. The culmination is a stage of synthesis where the student structures knowledge in his own way, for his own purposes.

There are many who fear that recent technological developments, and the growing interest in technological implications for education will serve as a check on the trend to emphasize the importance of logical procedures in the classroom. There are some, however, who maintain that technology is merely another avenue, perhaps a short-cut, toward the solution of a common problem. But whatever view one takes, the following discussion

---
[8] Robert H. Ennis, "A Concept of *Critical Thinking;* A Proposed Basis for Research in The Teaching and Evaluation of Critical Thinking Ability," *Harvard Educational Review,* XXXII (Winter 1962), 81–111.

regarding the technological revolution and the implications for education makes it clear that these are unalterable facts which must be seriously considered by educational philosophers and by educators.

The Instructional Revolution

American Technology

Americans have always placed a high value on those things which foster innovation and progress, and the most stable feature of American society is a continuum of change. In recent years the rate of change has been greatly accelerated by technological advances. It has been said that we are in the midst of a second scientific revolution that has permeated every area of living, a revolution that centers on atomic energy, automation, computers, and chemical materials. The accumulated techniques since the advent of the steam engine and the spinning machine have brought us to a technology that has altered, or has the potential of altering, all of our institutions.

Technology, in the broadest sense of the word, is the aspect of any culture which helps the members of a society to adjust to their environment. While every society then possesses a technology of sorts, American society, which is so developed that the basic adaptation to the physical environment is almost total, concentrates technological energies on solving social problems and on changing or expanding the physical environment. Many people have the idea that technology is a collection of gadgets or instrumentation, but it involves a great deal more. Over and above the products that result from advanced technology are the new techniques or procedures, the new ways of doing things that expand physical and intellectual horizons. Technology is a way of thinking that alters concepts of leisure and of work, and it has resulted in automation that has widespread effects throughout industry, government, and most of society.

Automation alters procedures in libraries, hospitals, factories, offices, and schools and affects workers, executives, and professionals. Industry and government spend billions of dollars each year on research and development, and yet we can only imagine some of the long-range effects of this aspect of our technological progress. As discoveries are made, they find their way to the public in no time at all. For instance, the materials originally developed for the nose cone of guided missiles were soon found in cookware and appliances in kitchens all over America. Miniature computers and other electrical equipment developed for the missiles were quickly adapted by private industry where they were even used to cut bikini patterns from a standard size model in order to make suits for the mass market, an undertaking that was previously a cut-and-fit, hand-done job requiring great skill.

Changes occur so rapidly that it is difficult for the layman and the professional to keep their own knowledge up to date, and as companies become more and more automated, the demand for the unskilled worker shrinks as new jobs come into being. New skills are needed that emphasize the mental rather than the physical aspect of the worker. New positions are created which require a larger degree of *creative* intelligence. It depends upon the schools to turn out individuals who are not only capable of understanding and using the tools of an expanding technology but who will have the necessary knowledge and skill to adapt to the changes generated by current innovations. Automation and our increasing reliance on advanced technological methods present education with one of the greatest challenges of all time and promise immeasurable rewards commensurate with the investments educators are willing to make of their time and personnel to support the necessary research. Yet many are still skeptical about the possibilities of instructional technology, and education continues to lag as the most primitive sector of American technology.

The Technological Lag in Education

There are a number of reasons why educators have been slow to accept the implications of technology for education. First, the teaching profession is characterized by an innate conservatism which discourages progress in educational techniques and methods and which exhibits a marked reluctance to question traditional attitudes. Some teachers, fearing that they will be replaced by a machine, see automation as a threat to their livelihood, if not to their very reason for being. Many believe that automation will inevitably result in a dilution of quality, and teachers and parents alike, who confuse programed education with industrial automation, recoil from the idea of assembly-line technology that they see as a threat to individualism.

Secondly, there are those, including many outstanding scholars, who tend to "throw the baby out with the bath water." They criticize, often with good reason, one aspect or implication of an innovation. Unfortunately, the weight and magnitude of their prestige frequently carries sufficient influence to contribute to the retardation of concepts that have a good deal to offer. For instance, George Kneller, a professor of education at U.C.L.A., warns against programed instruction with the following statement. He says, "If we seek exact responses and reward only those who conform to the demands of the machine, we are likely to snuff out the precious spark of revolt that is necessary to healthy growth and activity." Certainly one can find little reason to quarrel with the statement, granting the assumption that the proponents of programed instruction advocate its use to the exclusion of all other techniques. However, those who are informed about programing techniques know that they are not intended to be a substitute for textbooks, laboratories, lectures, or other valuable learning experiences.

Benjamin Fine, in his book on *Teaching Machines,* makes a statement that expresses an attitude similar to Kneller's. He writes that, "Dr. Skinner has developed a program to help a student memorize a long poem, but he has not yet found one which will teach a student to enjoy poetry!" Since any good teacher knows that a love of poetry does not necessarily follow from rote memorization, regardless of how it is accomplished, the statement hardly seems germane to a criticism of programed instruction. Nor does the remark made by another professor of education, Lee J. Cronbach, who has said that, "It is difficult to see how a program can contribute to divergent thinking and creative imagination. . ." Certainly the innate limitations of programed instruction should be considered when one attempts an evaluation of its potential as a teaching resource; but its unique possibilities should receive equal consideration. It is not the purpose here to defend nor to attack programed instruction. But it is relevant to our concern for the philosophic enterprise to point out the error of judging a whole by one of the parts or of making an assessment without sufficient information.

Data Processing in Schools

Since the 1930's there has been a slow development and use in some schools of instruments and materials that are the conventional audio-visual devices, and since 1950 there has been in scattered instances, some use of television, electronic learning laboratories, various types of teaching machines and computers. For the most part, however, these efforts have been viewed as mere "tinkering" in comparison to the "real concerns" of education, and computers and electronic accounting machinery have been used in schools only to make traditional systems more efficient. Some of the larger school districts converted to accounting machinery for routine bookkeeping, for preparation of class schedules, or in their libraries, but through the 1960's the available computer technology and programing techniques were still practically untapped.

Data processing came into the school office in the early 60's by way of modern business operations. For obvious reasons, the programs were initially introduced and adopted in crowded urban areas where the school system was able to take advantage of available equipment on a local basis, either by way of a local business firm willing to handle data processing on a service basis, or by renting the basic equipment. As the pioneering efforts of the larger systems continue to be efficacious, the smaller systems may eventually become inspired to a regional pooling of resources, or perhaps to combining school use with local government utilization, or to finding some other solution to the lack of available equipment.

Data processing was not introduced into the school office without its attendant problems, but they have been problems that can be met in a situation open to experimentation, and reports from schools where data processing has been tried are on the credit side. Data processing equipment has been used effectively to accomplish many tasks ordinarily handled by professional school personnel. It has been applied to attendance keeping, grade reporting, scheduling of pupil classes, recording and analysis of health data, and relevant information for guidance counselors. School business managers have used data processing for check writing, census taking, accounting, bus lists, and other details of school operation. The process is basically simple, for the data processing operation must be reduced to the binary simplicity of a "yes" or "no" kind of sequence. Each operation is reduced to its simplest components, which is a challenge comparable to the one that the author of a linear program for programed instruction faces.

As a matter of fact, by the late 1960's, many educators who had been slow to accept the implications of the new technology for education began to see data processing in the schools as being important not only in its own right but as a significant step towards a more objective view of programed instruction. Subjectivity often places the largest stumbling blocks in the way of progress, and nothing clears the path more effectively than the empirical data from schools where data processing has been successfully adopted. The school office may well prove to be the shortest route into the classroom for the computer, for many of the objections to data processing which have been invalidated, are the same objections that have been made against programed instruction.

Data processing in school offices has convinced many who subscribed to the machine mythology that the computer may take over all thought processes that their fears are groundless. Those who have worked with data processing equipment have experienced its limitations, as they have benefitted from its capabilities, and they have no illusion that the entire man or woman could ever be replaced by a machine. Teachers who have been relieved of routine and uncreative clerical tasks that can be accomplished by machinery have found more time and energy for the creative thinking that is essential for superior teaching. These teachers no longer fear that they will be replaced by the teaching machine, but realize that programed instruction will simply mean a redefinition of their role. They realize that it is as foolish to predict teacher replacement by machinery as it would be to fear that the surgeon will be replaced by the laser beam. The fear of change that was a threat to many educators, becomes a challenge for the informed to seek out additional ways to release professionals from the tyranny of trivia so that they will be free for the more important task of evaluating and planning their own teaching.

Programing Techniques

The idea behind programed instruction is as old as the Socratic method that we found in Plato's *Meno*. We saw how Socrates led the ignorant slave boy step by step, from simple to more complex facts, to the objective that he had in mind—the solution of a particular mathematical problem. We have seen that throughout the history of education, good teachers have used this technique—asking questions, leading the student from error toward truth, forcing him to be responsive, and allowing him to move at his own rate of speed in a one to one relationship. Even though the most noted educational theorists do not claim to have any definitive answers about *how* a child learns, most do agree that the ideal teaching situation for children is one of individual tutoring, a system where each child can be approached according to his particular needs and abilities. Unfortunately, this is possible for only a privileged few, for such a system is not practical in public school systems which must serve millions upon millions of children.

However, results obtained in computerized classrooms such as those in the Brentwood Elementary School, and the Walter Hays School—both in Palo Alto, California—indicate that the computer may be a likely substitute for the tutor. In both cases, the child learns by doing and reacting for himself. His mistakes are corrected at once so that wrong answers cannot become a lasting part of his experience, and correct answers are immediately reinforced by other similar problems. The risk of boredom is minimized, because as soon as the child has mastered the problem at hand, he moves directly to a more difficult problem. The child is not held back by slower students, nor is he forced to move ahead before he is ready, for each progresses at his own rate. As individual tutoring must be supplemented by social experiences among other children, it should go without saying that the machine is only *one* aspect of the total educational experience of a child. Used for "drill and practice," or for what has been called "conceptual teaching," there is little difference between the question and answer technique used by the human tutor and the "computer-tutor." In both cases the heart of the technique is the program, and in both cases the program is developed by a human teacher or by a human programer. There is no way for a computer to deal with intuitive insights or with creative thinking, and this makes the task of the programer an exacting one. The programer is forced to analyze the subject matter in advance more carefully than a teacher who is using the question and answer technique. The programer must be fully aware of the objectives, and the questions must be constructed in advance so that correct answers are not possible if the student does not understand the material. Properly used, the computerized tutoring and drilling can free the teacher to concentrate on developing the use of the creative aspects of language and math.

It should be noted that the computer is not just an ordinary machine that can serve only one person at a time. A talking computer can give individual attention to as many as sixteen children, and only one computer can drill and practice as many as thirty children at a time. Nor do the children have to be at the same place as the computer, as the machines used for drill and practice can be connected to a computer thousands of miles away by telephone lines. It is regrettable that the machinery of programed instruction attracts more public attention than the methods, for the machine itself is less complicated than many of the educational toys that utilize the mechanical principles of the simple teaching machine. The program (subject matter) and the programing (the arrangement of the materials) are the crucial aspects of this sort of instruction. The programing varies according to the subject, but generally speaking the material is presented in small steps beginning with the simple, easy to understand concepts, and building to the complex. At each step a check is made to substantiate the learner's understanding and comprehension of the material before proceeding to the next step or question. The psychological basis for programed instruction is the principle of immediate reinforcement. The technique encourages an orderly and controlled development of individual skill, and the flexibility and adjustment to individual differences is a safeguard against the assembly line prototypes that many fear.

There are three distinct philosophic attitudes among the pioneers of program techniques, and these are best exemplified by the developments of S. L. Pressey, B. F. Skinner, and N. A. Crowder. The first of these men, S. L. Pressey, regarded the program as a supplement rather than a substitute for other techniques. Pressey's idea was that teaching machines should function as quiz devices to help consolidate materials learned from other sources, such as the textbook, lectures, or the laboratory. His devices employed the principles of continuous activity of the student, reinforcement, and individual rate of progress and relied upon the multiple-choice type of question. This type of programing where the activity moves from question to learning material and back to questions is called "branching."

B. F. Skinner's programed learning, in sharp contrast to branching, is linear where reinforcement is the primary basis of learning. Here the subject matter is developed in small steps and the pupil is rewarded by each success. At the same time, his knowledge is reinforced. The pupil is motivated by the reward for correct answers, and the sequence of questions is tight and carefully constructed in order to minimize incorrect responses. This type of programing is especially suited for drill and practice teaching.

Crowder's approach is associated with intrinsic programing, and like Pressey, he relies upon multiple choice items. The pupil answers a question, and when he makes an error he is referred to correct sources of information. He can proceed only when the mistake has been eliminated. This too, is a branching procedure, but when the student meets an obstacle he is helped by a specific direction. The method of programing necessitates an insight into how the pupil can be expected to think and to respond. The anticipated incorrect answers are used to help build knowledge and skill. All teachers who use cogent reasoning and well-conceived questions to encourage student answers utilize the branching technique, but the use of the machine enables the student to receive more individual instruction than is possible otherwise.

The Computer-Based Classroom — Pros and Cons

Results from computer-based classrooms are still by no means conclusive, but for the most part the findings have been encouraging. At Walter Hays School, special groups of children with an average IQ of 137 were chosen to participate in computer education programs. On the other hand, the children involved in the programs at Brentwood Elementary School had an average IQ of 82 and came from disadvantaged homes. In both cases, improvement in the rate of learning was significant, and both the bright students and the dull ones made considerable progress. One of the most significant findings was that computer instruction seemed to eliminate the difference in learning rates between the sexes. Educators have long been aware that girls have less trouble learning spelling, grammar, and word usage than boys, but in the computer-based classrooms the learning leap of the boys—bright and dull—was great enough so as to wipe out the difference. Further, bright and dull children of both sexes in the computer-based classrooms tested notably higher on standard achievement language tests than those students in a "control group" who had not been taught by the computer.

Patrick Suppes, a Stanford professor who developed the mathematic curriculum for the computer, found the significant result of math instruction by computer to be that the children who started out ranking the lowest made the greatest leaps. His findings lead him to believe that at least initially, computer-based instruction has the greatest impact on the bottom twenty-five per cent and on the top twenty-five per cent of the students. This is probably due to the fact that in computer-based classrooms bright students are not held back, and slow students are not forced beyond their present level of comprehension and understanding. The computer is able to keep a running account of all questions and answers, and so it can make an exact determination as to when a child should be moved forward or held back in his lessons. It can also search out *patterns* of errors so that a child can be individually drilled according to his personal problems. Furthermore, the computer is capable of compiling a record of its own effectiveness while it is teaching, and it is flexible enough so that necessary changes can be made overnight. It seems that without exception, those who have actively worked with children in computer-based classrooms are convinced that it is the best method for teaching children to read and to figure, because it does work.

We have already noted some of the reasons why there are not more computer-based classrooms, but perhaps the prime factor is a lack of sufficient funds to finance such programs. For instance, the program at the Brentwood Elementary School for just one year cost more than a million dollars. The cost of a single console, installed and connected to a computer at a central district office, is more than two thousand dollars. Even if mass production should reduce this cost to less than a thousand dollars, it would still cost upward of a billion dollars to put the consoles into most classrooms in America. It could be that another teaching device, the Talking Typewriter developed by Omar K. Moore, will prove to be more practical on a large scale. The Talking Typewriter does not have the research capacity of the computer, nor can it keep the same sort of running records. But there is considerable evidence that it *can* teach, and the cost of installation is considerably less than the computer consoles.

In any event, the application of technology to education seems inevitable if we are going to solve the many problems that have been created by the increased rate at which our store of knowledge is growing. We can be sure that if technology, with its systems and organizational patterns, is applied to instruction a different and tighter organization than the usual instructional systems will be necessary. We can be equally sure that many of our traditional ideas of curriculum, grading, promotion, and retention will be altered, and that the changes will inevitably call for a redefinition of the role of the teacher.

Teaching and Society

N. L. Gage has defined teaching in the context of research as follows:

> By teaching, we mean, for the present purpose of defining research on teaching, any interpersonal influence aimed at changing the ways in which other persons can or will behave. The restriction to "interpersonal" influence is intended to rule out physical (e.g., mechanical), physiological, or economic ways of influencing another's behavior, such as pushing him, drugging him, or depriving him of a job. Rather the influence has to impinge on the other person through his perceptual and cognitive processes, i.e., through his ways of getting meaning out of the objects and events that his senses make him aware of.[9]

The definition by Gage emphasizes the cognitive domain of the teaching-learning continuum where remembering information and synthesizing are both important. Two dimensions of teaching that have an impact upon society are implicit in the definition. The first concerns the kinds of attitudes, values, and competencies that graduates should have, regardless of which level in the educational structure graduation takes place. The second dimension deals with the teachers individually and as an occupational group within the societal complex. These two dimensions are obviously related. Note, for example, the reciprocal relation between student militancy and teacher dissatisfaction.

Teaching and the Student

Beginning with the Sophists we could document the irrascible and perhaps irresponsible behavior of the young. The medieval university student has been reported to have been a carousing, bullying, nonstudying disrupter of society. The exact cause of such actions is difficult to pinpoint, but one can be sure that at least part of the unrest stemmed from inadequate teaching. We can note similar disruptions and dissatisfaction in our own history which culminate in the present state of rebellion of high school and college students. Among other things, students complain about poor teaching, irrelevant content, and inadequate facilities. A graduating senior at the University of Illinois made the following statement which was printed as part of an editorial published in the September 1968 issue of the **Phi Delta Kappan** journal:

---

[9] N. L. Gage, "Paradigms for Research on Teaching," *Handbook of Research on Teaching*, N. L. Gage, ed. (Chicago: Rand McNally Co., 1963), p. 96.

By the most important standard, the development of critical minds, this university has failed us. It has led many students to really believe the recent industrial recruiting ad which said: "college is a waste of time unless you find a job that turns you on." But *I* am not looking so much for a job as for some guidance in solving for myself the critical question of my duty to my society and to myself. . .

Formal classroom structures are out of phase with reality. And we students are painfully aware of this. You teachers feel that the questions of your era are important today. It isn't so. We students want to be heard. We cry out to you in our need. And we see no one listening. . . .[10]

One need not look far to see that students and teachers are not only engaged in a conflict with each other but with the society which spawns them. Groups of students who rebel and attempt to establish "Free Universities" within the larger structure claim that they are motivated by a concern for different values, attitudes, and competencies. Some teachers indicate their dissatisfaction with the *status quo* by contributing their time and talents in this regard. Some are becoming actively involved in politics, and others unite to express their demands for change by way of strikes.

Speculation about the possible causes of the general unrest, which is reflected by student protest demonstrations and by student withdrawal, has prompted thousands of articles in journals, magazines, and newspapers. One of the most searching of these is a review of a University of Wisconsin professor of psychiatry, S. L. Halleck, M.D., which appeared in the September 1968 edition of the *Phi Delta Kappan*.[11] Professor Halleck begins his article with a description of the activist and of the alienated student who take different ways to demonstrate their rejection of societal values. He tells us that student activists are prone to attack the political and economical *status quo* vigorously and to insist that our social structure must undergo radical changes. The alienated students are equally disillusioned with the *status quo* and reject the "Western ethics of hard work, self-denial, success, and responsibility." But they make no attempt to bring about changes and are inclined to be withdrawn and passive. Both the activists and the alienated are peer-conscious and find it impossible to relate with the adult generation which they find to be hypocritical.

It is Professor Halleck's view that, although no one hypothesis is more than a partial explanation of a highly complex phenomenon, all should be considered as possible guide lines to help educators who must deal with activism and alienation. He makes a penetrating analysis of the hypotheses, both critical and sympathetic, which have been advanced to explain what is happening to the younger generation. The critical hypotheses include the following: Permissiveness; nonresponsibility; affluence; and family pathology.

---

10 Paul Schroeder, *Phi Delta Kappan*, XL, No. 1 (September 1968), 1.
11 S. L. Halleck, "Hypotheses of Student Unrest," *Phi Delta Kappan*, XL, No. 1 (September 1968), 2–9.

The sympathetic theories are: the two-armed-camp hypothesis which stresses education and competition; the war-in-Vietnam hypothesis; the deterioration-in-the-quality of life hypothesis; the civil rights hypothesis; the neutral hypotheses where explanations center on impersonal processes; the technology hypothesis; and finally, the wide range of mass media hypotheses.

Professor Halleck advances the suggestion that the new media, especially television, may be affecting the character of young people by bringing them face to face with the worst aspects of our social order before they have the experience and the emotional maturity to cope with such harsh realities. He suggests that when youngsters are presented with the "cruel facts of life" too early in their developmental process, a decline in respect for authority is likely to follow. Halleck propounds the theory that man is an animal requiring dependency upon others during the initial stages of growth and development. A child, therefore, relies extensively upon others for structure and order in his life. Accordingly, in order to develop a sense of identity it is necessary to make commitments to some authority, such as church, family, government, or an ideology. Although one must eventually come to terms with authority, the very young need their myths, their illusions, and their fantasies until they have reached a degree of maturity. If they are deprived of these too soon, they will be inclined to rebel or to withdraw.

Certainly the view is not shared by the developers of a new reading program which has been the cause of a great deal of controversy. Project Read was developed at the Behavioral Research Laboratories in Palo Alto, California by Dr. M. William Sullivan, a linguist and authority on reading skills, and Dr. Alvin D. Calvin, a learning theorist. The program is based on the theory that children learn better and faster if they relate to something familiar which according to the developers of Project Read include such things as darts, guns, clubs, cops, robbers, fighting, war, and prisons! The program was originally introduced in 1968 in schools in selected areas, mostly poverty pockets, in New York, San Francisco and Ravenswood, California; Miami-Dade County and Fort Lauderdale, Florida; St. Paul, Minnesota; Detroit and Flint, Michigan; New Haven, Connecticut; Vicksburg, Mississippi; and Akron, Ohio.

There are twenty-four workbooks in the teaching series, each of about one hundred pages with eight illustrations on each page. There are also twenty-eight reading books. Children complete the workbooks in a series of five and then are ready for a storybook. The learners supply the missing letters in the key words from the exposition explaining each picture. For instance, there is a picture of a child's arm with a dart stuck in it, with the following sentences: "Did the dart hit Art? It hit him in the arm." The next picture shows Art standing by the target holding his arm where he has been hit by the dart. Blood drips from the wound, and we read that "Art's arm is sore. He can't toss his darts and win the bet." The following illustration shows Art peering around a corner, and the sentences read,

" 'If Ned starts to toss more darts,' Art thinks, 'I'll have to get a gun.' " Other examples are "A man can rob" and "Bob can rob a man." "These men are at war," and "At the end of the truce the men go back to war." "This cop grips a club in his hand," and "Pat plans to grab Nell's bag," and "Pat grabs the bag," and "Nell slaps Pat," and "Pat runs as fast as he can," and "The cop grabs Pat." The executive vice-president of Behavioral Research Laboratories, George H. Stern, said, "I don't think the violence is extreme. It's available at every turn in life. This series is something the child has heard, seen, or can identify with clearly." Richard White, director of special reading services for Dade County school system made the public statement that "the material is designed to give students a picture image that will cause a memory implant. These are the types of things they see on television, read in newspapers and see in cartoons. They are references they can latch on to."

The controversy over Project Read began in October 1968 when a mother of two registered her protest against the program to the school principal of Coconut Grove Elementary School in Miami. Mrs. Ellen Morphonios, chief of the criminal division in the Florida State's Attorney's office, emphatically agreed that the material should not be used in the schools. She made the following statement:

> It's terrible. Illustrations depict masked robbers holding people at gunpoint, even a bank robbery. The question is asked, for example, "Did Red rob a man?" In the book the correct answer is "yes." A child who answers "no," is graded wrong. If this isn't subversive and deliberately done as part of a master plan, only a sick mind could have produced it.[12]

Still nothing was done until, through the news media, the matter was finally brought to the attention of the Florida Textbook Inquiry Commission which called a public hearing in Miami.

The most disturbing aspect of the whole affair, one which should concern all educators, is that almost nobody except the children had bothered to read the workbooks after they came from the publishers! Here was an expensive program (Dade County paid $40,000 to instruct 4,000 students.), yet no one seemed to have bothered to investigate what they were getting for the money. The books were not on the approved list of the state commission which is supposed to review all textbooks. Dade County School Superintendent, E. L. Whigham, testified he hadn't read them, and members of the Dade County School Board acknowledged they had not. Even Dr. Tod Mikuriya, who was sent from San Francisco by the laboratories to speak for the books, told the commission he had only "skimmed through" a few and had not seen most. He admitted that the "dart-gun" pictures might be harmful to some children. Only a few of the parents had read the books,

---

[12] *National Enquirer*, XLIII, No. 21 (January 26, 1969), 3.

and some did not oppose them saying that violence is an everyday occurrence and a fact of life seen daily on television and in comic books.

The result of the hearings was a temporary withdrawal of Project Read in Dade County. But it was soon back with a few revisions, and some five million children in public schools from coast to coast are still being taught to read with picture books of violence. It is a curious situation when one can pick up a morning paper with the headline: "U.S. Violence Blamed Largely on Youth." The headline was prompted by a report from the National Commission on Violence headed by Dr. Milton Eisenhower. The progress report stated that: "Better control of illegitimate violence in our democratic society" can and must be achieved. The report contained several themes of challenge, but placed greatest emphasis on the following:

> The key to much of the violence in our society seems to lie with the young.
> Our youth account for an ever-increasing percentage of crime, greater than their increasing percentage of the population. The thrust of much of the group protest and collective violence—on the campus, in the ghettos, in the streets—is provided by our young people.
> It may be here, with tomorrow's generation, that much of the emphasis of our studies and the national response should lie.[13]

Dr. Halleck tells us that those who are concerned about educating, understanding, and helping students need to take an objective approach. He does not believe that students need more paternalism and coddling but that they do need adult understanding and guidance. He says that: "They can still learn much from adults who are committed to the pursuit of ideals in a climate of tolerance, compassion, and responsibility." But how responsible are adults who spend so much of their resources and energies on speculation about the possible causes of student uprising all over the country while we continue to add to their numbers by way of our public elementary and secondary schools?

Throughout all of the investigations, all of the reports, all of the articles, runs a common thread, the question of values. Yet, apart from a relatively minor controversy in Florida, who is questioning the valuational impact of Project Read on the five million children who are being taught to read with examples of violence simply because they can relate with violence? When he announced the introduction of Project Read to 40,000 schoolchildren in New York City (at a cost of $600,000) Superintendent of Schools, Bernard E. Donovan, said: "The innovative aspects of the programed linguistic materials have special appeal to the underachiever since the materials have a built-in 'success' factor that gives the pupils confidence in their ability to succeed and contribute to their self-image." Where does the responsibility lie for the contribution Project Read is making to the self-image of the next generation? Some 55,000 New York teachers went on

---

[13] *National Commission on Violence.*

strike for two weeks during the 1968–1969 school year. They were insistent in their demands for better working conditions and for job security. But it was left to one concerned mother in Dade County, Florida, to protest the stamp of approval on violence that is implied by the subject matter of Project Read. There seems to be good and sufficient reason to question the degree of our real concern for the student within the total educational complex.

Teaching and the Teacher

Teaching is probably one of the most complex and all-encompassing operations in contemporary society, for the teacher is responsible to self, the student, the community, the larger social order, and the teaching profession. Her responsibilities extend into three separate areas, her personal life, the classroom, and her public life. Generally speaking, the totality of her activities in these diverse areas contribute to or detract from her effectiveness as a teacher. More than in any other occupation, the "whole person" is involved in teaching. It has been said that whatever a teacher's style, whether she is authoritarian or permissive, active or passive, voluble or quiet, she must first and foremost, be confidently herself.

There was a time when a teacher was forced to operate within strict guide lines which were laid down for her personal, public, and classroom conduct. Today, once the neophyte has finished her training and has accepted a teaching position, she is more or less on her own. But the teacher's responsibility has increased in proportion to her new freedom, and the demands upon her personal and intellectual capabilities are greater than at any other period in our history. The validity of this statement is underscored by N. L. Gage's definition of teaching as "any interpersonal influence aimed at changing the ways in which other persons can or will behave."

The teacher's personal life has long been considered a legitimate matter for public concern. The colonial teacher was forced to conform to the dictates of those fearful and anxious citizens who clung determinedly to their strict religious and moral orthodoxies. Even through the nineteenth century and into the first decades of the twentieth century, the teacher was subjected to stringent rules and regulations set forth by school boards and citizens' councils. The following set of rules governing special classroom duties and personal conduct, were posted by a New York principal in 1872:

Rules for Teachers

1. Teachers each day will fill lamps, clean chimneys, and trim wicks.
2. Each teacher will bring a bucket of water and a scuttle of coal for the day's session.
3. Make your pens carefully. You may whittle nubs to the individual taste of pupils.

4. Men teachers may take one evening each week for courting pur-poses, or two evenings a week if they go to church regularly.
5. After ten hours of school, the teachers spend the remaining time reading the Bible or other good books.
6. Women teachers who marry or engage in unseemly conduct will be dismissed.
7. Every teacher should lay aside from each pay a goodly sum of his earnings for his benefit during his declining years so that he will not become a burden on society.
8. Any teacher who smokes, uses liquor in any form, frequents pool or public halls, or gets shaved in a barber shop will give good reason to suspect his worth, intentions, integrity, and honesty.
9. The teacher who performs his labors faithfully and without fault for five years will be given an increase of 25 cents per week in his pay providing the Board of Education approves.

The following rules taken from the 1923 edition of the Idaho Teach-ers' Handbook, are only slightly less restrictive to the personal life of the teacher:

1. Don't get married, and don't keep company with men.
2. Don't be away from home between the hours of 8 p.m. and 6 a.m.
3. Don't loiter in ice cream parlors.
4. Don't smoke cigarettes, and don't drink beer, wine, or whiskey.
5. Don't leave town without permission.
6. Don't ride in a carriage or automobile with any man except your father or brother.
7. Don't dress in bright colors, dye your hair or use face powder, mascara, or lipstick.

There are still some communities where there is an attempt to regu-late the personal life of the teacher, but it is usually done through the ad-ministrator, who feels the greatest pressure of public opinion. For the most part, the individual teacher must decide to what extent she is able to conform with the community mores and taboos. A teacher who forsakes her own values simply to avoid any community disapproval is not being "confidently herself," and studies show that, contrary to popular opinion, her effectiveness as a teacher will be lessened. Student respect for the teacher is surely an important aspect of good teaching, but a teacher who acts out of fear of being different, rather than from personal conviction, merits neither the confidence nor the respect of her student.

On the other hand, excessive extremism in social beliefs can also handicap effective teaching, and it depends upon the individual teacher to determine social patterns that will be acceptable without inhibiting indi-vidual differences and genuine individuality. The emphasis on individual determination in regards to the social behavior of the teacher is reflected in the changes of the 1952 NEA Code of Ethics that were made and adopted in July 1963. The principle suggesting that teachers "adhere to any reasonable pattern of behavior accepted by the community for professional persons" was dropped from the code, and there are no suggested guidelines for the social behavior patterns in the revised code. Certainly the trend is to question seriously the validity of superficial and nonprofessional criteria for measuring teaching success.

There have also been considerable changes during the past decade in classroom procedures. Here too, the teacher is accorded far more personal and professional latitude and is gradually being emancipated from traditional approaches that are no longer profitable. We have noted many of the classroom changes brought about by new technological developments, but we have made no mention yet of a device which promises a high degree of success in the improvement of teaching methods.

The device is instant-replay television or what is sometimes called "mirror feedback." The video project involves the use of demonstration video tapes which illustrate cognitive and affective objectives. After viewing the tapes, the teacher makes decisions about objectives and method, and her own class performance is then taped. The playback, along with data processing information, is then evaluated. The teacher is able to make an accurate assessment of her class performance and can make any necessary changes in her procedure. Again, the burden of responsibility for her effectiveness in the classroom depends upon the teacher, but the video technique enables her to make a more objective evaluation of both her strong points and her weaknesses than would be possible otherwise.

But regardless of the teaching advantages modern technology affords, the attitudes, values, and beliefs of the teacher make the greater difference in classroom procedures. A constant factor in teaching has always been that the view one has of educational goals and purpose determine the nature of the teaching-learning activities. We have seen the historical panorama of educational goals that have been influenced by philosophical views which range from Plato's ideas about the rational soul to the experientially based investigations of recent pragmatic and analytical philosophers. Today the greatest emphasis is on notions of inquiry, discovery, and discipline, and knowledge of subject matter alone is insufficient for effective classroom procedures. More than ever before, the teacher needs a well-developed, viable philosophy of education and needs to understand the close functional relationship between philosophy and practice in education.

The third operational area where teacher involvement affects the totality of her contribution to the educational scene is that of public affairs. The public interests and commitments of teachers and the manner in which these concerns are pursued are not only public statements of how teachers view themselves and their occupation, but are important factors in reshaping the public view of teaching. Where once teachers were thought to be little more than public servants who may be seen but not heard outside of the classroom, they have gradually come to be recognized individually, as self-assertive and self-confident members of the community and collectively as a force to be reckoned with. Teachers today make no secret of their concern about social reform and political movements, and their involvements in politics, protest demonstrations, and strikes is unprecedented and would not have been tolerated even a few years ago.

Teachers are beginning to rebel against the ambiguous role imposed upon them where they are charged with the intellectual and often moral development of young America yet are denied the autonomy necessary for making educational choices. They rebel against the ambiguity of substandard salaries for their performance of a unique and socially important function in the dominant national enterprise. They insist on professional status for teachers who have undergone a period of specialized training, who have acquired a special learned body of knowledge, who have a code of ethics, autonomy in their teaching, and a sense of social service. Teachers are making their demands heard through the National Educational Association, which stresses the professional idea of teaching, or through the American Federation of Teachers, which stresses labor affiliation. There has been considerable conflict between the professional-minded and the worker-oriented, but there is every indication of a merger of the AFT and the NEA in the near future.

It is important, however, to make the point here that our sketch of the militant teacher is no more the general rule than our sketch of the professional. The important thing is that the trend is in the direction of a combination of militancy and professionalism by self-assertive, sophisticated, and knowledgeable specialists who represent the new breed of teachers. If such a combination seems dichotomous, it is surely no more so than the wide range of demands the public makes of its teachers.

Tomorrow's Teachers

How does one conclude the closing chapter of a study such as ours? Concluding statements about teachers and their responsibilities to the student, the profession, and society are apt to sound lofty and platitudinous, more like a coach's half-time pep talk to his losing team: let's fight harder for the old school colors; don't forget your team spirit; loved ones are watching you; and perhaps even a moment of silent prayer for the strength to return to the field (one can hardly resist the temptation to say the field of life!) and win!

Certainly teachers have more at stake than a football team, as they are fighting for a way of life—professional recognition, status in the community and the larger society, financial security, a measure of control over educational choices and decisions—for all of these and more. The point is, how can these ideals of today become the realities of tomorrow? The American tradition says by perseverance and hard work. But we have seen through the course of our study that perseverance and hard work alone are insufficient, for these must have direction. Unfortunately, we have seen that all too often we lose track of our concern for direction somewhere in the never-never land between educational theory and educational practice.

The practicing educator has been prone to assume that when educational theorists talk about direction or purpose they refer to traditional attitudes about ultimates, which are not especially relevant to classroom procedures. But today the gap between theory and practice is narrowing. Current stress on the use and clarification of language and on logical procedures in the classroom, on the one hand, and philosophical investigations of the implications of data processing and programed instruction, on the other hand, promise to bridge the gap between the teacher and the educational theorist. Plato wrote: "Until philosophers are kings, or the kings and princes of this world have the spirit and power of philosophy . . . then only will this our State have a possibility of life and behold the light of day." With apologies to Plato, let us conclude our study with the suggestion that when teachers become theorists to the extent of being able to combine "the spirit and power of philosophy" with the act of teaching, they will have discovered the means to achieve their goals, and America will be insured of a vital educational system.

ISRAEL SCHEFFLER

Philosophical Models of Teaching*

It seems particularly appropriate to conclude our study with a discussion of the philosophical models of teaching, for here is a perfect mating of philosophy with educational theory and practice. Israel Scheffler's "Philosophical Models of Teaching" has been selected for this final reading, as there can be little doubt that he is a highly qualified spokesman in both respects. The ideal of successful teaching, a topic for much discussion of late, has been a directing force of our study, and Israel Scheffler is in the forefront of those who hold the view that principled thought is fundamental to good teaching. His article, with its emphasis upon models of teaching, brings together philosophical and theoretical orientations as they bear upon the activities associated with teaching, and in that manner functions as a "summing-up" of the underlying prin-

* Israel Scheffler, "Philosophical Models of Teaching," *Harvard Educational Review*, XXXV, Spring 1965, 131–143. Copyright © 1965 by President and Fellows of Harvard College.

ciples of our study. Scheffler's distinction between learning *to teach and* understanding *what teaching is about is an important one. If one does more than to emulate one's own teachers (or to reject them, I suppose) it is necessary to consider the task of teaching through theoretical categories so that the practice of teaching will rise above the mere shaping of youthful behavior. Whether or not one agrees with Israel Scheffler that "Our teaching needs thus to introduce students to those principles we ourselves acknowledge as fundamental, general, and impartial in the various departments of thought and action," one will benefit immeasurably from a careful study of the three models he presents for our consideration.*

I. Introduction

Teaching may be characterized as an activity aimed at the achievement of learning, and practiced in such manner as to respect the student's intellectual integrity and capacity for independent judgment. Such a characterization is important for at least two reasons: First, it brings out the intentional nature of teaching, the fact that teaching is a distinctive goal-oriented activity, rather than a distinctively patterned sequence of behavioral steps executed by the teacher. Secondly, it differentiates the activity of teaching from such other activities as propaganda, conditioning, suggestion, and indoctrination, which are aimed at modifying the person but strive at all costs to avoid a genuine engagement of his judgment on underlying issues.

This characterization of teaching, which I believe to be correct, fails, nevertheless, to answer certain critical questions of the teacher: What sort of learning shall I aim to achieve? In what does such learning consist? How shall I strive to achieve it? Such questions are, respectively, normative, epistemological, and empirical in import, and the answers that are provided for them give point and substance to the educational enterprise. Rather than trying to separate these questions, however, and deal with each abstractly and explicitly, I should like, on the present occasion, to approach them indirectly and as a group, through a consideration of three influential models of teaching, which provide, or at any rate suggest, certain relevant answers. These models do not so much aim to *describe* teaching as to *orient* it, by weaving a coherent picture out of epistemological, psychological, and normative elements. Like all models, they simplify, but such simplification is a legitimate way of highlighting what are thought to be important features of the subject. The primary issue, in each case, is whether these features are indeed critically important, whether we should allow our educational thinking to be guided by a model which fastens upon them, or whether we should rather reject or revise the model in question. Although I shall mention some historical affiliations of each model, I make no pretense to historical accuracy. My main purpose is, rather, systematic or dialectical, that is, to outline and examine the three models and to see what, if anything, each has to offer us in our own quest for a satisfactory conception of teaching. I turn, then, first to what may be called the "impression model."

II. The Impression Model

The impression model is perhaps the simplest and most widespread of the three, picturing the mind essentially as sifting and storing the external impressions to which it is receptive. The desired end result of teaching is an accumulation in the learner of basic elements fed in from without, organized and processed in standard ways, but, in any event, not generated by the learner himself. In the empiricist variant of this model generally associated with John Locke, learning involves the input by experience of simple ideas of sensation and reflection, which are clustered, related, generalized, and retained by the mind. Blank at birth, the mind is thus formed by its particular experiences, which it keeps available for its future use. In Locke's words (Bk. II, Ch. I, Sec. 2 of the *Essay Concerning Human Understanding*):

> Let us then suppose the mind to be, as we say, white paper, void of all characters, without any ideas: how comes it to be furnished? Whence comes it by that vast store, which the busy and boundless fancy of man has painted on it with an almost endless variety? Whence has it all the materials of reason and knowledge? To this I answer, in one word, From experience; in that all our knowledge is founded, and from that it ultimately derives itself. Our observation, employed either about external sensible objects, or about the internal operations of our minds, perceived and reflected on by ourselves, is that which supplies our understandings with all the materials of thinking. These two are the fountains of knowledge, from whence all the ideas we have, or can naturally have, do spring.

Teaching, by implication, should concern itself with exercising the mental powers engaged in receiving and processing incoming ideas, more particularly powers of perception, discrimination, retention, combination, abstraction, and representation. But, more important, teaching needs to strive for the optimum selection and organization of this experimental input. For potentially, the teacher has enormous power; by controlling the input of sensory units, he can, to a large degree, shape the mind. As Dewey remarked,[1]

> Locke's statements . . . seemed to do justice to both mind and matter. . . . One of the two supplied the matter of knowledge and the object upon which the mind should work. The other supplied definite mental powers, which were few in number and which might be trained by specific exercises.

The process of learning in the child was taken as paralleling the growth of knowledge generally, for all knowledge is constructed out of elementary units of experience, which are grouped, related, and generalized. The teacher's object should thus be to provide data not only useful in themselves, but collectively rich enough to support the progressive growth of adult knowledge in the learner's mind.

The impression model, as I have sketched it, has certain obvious strong points. It sets forth the appeal to experience as a general tool of criticism to be employed in the examination of all claims and doctrines, and it demands that they square with it. Surely such a demand is legitimate, for knowledge does rest upon experience in some way or other. Further, the mind is, in a clear sense, as the impression model suggests, a function of its particular experiences, and it is capable of increased growth with experience. The richness and variety of the child's experiences are thus important considerations in the process of educational planning.

---

[1] John Dewey, *Democracy and Education*. New York: The Macmillan Company, 1916, p. 72.

The impression model nevertheless suffers from fatal difficulties. The notions of absolutely simple ideas and of abstract mental powers improvable through exercise have been often and rightly criticized as mythological:[2] Simplicity is a relative, not an absolute, concept and reflects a particular way of analyzing experience; it is, in short, not given but made. And mental powers or faculties invariant with subject matter have, as everyone knows, been expunged from psychology on empirical as well as theoretical grounds. A more fundamental criticism, perhaps, is that the implicit conception of the growth of knowledge is false. Knowledge is not achieved through any standard set of operations for the processing of sensory particulars, however conceived. Knowledge is, first and foremost, embodied in language, and involves a conceptual apparatus not derivable from the sensory data but imposed upon them. Nor is such apparatus built into the human mind; it is, at least in good part a product of guesswork and invention, borne along by culture and by custom. Knowledge further involves *theory,* and theory is surely not simply a matter of generalizing the data, even assuming the data are organized by a given conceptual apparatus. Theory is a creative and individualistic enterprise that goes beyond the data in distinctive ways, involving not only generalization, but postulation of entities, deployment of analogies, evaluation of relative simplicity, and, indeed, invention of new languages. Experience is relevant to knowledge through providing tests of our theories; it does not automatically generate these theories, even when processed by the human mind. That we have the theories we do is, therefore, a fact, not simply about the human mind, but about our history and our intellectual heritage.

In the process of learning, the child gets not only sense experiences but the language and theory of his heritage in complicated linkages with discriminable contexts. He is heir to the complex culture of belief built up out of innumerable creative acts of intellect of the past, and comprising a patterned view of the world. To give the child even the richest selection of sense data or particular facts alone would in no way guarantee his building up anything resembling what we think of as knowledge, much less his developing the ability to retrieve and apply such knowledge in new circumstances.

A *verbal* variant of the impression model of teaching naturally suggests itself, then, as having certain advantages over the *sensory* version we have just considered: What is to be impressed on the mind is not only sense experience but language and, moreover, accepted theory. We need to feed in not only sense data but the correlated verbal patterning of such data, that is, the *statements* about such data which we ourselves accept. The student's knowledge consists in his stored accumulation of these statements, which have application to new cases in the future. He is no longer, as before, assumed capable of generating our conceptual heritage by operating in certain standard ways on his sense data, for part of what *we* are required to feed into his mind is this very heritage itself.

This verbal variant, which has close affinities to contemporary behaviorism, does have certain advantages over its predecessor, but retains grave inadequacies still, as a model of teaching. To *store* all accepted theories is not the same as being able to *use* them properly in context. Nor, even if some practical correla-

---

2 Dewey, *ibid.*, "the supposed original faculties of observation, recollection, willing, thinking, etc., are purely mythological. There are no such ready-made powers waiting to be exercised and thereby trained."

tion with sense data is achieved, does it imply an understanding of what is thus stored, nor an appreciation of the theoretical motivation and experimental evidence upon which it rests.

All versions of the impression model, finally, have this defect: They fail to make adequate room for radical *innovation* by the learner. We do not, after all, feed into the learner's mind all that we hope he will have as an end result of our teaching. Nor can we construe the critical surplus as generated in standard ways out of materials we do supply. We do not, indeed cannot, so construe insight, understanding, new applications of our theories, new theories, new achievements in scholarship, history, poetry, philosophy. There is a fundamental gap which teaching cannot bridge simply by expansion or reorganization of the curriculum input. This gap sets *theoretical* limits to the power and control of the teacher; moreover, it is where his control ends that his fondest hopes for education begin.

III. The Insight Model

The next model I shall consider, the "insight model," represents a radically different approach. Where the impression model supposes the teacher to be conveying ideas or bits of knowledge into the student's mental treasury, the insight model denies the very possibility of such conveyance. Knowledge, it insists, is a matter of vision, and vision cannot be dissected into elementary sensory or verbal units that can be conveyed from one person to another. It can, at most, be stimulated or prompted by what the teacher does, and if it indeed occurs, it goes beyond what is thus done. Vision defines and organizes particular experiences, and points up their significance. It is vision, or insight into meaning, which makes the crucial difference between simply storing and reproducing learned sentences, on the one hand, and understanding their basis and application, on the other.

The insight model is due to Plato, but I shall here consider the version of St. Augustine, in his dialogue, "The Teacher,"[3] for it bears precisely on the points we have dealt with. Augustine argues roughly as follows: The teacher is commonly thought to convey knowledge by his use of language. But knowledge, or rather *new* knowledge, is not conveyed simply by words sounding in the ear. Words are mere noises unless they signify realities present in some way to the mind. Hence a paradox: If the student already knows the realities to which the teacher's words refer, the teacher teaches him nothing new. Whereas, if the student does not know these realities, the teacher's words can have no meaning for him, and must be mere noises. Augustine concludes that language must have a function wholly distinct from that of the signification of realities; it is used to *prompt* people in certain ways. The teacher's words, in particular, prompt the student to search for realities not already known by him. Finding these realities, which are illuminated for him by internal vision, he acquires new knowledge for himself, though indirectly as a result of the teacher's prompting activity. To *believe* something simply on the basis of authority or hearsay is indeed possible, on Augustine's view; to *know* it is not. Mere beliefs may, in his opinion, of course, be useful; they are not therefore

---

[3] *Ancient Christian Writers*, No. 9, St. Augustine, "The Teacher," edited by J. Quasten and J. C. Plumpe, translated and annotated by J. M. Colleran, Newman Press, Westminster, Md.: 1950; relevant passages may also be found in Kingsley Price, *Education and Philosophical Thought*, Boston: Allyn and Bacon, Inc., 1962, pp. 145–159.

knowledge. For knowledge, in short, requires the individual himself to have a grasp of the realities lying behind the words.

The insight model is strong where the impression model is weakest. While the latter, in its concern with the conservation of knowledge, fails to do justice to innovation, the former addresses itself from the start to the problem of *new* knowledge resulting from teaching. Where the latter stresses atomic manipulable bits at the expense of understanding, the former stresses primarily the acquisition of insight. Where the latter gives inordinate place to the feeding in of materials from the outside, the former stresses the importance of firsthand inspection of realities by the student, the necessity for the student to earn his knowledge by his own efforts.

I should argue, nevertheless, that the case offered by Augustine for the prompting theory is not, as it stands, satisfactory. If the student does not know the realities behind the teacher's words, these words are, presumably, mere noises and can serve only to prompt the student to inquire for himself. Yet if they *are* mere noises, how can they even serve to prompt? If they are not understood in any way by the student, how can they lead him to search for the appropriate realities which underlie them? Augustine, furthermore, allows that a person may believe, though not know, what he accepts on mere authority, without having confronted the relevant realities. Such a person might, presumably, pass from the state of belief to that of knowledge, as a result of prompting, under certain conditions. But what, we may ask, could have been the content of his initial belief if the formulation of it had been literally unintelligible to him? The prompting theory, it seems, will not do as a way of escaping Augustine's original paradox.

There is, however, an easier escape. For the paradox itself rests on a confusion of the meaning of *words* with that of *sentences*. Let me explain. Augustine holds that words acquire intelligibility only through acquaintance with reality. Now it may perhaps be initially objected that understanding a word does not always require acquaintance with its signified reality, for words may also acquire intelligibility through definition, lacking such direct acquaintance. But let us waive this objection and grant, for the sake of argument, that understanding a word *always* does require such acquaintance; it still does not follow that understanding a true sentence similarly requires acquaintance with the state of affairs which it represents. We understand new sentences all the time, on the basis of an understanding of their constituent words and of the grammar by which they are concatenated. Thus, given a sentence signifying some fact, it is simply not true that, unless the student already knows this fact, the sentence must be mere noise to him. For he can understand its meaning indirectly, by a synthesis of its parts, and be led thereafter to inquire whether it is, in reality, true or false.

If my argument is correct, then Augustine's paradox of teaching can be simply rejected, on the ground that we *can* understand statements before becoming acquainted with their signified realities. It follows that the teacher can indeed *inform* the student of new facts by means of language. And it further seems to follow that the basis for Augustine's prompting theory of teaching wholly collapses. We are back to the impression model, with the teacher using language not to prompt the student to inner vision, but simply to inform him of new facts.

The latter conclusion seems to me, however, mistaken. For it does *not* follow that the student will *know* these new facts simply because he has been *informed;* on this point Augustine seems to me perfectly right. It is knowing, after all, that Augustine is interested in, and knowing requires something more than the receipt and acceptance of true information. It requires that the student earn the right to his assurance of the truth of the information in question. New *information,* in short, can be intelligibly conveyed by statements; new *knowledge* cannot. Augustine, I suggest, confuses the two cases, arguing in effect for the impossibility of conveying new knowledge by words, on the basis of an alleged similar impossibility for information. I have been urging the falsity of the latter premise. But if Augustine's premise is indeed false, his conclusion as regards knowledge seems to me perfectly true: To *know* the proposition expressed by a sentence is more than just to have been told it, to have grasped its meaning, and to have accepted it. It is to have earned the right, through one's own effort or position, to an assurance of its truth.

Augustine puts the matter in terms of an insightful searching of reality, an inquiry carried out by oneself, and resting in no way on authority. Indeed, he is perhaps too austerely individualistic in this regard, rejecting even legitimate arguments from authority as a basis for knowledge. But his main thesis seems to me correct: One cannot convey new knowledge by words alone. For knowledge is not simply a storage of information by the learner.

The teacher does, of course, employ *language,* according to the insight model, but its primary function is not to impress his statements on the student's mind for later reproduction. The teacher's statements are, rather, instrumental to the student's own search of reality and vision thereof; teaching is consummated in the student's own insight. The reference to such insight seems to explain, at least partially, how the student can be expected to apply his learning to new situations in the future. For, having acquired this learning not merely by external suggestion but through a personal engagement with reality, the student can appreciate the particular fit which his theories have with real circumstances, and, hence, the proper occasions for them to be brought into play.

There is, furthermore, no reason to construe adoption of the insight model as eliminating the impression model altogether. For the impression model, it may be admitted, does reflect something genuine and important, but mislocates it. It reflects the increase of the culture's written lore, the growth of knowledge as a public and recorded possession. Furthermore, it reflects the primary importance of conserving such knowledge, as a collective heritage. But knowledge in this public sense has nothing to do with the process of learning and the activity of teaching, that is, with the growth of knowledge in the individual learner. The public treasury of knowledge constitutes a basic source of materials for the teacher, but he cannot hope to transfer it bit by bit in growing accumulation within the student's mind. In conducting his teaching, he must rather give up the hope of such simple transfer, and strive instead to encourage individual insight into the meaning and use of public knowledge.

Despite the important emphases of the insight model which we have been considering, there are, however, two respects in which it falls short. One concerns the simplicity of its constituent notion of insight, or vision, as a condition of knowing; the other relates to its specifically cognitive bias, which it shares with the impression model earlier considered. First, the notion that what is crucial in knowledge is a vision of underlying realities, a consulting of what is found within the mind, is far too simple. Certainly, as we have seen, the knower must satisfy *some* condition beyond simply being informed, in order to have the right to his assurance on the matter in question. But to construe this condition in terms of an intellectual inspection of reality is not at all satisfactory. It is plausible only if we restrict ourselves to very simple cases of truths accessible to observation or introspection. As soon as we attempt to characterize the knowing of propositions normally encountered in practical affairs, in the sciences, in politics, history, or the law, we realize that the concept of a *vision of reality* is impossibly simple. Vision is just the wrong metaphor. What seems indubitably more appropriate in all these cases of knowing is an emphasis on the processes of deliberation, argument, judgment, appraisal of reasons *pro* and *con,* weighing of evidence, appeal to principles, and decision-making, none of which fits at all well with the insight model. This model, in short, does not make adequate room for principled deliberation in the characterization of knowing. It is in terms of such principled deliberation, or the potentiality for it, rather than in terms of simple vision, that the distinctiveness of knowing is primarily to be understood.

Secondly, the insight model is specifically cognitive in emphasis, and cannot readily be stretched so as to cover important aspects of teaching. We noted above, for example, that the application of truths to new situations is somewhat better off in the insight than in the impression model, since the appropriateness of a truth for new situations is better judged with awareness of underlying realities than without. But a judgment of appropriateness is not all there is to application; habits of proper execution are also required, and insight itself does not necessitate such habits. Insight also fails to cover the concept of character and the related notions of attitude and disposition. Character, it is clear, goes beyond insight as well as beyond the impression of information. For it involves general principles of conduct logically independent of both insight and the accumulation of information. Moreover, what has been said of character can be applied also to the various institutions of civilization, including those which channel cognition itself. Science, for example, is not just a collection of true insights; it is embodied in a living tradition composed of demanding principles of judgment and conduct. Beyond the cognitive insight, lies the fundamental commitment to principles by which insights are to be criticized and assessed, in the light of publicly available evidence or reasons. In sum, then, the shortcoming of the insight model may be said to lie in the fact that it provides no role for the concept of *principles,* and the associated concept of *reasons.* This omission is very serious indeed, for the concept of principles and the concept of reasons together underlie not only the notions of rational deliberation and critical judgment, but also the notions of rational and moral conduct.

IV. The Rule Model

The shortcoming of the insight model just discussed is remedied in the "rule model," which I associate with Kant. For Kant, the primary philosophical emphasis is on reason, and reason is always a matter of abiding by general rules or principles. Reason stands always in contrast with inconsistency and with expediency, in the judgment of particular issues. In the cognitive realm, reason is a kind of justice to the evidence, a fair treatment of the merits of the case, in the interests of truth. In the moral realm, reason is action on principle, action which therefore does not bend with the wind, nor lean to the side of advantage or power out of weakness or self-interest. Whether in the cognitive or the moral realm, reason is always a matter of treating equal reasons equally, and of judging the issues in the light of general principles to which one has bound oneself.

In thus binding myself to a set of principles, I act freely; this is my dignity as a being with the power of choice. But my own free commitment obligates me to obey the principles I have adopted, when they rule against me. This is what fairness or consistency in conduct means: if I could judge reasons differently when they bear on my interests, or disregard my principles when they conflict with my own advantage, I should have no principles at all. The concepts of *principles, reasons,* and *consistency* thus go together and they apply both in the cognitive judgment of beliefs and the moral assessment of conduct. In fact, they define a general concept of rationality. A rational man is one who is consistent in thought and in action, abiding by impartial and generalizable principles freely chosen as binding upon himself. Rationality is an essential aspect of human dignity and the rational goal of humanity is to construct a society in which such dignity shall flower, a society so ordered as to adjudicate rationally the affairs of free rational agents, an international and democratic republic. The job of education is to develop character in the broadest sense, that is, principled thought and action, in which the dignity of man is manifest.

In contrast to the insight model, the rule model clearly emphasizes the role of principles in the exercise of cognitive judgment. The strong point of the insight model can thus be preserved: The knower must indeed satisfy a further condition beyond the mere receiving and storing of a bit of information. But this condition need not, as in the insight model, be taken to involve simply the vision of an underlying reality; rather, it generally involves the capacity for a principled assessment of reasons bearing on justification of the belief in question. The knower, in short, must typically earn the right to confidence in his belief by acquiring the capacity to make a reasonable case for the belief in question. Nor is it sufficient for this case to have been explicitly taught. What is generally expected of the knower is that his autonomy be evidenced in the ability to construct and evaluate fresh and alternative arguments, the power to innovate, rather than just the capacity to reproduce stale arguments earlier stored. The emphasis on innovation, which we found to be an advantage of the insight model, is thus capable of being preserved by the rule model as well.

Nor does the rule model in any way deny the psychological phenomenon of insight. It merely stresses that insight itself, wherever it is relevant to decision or judgment, is filtered through a network of background principles. It brings out thereby that insight is not an isolated, momentary, or personal matter, that the growth of knowledge is not to be construed as a personal interaction between teacher and student, but rather as mediated by general principles definitive of rationality.

Furthermore, while the previous models, as we have seen, are peculiarly and narrowly *cognitive* in relevance, the rule model embraces *conduct* as well as cognition, itself broadly conceived as including processes of judgment and deliberation. Teaching, it suggests, should be geared not simply to the transfer of information nor even to the development of insight, but to the inculcation of principled judgment and conduct, the building of autonomous and rational character which underlies the enterprises of science, morality and culture. Such inculcation should not, of course, be construed mechanically. Rational character and critical judgment grow only through increased participation in adult experience and criticism, through treatment which respects the dignity of learner as well as teacher. We have here, again, a radical gap which cannot be closed by the teacher's efforts alone. He must rely on the spirit of rational dialogue and critical reflection for the development of character, acknowledging that this implies the freedom to reject as well as to accept what is taught. Kant himself holds, however, that rational principles are somehow embedded in the structure of the human mind, so that education builds on a solid foundation. In any event, the stakes are high, for on such building by education depends the prospect of humanity as an ideal quality of life.

There is much of value in the rule model, as I have sketched it. Certainly, rationality is a fundamental cognitive and moral virtue and as such should, I believe, form a basic objective of teaching. Nor should the many historical connotations of the term "rationality" here mislead us. There is no intent to suggest a faculty of reason, nor to oppose reason to experience or to the emotions. Nor is rationality being construed as the process of making logical deductions. What is in point here is simply the autonomy of the student's judgment, his right to seek reasons in support of claims upon his credibilities and loyalties, and his correlative obligation to deal with such reasons in a principled manner.

Moreover, adoption of the rule model does not necessarily exclude what is important in the other two models; in fact, it can be construed quite plausibly as supplementing their legitimate emphasis. For, intermediate between the public treasury of accumulated lore mirrored by the impression model, and the personal and intuitive grasp of the student mirrored by the insight model, it places general principles of rational judgment capable of linking them.

Yet, there is something too formal and abstract in the rule model, as I have thus far presented it. For the operative principles of rational judgment at any given time are, after all, much more detailed and specific than a mere requirement of formal consistency. Such consistency is certainly fundamental, but the way its demands are concretely interpreted, elaborated, and supplemented in any field of inquiry or practice, varies with the field, the state of knowledge, and the advance of relevant methodological sophistication. The concrete rules governing inference and procedure in the special sciences, for example, are surely not all embedded in the human mind, even if the demands of formal consistency, as such, *are* universally compelling. These concrete rules and standards, techniques and methodological criteria evolve and grow with the advance of knowledge itself; they form a live tradition of rationality in the realm of science.

Indeed, the notion of tradition is a better guide here, it seems to me, than appeal to the innate structure of the human mind. Rationality in natural inquiry is embodied in the relatively young tradition of science, which defines and redefines those principles by means of which evidence is to be interpreted and meshed with theory. Rational judgment in the realm of science is, consequently, judgment which accords with such principles, as crystallized at the time in question. To teach rationality in science is to interiorize these principles in the student, but furthermore, to introduce him to the live and evolving *tradition* of natural science, which forms their significant context of development and purpose.

Scholarship in history is subject to an analogous interpretation, for beyond the formal demands of reason, in the sense of consistency, there is a concrete tradition of technique and methodology defining the historian's procedure and his assessment of reasons for or against particular historical accounts. To teach rationality in history is, in effect, here also to introduce the student to a live tradition of historical scholarship. Similar remarks might be made also with respect to other areas, e.g. law, philosophy and the politics of democratic society. The fundamental point is that rationality cannot be taken simply as an abstract and general ideal. It is embodied in *multiple evolving traditions,* in which the basic condition holds that issues are resolved by reference to *reasons,* themselves defined by *principles* purporting to be impartial and universal. These traditions should, I believe, provide an important focus for teaching.

V. Conclusion

I have intimated that I find something important in each of the models we have considered. The impression model reflects, as I have said, the cumulative growth of knowledge in its *public* sense. Our aim in teaching should surely be to preserve and extend this growth. But we cannot do this by storing it piecemeal within the learner. We preserve it, as the insight model stresses, only if we succeed in transmitting the live spark that keeps it growing, the insight which is a product of each learner's efforts to make sense of public knowledge in his own terms, and to confront it with reality. Finally, as the rule model suggests, such confrontation involves deliberation and judgment, and hence presupposes general and impartial principles governing the assessment of reasons bearing on the issues. Without such guiding principles, the very conception of rational deliberation collapses, and the concepts of rational and moral conduct, moreover, lose their meaning. Our teaching needs thus to introduce students to those principles we ourselves acknowledge as fundamental, general, and impartial, in the various departments of thought and action.

We need not pretend that these principles of ours are immutable or innate. It is enough that they are what we ourselves acknowledge, that they are the best we know, and that we are prepared to improve them should the need and occasion arise. Such improvement is possible, however, only if we succeed in passing on, too, the multiple live traditions in which they are embodied, and in which a sense of their history, spirit, and direction may be discerned. Teaching, from this point of view, is clearly not, as the behaviorists would have it, a matter of the teacher's shaping the student's behavior or of controlling his mind. It is a matter of passing on those traditions of principled thought and action which define the rational life for teacher as well as student.

As Professor Richard Peters has recently written,[4]

> The critical procedures by means of which established content is assessed, revised, and adapted to new discoveries have public criteria written into them that stand as impersonal standards to which both teacher and learner must give their allegiance. . . . To liken education to therapy, to conceive of it as imposing a pattern on another person or as fixing the environment so that he "grows," fails to do justice to the shared impersonality both of the content that is handed on and of the criteria by reference to which it is criticized and revised. The teacher is not a detached operator who is bringing about some kind of result in another person which is ex-

---

[4] *Education as Initiation,* an inaugural lecture delivered at the University of London Institute of Education, 9 December 1963; published for The University of London Institute of Education by Evans Brothers, Ltd., London.

ternal to him. His task is to try to get others on the inside of a public form of life that he shares and considers to be worthwhile.

In teaching, we do not impose our wills on the student, but introduce him to the many mansions of the heritage in which we ourselves strive to live, and to the improvement of which we are ourselves dedicated.

A Selected Bibliography

Abbott, Edwin A. FRANCIS BACON: AN ACCOUNT OF HIS LIFE AND WORKS. London: Macmillan & Co. Ltd., 1885.

Aiken, Henry D. THE AGE OF IDEOLOGY. Boston: Houghton Mifflin Company, 1957.

Association for Supervision and Curriculum Development. LEARNING AND MENTAL HEALTH IN THE SCHOOL. Washington, D.C., 1966.

Bakewell, Charles M. SOURCE BOOK IN ANCIENT PHILOSOPHY. New York: Charles Scribner's Sons, 1907.

Bayles, Ernest E. DEMOCRATIC EDUCATIONAL THEORY. New York: Harper & Brothers, 1960.

Beck, Lewis White. A COMMENTARY ON KANT'S CRITIQUE OF PRACTICAL REASON. Chicago: University of Chicago Press, 1960.

Becker, Carl L. THE HEAVENLY CITY OF THE EIGHTEENTH-CENTURY PHILOSOPHERS. New Haven, Connecticut: Yale University Press, 1959.

Belth, Marc. EDUCATION AS A DISCIPLINE. Boston: Allyn & Bacon, Inc., 1965.

Benjamin, A. Cornelius. SCIENCE, TECHNOLOGY, AND HUMAN VALUES. Columbia, Missouri: University of Missouri Press, 1965.

Bigge, Morris L. LEARNING THEORIES FOR TEACHERS. New York: Harper & Row, Publishers, 1964.

Boring, Edwin G. A HISTORY OF EXPERIMENTAL PSYCHOLOGY, 2nd ed. New York: Appleton-Century-Crofts, 1950.

Boynton, Paul L. INTELLIGENCE, ITS MANIFESTATIONS AND MEASUREMENTS. New York: D. Appleton & Company, 1933.

Bruner, J.; Goodnow, J.; and Austin, G. A STUDY OF THINKING. New York: John Wiley & Sons, Inc., 1956.

Bruner, Jerome. "Education as Social Invention," THE JOURNAL OF SOCIAL ISSUES, XX, No. 3 (July 1964), 21–33.

Bruner, Jerome. THE PROCESS OF EDUCATION. Cambridge, Massachusetts: Harvard University Press, 1960.

Bruner, Jerome. TOWARD A THEORY OF INSTRUCTION. Cambridge, Massachusetts: Harvard University Press, 1966.

Burnet, J. ARISTOTLE ON EDUCATION. Cambridge: Cambridge University Press, 1903.

Butler, J. Donald. FOUR PHILOSOPHIES AND THEIR PRACTICE IN EDUCATION AND RELIGION. New York: Harper & Brothers, 1951.

Butler, R. J., ed. ANALYTICAL PHILOSOPHY. New York: Barnes & Noble, Inc., 1962.

Caird, Edward. THE SOCIAL PHILOSOPHY AND RELIGION OF COMTE. Glasgow: James Maclehose and Sons, 1893.

Cassirer, Ernst. AN ESSAY ON MAN. New Haven, Connecticut: Yale University Press, 1944.

Cassirer, Ernst. THE PROBLEM OF KNOWLEDGE, trans. William H. Woglom and Charles W. Hendel. New Haven, Connecticut: Yale University Press, 1950.

Cassirer, Ernst; Kristeller, Paul Oskar; and Randall, John Herman, Jr., eds. THE RENAISSANCE PHILOSOPHY OF MAN. Chicago: University of Chicago Press, 1948.

Childs, John L. EDUCATION AND MORALS. New York: Appleton-Century-Crofts, 1950.

Collins, James. A HISTORY OF MODERN EUROPEAN PHILOSOPHY. Milwaukee, Wisconsin: The Bruce Publishing Company, 1954.

Commager, Henry Steele. THE AMERICAN MIND. New Haven, Connecticut: Yale University Press, 1950.

Copleston, Frederick, S.J. A HISTORY OF PHILOSOPHY. The Bellarmine Series VII. London: Burns, Oates & Washbourne, Ltd., 1960.

Copleston, Frederick, S.J. A HISTORY OF PHILOSOPHY, vol. 1. Westminster, Maryland: The Newman Press, 1957.

Copleston, Frederick, S.J. A HISTORY OF PHILOSOPHY, vol. 2. Westminster, Maryland: The Newman Press, 1957.

Copleston, Frederick, S.J. A HISTORY OF PHILOSOPHY, vol. 5. Westminster, Maryland: The Newman Press, 1964.

Copleston, Frederick, S.J. CONTEMPORARY PHILOSOPHY. London: Burns, Oates & Washbourne, Ltd., 1956.

Cornford, Francis M. THE REPUBLIC OF PLATO. New York: Oxford University Press, 1956.

Cremin, Lawrence A. THE TRANSFORMATION OF THE SCHOOL. New York: Vintage Books, 1964.

Curtis, S. J., and Boultwood, M. E. A. A SHORT HISTORY OF EDUCATIONAL IDEAS. London: University Tutorial Press Ltd., 1958.

De Garmo, Charles. HERBART AND THE HERBARTIANS. New York: Charles Scribner's Sons, 1912.

Dennis, Wayne, et al. CURRENT TRENDS IN PSYCHOLOGICAL THEORY. Pittsburgh: University of Pittsburgh Press, 1951.

Dessoir, Max. OUTLINES OF THE HISTORY OF PSYCHOLOGY, trans. Donald Fisher. New York: The Macmillan Company, 1912.

Dewey, John. ART AS EXPERIENCE. New York: Minton, Balch & Company, 1934.

Dewey, John. DEMOCRACY AND EDUCATION. New York: The Macmillan Company, 1916.

Dewey, John. EXPERIENCE AND NATURE. New York: W. W. Norton & Co., Inc., 1929.

Dewey, John. HOW WE THINK. Boston: D. C. Heath and Company, 1933.

Dewey, John. INDIVIDUALISM OLD AND NEW. New York: Minton, Balch & Company, 1930.

Dewey, John. INTELLIGENCE IN THE MODERN WORLD, ed. J. Ratner. New York: Modern Library, 1939.

Dewey, John. LOGIC, THE THEORY OF INQUIRY. New York: Henry Holt & Company, 1938.

Dewey, John. MY PEDAGOGIC CREED. E. L. Kellog Pamphlet, 1897.

Dewey, John. RECONSTRUCTION IN PHILOSOPHY. New York: New American Library of World Literature, 1950.

Dewey, John. "Some Questions About Value," THE JOURNAL OF PHILOSOPHY, XLI, No. 17 (August 17, 1944), 449–455.

Dewey, John. "Theory of Valuation," INTERNATIONAL ENCYCLOPEDIA OF UNIFIED SCIENCE, II, No. 4. Chicago: The University of Chicago Press, 1939.

Dewey, John. THE CHILD AND THE CURRICULUM. Chicago: University of Chicago Press, 1902.

Dewey, John. THE SCHOOL AND THE SOCIETY. Chicago: University of Chicago Press, 1900.

Dewey, John. THE QUEST FOR CERTAINTY. London: George Allen & Unwin Ltd., 1929.

Dierenfield, Richard B. RELIGION IN AMERICAN PUBLIC SCHOOLS. Washington: Public Affairs Press, 1962.

Dunkel, Harold B. WHITEHEAD ON EDUCATION. Columbus, Ohio: Ohio State University Press, 1965.

Edwards, Paul. THE LOGIC OF MORAL DISCOURSE. New York: The Free Press, 1955.

Ehlers, Henry, ed. CRUCIAL ISSUES IN EDUCATION. New York: Henry Holt and Company, 1955, 1959.

Elam, Stanley, ed. EDUCATION AND THE STRUCTURE OF KNOWLEDGE. Chicago: Rand McNally & Company, 1964.

Ewing, A. C. A SHORT COMMENTARY ON KANT'S CRITIQUE OF PURE REASON. London: Methuen & Company, Ltd., 1961.

Felkin, Henry, and Felkin, Emmie. HERBART'S SCIENCE AND PRACTICE OF EDUCATION. Boston: D. C. Heath and Company, 1898.

Fisch, Max H., ed. CLASSIC AMERICAN PHILOSOPHERS. New York: Appleton-Century-Crofts, 1951.

Flugel, J. C. A HUNDRED YEARS OF PSYCHOLOGY, 2nd ed. London: Gerald Duckworth & Co., Ltd., 1951.

Ford, G. W., and Pugno, Lawrence, eds. THE STRUCTURE OF KNOWLEDGE AND THE CURRICULUM. Chicago: Rand McNally & Company, 1964.

Friedrich, Carl, ed. THE PHILOSOPHY OF HEGEL. New York: Random House, Inc., 1954.

Fuller, B. A. G., and McMurrin, Sterling. A HISTORY OF PHILOSOPHY. 2 vols. New York: Holt, Rinehart & Winston, Inc., 1955.

Gagne, Robert M. PSYCHOLOGICAL PRINCIPLES IN SYSTEMS DEVELOPMENT. New York: Holt, Rinehart & Winston, Inc., 1962.

Gardner, John W. SELF-RENEWAL, THE INDIVIDUAL AND THE INNOVATING SOCIETY. New York: Harper & Row, Publishers, 1963.

Gay, Peter, ed. JOHN LOCKE ON EDUCATION. New York: Bureau of Publications, Teachers College, Columbia University, 1964.

Gibson, James. LOCKE'S THEORY OF KNOWLEDGE AND ITS HISTORICAL RELATIONS. Cambridge: Cambridge University Press, 1917.

Gilbert, Neal W. RENAISSANCE CONCEPTS OF METHOD. New York: Columbia University Press, 1960.

Gilby, Thomas. ST. THOMAS AQUINAS, PHILOSOPHICAL TEXTS. London: Oxford University Press, 1952.

Gordon, Ira. HUMAN DEVELOPMENT. New York: Harper & Row, Publishers, 1962.

Greene, Theodore Meyer, ed. KANT SELECTIONS. New York: Charles Scribner's Sons, 1957.

Guilford, J. P.; Merrifield, P. R.; and Cox, Anna B. "Creative Thinking in Children at the Junior High School Levels." REPORTS FROM THE PSYCHOLOGICAL LABORATORY, No. 26. U.S. Office of Education, Cooperative Research Project No. 737. Los Angeles: The University of Southern California, September 1961.

Hall, Everett W. MODERN SCIENCE AND HUMAN VALUES. Princeton, New Jersey: D. Van Nostrand Company, Inc., 1956.

Hare, R. M. THE LANGUAGE OF MORALS. New York: Oxford University Press, 1964.

Harris, E. E. NATURE, MIND AND MODERN SCIENCE. London: George Allen & Unwin Ltd., 1954.

Hartshorne, Charles, and Weiss, Paul, eds. COLLECTED PAPERS OF CHARLES SANDERS PEIRCE. Cambridge, Massachusetts: Harvard University Press, 1931–1935.

Harvey, O. J.; Hunt, David E.; and Schroder, Harold M. CONCEPTUAL SYSTEMS AND PERSONALITY ORGANIZATION. New York: John Wiley & Sons, Inc., 1961.

Hawkes, Jacquetta, and Wooley, Sir Leonard. HISTORY OF MANKIND, PREHISTORY AND THE BEGINNINGS OF CIVILIZATION, vol. 1. New York: Harper & Row, Publishers, 1963.

Hazard, Paul. EUROPEAN THOUGHT IN THE EIGHTEENTH CENTURY FROM MONTESQUIEU TO LESSING. New Haven, Connecticut: Yale University Press, 1954.

Hegel, Georg W. THE PHENOMENOLOGY OF MIND, trans. J. B. Baillie. 2 vols. New York: The Macmillan Company, 1910.

Hegel, Georg W. THE PHILOSOPHY OF HISTORY. New York: The Colonial Press, 1900.

Heilbroner, Robert L. THE FUTURE AS HISTORY. New York: Harper & Brothers, 1960.

Heilbroner, Robert L. THE WORLDLY PHILOSOPHERS. New York: Simon & Schuster, Inc., 1953.

Hibben, John Grier. THE PHILOSOPHY OF THE ENLIGHTENMENT. Epochs of Philosophy. New York: Charles Scribner's Sons, 1910.

Hocking, Richard Boyle O'Reilly, and Hocking, William E. TYPES OF PHILOSOPHY. New York: Charles Scribner's Sons, 1959.

Hocking, William Ernest; Blanshard, Brand; Hendel, Charles William; and Randall, John Herman, Jr. PREFACE TO PHILOSOPHY: TEXTBOOK. New York: The Macmillan Company, 1946.

Hodenfield, G. K., and Stinnett, T. M. THE EDUCATION OF TEACHERS. Englewood Cliffs, New Jersey: Prentice-Hall, Inc., 1961.

Hook, Sidney. MARX AND THE MARXISTS, THE AMBIGUOUS LEGACY. Princeton, New Jersey: D. Van Nostrand Company, Inc., 1955.

Hook, Sidney. TOWARD THE UNDERSTANDING OF KARL MARX. New York: The John Day Co., Inc., 1933.

Hospers, John. AN INTRODUCTION TO PHILOSOPHICAL ANALYSIS. Englewood Cliffs, New Jersey: Prentice-Hall, Inc., 1953.

Hunt, Joseph McVicker. INTELLIGENCE AND EXPERIENCE. New York: The Ronald Press Company, 1961. Chapter V.

Hutchins, Robert M. EDUCATION FOR FREEDOM. Baton Rouge, Louisiana: Louisiana State University Press, 1943.

Hutchins, Robert M. FREEDOM, EDUCATION AND THE FUND. New York: Meridian Books, 1956.

Hutchins, Robert M. THE HIGHER LEARNING IN AMERICA. New Haven, Connecticut: Yale University Press, 1936.

Hutchins, Robert M. THE UNIVERSITY OF UTOPIA. Chicago: University of Chicago Press, 1953.

INNOVATION AND EXPERIMENT IN EDUCATION. A Progress Report of the Panel on Educational Research and Development to the U.S. Commissioner of Education, the Director of the National Science Foundation, and the Special Assistant to the President for Science and Technology. Washington, D.C.: U.S. Government Printing Office, March 1964.

Jacob, Philip E. CHANGING VALUES IN COLLEGE. New York: Harper & Brothers, 1957.

James, William. PRAGMATISM, A NEW NAME FOR SOME OLD WAYS OF THINKING. New York: Macmillan and Company, 1907.

James, William. TALKS TO TEACHERS ON PSYCHOLOGY. New York: Holt, Rinehart & Winston, Inc., 1899.

Joad, C. E. M. A CRITIQUE OF LOGICAL POSITIVISM. Chicago: University of Chicago Press, 1950.

Jowett, B. THE DIALOGUES OF PLATO. New York: Random House, Inc., 1937.

Kant, Immanuel. CRITICK OF PURE REASON, trans. Francis Haywood. London: William Pickering, 1848.

Kant, Immanuel. EDUCATION. Ann Arbor, Michigan: The University of Michigan Press, 1960.

Kant, Immanuel. PROLEGOMENA TO ANY FUTURE METAPHYSICS. The Little Library of Liberal Arts. New York: The Liberal Arts Press, 1950.

Kaufman, Gordon D. RELATIVISM, KNOWLEDGE AND FAITH. Chicago: University of Chicago Press, 1960.

Kaufmann, Walter, ed. EXISTENTIALISM FROM DOSTOEVSKY TO SARTRE. New York: Meridian Books, 1956.

Kaufmann, Walter, ed. PHILOSOPHIC CLASSICS: BACON TO KANT. Englewood Cliffs, New Jersey: Prentice-Hall, Inc., 1962.

Kierkegaard, Sören. STAGES ON LIFE'S WAY, trans. Walter Lowrie. Princeton, New Jersey: Princeton University Press, 1940.

Kline, George L. ALFRED NORTH WHITEHEAD, ESSAYS ON HIS PHILOSOPHY. Englewood Cliffs, New Jersey: Prentice-Hall, Inc., 1963.

Kneller, George F. EXISTENTIALISM AND EDUCATION. New York: Philosophical Library, Inc., 1958.

Kneller, George F. LOGIC AND LANGUAGE OF EDUCATION. New York: John Wiley & Sons, Inc., 1966.

Knight, Douglas M. THE FEDERAL GOVERNMENT AND HIGHER EDUCATION. Englewood Cliffs, New Jersey: Prentice-Hall, Inc., 1960.

Lambert, P. M.; Miller, D. M.; and Wiley, D. E. "Experimental Folklore and Experimentation: The Study of Programmed Learning in the Wauwatosa Public Schools," JOURNAL OF EDUCATIONAL RESEARCH, LV, No. 9 (June 1962), 485–494.

Lamont, Corliss. DIALOGUE ON JOHN DEWEY. New York: Horizon Press, 1959.

Lamprecht, Sterling P., ed. LOCKE SELECTIONS. New York: Charles Scribner's Sons, 1956.

Larrabee, Harold. RELIABLE KNOWLEDGE, rev. ed. Boston: Houghton Mifflin Company, 1964.

Lepley, Ray, ed. THE LANGUAGE OF VALUE. New York: Columbia University Press, 1957.

Lepley, Ray. VALUE: A COOPERATIVE INQUIRY. New York: Columbia University Press, 1949.

Levi, Albert William. PHILOSOPHY AND THE MODERN WORLD. Bloomington, Indiana: Indiana University Press, 1959.

Levy-Bruhl, L. THE PHILOSOPHY OF AUGUSTE COMTE. London: Swan Sonnenschein and Company Ltd., 1903.

Locke, John. AN ESSAY CONCERNING HUMAN UNDERSTANDING, vol. 2, ed. Alexander Campbell Fraser. London: Clarendon Press, 1894.

Lowrie, Walter, and Swenson, David, trans. KIERKEGAARD'S CONCLUDING UNSCIENTIFIC POSTSCRIPT. Princeton, New Jersey: Princeton University Press, 1941.

Mackenzie, Millicent. HEGEL'S EDUCATIONAL THEORY AND PRACTICE. London: Swan Sonnenschein and Company Ltd., 1909.

MacVannel, John Angus. THE EDUCATIONAL THEORIES OF HERBART AND FROEBEL. New York: Columbia University Press, 1906.

Mager, Robert F. PREPARING INSTRUCTIONAL OBJECTIVES. San Francisco, California: Fearon Publishers, Inc., 1962.

Martineau, Harriet. THE POSITIVE PHILOSOPHY OF AUGUSTE COMTE. London: John Edward Taylor, 1853.

Marx, Karl. KARL MARX SELECTED WORKS, vols. 1 and 2. New York: International Publishers Co., Inc., 1937.

Marx, Karl. SELECTED WRITINGS IN SOCIOLOGY AND SOCIAL PHILOSOPHY. London: C. A. Watts & Co. Ltd., 1956.

Mayer, M. H. THE PHILOSOPHY OF TEACHING OF ST. THOMAS AQUINAS. Milwaukee, Wisconsin: The Bruce Publishing Company, 1929.

McKeon, Richard, ed. THE BASIC WORKS OF ARISTOTLE. New York: Random House, Inc., 1941.

McKinney, J. F. THE CHALLENGE OF REASON. Brisbane, Australia: The Mountain Press, 1950.

Miller, James G. "Information Overload," in SELF-ORGANIZING SYSTEMS, ed. M. C. Yovits. Washington, D.C.: Spartan Books, Inc., 1962.

Montagu, Basil, ed. THE WORKS OF FRANCIS BACON, vol. 1. Philadelphia: Parry and McMillan, 1854.

Montagu, Basil, ed. THE WORKS OF FRANCIS BACON, vol. 2. Philadelphia: Parry and McMillan, 1854.

Montague, William Pepperell. THE WAYS OF KNOWING. New York: The Macmillan Company, 1958.

Morris, C. W. SIX THEORIES OF MIND. Chicago: University of Chicago Press, 1932.

Müller, F. Max, trans. IMMANUEL KANT'S CRITIQUE OF PURE REASON. New York: The Macmillan Company, 1911.

Muller, Herbert J. FREEDOM IN THE ANCIENT WORLD. New York: Harper & Brothers, 1961.

Murphy, Gardner. HISTORICAL INTRODUCTION TO MODERN PSYCHOLOGY, rev. ed. New York: Harcourt, Brace & Co., Inc., 1949.

Oates, Whitney J. BASIC WRITINGS OF SAINT AUGUSTINE. New York: Random House, Inc., 1948.

O'Connor, D. J. AN INTRODUCTION TO THE PHILOSOPHY OF EDUCATION. New York: Philosophical Library, Inc., 1957.

Olivet, Regis J. INTRODUCTION TO KIERKEGAARD. London: Frederick Muller Ltd., 1950.

Osborne, H. FOUNDATIONS OF THE PHILOSOPHY OF VALUE. London: Cambridge University Press, 1933.

Pareti, Luigi; Brezzi, Paolo; and Petech, Lucians. HISTORY OF MANKIND, vol. 2. New York: Harper & Row, Publishers, 1965.

Patrick, J. Max. FRANCIS BACON. London: Longmans, Green & Co. Ltd., 1961.

Pegis, Anthony C., ed. BASIC WRITINGS OF SAINT THOMAS AQUINAS, vol. 1. New York: Random House, Inc., 1945.

Pegis, Anthony C., ed. INTRODUCTION TO SAINT THOMAS AQUINAS. New York: The Modern Library, 1948.

Phenix, Philip. REALMS OF MEANING. New York: McGraw-Hill Book Company, 1964.

Price, Kingsley. EDUCATION AND PHILOSOPHICAL THOUGHT. Boston: Allyn & Bacon, Inc., 1962.

Prichard, H. A. KANT'S THEORY OF KNOWLEDGE. Oxford: The Clarendon Press, 1909.

Rand, Benjamin, ed. MODERN CLASSICAL PHILOSOPHERS. Boston: Houghton Mifflin Company, 1936.

Reese, William. THE ASCENT FROM BELOW. Boston: Houghton Mifflin Company, 1959.

Reichenbach, Hans. THE RISE OF SCIENTIFIC PHILOSOPHY. Berkeley: University of California Press, 1957.

Ripple, R. E., and Tockcastle, V. N., eds. PIAGET REDISCOVERED. Ithaca, New York: School of Education, Cornell University, 1964.

Rockwood, Raymond O. CARL BECKER'S HEAVENLY CITY REVISITED. Ithaca, New York: Cornell University Press, 1958.

Ross, Sir David. PLATO'S THEORY OF IDEAS. London: Oxford University Press, 1951.

Russell, James E. CHANGE AND CHALLENGE IN AMERICAN EDUCATION. Boston: Houghton Mifflin Company, 1965.

Scheffler, Israel. THE LANGUAGE OF EDUCATION. Springfield, Illinois: Charles C. Thomas, Publisher, 1960.

Scheffler, Israel. PHILOSOPHY AND EDUCATION, 2nd ed. Boston: Allyn & Bacon, Inc., 1966.

Scott, C. Winfield; Hill, Clyde M.; and Burns, Hobert W., eds. THE GREAT DEBATE. Englewood Cliffs, New Jersey: Prentice-Hall, Inc., 1959.

Sears, P., and Hilgard, E. "The Teacher's Role in the Motivation of the Learner," THEORIES OF LEARNING AND INSTRUCTION, NSSE 63rd Yearbook, Part I, ed. Ernest Hilgard. Chicago: University of Chicago Press, 1964.

Shore, Maurice. SOVIET EDUCATION. New York: Philosophical Library, Inc., 1947.

Simon, Walter Michael. EUROPEAN POSITIVISM IN THE NINETEENTH CENTURY. Ithaca, New York: Cornell University Press, 1963.

Smart, Harold R. PHILOSOPHY AND ITS HISTORY. La Salle, Illinois: Open Court Publishing Company, 1962.

Smith, A. H. A TREATISE ON KNOWLEDGE. Oxford: The Clarendon Press, 1943.

Smith, B. Othanel, and Ennis, Robert H., eds. LANGUAGE AND CONCEPTS IN EDUCATION. Chicago: Rand McNally & Company, 1961.

Smith, B. Othanel, and Meux, Milton O. A STUDY OF THE LOGIC OF TEACHING. Urbana, Illinois: Bureau of Educational Research, University of Illinois, 1962.

Smith, Norman Kemp. A COMMENTARY TO KANT'S CRITIQUE OF PURE REASON. London: Macmillan & Co. Ltd., 1923.

Snider, Denton J. THE LIFE OF FREDERICK FROEBEL. Chicago: Sigma Publishing Co., 1900.

Spicer, E. E. ARISTOTLE'S CONCEPTION OF THE SOUL. London: University of London Press, 1934.

Stace, W. T. THE PHILOSOPHY OF HEGEL. London: Macmillan & Co. Ltd., 1924.

Stevenson, Charles L. ETHICS AND LANGUAGE. New Haven, Connecticut: Yale University Press, 1944.

Stoddard, George D. THE MEANING OF INTELLIGENCE. New York: The Macmillan Company, 1943.

Stolurow, L. M., and Walker, C. C. "A Comparison of Overt and Covert Response in Programmed Learning," JOURNAL OF EDUCATIONAL RESEARCH, LV (1962), 421–429.

Suppes, P. "Modern Learning Theory and the Elementary School Curriculum," AMERICAN EDUCATIONAL RESEARCH JOURNAL, L (1964), 79–94.

Taba, H.; Levine, S.; and Freeman, F. E. THINKING IN ELEMENTARY SCHOOL CHILDREN. U.S. Office of Education, Cooperative Research Project No. 1574. San Francisco, California: San Francisco State College, 1963.

Tiedt, Sidney W. THE ROLE OF THE FEDERAL GOVERNMENT IN EDUCATION. New York and Ontario: Oxford University Press, 1966.

Titus, Harold H. LIVING ISSUES IN PHILOSOPHY. New York: American Book Company, 1959.

Veitch, John, trans. THE MEDITATIONS AND SELECTIONS FROM THE PRINCIPLES OF RENÉ DESCARTES. La Salle, Illinois: Open Court Publishing Company, 1955.

Vygotsky, L. S. THOUGHT AND LANGUAGE. Cambridge, Massachusetts: Massachusetts Institute of Technology Press, 1962. Reprinted from THOUGHT AND LANGUAGE by Lev Vygotsky, translated by Eugenia Hanfmann and Gertrude Vakar by permission of the M.I.T. Press, Cambridge, Massachusetts.

Wallace, William. HEGEL'S PHILOSOPHY OF MIND. Oxford: The Clarendon Press, 1894.

Walsh, W. H. PHILOSOPHY OF HISTORY. New York: Harper & Row, Publishers (Harper Torchbooks), 1960.

Watson, John. COMTE, MILL, AND SPENCER. New York: Macmillan and Company, 1895.

Weldon, T. D. KANT'S CRITIQUE OF PURE REASON. Oxford: The Clarendon Press, 1958.

Werkmeister, W. H. THE BASIS AND STRUCTURE OF KNOWLEDGE. New York: Harper & Brothers, 1948.

Whipple, G. M., ed. INTELLIGENCE, ITS NATURE AND NURTURE. 39th Yearbook of the National Society for the Study of Education. Bloomington, Illinois: Public School Publishing Company, 1940.

White, Morton. THE AGE OF ANALYSIS. Boston: Houghton Mifflin Company, 1955.

White, Morton. THE ORIGINS OF DEWEY'S INSTRUMENTALISM. New York: Columbia University Press, 1943.

Whitehead, Alfred North. THE AIMS OF EDUCATION AND OTHER ESSAYS. New York: The Macmillan Company, 1929.

Whitehead, Alfred North. SCIENCE AND PHILOSOPHY. Paterson, New Jersey: Littlefield, Adams & Co., 1964.

Whitehead, Alfred North. SCIENCE AND THE MODERN WORLD. New York: The Macmillan Company, 1925.

Wiener, Philip P. EVOLUTION AND THE FOUNDERS OF PRAGMATISM. Cambridge, Massachusetts: Harvard University Press, 1949.

Wolff, Robert Paul. KANT'S THEORY OF MENTAL ACTIVITY. Cambridge, Massachusetts: Harvard University Press, 1963.

Woodworth, Robert S. CONTEMPORARY SCHOOLS OF PSYCHOLOGY, rev. ed. New York: The Ronald Press Company, 1948.

Woozley, A. D. THEORY OF KNOWLEDGE. London: Hutchinson University Library, 1962.

Wynne, John P. THEORIES OF EDUCATION. New York: Harper & Row, Publishers, 1963.

Yolton, John W. JOHN LOCKE AND THE WAY OF IDEAS. London: Oxford University Press, 1956.

Index